The Handbook of Human Resource Management

4

B

Human Resource Management in Action Series
Edited by Brian Towers

The Handbook of Human Resource Management

Second Edition

Edited by Brian Towers

Copyright © Blackwell Publishers Ltd 1992, 1996
Editorial organization © Brian Towers 1992, 1996

First published 1992
Reprinted 1993, 1994, 1995
Second edition 1996
Reprinted 1997, 1998

Blackwell Publishers Ltd
108 Cowley Road
Oxford OX4 1JF, UK

Blackwell Publishers Inc
350 Main Street
Malden, Massachusetts 02148, USA

British Library Cataloguing in Publication Data
A CIP catalogue record for this book is available from the British Library

Library of Congress Cataloging in Publication Data
The handbook of HRM / edited by Brian Towers. — 2nd ed.
p. cm. — (Human resource management in action)
Rev. ed. of: The Handbook of human resource management. 1992.
'Blackwell business.'
Includes bibliographical references and index.
ISBN 0–631–19851–2 (alk. paper)
1. Personnel management—Handbooks, manuals, etc. 2. Personnel
management—Case studies. I. Towers, Brian. II. Title: Handbook of
human resource management. III. Series.
HF5549.H2964   1996   96–5367
658.3—dc20   CIP

Typeset in 11 on 13pt Plantin
by Graphicraft Typesetters Limited, Hong Kong
Printed and bound in Great Britain
by MPG Books Ltd, Bodmin, Cornwall

This book is printed on acid-free paper

Contents

Part III: Cases

Figures

Tables

Contributors

Gordon C. Anderson is Professor and Head of Business Administration at Glasgow Caledonian University, having formerly been Chairman and director of MBA Programmes at the University of Strathclyde. His books include *Managing Performance Appraisal Systems* (Blackwell 1993). His current research centres on the design and implementation of performance appraisal and performance management systems.

Greg J. Bamber is Professor and Director, Graduate School of Management, Griffith University, Brisbane. His publications include (with Ed Snape and Tom Redman) *Managing Managers* (Blackwell 1994) and (with Russell Lansbury) *International Perspectives on Human Resources and Industrial Relations* (Routledge 1989).

P.B. Beaumont is Professor of Employee Relations in the Department of Social and Economic Research, University of Glasgow. He has published widely, including *The Future of Employment Relations* (Sage 1995).

Paul Blyton is Professor of Industrial Relations and Industrial Sociology at Cardiff Business School, University of Wales, Cardiff. His books include (with Peter Turnbull) *The Dynamics of Employee Relations* (Macmillan 1994) and (with M. Noon) *The Realities of Work* (Macmillan, forthcoming).

Paul Dobson is Lecturer in Organizational Behaviour at the City University Business School, and a member of the Centre for Personnel Research and Enterprise Development. His publications include the co-authored *Changing Culture* (2nd edition, IPD 1993). Current research interests focus on organizational change and managerial competencies.

Katherine M. Gardiner is Lecturer in Human Resource Management and Organizational Behaviour, Sheffield Business School. Her current research interest is the influence of culture on managerial work.

John Gennard is Institute of Personnel and Development Professor of Human Resource Management in the Department of Human Resource Management, University of Strathclyde. His most recent publication is *The History of the Society of Graphical and Allied Trades* (Routledge 1995).

Ward Griffiths is Corporate Resource Director and Deputy Chief Executive of Kent County Council. He is Vice-President of the Institute of Personnel and Development and has published widely on personnel and human resource management themes including 'Kent County Council: a case of local pay determination', *Human Resource Management Journal*, 1(1), 1990.

David Guest is Professor of Occupational Psychology at Birkbeck College, University of London. He has written and researched extensively on developments in HRM and personnel management and is also working on related issues of culture change and organizational commitment.

Laurie Hunter is Professor in Applied Economics in the Department of Social and Economic Research, University of Glasgow. His current research relates to the interface between industrial relations, human resource management and labour economics, e.g. labour market flexibility, customer supplier relations.

Jeff Hyman is Senior Lecturer in Industrial Relations in the Department of Human Resource Management at the University of Strathclyde. The most recent of his publications (co-authored with Bob Mason) is *Managing Employee Involvement and Participation* (Sage 1995).

James Kelly is Senior Lecturer in the Department of Human Resource Management, University of Strathclyde. He has written several articles on personnel management-related research.

Paul Kirkbride is Managing Director of The Change House, a Retained Associate at Ashridge Management College, and a Visiting Professor at the University of Hertfordshire. His consulting and research interests include strategic human resource management, international human resource management, international/cross-cultural management and organizational change and development. His recent publications include *Human Resource Management in Europe: Perspectives for the 1990s* (Routledge 1994).

Cliff Lockyer is Senior Lecturer in the Department of Human Resource Management at the University of Strathclyde. He worked as an industrial relations officer in the car industry before returning to academic life. For the past five years he has run a large quarterly survey of Scottish business and labour market trends. This has formed the basis for a series of research studies of skill shortages, employment trends, and training and selection practices.

Helen D. McIntosh is Lecturer in the Department of Business and Information Management, Napier University, Edinburgh, teaching mainly in the area of information management. Her research interests include women and new technology training, and supervised work experience for undergraduate students.

Alan McKinlay is Professor of Corporate Strategy, University of Stirling. His research interests include business history, the social history of work and contemporary changes in work organization. His most recent book is *The British Motor Industry* (Manchester University Press 1995).

Paul Miller is Lecturer in Business Policy and Director of the MBA Programme at the University of Newcastle upon Tyne. He has written on the intregration of HRM with business policy and also on economic development in small firms.

Chris Moore is Senior Lecturer in Public Management in the Department of Human Resource Management at the University of Strathclyde. His teaching and research interests are in various areas of public policy and in the development of public sector management. He has written several articles on these areas and is the co-author of two books: *Managing Competition* (Clarendon Press 1989) and *Local Partnership and the Unemployment Crisis in Britain* (Unwin Hyman 1989).

Nick Oliver is a Lecturer in Management Studies at the Judge Institute of Management Studies, University of Cambridge. His research interests include the operation of lean production systems in Japan and the West, and Japanese overseas investment. He is co-author (with Barry Wilkinson) of *The Japanization of British Industry* (Blackwell 1988), and has been involved in a number of benchmarking studies which have covered both manufacturing and new product development.

Harvie Ramsay is Professor of International Human Resource Management in the Department of Human Resource Management at the University of Strathclyde. He is co-author of *People's Capitalism: A critical analysis of profit sharing and employee share ownership* (Routledge 1989), and co-editor of *Information Technology and Workplace Democracy* (Routledge 1992).

Richard B. Sappey teaches Industrial Relations in the Faculty of Business at the Queensland University of Technology. He is co-author (with Marianne Winter) of *Australian Industrial Relations Practice* (Longman Cheshire). He has worked in the training and industrial relations fields with unions and international aid organizations.

Dora Scholarios is Lecturer in Organizational Analysis in the Department of Human Resource Management at the University of Strathclyde. She teaches and researches in the general areas of selection and assessment, psychometrics, and work and organizational psychology.

Ramsumair Singh is Lecturer in Industrial Relations at the University of Lancaster. He is a Chartered Electrical Engineer and Economist, with training and work experience with the General Electric Company and Texaco Trinidad. He has published on third-party intervention and industrial disputes and is an ACAS Arbitrator. His research interests include the impact of European Union law on industrial relations and he has published several articles in this field.

Ken Starkey is Professor of Corporate Strategy, University of Nottingham. He has published widely in corporate strategy and organizational theory. His most recent book (with Alan McKinlay) is *Strategy and the Human Resource: Ford and the search for competitive advantage* (Blackwell 1993).

George Strauss is Professor of Business Administration in the Department of Business Administration at the University of California, Berkeley, California, USA. Former president of the US Industrial Relations Research Association, he has written widely in the HRM field, his latest being 'Is the New Deal system collapsing? With what might it be replaced?', *Industrial Relations*, 34(2), 1995.

John A. Taylor is Professor of Management, Glasgow Caledonian University, where he helps to direct research in the Business Faculty. He has worked extensively on themes and issues related to the adoption by organizations of information and communication technologies. He has contributed to many books on this subject and has published in several academic journals, particularly those related to public policy and management. His forthcoming book is entitled *Government in the Information Age*.

Phil Taylor is a Research Fellow in the Department of Human Resource Management at the University of Strathclyde, currently engaged in an investigation of Sick Building Syndrome. He has recent joint publications on this subject and on industrial relations in the British shipbuilding industry.

Brian Towers is Professor of Industrial Relations in the Department of Human Resource Management, University of Strathclyde. He is founder and editor of the *Industrial Relations Journal* and editor of this *Handbook* and the *Handbook of Industrial Relations Practice*.

Barry Wilkinson is Professor of International Business, School of Management, University of Bath. He co-authored (with Nick Oliver) *The Japanization of British Industry* (Blackwell 1988). His area of research interest is the social impact of Japanese direct investment in the UK and elsewhere.

Allan Williams is Professor of Organizational and Occupational Psychology and Head of the Department of Business Studies at the City University Business School. He is also Director of the Centre for Personnel Research and Enterprise Development. His publications include the co-authored books *Changing Culture* (2nd edition, IPD 1993) and *The Competitive Consultant* (Macmillan 1994). Current research interests focus of organizational change and managerial competencies.

Jean Woodall is Reader in Human Resource Management at Kingston Business School. Her research interests include management development, and the implications of organizational restructuring for managerial careers. She is co-author (with Diana Winstanley) of *Management Development: strategy and practice* to be published by Blackwell in 1996.

Young-Ha Lee is Training Programme Manager, Seoul Training Centre, Korea Electric Power Co., Seoul, Korea. He completed his PhD, 'A Cross-cultural Comparison of Work Activities between Korean and Western Managers' at Glasgow University in 1994.

Foreword

WARD GRIFFITHS

The pace of change in the labour market and the world of work quickens. Organizations become more complex. In this country, as elsewhere, increasing numbers of employees encounter new working practices, restructuring and the pervasive effects of new technology. Trends suggest there will be more employees on temporary contracts and part-time work, particularly in the service sector. Women's employment continues to grow. There is a higher proportion of managerial and professional work. Contracting-out and outsourcing has mushroomed. The TUC General Secretary acknowledges that 'the speed of some of these changes has left trade unions gasping'.

In these circumstances the influence of the human resource management approach to employment relationships seems unlikely to recede. Never a wholly precise or definitive model, characteristics typical of HRM include line responsibility for people management; an integrating, 'business-based' approach to human resource processes; individualism rather than collectivism; and proactive people strategies aiming, for example, to develop increased employee commitment and morale. These are themes which many would feel are highly relevant to current trends in the labour market and the management of organizations.

There remains a continuing unease, even hostility in some quarters, to people practices and concepts which spring from the resource-based concept of the organization. Thus, if employees are viewed principally as an economic resource, concerns can arise over possible neglect of the total person; if HRM is mainly a vehicle for managerial control, what of this country's institutional traditions and patterns of joint regulation and collective bargaining? Yet previous challenges to

HRM in the UK as an ephemeral, fashion-led theory now seem to be less frequent, and no one denies that there are significant shifts in the nature of the employment relationship. Pragmatically, therefore, the best of HRM and of professional personnel management can inform one another in making progress towards securing new and effective 'psychological contracts' at work.

Trade unions certainly recognize HRM when they see it – and it has faced them with huge challenges. Typical has been the individualist forms of managing people, and the impact on employees of 'lean organization' techniques. The emergence from economic recession may refresh our collective bargaining and industrial relations/procedural frameworks. The TUC calls for the adoption of an agenda of social partnership. Yet many unions also pragmatically engage with HRM. They recognize it is an established, not transitory, manifestation of changed approaches to the management of employees.

The influence of HRM does seem to be having a continuing and significant impact on employment practices in this country. The relentless drive for performance improvement in pursuit of business goals suggests that HRM will be ubiquitous, in both unionized and non-unionized environments, in an increasingly fractionalized labour market.

All the more reason, therefore, to look for and define the movement's successes, and to track evidence of its positive impacts on the management of people at work. A vital need is to find ways of creating and sustaining continuous individual and organizational learning. Learning companies, recognizing the potential of sensitively and imaginatively applied HRM approaches, can position themselves for optimum employee motivation, performance and successful business outcomes.

For many practitioners in the UK the debate over whether HRM is a new and different model of people management, as opposed to an evolution of established personnel management trends, may be a relatively distant matter. But for all managers – whether in the line or in the personnel field – there is a need for well-researched, current and comparative information on positive developments in effective people management.

Once again Brian Towers and the contributors to this *Handbook* address that need. As in the earlier edition, they provide a comprehensive and well-informed resource combining contextual analysis, international perspectives and practical case studies. This book makes a positive contribution to understanding how best to take forward the continuing search for balance and compatibility between the interests of employers and employees.

Ward Griffiths
Corporate Resource Director and Deputy Chief Executive
Kent County Council

Vice-President
Organisation and Human Resource Planning
Institute of Personnel and Development

Introduction
Human Resource
Management: Into Maturity?

BRIAN TOWERS

The word 'maturity' also implies decline, senescence and eventual demise. Human resource management (HRM) may be seen as just another management fad – of limited life with others to follow – especially associated with the United States and prone to adopt its excesses without its virtues. It can even be argued, and has been, that HRM has been 'talked-up' by leading and influential academics in personnel management and industrial relations as a job-creation exercise for themselves and their colleagues; that is, through exaggerating the shift in business away from styles and policies rooted in a pluralist conflictual perspective of the employment relationship. This charge is also an exaggeration although academics do have some of this supposed influence as witness the rise and rise of peripatetic business school pundits with beguiling easy solutions to complex organizational problems.

Is HRM, therefore, made of enduring stuff? More specifically, how far does it describe a management strategy, or paradigm, associated with a defining set of practices which is both widespread in its incidence and distinguishable from other paradigms and practices? The answer to this question, which justifies the second edition of this volume, is positive but also qualified, not least because HRM does not always travel well, or remain the same, outside its American birthplace.

In the USA it is associated with non-unionism. But this need not be one of its distinguishing features since non-unionism is so widespread in that country that the overwhelming majority of locational decisions can be taken without considering the union option. Outside the USA the story is usually different. In countries with much stronger union presences HRM is far more likely to be the driving strategy in unionised operations – as research increasingly reveals. Management, in Britain for example, frequently chooses a dual, individualist/collectivist strategy rather than attacking unions or by-passing them (Storey 1992; Clark and Winchester 1994). In countries with a 'social partner' culture, for example Germany, the introduction of HRM-style practices (such as teamworking in the auto industry) can destabilize, or change, the roles and functions of works councils and shop stewards but without by-passing them. Indeed, the legitimation of German works councils formally prevents this, illustrating the force of different political, legal and institutional contexts in explaining the variety of the international experience of HRM (Turner 1991). Beyond Europe, to an even greater extent the lingua franca of HRM may use the same words but sometimes with different meanings and a sensitivity to national and regional variations in culture (Pieper 1990).

Yet there has been a search among academics for some commonality. Many commentators have followed the simple 'hard' and 'soft' dichotomy but this may have more resonance among the necessary simplicities of the lecture hall and the textbook than in the complexities and contradictions of the workplace. There, 'hard' may even have little connection with HRM and may better describe situations in which employees are treated as 'factors of production' (Millward 1992) rather than precious assets. Hence the more pragmatic, empirically based 'models' may be of more value, such as the 'shopping list' (Storey 1992); or the application of tests to assess HRM-proneness, for example, David Guest's (1987) essential goals of integration, commitment, flexibility and quality, which he again uses to good effect in the opening chapter of this volume – as well as Jean Woodall in chapter 15 on HRM and women.

As to the charge that academics have talked-up the growth of a new paradigm, it must be noted that there actually has been a transformation in management practices and industrial relations in the USA (Kochan et al. 1986). Unions and collective bargaining have been beating a disorderly retreat before advancing, aggressive management for over forty years. In the UK, too, unions and collective bargaining have been in rapid and continuing decline since 1979 (as is well known), although for reasons less clearly related to macho management styles – unlike in the USA.

To be sure, the 'subject' of HRM has developed rapidly since the first (1992) edition of this volume. It has been reinforced by the publication of numerous textbooks; the establishment of two specialised journals – one with 'international' in the title; and the publication of popular, widely disseminated articles in magazines such as *Personnel Management*, now significantly remodelled and renamed as *People Management*.

These academic developments are reflected in this volume but, as a 'handbook', it keeps to its own, practical, knitting – mainly, in the 'Practice' and 'Cases' sections. Here all the contributions have been revised, some extensively, and new chapters have been included, such as those on the public sector and information technology in Part II, and two new British case studies in Part III as well as two others on the widely differing experiences of managing in the national cultures of Ghana and Korea.

The growing maturity of a set of management practices that make special claims to merit and invite imitation should also increasingly attract sceptical appraisals and trenchant critiques – as in the revised 'sceptical' contribution by Ramsumair Singh and the new chapter by Jean Woodall which charge HRM with the neglect of the 'dimensions of employment diversity', that is, ethnicity, age, disability and gender. Alan McKinlay and Phil Taylor also tell a remarkable story, again in a new chapter, of worker resistance to, and adaptation of, HRM practices that threaten their natural collectivism. Additionally, an ethical perspective – now fashionable in some businesses and many business schools – is carefully developed and applied to HRM in Paul Miller's revised chapter.

Practice, though, has to be placed in its wider contexts with assessments as to how far those contexts are changing, and interacting with, organizations. This is the continuing purpose of Part I. All the chapters have been fully revised to reflect significant developments in the UK, other European countries, the USA and Australia between 1992 and 1996. Together, they also confirm the diversity and changing nature of HRM; and if it has reached maturity the next revised edition may begin to suggest the beginnings of old age. At all stages, though, it is the duty of both academics and practitioners to subject management innovations to critical evaluation and close scrutiny. This is the main purpose of this *Handbook of HRM*.

References

Clark, J. and Winchester, D. 1994: Management and trade unions. In Keith Sisson (ed.), *Personnel Management in Britain*, Oxford: Blackwell.

Guest, D. 1987: Human resource management and industrial relations. *Journal of Management Studies*, 24(5), 503–21.

Kochan, T.A., Katz, H.C. and McKersie, R.B. 1986: *The Transformation of American Industrial Relations*. New York: Basic Books.

Millward, N. 1994: *The New Industrial Relations*. London: Policy Studies Institute.

Pieper, R. 1990: *Human Resource Management: an international comparison.* Berlin and New York: de Gruyter.

Storey, J. 1992: *Developments in the Management of Human Resources.* Oxford: Blackwell.

Turner, Lowell 1991: *Democracy at Work: changing world markets and the future of labor unions.* Ithaca, N.Y., and London: Cornell University Press.

Part I
Contexts

1

Human Resource Management in the United Kingdom

DAVID GUEST

Introduction

We have now lived for a decade or more with the concept of human resource management (HRM). The term came to prominence in the UK during the 1980s, especially the second half of the decade. It aroused considerable interest in the academic community because it offered a potentially distinctive new approach to replace the traditional system of British industrial relations which, in any case, was under heavy attack from the government. And for industry it was an approach to management that seemed to fit comfortably with the spirit of the times. Now, well into the 1990s, the initial euphoria has disappeared, research data have begun to pour in and we are in a much better position to assess the impact of HRM in the UK.

An initial finding is that apparently many people in industry and commerce are deeply sceptical about the rhetoric and the language of HRM. In particular, they are unenthusiastic about the term 'human resource management'. The 1990 Workplace Industrial Relations Survey, an authoritative and comprehensive source of information about policy and practice, found that less than 1 per cent of workplace managers responsible for the management of human resources had adopted the title of human resource manager (Guest and Hoque 1993). When we look at the corporate centre in larger organizations, the picture changes a little. Marginson et al. (1993) in their company-level industrial relations survey found that 9 per cent used the human resource title. Other company-level surveys have reported a figure closer to 20 per cent. However, even this figure is lower than we might expect. It seems that connotations of manipulation and the view that human resources are like other resources, to be utilized or dispensed with as appropriate, does not appeal to the values of those responsible for managing people at work. Symbolically, the journal of the Institute of Personnel and Development has reflected this in its change of title, not to *Human Resource Management*, but to *People Management*.

There is something of a paradox in the antipathy to the term 'human resource management' since it appears to reflect a recognition that management of human resources should be closely integrated with business concerns and this is precisely what has been advocated for many years by professionals in the field, not least among the leading figures in the Institute of Personnel and Development. When an approach, supported by the language and rhetoric to reinforce it, becomes available, a sudden coyness appears. Perhaps it is not surprising that other managers sometimes display ambivalence about the business contribution of their colleagues in personnel departments.

In a post-modernist world, it would be dangerous to dismiss out of hand the rhetoric of language and job titles, but they reduce in importance if there is evidence that the work undertaken is effective. The endless debates about the nature of human resource management still seem to indicate that it is concerned with a set of policies and practices designed to achieve strategic integration, high employee commitment to the organization, a high degree of workforce flexibility and a high-quality workforce (Guest 1987). The policies and practices cover all aspects of personnel management, the key being how they are conceived and applied and the goals they are designed to achieve. For example, all jobs have to be designed in some way; the key is the assumptions about how to design jobs and the purposes behind a particular approach to job design. The expectation, or at least the working hypothesis, is that if the policies and practices achieve high integration, commitment, quality and flexibility, the result will be more-effective performance outcomes. The extent to which this is indeed the case provides one of the major contemporary research questions in the field. One way of assessing the current state of HRM in the UK is to determine how far we have progressed towards these four goals. In this chapter, we shall look briefly at each of these in turn.

Strategic Integration

Strategic integration, or what is sometimes called 'fit', lies at the heart of HRM. It is a complex issue covering a number of aspects.

The first concerns the link between the business strategy and HRM. The second aspect is the extent to which the various personnel policies and practices cohere and provide a consistent and comprehensive focus. The third is ownership of personnel policy and practice and in particular the extent to which it is integrated into the values of the organization and 'owned' by line managers. Strategic integration also implies that the policy goals of commitment, flexibility and quality are all pursued in a complementary way.

Integration of HRM strategy and business strategy

Brewster's (1994) evidence from the Cranfield/Price Waterhouse survey, which explores HRM policy and practice in most European countries, found that the HR function is represented at board level in 49 per cent of organizations (he only looked at those employing 200 or more). In the majority of cases, the personnel function claims to be involved in strategy development. The second Company Level Industrial Relations Survey (CLIRS2) (Marginson et al. 1993) found that there was a main board personnel director in 30 per cent of the companies although rather more used the title of 'director'. The data from the third Workplace Industrial Relations Survey (WIRS3) (Millward et al. 1992), however, notes that there was a small decline in board representation by personnel specialists in the second half of the 1980s. CLIRS2 confirms that personnel issues are often considered in key strategic decisions (usually in more than 75 per cent of the cases) but this does not necessarily mean involvement by personnel specialists. Not unexpectedly, there was some disagreement between finance and personnel directors about the amount of personnel department influence. CLIRS2 also revealed that personnel influence was markedly greater where there was a main board personnel director and that this was much more likely to be the case in foreign-owned as opposed to UK-owned companies.

It seems that personnel department involvement in strategic decisions is patchy and is probably not increasing much, even if personnel issues are more often considered. However, the company-level survey also suggests that the decisions are often concerned with implementation rather than formulation of strategy, a point reinforced by Purcell and Ahlstrand (1994) in their study of HRM in multi-divisional firms. Whatever the nature of the personnel department contribution, a study by Doherty, Tyson and Viney (see Guest et al. 1995) suggests that it is more highly valued in successful companies, although it would be presumptuous to assume any cause and effect.

Alongside these surveys concerning the role of personnel departments and personnel issues in strategy formulation and implementation, case study analysis raises doubts about how sensible it is to try to analyse strategic 'decisions'. The detailed case studies by Pettigrew and his colleagues in some of the better-known UK companies (Hendry and Pettigrew 1992; Pettigrew and Whipp 1991) and the more recent work by Tyson (1995) in a number of apparently successful companies reveal that the strategy process is complex, emergent and opportunistic – or what is sometimes described as 'flexible' and 'pragmatic'. In most cases there is no clear point where an HRM strategy is written, presented and agreed as a formal basis for action. This, at least, is the pattern among typical UK-owned companies. As Marginson et al. highlight with CLIRS2 data, it is possible to have a more consistent HRM strategy but it is the foreign-owned companies operating in the UK that are more likely to achieve this.

Despite the apparent preference for flexibility among UK organizations, there do appear to be circumstances in which it is helpful to give some systematic thought to HRM strategy, or at least to policy. A study by Guest and Peccei (1994), using an extensive sample of trusts and districts in the National Health Service, explored how far a range of personnel policies had been written down and actively endorsed or 'signed off' by the board. There was a considerable range of response. The issue assumed significance as one of the few indicators of HRM effectiveness. The more that policy areas had been actively endorsed by the board, the more positive were the ratings of HRM effectiveness by both senior personnel and line managers.

The implication of the work by Tyson on successful firms is that they can do very nicely without a formal or coherent strategic approach to HRM. Furthermore, such firms are driven by rather short-term financial market considerations, making flexibility a virtue. Recent American research has sought to demonstrate a link between strategic fit and performance. In particular it has tried to show that following the strategic prescriptions offered, for example, by Miles and Snow (1984), to link business strategy and HRM strategy, will result in superior performance (Huselid 1995). There is some evidence in one UK study, by Fox and McLeay (1992), which found a positive link between a strategic approach to HRM and firm performance, to suggest that it may be sensible to follow the foreign-owned firms in at least seeking some consistency in the strategic approach to HRM.

Integration of HRM policy and practice

There is less evidence about internal fit, the pattern of consistency among HRM policies. The evidence of Huselid and others in the USA suggests that there is a link between the use of more 'high-performance' HRM practices and company performance. However, there is some dispute about which variables should be included in the list of practices. The 1990 WIRS3 painted a rather gloomy picture about the use of HRM practices. The focus of the survey was on employee relations issues rather than the full range of HRM. Nevertheless, it found no establishment that claimed to have adopted the full range of employee relations practices included in the survey. In his more detailed analysis, Millward (1994) confirms that there has been some growth in the use of HRM practices but cautions against any assumption that there has been a widespread adoption of a full range of them.

Guest and Hoque (1994), looking more narrowly at greenfield sites, found quite a widespread adoption of HRM practices and no clear indication that UK-owned establishments were more reluctant to use them. There was also some evidence that establishments which had a strategic approach to an integrated set of practices reported better human resource and employee relations outcomes. The finding about the take-up of HRM in UK establishments needs to be replicated before we can have confidence in this conclusion. There are also of course problems in general surveys of this sort in determining what it means to be using practices such as quality circles or tests in selection. So while they might indicate an increase in interest in HRM practices they do not in themselves show effective integration.

Integration of line managers and HRM

The thinking behind this sort of integration is that, since line managers must do the day-to-day managing of employees, it is essential that they accept the values underpinning HRM and support HRM policy and practice. This is extremely difficult to assess. However, the case study evidence presented by Pettigrew and his colleagues and by Storey (1992) indicates that a large number of line managers do seem to be taking human resource issues seriously; and although it is difficult to demonstrate, the implication is that they are taking them more seriously. On the other hand, in contexts such as company take-overs, human resource issues still seem to be neglected until after the event. Tyson's work is more encouraging in the sense that the human resource contribution appears to be valued in successful companies. There is also evidence from sources such as the surveys by Poole and Mansfield (1993) of Institute of Management members to indicate that views about employee relations and about how to manage the workforce have been modified and come somewhat closer to the values associated with HRM over the decade of the 1980s.

The values of line managers become more of an issue as the possibility of decentralizing, devolving or giving away to line managers a range of personnel decisions becomes fashionable. As Wilkinson and Marchington (1994) note, this may indicate that responsibilities are being taken away rather than given away. On the basis of the limited amount of information available (see, for example, Adams 1991) it seems that decentralization to local personnel managers rather than to line managers is more likely to have occurred. It is, of course, possible that line managers are reluctant to take over activities they do not value highly. Nevertheless specific examples of major changes in values across a significant group of managers, such as that which has occurred at Rover, indicates the potential impact of line management's incorporation of a new set of values.

In summary, there has been much discussion about HRM strategy; there is some indication that human resource issues are more widely considered in strategic decisions. However, in many organizations there is no clear and consistent strategy. The judgement of UK firms seems to be that flexibility and speed of reaction to a rapidly changing external environment are the key to success. Purcell's (1989) conclusion at the end of the 1980s, that HRM is a second- or third-order strategic issue, still seems to hold good in many cases. Similarly, there has been a modest increase in the use of human resource practices but no rush to embrace them or to adopt a complete set of practices. Line managers seem more aware of human resource issues but there is little evidence that they are more committed to any set of values associated with HRM. Set against this, there are exceptions, more often found in foreign-owned firms, and there is a steady accumulation of evidence, none of it convincing on its own but beginning to combine into a consistent picture, suggesting that a more strategic approach, a fuller range of HRM practices and a greater valuing of HRM issues may be associated with more-successful firm performance.

Quality

The second element in the model of HRM, and one where the sustained interest might lead us to expect to see some progress, is quality. The 'quality movement' has been a part of the work scene for almost as long as HRM and contains a variety of elements. Some of these, such as just-in-time working and various forms of process control, can be singularly task- and production-focused. Arguably, they reflect a return to aspects of Taylorism and intensification of work, by-passing the rhetoric of HRM. However, there is another 'softer' dimension of quality which suggests that it is achieved through people and in which HRM is central. This perspective has three main elements. The first is the quality of the workforce, which will often be a function of the selection and training and development policies. The second is the quality of the management of the workforce, which is likely to be more deeply embedded in the culture and in particular the reward systems for managers. The third is the quality of the HRM policy and practice and the reputation the firm gains for its management of the workforce. There is, of course, the overriding concern for the quality of work undertaken, of the goods and services provided and therefore the satisfaction of customer requirements. Arguably, quality of customer service will be partly a function of the quality of management of human resources.

HRM is closely linked to quality through the issues of quality of employees and management of the quality system and wider organization system. Giles and Williams (1991) have suggested that quality provides 'a chance in a lifetime for personnel managers'. The obvious input, although it is not what Giles and Williams were referring to, is through training and improving the quality of the workforce. In recent years, training issues have figured quite highly in the national debate. There has been an attempt to raise general standards through a national system of technical qualifications and competencies. The various Lead Bodies have devised standards of progressive qualification which have been slowly if not enthusiastically adopted. There has been some indication of increased expenditure on training and development. On the other hand, we must be cautious about placing too much emphasis on financial data. Japanese companies typically report low training expenditure because training is built into the job of the supervisor or superior. In the UK, there is a growing realization of the need to create an environment in which training and learning can flourish. The chief manifestation of this is the concept of 'The Learning Organization'. Ideally, this is an organization in which learning is a continuous process. While this is an appealing idea, such evidence as is available suggests that the concept of the learning organization is more rhetoric than reality.

Another potentially strong link between HRM and quality comes through TQM, or Total Quality Management. This is a more embracing approach to quality which, as Hill (1991), for example suggests, involves a change in organizational culture and in mind set if it is to succeed. One of the changes required is from external to internal control and commitment to quality. Hill, on the basis of his case study analysis, believes that it has a reasonable chance of succeeding as an approach. One of the key ways in which this links with HRM is in the need for a shift in the underlying values from an approach based on control of a compliant workforce by management to a workforce exercising self-control and committed to organizational values and high quality. A key element in the success of quality and HRM initiatives will therefore be the commitment of senior and middle management to a style of managing that reflects this approach. Where this can be achieved, there is a real chance of significant culture change.

Case study evidence presented by Wilkinson and Marchington (1994) shows a range of personnel contributions to TQM. However, the personnel managers they studied generally operated with a restricted view of the goals of TQM. Their cases show that TQM is not based on significant culture change and commitment but on pragmatic steps to improve local performance within existing hierarchies. This is closer to the 'hard' version of TQM and reflects the role of personnel managers as what Legge (1978) termed 'conformist innovators'. This is reinforced in an earlier paper (Wilkinson et al. 1992) which shows that the typical UK view of TQM is as a top-management-controlled initiative driven by business concerns based around greater customer focus. In this view, the need to improve the human resource dimension is given relatively low status. Employee involvement is limited and the emphasis on trust, commitment and self-control is neglected. It is therefore not too surprising that, after initial enthusiasm, such TQM initiatives run into the sand, managers are disappointed about lack of progress and employees are disappointed about the lack of real involvement.

On the basis of this evidence, the potential for TQM noted by Hill is not being realized. The human resource dimension and the related cultural change is not being considered sufficiently and the commitment of management is short-term and partial. Even those companies that explicitly claim to be pursuing culture change linked to TQM run into difficulties. The route to culture change typically adopted is through training, often using an imported package. Organizations such as British Rail invested many millions of pounds in these programmes at a time when they were going though many other changes, so quality was not uppermost in the minds of many managers. It appears that such investments are often likely to be wasted. Successful TQM requires a major long-term investment – a long-term strategy. It may be no coincidence that up to and including 1995, all the winners of the European Quality Award have been non-European companies with a long-term investment in quality.

At an individual level, it is possible to model what training for quality entails. An interesting attempt to do this has been reported by Peccei and Wood (1995), who explored the antecedents of the concept of 'quality consciousness', defined broadly as a positive approach towards taking quality issues seriously. In their study, they found that a supportive quality-orientated organizational climate was the best predictor of quality consciousness. They explored this concept in the context of a training intervention. They found that training in quality-related issues had an impact only if the employee evaluated the training experience positively. However, since that evaluation might be shaped by expectations derived from the existing quality climate in the organization, a positive evaluation could be blocked by the very feature the training is partly intended to change: the state of the general organizational climate as it affects quality. It may not matter how good the training is if people do not see it as relevant or applicable. In such contexts, reactions will be negative, resulting in a failure to transfer any learning. Certainly, the view of those who have explored UK experience of quality initiatives (see, for example, Dale and Cooper 1992) are highly critical of the failure to follow up and reinforce training. Wilkinson and Marchington (1994) take a similar view.

The picture emerging in the UK is one in which the importance of taking seriously issues such as training and quality of management of human resources is widely acknowledged. The 'our people are our most important asset' cliché is still frequently displayed in company reports. Yet the practice shows that in most cases the steps towards this become bureaucratized and channelled into formal training without the cultural change to support it. And the model of quality is too narrow and task-orientated to be effective. Greater organization-wide cultural change is necessary if quality initiatives are to have a lasting impact. The HRM dimensions of quality must be part of the strategic integration to ensure that a high-quality workforce and management of the workforce has a positive impact on performance. To date, this has too rarely been the case.

Flexibility

The third human resource outcome is a highly flexible workforce. During the 1980s the subject of flexibility became a topic of considerable debate, partly shaped by the influential Institute of Manpower Studies (now Employment Studies) model (Atkinson 1984). Based on this, it is possible to identify various types of flexibility which, it was suggested, could be combined to form part of a coherent strategy – what became known as the flexible firm.

Four main types of flexibility are usually identified. The first is flexibility of work time and in particular the use of a stock of part-time workers. The second is contract flexibility, the opportunity to employ people on very short-term or fixed-term contracts or even to employ significant numbers of temporary workers. The third aspect is flexibility of rewards, increasing the proportion of variable pay but also examining the possibility of broadening the concept of reward and deferring some aspects of rewards. The final type of flexibility is functional flexibility. This implies designing jobs or groups of jobs in such as way as to make full use of human resources. It might imply broadening and deepening the range of activities required of an employee.

Although all aspects of flexibility are relevant to personnel management, it is functional flexibility which is particularly relevant to HRM. However, it is the others that have attracted the most attention. In part this reflects a difference of priority between those who want to improve efficiency by increasing the proportion of labour and labour costs that are variable rather than fixed and those who are more interested in making full use of existing resources. Of course, the two approaches are not necessarily incompatible, but there are potential problems in trying to reconcile them. The way of reconciling them advocated by Atkinson is to create a flexible firm by separating out the core from the peripheral workforce. Functional flexibility could then be applied to the core workforce. However, it is sometimes difficult to identify the appropriate boundary between the core and periphery and there is a risk that the core may not feel comfortable in an environment where they work alongside temporary or fixed-term contract staff; it may alter their perceived psychological contract and hence their commitment to the organization.

There is little evidence that firms have adopted a strategy which corresponds in any way to the core/periphery distinction. In the late 1980s, Hakim (1990) found that very few firms had deliberately adopted a strategy of workforce flexibility. Where it was being pursued, it was opportunistically rather than strategically. A year or two later, Hunter and his colleagues (Hunter et al. 1993) reported a similar finding. They were unable to demonstrate a growth in adoption of an integrated, carefully thought through strategy on flexibility, designed to fit with the direction of the business.

Even at the national level, the growth of flexible forms of working should not be overstated. For example the Conservative government opted out of the Social Chapter partly to permit greater flexibility of work practices and the opportunity to copy America in creating more jobs. Yet the evidence is that the UK has been rather unsuccessful in creating jobs over the past two decades. Furthermore, it is clear that some European countries still make greater use than the UK of part-time and temporary workers. The Cranfield/Price Waterhouse surveys have consistently shown that the UK is well behind some of its European partners in its practice of some forms of flexibility; EU statistics confirm this pattern.

Trends in flexible working are well summarised by Beatson (1995). He reports that the proportion of part-time jobs, defined as those involving 30 hours a week or less, rose from 19 per cent of all jobs in 1978 to 28 per cent in 1994. Contrary to popular belief, growth in part-time working was greater in the 1970s than in the 1980s. Furthermore, the increase is not evenly spread. It has occurred mainly in a limited range of service jobs, particularly in retailing. In hotels and catering the figure has always been high, while in manufacturing there is no real evidence of any increase in part-time working during the 1980s and into the early 1990s. Indeed, about three-quarters of the growth in the 1980s can be accounted for by structural changes in employment. There has been little overall growth in such things as fixed-term contracts, temporary work, home or teleworking, or other much-debated approaches. There appears to have been an increase in subcontracting, outsourcing and the use of contract staff, determined partly by the government's insistence on the use of compulsory competitive tendering in parts of the public sector, but there are no good data on how extensive this is. There has been some growth in the use of flexitime and of annualized hours, and overtime remains as popular as ever. Finally, we know that there has been a growth in the use of incentive payment schemes, including profit-sharing and employee share ownership. However, it is not clear that there has been a marked increase in the amount of basic pay that is at risk, which is perhaps the key indicator of flexibility.

There is very little comprehensive evidence about the growth of functional flexibility. However, there are a number of sources of indirect evidence. The first is that it is apparent that there has been a steady intensification of work among those in employment. The second is that the early 1980s saw a series of flexibility agreements which resulted in a short-term boost in productivity (Marsden and Thompson 1990). Since then there have been further, less highly publicized agreements and a range of company policies to break down remaining demarcations between classes of job. The whole concept of process re-engineering is an extension of this approach.

The logical point to reach in the pursuit of functional, flexibility is reflected in Bridge's (1995) notion of 'Jobshift' or the idea of the end of the job. Although he overstates his case, the idea is that multi-skilled people work in flexible project teams. Their employment is built around the project, and their continued employment depends on demonstrated ability to contribute to the successful completion of the project. This model has existed for many years in fields such as management consultancy, in research and development work and in a number of service areas such advertising. There is some doubt about how far we can take this into other areas of work.

Watson and Fothergill (1993) have explored employee reactions to aspects of flexible working. They found that most part-time work-ers choose that work for a variety of reasons related to their lifestyle. They distinguished between voluntary part-timers, much the largest category, involuntary part-timers who would prefer full-time work, and involuntary part-timers who needed the money. Using evidence from the 1994 labour Force Survey, it appears that only 13 per cent were part-timers because they could not find full-time employment, implying that the trends reflect more than company strategy; they are also a response to supply-side factors among the workforce. Temporary work is rather different: 43 per cent said they were en-gaged in temporary work because they could not find permanent work. The statistics also show that the growth in self-employment has been driven largely by a desire of people to have more freedom and autonomy: only 13 per cent said they had become self-employed as a result of becoming unemployed. Even allowing for some under-statement, this is a low response and again suggests that firms are not pursuing an aggressive policy of flexibility which they impose on a reluctant workforce.

WIRS3 asked few questions relating to functional flexibility. However, it did explore increases in employee involvement and asked about specific types of initiative. Among the 43 per cent who had taken some sort of initiative in the past three years, only 2 per cent mentioned autonomous work groups and 2 per cent mentioned quality circles. None of the other types of initiative could be construed as potentially leading to greater functional flexibility. A survey by Guest and Hoque (1994) of developments in greenfield sites and in a comparison group of older establishments found a more positive picture, perhaps because the topics were raised explicitly. Across both greenfield and older sites, over 75 per cent claimed to have flexible job descriptions not linked to one specific task. Over 44 per cent claimed to deliberately design jobs to make full use of workers' skills and abilities; and over 67 per cent claimed to organize work around teams for the majority of staff. If these figures are correct, they indicate a large level of functional flexibility. They do not, of course, show that this is part of a coherent strategy.

In summary, there is evidence of some moves to increase various types of flexibility. However, there is little sign that this reflects a coherent company strategy. Indeed, it seems to reflect either a desire to increase efficiency by cutting costs in an opportunistic and piece-meal way or a tendency to follow fashion. In all but a few cases, changes have been relatively limited and it is important not to be misled into believing that increases in part-time working, fixed-term contracts and self-employment represent a dramatic shift in employment practice. It also follows that the kind of functional flexibility most closely associated with a model of HRM that gives weight to full utilization of human resources has not received the priority that advocates of HRM or enthusiasts like Bridges believe it deserves.

Organizational Commitment

The final human resource outcome we might look for is evidence of increasing commitment to the organization among employees. The logic of this is that investment in high employee quality will only be repaid by long tenure among functionally flexible workers. This can more easily be achieved if employees display high commitment to the organization. Antecedents of commitment include perceptions of fairness, met expectations and an opportunity to exercise responsibility. In an environment where the fashion is to promote flexibility of contracts and to reduce security, it might be argued that the expectations associated with the traditional psychological contract are being transgressed.

There is very little evidence about changes in levels of commitment among UK workers. In one of the few surveys across organizations, Fletcher and Williams (1992) report relatively low levels of commitment in nine organizations. Similarly, in a comparative study in the electronics industry, Guest and Dewe (1991) found that the typical employee response was to display low commitment to both company and union. This contrasts with the higher levels of commitment displayed in countries such as Sweden and Germany. An evaluation of an explicit attempt to enhance organizational commitment through employee involvement in British Rail, based on careful longitudinal analysis using control groups, revealed no significant change in commitment (Guest and Peccei 1995). One implication of this is that after the initial entry phase into an organization, organizational commitment is relatively stable. On the other hand, Morris et al. (1993), using a management sample, suggest that HRM policy and practice can modify organizational commitment, and that career prospects are particularly influential.

The typical routes to change in organizational commitment are either by changing corporate culture or by increasing employee involvement. A variety of initiatives to increase employee involvement have been introduced in the UK in the past decade. Various forms of financial participation have been particularly encouraged by the government. As noted earlier, WIRS3 found that 43 per cent of establishments had introduced an employee involvement initiative in the previous three years. Much the most widely reported concerned either one-way or two-way communication and flow of information. This type of involvement seems more likely to be directed at commitment rather than flexibility. Marchington et al. (1993) conducted a careful evaluation of a number of these initiatives. The best were able to show a modest positive impact on general employee attitudes. However, the researchers were somewhat sceptical about the motives behind many of the initiatives. They showed that they quite often stemmed from a desire by particular managers to further their careers by promoting a currently fashionable idea and thereby demonstrating their ability to innovate at the leading edge of current thinking. The particular form of employee involvement adopted seemed to reflect the latest fad and the whole process was driven less by a deep interest in employee involvement than by a desire for career advancement. Not surprisingly, such initiatives quickly faded either when the ploy succeeded and the manager moved on or when the fashion changed and a new fad arrived.

Changes in organizational culture are even more difficult to assess. There is some general indication from a few well-publicized cases, such as British Airways or Rover, that culture change can lead to a more committed workforce; and in these cases the type of HRM intended to promote quality, flexibility and commitment has been both an objective of the change and a part of the process of change. But there are too few cases where there is convincing evidence of a change in organizational commitment for us to have confidence that this is a generally feasible route to follow.

At managerial levels we can expect to see a reduction in organizational commitment as ideas about a new psychological contract become more widespread and individuals are expected to display more self-reliance in managing their own careers, rather than rely on the company to provide the traditional career path. In this context, it is the most effective and resilient workers who will transfer commitment to their own personal careers rather than to the company. The suggested answer is to provide a new psychological contract in which the experience in the company provides the individual with development opportunities, with challenging work, and thereby with greater career marketability. To date, it is not clear that many organizations have developed policies which allow this approach to be put into practice.

In summary, although we have seen steps taken to increase organizational commitment, there is little good evidence that it has changed. One factor may be the wider economic climate. The typical strategy of increasing competitiveness by cutting back on staff costs engenders a sense of insecurity and is unlikely to encourage a sense of trust and commitment in a company. It requires very special long-term action demonstrating reciprocal commitment before employees display increased levels of commitment to their employing organization. To date, too many of the initiatives have been one-way or have focused on a limited view of commitment tied to financial inducements.

The Impact of Human Resource Management

The previous sections have revealed progress towards achieving HRM goals that could be described as piecemeal at best. Broadly, concern for efficiency has overridden concern for effectiveness and full utilization. There is little sign of strategic intent to seek a more integrated approach to effective management of the workforce. We might therefore expect to see little evidence that HRM has had a positive impact on performance.

Inevitably evidence is hard to come by, mainly because it is difficult to establish cause and effect. One way around this is to introduce statistical controls for as many variables as possible. This is the approach which has sometimes been adopted when using major surveys such as WIRS3, although doing so has not been without controversy. WIRS3 is not ideally suited to any assessment of the impact of HRM since it concentrates on issues more typically associated with employee relations and it omits most aspects of strategic integration. Fernie and Metcalf (1995) have marshalled the data and conclude that there is no consistent evidence that those measures more associated with HRM are in turn associated with superior outcomes. A slightly more positive, albeit cautiously positive, conclusion is reached in a separate and somewhat different analysis of the same data by Guest and Hoque (see Guest et al. 1995). They also reach a more positive conclusion based on their analysis of greenfield sites. Those with a clear strategy and a high uptake of HRM practices report better HRM outcomes, such as commitment and quality, and better industrial relations outcomes, such as less industrial conflict. However, the performance outcomes, while tending to be superior, are not significantly so. In using these studies care must be taken because the outcomes are measured using self-report data. As a result, the jury is still out on the impact of HRM on organizational performance in the UK.

Conclusions

This brief review suggests that progress in HRM in the UK has been slow and rather crab-like. Companies have approached the issue tentatively rather than throwing caution to the wind and embracing HRM wholeheartedly. Yet most movement has been positive, including some which this survey has not revealed. One factor is the change in attitude of the trade unions, which are now much more open and sometimes even positive about HRM, as long as they have a part to play in its introduction and operation. We know from WIRS3 that unionized workplaces are more likely to have adopted certain types of HRM.

Another important advance is the increase in the number of demonstration cases. Of course, successful illustrations of the impact of HRM are highly atypical. But they do show what can be done and, if we avoid the hyperbole that is sometimes associated with such cases, we can learn much from them. HRM can be introduced in the UK and it can have a positive impact. However, as long as senior managers retain their short-term perspective and display limited enthusiasm for any notion of a consistent strategy, then it is unlikely to have much impact across the field of industry. It will remain a subject of fads and fashions and a focus of justifiable scepticism.

References

Adams, K. 1991: Externalization vs specialization: what is happening to personnel? *Human Resource Management Journal*, 1(4), 40–54.

Atkinson, J. 1984: Manpower strategies for flexible organizations. *Personnel Management*, 16, August, 20–4.

Beatson, M. 1995: *Labour Market Flexibility*. Employment Department Research Series no. 48. Sheffield: Employment Department.

Brewster, C. 1994: The integration of human resource management and corporate strategy. In A. Hegewisch and C. Brewster (eds), *Policy and Practice in European HRM*, London: Routledge.

Bridges, W. 1995: *Jobshift*. London: Nicholas Brealey.

Dale, B. and Cooper, C. 1992: *Total Quality Management and Human Resources: an executive guide*. Oxford: Blackwell.

Fernie, S. and Metcalf, D. 1995: Participation, contingent pay, representation and workplace performance: evidence from Great Britain. *British Journal of Industrial Relations*, 33(3), 379–415.

Fletcher, C. and Williams, R. 1992: Organizational experience. In S. Bevan, M. Thompson, C. Fletcher and R. Williams, *Performance Management in the UK*, London: IPM.

Fox, S. and McLeay, S. 1992: An approach to researching managerial labour markets: HRM, corporate strategy and financial performance in UK manufacturing. *International Journal of Human Resource Management*, 3(3), 523–54.

Giles, E. and Williams, R. 1991: Can the personnel department survive quality management? *Personnel Management*, April, 28–33.

Guest, D. 1987: Human resource management and industrial relations. *Journal of Management Studies*, 24(5), 302–21.

Guest, D. and Dewe, P. 1991: Company or trade union: which wins workers' allegiance? A study of commitment in the UK electronics industry. *British Journal of Industrial Relations*, 29(1), 75–96.

Guest, D. and Hoque, K. 1993: The mystery of the missing human resource manager. *Personnel Management*, June, 40–1.

24   *Contexts*

Guest, D. and Hoque, K. 1994: *Human Resource Management in Greenfield Sites: preliminary survey results*, Working Paper no. 530. London: London School of Economics.

Guest, D. and Peccei, R. 1994: The nature and causes of effective human resource management. *British Journal of Industrial Relations*, 32(2), 221–42.

Guest, D. and Peccei, R. 1995: A test of the feasibility of changing organizational commitment. London: Birkbeck College, Dept of Organizational Psychology, mimeo.

Guest. D., Tyson, S., Doherty, N., Hoque, K. and Viney, C. 1995: *The Contribution of Personnel Management to Organizational Performance: moving the debate along*, IPD Research Issues no. 9. London: IPD.

Hakim, C. 1990: Core and periphery in employers' workforce strategies; evidence from the 1987 ELUS survey. *Work, Employment and Society*, 4(1), 157–88.

Hendry, C. and Pettigrew, A. 1992: Patterns of strategic change in the development of human resource management. *British Journal of Management*, 3(3), 137–56.

Hill, S. 1991: Why quality circles failed but total quality management might succeed. *British Journal of Industrial Relations*, 29(4), 541–68.

Hunter, L., McGregor, A., MacInnes, J. and Sproull, A. 1993: The 'flexible firm': strategy and segmentation. *British Journal of Industrial Relations*, 31(3), 383–407.

Huselid, M. 1995: The impact of human resource management practices on turnover, productivity and corporate financial performance. *Academy of Management Journal*, 38, 635–70.

Legge, K. 1978: *Power, Innovation and Problem-solving in Personnel Management*. London: McGraw-Hill.

Marchington, M., Wilkinson, A., Ackers, P. and Goodman, J. 1993: The influence of managerial relations on waves of employee involvement. *British Journal of Industrial Relations*, 31(4), 553–76.

Marginson, P., Armstrong, P., Edwards, P., Purcell, J. and Hubbard, N. 1993: *The Control of Industrial Relations in Large Companies: an initial analysis of the second company level industrial relations survey*, Warwick Papers in Industrial Relations no. 45. Coventry: IRRU, University of Warwick.

Marsden, D. and Thompson, M. 1990: Flexibility agreements and their significance in the increase in productivity in British manufacturing since 1980. *Work, Employment and Society*, 4(1), 83–104.

Miles, R. and Snow, C. 1984: Designing strategic human resource systems. *Organizational Dynamics*, Summer, 36–52.

Millward, N. 1994: *The New Industrial Relations*. London: PSI.

Millward, N., Stevens, M., Smart, D. and Hawes, W. 1992: *Workplace Industrial Relations in Transition*. Aldershot: Dartmouth.

Morris, T., Lydka, H. and Fenton O'Creevy, M. 1993: Can commitment be managed? A longitudinal analysis of employee commitment and human resource practices. *Human Resource Management Journal*, 3(3), 21–42.

Peccei, R. and Wood, S. 1995: The impact of total quality management on quality consciousness. London: London School of Economics, Department of Industrial Relations, mimeo.

Pettigrew, A. and Whipp, R. 1991: *Managing Change for Competitive Success.* Oxford: Blackwell.

Poole, M. and Mansfield, R. 1993: Patterns of continuity and change in managerial attitudes and behaviour in industrial relations 1980–1990. *British Journal of Industrial Relations,* 31(1), 11–35.

Purcell, J. 1989: Corporate strategy and human resource management. In J. Storey (ed.), *New Perspectives on Human Resource Management.* London: Routledge.

Purcell, J. and Ahlstrand, B. 1994: *Human Resource Management in the Multi-divisional Company.* Oxford: Oxford University Press.

Storey, J. 1992: *Developments in the Management of Human Resources.* Oxford: Blackwell.

Tyson, S. 1995: *Human Resource Strategy: towards a general theory of human resource management.* London: Pitman.

Watson, G. and Fothergill, B. 1993: Part-time employment and attitudes to part-time work. *Employment Gazette,* May, 213–20.

Wilkinson, A. and Marchington, M. 1994: TQM: instant pudding for the personnel function? *Human Resource Management Journal,* 5(1), 33–49.

Wilkinson, A., Marchington, M., Goodman, J. and Ackers, P. 1992: Total quality management and employee involvement. *Human Resource Management Journal,* 2(4), 1–20.

2

Human Resource Management in the USA

GEORGE STRAUSS

This is a brief sketch of the main issues facing human resources management (HRM) in the United States during the late 1990s. It will focus on policy issues rather than techniques, though the latter are of great importance to practitioners. Three themes run through this discussion. The first is the tension between the ideal of high-commitment management (based on employee involvement) and the growing emphasis on lean and mean management (concerned chiefly with continual cost-cutting). The second relates to the public regulation of the HR function. And the third looks at the search for new forms of compensation and the necessity for dealing with increasingly costly fringe benefits.

Please note that the term 'HRM' is used in the broad, American sense, to cover employment relations generally, rather than in the more restricted sense, sometimes common in the United Kingdom, as a managerial counterpart of Thatcherism.

Managerial Policies

Historical background

Personnel, as a function, can be traced back to before 1900 (Jacoby 1985). It grew in status during the 1930s and 1940s largely because of the wartime labour shortage, the union threat and the later need (in many companies) to adjust to being unionized. Then as union–management relations 'matured' and became routinized, other, seemingly more pressing functions, such as production, marketing, finance and law, began to receive the bulk of top management's attention.

In the early 1970s things began to change again. New laws, dealing with equal employment opportunities, safety and the like, forced radical changes in HR procedures. These developments in turn raised HR specialists' status and budget. In the late 1970s, as the economic climate turned sour, many top managements began to view HR policies as critical for reducing costs, increasing organizational flexibility and even insuring survival. Industrial relations, personnel and organization development policies became increasingly closely co-ordinated (Kochan and Cappelli 1984).

In some cases this meant using hard-ball tactics to keep unions out of non-union worksites and to extract deep economic concessions at locations where unions already existed. In other instances, it involved developing co-operative high-commitment workplaces. Regardless of strategy, management's purpose was to increase efficiency and soften the effects of rigid work rules, often developed for an earlier technology. In general, however (particularly where the companies employed few blue-collar workers), policy toward unions was subsidiary to broader interests, especially efficiency and flexibility. Indeed – a point to be stressed – HRM in most companies is primarily concerned with managers and other white-collar employees, not the declining numbers of blue-collar workers.

Many of the new initiatives came from top management. As top management demonstrated greater interest in HR *policies*, the status and perhaps the clout of the newly named human resources *departments* seemed to grow, at least for a while. As a consequence, according to a *Wall Street Journal* article (27 April 1983, p. 1), former personnel workers received 'at least 30 per cent higher pay . . . if the company uses the trendy "human resources" title'.

Meanwhile, two somewhat conflicting HRM philosophies – *high commitment* and *lean and mean* – began to contend for management's support. The victory of lean and mean often meant the displacement of HR personnel, who were viewed as insufficiently committed to the new policies of 'slash and burn' job-cutting.

High-commitment policies

Beginning in the 1980s there was much discussion of 'high-commitment' policies, though perhaps more talk than practice. These policies were designed to develop broadly trained employees who identified with their organization and who were prepared and trusted to exercise high orders of discretion (Lawler 1986). In return for this, presumably, came a commitment from the firm to provide employment security and the opportunity to develop a satisfying *career* (not just a job). Key components of this strategy included participation, employment security, career flexibility, individual job rights and performance-based compensation. Indeed, some argued that these policies could be effective only if linked together in a 'cluster' or 'bundle' of policies which were consistent both with each other and with the firm's strategy and technology (Levine 1995). For example, the policies would work better in firms which stressed quality rather than cost.

High-commitment policies required heavy investment in human capital and, in some ways, were like the stereotype of Japanese management. But unlike Japanese management, they gave employees a considerable amount of free choice and individual rights.

An advantage of these policies was that they gave management the flexibility to move employees from one job to another. A disadvantage was that the emphasis on employment security tended to convert employment costs into fixed costs, thus reducing management's overall flexibility.

Some of the early leaders in this development, IBM and Hewlett-Packard, for example, were non-union. However, General Motors' new Saturn Division, NUMMI (the GM–Toyota joint venture) and Xerox showed that equally innovative plans could be adopted in genuine collaboration with unions. After all, there is nothing basically inconsistent between high-commitment HR and collective bargaining. In fact, the chances of non-union firms backsliding from their good intentions are much reduced if they are unionized.

Mean and lean policies

Some call high-commitment organization the wave of the future; others see it as the fad of the month. But if it is the wave of the future, this wave has hit some big rocks. These take the form of the recent stress on 'lean and mean' management (Harrison 1994) which is more concerned with cutting costs than developing human resources.

American corporations have gone through a series of hostile takeovers and leveraged buyouts. Quite often these organizations have emerged with high debt levels and a desperate need or cash flow. On top of this, as major US companies began posting lacklustre profits, once-docile boards of directors became restless. Show better results, they told their CEOs, or be fired. And many were fired, including the CEOs of IBM, GM, American Express, Westinghouse and Kodak. So the message went out: cost-cutting comes before human resources development. Firm after firm has sought to become 'mean and lean' through almost continual 'restructuring' and 'downsizing'. GM reduced its employment by over 200,000, IBM by 175,000. Total employment in major (Fortune 500) companies dropped by 30 per cent. Managerial positions, which once were viewed as sacrosanct, have become just as much at risk as blue-collar jobs. In many cases career employees have been replaced with contingent ones (see discussion below, p. 32) or work has been subcontracted. In the process, labour (even managerial labour) has been made a variable cost. Indeed, downsizing has resulted in heavy cuts in 'fringe' activities, including HRM.

As we shall see, some firms have attempted to salvage what's left of their high-commitment culture. At the moment, however, disinvestment in human resources seems to predominate over high commitment. In the long term this trend may switch.

Employee involvement and participation

Expanded employee involvement (EI) is at the heart of the high-commitment strategy, and there has been much experimentation with various forms of participation, even in firms which otherwise are 'mean and lean' (Strauss 1992). EI, it is hoped, will increase employee satisfaction and commitment *as well* as organizational effectiveness. If successful, all parties gain.

EI is hardly new. Informal participation, as a style of consultative management, has been preached for a long time, but the last few years have seen a considerable increase in *formal* participation schemes. These schemes can be grouped under four heads: (a) problem-solving groups such as quality circles, which make recommendations to management; (b) work teams, which enjoy various degrees of autonomy in making decisions; (c) total quality management; and (d) representative joint union–management or employee–management committees (see Ramsay, chapter 11). The first three seem to have proliferated more widely in the USA than in Britain (compare Millward et al. 1992 with Osterman 1994). For example, according to a 1992 survey, at least half the workforce participated in teams in 41 percent of the establishments surveyed. Representative committees exist primarily in the unionized sector since such committees are legally suspect in non-union plants if they 'deal' with management regarding 'working conditions'.

One of the most successful recent turnabouts in American industry occurred at NUMMI, the joint GM–Toyota venture located at GM's former drugs–absenteeism–poor-labour-relations plagued Fremont, California, plant. Using almost the same technology and employees as the old plant, NUMMI has now zoomed close to the top in productivity and lowest in absenteeism. Here 'work teams' are responsible for planning job rotation, balancing work assignments to equalize work loads and engaging in *kaizen* (continuous job improvement). Team leaders, who remain union members, are selected on the basis of recommendations of a joint union–management committee (Adler 1992).

According to the limited research to date, most EI schemes in the USA succeed in bettering *something*. They increase satisfaction, productivity or quality, or they improve turnover, safety or union–management relations. A problem in the USA, as in the UK (MacInnes 1985), is that many of these schemes are short-lived. They succumb to a variety of ills: opposition (or merely half-hearted support) by unions, workers, supervisors or top management; problems with regards to equitable compensation; and distrust, too-high expectations and burnout. For example, management may give work teams too little discretion. Multi-skilling, which often accompanies the use of work-teams, may merely give management greater flexibility to move employees arbitrarily. Indeed, EI is not totally inconsistent with 'lean and mean'. Workers are told in effect: Cut costs participatively – or lose your jobs! Often the main purpose of teams is to permit the elimination of a layer of supervisors.

In any case EI appears to be more than a fad. Teamwork, at least, seems to be here to stay.

Work schedules and careers

Many workers are more concerned with *when* they work than in participating *at* work. This is shown by the considerable interest in new approaches to work scheduling, such as the compressed work week, flexitime and job sharing, as well as the expansion of an older arrangement: part-time work. And 'telecommuting', the opportunity to work at home via computers, has become more popular. Oldsmobile, for example, has eliminated many of its sales offices, and require their salespersons to do their clerical work at home.

For some workers, these new schedules represent a changing lifestyle which downgrades work as a source of satisfaction. But for many women and some men it is important chiefly as an opportunity to combine work with family life. Indeed, work schedules have become a major issue for some women's groups.

The demand for change is expressed most frequently by university graduates and MBA-trained women who are competing with men for managerial careers. For some women the 'mummy track', which slows the promotion timetable enough to allow for family obligations, meets the need. For others it does not. Lately, neo-feminists have become interested not just in equality on the job, but in equality *plus* the chance to bring up a family without undue harm to career.

Beyond flexitime, there are open, flexible career systems. These include the freedom to move back and forth from full- to part-time to zero-time work (especially in response to family demands) – and to do so without jeopardizing the employee's status as a permanent employee. It also involves the right to a phased retirement (a right especially important since mandatory retirement has become illegal in the USA).

In 'open career systems' individuals are given considerable freedom to manage their own careers. In such settings we find features such as realistic job previews (RJP, a procedure in which job applicants are frankly told a job's disadvantages), a chance to bid on jobs and training opportunities, and the freedom to accept or decline transfers. Assisting employees to make wise career choices requires assessment centres to evaluate skills, as well as more opportunities for counselling.

Although demand for career flexibility comes chiefly from the women's movement, it is of interest to men, too, and particularly to professionals and managers. Flexible career systems are certainly consistent with the philosophy of participation and high commitment. On the other hand, flexibility may be hard for organizations to provide. Individual and organizational needs often mesh quite badly. The Utopia in which everyone does his or her own thing may be far off. As yet, open career systems are more talked about then practised. Further, such systems are often accompanied by reduced job security. Lean and mean provides another form of flexibility, but it is flexibility at management's discretion, not the employee's.

Job security and contingent employment

One of the formal objectives of high-commitment companies is to provide something akin to Japanese-style lifetime employment. In this, their objectives are much like those of unions, which typically insist that their members receive a constant stream of income from the day they are hired to the day they die: they get it in the form of wages, vacations, sick leave, unemployment benefits, pensions and the like. To the extent that this occurs, the major economic uncertainties of life are transferred from the employee to the employer.

During the 1980s job security became a major union objective, often given higher priority than wage increases. When long-time unionized employees in the US auto and steel industries are made redundant, they now enjoy guaranteed income streams equalling or nearly equalling their pre-redundancy pay. In some cases these streams continue until the worker is ready for retirement. To support this programme General Motors has committed more than US$5 billion over the years.

Maintaining lifetime employment, in the face of the vagaries of the market, is difficult for many businesses. An increasingly common solution is to do this in the traditional Japanese way; that is, by absorbing peak workloads through overtime, subcontracting and hiring 'peripheral' or 'contingent' employees, who work on a part-time, temporary or on-call basis, as well as 'agency temporaries' supplied by firms specializing in providing temporary employees. In slack times these firms protect their core employees by reversing this process, that is by eliminating overtime and dismissing peripheral workers.

In lean and mean firms the number of contingent employees has grown considerably. Subcontracting has also increased. The kind of work subcontracted ranges from caretaking and equipment maintenance to top-management decision-making (in the latter case the subcontractors are called management consultants). American Airlines does its data processing in the Barbados where labour is cheaper, for instance, rather than in the USA. 'Networks' are increasingly common. They consist of legally independent firms which maintain close relations with each other, and are quite common, for example, in Silicon Valley and the clothing industry (Miles and Snow 1994).

Some people like the independence of being subcontractors. Many employees (especially working mothers) dislike being tied down to full-time permanent jobs and prefer flexibility. But few of these contingent workers enjoy much security. Generally they are low-paid, have meagre fringe benefits, most of them are women, and few are unionized. A high percentage of part-time workers, possibly a majority, would prefer full-time regular employment. At least, they might like the choice whether to be full-time or part-time to be their's, not their employer's.

Thus, the growing distinction between core and other employees accentuates what economists call the 'segmented labor market' and creates serious social dilemmas. The relative job security enjoyed by core employees merely accentuates the insecurity suffered by the rest. A severely disadvantaged secondary labour force consisting more than proportionally of racial minorities is the ugly backside of high-commitment policy.

Downsizing and outplacement

When business is seriously depressed, there is too little work for even core employees. When this occurs, high-commitment firms tend to follow the policy of delay. They search for temporary assignments for surplus workers and perhaps provide them with special training or subsidize their transfer to other plants. If business gets still worse they accelerate attrition through fairly lavish voluntary early retirement schemes. Indeed, early retirement has become a favourite downsizing strategy. In effect, workers are bribed to quit.

As lean and mean policies spread, companies have become less generous. IBM avoided involuntary layoffs for many years, providing bonuses for voluntary resignation or early retirement instead. But as cost-cutting pressures increased, the firm went through several rounds of involuntary layoffs with progressively reduced severance pay.

What distinguishes current 'outplacement' from the earlier 'sack' is the delicacy with which it is done. A whole new art of firing people has been developed. Aside from the considerable expenses which are incurred to induce older employees to accept early retirement, some companies finance training for new occupations, subsidize job-finding trips, continue employee pay and benefits and give them time off to look for a new job. Outplacement counsellors listen to outplaced workers' emotional traumas, assist in writing job applications, coach interview skills and generally help in the job search.

These enlightened HR policies are not uniformly followed, of course. A large percentage of employers do little or nothing to cushion the shock of layoffs. Often employees receive only limited government-financed unemployment insurance (the dole) at a rate of no more than half the employee's pre-redundancy pay for no more than 26 weeks.

There are few legal restrictions on employees' right to make layoffs. In 1988 Congress passed a law requiring 60 days notice before making 'mass layoffs' or closing down a plant. Experience to date suggests that complying with the law is less of a burden than management had feared; on the other hand, it has done less than its proponents had hoped to reduce unemployment or to ease the transition to new jobs.

Labour relations

What about unions, the reader might ask? In fact, they are no longer very relevant. In a process not much different from that occurring in the United Kingdom, US unions have become substantially weaker

(Chaison and Rose 1991). From a 1955 peak of approximately 33 per cent of the labour force, union density declined to 15 per cent in 1995. The decline in the private sector was even greater, from over 35 per cent in 1955 to about 10 per cent today (and the percentage continues to drop). Meanwhile, the public sector has assumed an increasingly important union role. Public-sector unionism was minimal in 1955; today, close to 38 per cent of government employees belong to unions and this figure is holding constant.

Why the private-sector decline? One reason is that traditionally unionized industries, especially manufacturing, mining, transportation and utilities, have grown much less rapidly than the non-union industries, such as trade and services. Factories have moved to the non-union southern states. Additionally, non-union employers have adopted tougher, more sophisticated and more effective techniques to keep their organizations 'union free'. Often they compete with unions through the adoption of high-commitment policies. Further, in government-run elections designed to determine whether workers want union representation, employers campaign vigorously, taking advantage of every technicality the law allows. Often their tactics skirt or even violate the law, since the penalties for doing so are minimal.

An increasing (though still small) number of already unionized firms have rid themselves of unions altogether. A common technique is to adopt such a hard line in bargaining that the union members go on strike. Management then replaces the striking workers with new employees. More commonly, management has sought to negotiate 'concessions', new contracts which provide fewer benefits than those which are expiring. They often threaten to close the plant in question and move its work to another plant, either in the USA or overseas. Bargaining as a whole has become much more decentralized. As union strength has declined, so have the number of strikes.

On the other hand, a considerable number of union–management relations could be characterized as being relatively co-operative. Unions and managements in the steel, automotive and a few other industries have sought to work together. Though the adversarial aspects of their relationship will never be eliminated, numerous joint efforts have been undertaken to resolve common problems such as productivity, substance abuse and the like.

Though unions are still significant in some industries, their role in HRM generally is much reduced. Forty years ago it was the union movement which took the initiative in proposing new HR ideas – and management reacted. Today management has the upper hand. Indeed, the women's groups and the government may have more influence than unions. Among the issues derived from the women's agenda (if not from the women's movement itself) are the following: comparable worth, flexitime, child care, elder care and the freedom to move in and out of the labour force. The role of government and the law is discussed below.

Government and the Law

At one time a sharp contrast could be drawn between the HR practices in the USA and those in continental Europe: continental practices were tightly regulated by law while those in the USA were comparatively unfettered. This began to change during Roosevelt's New Deal (1933–41) when laws were passed which protected unionization and established some fairly minimum wages. The New Deal also introduced tax-supported unemployment and old-age (superannuation) benefits. But, aside from union–management collective bargaining agreements, HR practices remained relatively unregulated.

Beginning in the 1960s, however, a series of major laws were enacted which dealt with such topics as occupational safety, employer-funded superannuation funds, discrimination, and equal employment. These laws have had some major impacts, as we shall see.

In 1980 President Reagan was elected on a platform that called for deregulation. His administration was marked by a considerable slackening in the rigour with which the executive branch enforced the laws, a policy followed to a lesser extent by George Bush, his successor. Nevertheless, none of the old legislation was repealed or significantly weakened. Indeed, a series of new laws were enacted, some strengthening previous laws (for example, those relating to discrimination against the aged and disabled) and others branching out into completely new directions, for example severely restricting employers' use of polygraphs (lie detectors). No single recent law has had a major impact, but their cumulative effect was substantial.

Less was accomplished than might have been expected during the first Clinton years, in large part because of Congressional deadlock. Congress passed only one significant new law: a requirement that employers provide a minimum of 12 weeks maternity leave, but with no requirement that employees be paid during this period (hardly a generous provision by European standards). The Republican Congress, elected in 1994, launched a major attack on all forms of government regulation, but more attention was given to environmental issues than to those affecting HRM.

The legal push comes not just from the federal Congress. As is permitted in the federal system, state legislatures have been passing laws on similar topics. Further, the USA is a litigious society, and state courts have been actively expanding employee rights and creating a new body of common law, especially with regards to employers' ability to discharge employees 'at will' (more on this below, p. 43). The net effect is much broader government intervention in HR practices, from hiring to discharge. Some call this the Europeanization of American HRM. Republicans may slow down and even temporally reverse this process. My guess is that this will not be for long.

These relatively new legal developments have considerably affected HR decision-making processes, which have become more formal, more time-consuming and more bound by paper work. All this helped to link the HR function more closely with the corporate legal department.

Equal employment – ethnicity and gender

Equal employment – not collective bargaining – was the most significant HR issue in the United States since the mid-1960s, at least until recently. A series of state and federal laws now ban discrimination on the basis of ethnic origin, religion, gender, age and physical disability. These laws and their interpretation are complex and technical and have provided employment for numerous lawyers and testing experts.

Such laws have real teeth. They are enforced in a number of ways: through action by the federal Equal Employment Opportunities Commission or its state counterparts; through special regulations applying to government contractors; and thorough class-action suits filed on behalf of categories of job applicants or employees alleged to have suffered from discrimination. Settling these suits has cost companies substantial sums of money, in some cases over US$100 million.

Equal employment regulations cover most aspects of employment: hiring, promotions, redundancies, compensation and even training opportunities. As the US Supreme Court put it, the law 'proscribes not only overt discrimination but also practices that are fair in form, but discriminatory in operation. The touchstone is business necessity. If an employment practice operates to exclude [minorities] and cannot be shown to be related to job performance, the practice is prohibited.' This means that if selection practices (such as a recruitment procedures, tests, interview protocols or weight requirements) screen out proportionally more individuals from any one ethnic or gender category, then the 'business necessity' of these procedures must be validated. For example, job applicants' test scores must be statistically correlated with relevant aspects of work performance. In practice, too, the regulatory process often requires 'goals' and 'time tables' and even flexible 'quotas' ('affirmative action'), especially where the employer has discriminated in the past.

These requirements forced radical changes in the procedures used to select, evaluate and promote employees at all levels. There have been important new technical, psychometrically validated developments in testing and performance evaluation. 'Work sample' tests have been introduced which test the specific skills required for the job in question. Applicants for the job of customer service representative, for example, may be evaluated in terms of how they respond to simulated customer telephoned complaints. Performance appraisal procedures have been overhauled to reflect actual behaviour rather than attitudes or traits. Promotional ladders have been redesigned to insure that women are not held down by 'glass ceilings'. Considerable efforts were made to recruit minorities, including offering university scholarships to promising candidates.

As a consequence of these efforts there has been significant increases in the employment of women and ethnic minorities in occupations that were once entirely white and male. Nevertheless, wide disparities in employment and earnings remain. Women may have gained more ground than blacks. A large black underclass is only marginally in the labour force. None the less, real progress has occurred.

By now the legally mandated adjustments in company policy have largely been made. Organizations have learned how to live under equal employment rules and yet preserve a degree of flexibility. For this reason, big business showed little interest in following the Reagan administration's call to dismantle the regulatory machinery.

In sum, equal *employment* for women and minorities is much less an issue for business than it was in the 1970s. The political clout of minority groups has declined considerably. HR managers talk much more about 'accommodating to cultural diversity' (a common topic for training programmes in the mid-1990s) than they do about quotas or equal employment. The main undecided questions today relate to promotion and to the aged, disabled, homosexuals (in some jurisdictions) and opportunities for women to combine maternity and careers. In mid-1995 several major candidates for the Republican presidential nomination came out for the elimination of all forms of preference for ethnic minorities or women. Senator Dole, for example, reversed his previous position supporting affirmative action. Opposition to affirmative action appears to be directed chiefly to white working-class males and to small businesses. Big Business gives higher priority to other forms of deregulation.

Comparable worth

'Comparable worth' is an issue which received more attention in the mid-1980s than it does now. Current law requires that men and women be paid equally when they perform the same or closely similar jobs. But women's groups have argued that jobs which are performed primarily by women should be paid wages equal to those of male jobs of 'comparable worth', even if the jobs are not closely similar. They object, for example, to the common practice of paying truck drivers and electricians more than nurses, even though nurses require considerably more training and bear much more responsibility. In effect, comparable-worth advocates seek a major reorganization of wage-setting in American industry. Meeting their demands would require a massive job evaluation scheme in which the requirements of every job would be compared to every other.

Understandably this proposal met considerable resistance. Arguing that an unfair wage structure constitutes a form of discrimination, women's groups made some progress in a few lower courts, but higher courts hesitated to become involved in the difficult process of wage determination. In some states, female government employees won major adjustments, either through legislation or collective bargaining. At the moment, however, comparable worth is making little headway.

Age discrimination

Mandatory retirement is now prohibited in most occupations. Likewise, discrimination on the grounds of age (over 40) is illegal. Together these provisions make it difficult for employers to replace older, presumably less-energetic employees, with younger, possibly more-enthusiastic ones. Elaborate documentation of poor performance is required before older employees may be demoted or replaced.

Many of the key legal cases here have involved top executives. This is understandable: evaluations of executive performance are inevitably subjective and liable to dispute. Displaced executives can better afford to hire lawyers than can low-paid production workers. Additionally, juries may grant punitive as well as remedial damages in age-discrimination cases, thus making them attractive to lawyers seeking large fees. There have been some dramatic awards (many reduced on appeal). In some of these cases employees have produced 'smoking guns' that confirm the employer's purpose; for example, a memo stating an intent to 'rejuvenate the organization and bring in fresh, young blood'.

In recent years, companies have learned to avoid obviously discriminatory statements. Instead, they document performance, provide periodic performance appraisals and give employees opportunities to improve their performance before firing them. As a result the number of cases won by plaintiffs has declined.

The disabled

Over 40 million Americans suffer from some form of mental or physical disability, and a high percentage of disabled individuals are unemployed. In 1990 the Americans with Disabilities Act strengthened previous legislation designed to protect this disadvantaged minority. The new law – which had the strong support of President Bush and Senator Dole (himself a badly injured war veteran) – prohibits employers from discrimination in hiring disabled persons, provided that with 'reasonable accommodation' they can perform the essential functions of the job in question.

The meaning of 'reasonable accommodation' has led to extensive litigation. For example, variations in the way the job is done may be required. Special equipment may have to be provided. But accommodation is required only as long as it doesn't cause 'undue hardship' to the employer. In determining 'undue hardship' (a fuzzy term) the cost of the accommodation must be balanced against the employer's size.

Experience suggests that large employers can make necessary accommodations relatively easily, provided they show flexibility and imagination. Perhaps the most noticeable change is an increase in the number of ramps and toilets suitable for the wheelchair-bound. But small employers, in particular, object to the cost and seeming pettiness of some regulations.

Occasionally even big businesses slip up. In 1995 a jury awarded US$7.1 million to a former Coca Cola executive who was fired after he informed management that he was being treated for alcoholism. It was held that this was a form of occupational disability. In its unsuccessful defence the company claimed that the executive was dismissed for 'dangerous behavior including threatening remarks' at a company-sponsored party.

Individual job rights

Recent years have shown a growing concern for individual job rights. By contrast with participation and flexible career systems, both of which give individuals the freedom to make choices *within* the organization, the rights to be discussed here protect the individual *from* the organization and its members. In effect they say that the organization can go so far – and no further. Some of these rights have been obtained primarily through legislation, others through court decisions or union contracts. Many raise controversial questions. For example:

- What rights does a professor have to see confidential peer evaluations of his or her work? What rights does anyone have to prevent dissemination of material in one's file to others?
- Who can have access to reports prepared by company doctors and psychiatrists? Under what circumstances can a supervisor search an employee's desk or clothes locker?
- What freedom of dress and hairstyle does one have on the job? Under what circumstances can an employer inquire about one's sexual or political behaviour off the job?
- What rights does an employee have to smoke on the job? What rights does one have not to be bothered by other people's smoking?
- Do polygraphs (lie detectors) or testing for AIDs or for genetic defects violate individual privacy?
- Are AIDS, alcoholism, drug addition and obesity 'occupational handicaps' to which the employer must make a 'reasonable accommodation'?
- May clerical workers place pictures of their family on their work desks? Is it sexual harassment for employees to pin 'nudie' pictures in locations where women can see them? (A court has ruled that it is.)

For the most part these are new, recently articulated issues. For instance, they were not on traditional union agendas, and indeed, they stem largely from changes in overall social values. Much controversy relates to drug testing. Can/should the employer test everyone? Only those in critical jobs, such as aircraft pilots, who might do serious harm if they *were* influenced by drugs? Or only those who demonstrate overt signs of being *currently* drugged? What deductions can the employer draw from a single positive test (since false positives are common)? Suppose the test is accurate, what is the employer's obligation: to inform the police? to discharge the employee quietly? or to send him for an expensive, employer-paid cure?

Controversy has been greatest with regard to random testing: civil libertarians argue that employees should not be penalized for off-the-job drug use as long as it does not demonstrably affect their on-the-job performance. Unions have been ambivalent on the drug-testing issue, fearing to be seen as supporting drug use. For the most part they have insisted on procedural safeguards and that drug users receive treatment rather than discipline.

In 1989, after a serious train accident was blamed on employees being 'stoned', a new federal regulation made 'safety-sensitive' transportation employees subject to random testing. Similar regulations have been applied to a variety of 'sensitive' government employees, such as customs officers. With this precedent, testing spread rapidly to other industries. Today a majority of large companies use one form of drug testing or another (*AFL-CIO News*, 22 July 1991).

Most uses of polygraphs (lie detectors) are now illegal. Challenges are being mounted against paper-and-pencil 'honesty' and personality tests on the grounds that they are often invalid and that the latter frequently probe sexual preferences and political and religious values.

With union endorsement, bills have been introduced into Congress and state legislatures which would restrict electronic monitoring in the office and the use of undercover agents to check on sales clerks. For example, they would prohibit assessing job performance by counting the number of key strikes an employee makes on a computer keyboard, or through listening into telephone conversations with customers. Unions argue that these practices place workers under excess stress.

Standards are unclear here, and they are rapidly changing. Until recently, for instance, the right to smoke on the job was generally recognized, and non-smokers had to accommodate themselves as best they could. Now the reverse is the case. Limitations on smoking have spread widely. The Occupational Safety and Health Administration has declared tobacco smoke a workplace hazard. Employees have won damages from employers for injuries to health caused by being forced to work in smoke-filled places. An increasing number of communities ban smoking on the job. A few employers go further: they forbid employees to smoke (or even to drink alcohol) *off* the job on the grounds that this increases health costs. Counterattacking, smokers and tobacco companies have lobbied for laws providing a 'smokers' bill of rights' to prohibit discrimination against smokers.

Emotions over such issues run high. All of them invite the legislature or the courts to set general standards, although neither management nor civil libertarians may be happy with the results. Clearly, management has less freedom in these areas than it had a few years ago.

Sexual harassment

In October 1991 the American people were treated to a televised real-life soap opera: Anita Hill's charge to a Senate committee that she had been sexually harassed by Clarence Thomas, her former boss and then a Supreme Court nominee. Eventually Thomas was confirmed. Yet the case dramatized the sexual harassment issue. In the face of this publicity, many women, from all walks of life, confirmed that they too had been subjected to harassment, but had been too embarrassed to admit it.

As much as any issue, the sexual harassment controversy illustrates the changes in values. Forty years ago 'hanky-panky' (as it was then known) was common in many offices. Women coped with it as best they could and, if things got too bad, they quietly quit. Sexual banter was widespread in blue-collar work. Those who could not find other jobs bore the insults in silence. Thus sexual harassment is nothing new, but to have women publicly objecting to it is.

The law recognizes two chief forms of harassment. The first involves 'quid pro quo' harassment or sexual extortion, in which the supervisor takes advantage of his position to seek sexual favours. In situations like this, the company can be held liable even if top management is unaware of what is happening and the supervisor's behaviour violates company policy. The second form of harassment occurs when either the boss or fellow employees create an 'intimidating, hostile, or offensive working environment'. In a case where an employee had to run 'what she described as virtual obstacle course of pornographic pinups and sexual demeaning cartoons' a federal judge ordered that sexually oriented pin-ups and magazines be removed from the work premises. When environmental harassment occurs, the organization can be held liable if it 'knows or *should have* known' of the conduct in question 'unless it can be shown that it took immediate and appropriate corrective action'.

In 1994 a California jury awarded a secretary US$8.1 million in damages from a law firm for permitting sexual harassment. A partner had dropped candies down her blouse and attempted to fondle her breasts. What antagonized the jury was that the organization had ignored her complaints.

Due process

Formal due process procedures to protect job rights are becoming increasingly common. There is growing use of ombudsmen, formal grievance and appeals procedures, and binding arbitration in non-union companies.

Along with this, employees are having easier access to the courts. Judicial decisions are rapidly eroding the traditional common law view that employment is 'at will' and can be terminated for any reason – or none. Courts are increasingly treating company handbooks and even 'implicit' contracts (such as, 'if you work hard, you have a job here for life') as legally binding (Edwards 1993). Under these circumstances employers must generally bear the burden of proving 'just cause' when they discipline. In some states courts now prohibit discharges which violate 'public policy' or implicit covenants of 'good faith and fair dealing'. Further, unless a company is careful about how it fires an employee, it may be subject to defamation or libel suits. Finally, when an employer discharges a woman, a member of an ethnic minority or an older worker, it may be subject to a discrimination suit.

While courts are unlikely to defer entirely to the company's internal adjudication process, the existence of such a process may constitute a defence against charges of procedural, if not substantive, unfairness. In 1994 the Supreme Court went further, holding that once an employee agreed to binding arbitration of an employment dispute, that employee forfeited other forms of legal recourse.

Thus US workers are gradually gaining the protections provided to British workers under the industrial tribunal scheme, the main differences being that the grounds according to which American workers can appeal are somewhat different than they are in the United Kingdom, and the damages awarded to a successful complainant can be considerably more liberal. But these protections are of little value to contingent employees.

Compensation

There is a growing dissatisfaction with traditional compensation practices, which, for US blue-collar workers, are typically based on job classifications and seniority, adjusted by cost-of-living changes. It is argued that this system is inflexible (especially in bad times), rewards longevity rather than performance, and discourages teamwork and job-switching. As a consequence there is considerable experimentation with alternative compensation schemes, most of which place a considerable part of the employee's earnings 'at risk'. Taken as a whole, these new approaches to compensation seek to reward teamwork and performance and to provide the employer a more flexible wage bill, one which is responsive to fluctuations in the business cycle. Among others, the most common new approaches are (Conference Board 1990; Roomkin 1990):

- the abandonment of individual piecework payment plans and greater use of gainsharing programmes based on departmental, plant or organization-wide performance;
- profit-sharing and Employee Stock Ownership Plans (ESOPs); by 1994 these plans had assets totalling US$800 billion;
- for blue-collar workers, pay for knowledge; that is, pay based on the number of skills learned rather than the particular job classification the employee is in;
- greater use of one-time awards and bonuses which provide recognition for meeting specific goals but which don't enter into base pay (lump-sum bonuses have taken the place of wage increases in many recent labour–management contracts);
- basing individual managers' pay on the contribution which they (or the unit under their direction) make to overall organizational performance;
- and finally, tying top management compensation to changes in the value of company stock.

Each of these approaches has its problems and limitations. Some, such as ESOPs, have been introduced primarily for tax reasons. Others represent symbolic quid pro quos given in return for blue-collar pay cuts. Attempts to extend top management bonus systems to lower levels of management have frequently caused much dissatisfaction and charges of unfairness. In a period when the real wages (after inflation) of American workers have dropped, total top management compensation (including bonuses and stock options) has increased rapidly, even in unprofitable companies. The ratio between total top management compensation and that of ordinary workers is much higher in the USA than in other countries. All this has led to considerable criticism.

Profit-sharing, ESOPs, various bonus and gainsharing systems, all shift some of the risk of employment from the company to the employee, and for this reason often meet union and worker resistance. Still, by emphasizing the fact that company and employee somehow share a common fate, they remain consistent with the high-commitment philosophy. On the up side, they reward participative efforts. And they are also consistent with the lean–mean approach of getting everybody to work harder.

Fringe benefits

The costs of fringe benefits – forms of compensation other than pay and bonuses – are increasing faster in the USA than are wages. Understandably they lead to considerable controversy. Although vacations are shorter in the USA and holidays less frequent than in many European countries, the total cost of fringe benefits to employers is greater because pension (superannuation) and health costs are privately financed to a larger degree than in Europe.

The USA has nothing like the British National Health Service. The federal government pays part of the medical costs for the very poor and those aged 65 and over. The bulk of the population, however, relies on employer-financed health insurance. The adequacy of this protection varies widely, and some 41 million Americans are not covered by any scheme, public or private (and this figure is growing). Many small employers do not offer health insurance and few contingent employees receive it. Those not covered are usually people on low income to begin with. Once taken ill, they can quickly exhaust their meagre savings, and are then dependent on charity.

Another problem: health costs have increased dramatically. Today they consume 12 per cent of GDP in the USA, compared with 6 per cent in the UK and 9 per cent in France. Some of the causes for high costs are common throughout the world: an ageing population and increasingly expensive medical technology (a liver transplant can cost over US$300,000). But one source of expense is uniquely American: the cost of malpractice suits filed against hospitals and doctors whenever a mistake is apparently made. Not only is malpractice insurance terribly expensive but, to prevent suits, doctors engage in 'defensive medicine', for instance, they order an excessive number of expensive tests. Adding further to the costs, neither doctors nor patients have much incentive to keep expenses down. Under traditional insurance plans charges are easily passed on to either insurance funds or employers. Finally, the expense of administering this cumbersome scheme adds 10–20 per cent to overall cost.

In 1994 to deal with these problems President Clinton introduced a plan designed both to hold down expenses and to provide medical cover for the uninsured. The plan was complex, difficult to explain and strongly opposed by special interest groups such as doctors, insurance companies and small businesses. Rather than expand health-care coverage, the 1955 Republican Congress voted substantial cuts in the health-care funds available for both the very poor and the aged.

Meanwhile, there has been some progress in controlling medical costs. 'Managed care' plans have spread rapidly and now cover half the workforce; employers and insurers negotiate with doctors and hospitals to provide medical care for plan members for fixed fees, usually somewhat lower than those previously charged. To be fully reimbursed for their medical bills, plan members must use health-care providers who accept these arrangements (and thus plan members lose some 'freedom of choice'). Often second opinions may be required before non-urgent operations are undertaken, and medical bills are closely monitored. Thus managed care plans are akin to a set of competitive, privatized British National Health Services. At least during 1992–5 managed care succeeded in slowing the spiralling cost of health care.

As the population ages, pension costs will also increase. The problem has lessened for the moment because pension funds are heavily invested in stocks, and until recently stock prices increased faster than pension costs, thus providing a financial buffer. This windfall is unlikely to continue for long. There are other problems: some employers have under-contributed to their funds; others have 'recaptured' allegedly excessive contributions; and still others have inappropriately invested them or have used these funds in struggles for corporate control.

Over time, both pensions and health-care benefits will consume an increasing portion of national income. As resources get tighter, tensions may increase. Already we see some conflict between childless people and those with large families, and between younger people who want income *now* and older people who want improved pensions and medical care.

Additional problems derive from the fact that our US benefit systems were developed to meet the needs of a traditional family with a working husband and a non-working wife. Problems arise when both spouses work and the family acquires children. Immediately, there is a demand that the employer provide child-care (one of the most difficult HR issues today).

Beyond this, maternity leave, which initially covered only the wife's period of confinement (if that), has been frequently extended to include the first few weeks after the new baby comes home. But children are occasionally ill, and some employers now allow employees to use sick-leave time to take care of their ailing offspring. And if it can be used for sick children, how about for dependent, elderly parents? Or a sick spouse or 'significant other'? As time goes by the distinction between vacations and sick leave may decline. Eventually it may be eliminated.

All this points to the greater use of 'cafeteria plans' which give employees a choice of which fringe benefits they use. The range of possible benefits will increase but a reasonably firm cap will be placed on their total cost. The employer will pass the buck to the employee to make the difficult choice among the many benefits available.

But this will do little to resolve another issue: the widening differences between core employees and the remainder of the population in terms of the benefits, especially retirement and health benefits, enjoyed by the two groups. The only reasonable solution is for fewer benefits to be provided privately and more by the state, either directly or through legally established minimum standards. Movement in this direction seems unlikely in the present political climate.

Conclusion

It is difficult to generalize about HR developments in the USA, so much is happening. But at the risk of drawing too simple a picture, let me suggest several trends.

There was a time in the USA when employers were almost entirely unregulated, either by unions or by the government. Employees were looked upon as commodities. The employer had no obligation towards them except to pay their regular wages. The financial burden of life's risks – illness, unemployment, old age, death – were borne exclusively by the employee. The employee's only right was to quit; a right more than counterbalanced by the employer's right to discharge the employee at will.

Unions arose to redress this balance. They gave workers a series of rights, defended by the grievance procedure. Strong unions also won a comprehensive stream of benefits for their members. These shifted the risks to the employer. Though unions have now been greatly weakened, the reforms they introduced have been widely adopted, particularly by large, 'progressive' companies.

High-commitment policies offer workers many (certainly not all) of the advantages of unionism. However, it is an oversimplification to think of the two as substitutes. In principle, high-commitment policies offer benefits beyond those provided by the average union contract, especially opportunities for participation, creativity and personal development. Indeed, in some instances unions have played a critical role in the development of high-commitment programmes.

A major drawback of high-commitment programmes, from management's viewpoint, is the expense of guaranteeing job security and the inflexibility this causes. Strong economic forces require employers to be more flexible. Career employees are being replaced by contingent ones. As a form of motivation, performance-based pay and fear of discharge is displacing organizational commitment (but let's not exaggerate the extent to which organizational commitment ever existed in large companies). Workplace employee involvement, such as teams, may continue in 'lean and mean' companies, but broader forms of participation, such as unions, are out.

With unions in decline and few companies giving more than lip service to high-commitment policies, many companies have become as arbitrary as of old. In the face of growing public pressures to deal with the most obvious inequities, Congress and the courts have gradually begun fashioning new rights and regulations. For some companies, these do little more than formalize what they already feel to be good HR policies. For others, adjustment is proving difficult, but rarely impossible.

As for the intermediate future, the full range of high-commitment policies are likely to be implemented fairly infrequently. On the other hand, excessive 'mean and lean' cost-cutting may prove counter-productive. Meanwhile, industrial giants, such as GM, will play a lesser role. There will be some slowdown in the growth of legal regulation (but for how long?). There will be fewer permanent jobs and greater mobility and insecurity. HR departments will continue to perform a significant function, but they are unlikely to follow a single set of policies or to play a major role in setting corporate strategy.

References

Adler, Paul 1992: The 'learning bureaucracy': New United Motor Manufacturing, Inc. *Research in Organizational Behavior*, 15, 111–94.
Chaison, Gary and Rose Joseph, 1991: The macrodeterminants of union growth and decline. In George Strauss, Daniel Gallagher and Jack Fiorito (eds), *The State of the Unions*, Madison, Wis.: Industrial Relations Research Association, pp. 3–45.
Conference Board 1990: *Variable Pay: new performance rewards*, Research Bulletin no. 264. New York: Conference Board.
Edwards, Richard 1993: *Rights at Work*. Washington, D.C.: Brookings Institution.
Harrison, Bennett 1994: *Lean and Mean: the changing landscape of corporate power in the age of flexibility*. New York: Basic Books.
Jacoby, Sanford 1985: *Employing Bureaucracy: managers, unions, and the transformation of work*. New York: Columbia University Press.
Kochan, Thomas A. and Cappelli, Peter 1984: The transformation of the

industrial relations and personnel function. In Paul Osterman (ed.), *Internal Labor Markets*, Cambridge, Mass.: MIT Press.

Lawler, Edward E. 1986: *High Involvement Management*. San Francisco, Cal.: Jossey-Bass.

Levine, David 1995: *Reinventing the Workplace*. Washington, D.C.: Brookings Institution.

MacInnes, John 1985: Conjuring up consultation: the role and extent of joint consultation in post-war private manufacturing industry. *British Journal of Industrial Relations*, 23, 93–114.

Miles, Raymond and Snow, Charles 1994: *Fit, Failure and the Hall of Fame: how companies succeed or fail*. New York: Free Press.

Millward, Neil, Stevens, Mark, Smart, D. and Hawes, W.R. 1992: *Workplace Industrial Relations in Transition*. Alderdershot, Hants.: Dartmouth.

Osterman, P. 1994: How common is workplace transformation and who adopts it? *Industrial and Labor Relations Review*, 47, 173–88.

Roomkin, Myron (ed.) 1990: *Profit Sharing and Gain Sharing*. New Brunswick, N.J.: IMLR Press/Rutgers University.

Strauss, George 1992: Workers' participation in management. In Jean Hartley and Geoffrey Stephenson (eds), *Employment Relations: the psychology of influence and control at work*. Oxford: Blackwell.

3

Human Resource Management in Japanese Manufacturing Companies in the UK and USA

BARRY WILKINSON AND NICK OLIVER

Introduction

In the 1980s and 1990s the major Japanese manufacturing corporations have played a leading role as a model for new patterns of manufacturing management and work organization in the West. This role has been increasingly assumed by inwardly investing Japanese companies in North America and the UK, many of whom now confront indigenous manufacturers on their home ground. Although the Japanese have clearly not attempted a wholesale transfer of the methods which they use in Japan (Abo 1994) they have selectively applied some of their key management tools and introduced and modified others. Large numbers of non-Japanese companies in America and the United Kingdom are also applying management methods which look suspiciously Japanese. Many of these deny that their experiments with just-in-time production, total quality control and employee relations practices, such as harmonization, flexible work roles and single union deals, owe anything to the Japanese model, a position which some commentators have ascribed to Western fears of 'cultural violation' (Kelman 1990).

The distinct configuration of manufacturing, supplier relations and human resource management techniques found in their purest form in the major Japanese corporations carries a variety of labels, including 'Japanization' (Oliver and Wilkinson 1992), 'world class manufacturing' (Schonberger 1986), 'lean manufacturing' (Womack et al. 1990), and the 'Toyota production system' (Monden 1983; Wood 1992). Therefore the activities of Japanese manufacturing companies in the West are of considerable practical and theoretical significance. In setting up on greenfield sites and using state-of-the-art management methods these companies are indicative of the direction in which many indigenous companies would like to go. The operations of these companies are also a fascinating test case of the transferability of management methods across different industrial cultures. Do these methods represent a universal set of management principles which, properly implemented can work anywhere? Or are they a response to the unique set of historical, economic and market conditions in which the major Japanese companies found themselves in the latter part of the twentieth century?

This chapter describes the management practices used by Japanese manufacturing companies in the UK and USA, focusing in particular on their human resource management (HRM) activities. We do not follow a specific definition of HRM, but use the term to cover a range of practices concerning employee relations and work organization. These practices are contrasted with those found in Japan itself and with traditional British and American practices.

Human Resource Management in Japan

In the search by Western pundits for the 'secret' of Japan's economic success during the 1970s and 1980s, several best-sellers emerged which focused on HRM in Japan (Ouchi 1981; Pascale and Athos 1982). These accounts centred on the provision of lifetime employment, company welfareism, seniority-based wages and promotion and enterprise unionism. It is alleged that these confer a high level of legitimacy on management actions and generate a commitment and loyalty to the company not typically found in the West. Company paternalism in Japan was underpinned by the ideology of loyalty to one Lord, as derived from Japanese Confucianism and the feudal legacy (Morishima 1982; Nakane 1973; Dore 1973), though such practices emerged as responses to specific labour market problems prevailing earlier this century (Littler 1982; Sethi et al. 1984). Enterprise unions, on the other hand, developed as late as the 1950s following the suppression of independent trade unions (Cusumano 1986; Littler 1982). Many Western commentators chose to interpret these conditions from a crude human relations perspective. The paternalism of the Japanese corporations showed that they were 'good' to their workers; if Western companies did the same then they too might enjoy enhanced commitment and motivation from their employees and therefore enhanced business performance.

During the 1980s the strong yen, trade friction with the USA and Europe, competition from other East Asian producers, increased labour costs and an ageing population have placed a variety of pressures on Japanese manufacturers. One effect has been that lifetime employment obligations have not always been met. Some companies, especially in the declining coal, steel and shipbuilding industries, have been forced to shed labour, whilst others are attempting to eliminate, or at least dilute, seniority-dominated pay and promotion systems in favour of performance-related ones (Japan Institute of Labour 1984; Sakasegawa 1988). In the early 1990s Japan slid into a major recession and again faced this problem, particularly in the financial sector, where significant downsizing occurred. Reports appeared in the Japanese press of older employees being pressed into early retirement, undermining the confidence of younger employees that they really had a job for life.

Given the expectation of lifetime employment (at least for an elite of core workers – women and peripheral workers are largely excluded from the system), it is not surprising that recruitment and selection by the major Japanese corporations is a careful process. The major corporations recruit direct from the educational institutions with the best reputations and look for potential rather than specific skills. Careful screening, sometimes with the assistance of private investigators, is used to eliminate radicals or 'unbalanced personalities' and to ensure the recruitment of candidates likely to endorse company values and philosophy (Pucik 1985; Robbins 1983). Job training is typically provided by the company, and is preceded by induction programmes more akin to those provided by religious orders or military schools, which familiarize the recruit with the philosophy and ways of the company (Azumi 1969; Ishida 1977; Naylor 1984). Training and socialization continue throughout the employee's career, typically on-the-job and involving frequent rotation. This, together with symbols of common purpose such as a common uniform, encourages an acceptance of flexible work roles. Managerial job rotation encourages managers to have a company-wide orientation and makes them generalists rather than specialists (Clegg 1986).

In Japanese manufacturing industry work is typically organized around work teams which have a high degree of internal flexibility with a team leader who has significant production planning, quality and other responsibilities. The stereotype held by many Western observers is of Japanese production operators being 'empowered' and carrying more responsibility than their Western counterparts (Womack et al. 1990), although some studies have found that Japanese operators are actually given *less* discretion than those in the West (Andersen Consulting 1994). White-collar workers also often find themselves working in teams and open plan offices are commonplace. Consultation and communication in the form of team briefings and problem-solving activities such as quality circles are extensive.

These HRM practices need to be viewed in relation to the manufacturing methods of total quality control and just-in-time production which evolved in Japan from the early 1950s onwards. Just-in-time requires a production system run with minimal stocks. This means that material passes through the system very quickly, but this carries a price; the system is inherently fragile and vulnerable to disruption. This may be due to the unreliability of the process, to a lack of diligence or skill on the part of labour, or to suppliers who fail to deliver on time or to the right quality. Total quality control is an umbrella term covering a range of practices: an emphasis on error prevention; responsibility for quality at the point of production; and continuous improvement. The net effect of these methods is to heighten the strategic position of labour in the production process. In the major Japanese corporations, HRM practices and manufacturing practices appear to have found a happy 'fit', in that the labour relations required by the manufacturing methods are precisely what Japanese HRM policy delivers.

Japanese Manufacturers Move Overseas

Overseas investment by Japanese companies grew markedly in the 1970s, then surged in the 1980s under strong political and economic pressure from the West. The surge was particularly strong in Europe and America as the Japanese sought locations within the major markets for their products (Morris 1988; Perucci 1994). In the late 1980s North America received some 46 per cent of Japanese overseas manufacturing investment, the corresponding figure for Europe being 18 per cent (Oliver and Wilkinson 1992). Within Europe, the UK has been the favoured location, absorbing about one-third of Japanese investment in Europe (ibid.). By 1994 there were 206 Japanese manufacturing plants in the UK, compared to just 15 in 1983 (JETRO 1994). The biggest surge occurred in the period 1987–91, after which the rate of increase slowed dramatically. According to Dillow (1989), the UK is the favoured location because of a warm political welcome

(France and other EU countries have occasionally expressed hostility), low wages and relatively weak trade unions. In the USA, by 1988 there were over 300 Japanese manufacturing plants in the auto assembly and component sectors alone, and hundreds more in a range of other sectors. Dillow (1989) estimated that by the turn of the century Japanese companies would employ over 100,000 in the UK and somewhere between 850,000 and one million in the USA (Rehder 1990). In 1993 JETRO (1994) figures indicated that between 60,000 and 70,000 people worked for Japanese manufacturers in the UK.

Hence Japanese companies are a phenomenon worthy of study in their own right, though the greater significance of Japanese investment may be the lead that Japanese companies have offered in providing a model of human resource management for indigenous companies to follow. Indeed, Ford UK went so far as to call its productivity campaign of the early 1980s the 'After Japan' campaign, because of its avowed intention to be 'best of the rest – after Japan' (BBC 1986).

Human Resource Management in Japanese Companies in the UK and USA

The first point to note is what the Japanese have not brought with them to Western shores. Omissions are the extensive paternalistic welfare provisions and seniority-based pay and promotion systems which, as noted above, have recently become problematic in Japan itself. Similarly, promises of lifetime employment have not been in evidence, though the objective of long-term employment has frequently been expressed (Brown and Reich 1989; Gleave and Oliver 1990; Yu and Wilkinson 1989). What they have brought is an approach to organization based on teamwork and devolved responsibility, careful selection procedures, extensive and intensive consultation and communications, appraisal-based pay, and employee relations systems designed to safeguard managerial prerogatives and minimize the likelihood of industrial action.

Selection, induction and training

Recruitment into Japanese companies in Britain and America is characterized by careful selection procedures which emphasize attitude and potential rather than experience and acquired skills. The type of recruitment practice varies according the operations of the companies concerned. In the UK, about 32 per cent of the jobs created up to 1994 were in the consumer electronics field (JETRO 1994), the majority of these involving light, relatively low-skill assembly work. These companies have chosen young, female labour, on the grounds that such workers possess the speed and dexterity necessary for electrical assembly work. Thus, recruitment practices appear to reflect both Japanese preferences *and* the nature of the work.

Many companies have tended to recruit people straight from school or college with no previous work experience. As many of the inward investors set up on greenfield sites in areas of high unemployment, they have largely been able to recruit those with no experience of the industry in question (Oliver and Wilkinson 1992). At Komatsu (manufacturers of earth-moving vehicles) in the north-east of England candidates undergo skills, numeracy and dexterity tests, and throughout the whole selection procedure there is emphasis on teamwork ability and co-operative attitudes. Those with team leader potential undergo psychological tests to explore abilities for teamwork, flexibility and responsibility (Gleave and Oliver 1990). At Toyota's new Kentucky plant in the USA the first 1,700 recruits were selected from 100,000 applications after more than 20 hours of tests spread over several months. Adaptability and the ability to learn and to work in teams were primary criteria (Economist Intelligence Unit 1989). On-the-job training is typically preceded by induction: at Komatsu new recruits undergo a ten-week induction period during which there are five formal and five informal sessions, including Japan familiarization classes, a common feature across many companies. It is usual for those recruited to supervisory grades or above to be sent on trips to parent plants in Japan itself.

Job training is typically provided internally, though at least in the early stages of operations there has been a tendency to buy-in managerial talent (Pang 1987). However, British and American managers in Japanese transplants do not always enjoy the degree of autonomy they might wish for. Pucik (1989) alleges tight control of US subsidiaries by their Japanese parents, and complaints of career 'ceilings' for non-Japanese managers are commonplace (Gleave and Oliver 1990), although this is clearly not a complaint which is exclusive to Japanese multinationals. Similar reports also emanate from Japanese companies in the USA (Fucini and Fucini 1990). In the UK Lowe and Oliver (1990) report the use of 'shadow systems' in Japanese companies, whereby British managers were shadowed by Japanese counterparts, who regularly report back to Japan. Fucini and Fucini (1990) report a similar arrangement at Mazda's Flat Rock plant in the USA.

Teamwork

As described above (p. 52), the team concept is an important component of the Japanese manufacturing package, and involves vesting a high degree of 'ownership' of the process in the hands of relatively self-contained teams. Processes of selection and induction typically emphasise abilities to work in teams and to accept responsibility and flexible work roles. These working practices are directly imported from Japan, and are part and parcel of Japanese total quality philosophy. Team organization typically places the team leader in a much more demanding role than has traditionally been the case in either the USA or the UK, and international comparisons of the responsibilities of team leaders consistently show that team leaders in Japan shoulder the lion's share of shopfloor responsibility in Japanese factories (Andersen Consulting 1993, 1994).

At Nissan in the north-east of England, supervisors select their own staff and take responsibility for on-the-job training, communication, some maintenance, and for capitalizing on workers' ingenuity in improving quality and production processes (Kirosingh 1989). The number of specialists such as maintenance and inspection staffs is minimized, and those remaining may be brought under the jurisdiction of the team leader. Public displays of individual and group performance and a meticulous attention to detail are characteristic of the approach, as is the maintenance of strict discipline and bell-to-bell working (Brown and Reich 1989; Graham 1994; Morris et al. 1993; Rehder 1990; Slaughter 1987; Takamiya 1981; Wickens 1987). Some trade unionists in both the USA (Brown and Reich 1989; Holmes 1989) and the UK (Oliver and Wilkinson 1992) have themselves accepted the need for such discipline. A senior official from the UK electricians' union who had negotiated a number of agreements with Japanese firms commented to the authors:

> The Japanese believe in bell-to-bell working. They cannot understand the mentality of the British people where they have to go to the toilet at times other than their natural break because they have conditioned themselves to do that. They can't understand why they are not prepared to co-operate with the company and give back to the company the two and a half minute washing time before the end of the bell because the Japanese say 'Well it's our company and that two and a half minutes, if added up throughout the week is 70 television sets.' Whichever way you look at it they are absolutely right.   (Oliver and Wilkinson 1992)

Fucini and Fucini (1990) describe how the team system at Mazda's Flat Rock plant created a 'self-regulating attendance system' which relied on peer pressure to discourage tardiness and absenteeism. The Big Three US vehicle producers keep a reserve pool of labour to fill in for absentees. Thus it is the absentee alone (and indirectly the company) who pays for the transgression:

> To his fellow workers [the absentee] is the other driver, pulled off to the side of the road for speeding. His problems are not theirs. This is not the case at Mazda. The speeding driver is not ticketed at the side of the road, but in the middle, forcing all traffic to come to a halt. The transgression of one team member creates problems for all team members. When one team member is absent, his team mates will have to work that much harder to pick up the slack.   (Fucini and Fucini 1990: 136–7)

Similar arguments apply to production errors or problems with work rate – a worker's team mates suffer the consequences if someone is slow or error-prone by having to perform more rectification work, or having to work overtime to meet production quotas.

While both the advocates and critics of Japanese-style teamwork agree that expectations on workers regarding quality, productivity and attendance are higher under the team system, there is debate as to whether the result is best characterized as an improvement in working conditions (Womack et al. 1990) or 'work intensification'   (Garrahan and Stewart 1992).

Consultation and communication

Frequent feedback of information on quality, productivity, and so on to work teams and Japanese managers' common practice of spending time on the shopfloor (White and Trevor 1983) means that day-to-day management–worker communication is frequent and direct. Typically this is backed up by formal consultation and communication groups such as team briefings, *kaizen* (continuous improvement) groups, quality circles and company advisory boards. Team briefings are typically used for the transmission of detailed information to work teams regarding output and quality levels, and are often an opportunity to set targets for the shift, the week or the month. Company advisory boards are similar to works councils and provide a forum for managers and workers' representatives (who need not be trade unionists) to discuss a wide range of issues, such as company performance, markets and a range of company policies. *Kaizen* groups and quality circles are examples of formal sessions where employees are encouraged to generate and pursue ideas for the improvement of productivity and quality in their work areas.

Authors such as Wickens (1987), Trevor (1988) and Morton (1994) stress the positive points of the two-way sharing of information and the involvement of workers in Japanese transplant operations. Garrahan and Stewart (1992), on the other hand, have pointed to the problems trade unions can face when communication from management to workforce bypasses the shop steward. Rehder (1990), describing Japanese transplants in the USA, argues that the *kaizen* process can mean that the ingenuity of informal work groups is brought under management control, thereby reducing waste but at the cost of intensifying work.

Single status and harmonization

Japanese transplants in the USA and the UK have facilitated flexible work practices by using relatively few job classifications, and by reducing visible status distinctions, especially between blue- and white-collar workers. Company uniforms, common car parks and canteen and toilet facilities, and clocking on for all (or none), sometimes followed by group exercises and/or team briefings at the start of the shift, are commonly found (Pang and Oliver 1988; Gleave and Oliver 1990; Morris et al. 1993). The risk of demarcation disputes is also reduced if there are few job classifications. The extent of change from traditional Western practices is well-illustrated by Toyota's joint venture with GM at the NUMMI plant in California. Prior to Toyota's involvement there were over 80 blue-collar job classes and more than 200 overall. This was reduced to one job class for production workers and four overall (Brown and Reich 1989). At Nissan in the north-east of England, a greenfield site, there are only two blue-collar job titles – 'manufacturing staff' and 'manufacturing technician' (Wickens 1987). Elsewhere in the UK and the USA many companies have attempted to reduce the number of job classes and to harmonize terms and conditions in order to gain more flexibility, though in some cases this has proved difficult; the attempted violation of job demarcations was probably the central issue behind the Ford UK strike in 1988 – Ford's first national strike for over a decade (Wilkinson and Oliver 1990).

Reward systems are also designed to encourage flexible working practices. Instead of linking pay to an elaborate and complex system of job classes and job evaluation, remuneration systems in Japanese transplants pay workers to be flexible. At Toshiba in Plymouth, for instance, there are 18 recognized production skills, and increments are paid for each one mastered. A formal assessment of each employee is carried out annually.

Pay and appraisal

It is in the area of reward systems that we find the most marked divergence from practices which are common in Japan. As noted above, company provision of housing, health and educational facilities is typically left behind. Further, seniority carries relatively little weight in consideration of decisions on pay and promotion. Japanese companies have not, however, gone for large-scale job evaluation exercises typical in many US and UK companies at least up until the 1980s.

In the UK, in the labour markets in which many Japanese manufacturing companies operate – relatively low-skill light assembly work – the companies themselves report that they pay average or above average wages (Pang and Oliver 1988; Yu and Wilkinson 1989). Wage levels are generally determined by the company in relation to industry and regional labour markets; many companies in both the USA and the UK have avoided unionization and hence wage bargaining, and even some of those companies in Britain which recognize single unions claim that collective bargaining has no influence on wages. Rather, wages are often established via the recommendation of the company advisory board or company council – a company institution in which union officials often play only a minor role.

A striking aspect of pay systems in Japanese companies in the UK is the widespread use of formal performance appraisal schemes. Although more common in the USA, appraisal in the UK has typically been restricted to managerial and white-collar staffs. In contrast, surveys show that virtually *all* Japanese firms employing over 200 people use performance appraisals. Nearly all apply these schemes to all grades of staff, including blue-collar staff, and the great majority indicate an influence of appraisal results on job grades, wage level, promotion and task allocation (Yu and Wilkinson 1989). This has been compared by Nissan's personnel director with traditional British practice, where 'frequently the only use to which [appraisals] are put is as a reference document for the next review' (Wickens 1987: 123).

Of 13 sets of Japanese companies' appraisal documentation recently collected by the authors, 11 included forced-choice questionnaires inviting the appraiser (typically the immediate superior or team leader) to grade the appraisee against a range of criteria. These criteria are

Table 3.1   Appraisal criteria in Japanese companies in the UK

Criteria	No. of companies using criteria
Teamworking ability, co-operation	11
Self-organization, problem-solving skills	10
Leadership, persuasiveness	9
Attendance, punctuality	8
Quantity of work, efficiency, productivity	8
Communication skills	7
Job knowledge	7
Accuracy, attention to detail	7
Attitude, motivation, loyalty	7
Creativity, initiative	6
Flexibility, adaptability	5
Quality of work	5
Ability to work under pressure	4
Enthusiasm, willingness to work	4
Safety, housekeeping	4
Reasoning, analytical skills	4
Persistence, determination	3
Work skills	3

Source: Yu and Wilkinson (1989)

indicated in table 3.1. The criteria, a mix of task performance indicators and personal qualities, are striking for the frequent use of factors such as teamwork, communications, co-operation and attitude. This orientation fits the Japanese emphasis on flexibility and teamwork, serving constantly to reinforce the message initially given in selection and induction. Whether judging people on their co-operation serves to resolve the apparent contradiction between individualized appraisal and reward on the one hand and co-operation and teamwork on the other is an open question.

Employee relations

In the UK, apart from a few joint ventures or where the Japanese company has taken over a going concern, the norm has been the avoidance of trade unions by locating in new towns and semi-rural locations, or the recognition of only one union in established industrial areas; for instance, only two out of 26 Japanese manufacturers in

Wales in 1992 did not recognise a trade union (Wilkinson et al. 1993). Many non-Japanese companies setting up on greenfield sites have also had success with the single-union option in the 1980s (Bassett 1986; Oliver and Wilkinson 1992).

The advantages to companies of single union recognition are primarily: the facilitation of flexible working in the absence of union demarcation lines; the reduced likelihood of industrial disputes 'spilling over' from plant to plant; and the simplification of bargaining and consultation structures and procedures. In itself single-union recognition is hardly new to the UK, as the trade union defenders of such deals have pointed out. However, when we look closely at the additional features of the single-union deals signed at Toshiba and other companies in the 1980s, a marked departure from traditional UK practice is evident. This is because the deals typically incorporate most or all of the following: company advisory boards; binding arbitration; specific clauses on flexible working; and strongly unitarist language and sentiments.

Company advisory boards come under a variety of names such as staff councils, company councils and advisory committees. Like many traditional joint consultative committees, members are not necessarily trade union officers, or even trade union members, but the boards' responsibilities typically extend to areas normally the preserve of collective bargaining, including pay and terms and conditions. In addition, such boards are important mechanisms for the transmission of company information. At Toshiba UK, manufacturers of colour televisions, union representatives are requested to sign a form stating:

> It is recognized that the company advisory board is the best and first means of resolving all collective issues between the company and its employees, and the representative fully supports and encourages the role of the Company Advisory Board in the conduct of relationships between the company and its employees.

The shift of responsibilities from shop stewards to worker representatives on advisory boards poses a threat to the traditional role of the shop steward. Describing Nissan UK's agreement with the engineering union, the AEU, Crowther and Garrahan (1988: 57) argue that 'it allows virtually no independent role for shop stewards, and whilst it appears that the company does not intend to actively obstruct union activities, the mechanisms for representation are highly supportive of non-union participation'. This is one explanation suggested by Crowther and Garrahan for the low union membership at Nissan.

At other Japanese companies in Britain, however, strong support of union membership from management helps membership levels to be similar to those for the rest of British manufacturing industry (Oliver and Wilkinson 1992).

Some single-union agreements incorporate a binding arbitration clause, and all those deals seen by the authors include procedures which greatly reduce the likelihood of an official dispute. 'Signing away the right to strike' has been vehemently criticized, though collective agreements are not legally binding in the UK. What is important is that dispute procedures in such deals may contribute, at least symbolically, to the industrial relations stability which is so important to the vulnerable Japanese system of production (Wilkinson and Oliver 1989).

Specific flexibility clauses are typical in these agreements. These generally assert in unambiguous terms the managerial prerogative over labour deployment, reinforcing the potential for flexible working that comes with single-union recognition. The agreement between Hitachi and the electricians' union (now merged with the Engineering Union) in the UK, for instance, reads:

> All company members will agree the complete flexibility of jobs and duties within and between the various company functions and departments. The main flexibility principle will be that when necessary to fit the needs of the business, all company members may be required to perform whatever jobs and duties are within their capability.

The language of 'harmony', 'mutual benificence' and 'commitment to company success' features prominently in many of the agreements between Japanese companies and unions, on both sides of the Atlantic. This indicates a redefinition of the role of the trade union as 'partner' rather than 'adversary'. Attitudes of trade unionists to the new style of employee relations (which, it must be stressed are not the exclusive preserve of Japanese companies) have been mixed.

In the UK some trade unionists have been critical of the employment practices of Japanese companies, and against those unions which have been party to agreements with these companies. In the USA some trade unionists have also been vocal in their denunciation of the Japanese approach to industrial relations. Following one dispute in 1989 between workers and the Japanese construction company Ohbayashi, labour leaders announced an anti-Japanese investment rally on the 7 December, Pearl Harbor Day (Kane 1989). (The dispute was settled before the rally took place when Ohbayashi agreed that the

AFL-CIO (the American Federation of Labor and Congress of Indus-trial Organizations) could play the role in labour assignments it wished.)

In the UK, in the context of declining trade union membership inter-union competition was the response of the trade union movement to the new industrial relations strategies of newly investing companies, and some trade unions, notably the EETPU (Electrical, Electronic, Telecommunications and Plumbing Union), the AEU (Amalgamated Engineering Union) and MATSA (Managerial Administrative Tech-nical Staff Association), took a proactive approach in offering model agreements on the above lines to potential investors. In the well-rehearsed debate, the advocates of the new unionism claim 'realism' and 'mutual benefit', the critics complain of a 'beauty contest' syn-drome resulting in 'sweetheart deals'. What is clear is that the unions party to such deals are explicitly accepting a *collaborative* rather than an *adversarial* role, a role which implies a new kind of trade unionism with similarities to Japanese company unionism.

In the USA, the majority of Japanese manufacturers have avoided the recognition of trade unions altogether, with employee relations being conducted through the various consultative and communication mechanisms described earlier. However, in those situations where unionization has occurred, similar issues have surfaced. The GM–Toyota joint venture, NUMMI in California, is instructive in this respect, and it is worth explaining the implications for industrial re-lations in the US auto industry.

In the context of fierce competition from the Japanese, it was as early as the late 1970s that the desire on the part of auto sector em-ployers in the USA to shift from 'pattern bargaining' was being strongly expressed. Pattern bargaining was a well-established system of bar-gaining in the Canadian as well as the US automotive industry which more or less ensured standard industry-wide wages, conditions and working practices. The desire was to move towards company- or even plant-level bargaining. In the early 1980s, with several Japanese as-semblers moving into non-union plants on greenfield sites in the Mid-West, the pressure grew even greater. According to Holmes (1989: 21–2): 'by 1985 the top UAW [United Automobile Workers] leadership . . . were implicitly endorsing the team concept as a strategy to make the US auto industry competitive . . . It involves a shift to-wards enterprise unionism where the union views itself as a partner in management.'

Since the mid-1980s the team concept and local bargaining have become widely established in the USA, and are making inroads into the Canadian auto industry as well. Florida and Kenney (1991) comment that the Japanese auto makers were large and powerful enough to mould their environment rather than simply adapt to it.

The Toyota–UAW local agreement at NUMMI was probably the single most important deal, since when NUMMI has provided a model of management–union relations as well as work practices in GM and other plants across America. Toyota Motor Corporation President, Soichiro Toyoda, was directly involved in 'efforts to communicate to the UAW our wish to introduce Japanese methods to the greatest possible degree ... in my opinion the most critical area is labour–management relations' (quoted in *Productivity Digest*, Singapore, 3–11 January 1985).

In the UK Toyota was a relatively late investor, and commenced production in late 1992. Toyota's chosen site is in Derbyshire, outside the traditional car-producing areas of the UK, and the company signed a single-union agreement with the Engineers' Union. Honda, in contrast, are pursuing a non-union route at their plant at Swindon in Wiltshire (the only non-union car plant in the UK). Local producers are alarmed at the cost advantages they fear the Japanese will have, and are attempting to move towards the Japanese model themselves. Being on established sites, the indigenous producers are finding this a slow and difficult process.

Summary and Conclusions

Comparison between the UK and USA experiences with Japanese companies reveals some differences but many similarities. What is less than clear is the extent to which these companies are reflecting current 'international' perceptions of best management practice versus their Japanese origin. Certainly the fact that they are setting up on greenfield sites gives them a scope for experimentation not open to companies on established sites. Moreover, it is clearly mistaken to regard inwardly investing 'Japanese companies' as a homogeneous mass; although there are some similarities in HRM style between these companies, there are also important differences which are mediated by a whole variety of locational and technological factors. The nation of origin is only one of many factors which impacts on management practice (Elger and Smith 1994).

When the inwardly investing companies are considered relative to those operating in Japan itself, there are clear differences. Left behind in Japan are the extensive welfare provision, lifetime employment and seniority wages and promotion. The Japanese manufacturers have brought total quality and just-in-time manufacturing systems and the team concept which goes with them.

On both sides of the Atlantic Japanese human resource management policies entail careful attention to selection, training, consultation and communication, single-status facilities, harmonized terms and conditions, the minimization of job classes, and individual appraisals emphasizing co-operation, teamwork and flexibility. Such practices underwrite an efficient manufacturing system dependent on teamwork, strict discipline, flexibility and attention to detail. The productivity and quality performance of Japanese transplants is a moot point. Individual companies have publicly claimed that the performance of their transplants meets that of the mother factories in Japan; international benchmarking studies do not wholly support this claim (Womack et al. 1990; Andersen Consulting 1994).

The context in the 1980s and 1990s, however, for both the USA and UK, has been one of high unemployment, weakening trade union strength, and a political climate hostile to labour movements and organized industrial action. This context, together with the fact that many (in the USA) or most (in the UK) Japanese companies are setting up on greenfield sites without the baggage of established organizational cultures and traditions, probably helps to account for the apparent ease with which Japanese companies have established new practices. In both countries, too, most Japanese manufacturers have been welcomed by local trade union leaders, businessmen and civic dignitaries for the new life they promise to put into communities suffering from the decline of their traditional industries.

In the 1980s and early 1990s, there was a clear 'honeymoon' effect surrounding many of these investments. The extent to which the HRM practices we have discussed will be sustained in the longer term and the extent to which they will be modified in the light of local conditions remains an open question.

References

Abo, T. (ed.) 1994: *Hybrid Factory*. New York: Oxford University Press.

Andersen Consulting 1993: *The Lean Enterprise Benchmarking Project*. London: Andersen Consulting.

Andersen Consulting 1994: *The Worldwide Manufacturing Competitiveness Survey*. London: Andersen Consulting.

Anglo-Japanese Economic Institute 1991: *Japanese Addresses in the UK*. London: AJEI.

Azumi, K. 1969: *Higher Education and Business Recruitment in Japan*. New York: Columbia University Press.

Basset, P. 1986: *Strike Free: New Industrial Relations in Britain*. London: MacMillan.

British Broadcasting Corporation (BBC) 1986: Process capability and control. In *Quality Techniques*, PT 619. Milton Keynes, Bucks.: Open University/BBC Productions [film].

Brown, C. and Reich, M. 1989: When does union–management co-operation work? A look at NUMMI and GM–Van Nuy's. *California Management Review*, 31(4), 26–44.

Clegg, C. 1986: Trip to Japan: a synergistic approach to managing human resources. *Personnel Management*, August, 35–9.

Crowther, S. and Garrahan, P. 1988: Invitation to Sunderland: corporate power and the local economy. *Industrial Relations Journal*, 19(1), 51–9.

Cusumano, M. 1986: *The Japanese Automobile Industry: technology and management at Nissan and Toyota*. Cambridge, Mass.: Harvard University Press.

Dillow, C. 1989: *A Return to Trade Surplus? The impact of Japanese investment in the UK*. London: Nomura Research Institute.

Dore, R. 1973: *Origins of the Japanese Employment System*. London: Allen & Unwin.

Economist Intelligence Unit 1989: *Japanese Motor Business*, no. 19, March.

Elger, A. and Smith, C. 1994: Global Japanization? Convergence and competition in the organization of the labour process. In A. Elger and C. Smith (eds), *Global Japanization?*, London: Routledge, pp. 31–59.

Florida, R. and Kenney, M. 1991: Transplanted organizations: the transfer of Japanese industrial organization to the US. *American Sociological Review*, 56, 381–98.

Fucini, J.J. and Fucini, S. 1990: *Working for the Japanese*. New York: Free Press.

Garrahan, P. and Stewart, P. 1992: *The Nissan Enigma*. London: Mansell.

Gleave, S. and Oliver, N. 1990: Human resources management in Japanese manufacturing companies in the UK: five case studies. *Journal of General Management*, 16(1), 54–68.

Graham, L. 1994: How does the Japanese model transfer to the United States? A view from the line. In A. Elger and C. Smith (eds), *Global Japanization?*, London: Routledge.

Holmes, J. 1989: *From Uniformity to Diversity: changing patterns of wages and work practices in the North American automobile industry*. Paper presented to the Annual Employment Research Unit Conference, Cardiff Business School, University of Wales College of Cardiff, 19–20 September.

Ishida, H. 1977: *Exportability of the Japanese Employment System*. Tokyo: Japan Institute of Labour.

Japan Institute of Labour 1984: *Wages and Hours of Work*. Japanese Industrial Relations Series, no. 3. Tokyo: Japan Institute of Labour.

JETRO (Japan External Trade Organization) 1994: *The 10th Survey of*

European Operations of Japanese Companies in the Manufacturing Sector. London: JETRO

Kane, M. 1989: *Regional Underpinnings of the US–Japan Partnership Commonwealth of Kentucky: a case study*. Lexington, KY: University of Kentucky.

Kelman, S. 1990: The Japanization of America. *Public Interest*, 98, 70–83.

Kirosingh, M. 1989: Changed work practices. *Employment Gazette*, 97(8), 422–9.

Littler, C. 1982: *The Development of the Labour Process in Capitalist Societies*. London: Heinemann.

Lowe, J. and Oliver, N. 1990: *New Look Employee Relations: the view from the inside*. Paper presented to the Employment Research Unit Conference on Employment Relations in the Enterprise Culture, Cardiff Business School, University of Wales College of Cardiff, 18–19 September.

Monden, I. 1983: *Toyota Production System*. London: Industrial Engineering and Management Press.

Morishima, M. 1982: *Why Has Japan 'Succeeded'? Western technology and the Japanese ethos*. Cambridge: Cambridge University Press.

Morris, J. 1988: The who, why and where of Japanese manufacturing investment in the UK. *Industrial Relations Journal*, 19(1), 31–40.

Morris, J., Munday, M. and Wilkinson, B. 1993: *Working for the Japanese: the economic and social consequences of Japanese investment in Wales*. London: Athlone.

Morton, C. 1994: *Becoming World Class*. London: Macmillan.

Nakane, C. 1973: *Japanese Society*. Harmondsworth, Middx: Penguin.

Naylor, L. 1984: Bringing home the lessons. *Personnel Management*, 16(3), 34 7.

Oliver, N. and Wilkinson, B. 1992: *The Japanization of British Industry*, 2nd edn. Oxford: Blackwell.

Ouchi, W. 1981: *Theory Z: how American business can meet the Japanese challenge*. Boston, Mass.: Addison-Wesley.

Pang, K.K. 1987: *Japanese Management Practices in Overseas Subsidiaries: a case approach*. MBA dissertation, Cardiff Business School, University of Wales College of Cardiff.

Pang, K.K. and Oliver, N. 1988: Personnel strategy in eleven Japanese manufacturing companies in the UK. *Personnel Review*, 17(3), 16–21.

Pascale, R. and Athos, A. 1982: *The Art of Japanese Management*. Harmondsworth, Middx: Penguin.

Perucci, R. 1994: *Japanese Auto Transplants in the Heartland: corporatism and community*. New York: Aldine/de Gruyter.

Piore, M. and Sabel, C. 1984: *The Second Industrial Divide*. New York: Basic Books.

Pucik, V. 1985: Managing Japan's white collar workers. *Euro-Asia Business Review*, 4(3), 16–21.

Pucik, V. 1989: *Management Culture in Japanese-owned US Corporations*. Tokyo: Egon Zehnder International.

Rehder, R. 1990: Japanese transplants: after the honeymoon. *Business Horizons*, January–February, 87–98.

Robbins, S. 1983: Theory Z from a power-control perspective. *California Management Review*, 25(2), 67–75.

Sakasegawa, K. 1988: Technological innovation and wage systems: the Japanese experience. In International Labour Office (ed.), *Technological Change, Work Organization and Pay: lessons from Asia*, Labour–Management Relations Series no. 68, Geneva: ILO, pp. 171–84.

Schonberger, R. 1986: *World Class Manufacturing*. New York: Free Press.

Sethi, S., Namiki, N. and Swanson, C. 1984: *The False Promise of the Japanese Miracle*. London: Pitman.

Slaughter, J. 1987: The team concept in the US auto industry. Paper presented to the Conference on the Japanization of British Industry, Cardiff Business School, University of Wales College of Cardiff, 17–18 September.

Takamiya, M. 1981: Japanese multinationals in Europe: international operations and their public policy implications. *Columbia Journal of World Business*, Summer, 5–17.

Trevor, M. 1988: *Toshiba's New British Company*. London: Policy Studies Institute.

White, M. and Trevor, M. 1983: *Under Japanese Management*. London: Heinemann.

Wickens, P. 1987: *The Road to Nissan*. London: Macmillan.

Wilkinson, B. and Oliver, N. 1989: Power, control and the *kanban*. *Journal of Management Studies*, 26(1), 47–58.

Wilkinson, B. and Oliver, N. 1990: Obstacles to Japanization: the case of Ford UK. *Employee Relations*, 12(1), 17–22.

Wilkinson, B., Morris, J. and Munday, M. 1993: Japan in Wales: a new IR. *Industrial Relations Journal*, 24(4), 273–83.

Womack, J.P., Jones, D.T. and Roos, D. 1990: *The Machine that Changed the World: the triumph of lean production*. New York: Rawson Macmillan.

Wood, S. 1992: Japanization and/or Toyotaism? *Work, Employment and Society*, 5(4), 567–600.

Yu, C. and Wilkinson, B. 1989: *Pay and Appraisal in Japanese Companies in Britain*. Japanese Management Research Unit Working Paper no. 8. Cardiff: University of Wales College of Cardiff.

4

Human Resource Management: the European Dimension

PAUL KIRKBRIDE

Introduction

While it might be expected that this chapter will simply represent an interesting and uncontroversial excursion from the detail of HRM to the geo-political dimension of Europe, in fact it immediately raises a number of definitional and semantic questions. First, the use of the term 'Europe' begs the question as to what really constitutes Europe. There are, of course, a series of potential answers to this enquiry. Increasingly there has been a tendency to use the term 'Europe' loosely to refer to the European Union (EU). This is not surprising in that the 40 years since the Treaty of Rome in 1957 has seen the Community expand from the initial six (Belgium, France, Italy, Luxembourg, Netherlands and West Germany) through the additions of Denmark, Ireland and the United Kingdom (1973), Greece (1981), Portugal and Spain (1986) and Austria, Finland and Sweden (1994), to the current 15 as of 1995. The EU has come to dominate Western Europe in both economic and political terms during this period.

These trends have been reinforced by the then EC decision in 1985 to create a Single European Market or a 'Europe without frontiers'. This came into effect on 31 December 1992 and aims to remove almost all physical, technical and fixed barriers to competition and internal trade. Closely associated with this initiative is the concept of the establishment of economic and monetary union (EMU) which would allow a single market to operate more efficiently via the development of a Community Central Bank and a common currency. Initially progress in this direction involved the establishment of the European Monetary System (EMS) and associated Exchange Rate Mechanism (ERM). The European Commission, then under President Jacques Delors, envisaged a series of steps towards full EMU, starting with the completion of the Single Market and moving, via a tightening of the ERM, to a system of fixed and locked exchange rates and the establishment of a single currency. However, events during recent years, such as the near-collapse of the ERM, the political furore over the failure of Denmark to ratify the Maastricht Treaty, the United Kingdom's perceived delaying tactics over progress to EMU, the change of EU presidency and a less federalist mood, must cast some doubts on the suggested timetable for progress to EMU, if not on its final achievement.

A politically important aspect of the EU, particularly relevant to human resource management, is the social dimension represented by the Charter of Fundamental Social Rights and its associated draft directives. Together these initiatives represent a move towards a comprehensive system of European employment law. It is therefore clear that the EU raises some pressing and far-reaching issues, problems and opportunities for human resource practitioners, such as the need for harmonization of employment conditions; the need to meet EU statutory requirements; the need to deal with increased cross-border mobility (transfers and hiring); and the need to develop new 'pan-European' managers for pan-European organizational structures.

However, despite its comparative dominance, Europe should not be conflated with the EU. A few European countries are currently not members of the EU, although these are at the time of writing considering membership. In addition, and perhaps more importantly, our conception of Europe has been greatly widened since the collapse of the Iron Curtain by the 'opening-up' of what was previously Eastern Europe. Thus a greater Europe would now include countries such as Albania, Bulgaria, the Czech Republic, Estonia, Hungary, Latvia, Lithuania, Poland, Romania, Slovakia and the individual components of the former Yugoslavia. A wider definition would also include the individual republics of the former USSR. The opening up of 'poorer' Eastern European countries has created a set of issues, problems and tensions which have yet to be addressed and resolved, but are currently being perhaps most keenly felt in the new united Germany. An additional trend to note is the beginning of a drift to the Mediterranean, with Cyprus and Turkey being considered for membership, Malta looking for closer ties, and the potentially pivotal role to be played by Israel.

Europe then may be said to be currently in a state of flux. At the same time that Western Europe appears to be slowly, and rather unsurely, moving towards greater economic and political integration, another very different integrated bloc has crumbled, leaving a legacy of serious economic problems. The key issues for the countries of Eastern Europe to resolve include the transition to a market economy, the privatization of state industries, dealing with rising inflation, creating currency convertibility, maintaining productivity and avoiding hyper-unemployment. The implications and problems for human resource professionals in these countries are both urgent and stark.

A second definitional and semantic issue concerns the use of the term 'human resource management' (HRM) and its applicability to Europe. This concept has become the subject of extensive, and often negative, theoretical debate in the academic literature (Blyton and Turnbull 1992). In the practitioner sphere, on the other hand, the term has been accepted fairly positively and without critical comment. Part of the debate concerns the applicability of what was originally an American map, model or theory (Noon 1992) to the European context. To what extent does Europe represent a distinct context for the operation of HRM? Obviously we have already alluded to potential specificities in the economic and political spheres, but another major potential differentiator remains the cultural context. Here there are several questions. To what extent can we discern a pan-European culture and thus suggest that a pan-European model of HRM might emerge (Thurley and Wirdenius 1989) which would be distinctive from both American and Japanese models of HRM? Or is it the case that the countries of Europe are so culturally diverse that HRM becomes almost country-specific? Or can we identify regions within Europe where sufficient cultural homogeneity exists to suggest that common patterns of HRM practice and approach may occur?

The structure of the chapter is as follows. First, we seek to locate the concept of HRM within a cultural framework by describing, in outline, the cultural contours of Europe. We shall then consider to what extent European HRM is different from American HRM in cultural, but also political and economic terms. Drawing heavily on the Price Waterhouse/Cranfield Project on European Human Resource Management we shall then attempt to outline the current key trends in HRM in Europe. Finally, we turn our attention to recent attempts to create pan-European managers to meet the increased 'Europeanization' of large organizations.

The Cultural Context

One of the great problems in describing 'European human resource management' is that HRM practices are obviously partially determined by the wider environment within which they take place. The countries of Europe, despite some convergence, still have specific and particular political, economic, legal and social environments. Previous studies of HRM in Europe have tended to focus on the political and legal differences and the increasing relevance of EU directives and codes. However, it is obvious that for HRM the cultural context is particularly salient and we shall focus on this dimension in our examination of European HRM.

Important cultural differences exist between the northern and southern components of what is commonly referred to as Western Europe and between the various parts of what was once the Eastern European communist bloc. Unfortunately, the difficulties of research access since the Second World War has meant that much more is known about cultural differences in the former than in the latter. Culture has been expressed as the special 'collective programming of the mind of members of a group, which is reflected in its particular assumptions, perceptions, thought patterns, norms and values' (Hofstede 1991: 8). Values are considered particularly significant in terms of the tendency of individuals (considered collectively as a culture) to prefer certain conditions or states of affairs to others. Individuals acquire values as part of the general socialization process involved in growing up in a country, region and family group. Values are associated with the national culture of a country as boundaries encourage interaction and socialization within them. However, the movement of peoples across national boundaries, the periodic changing of frontiers, the preservation by particular groups of a culture different from the mainstream culture, and differences in social and economic experience mean that subcultures exist in all countries. Consequently, whatever are described as the mainstream cultural traits are best considered as a central tendency or average. Individuals will differ in the extent to which they share the values associated with any particular country.

Context

Context refers to 'the information that surrounds an event; it is inextricably bound up with the meaning of that event' (Hall and Hall 1990: 6). Cultures can be compared on a scale from high to low context:

A high context (HC) communication or message is one in which *most* of the information is already in the person, while very little is in the coded, explicit, transmitted part of the message. A low context (LC) communication is just the opposite; i.e., the mass of information is vested in the explicit code. (Quoted in Hall and Hall 1990: 6; emphasis in original)

Low-context peoples, such as Germans, Swiss, Scandinavians and other Northern Europeans, appreciate explicit, clear, written forms of communication as provided by computers, books, reports and letters. In contrast, high-context peoples, such as Southern Europeans, divulge less information officially in written forms, but tend to be better informed than low-context people, since they develop extensive informal networks for exchanging information verbally face-to-face or by telephone. High-context people are also more adept at interpreting non-verbal aspects of communication and seeing the significance of what is implicit or not said: pauses, silence, tone and other subtle signals. Information is also said to spread unofficially more rapidly in high-context countries.

Low-context peoples tend not to mix work and social topics when in negotiations, and to compartmentalize their work and personal relationships. High-context peoples are more flexible or elastic in the management of their work or that of others. Business and pleasure may be mixed, and time spent on rapport-building during meetings. In such circumstances it is argued that deadlocks in business will not be broken nor problems solved unless people allow time to develop correct interpersonal relations. Once these are attained, it becomes easier to solve technical problems. Engagements and agendas at meetings may be modified quickly as circumstances change.

Hofstede's four dimensions

Perhaps the major contribution to the 'mapping' of cultural values on a world-wide scale was that of Hofstede (1980). From a factor analysis of his extensive database of 116,000 IBM respondents over two time periods he was able to delineate four dimensions which seemed to identify key cultural differences. These dimensions were: power distance (low to high); uncertainty avoidance (weak to strong); individualism/collectivism; and masculinity/femininity. His empirical data allowed countries to be scored and located on each of these four dimensions. For the location of key European countries on these dimensions see table 4.1.

The power distance index (low to high) measures 'the extent to

Table 4.1   Scores of European countries on Hofstede's cultural dimensions

Country	Power distance	Uncertainty avoidance	Individualism/ collectivism	Masculine/ feminine
Austria	11	70	55	79
Belgium	65	94	75	54
Denmark	18	23	74	16
Finland	33	59	63	25
France	68	86	71	43
Germany (W.)	35	65	67	66
Greece	60	112	35	57
Ireland	28	35	70	68
Italy	50	75	76	70
Portugal	63	104	27	31
Spain	57	86	51	42
Sweden	31	29	71	5
Turkey	66	85	37	45
UK	35	35	89	66
Mean[a]	51	64	51	51

[a] These values represent the means of the scores of the 39 countries in Hofstede's original survey.

Source: Hofstede (1980: 315)

which the members of a society accept that power in institutions and organisations is distributed unequally' (Hofstede 1985: 347). In all Northern European EC countries (Finland, Denmark, Ireland, Germany, Netherlands, Sweden and the UK) as well as other non-EU Northern European countries (Norway), Hofstede's findings were that power distances were relatively small. The consequences for organizations in such societies are that one can expect to find: flat hierarchies; bureaucracy minimized; tasks delegated; a belief that power should be used legitimately; consultative management styles; and a degree of autonomy for subordinates (Hofstede 1991: 27–8). Hofstede found that EU countries in Southern Europe (Belgium, France, Greece, Italy, Portugal, Spain) had large or medium power distances (ibid.: 141). Characteristics of high power distance organizations include: steep hierarchies; autocratic, directive or paternalist management; special privileges and status symbols for senior staff; and an ambivalent attitude of employees to management. While subordinates tend to have a dependency relationship with superiors, being afraid to disagree with them, they sometimes reject managers they disrespect; a behaviour which Hofstede calls counter-dependence (ibid.: 27).

Hofstede defines uncertainty avoidance (from strong to weak) as society's fear of the unknown and the extent to which 'a culture programs its members to feel either uncomfortable or comfortable in unstructured and ambiguous situations' (Hofstede 1992: 6). Characteristics of low uncertainty avoidance (UA) societies, which include Denmark, Holland, Ireland and the UK, are: tolerance of differing views; limited influence of experts; informality; few rules; control of one's emotions (Hofstede 1991: 111–12). These values are expressed in UK organizations by a preference for those managers who are outward-going, decisive and practical and geared towards action or taking decisions fairly rapidly. Less store has been placed on intellectual skills, qualifications or specialism. All Southern European countries (France, Greece, Italy, Portugal, and Spain) rank high on uncertainty avoidance, indicating a desire to minimize ambiguity and anxiety and to control the future. Characteristics of high uncertainty avoidance societies include emphasis on laws and rules to cover all eventualities, safety and security measures, desire for long careers in the same business, and focus on formal procedures (ibid.: 116). Hofstede points out that the need for rules and laws in Latin countries can lead to the growth of nonsensical or dysfunctional rules. People seem less concerned about what happens in reality since some rules are only formally followed, having been divested of any practical meaning (ibid.: 121).

Hofstede defines individualism as societies where ties are loose, where everyone is expected to care for himself/herself and immediate family only, and where emphasis is placed on individual achievement, identity and decision-making. Managers prefer to keep a distance from subordinates both professionally and personally. Organizations exert control by inducing 'guilt' feelings in potential violators of rules. Hofstede describes collectivist cultures as associated with strong extended family units, individual dependence on the group which protects members in exchange for loyalty, a strong 'in-group'–'out-group' dichotomy; and sophisticated networks and alliances (relations, close friends and associates) which bind 'in-groups'. Key values include achieving harmony at work, consensus in meetings, face-saving in work and social situations, and group decision-making. Inducing 'shame' is a means of group control over individuals who may violate group norms. People are high-context and polychronic and are motivated by involvement in achieving group aims rather by seeking self-advancement. In Hofstede's findings, all of Western Europe is individualist except

Portugal and Greece, with the UK ranked as the second-highest individualist country world-wide after the USA (Hofstede 1991: 53).

The masculinity–femininity dimension is the only one for which Hofstede claims that a significant difference exists between the scores of men and women. In masculine countries he argues that gender roles tend to be fairly strictly demarcated and that stereotypically male values such as competitiveness, individual advancement, materialism, profit, assertiveness, strength and action-focused activities tend to be appreciated. Masculine countries in his data sample include Germany, Greece, Italy, Spain and the UK. In feminine countries (Denmark, Finland, Norway, Portugal and Sweden) more appreciation is given to stereotypically female values such as co-operation, warm relationships, caring and nurturing, the quality of life, while less differentiation exists between male and female roles.

Universalism and particularism

Universalism and particularism are concepts which are fairly well established in the cross-cultural literature (Alder 1991). Universalism (societal obligation) implies that people generally apply the same rules and standards, or act in a similar manner towards other members of society whatever the circumstances. No rigid distinction tends to be made between the public or private domain or between 'in-group' (family and close friends) and 'out-group' relations. In such 'inclusive' cultures everyone is considered a potential friend or enemy to a higher degree than in particularist 'exclusive' cultures. Both the USA and the UK have been cited as good examples of countries where universalistic norms apply (Peabody 1985: 208).

Particularism (personal obligation) implies that people operate different codes depending on who they are dealing with. They operate two codes, one governing behaviour within the private domain (relations, close friends and associates) and another governing relationships with others. In societies which make important or rigid 'in-group' – 'out-group' distinctions such as Greece, Italy and to a lesser extent France, outsiders may be regarded with suspicion or mistrust (Barzini 1968: 205; Fleury 1990: 129; Peabody 1985: 139–40). Within such cultures (universalistic) rules, as created by the state or any other organization or body, may be modified according to circumstances or situations, by people acting on a particularistic basis. It is this value which illuminates the apparent paradox in high uncertainty avoidance cultures of having a plethora of rules and then ignoring them.

European country clusters

Our analysis of dimensions of cultural difference has perhaps demon-strated that on most dimensions countries are not spaced equally, but instead form clusters. This has been noted by several of the leading commentators on culture and comparative management (Hofstede 1980, 1991; Ronen 1986). We suggest that it is perhaps at the level of the country cluster that cultural differences have their greatest explanatory power. One blunt but informative distinction is the differ-ence, noted by many commentators, between a Northern European cluster and a Southern European cluster (Madariaga 1952: 61). If we go beyond the crude North–South dichotomy we can distinguish a number of reasonably clear country clusters. These include:

1   Scandinavian: Denmark, Finland, Norway, and Sweden;
2   Anglo: Ireland and the UK in Europe but also other English-speaking countries such as Australia, New Zealand and Canada (excluding Que-bec), and the United States;
3   Germanic: Austria, Germany and Switzerland;
4   Latin and Mediterranean: Italy, Portugal and Spain;
5   Northern (quasi) Latin: France and Belgium, which have frequently been placed in a separate cluster of two; however, France is often also put in the Latin and Mediterranean group.

Is there a 'European' Model of HRM?

A legitimate follow-on question from our discussion of the cultural 'map' of Europe is: to what extent can a specifically 'European' model of human resource management be delineated? This is a rather com-plex question in that any answer requires discussion and debate of the origins and nature of HRM as well as the distinctive 'European' at-tributes of practices.

The precise meaning of the term 'HRM' is far from clear and the concept remains differentiated and fluid (Brewster 1994, 1995). Defi-nitions and models range from the Harvard four-fold typology (Beer et al. 1985) to models which identify distinctive HRM areas (DeCenzo and Robbins 1988) to models which propose sequential processes of HR activity (Fombrun and Devanna 1984). Despite their differences, these models have come to be seen as the vanguard of an 'HRM' move-ment or school and have been subject to common critiques. It has been suggested that the HRM concept relies too heavily on specific aspects of Japanese practice, on examples drawn from a small number of private sector firms, and for failing to link theory to general practice (Beaumont 1991; Pieper 1990; Poole 1990).

A common thread running through all these models of HRM is the notion of organizational independence and autonomy. As Brewster (1995: 2) notes, 'Defining and prescribing HRM strategies for organisations implies that the organisations concerned are free to develop their own strategies.' Yet we may argue that this view is at once representative, if not actually iconic, of US culture and, in fact, atypical of most European countries. Guest (1990) has noted that this view of organizational freedom and autonomy in HRM is particularly American and redolent of 'land of opportunity', 'rugged individualist' and 'frontiers' mentalities. These ideals are reflected in the 'private enterprise' culture of the USA which consists of expressions of the right to manage, antipathy to organized labour and comparatively low levels of state support and control in HR issues.

Yet we may argue that Europe is different to the USA and that European organizations face a different cultural backdrop and experience less freedom and autonomy. Most comparative empirical studies of national cultural differences agree that the US culture is more individualistic and more achievement-orientated than most other cultures in the world (Hofstede 1980; Trompenaars 1993). Yet, as we have seen, Europe is much more heterogeneous. The Scandinavian cluster is characterized by high femininity scores and less achievement orientation. The Latin–Mediterranean cluster is characterized by a greater collectivism and much greater power distance. Even countries in the Anglo cluster (Ireland, UK) are not as extreme as the USA in terms of their individualism and achievement orientation.

These cultural differences are reflected, more practically, in the areas of legislation, business structure and employee involvement. As Pieper (1990: 8) notes, 'the major difference between HRM in the US and in Western Europe is the degree to which [HRM] is influenced and determined by state regulations [in Europe]. Companies have a narrower scope of choice in regard to personnel management than in the US.' European companies are constrained by legislation on hiring, dismissal, pay, health and safety, and working hours, to name but a few. In addition to national legislation, European firms are also increasing subject to supranational EU legislation on HRM via the European Social Charter. The result is, as Brewster (1995: 5) notes, that 'governments in Europe and the overall European Union tend to have more of a controlling function (through legislation) and supporting (through finance) role in HRM than is the case in the United

States. The corollary is the employers are less autonomous vis-à-vis the State.'

Patterns of business ownership and structure in Europe also vary widely from those found in the United States. Despite the recent trend towards denationalization within Europe (and particularly the United Kingdom), public ownership is still more widespread than in the United States. In the private sector there are also crucial differences between the US model and Europe. Brewster cites, for example, the family control of major companies in Southern Europe and the degree of interlocking control of large German companies by a small number of major banks. Another area of major difference is that of trade union representation and employee involvement. While HRM has often been linked in the USA to non-unionism (Kochan et al. 1984), the situation in Europe is rather different. Both trade union density and trade union recognition remain greater in Europe as a whole than in the USA. As Brewster notes:

> Trade unionism remains widespread and important in Europe, an importance that current EU-level approaches may well enhance. Furthermore, in most European countries, many of the union functions in areas such as pay bargaining, for example, are exercised at industrial or national levels – outside the direct involvement of managers within individual organisations – as well as at establishment levels.   (Brewster 1995: 7)

In addition, in the area of employee involvement, many European countries have adopted systems of works councils and board-level representation (including two-tier management boards) which limit managerial freedom and autonomy.

As a result,

> European organisations operate with restricted autonomy; constrained at international (European Union) level and at the national level by culture and legislation, at the organisational level by patterns of ownership, and at the HRM level by trade union involvement and consultative arrangements. There is a need, therefore, for a model of HRM that goes beyond seeing these features as external constraints, and integrates them into the concept of HRM.   (Brewster 1995: 3)

What would such a model look like? At a general level Thurley and Wirdenius (1991) attempted to characterize a European approach to management as:

Environment   Organization

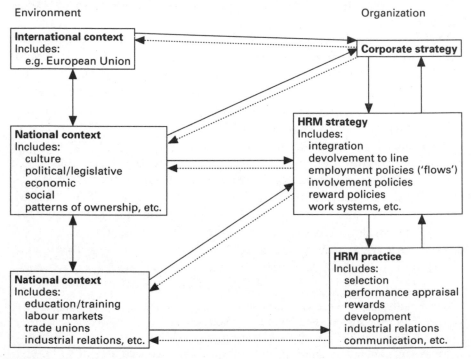

Figure 4.1   'European' (contextual) model of human resource management
Source: Brewster (1995)

- emerging, but not fully in existence except in limited circumstances;
- broadly linked to the idea of European integration which is continually expanding;
- reflecting key values such as pluaralism and tolerance; and
- associated with a balanced stakeholder philosophy and the concept of social partners.

Brewster (1995) proposes a European model of human resource management which follows the American models in depicting HR strategies as interacting with business strategies (figure 4.1). However, it also shows, in outline form, that the business strategy, HR strategy and HR practice of an organization interact with an external environment which comprises national culture, legislation, employee representation and other factors that we have discussed earlier. The key difference between Brewster's model and that of previous commentators is that it considers the sets of factors external to the organization as an integral part of the HRM model and system, rather than simply as an external influence or constraint upon the organizationally tied HRM system.

Trends in European HR Practice

Now that we have considered the conceptual basis of 'European HRM' we can turn our attention to some of the trends that can be identified across Europe in terms of both HR role and HR practices. Perhaps the best source of such data, and certainly the largest empirical study to date, is the Price Waterhouse/Cranfield Project on European Human Resource Management conducted at the Centre for European Human Resource Management, Cranfield, under the direction of Professor Chris Brewster. The results of these studies have been published extensively (Brewster 1994; Brewster et al. 1994; Brewster and Hegewisch 1994) and we shall only seek to extract some key trends for consideration here.

One issue concerns the power, influence and visibility of the HR function across Europe. There are several ways of measuring this, including: HR specialist involvement in the main strategy-making forum (board or equivalent); HR involvement in the development of overall business strategy; and operationalization of HR strategies and evaluation of the HR function. Whilst there are, of course, national variations the Cranfield data show that the majority of European companies have an HR presence at board level and that this appears to be an increasing trend. Secondly, the data show that in most countries the HR function is involved from the earliest stage in the development of corporate strategy and has a written formal HR strategy. However, fewer organizations actually implement their HR strategies into work programmes or are systematically evaluated (Brewster 1994). However, the greatest variability concerns the devolution of HR activities to line managers. As Brewster et al. (1994: 128) note:

> the results show that in Denmark and Switzerland devolvement is the norm for most organizations . . . Sweden and the Netherlands are also above the 'devolution average'. Five out of the ten countries [Germany, Spain, France, Norway and the UK] fall in a cluster at or below the 'devolution average'. Variations within the group of five do exist despite the close overall ranking. Somewhat of a surprise to many commentators is the position of the UK. It is one of the least devolved countries in our sample. Italy . . . stands on its own and has by a clear majority the fewest organisations devolving issues to the line.

To sum up, it appears 'that in Europe there may be a higher degree of integration of HRM at the top levels of organisations than there is in the USA: especially when the extra-organizational cultural and legislative influences are included' (Brewster 1994: 76).

What of more substantive aspects of HR practice? Are there any key trends here that can be discerned across Europe? Three issues are particularly worthy of mention, two concerning payment and one concerning training. One clear trend across Europe has been the gradual decentralization of bargaining structures to the extent that pay is increasingly determined at company or workplace level rather than at national or industry levels. This is true both for those countries which still have a predominantly centralized system (such as the Scandinavian countries) as well as those which have moved to predominantly decentralized systems (France and the UK). Least movement can be discerned in Germany where industry agreements remain the norm for over 90 per cent of workers, although these do allow for company-level bargaining over implementation. The Scandinavian countries remain fairly centralized, with over 60 per cent of employers still bargaining at national or industry levels, despite trends towards the industry level (from the national) and company-level supplementary negotiation (Hegewisch 1991). At the other extreme, in the UK national or industrial bargaining is now largely a public sector practice: only 22 per cent of private sector employers negotiate at industry level for manual workers while 82 per cent of public sector employers implement national agreements (Brewster et al. 1994).

A second major payment trend concerns the increasing use of variable merit- or performance-related payment across Europe. There are several reasons for this. Human resource management theories of the last ten years have tended to stress the need to link payment more directly to employee performance. Lower inflation has enabled companies to introduce performance-related elements on top of, or in lieu of, cost-of-living increases. However, whatever the reason, the data show that in all countries in the Cranfield survey, except the Netherlands and Norway, the majority of organizations increased variable pay during the period 1988–91. While there is a discernible trend to performance-related pay, European countries vary radically in their relative usage. As Brewster et al. (1994: 117) note:

> the practice of merit or performance related pay is least common in the Scandinavian countries; even for managerial staff less than a fifth of organisations in Norway and less than a sixth in Denmark and Sweden use this approach ... In France, Italy and the UK over two-thirds of

organisations use merit pay for managerial staff and, at least in France and Italy, a third and more do so for manual workers.

In terms of company-level performance payments, there is again strong variability, with profit-sharing for managers common in France and Germany but less so in the Netherlands and the UK, while, conversely, employee share options have become fairly widespread in the UK (to over 40 per cent of managerial staff) but much less common elsewhere in Europe.

A final notable trend concerns training and development. The Cranfield data show a Europe-wide increase in training at all levels, but particularly for managerial and professional staff, despite variations from country to country in terms of the absolute level of provision and the extent of government intervention and support. Training and development is increasingly seen as a critical part of an organization's HR strategy. Particular issues of common concern include: providing a substitute to difficult and costly external recruitment; providing new skills required by technological and organizational change; and enabling management succession and career path planning. Companies in Europe are spending between 2 per cent and 4 per cent of payroll on training and in eight out of the ten countries in the Cranfield survey more than 10 per cent of organizations devote five or more days to the training of manual workers (normally the least-trained group). Despite these trends national variations do exist. Countries with poorer state education systems such as Spain allocated more days to manual worker training than did those with a superior state education system such as Germany.

Creating the Pan-European Manager

One of the most interesting aspects of the increasing 'Europeanization' of organizations is the need to develop 'pan-European' managers. Why is this deemed necessary? First, because the effective management of human resources is increasingly seen as a major determinant of success or failure in international business and because the quality of an organization's management capability seems even more salient and critical in the international as opposed to the domestic arena (Tung 1984). Secondly, because shortages of such 'international managers' is becoming an increasing problem for European firms. A survey of 440 European executives claimed that such shortages were the single most important factor hindering efforts to expand abroad, and over one-third of respondents had experienced difficulties in finding managers with the necessary international experience and orientation (*International Management*, November 1986). More recently, in a study of 45 British and Irish firms, Scullion (1992) reports that 67 per cent of the firms had experienced shortages of international managers and over 70 per cent indicated that future shortages were anticipated. Of the respondents, 75 per cent cited the increasing pace of internationalization as the primary reason for the shortages. Scullion also asked his respondents to identify the main HRM challenges posed by the advent of the Single European Market (SEM). For over 80 per cent of the firms the main challenge was seen as the need to secure an adequate supply of international managers, while a majority of respondents also pointed to the need to upgrade managerial skills and competencies in order to compete effectively in Europe (Scullion 1992).

What then are the core competencies of such international managers? A recent study from Ashridge (Barham and Wills 1992; Barham and Berthoin Antal 1994) conducted in-depth qualitative research with nine global/international organizations. The results point to two sets of related competencies. The first, the 'doing' competencies, suggest that the effective international manager:

• champions international strategy;
• operates as a cross-border coach and co-ordinator;
• acts as an inter-cultural mediator and change agent; and
• manages personal effectiveness for international business.

However, in order to fulfil all these roles the successful international manager requires some special 'being' competencies. Barham and Wills (1992) argue that the first of these is cognitive complexity. This is 'the ability to see several dimensions in a situation rather than only one and to identify relationships and patterns between different dimensions' (Barham and Berthoin Antal 1994: 235). It is argued that because of the competing perspectives and expectations which exist in international work, successful managers need the ability to see situations from multiple perspectives and to question their 'in-culture' viewpoint. Associated with this competency are a number of related factors such as a sense of humility, cultural empathy and an active listening style. These all support the overall competence and suggest that they are the 'open' and 'sensitive' behavioural outcomes of an understanding of potential differences.

The second 'being' competence identified by Barham and Wills (1992) was emotional energy: 'International managers bring to their work a great deal of emotional energy. They have developed an emotional resilience that allows them to take risks and deal with personally uncomfortable or stressful situations. This is often fostered through earlier career experience abroad' (Barham and Berthoin Antal 1994: 236). This competency can be broken down into a number of subfactors. The successful international manager requires an understanding of his/her own emotional make-up and a great deal of general self-understanding. He/she also requires a certain emotional resilience and often the emotional support of the family.

The final 'being' competence is that of psychological maturity, which can be split into three core values. First, successful international managers must have a strong curiosity to learn about other cultures and other styles of behaviour. Secondly, successful international managers live in the 'here and now', focusing upon and applying energy to the problem of unravelling current complexities and difficulties. This is in stark contrast to less-successful international managers, who tend to 'look backward' in order to make sense of a current cross-cultural situation by reference to historic data which are often used to confirm their previous conclusions (Ratiu 1983). Finally, it is argued that successful international managers tend to develop a strong personal morality, probably as a mechanism for preserving a solid 'self' against both the need to be flexible and the diversity of viewpoints in the international arena.

If these are the core competencies of potential pan-European managers, how are we going to train managers to meet the present and expected shortfall in supply? The first point to make is that we need to be clear that we are seeking to develop 'international' managers and not simply seeking to impose a home-country model on third-country nationals in overseas operations (Scullion 1994). Barham and Berthoin Antal (1994) argue that effective development processes for international managers would be long term in orientation; focused on development experiences rather than simply training interventions; and focused on teams, as teamwork is a key competence required of international managers (see also Barham and Wills 1992).

One practical example is work being currently undertaken by Volkswagen AG. Here an organization that seeks to maintain and expand a global presence in the market place has deliberately set out to identify and develop high-potential global managers for the future. This led to the creation of the VW Group Junior Executive Programme. This takes 30–36 high-potential middle managers from around the world (including participants from Belgium, Brazil, Canada, the Czech Republic, Italy, Japan, Mexico, Slovakia, South Africa, Spain, the UK and the US, as well as Germany) and develops them over a nine-month period. The programme consists of three taught modules, but the major learning and development vehicle is a major strategic project. Participants are allocated to multi-cultural, multi-company, multi-functional teams and each team is allocated a strategic project sponsored either by the group board or a brand board. Each team has a budget and must spend a minimum of 40 days during the year working on the project prior to a presentation to board members at the final module. Projects are chosen for their difficulty, strategic importance, implementability and above all multi-national scope and ramifications. Volkswagen believes that the process of working under great stress over an extended period in multi-cultural teams on real projects ensures the maximum amount of development in terms of international competencies.

Conclusion

In this chapter we have sought to illuminate the cultural context, conceptual status and key trends of HRM in Europe. We can now conclude with comments on some of the key issues that emerge from any discussion of 'European HRM'.

One issue is the 'transfer' of various forms of HRM theory, processes and practices. The first, and oldest, form is the transfer of managerial theory and HR knowledge from the USA to Europe. It is widely acknowledged that the majority of modern managerial theory in many diverse fields has its origins in the USA. Historically, business and management education, and thus an academic business profession, occurred much earlier and on a much greater scale there than anywhere else in Europe. As a result the bulk of management thought currently taught in business schools throughout Europe is either directly American in origin or is indirectly heavily influenced by American work. There is very little which is distinctly 'European' or indigenous to a particular European country.

Examples of this process of 'transfer' from the USA to Europe include leadership theory, HRM models and HRM practices. Of course, there is nothing intrinsically *wrong* with such transference. Indeed, the transfer of a model or practice from one context to another which shares the same environment can be applauded as a learning process and a refusal to 'reinvent the wheel'. However, the key issue is that the environmental contexts have to be the same. Yet neither the cultural nor the political, economic and legal environments are the same in Europe as they are in the United States. Indeed, they are not even the same *within* Europe. Thus either the models and practices have to be adapted for use in a new environment or indigenous models and practices have to be developed within the new environmental contexts.

The second, and most recent, form of such transference is that which is increasingly occurring between 'West' and 'East'. Here we appear, with a sense of *déjà vu*, to be witnessing history repeating itself. Several commentators (Krulis-Randa 1990; Woodall 1994) have identified an explosion in terms of the transfer of 'American' and 'Western European' theories, models and practices to Eastern Europe. While this process may be seen as a necessity, given the rapid collapse of the Eastern bloc system and the serious economic problems which Eastern European nations find themselves in, there is obviously still a need for both cultural and environmental sensitivity in the process. Put simply, solutions to a set of issues and problems pertaining in one context do not necessarily resolve very different sets of issues and problems in another context.

Another key trend concerns the development of new organizational structures. Changing structures and forces with the European Union have contributed to the already increased incidence of European joint ventures and what are variously referred to as 'European multi-national corporations', 'pan-European companies' and 'transnational' or 'global' organizations. It may be suggested that such organizations have distinct and different sets of problems and issues to those which are domestic in orientation. Of particular relevance to HRM are the problems of cultural compatibility between European joint-venture partners and the difficulties in sourcing and developing the new breed of 'international' or 'European' managers required to operate in this complex cultural context and new structural configurations.

What of the prospects for the future? A key theoretical debate is that of cultural convergence versus cultural divergence. To what extent are European countries beginning to coalesce towards a common 'European' culture? Or are the very different cultures of Europe proving resistant to pressures to change? On the one hand, it may be argued that there is evidence of the strong pressures to convergence which include the economic and political pressures of the EU, the development of a European labour market, and the increased incidence of European multinational corporations and international joint ventures. There is some evidence that it may be possible, at the appropriate level of abstraction, to delineate the contours of a European theory of management or a European model of HRM. On the other hand, there is evidence of the problems caused by the clash of different European cultures for pan-European operation (see, for example,

Lichtenberger and Naulleau 1994). On a more qualitative level, we hear this issue raised continually by organizations operating on a pan-European basis. It has also been suggested that it is at the level of cultural 'clusters' that the key implications for differences in HRM practices and leadership styles are located (Durcan and Kirkbride 1994). Overall, as a tentative conclusion to an on-going debate, we can say that the persistent human-level problems seem to be a constraint on the structural-level ambitions of both states and organizations.

References

Adler, N.J. 1991: *International Dimensions of Organizational Behavior*, 2nd edn. Boston, Mass.: PWS Kent.

Barham, K. and Berthoin Antal, A. 1994: Competencies for the pan-European manager. In P.S. Kirkbride (ed.), *Human Resource Management in Europe: perspectives for the 1990s*, London: Routledge.

Barham, K. and Wills, S. 1992: *Management Across Frontiers*, Berkhamsted, Herts.: Ashridge Management Research Group and Foundation for Management Education.

Barzini, L.C. 1968: *The Italians*. Harmondsworth, Middx: Penguin Books.

Beaumont, P.B. 1991: The US human resource management literature: a review. In G. Salaman (ed.), *Human Resource Strategies*, Milton Keynes, Bucks.: Open University.

Beer, M., Spector, B., Lawrence, P., Mills, Q. and Walton, R. 1984: *Managing Human Assets*. New York: Free Press.

Blyton, P. and Turnbull, P. (eds) 1992: *Reassessing Human Resource Management*. London: Sage.

Brewster, C. 1994: European HRM: reflection of, or challenge to, the American concept. In P.S. Kirkbride (ed.), *Human Resource Management in Europe: perspectives for the 1990s*, London: Routledge.

Brewster, C. 1995: towards a 'European' model of human resource management. *Journal of International Business Studies*, 26(1), 1–21.

Brewster, C. and Hegewisch, A. 1994: *Policy and Practice in European Human Resource Management: the evidence and analysis from the Price Waterhouse Cranfield survey*. London: Routledge.

Brewster, C., Hegewisch, A. and Mayne, L. 1994: Trends in European HRM: signs of convergence? In P.S. Kirkbride (ed.), *Human Resource Management in Europe: perspectives for the 1990s*, London: Routledge.

DeCenzo, D.A. and Robbins, S. 1988: *Personnel/Human Resource Management*, 3rd edn. Englewood Cliffs, N.J.: Prentice-Hall.

Durcan, J.W. and Kirkbride, P.S. 1994: Leadership in the European context: some queries. In P.S. Kirkbride (ed.), *Human Resource Management in Europe: perspectives for the 1990s*, London: Routledge.

Fleury, P. 1990: Au-delà des particularismes ... Quels fonds commun universel? *Intercultures*, 8 (December 1989–January 1990), 119–30.

Fombrun, C. and Devanna, M.A. 1984: *Strategic Human Resource Management*. New York: John Wiley.

Guest, D. 1990: Human resource management and the American dream. *Journal of Management Studies*, 27(4), 377–97.

Hall, E.T. and Hall, M.R. 1990: *Understanding Cultural Differences*. Yarmouth, Mass.: Intercultural Press.

Hegewisch, A. 1991: The decentralisation of pay bargaining: European comparisons. *Personnel Review*, 20(6), 28–35.

Hofstede, G. 1980: *Culture's Consequences: international differences in work-related values*. Beverly Hills, Cal.: Sage.

Hofstede, G. 1985: The interaction between national and organizational value systems. *Journal of Management Studies*, 22(4), 347–57.

Hofstede, G. 1991: *Cultures and Organizations*. Maidenhead Berks.: McGraw-Hill.

Hofstede, G. 1992: The reintegration of Eastern Europe in the family of nations. Plenary speech at SIETAR International's XVIII Annual Congress, Montego Bay, Jamaica, 8–13 May.

International Management 1986: Expansion abroad: the new direction for European firms, 41(11), 21–5.

Kochan, T.A., McKersie, R.B. and Capelli, P. 1984: Strategic choice and industrial relations theory. *Industrial Relations*, 23, 16–39.

Krulis-Randa, J. 1990: Strategic human resource management in Europe after 1992. *Human Resource Management*, 1(2), 136.

Lichtenberger, B. and Naulleau, G. 1994: Cultural conflicts and synergies in the management of French–German joint ventures. In P.S. Kirkbride (ed.), *Human Resource Management in Europe: perspectives for the 1990s*, London: Routledge.

Madariaga, S. de 1952: *Portrait de l'Europe*, Paris: Calman Levy.

Noon, M. 1992: HRM: a map, model or theory? In P. Blyton and P. Turnbull (eds), *Reassessing Human Resource Management*, London: Sage, pp. 16–32.

Peabody, D. 1985: *National Character*. Cambridge: Cambridge University Press.

Pieper, R. (ed.) 1990: *Human Resource Management: an international comparison*. Berlin: Walter de Gruyter.

Poole, M. 1990: Human resource management in an international perspective. *International Journal of Human Resource Management*, 1(1), 1–15.

Ratiu, I. 1983: Thinking internationally: a comparison of how international executives learn. *International Studies of Management and Organization*, xiii (1–2), 139–50.

Ronen, S. 1986: *Comparative and Multinational Management*. New York: John Wiley.

Scullion, H. 1992: Strategic recruitment and development of the international manager. *Human Resource Management Journal*, 3(1), 57–69.

Scullion, H. 1994: Creating international managers: recruitment and development issues. In P.S. Kirkbride (ed.), *Human Resource Management in Europe: perspectives for the 1990s*, London: Routledge.

Thurley, K. and Wirdenius, H. 1989: *Towards European Management*. London: Pitman Publishing.

Thurley, K. and Wirdenius, H. 1991: Will management become 'European'? Strategic choices for organisations. *European Management Journal*, 9(2), 127–34.

Trompenaars, F. 1993: *Riding the Waves of Culture: understanding cultural diversity in business*. London: Nicholas Brealey.

Tung, R.L. 1984: Strategic management of human resources in the multinational enterprise. *Human Resource Management*, 23, 129–43.

Woodall, J. 1994: The transfer of managerial knowledge to Eastern Europe. In P.S. Kirkbride (ed.), *Human Resource Management in Europe: perspectives for the 1990s*, London: Routledge.

5

Industrial Relations Reform and Organizational Change: Towards Strategic Human Resource Management in Australia

GREG J. BAMBER AND RICHARD B. SAPPEY

Is strategic human resource management (HRM) being practised in Australian workplaces? What are the links between HRM strategies, industrial relations (IR) reform, organizational change and business strategies? In confronting such questions, it is helpful to distinguish between three levels of decision-making about IR and HRM issues: first, a macro (national) level; secondly, a micro (workplace) level; and thirdly, an intermediate level, the enterprise (cf. Kochan et al. 1987).

In many larger enterprises, there used to be a demarcation line between IR and personnel management. Few Australian enterprises still observe such a demarcation. By the 1990s, they generally treated IR as one aspect of the broader field of HRM. Most practitioners use the term HRM in a broad sense, then, as a generic label which subsumes much of traditional personnel management (and also most aspects of IR).

Australian experiences can inform international debates about HRM. Many of these debates are concerned with the interface between personnel management and IR, and between HRM and organizational change, as well as with notions of strategy (cf. Fombrun et al. 1984; Hendry and Pettigrew 1990), so the present discussion also comments on such issues. It starts, however, with an introduction to the Australian context.

The Australian Context

With a population of only 18 million, Australia's economy is strongly influenced by international businesses whose head offices are in Europe, North America and Japan. Fifty-two per cent of private-sector workplaces with more than 500 employees are partly or wholly foreign owned (Callus et al. 1991: 27). Therefore to a considerable extent Australia has imported, but has also adapted, HRM techniques from overseas.

Compared with the UK and other 'unitary' countries, *political power* is more devolved in Australia, which is a federation of states. Despite constitutional constraints on federal governments, most IR arrangements are still more centralized in Australia than in the UK.[1] From 1983 to 1996 there was a social-democratic Australian Labor Party (ALP) federal government. In this period, the Australian Council of Trade Unions (ACTU) was much more influential in the Australian polity and economy than its British equivalent the Trades Union Congress (TUC) was in the UK under a conservative government. Unlike the TUC, the ACTU was dealing with a national government that was generally sympathetic to union and employees' interests.

The close connection between the ACTU and the ALP allowed them to attempt to introduce a more consensual approach to national policy-making by forging the post-1983 ALP–ACTU Accord on prices and incomes, the economy and social issues. Its advent marked a change of direction from the adversarial approaches of earlier governments. The Accord had some similarities with the post-1974 UK Social Contract between the Labour government and the TUC, but the Accord lasted much longer than the Social Contract and appears to have been more successful (Chapman and Gruen 1990). Unlike in the UK, the USA and Japan, then, in this period unions exerted considerable influence at national policy-making level in Australia. This influence was despite a continuing decline in union density from 56 per cent of employees in 1979 to 35 per cent in 1994 (ABS 1995), which paralleled the decline in the UK.

The Accord did not formally embrace employers, who have been less united and appear to have had less explicit influence on the ALP government than the ACTU. However, the ALP government also listened to, and took heed of, employers' views, particularly those of the larger enterprises, most of which belong to the Business Council of Australia (BCA), and those of the engineering employers represented by the Metal Trades Industry Association (MTIA).

The ALP government was not radical; it attempted to pursue relatively modest social-welfare policies which generally kept the unions satisfied, whilst attempting also to induce economic restructuring (and, arguably, positioning the economy for long term growth of income and jobs). None the less, in the 1996 general election, Australians resoundingly rejected the ALP government. The post-1996 government is a coalition of two conservative parties. Its advent terminated the ALP–ACTU Accord. However, the Accord left a legacy that has continuing relevance in Australia and other countries, so this chapter includes discussion of its key details. The conservative government has pursued a policy of greater workplace bargaining between employers and employees while trying to minimise interventions by unions and other agencies.

In contrast with earlier British traditions of voluntary collective bargaining, Australian employment relationships have long been regulated by legally binding arbitrated industrial awards.[2] Many of these are, in effect, voluntary collective agreements, but are subsequently endorsed either by the federal Australian Industrial Relations Commission (AIRC), a state arbitration commission, or the equivalent. To a greater extent than in the UK, corporate chief executives still see IR issues as important. This perception may have been reinforced because IR reform has remained high on most public-policy agendas.

Although such contrasts exist, compared with most countries Australian IR shows more similarities than differences with the UK. Australia inherited a British legacy of unions with craft foundations and labourist ideologies. In both countries, much management is characterized by short-termism and there is fragmentation among the employers' organizations. There are long traditions of adversarialism, rather than social partnership. The national political spectrum is broadly similar in both countries, with governments alternating periodically between Labour and Conservative.[3] The ALP's policies since 1983 exhibit a greater similarity to those of the British Labour Party of the mid-1990s than those of a decade earlier.

In Australia (as in the UK), there are occasional and much publicized examples of confrontational unionism and employerism, including serious industrial disputes and legal action, much media coverage and threats of dismissals. However, 72 per cent of Australian workplaces (with at least five employees) have never experienced any industrial action (Callus et al. 1991: 62).

Union Policies[4]

Some influential leaders of the Australian labour movement have focused particularly at a macro level of human resources (HR) policy, although they generally would not use the term HR. It is such an approach – linking labour, HR and economic policies – that Kochan and McKersie (1989: 229) propose as a suitable strategy option for the (American) nation. In recent years there have been fewer signs of such explicit macro-level HR strategies by policy-makers in the USA or the UK.

Perhaps because it was closer to the centre of its political stage in the post-1983 period than was the TUC, the ACTU developed relatively more coherent economic strategies, notably the Accord. The industrial and political wings of the Australian labour movement thereby aimed to ensure that living standards of employees and non-income-earning sectors of the population requiring protection would be maintained and, over time, increased with movements in national productivity. The ALP government would: introduce national health insurance and fairer taxation; increase expenditure on social security, public services and education; change the elements of labour law most disliked by the unions; improve policies on occupational safety and health, HR planning, industrial and technological development, multi-culturalism, regulation of prices, employee participation and industrial democracy.[5] In exchange for such government action, apart from its 'national wage case' claims arbitrated by the AIRC on approximately an annual basis, the ACTU agreed to make no extra claims (except when there were extraordinary circumstances). This was a remarkable concession in view of Australia's adversarial legacy.

Concern about revitalizing Australia's economy prompted the ACTU in 1986 to send a senior delegation on a mission to Europe. The mission's objectives included a consideration of 'the implications of technology, work organizations, education and productivity for international competitiveness' (Australia 1987: xi). In spite of Australia's links with the UK, the mission's influential report, *Australia Reconstructed*, saw the UK as providing an inappropriate model which Australia should avoid. It observed that the UK's contemporary policies 'had been pursued in a socially disruptive and inefficient way, and had resulted in disastrous levels of unemployment and high social and regional inequality'. In addition, the report was critical of Australia's 'passive' approach to labour market policy and its approach to corporate planning (for example, the accent on short-term returns versus longer-term planning and investment) (ibid.: xii–xiii).

On the other hand, the mission was especially influenced by its observations of tripartite HR policies in Sweden and Austria 'where low inflation, reasonable growth and improved balance of payments have been accompanied by low unemployment, social cohesion and more balanced regional growth' (ibid.: xii). The mission saw such countries as models to emulate, particularly as in general their experiences seemed to reinforce the Accord (and such countries had relatively high union densities). The mission's recommended strategies included developing a national economic and social objective, negotiated and supported on a tripartite basis. This 'should aim to achieve full employment, low inflation and rising living standards which are equitably distributed . . . an innovative, positive and consensual approach to the management of change and to the removal of all impediments to achieving these objectives . . . [and] the generation of productive investment' (ibid.).

It is worth illustrating the implementation of such union strategies. First, federal and state governments legislated to promote equal employment opportunity, occupational health and safety, and more flexible educational arrangements; for example, to establish a 'unified national system' of higher education, which included abolishing the distinction between universities and colleges of advanced education (polytechnics) and promoting credit transfer and articulation arrangements between institutions, embracing those in technical and further education, as well as the higher education sector.

The government also initiated a workplace reform agenda which aimed to improve the quality of products and services, for example, by promoting benchmarking and best practice.

Historically, Australia has devoted relatively little funding to skill formation. Neither its general workforce nor most of its managers appear to be highly skilled, in comparison with its foreign competitors. Hence the government promoted several training initiatives. Following a Task Force Report *Enterprising Nation* (Karpin 1995), there is also much rhetoric among employers about improving management development, especially in terms of people-management skills. However, the realities of most enterprises' management development do not yet match up to the rhetoric.

The AIRC has been involved in another mode for implementing union policies. In 1988 it endorsed a fundamental programme of workplace change to restructure Australia's numerous antiquated industrial awards. Such restructuring was long overdue, for some awards had their origins in the early twentieth century. Many newer awards copied the concepts of the older ones. These had reflected nineteenth-century craft demarcations and fragmented forms of work organization, with outdated management and union structures.

Under this programme to enhance 'structural efficiency', employers and unions were obliged to engage in a form of productivity bargaining. To a greater extent than most UK experiences of the 1960s and subsequently, however, there were more explicit aims in Australia to move away from Taylorist forms of management and work organization. These aims included:

- establishing skill-related career paths which provide an incentive for workers to participate in skill formation;
- eliminating impediments to multi-skilling and broadening the range of tasks which a worker may perform;
- ensuring the working patterns and arrangements enhance flexibility and . . . efficiency;
- developing appropriate consultative procedures.   (AIRC 1989; see also CAI 1990)

Employer Policies

Although the ACTU leadership played a catalytic role in initiating the above policies before 1996, much of the responsibility for implementing them inevitably involved employers. Subsequently, employers were in a position to regain much of the initiative, in partnership with the post-1996 conservative coalition government. How did employers (and unions) attempt to implement such policies? Two contrasting ideal types of approach can be identified: a cost minimization approach (CMA); and a productivity enhancement approach (PEA). Enterprises that are most exposed to international competition are more likely to adopt a PEA, as they endeavour to compete with their rivals. Conversely, those that are most sheltered (for example, by tariffs) are more likely to adopt a CMA. Those that compete in terms of quality and higher added value will tend to adopt a PEA while those that compete in terms of price will tend to adopt a CMA (Curtain and Mathews 1990). Variants of either approach are likely to be adopted in particular enterprises depending on the knowledge, imagination, effort, mutual trust and political capacity shown by key players.

The policies mentioned above and the moves towards structural efficiency could precipitate a step away from adversarial IR, especially in cases that approximate to the PEA type. These moves have an *integrative* potential (cf. Walton and McKersie 1965); besides institutional IR issues they also embrace the management of the labour process (work organization, job classifications and work procedures), and other aspects of HRM (selection, skill formation, career development, performance appraisal and productivity-linked pay systems).

The Accord appeared to bring relative industrial peace and reductions in real wages, despite being accompanied by increases in managerial salaries (especially for senior executives). The 1983–96 ALP government's negotiated-corporatist approaches initially were welcomed by many opinion leaders and most managers, particularly those in larger enterprises.[6]

In 1983, the chief executives of about 80 of these began meeting regularly as the Business Council of Australia (BCA). It established a Study Commission chaired by Professor Fred Hilmer:[7] 'to identify means of achieving changes to the current industrial relations system that will improve the way people work together . . . to increase the competitiveness and performance of Australian enterprises' (BCA 1989: x).

The Commission developed a series of policies designed to accelerate a shift from an IR to an employee-relations (ER) mind-set and to replace macro-level negotiated corporatism with a deregulated (or, as Hilmer puts it, a 'self-regulated') approach at the enterprise level.[8] This approach includes: promoting enterprise unionism (rather than occupationally based unionism); devolving ER responsibilities from staff specialists to line managers; flattening organization structures; opening up management–employee communications; encouraging training and skills development; and installing performance appraisal, incentive pay schemes and improved grievance procedures (Hilmer 1989).

To What Extent Are Union and Employer Policies Compatible?

Restructuring unions was a keystone of the policies developed by the ACTU and the BCA. Both concluded that the UK legacy of occupationally structured unions was no longer appropriate. In proposing a change towards about 20 large industry unions, the ACTU was inspired by the Nordic and Austro-German examples. In proposing enterprise unionism, the BCA was inspired by the Japanese (and to a lesser extent American) examples.

Progress has been made towards both objectives. Within a few years, the plethora of unions had been significantly rationalized. Most union mergers were determined almost as much by ideological considerations as by industrial logic. Nevertheless, at a micro level, there has been progress towards a form of enterprise unionism, albeit within larger union structures. 'Single-union deals' are being agreed at some new establishments. For instance, although the Australian Manufacturing Workers' Union is a large conglomerate union, it is in effect an enterprise union for the new Toyota plant in Melbourne. Similarly, the UK Amalgamated Engineering and Electrical Union is an enterprise union for Nissan's plant in north-east England (although Toyota Australia has a higher union density).

By the late 1980s there was some common ground between union and employer positions. Each aimed to promote some devolution of job regulation, or 'managed decentralism', as one of the most influential employers' organizations, the MTIA, put it (Evans 1989, after McDonald and Rimmer 1989), whereby there would continue to be centralized pay regulation, but increasing scope for enterprise bargaining.

The early 1990s versions of the Accord promoted enterprise pay bargaining; invariably this involved minimum rates being set at industry level, but employers and unions were able to negotiate additional payments depending on enterprise productivity improvements. This could be seen as an 'Australian model' of regulated flexibility – an alternative to the form of 'unregulated flexibility' developed at enterprise level in the UK and USA (Mathews 1989).

The ACTU generally seeks to promote workers' interests and adopts a macro-orientation with a pluralist/collective perspective, while the BCA generally seeks to promote employers' interests and adopts more of a micro-orientation with a unitary/individualistic perspective (cf. Fox 1966; Purcell 1987; Sutcliffe and Sappey 1990). Despite these different sets of general objectives, perspectives and values, the differing emphases on macro- and micro-level reforms are complementary and there are overlaps between the two policies. Both parties are seeking to move away from Australia's traditional reliance on external labour markets, towards a more highly skilled workforce, which would be more likely to be developed in internal labour markets (cf. Curtain and Mathews 1990). Both are aiming towards several other similar goals: greater productivity and international competitiveness through improved work organization and HRM, particularly at workplace level.[9] Both parties' policies are ahead of their constituents' views, rather than merely reflecting them.

Through its post-1987 industrial relations legislation, the federal ALP government aimed to maintain the union's support and to promote productivity. Part of the legislation was based upon the belief that the international economy had changed to such an extent that it was no longer appropriate to rely upon agricultural, extractive and mass-production manufacturing industries, some of which were protected by tariffs and other forms of industry protection. By themselves these industries would not provide sufficient jobs for future generations nor provide a standard of material living sufficiently high for stability. The ALP government amended its legislation several times in the early 1990s, in an attempt to encourage more flexible workplace bargaining (and to meet some of the employers' criticisms of its earlier legislation which regulated dismissals). This extended the range of possibilities for enterprise bargaining between employers and employees.

Apart from traditional awards, greater flexibility could be achieved through 'certified agreements' (between unions and employers), enterprise flexibility agreements (which did not involve unions), and enterprise flexibility clauses in existing awards. These changes enabled conditions such as hours of work (particularly night and weekend work) to be made more flexible to suit customer demand and technological efficiency criteria. Some of these changes had the potential to marginalize union involvement, but by 1996 this had occurred only to a relatively limited extent.

Awards, and particularly agreements, increasingly include issues that hitherto were invariably seen as managerial prerogatives including: quality assurance; performance indicators; training; consultative arrangements; job evaluation; work organization; teamwork; and union representation on selection panels. Especially in the public sector and to a lesser extent in large-scale private-sector enterprises, there was also a developing alignment between IR processes and performance appraisal schemes, particularly where these involved individual or collective bonus systems and/or promotion arrangements (DIR 1994: 9; DEVETIR 1994: 1).

Strategic Human Resource Management at Workplaces?

As in the USA and the UK, in Australia some writers seek to distinguish HRM from personnel management, on the grounds that HRM implies specifically a move away from seeing employees merely as a cost (to be cut), towards an 'investment orientation' and a more innovative and strategic view of the management of people (Boxall and Dowling 1990: 158; Blunt 1990: 48). When referring to such a specific implication, enthusiasts add the prefix 'strategic' HRM. There is no general agreement on the characteristics of strategic HRM. However, there are some demanding claims about it which emphasize, among other things, links with business strategies and organizational change, and use of such techniques as: productivity measurement, performance appraisal, training, performance-related pay, profit-sharing and share ownership schemes, and job redesign, with a management philosophy that espouses teamwork, consultation, communications and information-sharing. To what extent are these techniques found in practice?

Several studies have attempted to show how HRM is practised in Australia, for instance Dunphy and Stace (1990). They found three trends in all the medium- to high-performing enterprises in their sample. First, a decentralization of the HRM function to business units, away from central HRM departments. Secondly, there was a trend for enterprises to move to a more strategic orientation in the way that HRM policy is instigated, considered and linked into the corporate planning process; they found the most senior HRM executives reporting directly to the chief executive, and an increasing importance of HRM issues in formulating business plans. Thirdly, these enterprises had developed comprehensive performance management systems as an integrated form of a management-by-objectives approach to goal-setting, appraisal, development and reward structures.

In the early 1980s none of these trends would have been widely observed, as most personnel departments were centralized, personnel policies were precedent-based, rather than strategically focused, and performance management was either absent or control-based (that is, an appraisal, rather than an appraisal–training–reward, orientation). Such trends may reflect changing circumstances. However, another inference from these trends is that there are fashions in HRM as in other fields of management.

As well as the above trends, Dunphy and Stace found four distinct types of HRM strategies, as illustrated in table 5.1. First, the 'structural' HRM strategy type 'was characteristic of the majority of enterprises' in their sample. The HRM orientation of these enterprises appeared 'to cluster around business unit, work team and job redesign; functional skills training; lateral recruitment as a norm' rather than the exception, and greater emphasis on HRM systems driven by line managers than by corporate staff.

Secondly, the 'developmental' HRM strategy appeared compatible with arguments in much of the current HRM literature; it was characteristic of a few medium- to high-performing enterprises in the sample. These placed strong emphasis on workforce and organizational change

Table 5.1 Contrasting types of HRM strategy

Structural HR strategies[a]
HR strategy is strongly focused on the business unit

Features:
- strong bottom line orientation;
- emphasis on workforce planning, job redesign and work practice reviews;
- focus on tangible reward structures;
- internal or external recruitment;
- functional skills training and formalized multi-skilling;
- formalized IR/ER procedures;
- strong business unit culture.

Turnaround HR strategies
HR strategy is driven for a short period by the executive leadership, characterized by challenging, restructuring or abolishing HR systems, structures and methodologies

Features:
- major structural changes affecting the total organization and career structure;
- downsizing, retrenchments;
- lateral recruitment of key executives from outside;
- executive team-building;
- breaking with the old culture.

Developmental HR strategies[a]
HR strategy is jointly actioned by the corporate HR unit and business units

Features:
- emphasis on developing the individual and the team;
- internal recruitment, where possible;
- extensive developmental programmes;
- use of intrinsic rewards;
- corporate organizational development given high priority;
- strong emphasis on corporate culture.

Paternalistic HR practices
HR practice is centrally administered

Features:
- centralist personnel orientation;
- emphasis on procedures, precedent and uniformity;
- organization and methods studies;
- inflexible internal appointments policy;
- emphasis on operational and supervisory training;
- industrial awards and agreements set the HR framework.

[a] Both of the above give high priority to performance management systems.
Source: Dunphy and Stace (1990: 126)

'in areas like personal development, management development, career management and culture management (internal marketing, culture surveys, employee communication strategies). In each case this type of HR strategy was associated with a consultative style of corporate change leadership.'

The structural and developmental strategies 'were not completely discrete categories: organizations with a dominantly structural' HRM orientation would often include some developmental HR policy in their HRM strategies and vice versa. The implication is that even when pursuing a structural strategy, some culture building and management development will be necessary. Similarly, a developmental HRM strategy should not avoid the difficulty of workforce and job restructuring.

Thirdly, the 'turnaround' HRM strategy type was characteristic of some of the enterprises 'in the period three years before the study', a time when they were undergoing a period of organizational change. These enterprises had substantially contracted, redefined or abolished their central personnel departments; 'were in the process of radically reviewing' their HRM systems and policies; were implementing voluntary or forced redundancies; and 'had opened their recruitment' to the external labour market at key executive and other levels.

The fourth HRM type, 'paternalistic', was associated with lower-performing enterprises that made change by fine tuning. A paternalistic HRM strategy exemplifies the 'traditional mechanistic' personnel management policies of the 1960s–1970s. It is strongly influenced by Tayloristic scientific management, standard IR practices and a wish by management to maintain the status quo. This paternalistic type featured a centralist approach to HRM, an emphasis on procedures, 'heavy reliance' on work study 'as a form of personnel/control, and formalistic employer–employee . . . relationships' (Dunphy and Stace 1990: 127–9).

What determines the type of HRM strategy adopted? Dunphy and Stace conclude that the type of HRM strategies adopted can potentially be related to the broader business strategy. But the type of organizational change is the important intervening variable which modifies the relationship. They found that an enterprise's organizational change strategy tends to drive its HRM strategy rather than vice versa, as illustrated in figure 5.1.

The inferences from this analysis reinforce the idea of contingency, that decision-makers should select that HRM strategy which is most compatible with an enterprise's business circumstances and organizational change strategies. A loose collection of non-customized HRM

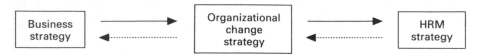

Figure 5.1　A model of relations between business strategy and HRM
strategy
Source: Dunphy and Stace (1990: 133)

interventions and gimmicks will not suffice if an enterprise is to develop
the internal synergies likely to be necessary for high performance.

The model summarized above helps our understanding of the complementary nature of IR issues, organizational change and HRM
policies. Corporate and change strategies are generally initiated by
senior executives, but HRM policies may be formulated by personnel
or HRM departments, then implemented by supervisors and line
managers. As Dunphy and Stace argue, it is important for us to
formulate a more integrated understanding of how various management choices interrelate. This is particularly so in relation to organizational change and HRM strategies, which are introduced into
some enterprises in ways that are mutually contradictory. Dunphy
and Stace's enterprise-level models are helpful conceptual tools to
sharpen the debates about types of organizational change, styles of
leadership and varieties of HRM policies. Besides providing a basis
for theory building, models like these can facilitate improved management practices.

Further inferences about the pervasiveness of HRM techniques may
be derived from the Australian Workplace Industrial Relations Survey
(AWIRS).[10] For instance, half its sample of workplaces admitted that
they did not measure labour productivity in a quantifiable way.[11] However, as many as 61 per cent of workplaces claimed to have performance appraisal schemes for their employees (Callus et al. 1991: 266).

Why might managers take the trouble to appraise their employees?
HRM textbooks indicate that the general purpose of these schemes is
to facilitate the choice of appropriate training and to link pay with
performance (see, for example, Schuler et al. 1992). Only 52 per cent
of the private sector workplaces claimed to provide formal off-the-job
training, in comparison with 71 per cent of those in the public sector.
A positive correlation between workplace size and training revealed
that proportionately more larger workplaces than smaller workplaces
offer such training (Callus et al. 1991: 303).

Table 5.2 Issues about which management regularly provides information to employees or their representatives, by sector

| | % of workplaces | | |
Issue	Public	Private	All
Future staffing plans	65	41	48
Marketing strategies	25	42	36
Investment/corporate plans	57	38	43
Financial position of workplace	54	38	43
None of the above	15	26	23

Population: Australian workplaces with at least 20 employees.
Figures are weighted and are based on responses from 2,004 workplace managers.
Source: Callus et al. (1991: 136)

Only 32 per cent of workplaces claimed to provide performance-related pay to any of their non-managerial employees. Such a form of pay was more common in the private (44 per cent) than in the public sector (8 per cent). It is more common (42 per cent) in small workplaces (5–19 employees) than in larger ones; performance-related pay is provided in only 31 per cent of workplaces with over 500 employees. Two sectors were particularly prone to provide this type of pay: retailing (61 per cent) and finance and property (52 per cent) (Callus et al. 1991: 243).

Only 8 per cent of private-sector workplaces had a profit-sharing scheme for non-managerial employees; 13 per cent had a share-ownership scheme to which any employee could belong. Within the previous five years, only 44 per cent of workplaces had implemented any job redesign.

Managers in only one-third of workplaces claimed that their employees were consulted about changes affecting them. Also, managers in only one-third of workplaces claimed to have a philosophy of teamwork/consultation. As an approximate index of employee communications, managers were asked: 'On which, if any, of these issues affecting this workplace does management regularly provide information to employees or their representatives?' As shown in table 5.2, on every issue listed, a majority of workplaces did not regularly provide information to employees.

HRM rhetoric also suggests that personnel decisions are increasingly decentralized from head office to workplaces, and from staff to line managers. Nevertheless, such devolution is not exclusively associated with modern HRM. Late-nineteenth-century foremen had a great deal of power to hire, fire and establish work rules (cf. Gospel 1983: 98), to a much greater extent than most contemporary supervisors and line managers, whose autonomy was constrained after the First World War, not least by the growth of personnel and IR departments. (This illustrates that historic reflections can be valuable in putting contemporary debates into a broader context.)

Renewed decentralization to supervisors and line managers is relatively recent. As yet, such managers have much less autonomy than their nineteenth-century predecessors. It can be inferred from the AWIRS data that, on average, only 14 per cent of the key personnel decisions were made by supervisors and line managers. Responsibility for such decisions is shared between managers within and beyond the workplace (Callus et al. 1991: 79–80).

The AWIRS data indicate uneven use of techniques commonly associated with strategic HRM. There does not yet appear to be a consistent pattern that might indicate which enterprises in particular sectors or size categories are more likely to adopt strategic HRM practices. Evidently, there has been less training, consultation, devolution and so on than is sometimes implied by the HRM textbooks.

However, it can also be inferred from these data that there has been a great deal of workplace change in recent years; 86 per cent of workplaces had experienced at least one type of significant change in the previous two years (Callus et al. 1991: 186). Many different approaches to change have been adopted, depending on the degree to which they embrace initiatives such as those discussed above. Moreover, there has been much proselytizing about ACTU and BCA policies. Their proponents each imply that their approach is *the* way in which to manage change in HR strategies, unions and employing organizations.

To analyse the notion of strategic choice, Deery and Purcell (1989) surveyed large Australian companies. This study sheds light on IR and HRM practices as well as on strategic choice. They found, *inter alia*, that joint consultation committees were more prevalent among manual (36 per cent) than white-collar (22 per cent) employees, and more common in the public sector (54 per cent) than in private sector foreign-owned firms (36 per cent) or Australian-owned firms (29 per cent). They infer that joint consultation has more to do with white-collar unionism than 'initiatives of well resourced personnel departments' (Deery and Purcell 1989: 472–3). Yet in the private sector where joint consultation has been established it has been less associated with the need to accommodate unions.

Lansbury and Marchington (1993) suggest that there has been an extension of consultative schemes with the tendency for them to be informal (for example, walkabouts), though some schemes do not last very long, indicating a faddish quality (e.g. suggestion schemes and some quality circles). McGraw and Palmer (1994) note the stimulus for consultation from the national IR system through enterprise bargaining. Their evidence suggests that it is not easy to integrate IR and HRM.

Kramar's (1992) comparative study of employment strategies in three large private sector enterprises raises questions about attempts to design and implement HRM strategies and the potential costs involved. Social and political factors in enterprises tend to compromise strategies and their implementation. Allan's report of one bank's strategy to establish HRM by excluding a union was one of the early examples which led to legal action, and illustrates that there can be continuing incompatibility between IR and HRM (Allan 1992). There is evidence, then, of subtle and overt manifestations of continuing industrial tension, in spite of the adoption and practice of HRM initiatives.

Other research has addressed the question of organization culture. Kabanoff's (1993) study of espoused culture in 98 organizations identifies key values as reflected in their communications and other documentation. He establishes a model of culture based upon a structural power which predisposes an enterprise to distributive equality or inequality, and a second dimension which either reinforces the structural tendency or compensates for it. His four consequent 'ideal types of culture' are: collegial, meritocratic, leader focused, and elite, which broadly run from egalitarian to inegalitarian. He concludes that the leader focused and the elite were the most common. This suggests that managerial approaches which are broadly compatible with assumptions of participative management styles in the prescriptive culture literature are not prevalent in Australian enterprises.

Summary and Conclusions

The above data throw light on the contours of employment relationships and change. None the less, when trying to explain the dynamics and processes of change, it is worth complementing surveys with other methods. Therefore, it is important also to consider organizational change explicitly and to draw on more intensive case study data.[12]

This contribution has discussed macro- and micro-level policies and their implementation (or lack of it) by employers, governments and unions. The approaches by ACTU, BCA and MTIA in the 1983–96 period each in its own way sought to achieve some form of consensus, albeit not to the extent of Nordic styles of tripartism. There are signs of strategic thinking about HR issues at the macro level, for instance, by the ALP and coalition federal governments (albeit with different emphases), the ACTU, BCA and MTIA. In the post-1983 period, there appear to have been more signs of strategic innovations from IR parties in Australia than in the UK or USA. However, national-level thinking in Australia has not yet been translated into consistent local-level practices.

In comparison with most other industrialized market economies, Australia has a high degree of foreign ownership of its large enterprises. Many of the most important decisions that induce organizational change in such enterprises are taken at corporate headquarters overseas. Based in Australia, it is difficult, even for champions of strategic HRM, to exert much influence on corporate strategies that are formulated elsewhere.

Nevertheless, certain enthusiasts claim that, in general, employers in Australia are implementing certain aspects of strategic HRM. We should remain sceptical about many of these claims, especially those that seem to regard a particular form of HRM as a universal managerial prescription. At a micro (workplace) level, it can be inferred that short-term, inconsistent and *ad hoc* forms of personnel and IR management have by no means been displaced by long-term, consistent and strategic HRM. At the first signs of a change in business circumstances, a reaction in many enterprises still seems to be to declare redundancies. This reaction seems to be prevalent among personnel and IR specialists, not least those in education and training. Such *short-term* responses are the antithesis of strategic HRM, with its notion of investing in people, over a *longer term*. In Australia, as in the UK, apart from in a few leading-edge enterprises, many claims about strategic HRM are exaggerated and rhetorical, rather than realistic and generally implemented (cf. Guest 1987; Legge 1989).

Some of the more enlightened HRM specialists who survive play a vital role as catalysts for and implementors of change. They are helping to restructure management, IR and work organization by rethinking and improving their policies and practices. To this end, they are also trying to learn, selectively, from the approaches promoted by policy-makers with a longer-term orientation, the ACTU and certain unions, some innovative enterprises and employers' associations, and others. If broadly defined and based on a realistic contingency approach, even if not necessarily strategic, contemporary HRM practices, then, have considerable potential to provide constructive and much-needed links between the formerly separate territories of business policy, personnel and IR, and also between national, enterprise and workplace perspectives. Interestingly, much of the stimulus came from Australia's tentative moves towards negotiated corporatism among its IR institutions in the 1983–96 period, providing opportunities for strengthening these links.

In the search for productivity improvements through increased flexibility, the reforms encouraged a more flexible approach to the management of people yet also enabled foundations to be laid for a greater degree of integration between HRM and IR, and for unions to challenge employers' clinging to managerial prerogatives.

Following the recent moves to decentralize the IR system, only a minority of employees are as yet covered by new-style agreements rather than the older notion of awards (ACTU 1995: 22–4). Important changes are being introduced at workplaces, but only a small proportion of them are being negotiated and agreed (DIR 1994, 1995). Despite much workplace change, the bargaining agenda may have narrowed. Further, the deregulation of IR in the federal and some state jurisdictions appears to have been used by employers to initiate contracts of questionable legality which provide working conditions below those stipulated in the relevant awards. Rapid changes in legislation have resulted in a degree of confusion and opportunism which will take time to address, particularly by inspection systems.

Apart from legislation dealing with the traditional IR system, other legislation has impacted upon the management of enterprises. Federal and state legislation primarily by ALP governments constructed a framework for equal opportunity and occupational health and safety. However, compliance and enforcement are patchy, and responses from employers and unions range from co-operation to conflict. There continues to be 'a wide variety of [HR/IR] polices and practices adopted by managers at the workplace level' (Wright 1991: 16). Despite the spread of HRM, then, some dimensions of people management are still significantly influenced by an IR context, especially in the public sector and in many of the larger private sector enterprises.

The post-1996 conservative government's changes promise to include:

- greater labour-market flexibility including easier dismissals and agreements with individuals;
- continuing decentralisation towards more enterprise-level bargaining;
- promoting 'freedom of association' including the right not to join a union;
- prohibiting strike pay, secondary boycotts and pre-entry 'closed-shop' arrangements.

As in the UK after 1979, such changes are weakening unions, which have had their institutional and regulatory protection reduced; weak unions are less able to defend or improve their members' living standards. Divisions between unions, and between the unions and the coalition government may detract from the continuation of some of the national labour-market initiatives discussed above which were primarily initiated in the 1983–96 period. More adversarial relations may be a consequence. If so, it is even less likely that IR practice would be consistent with the rhetoric about strategic HRM by the latter's advocates.

Acknowledgements

Dexter Dunphy and Doug Stace commented on an earlier draft and kindly permitted the reproduction of table 5.1 and figure 5.1. Brian Towers and several other colleagues, including Chris Baker, Richard Curtain, Ian Glendon, June Hearn, Keith Sisson and George Strauss, also made helpful comments on an earlier draft which were much appreciated.

Notes

1 For more background on Australian IR and HRM arrangements, see: Isaac (1989); Howard (1990); Sutcliffe and Sappey (1990); Schuler et al. (1992); Gardner and Palmer (1992); Lansbury and Davis (1993); Bamber and Davis (1995).
2 An award is a legally enforceable determination of employment terms and conditions in a firm or industry, which has been arbitrated or certified by an IR commission (see Sutcliffe and Callus 1994: 17). An award may apply at a national, state, industry, enterprise, workplace and/or occupational level.
3 In Australia, when conservatives form a federal government it is usually as a coalition between the Liberal and National parties.
4 It is appropriate to discuss union strategies before employer strategies because at least in the 1983–96 period Australian labour movement leaders seemed more likely to be the initiators of new strategies than many of their employer counterparts.
5 The Accord and related ACTU policies included many more elements about a wide range of important issues, for instance, macro-economic and trade policies; for details see ALP–ACTU (1983); Davis (1983).

6 Many of the recommendations in *Australia Reconstructed* were also accepted by the government, and some by certain employers' organizations, albeit less enthusiastically. But other employer interests strongly criticized it (see, for example, Nurick 1987).

7 A prominent management consultant who became Dean of the Australian Graduate School of Management, University of New South Wales.

8 While the BCA Study Commission was deliberating at national level, the New South Wales state government commissioned Niland (1989, 1990) to prepare two green papers on IR reform at the state level. He also proposed, among other things, the adoption of an enterprise focus, which, like the BCA's proposal, aroused much controversy (see, for example, Dabscheck 1990; Rimmer 1990).

9 However, some employers are also seeking to segment their workforce into core and peripheral components (Bamber 1990; Bamber et al. 1992).

10 This survey was completed shortly before implementation of the above-mentioned award restructuring scheme, so unfortunately we cannot evaluate the effects of such initiatives from the AWIRS data. Most of the data cited here are from Callus et al. (1991).

11 In spite of these data, it is inferred that many more workplaces did not measure productivity systematically. Respondents may offer socially desirable answers to such questions. To some extent these may reflect the current rhetoric about HRM, which appears to be widely accepted. Hence, if anything, this and the following paragraphs are likely to overstate the pervasiveness of HRM techniques in practice.

12 Apart from the differing objectives and methods between the extensive survey and intensive case studies, it is worth noting that the AWIRS 1989–90 survey adopted a broad view of IR and also covered HRM more generally. It was of randomly selected stratified samples of 2,353 workplaces with more than four employees from the whole Australian economy, except agriculture and defence. Most of the present comments draw upon the sample of 2,004 workplaces with at least 20 employees. The analysis by Dunphy and Stace was primarily based on 13 prominent employing organisations in 1988–9 and each organization was also researched retrospectively in an earlier period to give a total sample of 26 cases, which were all in service-sector industries that have been, or are being, confronted by deregulation. These organizations have their head offices in one of three Australian states. Their analysis also drew on their consulting experience. Therefore, AWIRS data provide a map of the contemporary terrain, while arguably, Dunphy and Stace identify and explain some prototypical trends.

References

Allan, C. 1992: Banking on a strategy. In M. Gardner and G. Palmer, *Employment Relations*, Melbourne: Macmillan, pp. 306–12.

Australia, Commonwealth of 1987: *Australia Reconstructed: ACTU/TDC mission to Western Europe. A report by the mission members to the Australian Council of Trade Unions and the Trade Development Council.* Canberra: Australian Government Publishing Service.

Australian Bureau of Statistics (ABS) 1994: *Trade Union Statistics Australia*, cat. no. 6203.0. Canberra: Australian Bureau of Statistics.

Australian Council of Trade Unions (ACTU) 1995: *Workplace.* Melbourne: Australian Council of Trade Unions, Summer.

Australian Industrial Relations Commission (AIRC) 1989: *National Wage Case Decision.* Melbourne: Australian Industrial Relations Commission (Print H9100).

Australian Industrial Relations Commission (AIRC) 1991: *National Wage Case Decision (October 1991).* Melbourne: Australian Industrial Relations Commission (Print K0300).

Australian Labor Party and Australian Council of Trade Unions (ALP–ACTU) 1983: *Statement of Accord by the Australian Labor Party and the Australian Council of Trade Unions Regarding Economic Policy.* Melbourne: Australian Labor Party and Australian Council of Trade Unions.

Bamber, G.J. 1990: Flexible work organization: inferences from Britain and Australia. *Asia-Pacific Human Resources Management*, 28(3), 28–44.

Bamber, G.J. and Davis, E.M. 1995: Industrial relations. In J. Henningham (ed.), *Institutions in Australian Society*, new edn, Melbourne: Oxford University Press, pp. 110–30.

Bamber, G.J., Boreham, P. and Harley, B. 1992: Economic and industrial relations outcomes of different forms of flexibility in Australian industry: an analysis of the Australian Workplace Industrial Relations Survey. In *Exploring Industrial Relations: further analysis of AWIRS*, Department of Industrial Relations, Industrial Relations Research Series, no. 4, November, Canberra, pp. 1–70.

Blunt, P. 1990: Recent developments in human resource management: the good, the bad and the ugly. *International Journal of Human Resource Management*, 1(1), 45–60.

Boxall, P. and Dowling, P.J. 1990: Human resource management: employee relations and the industrial relations tradition in Australia and New Zealand. In G. Griffin (ed.), *Current Research in Industrial Relations: proceedings of the 5th AIRAANZ Conference*, Sydney: Association of Industrial Relations Academics of Australia and New Zealand, pp. 152–68.

Business Council of Australia (BCA) 1989: *Enterprise-based Bargaining Units – a Better Way of Working: report to the Business Council of Australia by the Industrial Relations Study Commission, 1.* Melbourne: Business Council of Australia.

Callus, R., Morehead, A., Cully, M. and Buchanan, J. 1991: *Industrial Relations at Work: the Australian Workplace Industrial Relations Survey*. Canberra: Australian Government Publishing Service.

Chapman, B.J. and Gruen, F.H. 1990: *An Analysis of the Australian Consensual Incomes Policy: the Prices and Incomes Accord*. Canberra: Australian National University, Centre for Economic Policy Research, Paper 221.

Confederation of Australian Industry (CAI) 1990: *Award Restructuring: guidelines for employers*. Melbourne: Confederation of Australian Industry.

Curtain, R. and Mathews, J. 1990: Two models of award restructuring in Australia. *Labour and Industry*, 3(1), 58–75.

Dabscheck, B. 1990: Industrial relations and the irresistible magic wand: the BCA's plan to Americanise Australian industrial relations. In M. Easson and J. Shaw (eds), *Transforming Industrial Relations*, Sydney: Pluto/Lloyd Ross Forum, pp. 117–30.

Davis, E.M. 1983: The 1983 ACTU Congress: consensus rules OK! *Journal of Industrial Relations*, 25(4), 507–16.

Deery, S. and Purcell, J. 1989: Strategic choices: industrial relations management in large organizations. *Journal of Industrial Relations*, 31(4), 459–77.

Department of Employment, Vocational Education, Training and Industrial Relations (DEVETIR) 1994: *Industrial Relations Reform Act Overview*. Brisbane: Queensland Government.

Department of Industrial Relations (DIR) 1994: *DIRect Line*. Canberra: Australian Government Publishing Service.

Department of Industrial Relations (DIR) 1995: *Enterprise Bargaining in Australia 1994* (a summary of the annual report on developments under the Industrial Relations Reform Act). Canberra: Australian Government Publishing Service.

Dunphy, D. and Stace, D. 1990: *Under New Management: Australian organizations in transition*. Sydney: McGraw-Hill.

Evans, A.C. 1989: *Managed Decentralism in Australia's Industrial Relations*, 11th Sir Richard Kirby Lecture, University of Wollongong. Sydney: Metal Trades Industry Association.

Fombrun, C.J., Tichy, N.M. and Devanna, M.A. 1984: *Strategic Human Resource Management*. New York: John Wiley.

Fox, A. 1966: *Industrial Sociology and Industrial Relations*, Research Paper 3, Royal Commission on Trade Unions and Employers' Associations. London: HMSO.

Gardner, M. and Palmer, G. 1992: *Employment Relations: industrial relations and human resource management in Australia*. Melbourne: Macmillan.

Gospel, H. 1983: The development of management organization in industrial relations: a historical perspective. In K. Thurley and S. Wood (eds), *Industrial Relations and Management Strategy*, Cambridge: Cambridge University Press, pp. 91–110.

Guest, D.E. 1987: Human resource management and industrial relations. *Journal of Management Studies*, 24(5), 503–21.

Hendry, C. and Pettigrew, A.M. 1990: Human resource management: an agenda for the 1990s. *International Journal of Human Resource Management*, 1(1), 17–44.

Hilmer, F. 1989: *New Games, New Rules: work in competitive enterprises*. Sydney: Angus & Robertson.

Howard, W. 1990: Industrial relations and human resource management: different or differentiated products? In G. Griffin (ed.), *Current Research in Industrial Relations: proceedings of the 5th AIRAANZ Conference*, Sydney: Association of Industrial Relations Academics of Australia and New Zealand, pp. 192–200.

Isaac, J.E. 1989: The arbitration commission: prime mover or facilitator. *Journal of Industrial Relations*, 31(3), 407–27.

Kabanoff, B. 1993: An exploration of espoused culture in Australian organizations (with a closer look at the banking sector). *Asia Pacific Journal of Human Resources*, 31(3), 1–29.

Karpin, D.S. 1995: *Enterprising Nation: Renewing Australia's managers to meet the challenges of the Asia-Pacific century* (report of the Industry Task Force on Leadership and Management Skills: Chair D.S. Karpin). Canberra: Australian Government Publishing Service.

Kochan, T.A. and McKersie, R.B. 1989: Future directions for American labor and human resources policy. *Relations Industrielles*, 44(1), 224–44.

Kochan, T.A., Katz, H.C. and McKersie, R.B. 1987: *The Transformation of American Industrial Relations*. New York: Basic Books.

Kramar, R. 1992: Strategic human resource management: are the promises fulfilled? *Asia Pacific Journal of Human Resources*, 30(1), 1–15.

Lansbury, R.D. and Davis, E.M. 1993: Australia. In G.J. Bamber and R.D. Lansbury (eds), *International and Comparative Industrial Relations*, Sydney: Allen & Unwin, pp. 100–25.

Lansbury, R.D. and Marchington, M. 1993: Consultation and industrial relations: experience from Australia and overseas. *Asia Pacific Journal of Human Resources*, 31(3), 62–82.

Legge, K. 1989: Human resource management: a critical analysis. In J. Storey (ed.), *New Perspectives on Human Resource Management*, London: Routledge, pp. 19–40.

Limerick, D., Cunnington, B. and Trevor-Roberts, B. 1984: *Frontiers of Excellence*. Brisbane: Australian Institute of Management.

Marchington, M. 1992: The growth of employee involvement in Australia. *Journal of Industrial Relations*, 34(3), 472–81.

Mathews, J. 1989: *Towards an 'Australian Model' of Wages-linked Structural Adjustment*. Stockholm: Swedish Centre for Working Life.

McDonald, T. and Rimmer, M. 1989: Award restructuring and wages policy. *Growth*, 37, 111–34.

McGraw, P. and Palmer, I. 1994: Beyond tea towels and toilets? Lessons from a Top 500 company using joint consultative committees for enterprise bargaining. *Asia Pacific Journal of Human Resources*, 32(3), 97–104.

Niland, J. 1989: *Transforming Industrial Relations in New South Wales,* vol. 1. Sydney: NSW Department of Industrial Relations and Employment.

Niland, J. 1990: *Transforming Industrial Relations in New South Wales,* vol. 2. Sydney: NSW Department of Industrial Relations and Employment.

Nurick, J. 1987: Australia reconstructed: a review. *Economic Witness,* 19 August, 1–7.

Purcell, J. 1987: Mapping management styles in employee relations. *Journal of Management Studies,* 24, 533–48.

Rimmer, M. 1990: The Niland Green Paper: a critical review. In M. Easson and J. Shaw (eds), *Transforming Industrial Relations,* Sydney: Pluto/Lloyd Ross Forum, pp. 6–17.

Schuler, R.S., Dowling, P.J., Smart, J.P. and Huber, V.L. 1992: *Human Resource Management in Australia,* 2nd edn. Sydney: HarperCollins.

Shadur, M.A., Rodwell, J.J., Simmons, D.E. and Bamber, G.J. 1994: 'International best practice, quality management and high performance: inferences from the Australian automotive sector'. *International Journal of Human Resource Management,* 5(3), 613–36.

Still, L.V. and Mortimer, D. 1993: The effectiveness of award restructuring and the training levy in providing a more educated workforce: a comparative study. *International Journal of Employment Studies,* 1(1), 77–101.

Storey, J. and Sisson, K. 1990: Limits to transformation: human resource management in the British context. *Industrial Relations Journal,* 21, 60–5.

Sutcliffe, P. and Callus, R. 1994: *Glossary of Australian Industrial Relations Terms.* University of Sydney: Australian Centre for Industrial Relations Research and Teaching, and Queensland University of Technology, Brisbane: Australian Centre in Strategic Management.

Sutcliffe, P. and Sappey, R. 1990: Human resource management and industrial relations: towards a framework for analysis. In G. Griffin (ed.), *Current Research in Industrial Relations: proceedings of the 5th AIRAANZ Conference,* Sydney: Association of Industrial Relations Academics of Australia and New Zealand, pp. 201–21.

Walton, R. and McKersie, R. 1965: *A Behavioral Theory of Labor Negotiations.* New York: McGraw-Hill.

Wright, C. 1991: *The Origins of Australian Personnel Management: developments in employment, selection and training procedures in manufacturing industry, 1940–1960,* ACIRRT Working Paper no. 8. Sydney: Australian Centre for Industrial Relations Research and Teaching, University of Sydney.

6

Trade Unions and Human Resource Management

P.B. BEAUMONT

Introduction

The International Labour Organization's (ILO) *World Labour Report* for 1992 argued that the response of many trade unions to human resource management (HRM) had been inadequate, largely as a result of technical inadequacies and/or ideological reservations (cited in *European Industrial Relations Review*, no. 222, July 1992: 31). This being said, there have been definite signs of a changing response by unions to HRM in recent years, although a changing response does not necessarily mean an effective response.

Initially, unions were primarily concerned with the underlying principles and assumptions embodied in HRM practices, arguing that they were 'individualizing' industrial relations and thus could undermine union organization and collective bargaining arrangements. As we shall see, such concerns and reservations still remain, but in more recent years the unions have recognized the inevitability of the introduction (with or without their blessing) of such practices. As a consequence, they have come increasingly to concentrate on the processes and conditions by which HRM practices are introduced, arguing the case for a 'joint partnership' type of approach. In addition, the unions have increasingly recognized that such practices will have important implications for their internal decision-making structures/processes, for their training of officials and representatives, and for their communications arrangements with rank and file members. This changing orientation is well illustrated by the following observations of Bill Jordan of the Amalgamated Engineering and Electrical Union (AEEU) (cited in Taylor 1994: 120):

> Whether we like it or not, these practices amount to a modern industrial development that is here to stay. It must be our job to ensure that

they are introduced in a way that is of maximum benefit to our membership. A refusal to acknowledge HRM would give the opponents of social partnership an opportunity to cast the trade union movement as negative and as being stuck in the past. Frankly, in my view, there would be some justification to this charge. Our adoption of an oppositionalist line would also deny us the opportunity to differentiate between good and bad management. At present AEEU support for HRM in its form at Toyota, Nissan and Sony allows us to be critical of those companies that try to use these techniques as a cloak for attacks on their workforces. In reality, companies will introduce these techniques regardless of our opposition. Let us not leave our shop stewards with the unenviable task of trying to respond to change with no guidance or practical support from their union or from the wider trade union movement.

In short, the initial approach of ignoring HRM, condemning it as an across-the-board principle, or leaving local representatives to work out their own solutions has given way to a greater emphasis on the processes of introduction and the resulting internal (union) adjustments which are necessary. In this chapter we seek to chart this change in the union response by examining, in turn, developments in the USA, UK and Ireland.

Some Variation Across National Systems?

At this stage it is important to ask the question whether this sort of change in the union response to HRM is reasonably common across national systems of industrial relations. To some commentators HRM in the USA has posed much more of a threat to unions than has generally been the case in Europe (Brewster 1994). The variation in the threat presented by HRM practices (as perceived by unions in different national systems) is a function of differences in (a) the content of the practices; (b) the way in which they are introduced; and (c) the wider industrial relations environment in which they are located. For instance, the perceived threat to unions is likely to vary according to both the overall level and change in union organization and collective bargaining coverage in recent years. As table 6.1 indicates, there are considerable national differences in these regards.

The contents of table 6.1 suggest that a sizeable fall in union density (and to a lesser extent in collective bargaining coverage) is most strongly associated with industrial relations systems with the following features: a strong (almost exclusive) union reliance on collective

Table 6.1 Union density and collective bargaining coverage, selected OECD countries, 1980 and 1990 (%)[a]

Country	1980		1990	
	UD[b]	CBC[c]	UD[b]	CBC[c]
Australia	48.0	88	40.4	80
Canada	36.1	37[d]	35.8	38
Finland	69.8	95	72.0	95
France	17.5	85	9.8	92[d]
Germany	35.6	91	32.9	90
Great Britain	50.4	70	39.1	47
Japan	31.1	28	25.4	23
Netherlands	35.3	76	25.5	71
Portugal	60.7	70	31.8	79
Spain	25.0	67[d]	11.0	68
USA	22.3	26	15.6	18

[a] The above study did not provide any relevant figures for Ireland. However, a publication by Industrial Relations Services (1991) reported that the level of union density was 63.4% in 1980 and 58.4% in 1987. (For the early 1990s the figure is put at some 55%, which drops to 43–44% if the unemployed are included in the calculation.)
[b] UD = union density.
[c] CBC = collective bargaining coverage.
[d] 1985 figure.
Source: OECD, *Employment Outlook*, July 1994: 184–5

bargaining; a traditionally adversarial collective bargaining approach; decentralized collective bargaining arrangements; and the absence of mechanisms for extending the results and outcomes of collective bargaining. These are features of the countries examined here,[1] which suggests that they are likely to be those where HRM is perceived by the unions to pose an above-average threat to the existing structures of the industrial relations systems concerned. In short, these are systems where it is particularly important to achieve an effective union response to HRM, but at the same time it is likely to be particularly difficult to achieve. Certainly individual unions in these systems have not formulated anything like as rapid a proactive response to HRM as has been the case with, for instance, IG Metall in Germany, where the response to the development of team working arrangements includes:

- a broad assignment of varying tasks for the group (including long cycle times);
- group competence in decision-making in areas such as job rotation, division of the work, quality control, and training needs;
- decentralization of the plant decision-making structure;
- selection of production organization and technology suitable for group work (based on decentralized technology and production concepts);
- equal pay for group members;
- equal opportunity for all, including special training where necessary for the disabled and socially disadvantaged, to participate in group work;
- support for the personal and occupational development of individuals and the group;
- regular group meetings, at least one hour per week;
- representation of group interests within the established plant system of interest representation;
- voluntary participation in the groups;
- pilot projects to test the functioning of group work before broader implementation;
- a joint steering committee at the firm level, with equal labour and management representation, to oversee and co-ordinate the implementation of group work and the activities of the groups (see Turner 1991: 113–14).

Discussion of varying union responses to HRM across different national systems of industrial relations should not, however, obscure an important point: there may be at least as much variation between unions within single systems. The ILO *World Labour Report* for 1992 noted that unions had entered into consultation agreements concerning HRM in Thompson CSF in 1989 and Renault in 1990 (EIRR no. 94, p. 12; EIRR no. 202, p. 16), but it would clearly be highly questionable, to say the least, to conclude that these two cases were typical of the French system as a whole.

The Position in the USA

As the concept and practice of HRM originated in the USA, this country provides a logical starting point for our analysis of the nature of the union response to such practices. Throughout the 1980s the essence of the union position in the USA was basically as follows: (a) the union confederation (the AFL–CIO) did not explicitly endorse or criticize HRM practices; (b) most individual unions pursued a position of 'decentralized neutrality', which involved the individual locals of national unions deciding if they wanted to be involved in such arrangements; and (c) the locals which decided to become involved sought from management various quid pro quos for their involvement. These broadly took two forms: direct controls concerning the outcomes of the arrangements (for example, sharing financial gains; no lay-offs); and indirect influences over the processes of introduction and operation (such as full participation in planning; joint choice of consultants; and ensuring no overlap/conflict with the subject matter of collective bargaining).

More recently, there has been considerable change in the US system. As one recent study has put it: 'The locus of debate within unions . . . has largely shifted from whether to participate to *under what conditions* and *how*' (Appelbaum and Batt 1993: 18). Indeed, in 1994 the AFL–CIO actually endorsed the joint partnership approach to introducing new models of work organization and employee participation (Kochan and Osterman 1994: 164–6). But prior to this statement it was very much individual national unions (for example, communication workers, steelworkers, clothing and textile workers) which took the initiative in issuing statements and guidelines concerning a joint partnership approach towards HRM. This important change resulted from the increased introduction of HRM practices in unionized settings (Eaton and Voos 1992). In some cases these practices have involved 'high profile', joint partnership programmes introduced via the collective bargaining process.[2] A leading example along these lines was the 1992 collective agreement between the communication workers and the electrical workers and AT&T. The main features of this particular agreement were:

- the workplace model where local union officers and AT&T managers seek to develop new approaches to managing change. These co-operative models can variously involve employee participation initiatives, self-managed teams, information sharing, and so on;
- the business unit/division planning councils, which examine the development and implementation of new technologies and work structures;
- the Constructive Relationship Council (first established in the 1989 contract) which consists of four members (two from the company, two from the union) from each of the national bargaining committees. It oversees the functioning of initiatives at the workplace and business unit/division levels;
- the Human Resources Board, a panel consisting of two union officials, three AT&T executives, and two outside experts in HRM accepted by both company and union. The Board is concerned with longer-run strategic HRM issues and can make recommendations to relevant executive committees of AT&T.

All four components are underpinned by both parties' acceptance of certain general principles (which emphasize mutual agreement and information sharing), and a company commitment to provide the necessary training (see Bahr 1993).

Out of such experiences a number of important lessons have emerged, such as the following (Commission on the Future of Worker–Management Relations, *Fact-finding Report*, May 1994, ch. 2):

1 A prior history of 'good union–management' relationships facilitates union involvement in such initiatives.
2 A joint partnership approach to the introduction and operation of these arrangements assists the effective maintenance and performance of such practices over time.
3 A steady, incremental growth and build-up of HRM practices over time is more likely to be effective than the one-off introduction of a large-scale transformation exercise.

The latter does, however, inevitably mean that any attempt to keep separate the two subject areas of collective bargaining and HRM is not feasible or even, arguably, desirable (Kochan et al. 1986). The three conditions outlined above are potentially important in ensuring a complementary relationship between HRM practices and union representation/collective bargaining. However, they are not the end of the story from the union point of view. Some important, not to say tough, decisions still have to be taken with regard to internal union organization. For example, Appelbaum and Batt (1993: 19–20), commenting on the Communication Workers and AT&T 1992 agreement, note:

> This kind of structure, however, requires unions to re-organise internally and to strengthen leadership and administration capabilities at several levels. It requires large investments by the union in training staff to monitor decentralised agreements and to develop technical expertise to analyse and contribute to new technological and organisational strategies. Moreover, it requires shifting power in decision-making to lower levels of union leaders. Work team leaders, QWL facilitators, and worker representatives on operations and strategic management committees can threaten the authority of elected union leadership if they are not fully integrated into a revamped union structure.

In short, a proactive union agenda in relation to HRM practices will have major implications for training and levels of decision-making within individual unions. In addition, increased priority and attention must be given by unions to communicating with rank and file members in such circumstances. The importance of this follows from the likelihood of internal political tensions arising within the membership as the unions seek to engage in such practices. The extensive package of new communications arrangements used by the Union of Automobile Workers (UAW) local involved in the high-profile Saturn partnership arrangement includes:

- *congress* – twice-a-month meetings attended by all local union executive board members, union module advisors, crew co-ordinators and other key staff functional co-ordinators. The purpose of the Congress is to provide the local union with strategic direction and focus on specific issues;
- *leadership team* – approximately 50 members from union leaders, including elected officers, executive board members, and crew co-ordinators. It meets every week and conducts periodic workshops to discuss the partnership, union strategy and business issues;
- *work unit counsellors* – bi-monthly meetings are held between elected union officers and elected work unit counsellors to discuss their roles and responsibilities as both production team leaders and elected union representatives;
- *block meetings* – weekly meetings between module advisors, work unit counsellors and crew co-ordinators to provide communications and discuss operating problems and issues in each module;
- *rap sessions* – monthly meetings held in each business team between the local union president and union members in an open question-and-answer forum;
- *town hall* – monthly local union meetings held twice during the normal work day to facilitate participation by crews on both first and second shifts;
- *member-to-member survey* – this annual survey utilizes the team leaders to conduct formal 45-minute interviews with every individual union member (5,300 in 1992) on the issues, concerns or needs they would like to see addressed by the union. The 1991 member-to-member survey served as the basis for the union's negotiating platform in the contract renewal process that year (Rubinstein et al. 1993: 358).

Developments in Britain

In the first edition of this book this chapter suggested that the position of trade unions in Britain towards HRM was basically as follows:

- they were concerned that HRM developments could potentially undermine union organization and collective bargaining arrangements;
- product and labour market circumstances were such that they would inevitably lead some employers to favour such initiatives;
- the case for membership involvement (or not) must be made at the individual organization level on a situation-by-situation basis;

- local negotiators should be wary about such involvement through the inclusion of appropriate safeguards and the obtaining of certain quid pro quos: in particular the prime role of collective bargaining must be maintained.

Since then the following developments need to be noted. First, the 1990 Workplace Industrial Relations Survey has revealed that HRM practices, although generally diffusing slowly throughout the system, are to a greater degree a feature of the union, than the non-union, employment sector (Millward et al. 1992). Secondly, some case study research has suggested that HRM practices have rarely been introduced via a joint partnership approach, which has tended to reduce the management priority attached to the collective bargaining process (Storey 1992). And thirdly, some further analysis of the 1990 Workplace Industrial Relations Survey data has revealed that HRM practices in unionized establishments appear to have been stimulated as a 'reform measure' by management perceptions of the less than satisfactory state of existing employee–management relationships (Beaumont and Harris 1995).

These various research findings all point to the need for the unions to take on board HRM as a matter of some urgency. But John Edmonds of the General, Municipal, Boilermakers (GMB) has characterized the existing British union response to HRM as 'incoherent, tentative, anxious, befuddled and uncertain' (quoted in *Employment Trends*, no. 552, January 1994). The GMB, however, produced an important brochure on HRM in 1993. It was sceptical of the motives of some managements in introducing such practices and raised concerns about the implications of such practices for unions and collective bargaining. At the same time, however, it recognized the inevitability of change along these lines, acknowledged that they may produce some benefits for members and that local officers and members needed more information and guidance concerning an appropriate response. The latter concern was reflected by issuing briefing notes on team working, annualized hours, performance-related pay, job evaluation, profit-sharing and profit-related schemes, and total quality management. The briefing notes set out questions and answers, checklists and negotiating points. In general, the brochure urged local officials to keep abreast of developments and to improve communications with members. The union guidelines stated:

- It is important to identify new management techniques as early as possible and to try to secure implementation only on the basis of agreement. However, it may not be possible to prevent implementation, in which case securing benefits from the change will be important.

- Remember that these techniques may be seen as positive by members, especially if they offer a bigger say in decision-making, better training and an end to repetitive work.
- Do not allow the trade union role to degenerate into a token one. Argue for an increase in union representation and try to keep it as near the shop floor as possible. Be positive about the trade union agenda – better training, flexibility to suit workers, job security.
- Watch out for developments that enhance the role of supervisors or team leaders and/or attempt to undermine the collective identity of workers. This may involve keeping a close eye on the employer's wider objectives – especially attempts to persuade workers to identify their interests solely in terms of the company's.
- Keep the membership informed at all times. Advise them of the dangers, particularly to the role of the union and the local representative, but discuss with them any areas of potential benefit. (GMB 1993: 10)

The contents of the GMB document are indicative of a general change in British unions in recent years concerning HRM. Indeed, some commentators have claimed to detect a movement in the direction of unions adopting a more proactive stance, citing in support of this judgement the following evidence (see *IRR&R*, no. 511, May 1992):

- national union and TUC-level statements emphasizing the need for individual organizations increasingly to adopt product quality and innovation-based competitive strategies, with a consequent need to attach increased priority to such matters as workforce training, career development, and so on;
- increased instances of unions in individual organizations moving away from a position of boycotting or ignoring certain HRM developments, and instead seeking to 'positively engage' and shape such developments.

There is no question that the need to catch up with the reality of workplace-level practice has produced change in individual unions in recent years. For example, the 1991 Biannual Delegate Conference of the Transport and General Workers Union (TGWU) voted to move away from their position of principled opposition to HRM practices. More recently, the General Secretary of the Trades Union Congress (TUC) has gone on record as saying:

We do not fear the agenda of the human resource development manager. We prefer a people-orientated system to a money-orientated one with the accountant in the driving seat – as is the case in far too many British companies. I believe that unions can have their own distinctive agenda with the human resource development company; it is not a traditional agenda but lies, for example, in the areas of ensuring that training is linkable to external qualifications, of ensuring that women at work receive special attention, of reducing working time, of pointing up single-status issues, of keeping an eye on executive pay (which has reached obscene levels in some cases) and of raising questions about pay systems, management styles, and future plans. In all these, there is a rich and fertile territory for the creative union.   (Monks 1993: 233)

This statement is of particular significance in view of the recent reorganization and relaunch of the TUC. As part of this exercise a task group was established to develop 'trade union responses to the human resource management agenda'. The task force report, which was presented to Congress in 1994, made the following points:

1   The rhetoric of HRM frequently exceeds its reality, with such practices being adopted in an ad hoc, piecemeal fashion and in some cases being a 'smokescreen' for anti-union initiatives.
2   Individual elements of HRM are more evidently a feature of unionized, than of non-unionized workplaces.
3   A high-quality competitive strategy involving minimum labour standards, long-term continuing training and an end to the short-termism of capital markets is favoured.
4   Organizational change is inevitable and should be handled through a joint partnership route.
5   This joint partnership route should place considerable emphasis on employment security and a widened collective bargaining agenda. Training, health and safety, and equal opportunities should be major new elements in this agenda.
6   The collective bargaining process needs to become less adversarial in nature, requiring changes from both management and unions.
7   Full-time officer briefings and shop steward training needs to be increasingly provided to convey more information about HRM.

There are two final points to make at this stage. First, a number of individual unions, such as the Union of Shop, Distributive and Allied Workers (USDAW),[3] are currently producing (*à la* GMB) national-level guidelines concerning responses to HRM. Secondly, as one goes down the union hierarchy, the level of concern, scepticism and criticism concerning HRM practices appears to increase considerably. For instance, I recently participated in a one-day education/training session attended by 25–30 regional and district officers from a wide variety of unions on the subject of HRM. My impressions of this session were:

1   Predominantly the views expressed ranged from the cynical to hostile.
2   In general, HRM was viewed as 'authoritarian', cost-driven and with little real priority being attached to producing better employee–management relationships.

3 There was also a strong tendency to view the practices as essentially 'elitist' in nature; that is, designed to look after a small, core group of skilled employees.

4 At most there was some recognition of the fact that HRM practices were not necessarily a homogeneous group. For example, a (genuine) employer interest in improving quality was viewed as a desirable tendency.

5 Frequent reference was made to a number of specific problems/difficulties, in particular the role of team leaders in reducing the importance of shop stewards to union members.

6 A management presentation concerning HRM developments in a company resulted in responses along the following lines: information-sharing does not constitute real union involvement, and consultations after key decisions are made does little more than present the unions with a *fait accompli*.

7 One union presentation that was pro-HRM made the following points: (a) such practices were consistent with traditional union rhetoric (for example, they drew on the expertise of operators); (b) collective bargaining was too wage-centred relative to the expressed needs/priorities of members; (c) unions have two 'customers', namely members and employers. The audience response in particular stressed the likelihood that employers would not deliver on quid pro quos requested by unions.

Union Views in Ireland

In the early 1990s the Executive Council of the Irish Congress of Trade Unions commissioned two management consultants to examine changing forms of work organization and the implications for trade unions. This work included twelve case studies of organizations in Ireland and discussions with union representatives in Germany and Sweden. The report outlined five options for unions in responding to such organizational changes:

- opposition;
- allow for a local response (local representatives decide on a case-by-case basis);
- adopt a minimalist approach (union co-operation, given certain assurances);
- adopt a proactive approach;
- actively promote with own agenda.

The various benefits and risks associated with these differing options are set out in table 6.2.

The report rejected the opposition and local-response options and recommended a policy based on a choice from the last three options

Table 6.2 Benefits and risks associated with options for trade union response to organizational change

Option	Benefits	Risks
Opposition	Maintains traditional adversarial approach No need for union to adapt or change	Unions bypassed by management Members question relevance and value of union membership Missed opportunity to be involved in QWL Damage to Ireland's perception
Local response only	Allows issues to be addressed without having a formal policy Maintains adversarial position nationally, while presenting a 'positive' response locally No blurring of traditional IR agenda No need for unions to adapt or change	Wide variety of local practices No support or guidance from trade unions Reaching rather than influencing Management proposals QWL initiative remains with management
Minimalist approach	Provides clear policy and guidelines Provides framework for local officials and members Maintains uniformity of approach	Takes no account of local practices Existing relationships Reasons for and scope of initiatives Limits scope of local officials to develop optimum solution Could be perceived as negative, if conditional upon achieving 'upfront' agreements
Positive approach	Allows for tailor-made approach Allows unions to optimize their level of input Opportunity for greater involvement of members	Could blur traditional 'us and them' relationships Blurring of traditional bargaining agenda Undermining of union solidarity

Table 6.2   (cont.)

Option	Benefits	Risks
	Builds member identification with union More involved in shaping final outcomes	Variety of local outcomes
Actively promote with own agenda	More involved in setting the agenda Seen to address wider member needs Closely involved in ongoing monitoring	Could be perceived as 'doing management's job' Undermining of union solidarity

Source: Irish Congress of Trade Unions, *New Forms of Work Organization: options for unions*. Dublin: ICTU, p. 44

(minimalist, positive and active promotion) on a company-by-company basis, depending on (a) the current and historical relationship between management, employees and unions; (b) the business circumstances of the individual company; and (c) the quality, depth and probable level of management commitment to the new work organization.

The report then went on to identify and highlight the implications for unions of pursuing the recommended options. The major items included:

- trade union policy in areas such as rewards, work organization and participation;
- the need for high levels of involvement of local officials and individual members in the specific details of the policy agenda;
- the need to manage the interaction with companies in work organization in a flexible, problem-solving manner;
- the need to re-evaluate existing internal union structures and processes to ensure effective support for full-time officials and workplace representatives;
- development of the knowledge and skills of officials and members;
- development of additional and alternative methods of communication with their members.

This important union document in Ireland, which essentially argued that unions should be prepared to buy into HRM where there are (a) employment security commitments and (b) *real* employee involvement, was published as recently as January 1993, so it is clearly too early to evaluate its practical impact. However, a number of preliminary observations can still be usefully made now. First, the publication of the document needs to be seen against the background of a noticeable fall in the overall level of union density in the 1980s (from 55.2 per cent of the workforce in 1980 to 43.1 per cent in 1987);[4] furthermore, existing research indicates a sizeable presence of non-union firms among new, greenfield site operations (Gunnigle 1992, 1994). Secondly, the Irish Congress of Trade Unions is a federation dominated in decision-making terms by general unions and public sector unions. The policy document is viewed as having been principally instigated by the younger, better-educated leaders of these unions; the craft unions and some of the white-collar private sector unions were considerably less comfortable with the responses advocated. These 'internal reservations' about the approach are particularly apparent at the lower levels of the union hierarchy, at branch level and below (a view not inconsistent with the list on pp. 124–5).

At present there are virtually no instances of high-profile, joint partnership approaches to the introduction and operation of HRM in Ireland, such as was noted earlier in the USA (see p. 119). At one stage it appeared that TEAM–Aer Lingus may have provided something of a role model along these lines, but the bitter and protracted dispute there in 1994 (EIRR nos 246–9) has been a major setback to this particular initiative; the craft unions have certainly suffered a great deal in public relations terms from this dispute. The Electricity Supply Board may be an important test case for the viability of the joint partnership approach to HRM in Ireland in the near future. In this particular case quite extensive employee involvement arrangements have been introduced in a highly unionized setting, but management has recently announced that more than 25 per cent of the workforce is to be made redundant. It remains to be seen how well these HRM practices will survive the pressures generated by this redundancy announcement. This will be particularly important in the Irish context given that, as noted earlier, the unions have placed considerable emphasis on employment security commitments from management as a leading quid pro quo for their involvement in HRM initiatives.

Conclusions

In this chapter we have deliberately concentrated on three national systems where the overall level of union density has fallen noticeably in the 1980s, and where an effective union response to HRM is important but difficult to achieve. In all three cases the unions have recognized the inevitability of the introduction of HRM, and have been increasingly concentrating on the processes of its introduction and the resulting internal (union) adjustments to be made. There were, however, some notable differences between the systems. For instance, in the USA the union confederation has played a very limited role in orchestrating a response to HRM, whereas in the other two cases the confederation is seeking to play a more prominent role.

This chapter began with reference to the ILO *World Labour Report* for 1992 which argued that ideological reservations and technical abilities had limited the union response to HRM. In the three countries examined here it appears that ideological reservations (however reluctantly) are declining as a constraint on the union response process. However, questions still remain concerning the adequacy of technical abilities in the response process, questions that can only be answered over time. But more importantly, we must recognize that the ability of unions to respond effectively to HRM is not entirely within their control, as the receptivity of management to their responses (as well as developments in the external environment) will continue to play a major role in shaping how well HRM practices fit with existing collective bargaining arrangements and relationships.

Notes

1 The relatively centralized bargaining arrangements of Ireland obviously constitute something of an exception here.
2 Such examples should not obscure the facts that many more organizations have not introduced such practices, or else have introduced them via a 'hard bargaining' approach.
3 In mid-1995 the research department of USDAW was in the process of establishing a series of membership discussions at the individual branch level. This 'bottom-up' process, which is likely to result in the production of some national level guidelines, is designed to identify what is 'going on' at the local level and how members feel about these developments. This initiative has arisen from members' concerns about the content of 'customer care' programmes, and national negotiating officers' perceptions about management's increased interest in HRM.
4 Since then it has stabilized at around this level. (These figures include the unemployed in the calculations.)

References

Appelbaum, E. and Batt, R. 1993: Policy levers for high performance production systems. *International Contributions to Labour Studies*, 3, 1–30.

Bahr, M. 1993: The workplace of the future: an innovative labor relations initiative in telecommunications. *Looking Ahead*, XIV(4), 21–4.

Beaumont, P.B. and Harris, R.I.D. 1995: Good industrial relations, joint problem solving and HRM: issues and implications. Paper presented at the International Industrial Relations Association Conference, Washington, D.C.

Brewster, C. 1994: European HRM: reflection of, or challenge to, the American concept? In P.S. Kirkbride (ed.), *Human Resource Management in Europe*, London: Routledge, pp. 56–89.

Eaton, A. and Voos, P. 1992: Unions and contemporary innovations in work organization, compensation and employee participation. In L. Mishel and P. Voos (eds), *Unions and Economic Competitiveness*, Armonk, N.Y.: M.E. Sharpe, pp. 173–215.

General, Municipal, Boilermakers (GMB) 1993: *HRM/TQM*. London: GMB.

Gunnigle, P. 1992: Management approaches to employee relations in greenfield sites. *Journal of Irish Business and Administrative Research*, 13, 20–38.

Gunnigle, P. 1994: Collectivism and the management of industrial relations in greenfield sites. University of Limerick, mimeo.

Industrial Relations Service (IRS) 1991: *Collective Bargaining, Trade Unions and Employers Organizations in Europe*. London: IRS.

Kochan, T.A. and Osterman, P. 1994: *The Mutual Gains Enterprise*. Cambridge, Mass.: Harvard Business School Press.

Kochan, T.A., Katz, H.C. and McKersie, R.B. 1986: *The Transformation of American Industrial Relations*. New York: Basic Books.

Millward, N., Stevens, M., Smart, D. and Hawes, W.R. 1992: *Workplace Industrial Relations in Transition*. Aldershot, Hants.: Dartmouth.

Monks, J. 1993: A trade union view of WIRS 3. *British Journal of Industrial Relations*, 31(2), 277–34.

Rubinstein, S., Bennett, M. and Kochan, T. 1993: The Saturn partnership: co-management and the reinvention of the local union. In B.E. Kaufman and M.M. Kleiner (eds), *Employee Representation: alternatives and future directions*, Madison, Wis.: IRRA.

Storey, J. 1992: *Developments in the Management of Human Resources*. Oxford: Blackwell.

Taylor, R. 1994: *The Future of Trade Unions*. London: Deutsch.

Turner, L. 1991: *Democracy at Work*. Ithaca, N.Y.: Cornell University Press.

7

Human Resource Management: a Sceptical Look

RAMSUMAIR SINGH

Introduction

There have been considerable developments profoundly influencing human resource management and, indeed, industrial relations in the UK over recent years. First, the whole nature of the economy and of organizations has changed dramatically: the implementation of the Single European Market within the European Union with the consequent free movement of citizens, goods and services; the continuing shift of employment from the public to the private sector brought about by privatization; the increasing share of employment attributable to small firms; the establishment of more hospital trusts; the implementation of the Next Steps initiative in the Civil Service; contracting out and the like. Secondly, the supremacy of EU law has become even more important within the field of employment, both as a source of governing rules and also as a mechanism whereby aggrieved individuals can challenge not only their employers but also domestic government action. The European Court of Justice (ECJ) has given significant decisions in particular areas of employment such as equal pay, sex discrimination and part-time work. The Court has become more explicit as to its powers to protect employment rights and to fashion good principles of employment relations, and the case law concerning remedies has grown considerably within the past five years. These developments have all had an impact on the practice of human resource management (HRM) and, in particular, that of constraining the ambit of its development.

Within recent years, however, HRM has assumed considerable importance in both the theory and the practice of the management of organizations. Many firms have been implementing HRM strategies, and the claim is often made that they are spending more on the development of their human resources than ever before (Schuster 1986; Peters and Waterman 1982; Tichy et al. 1982). In a rapidly changing and competitive environment HRM is seen as a strategic factor in influencing not only the success of companies, but also that of nations (Zhong-Ming 1990). Universities have not been slow to respond to these developments. Many have established chairs in HRM and new courses have been introduced. Journals dealing specifically with HRM have been founded and there is a growing body of literature within the field. These developments are not confined to any particular country, but are found internationally in both developed and developing countries. This is not say that there is a universally applicable model of HRM. For, as with industrial relations, it is profoundly influenced by the particular traditions and circumstances of the countries in which it is practised. As Pieper (1990: 11) rightly noted: 'the industrialised nations of the Western world have developed characteristic approaches to HRM which do show some similarities but are different, often contradictory, in many respects'. It seems that, in practice, a single universal HRM concept does not exist.

However, Brewster (1995) has perceptively noted that at one level HRM is universal, because all organizations have to utilize and, hence, to manage human resources. Perhaps this could be put another way: all organizations need humans, resources and management. Organizations are, moreover, not autonomous entities as they must operate within national and, indeed, international constraints. In Europe, as already noted, the law is particularly important, especially the supremacy of EU law over national law in member states. Many writers have tried to account for the similarities and divergences of HRM systems between countries. Filella (1991) argues that HRM systems may be related to stages of socio-economic development, with the Nordic countries at the top, the Latin countries at the bottom, and other countries in between. There also appears to be a correlation between how seriously countries take 'people issues' in the management of enterprises and their economic success (Porter 1991; Brewster and Larsen 1992). What can be said with certainty, however, is that HRM has now become a fashionable area of study and attention for both the practitioner and the theorist concerned with the management of organizations.

The unprecedented expansion of human resource management has inspired a rich academic literature. Writers have analysed the changes in HRM from a variety of perspectives. Some have produced detailed analyses of its practice, while others have urged a wider approach to the subject with greater emphasis on alternative mechanisms for the regulation of the employment relationship. At the same time the theories and assumptions underlying HRM have been subjected to extensive scrutiny and the literature and specific techniques have expanded. Any student of HRM who wishes to acquire a comprehensive view of the subject must, therefore, consult a wide variety of sources and grapple with a sometimes bewildering range of approaches.

While there are many advocates of HRM, it has not been embraced with open arms by a number of influential commentators (Legge 1989, 1995a; Keenoy 1990; Storey 1995). There is an increasing scepticism about the practice and theoretical underpinning of HRM. Indeed, some writers are hostile to its underlying philosophy. Burawoy (1985) has argued that HRM is a fundamental attack on established rights and is nothing more than a confidence trick by employers. Hart (1993: 29) went further: 'I believe HRM to be amoral and anti-social, unprofessional, reactive, uneconomic and ecologically destructive.' To be sure, there is a wide and continuing debate about HRM but, as Torrington (1993: 41), in a reply to Hart, noted: 'What is interesting is the relative acceptance of HRM by academics.'

Even the extent of the application of HRM is questionable. Guest (1990: 377), in his recent study of HRM in the USA, noted that 'the evidence casts some doubt upon any assumptions that HRM is widely applied in the USA. Indeed, as far as we can judge from published evidence, it appears to be limited to a small number of well-known cases. This raises questions about how we can reconcile the enthusiasm and the "talking up" with substance.' If this be true of the USA – the home of HRM – then clearly a pertinent question is: why all this fuss about HRM? Or, to pose a question raised by Storey (1995): is human resource management still marching on or marching out?

The Nature and Purpose of Human Resource Management

What is HRM? With so much at stake we should hope for a precise definition. Yet a perusal of the literature soon reveals a considerable diversity of opinion. Description and prescription are not easily separated. Some authors argue that HRM is a modern term for what has been traditionally referred to as personnel administration or personnel management (Byars and Rue 1987). Others use this term in addition to personnel management; this is reflected in the fact that there are now several textbooks on personnel and human resource management (PHRM) (Schuler 1987; Leap and Crino 1989). Yet others see the integration of the traditional personnel function into strategic management as the major difference between personnel management and the concept of HRM and the term 'strategic human resource management' (SHRM) is gaining a foothold in the literature. Most authors are agreed that the key to competitive advantage for an organization lies in making optimal use of human resources and in fostering cooperation between employer and employees in the pursuit of organizational goals.

According to this analysis, HRM has been defined as consisting of the following elements:

* traditional personnel administration (staffing, rewarding, work design);
* a specific management philosophy that values labour as the major asset of an organization and that regards human beings as being able and willing to grow and develop;
* the integration of the personnel function into strategic management (see Pieper 1990: 13).

Whilst it is not intended here to give a critical evaluation of all the approaches in the pursuit of a definition of HRM, nevertheless it is important to note that there has been a continuing controversy over the meaning of HRM which amply demonstrates the imprecision, ambiguity and contradiction associated with its theory and practice. Some writers seem to argue that the whole point of HRM is that it is designed to inspire and that 'to explain it is to destroy it' (Keenoy and Anthony 1992: 238). Others, notably Legge (1995), distinguish the rhetoric from the realities of HRM and expose its many contradictions. Legge has argued that the new enterprise culture of the UK is 'one that demands management's rights to manipulate and ability to generate and develop resources'. For her, HRM is, in many cases, a 'new label' as personnel management evokes images of do-gooding specialists (Legge, 1989: 40; 1995b). Keenoy (1990) in a perceptive article posed the question 'HRM: a case of the wolf in sheep's clothing?' Another writer asks whether HRM is a map, a model or a theory (Noon 1992). It seems that many analysts of HRM fasten not upon principles but upon opinions. The results have been unfortunate for a clear development of HRM. The list of sceptics is growing, and not without justification.

Advancing beyond this point involves recognizing that a description and analysis of HRM is necessary if the area of study is to advance and, in this context, Storey (1995: 5) proposed that 'Human resource management is a distinctive approach to employment management which seeks to achieve competitive advantage through the strategic deployment of a highly committed and capable workforce using an integrated array of cultural, structural and personnel techniques.'

None of these perceptions of HRM is right or wrong in any absolute sense; however, all are incomplete. An adequate understanding of the nature and purpose of HRM requires us to probe further into the way in which organizations are managed in society. At the most basic level it requires us to articulate more specifically the changes that are taking place in the society in which we live and to have some vision of the aspirations of that society as reflected in the ordering of the structures and processes of employment relations. The role of particular topics which constitute HRM, such as 'strategic integration' and 'strategic management' and the like, can be assessed only within such a framework. Concepts such as high quality, high commitment and high flexibility do not possess a unique interpretation and each must be analysed within its particular societal traditions and circumstances. The very meaning and importance of such concepts will differ depending upon the special characteristics of the country in which they subsist. Or to put the same point in a different way, every society will have some ideas about what it considers to be the nature and purpose of HRM, but these will differ depending upon the nature of that society.

All this is not to deny that HRM is a universal phenomenon and that there will be some commonalty of application of strategies and techniques in many countries and particularly those with multinational corporations. Yet a practice which is successful in, say, Japan may be inapplicable in the UK, where the traditions and circumstances are different. Likewise, some Third World Countries face very specific problems which cannot be compared with those of the advanced industrial countries. This is not to deny that countries can learn from each other's HRM practices. Indeed, it is imperative for them to do so: 'For all practical purposes, all business is global. Those individual businesses, firms, industries and whole societies that clearly understand the new rules of doing business in a world economy will prosper, those that do not will perish' (Mitroff 1987: ix). The point being made is that international transferability of HRM systems, no less than that of industrial relations systems, must be treated with the utmost caution.

Theory in Human Resource Management

While there has been a growth in the practice of HRM, however loosely defined, there has been very little theoretical development in the field. As Guest (1987: 509) noted: 'There is, as yet, no theory of human resource management.' Yet many authors have attempted to develop theory and, in particular, applicable theory. Although it is not the purpose here to review the various theoretical approaches, a brief review of some of the most important is necessary in any critical evaluation of HRM.

Beer et al. (1985) at Harvard proposed a model which they described as 'a broad causal mapping of the determinants and consequences of HRM policies' (p. 16). Attention has frequently been drawn to the fact that there are a number of difficulties with the Harvard framework. A central difficulty – which the authors themselves acknowledge – lies in the postulate that employees and unions be considered as 'stakeholders' in the organization; they also postulate individual well-being as an important outcome of their HRM model. The concept of 'stakeholder', as Guest (1987: 510) notes, 'owes more to idealism than to realism', and would be difficult to apply in many countries, and in particular in the UK, without new legislation relating to the ownership and control of firms.

In sharp contrast, the researchers of the Michigan group (Devanna et al. 1984) argue that strategic HRM should be seen as the overlapping part of both strategic or general management on the one hand and personnel management on the other. Such an integration of the personnel function into strategic management forms the major difference between traditional personnel management and HRM. As such, it is claimed, HRM becomes a particular approach to the management of organizations, distinct from other approaches (Fombrun et al. 1984).

There have been other influential attempts at theorizing in HRM: human asset accounting (Likert 1967); human capital theory (Schultz 1972); human resource (HR) indexing (Schuster 1986). The unifying feature of all these approaches is that they treat human labour as the most important asset of an organization rather than viewing it primarily as a cost factor. It is explicitly recognized that no organization can attain its goals without labour of the right quality and quantity. This is particularly true of those organizations concerned with high technology. Thus an organization must invest in the development of its human resources.

Not surprisingly, the quest for theoretical models to explain HRM continues unabated. Storey has proposed that there are so-called 'hard' and 'soft' versions:

The one [the 'hard' version] emphasises the quantitative, calculative and business strategic aspects of managing the headcounts resource in as 'rational' a way as for any other economic factor. By contrast, the 'soft' version traces its roots to the human-relations model. It emphasises communication, motivation and leadership. (Storey 1989: 8)

These two versions differ fundamentally in their view concerning the direction the transformation of an organization should take. The 'soft' version entails a range of specific policies and practices which are essentially people-centred. The 'hard' version admits anything that fits the business strategy. In other words it could result in low pay, harsh discipline and redundancy. Indeed, the impression is firmly given by the hard version that management can do, and should be able to do, anything it likes in the transformation of the organization. Yet, as already noted, this view is hardly compatible with the legal obligations of an employer and the corresponding rights of employees.

It is interesting to note that Storey in a later work posed the question: 'Is it possible that HRM is simply an elegant theory which has no basis in reality?' (Storey 1995: 8). Certainly the response to this is that a theory must explain the practice; if it cannot do so it is the theory that is deficient. In the 'real' world there is nothing so practical as a good theory. All this is not to deny that Storey and others are making considerable attempts to bridge the gap between the theory and practice of HRM.

Undoubtedly one of the most analytical and coherent portrayals of HRM is that of Brewster (1995). Drawing upon data from the Cranfield/Price Waterhouse survey of European countries, Brewster concludes that there is a convergence towards a HRM concept but within defined external boundaries which include a significant role for the state and trade unions. Thus, as Brewster perceptively notes, industrial relations can reclaim the area because it is essential to view HRM as covering a wider field than just managerial behaviour. All the evidence suggests that this trend will not only continue but will accelerate within the EU countries, as common policies, including that of employment, are uniformly introduced within them (Sparrow and Hiltrop 1995).

It is clear from this survey that theories about HRM are at a rudimentary stage. Yet HRM has proved to be a fertile field for employers, assisting them in the pursuit of their objectives, in many instances to the detriment of employees. As Sisson (1994: 15) noted: 'the rhetoric may be the people-centred approach of the "soft" version; the reality is the cost reduction approach of the "hard" version'.

A Framework for Analysing Human Resource Management Issues

Most of the literature on HRM takes the goals of the organization as its starting point and builds models primarily to help managers make and implement strategic decisions to achieve the firm's objectives. Yet it is evident that any model of HRM needs to go beyond the primary goals of management and consider the strategic interactions of other actors in the HRM system, notably individual workers, trade unions and, most importantly, society at large. Such a model is proposed in the hope that it will assist in the understanding and identification of national differences in HRM approaches. By its very nature, however, such a model is a heuristic device by means of which data may be analysed; it has no predictive capabilities.

A framework for the analysis of HRM issues is presented in figure 7.1. It is based on the fundamental premise that HRM processes and outcomes are determined by a continuously evolving dynamic inter-action of environmental factors and organizational responses to them. Of particular importance is the role of the external environment, its values, history and institutional structures, as is also the nature of the desired optimal HRM and performance outcomes.

A number of factors which are important in analysing HRM in particular countries are enumerated in the list headed 'External environment'; this list is by no means exhaustive but does draw attention to some of the critical variables. Since nations have different cultures, they consequently have different legal, political and industrial relations systems. Differences in the external environment profoundly affect HRM practices. Employers and workers have rights and obligations towards each other and this fidelity relationship is now recognized as bilateral. Thus the legal system is a particularly important determinant.

The parameters embodied in the desired optimum organizational goals of strategic integration, high quality, high flexibility and cost-effectiveness seem to be universal objectives of organizations; yet there are no universal solutions as to how to achieve them. The institutional structures and processes in pursuit of these objectives are undoubtedly

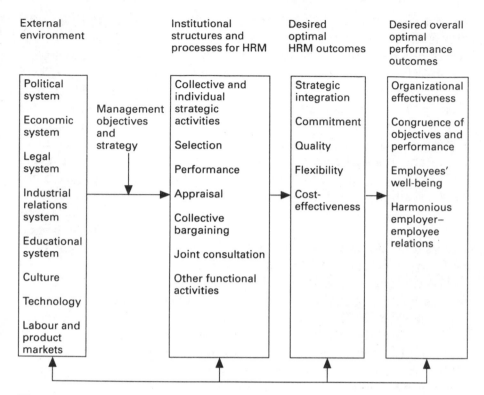

Figure 7.1 A framework for analysing human resource management issues

culture-bound. The HRM outcomes are, however, a means to an end: they are intended to achieve the overall optimum performance of the organization, not least the well-being of its employees.

The output from each component of the system helps to shape and balance the entire system. Some market forces, for example, may set in motion a series of responses from all the actors in the system. The interaction of market forces and the responses of employers, trade unions, workers and government policy together may determine the setting and the outcome of HRM strategies. Whether or not the organization achieves its objectives, the output of the system is fed back into the external environment and influences the environment itself.

While the framework does not constitute a fully developed new theory of HRM, there are several advantages in considering the relationship of the various elements of the system, and the roles played by environmental pressures and strategic choices. First, the framework recognizes the interrelationships among activities at different levels of the system and helps to explain any prevailing internal contradictions or inconsistencies among the various levels of HRM activities. For example, it helps us to understand how unions and workers have responded to the increased importance of decisions made unilaterally by employers. The framework also facilitates analysis of the effects that increased participation in workplace decisions by individuals and work groups have for the trade union movement and, indeed, for industrial relations. Since HRM policy-making with its concomitant effects on traditional collective bargaining have become increasingly important, researchers can no longer justifiably isolate the strategic levels of HRM into separate and isolated fields of study, any more than practitioners or policy-makers can segregate them into independent domains. The framework encourages analysis of the roles that management, trade unions, workers and the government play in each other's domain activities. In this way, HRM research, theory and policy or perspective analysis are brought together.

The test of whether the analysis provides a more insightful and useful understanding of the dynamics of HRM systems lies in the ability to explain why HRM evolved as it did and to identify the alternative choices the parties face as they shape the future of the system.

A combination of factors led to the development of HRM in the 1980s. A major factor was the increasing international competition faced by firms not only in the UK but also in other countries, notably the USA. The old models for the management of labour seemed not to be working effectively in a rapidly changing environment. The quest for new models became an urgent task for organizations. The climate of the period was fertile for the development of HRM. The impact of new technology, notably in manufacturing and office computerization, facilitated flexible working arrangements and new reward systems. Another significant development in the UK facilitating management initiatives in HRM was the diminishing power of trade unions coupled with a strong trend, encouraged by government policy, towards individual achievement. Trade unions have been losing their traditional membership reservoir, and thus their influence, as the coal, steel and manufacturing industries decline. Simultaneously and parallel with this development is the decline in the number of blue-collar workers as the services sector grows (Guest 1989). As a consequence the representation of such diverse groups has become difficult. Indeed, so strong has been this trend that the question was posed as to whether the working class can still be seen as a socially homogeneous group with shared interests and common values, lifestyles and political views (Pieper 1990). While new technology became available to all organizations globally the only variable parameter to give competitive advantage to organizations appeared to be labour. Within this context HRM appeared to offer something new which both management and workers could embrace. For most organizations the question posed was: how best to use our human resources?

Thus the acquisition of new technology is not the only important factor in determining economic success: a decisive determinant is whether people are educated and trained to a standard to use the new technology effectively. Technology, technological knowledge and finance for investment transcend national boundaries; by contrast, the workforce of a nation to a large extent remains within the nation to be educated, trained and employed. Whether a plant is built in the UK or in Japan, even if the same technology is used, the effectiveness of the plant would be profoundly affected by the quality of the labour force.

The economic and political circumstances of the UK are major determinants of the speed of introduction of HRM strategies in the 1980s by so many firms. The Conservative government was elected in 1979 and claimed that there was a need to create 'a climate in which enterprise can flourish, above all by removing obstacles to the market, especially the labour market' (HMSO 1985). In pursuit of this objective it introduced a number of statutes relating to employment relations. Ewing has suggested that intervention in the labour market has taken two distinct forms: the first has been to 'deconstruct' the edifice of collective labour law which had been introduced by the Labour government in the 1970s, thereby 'providing a surer and better-balanced framework of law for responsible and constructive industrial relations'; the second was to 'deregulate' the employment protection laws and to undermine the role played by Wages Councils which laid down minimum terms of employment for workers in some industries (Ewing 1990: 2). The Wages Councils introduced in 1909 were abolished in 1993.

An important strand of government policy, conducive to the introduction of HRM strategies, has been to weaken the collective power of trade unions in the areas where they continue to operate. This has been achieved by reducing the coercive power which trade unions have over workers, by means of legislation conferring rights on those not wishing to join trade unions. Secondly, the law has also been used to weaken the coercive power which trade unions have over their members. The statutory immunities relating to secondary picketing, secondary boycotts and other forms of sympathetic action have been removed. All industrial action must now be supported by a secret ballot, and unions are liable in damages if they fail to comply. The effect of the labour laws introduced in the 1980s and 1990s is to weaken the trade unions further, and thus make them more compliant to the HRM initiatives of employers.

The quest for new forms of management initiatives was further accelerated by the recession in the UK in the early 1980s. There were large job losses in a number of industries. Firms had to operate in an increasingly competitive environment both nationally and internationally. During this period many public corporations were privatized and as these firms moved into the private sector they implemented new policies for the management of labour. Cost-effectiveness and efficiency became the strategic objectives of organizations during this period. Traditional industrial relations, characterized by an adversarial relationship between management and unions, were of declining importance as they were associated with conflict and the decline of industry. Against this background there emerged what is loosely called 'the new industrial relations': a term used to describe industrial relations in the UK in the 1980s, one feature of which is closely associated with HRM.

Another factor, often overlooked when HRM is evaluated, is demographic change (Storey and Sisson 1990). In recent years there has been an increasing proportion of women in the workforce, many of them part-time workers. Young people also constitute a significant and growing proportion of those in employment. It is, therefore, of interest that in many firms in the electronics industry and in services, notably Toshiba and Marks & Spencer, where it is claimed that HRM is practised, there is a high proportion of women workers. Historically, women workers have been more difficult than men to organize into trade unions and more compliant with management initiatives.

Undoubtedly the most powerful influence in the introduction of HRM initiatives in the UK was the fact that in the 1980s a number of Japanese companies established plants in greenfield sites; this provided the opportunity for the introduction of new initiatives in the management of labour. Included in these initiatives, for example, is new machinery for the prevention and settlement of industrial disputes, notably pendulum arbitration (Singh 1986). There are several distinguishing characteristics of these companies which provide fertile ground for the introduction of innovative HRM practices: a highly professional management; a carefully selected and trained labour force and intrinsically rewarding work and security of employment. These companies actively pursue a careful and deliberate policy of marginalizing the influence of trade unions or of avoiding the need for them altogether. Management-led initiatives to achieve this result are commonplace in these organizations: quality circles, single status, staff consultative committees and the like. The outcome is that in these Japanese companies there is either no role for trade unions or, at best, one where unions are allowed to operate but on management's terms (Guest 1989, 1995).

These very successful Japanese companies have been trying to present a new vision of the employment relationship in contemporary society: a vision of unity, co-operation, purpose and inspiration and managerial wisdom unfettered within a compliant single-union or non-union environment. Not surprisingly, several writers have noted that there is a link between the competitive threat posed by Japanese companies and the interest in their HRM policies (Guest 1989, 1995). For the guiding principles of the new HRM strategies British firms have turned to Japan. The Japanese are viewed as leaders in modernization strategies, and managers in the UK are enthusiastically borrowing methods of control of the employment relationship from Japan, with little regard for the fact that Japanese society, in which these practices have their origin, differs from that of Britain. The Japanese approach to HRM appears to be characterized by a high commitment to quality, productivity, competitiveness and a philosophy of organizing the work environment to achieve these objectives. Convincingly, and with profitable results to justify their approach, these companies expound the virtues of their HRM techniques (Wickens 1987).

Conflict between the interests of employers and workers is seen as an aberration in these new-design organizations and so is the idea that workers organize into independent trade unions. The critical issues arising from the joint regulation of the employment relationship between management and workers are glossed over as too outmoded. HRM is based on a simple and seductive idea: harmony between the interests of employer and workers. Indeed, the paramount interests are the efficient production of high-quality goods at a competitive cost. Once this is understood any conflict between management and workers becomes superficial, a matter for HRM, not conflict of interest.

It is now almost a necessity for firms in the UK that want to appear modern and progressive to embark upon some form of HRM strategy. The primary concerns with productivity, quality and cost-effectiveness have posed serious questions about the ordering of the employment relationship. As already noted, traditional industrial relations have been blamed for the country's current industrial problems. A closer and more positive relationship between management and workers is widely advocated. Thus HRM would fill this gap, but likewise tremendous pressure has been put upon its practitioners to justify it.

The Legal System

Whereas economic, cultural and technological factors form a general framework for HRM, a country's legal system has to be seen as an all-important specific constraint since it determines the nature of the relationship between employers and employees. In many countries the legal environment for HRM is unique and closely tied to the country's history and structure But most countries are also bound by international laws and conventions as, for example, those of the International Labour Organization (ILO). And, of course, this is true for the UK.

It is therefore significant to note that some of the practices of HRM appear to be contrary to the spirit and purpose of both national and international law. The term 'human resource' is itself, in many respects, synonymous with 'human commodity', perceived as a cost of production. In 1944, in the Declaration of Philadelphia, the ILO adopted a declaration which defined the aims and the purposes of the organization and this was incorporated in the ILO Constitution. The declaration reaffirmed, in particular, that 'labour is not a commodity'; that 'freedom of expression and of association are essential to sustained progress' (Valticos 1985: 75).

One consequence of HRM policies has been the decline in the importance of industrial relations and, therefore, in the role of trade unions and their representatives in the workplace. Collective bargaining either has no role or only a marginal role in the organizations which claim to practise HRM. Whilst the Advisory Conciliation and Arbitration Service (ACAS) still has a general duty to promote the improvement of industrial relations, its duty 'to encourage the extension of collective bargaining' was abolished in 1993 (Turera 1993). In sharp contrast the ECJ has continued to raise the level of rights given to workers in the EU.

The doctrine of Community law supremacy has undoubtedly been one of the notable achievements of the ECJ and it has been the cornerstone in building a community legal order. The contributions made in recent years by EU law to the development of industrial relations in the UK have been enormous, particularly in the fields of sex discrimination, race discrimination, equal pay and rights for part-time workers. The UK government has been forced by the actions of the ECJ to bring UK law into line with EU law. While it is not intended here to review all such reforms, some of them are particularly important for HRM and require comment.

A major contribution of the ECJ to EU law has been through the development of the doctrine of direct effect. The concept allows individuals to bring actions in their own names within national courts in order to vindicate rights secured to them by EU law (*Francovich* 1991). It is in this sense a species of private enforcement. There is also the concept of 'indirect effect' whereby EU law is given effect through the intermediary of national law. In consequence, the fullest effect can be given to the principle that while, under the EU treaty, a directive leaves to national authorities the choice of focus and methods for its implementation in national law it is, none the less, binding upon member states as to the result achieved. The impact of this principle is enormous for constraining HRM and expanding IR within the EU: national courts are required to construe their own national law with this in mind. UK courts have, on the whole, shown themselves willing to construe national law in the light of EU law, and to give effect to the supremacy of the latter (Steiner 1994).

One of the interesting effects of these developments is that, although there has been a decline in trade union membership in the UK over recent years and a corresponding decline in the importance of collective bargaining, in sharp contrast there has been a rapid increase in the individual rights of workers conferred by the ECJ and by EU directives over the whole field of industrial relations. There has also been a greater willingness among workers to exercise their rights, as is evidenced by the sharp rise in industrial tribunal cases over recent years. Taking these factors together, a continued steady growth in industrial tribunal cases can be expected, thus severely constraining the development of HRM as at present practised, and forcing management to adopt more conventional industrial relations practices in conformity with EU law.

In 1992 the 12 members of the European Union signed the Treaty on European Union (Maastricht Treaty). The treaty incorporated the Community Charter of the Fundamental Social Rights of Workers which was adopted, in 1989, by eleven member states of the European Union. The United Kingdom did not adopt the Social Charter (Chapter), and also opted out of the Chapter in the Maastricht Treaty. Since the Treaty was signed the European Union has expanded to 15 members and the UK remains the only opted-out member.

The Agreement on Social Policy of the Maastricht Treaty is the cornerstone on which the social dimension of the European Union is based. It states:

> The Community and the Member States shall have as their objectives the promotion of employment, improved living and working conditions, proper social protection, dialogue between management and labour, the development of human resources with a view to lasting high

employment and the combating of exclusion. (Treaty on European Union 1992: 197)

Although the UK has opted out of the provisions of the Social Chapter, this does not mean that it can completely ignore them. The ECJ is the final arbiter on Treaty provisions, and its judgments must be given effect in all member states of the European Union. Secondly, many of the multinational companies give effect to directives based on the Chapter in their UK operations although they are not legally obliged to do so; for example, the implementation of the European Council Directive.

The Social Chapter provides the framework for the future development of the European 'social dimension'. The Chapter sets out 12 categories of 'fundamental social rights', and these form an essential part of the 'internal market' which came into being in 1992. The Chapter confers a number of rights for workers: equal pay for men and women; paid holidays; the right of association and collective bargaining; improvement in the working environment as regards the health and safety of workers; information, consultation and participation for workers; and freedom of movement within member states. Member states, excluding Britain, are required to implement the fundamental social rights in the Chapter because the social measures are 'indispensable to the smooth operation of the internal market as part of a strategy of economic and social cohesion' and to 'maintain the competiveness of the Community economy' (Treaty on European Union 1992: 197). Clearly, the Chapter represents a massive advance in employment protection, providing 'a floor of rights' on which working and living standards can be secured by new laws and new forms of relations between employers and employees across the European Union.

There can be little doubt that industrial relations, and with it HRM, are moving centrally into the field of human rights, and that human rights at the workplace are likely to assume greater importance than hitherto. The ILO conventions, the European Convention of Human Rights (ECHR) and EU laws are combining to extend the statutory rights of workers and to regulate and constrain HRM profoundly.

Evaluation

The rise of HRM in the 1980s seems to have taken most organizations and commentators by surprise. Yet resources, including human resources, have always been managed, although the forms of management have had to be adapted to changing economic, technological and social conditions. HRM has emerged as a pace-setter by emphasizing high employee commitment and flexibility in the utilization of labour. The great majority of firms can expect to continue to face intense foreign and international competition, and dramatic change in the way labour is managed may become a permanent feature of organizational life. The changing market and technological conditions will interact with equally important changes in the characteristics of the labour force and in the aspirations of workers.

Since the 1960s there has, moreover, been a great expansion in education at all levels in the UK. Thus the techniques of management control used in the past may not be appropriate to the changing environment. HRM strategies aimed at a better-educated and -trained labour force require more sophisticated methods of management. HRM manages 'power' and 'control'; in the present economic climate most workers accept management's edicts from a lack of choice. HRM requires a 'unitary' frame of reference; in this setting the possibility of conflict of interests is seldom recognized. Conflict does not originate inside the structures in organizations practising HRM; when it does appear – as it nearly always does – solutions are focused on the problems of individuals. It is the individual who has to be dealt with, not the organization.

Expansion of the areas of consensus between management and labour and reduction of the areas of conflict form a primary management task. To this end, HRM is a strategic management tool. The effective implementation of HRM policies calls for the training of line management in HRM strategy because they will find themselves at the leading edge of HRM implementation. At the same time, very few workers or trade union leaders are so trained. Management appears to have the competitive advantage in this regard.

Attention has been drawn to the recent developments in employment law, particularly those emanating from the EU. The impact of these laws is inhibiting the development of HRM strategies in the UK and there is a convergence of employment rights within EU countries. In most EU countries, for example, workers have rights which are guaranteed by law, such as a minimum wage and the right to strike. In the UK, workers, for the most part, have only immunities and as yet no minimum wage. In Germany, at company and plant levels, the system of legally guaranteed co-determination is a major determinant of the way in which trade unions become involved in the management of enterprises. Many multinationals, however, are establishing similar structures and processes for consultation throughout their European operations. In this context contemporary HRM may be just a passing fad.

If HRM is to be a respectable area of academic study it must develop theory and, so far, its exponents have demonstrably failed to do so. Its underpinning has been drawn from the attics and basements of other disciplines and, indeed, it could be characterized by 'what is true is not new and what is new is not true'.

The incursion of HRM into industrial relations has been restricted by law and practice in many countries, and certainly those within the European Union. Areas where the creativity of industrial relations has shown itself in recent years include equal pay, part-time work, sex and race discrimination, all of which restrict the rights of employers in the employment relationship. Industrial relations have consistently developed and found new fields of application over centuries. To paraphrase a famous dictum by Lord Denning: 'Industrial relations have not passed the age of child-bearing' (*Eves* 1975). The categories of principles and practices of industrial relations are never closed. In sharp contrast, HRM seems to lack potential for development.

Employers seem to treat HRM as a magic formula to transform their organizations, regardless of the rights or interests of their employees. All indications are that HRM will not develop further. It is well that this should be so; otherwise workers would be permanently insecure and this does not make for co-operative endeavour at the workplace. The most recent trends, as we have seen, favour a return to more orthodox principles of industrial relations. The legitimacy of HRM is at least suspect; at best it is a mutant from which further breeding should be discouraged.

References

Beer, M., Spector, B., Lawrence, P., Mills, D.Q. and Watton, R. 1985: *Human Resource Management: a general manager's perspective*. Glencoe, Ill.: Free Press.

Brewster, C. 1995: HRM: the European dimension. In J. Storey (ed.), *Human Resource Management: a critical text*. London: Routledge, pp. 309–31.

Brewster, C. and Hegewisch, A. (eds) 1994: *Policy and Practice in European Human Resource Management: the evidence and analysis from the Price Waterhouse Cranfield Survey*. London: Routledge.

Brewster, C. and Holt Larsen, H. 1992: Human resource management in Europe: evidence from ten countries. *International Human Resource Management Journal*, 3(3), 409–34.

Burawoy, M. 1985: *The Politics of Production: factory regimes under capitalism and socialism.* London: Verso.

Byars, L.L. and Rue, L.W. 1987: *Human Resource Management.* Homewood, Ill.: Irwin.

Commission for the European Communities (CEC) 1989: *Communication from the Commission Concerning its Action Programme Relating to the Implementation of the Community Charter of Basic Social Rights for Workers*, Com. (89), 568 Final, Brussels, 29 November.

Commission for the European Communities (CEC) 1990: *The Community Charter of Fundamental Social Rights for Workers*, Brussels.

Commission for the European Communities (CEC). Directorate-General for Employment, Industrial Relations and Social Affairs 1990: *Social Europe 1.90*, Brussels.

Devanna, M.A., Fombrun, C.J. and Tichy, N.M. 1984: A framework for strategic human resource management. In C.J. Fombrun, N.M. Tichy and M.A. Devanna (eds), *Strategic Human Resource Management*, New York: John Wiley, pp. 33–55.

European Works Council 1994: Council Directive 95/45/EC. Brussels: CEU.

Eves v. *Eves* [1975], 1 WLR 1388.

Ewing, K. 1990: Labour law under the 1980s Conservative government. Unpublished paper.

Filella, J. 1991: Is there a Latin model in the management of human resource?. *Personnel Review*, 20(6), 15–24.

Fombrun, C.J. Tichy, N.M. and Devanna, M.A. (eds) 1984: *Strategic Human Resource Management.* New York: John Wiley.

Francovich and Others v. *Italy*, Cases C6, C-9/90, Judgment of 19 November 1991.

Guest, D.E. 1987: Human resource management and industrial relations. *Journal of Management Studies*, 24(5), 503–21.

Guest, D.E. 1989: Human resource management: its implications for industrial relations and trade unions. In J. Storey (ed.), *New Perspectives on Human Resource Management*, London: Routledge, pp. 41–55.

Guest, D.E. 1990: Human resource management and the American dream. *Journal of Management Studies*, 27(4), 377–97.

Guest, D. 1995: Human resource management, trade unions and industrial relations. In J. Storey (ed.), *Human Resource Management: a critical text*, London: Routledge.

Hart, T.M. 1993: Human resource management: time to exorcise the militant tendency. *Employee Relations*, 15(3), 29–36.

Hartley, T.C. 1994: *The Foundations of European Community Law*, 3rd edn. Oxford: Clarendon Press.

Hepple, B. 1994: The implementation of the Charter of Fundamental Social Rights. *Modern Law Review*, 53, September, 643–54.

HMSO 1975: *Employment Protection Act 1975*, London: HMSO.

HMSO 1985: *Employment: the challenge for the nation*, Cmnd 9474, London: HMSO.

Keenoy, T. 1990: HRM: a case of the wolf in sheep's clothing? *Personnel Review*, 19(2), 3–15.

Keenoy, T. and Anthony, P. 1992: HRM: metaphor, meaning and morality. In P. Blyton and P. Turnbull (eds), *Reassessing Human Resource Management*, London: Sage, pp. 233–55.

Leap, T.L. and Crino, M.D. 1989: *Personnel/Human Resource Management*, New York: Collier-Macmillan.

Legge, K. 1989: Human resource management: a critical analysis. In J. Storey (ed.), *New Perspectives on Human Resource Management*, London: Routledge, pp. 19–40.

Legge, K. 1995a: HRM: rhetoric, reality and hidden agendas. in J. Storey (ed.), *Human Resource Management: a critical text*, London: Routledge, pp. 33–9.

Legge, K. 1995b: *Human Resource Management: rhetorics and realities*. London: Macmillan.

Likert, R. 1967: *The Human Organization*. New York: McGraw-Hill.

Mitroff, I.I. 1987: *Business Not as Usual*. San Francisco, Cal.: Jossey-Bass.

Noon, M. 1992: HRM: a map, model or theory? In P. Blyton and P. Turnbull (eds), *Reassessing Human Resource Management*, London: Sage.

Peters, T.J. and Waterman, R. 1982: *In Search of Excellence*. New York: Harper Row.

Pieper, R. (ed.) 1990: *Human Resource Management: an international comparison*. Berlin: Walter de Gruyter.

Porter, M. 1991: *The Competitive Advantage of Nations*. New York: Free Press.

Schuler, R.S. 1987: *Personnel and Human Resource Management*, St Paul, Minn.: West Publishing Co.

Schultz, T.W. 1972: *Investment in Education*. Chicago, Ill.: University of Chicago Press.

Schuster, F.E. 1986: *The Schuster Report: the proven connection between people and profit*. New York: John Wiley.

Singh, R. 1986: Final offer arbitration in theory and practice. *Industrial Relations Journal*, 17(4), 329–38.

Sisson, K. (ed.) 1994: *Personnel Management: a comprehensive guide to theory and practice in Britain*. Oxford: Blackwell.

Sparrow, P. and Hiltrop, J.-M. 1995: Redefining the field of European human management: a battle between national mindsets and forces of business transition? British Academy of Management Annual Conference, *Refereed Papers*, 345–65.

Steiner, J. 1994: *Textbook on EC Law*. London: Blackstone.

Storey, J. (ed.) 1989: *New Perspectives on Human Resource Management*. London: Routledge & Kegan Paul.

Storey, J. (ed.) 1995: *Human Resource Management: a critical text*. London: Routledge.

Storey, J. and Sisson, K. 1990: Limits to transformation: human resource management in the British context. *Industrial Relations Journal*, 21(1), 60–5.

Tichy, N., Fombrun, C. and Devanna, M.A. 1982: Strategic human resource management. *Sloan Management Review*, 23(2), 47–61.

Torrington, D. 1993: How dangerous is human resource management? A reply to Tim Hart. *Employee Relations*, 15(5), 40–53.

Treaty on European Union (Maastricht Treaty) 1992. Brussels: Commission for the European Communities.

TURERA 1993: *Trade Union Reform and Employment Rights Act*. London, HMSO.

Valticos, N. 1985: International labour law. In R. Blanpain (ed.), *Comparative Labour Law and Industrial Relations*, Antwerp: Kluwer, pp. 75–92.

Wichens, P. 1987: *The Road to Nissan*. London: Macmillan.

Zhong-Ming, W. 1990: Human resource management in China. In R. Pieper (ed.), *Human Resource Management: an International comparison*, Berlin: Walter de Gruyter, pp. 196–210.

Part II
Practice

8

Ethics, Strategy and Human Resource Management: Delivering Value to the Employee

PAUL MILLER

Introduction

There is a hotel not too far from where I work; it is a member of a group, itself a subsidiary of a much larger, publicly quoted corporation. In that hotel, the waiters are paid approximately £3 per hour until midnight. Of course, not too many people eat after midnight, but some do, in which case the waiters have to serve them and, after the last diners have left, they clear away and set the tables for breakfast. For hours worked after midnight the waiters are paid nothing. This needs clarifying. The job of 'waiting' in this hotel involves being in attendance until the last diner has left, clearing away and setting breakfast. Management assumes that these tasks will be completed by midnight; if they are not, the duties of a waiter are performed free of charge. Furthermore, if public transport is not available (which it isn't after midnight), waiters are expected to get home at their own expense and return by 7 a.m. to serve breakfast.

This hotel has a human resource manager. She reports to another at group level.

This chapter is about the ethics of human resource management. It is embedded in the literature on strategic human resource management because issues associated with the behaviour of corporations are clearly strategic ones. My purpose is to place a range of relatively well known HRM developments and issues in an ethical context. The reasons for this are simply stated. The first is that the ethical issues surrounding business are becoming of increasing interest to most sections of the community – fuelled by a range of high-profile cases in the United Kingdom. The second is that the employment of people gives rise to unique and important ethical considerations which have been largely ignored while those attaching to the environment have been well discussed, if not addressed. A glance at the indices of a range of current texts in human resource management will testify to the absence of considerations of 'ethics', 'morals', 'standards' and so on. And reference to material on 'policies' and 'procedure' are similarly bereft of ethical content (see, for example, Sisson 1994; Storey 1995; Armstrong 1992; Hendry 1995).

Systems, Procedures and Outcomes

What is wrong with the employment situation 'enjoyed' by the waiter described above? In order to identify the concerning factors, we must separate three issues. We call these 'system', 'procedure' and 'outcome' issues (Sheppard et al. 1992). A discussion of each will illuminate the broad reasons why many will feel concerned at the waiter's plight and relieved (if employed) that his or her own employment conditions are rather better.

System justice

This set of issues is concerned with 'fairness'. It is the issue upon which all others hinge, so I propose to consider it in some detail. The notion of fairness at work has a long history, and an evolving one. What used to be considered 'fair' no longer is. However, that is not to say that judgements about fairness are difficult to make. They are extremely easy, and this must be so because we make them all the time and very often. When we do, we are applying two broad principles. The first principle requires some notion of balance: the comparison of an action with some other action. The most common example is the rule of law and the scales of justice: the punishment must fit the crime.

In the example, the application of this principle suggests a comparison between the waiter's conditions of employment and those of other people. There are at least three things that tip the scales. The first is that the waiter is getting no reward at all for effort after midnight. There is *no* balance in other words. The second is that we have become used to a situation in which the majority of those working after a certain hour should in fact get more pay and not less. And the third feature that appears to tip the scales is that the employer makes no provision for the employee to get home if the latter, at the insistence of the former, has to work after public transport has stopped. Again, this conflicts with our understanding of what happens in other employment situations. Or does it?

As I have argued, the notion of balance requires a comparative judgement. This judgement changes over time and we had become used to the standards we apply becoming ever higher. We don't, for example, expect a horse thief to be hanged any longer; we don't expect an employee to be fined a week's wages for not saluting the boss. However, it is possible that the standards to which I referred earlier are no longer becoming higher in the context of employment and may indeed be lowering.

The second principle which we apply to help us reach a conclusion as to the fairness of something is that of 'correctness'. Whether an action is 'correct' encompasses aspects of consistency, clarity, procedural thoroughness and compatability with the morals and values of the times. The first three features are, of course, meat and drink to the human resource manager; the last is perhaps a little more unusual.

'Moral problems are concerned with the harms caused or brought to others, and particularly with [those that] are outside their own control' (Hosmer 1994: 19). Moral problems in management are often complex because harms to some groups are often accompanied by benefits to others; for example, the decision to transfer production from a high-wage economy to a low-wage one. In the case of our waiter, our judgement as to the 'correctness' of his conditions of employment returns us to the question of whether the (employment) morals and values of our times are somehow being eroded. Thus, the debate for our waiter might revolve around the choice between employment and unemployment; for the company, it might be said to revolve around the nature of the competitive environment. In other words, the dialogue in a modern economy has evolved in the last decade so that the boundaries of 'right' and 'wrong' in an employment context have been changed in ways that appear to do harms to employees. For example, the 'market' has often been used to justify drastic reductions in salaries – a phenomenon almost unheard of a decade ago and yet now so commonplace, it makes the news only when the directors of the same company award themselves significant increases at the same time.

Procedural justice

This is the second of the three issues, an understanding of which informs our decision as to the rightness or wrongness of the employment conditions faced by our waiter.

The issue in the definition of procedural justice is the presence of checks and balances against biased decisions and the unintended consequences of decision processes. Traditionally, the presence of strong, representative trade unions[1] ensured a measure of procedural justice, but as has been well recorded (see, for example, Clark and Winchester 1994), this role has been substantially eroded. Without appropriate substitutes, there is little prospect of procedural justice in the employment relationship. This suggests that other ways must be found in the search for it.

As in 'system' justice, the search for procedural justice requires correctness as well as balance. In traditional systems for the management of employees, organizations relied substantially on the procedural 'balance' conferred by trade unions. In a trade union-free environment, those concerned to display procedural justice must rely much more on the search for correctness. In our example, it is unlikely that the waiter is represented by a trade union (or at least one strong enough to have influence) and this means that the employer must use alternative ways to show procedural fairness. He does this by emphasizing the correctness of decisions. How does he do this?

There are three standards of procedural correctness: neutrality, trust and standing (Lind and Tyler 1988). Neutrality suggests a thorough information search which focuses on securing accurate data and permits monitoring and review. Trustworthiness suggest a procedure which is followed consistently; and finally, 'standing' suggests that individuals are treated in a manner consistent with their status. There is some limited empirical evidence for these principles (Sheppard et al. 1992) and for the related principle of 'correctability' in which the capacity to appeal a decision causes a related procedure to be perceived as more fair (Sheppard 1985).

An obvious example of these principles is the system for the determination of teachers' pay in the United Kingdom. Here is a situation in which trade unions were barred from the pay-determination process (denying procedural balance) and in which the government tried to replace it with procedural correctness. However, the system for procedural correctness does not meet the three criteria of neutrality, trust and standing. The party most affected (the teachers) are suspicious of the process and doubt its neutrality. They do not trust the process, partly because they do not believe it to be neutral (their representatives are absent from it) and partly because they do not believe it is consistently applied (for example, to others in the public sector), and finally, because the teachers do not believe it recognizes their status.

However, it is not difficult to imagine how a procedure that meets the needs of procedural correctness might be introduced. In a single organization, it is possible to imagine the human resource manager as pivotal in its design and instrumental in its maintenance. None of this is to deny the fact that systems for procedural balance are no longer important; it is merely to recognize the reality of the declining influence of collective representation for employees – whatever the reason might be. I shall return to this human resource management role.

Outcome justice

The notion of 'outcome justice' will perhaps be most familiar to human resource management practitioners. Traditionally, judgements about outcomes (and by this we mean reward, punishment and allocation) are based on comparisons with those of others. Our choice of 'other' is based on:

1 *similarity*: we tend to compare ourselves with others who have similar jobs, backgrounds, education and so on;
2 *proximity*: we compare ourselves with neighbours, people we work with and so on;
3 *salience*: we compare ourselves with people who come to mind quickly, either because we know them personally or because they are notable.

Festinger (1954) suggested that the need to compare ourselves with others is especially important in the absence of an absolute standard for making judgements, such as a yardstick for measuring length or a clock for measuring time. It is perhaps not a surprising thing to say to an audience of HRM professionals that there is no such absolute standard in the determination of outcome justice. However, we should recognize that others have made the attempt. Here we delve into the debate on 'distributive justice'. Because the HRM professional is concerned (perhaps above all) with the distribution of the organization's product, it is important to disentangle the elements of this organizational justice.

The core elements of distributive justice

There are some things upon which we can all agree when considering issues of distributive justice. For example, race, sex, IQ and rank are not grounds for just difference in the distribution of wealth and income. Part of the reason many of us agree about this is that people, by their own voluntary choices, cannot determine their own sex, IQ and so on: 'Properties can be the grounds for just discrimination between people, only if they have had a *fair opportunity* to acquire or avoid them' (Feinberg 1973; italics in the original). This leaves us with five possible reaons for justifying difference in the distribution of the organization's added value. These are:

* the principle of perfect equality;
* the principle of need;
* the principle of merit and achievement;
* the principle of contribution;
* the principle of effort.

The first two principles are fundamentally similar and are different from the last three. The former are concerned with 'need', the latter are concerned with 'desert'. The argument here is that, on the assumption that basic needs are met by the organization, the human resource manager should be concerned only with the distribution of added value based on contribution and effort.

Although I do not intend to argue it here, the principle of perfect equality is a difficult one to sustain beyond the fact that most of us would agree that all human beings have certain basic rights (to food, shelter and so on). Although there is no way to refute the principle, those who argue it usually base their argument on need or desert. The problem with basing an argument for equality on need is that, beyond the satisfaction of the basics, need is extremely elastic. It follows that the HRM manager would do well to avoid discussion of distribution based on need and concentrate upon issues of 'desert'. It follows that for most organizations, a minimum wage (an appropriate one) would mean the avoidance of discussion of distribution based on need.

Distribution of added value based on merit focuses not on what a person has done, but rather on what kind of person he is. This being so, we should recognize that the possession of native skill is ruled out as a basis for distributing reward because it is an inherited characteristic, like race and IQ. It should not be rewarded, therefore, any more than the racial characteristics of someone should be penalized. Of course, people may enhance the characteristics they inherit, but we should be clear that what we reward here is effort.

The principle of reward to contribution is a well-established one. It is stated in the form: A's share of X is to B's share of X as A's contribution to X is to B's contribution to X. This appears to be a very strong and plausible principle of distributive justice, BUT the difficulties of measuring contribution are severe; in other words, separating out luck, the contribution of demographics, of people now dead and so on.

The principle of effort is perhaps the one that meets most of our criteria most easily. Although we do not escape entirely the fact that people may be endowed with effort-type characterisitics, effort is something that is susceptible to measurement in individuals. Of course, the application of this principle does suggest that the gas showroom salesperson should get the same as the chief executive for the expenditure of the same effort. The fact that he or she does not, has nothing, however, to do with the application of the principle of distributive justice.

If we return to the case of our waiter, it is now clear why the example appears *so* offensive. Because the reward of effort is the one principle of distributive justice which we recognize (admittedly intuitively) has a sound basis, then clearly, when it is broken so thoroughly (the waiter gets nothing for working after midnight), we react severely.

When we combine our (workable) principles of distributive justice with the factors that we use to determine comparative fairness, we see that a another balance is necessary. To pursue the example from the gas industry. In this case, we cannot argue that people believe it right that the chief executive should earn more than the salesperson. All we can say is that the salesperson and the majority of us do not compare our situation with that of the chief executive. However, what the board of the gas company has asked us to do is make a new comparison: after the chief executive's salary has gone *up* and the salesperson's has gone *down*. Having made the comparison, we implicity recognize the issues to do with distributive justice; namely, that differences can logically only be based on effort differences and that (if anything) the efforts of the salesperson are rather more visible than those of the chief executive.

It is furthermore interesting that the salary issue in this company has not been justified by resort to relative contribution (because it is both difficult to sustain and insulting to the salesperson) but by resort to system justice issues. Thus, the justification put before the public has been that salaries of the magnitude paid to the British Gas chief executive are necessary in order to attract and retain high calibre people. However, as we have seen, this argument cannot be sustained, for two reasons. As an argument based upon system justice, it fails because we cannot judge the 'balance' between the chief executive's reward and the effort he puts into the job. The difficulty is compounded by the fact that most of us recognize that the company is a virtual monopoly and that conventional measures of success are inappropriate. The argument also fails because we are not convinced that it is 'correct'. I argued earlier that for the system to be thought just, it must be thought 'correct' – the argument must display 'consistency, clarity, procedural thoroughness and compatability with the morals and values of the times'. The argument that the salary of the chief executive must be high to retain him cannot easily be shown to be any of these things. It is an argument that is not applied to other occupations; it has not been demonstrated to be correct (and most of us recognize that it would be quite easy empirically to demonstrate the argument with examples); and it is not (yet) consistent with the morals and values of the time.

Unsurprisingly, in the absence of system justice in this area, the government has had resort to procedural justice. It has endorsed the committee established under the chairmanship of Sir Richard Greenbury to consider ways to police the salaries of directors. However, this mechanism fails both the tests for the display of procedural justice. I argued that for procedural justice to prevail there must be checks and balances against biased decisions and the unintended consequences of decision processes. The Greenbury Committee contains no such checks and balances.

Similarly, to ensure procedural correctness the system must be neutral, trustworthy and have standing (Lind and Tyler 1988). The Greenbury Committee will be unable to convince its audience of any of these things. It is also the case that the power vested in shareholders to correct unreasonable decisions of company boards is recognized to be very limited.

Ethical Analysis and Human Resource Management

The human resource manager has two roles to play in the context of the ethical management of organizations. They bring together what we might call the traditional role (to do with systems, procedures and so on) and a role to do with how people *should* be managed in an ethical organization.

The traditional role

It is not difficult to see the role of the human resource manager in the organization that wishes to establish procedures for the ethical treatment of its employees. The procedures would display 'balance' and they would be considered to produce outcomes considered 'correct'. A first question that is not possible to duck is the role of trade unions.

It was not too long ago that survey after survey showed the then personnel manager in favour of trade unions and the structures they brought to the organization – the 'closed shop' is an heroic example. There will have been many reasons for the encouragement of these systems and processes, not least the recognition that they brought legitimacy to much management decision-making, through the presumption of procedural balance. In a review of recent trade union history (Guest 1995), the conclusion is disappointing: 'trades unions have been a phenomenon of the twentieth century, displaced in the twenty first'. A strategy for the trade unions in these circumstances is difficult to determine and it may be that in the face of apparently terminal structural decline it is possible only to advise them to 'take an active role in the more positive aspects of HRM' (ibid.). However, it is important to note that the decline is primarily in their role of ensuring procedural balance in the employment relationship. The trade unions have not traditionally played a role in ensuring procedural correctness, and it is worth thinking about what that role might be and its potential relationship with human resource management.

The traditional roles of the personnel manager and the trade union official have mirrored one another. Within each occupational grouping, the negotiating role has been taken by the high-status sub-occupational group. The transition from personnel management to human resource management has altered significantly this traditional 'sub-hierarchy' within the professions. Clearly, the human resource manager has embraced this change more readily. For the trade union movement, embracing the change means involvement with the systems and processes associated with ensuring procedural correctness and abandoning their traditional role associated with ensuring balance. What would this mean?

It would mean bringing 'the back office' to the front. In other words, the research role, which has traditionally supported the bargaining role with information to 'correct' that flowing from management, would play the lead. There is some evidence that trade unions are assuming (albeit reluctantly) elements of this – for example, in seeking representation on TQM councils (Storey 1992). For the human resource manager, there are potential benefits to such a change in the trade union role, similar to those he has traditionally enjoyed. In other words, trade union involvement in ensuring procedural correctness would confer legitimacy – this time on the data, systems and so on that inform managerial behaviour. This contrasts with the earlier procedural role of trade unions which tended to revolve around the behaviour itself. Thus, the plea that management action was 'out of procedure' is a reference to proscribed management actions.

This is not to ignore the role of power in organizations and the limited extent to which trade unions have it in the absence of collective action. To some extent this is outside the realm of my argument here because it engages with the issue of control in a capitalist system. Little of the literature on ethics in business questions the economic system in which firms operate. This is unsurprising because this debate is a fundamentally different one. The literature on business ethics (to which this chapter is a minor contribution) engages the issue of how management (broadly defined) might become an ethical occupation within a capitalist system. The argument that it is not possible for it to be so, within such a system, is cogent and indeed potentially persuasive, but it is not one with which I can engage here.

The ethical management of organizations

Is human resource management an ethical occupation? Those who have been working as human resource managers for some time may reflect upon the changing nature of the role. In particular, the metamorphosis of the 'welfare officer' into the 'human resource manager' (passing through 'personnel manager' on the way). A moment's reflection will reveal how profound has been this transformation.

About 30 years ago, the professional literature on the role of the personnel manager indicated concern about the changes being made to it. Debate raged on whether or not the 'welfare officer' was actually a member of the organization's management or whether she (it was often a woman) was actually there in some sense to represent the views of the employees. Women were attracted to the profession because it was often seen as social work in an industrial context – a view presumably shared by those who recruited women to the role. Now we can argue about the reality of the role, but the perception was a real one. Indeed, that perception was buttressed by the then Institute of Personnel Management which talked of the personnel role as being to do with employee care and so on.

The change in the role through the 1980s has been cataclysmic. There is no question of the role of human resource manager being a management one, and indeed he or she is often the instrument of the kind of exploitation exemplified by the case referred to at the opening of this article. The story of this transition is not one with which I am concerned here but the extent to which the manager of human resources has been integrated into the organizational machine is indeed interesting. In the following, Morgan may well be describing the role of the modern human resource manager:

While we have advanced a long way from the naked exploitation found in slavery and in the developing years of the industrial revolution, the

same pattern of exploitation continues today in a more subtle form. . . .
Striking evidence of this [is found] in the way organisations structure
job opportunities to produce and reproduce the class structure of modern
societies; in the way organisations approach the problem of hazardous
work situations, industrial accidents and occupational disease; and in
the way organisations perpetuate structures and practices that promote
workaholism and associated forms of social and mental stress.   (Morgan
1986)

For some this transformation has been profoundly 'amoral' (Hart
1993) and fundamentally different from the traditions which informed
the practice of 'personnel management'. However, it is important to
recognize that not everyone believes the transformation to be that
great. Karen Legge (1989, 1995) in particular has argued consistently
that human resource management is little more than 'old wine in new
bottles'. If so, and the argument is persuasive, then the amorality
which Hart sees now has been around for quite a while.

And yet, mission statement after mission statement makes reference
to the enlightened treatment of employees:

- 'We have trust and respect for individuals [i.e. employees]'   (Hewlett
Packard)
- 'Human and ethical values play a pivotal role in the way FI Group conducts itself'   (FI Group)
- 'BICC strives to provide an open, challenging and involving environment
for all'   (BICC)
- '. . . practising always a concern for our staff'   (Portsmouth and Sunderland Newspapers)

It is also true to say that concerns about the ethical management of
organizations are not new. In his famous treatise on the functions of
the executive, Chester Barnard concluded by saying that the executive
process 'is not intellectual; it is aesthetic and moral involving a sense
of fitness, of appropriateness, of responsibility' (Barnard 1938).

The role of the human resource manager in this is viewed by many
practitioners as pivotal and benign both for the organization and its
employees. The full mission statements of which the examples above
are extracts reveal that organizations believe that realizing the potential of employees will be of benefit both to them and the organization.
Clearly, the practical implementation of HRM policies may be unethical
(in other words the gap is large between what the company says it
does and how it actually behaves). Alternatively, the theoretical pursuit
of HRM policies is, by definition, unethical. I should like to illuminate these issues by arguing a number of propositions.

Proposition 1 It is possible *objectively* to identify unethical employment practices.

I have argued earlier the reasons for our discomfiture with the employment conditions enjoyed by the waiter. They are to do with 'offences' against well-established principles of system, procedural and outcome justice. It is furthermore possible to imagine mechanisms which may be established to display procedural correctness in employment situations.

Proposition 2 'Management' (human resource, financial, marketing, production or strategic) is recognizably good and recognizably bad.

The evidence for this proposition is all around us in the failure of organizations, of products, in the acquisition of poorly performing companies, in the 'downsizing' or 'rightsizing' of companies, in the alienation that many people feel at work and which is evidenced in well-established ways such as sickness rates and turnover rates. On the other side of the equation, the evidence is there in the ability of companies to bring new products to the market place very rapidly, to win major contracts, to provide stable and enduring employment over considerable periods of time.

These sets of statements are not wholly to do with failures of, or fundamental discontinuities in, the capitalist mode of production. 'Management' (of which human resource management is but one facet) is necessary in all type of organization (universities, charities, public utilities and private ones) and in all socio-political systems (democratic, theocratic, autocratic). And in each of these organizations and societies there is management which is 'good' and management which is palpably awful.

The effects of good and bad management are many, but there is one thing that we can say with reasonable confidence and that is that they are visited upon the employees of the managed organization. Thus, the employees of a well-managed organization (perhaps innovative, perhaps proactive, perhaps just appropriately strategic) enjoy stable employment and a reasonable standard of living. (I use the term 'enjoy' advisedly.) Conversely, the employees of a badly managed organization are unlikely to enjoy decent wages and are likely, in the long run, to be out of a job altogether. It is also worth bearing in mind just who we mean when we speak of 'employees'. We are not usually talking about the board of directors suffering the consequences of its own lousy management; the generals are rarely shot.

The notion of human resource management and, in particular,

strategic human resource management, should therefore be thought of as associated with the 'good' management of organizations. This sounds like a cliché, but it appears to have been overlooked in the debate about what 'human resource management', and in particular, 'strategic human resource management', is or is not. So what is 'good' in this context?

Good management

Management is about 'deliverables'. It is about delivering dividends to shareholders; products to customers; harmless by-products into the environment; a water treatment plant in a Third World country; food, heat and light where it is wanted. However, given that we are concerned primarily with employment, I should like to suggest that the following four elements would be the deliverables that most of us (as employees) have the right to expect from an employer:

• employment for as long as we want it;
• terms and conditions of employment that do not deteriorate from those upon which we were originally engaged;
• a just distribution of added value;
• a reasonable level of enjoyment of the working day.

I suggest that these factors recognize two fundamental criteria associated with the ethical management of organizations. The first is that the ethical management of organizations is relative; in other words, the factors will change over time. The second is that the factors are indivisable. I argued earlier that, in the UK, we appear to have tolerated a diminution in our expectations of an employment contract. This will impact on one or two of the factors above, but a lowering across all four dimensions is not possible.

My argument here is that it is possible for the human resource manager to think ethically about what he or she must deliver to employees. I see nothing different here to the marketing or production manager thinking ethically about their constituencies. It is also worth emphasizing that it is possible to identify tools and techniques to assess the delivery of the 'goods'. I have suggested some earlier, but an armoury of opinion and attitude surveys is available.

Proposition 3   In order for good employment conditions to be delivered to employees, the organization must pursue a 'good' strategy. 'Good' HRM and 'bad' HRM are by-products of the management systems of which they are a subset.

It is not possible for employees to enjoy the benefits of 'good' human resource management unless the organization's strategy works. It has been argued elsewhere that strategic human resource management is a 'downstream' function dependent upon the organization's (market-driven) strategy (Miller 1987). There has been much debate about what exactly this might mean (see, for example, Boxall 1991) and a large degree of scepticism that a linkage or fit between human resource management and strategy exists or indeed is possible (see Purcell 1995: 36–7 for a summary of the problems).

Fit Revisited

What is fit? One way of thinking about it (Miller 1989) has been described as 'arguably the most extreme' (Sisson 1994). It is broadly that human resource management initiatives are *strategic* human resource management initiatives only if they are congruent with the organization's market-orientated strategy. Although 'extreme', this is not a million miles away from most people's understanding: 'all definitions of human resource management agree on one point: that there must be a link between a firm's strategy and the deployment and utilization of its human resource' (Purcell 1995). Purcell goes on to say, however (and this is often the nub of the theoretical criticism of the 'fit' argument), that 'it is relatively easy, but ultimately highly deceptive, to generate normative statements of what ought to happen and the way in which policies towards people at work should be constructed to maximise productivity, performance and ultimately profit'. And he goes on to say: 'there are no obvious roles for a corporate personnel department'.

This strikes me as a counsel of despair and I'm not convinced that Purcell himself thinks it is true because, about a page later, he does indeed identify three roles for a corporate personnel department. These include involvement with first-order decisions and the determination of budgets. The fundamental difference between these 'normative statements of what ought to happen' and the statements of what we might call the 'fit school' of HRM is that the former are prescriptions that are held to be strategic solely by virtue of their location in the organization's hierarchy. For HRM to be strategic, this is not good enough. This argument has been put before (Miller 1987) but it is worth restating.

An example will illustrate the issue. IBM is a company that many recognize to be a shadow of its former self. As a result of some

Table 8.1 Points of difference between personnel management and human resource management

Dimension	Personnel/IR	HRM
Nature of relations	Pluralist	Unitarist
Speed of decision	Slow	Fast
Key managers	Personnel	General/line
Pay	Job evaluation	Performance-related
Job categories	Many	Few
Communication	Restricted	Increased

Source: Storey (1992)

fundamental strategic errors, it has found itself in the position of having to 'downsize' substantially. It is certain that these decisions were taken corporately and it is possible that a personnel voice was party to them. These are 'first-order' decisions with 'budgetary' implications (Purcell 1995), BUT they are actions taken downstream of poor strategic decisions and visited upon a large number of employees, to their profound detriment. I don't see anything skilful, praiseworthy, *strategic* or *ethical* in a human resource manager implementing downsizing policies or wage reduction initiatives. Similarly, to draw distinctions between personnel management on the one hand and human resource management on the other is useful only in so far as it helps to tease out good management from bad.

To illustrate this point, consider the elements in table 8.1, a selection from 27 points of difference between personnel management and human resource management. Good management is not about positioning an organisation down the right or middle column, it is about determining, for example, pay, communication flow, decision making, and so on, in a way that is congruent with the needs of the business.

Consider a famous exemplar such as Hewlett Packard (HP). Here is a company whose business strategy appears to include bringing to the market an innovative product every nine months or so. We know also from work that has lengthy antecedents in industrial sociology (for example, Burns and Stalker 1961) that particular organizational forms are suited to this kind of environment. If HP had many job categories and restricted information flows it would not get innovations to the market place. On the other hand, it is a high-technology business and it is unlikely to succeed with a top-down, unitarist management style. Is HP an ethical company? To the extent that it meets the standards set earlier, then yes, it is. Is IBM? No, it is not. Could Hewlett Packard be an ethical company in human resource management terms if it does not establish a fit between its business strategy and its human resource management strategy? The answer is 'no' – not in the long term.

The long term v. the short term

The distinction between the short and long term is often mentioned but rarely considered. For organizations and individuals the difference has profound implications for behaviour. For example, consider a company whose manufacturing process expels a range of harmful chemical into the atmosphere, the accumulation of which will deplete the ozone layer. In the short term, the company says that it can't do anything because it can't afford it, or that its competitors do the same, or that the market won't sustain the cost, or whatever. In the long term, however, there won't be a company because the depleted ozone layer will destroy it (along with the rest of us).

A similar argument may be deployed for the short-term treatment of employees. John Towers, chief executive of Rover, commenting about the company's no-redundancy policy, tells us that it is not possible to introduce major organizational change if employees are concerned about job security.[2] In the long term, the ethical treatment of employees has profound strategic implications; considered in the short term, employees are as expendable as the ozone layer.

It will be clear from my argument that an organization which establishes an appropriate fit between strategy and HRM can be described as practising strategic human resource management. If the strategy is a good one, it is likely that the organization's human resource management will be ethical. A 'good' strategy is also likely to be an ethical one, although the argument for this is not one I can pursue here (see Hosmer 1994).

Catastrophe and Human Resource Management

It should follow from the preceding parargraphs that strategic human resource management should not be about the management of surprise. In the world I am describing, organizational catastrophe does not happen. It cannot happen, because an organization whose strategy is appropriately matched to its environment anticipates it. This is perhaps a revolutionary thought but it is one that several writers are beginning to address, most notably in work on organizational knowledge and learning (Senge 1990) and on the relationship of these characteristics to the resources available to the organization (Krogh et al. 1994). The challenge for human resource management is to find a role for itself in these developments. It is unlikely to do so without theoretical flights of fancy to generate a range of normative prescriptions of what the relationship might be between the management of human resources and, for example, the creation and preservation of those knowledge-based resources vital to the organization.

Conclusions

In this chapter, I have argued the case for an ethical approach to the management of human resources. The proposition has been put that it is both possible and desirable to establish procedures and mechanisms for the creation of procedural justice at work and that the ethical management of human resources is conditional upon an appropriate fit between it and the organization's strategy. Human resource management cannot be ethical unless it is strategic.

Notes

1   My use of the term 'trade unions' refers to all collectivities of employees. I do not imply solely 'craft' unions.
2   Quoted in *High Interest: The Car Wars*, a Channel 4 production, March 1994.

References

Armstrong, M. 1992: *Human Resource Management: strategy and action*. London: Kogan Page.

Barnard, C.I. 1938: *The Functions of the Executive*. Cambridge, Mass.: Harvard University Press.

Boxall, P.F. 1991: Strategic human resource management: beginning of a new theoretical sophistication. *Human Resource Management Journal*, 2(3), 60–79.

Burns, T. and Stalker, G.M. 1961: *The Management of Innovation*. London: Tavistock Publications.

Clark, J. and Winchester, D. 1994: Management and trades unions. In K. Sisson (ed.), *Personnel Management*. Oxford: Blackwell.

Feinberg, J. 1973: *Social Philosophy*. Englewood Cliffs, N.J.: Prentice-Hall.

Festinger, L. 1985: A theory of social comparison processes. *Human Relations*, 7, 117–40.

Guest, D. 1995: Trade unions and industrial relations. In J. Storey (ed.), *Human Resource Management*, London: Routledge.

Hart, T.J. 1993: Human resource management: time to exercise the militant tendency. *Employee Relations*, 15(3), 29–36.

Hendry, C. 1995: *Human Resource Management: a strategic approach to employment*. London: Butterworth.

Hosmer, L.T. 1994: Strategic planning as if ethics mattered. *Strategic Management Journal*, 15 (Summer), 17–35.

Jackson, N. and Carter, P. 1995: Organizational chiaroscuro: throwing light on the concept of corporate governance. *Human Relations*, 48(8), 875–89.

Keenoy, T. and Anthony, P. 1992: HRM: metaphor, meaning and morality. In P. Blyton and P. Turbull (eds), *Reassessing Human Resource Management*, London: Sage.

Krogh, G. von Roos, J. and Slocum, K. 1994: An essay on corporate epistomology. *Strategic Management Journal*, 15 (Summer), 53–72.

Legge, K. 1989: Human resource management: a critical analysis. In J. Storey (ed.), *New Perspectives on Human Resource Management*, London: Routledge.

Legge, K. 1995: HRM: rhetoric reality and hidden agendas. In J. Storey (ed.), *Human Resource Management*, London: Routledge.

Lind, E.A. and Tyler, T.R. 1988: *The Social Psychology of Procedural Justice*. New York: Plenum Press.

Miller, P. 1987: Strategic human resource management: distinction, definition, recognition. *Journal of Management Studies*, 24(4), 347–62.

Miller, P. 1989: Strategic human resource management: what it is and what it isn't. *Personnel Management*, February, 46–51.

Morgan, G. 1986: *Images of Organisation*, London: Sage.

Purcell, J. 1995: Corporate strategy and its link with human resource management strategy. In J. Storey (ed.), *Human Resource Management*, London: Routledge.

Purcell, J. and Ahlstrand, B. 1994: *Human Resource Management in the Multidivisional Company*. London: Oxford University Press.

Rawls, J. 1971: *A Theory of Justice*. Cambridge, Mass.: Harvard University Press.

Senge, P. 1990: *The Fifth Discipline*. New York: Doubleday Currency.

Sheppard, B.H. 1985: Justice is no simple matter. *Journal of Personality and Social Psychology*, 49, 953–62.

Sheppard, B.H., Lewicki, R.J. and Minton, J.W. 1992: *Organizational Justice*. New York: Lexington.

Sisson, K. 1994: *Personnel Management*. Oxford: Blackwell.

Storey, J. 1992: *Developments in the Management of Human Resources*. Oxford: Blackwell.

Storey, J. (ed.) 1995: *Human Resource Management*. London: Routledge.

Tucker, R. 1964: Marx and distributive justice. In ed. C.J. Friedrich and J.W. Chapman (eds), *Nomos VI: Justice*, New York: Aldine Atherton.

9

Human Resource Management and Selection: Better Solutions or New Dilemmas?

DORA SCHOLARIOS AND CLIFF LOCKYER

Introduction

The transition from the practice and language of personnel management to human resource management (HRM) is identified with a trend towards an increasingly systematic, sophisticated and strategic approach to staffing. The processes of job analysis, job specification and the 'locating of appropriate sources of supply of labour' (Livy 1988: 94) are more methodical in consideration of short- and long-term labour requirements and changing patterns of supply of 'qualified' job applicants (Johnston and Packer 1987). In the same vein, selection practice is seen as becoming more rigorous, with more reliable and job-relevant methods providing 'a careful questioning of the categories used to define both jobs and "acceptable" workers' (Goss 1994). The HRM approach, in general, has suggested a more coherent and strategic consideration of job and employee requirements and specifications (Mabey and Iles 1993).

The focus of this chapter is on identifying current UK trends in selection while highlighting some unfolding dilemmas embodied by the notion of 'strategic' HRM. Whilst recruitment policies are also a key component of staffing, this chapter concentrates on selection, where the lack of integration between HRM practice and developments in psychological research is arguably more apparent. In the HRM literature, selection is virtually universally identified as integral to effective 'strategic human resource management' (Townley 1989). Storey (1992: 35) lists selection as one of ten 'key levers' in HRM, arguing that whilst it is typically a 'separate, marginal task' in personnel and industrial relations, it is an 'integrated, key task' in HRM. 'It is perhaps not surprising to discover that the "excellent" companies place a great deal of emphasis on selection and socialisation of new recruits . . . reinforcing central values of the organisation' (Guest 1992: 12, quoting Waterman). Purcell notes the links between values stressing individualism and 'careful selection and recruitment systems' (1992: 67). The search for employee commitment 'rather than mere compliance on the part of the workforce' (Oliver and Wilkinson 1992: 175) also requires that 'considerable emphasis must be given to selection, socialisation and training as well as to mechanisms which are linked to employee involvement and commitment . . . in short they amount to a coherent and integrated human resource management strategy' (Guest 1992: 130). Others argue that selection of workers to match the needs of an organization is a 'core activity upon which most other HRM policies geared towards the development and motivation [of staff] could be built' (Keep 1992: 331). It is also equally relevant and evident in the public as well as private sector (Storey 1992: 49).

Reviews and case studies of HRM practice in the UK have claimed to reveal increasing elaboration in the selection function. As early as the First World War, Scott (1915) noted a move away from selection as the preserve of the foreman to being located in specialist departments. Sidney Webb in 1917 commented that 'appointments were, following American practice, increasingly being made by special employment departments or by relatively senior managers with special responsibilities for labour' (quoted by Gospel 1983). In 1943, the Institute of Labour Management, the forerunner to the Institute of Personnel Management (IPM), in a paper on modern personnel practices, noted the increasing use of psychological tests, replacing more traditional methods of staff selection. The introduction of the Civil Service and War Office selection procedures (Vernon 1950; Parry 1959, respectively) were widely followed by similar schemes in public utilities and large private companies (see, for example, Bray and Grant 1966; Moses 1973).

Recent reviews indicate varying levels of sophistication. Storey's (1992: 82) study of 15 large mainstream companies found that 12 had policies which indicated that selection was an integrated key task and the second most common 'key lever' in a range including increased communication, teamworking, marginalization of stewards, moves towards individual contracts, and performance-related pay. The Workplace Industrial Relations Surveys offer systematic evidence in support of this view. The 1990 survey indicated the importance of selection as a management activity, although the status and level of qualifications of personnel staff tended to be higher in the largest firms and in overseas-owned companies (Millward et al. 1992: 40).

Studies of UK subsidiaries of American and Japanese firms identify a far greater level of investment and sophistication in recruitment and selection (see, for example, Wickens 1987; White and Trevor 1983). 'Evidence in the UK shows a small but perceptible trend . . . whilst the practice of Japanese and American companies and their subsidiaries illustrates well developed policies in these areas' (Townley 1989: 92). Storey and Sisson's (1993) review of current methods of selection identifies increasing rates of adoption of 'a multi-method approach' to performance assessment using a range of selection tools. They identify new developments which are 'rather more systematic than the traditional interview', including the use of biodata, psychometric aptitude, ability and personality tests, or a range of methods, as in assessment centres. In general, Ballin (1986) identifies 'more concerted efforts to specify the skills, competencies, qualifications and qualities being sought from applicants'.

Notwithstanding this evidence, two distinct views of the degree and extent of greater sophistication in selection procedures are emerging in the HRM literature. A more optimistic group of writers claim evidence of this growing trend in the use of systematic selection and 'an increasing application of these procedures to sections of the workforce for whom this has not previously been the case' (Townley 1989: 92). Thus, reviews of company practice are drawn on to indicate that an increasingly diverse range of formal screening methods, ranging from application forms, references and recommendations to biodata, work samples and psychological tests, are being applied to select managerial and blue-collar entry-level employees, and for making promotion and career development decisions (see, for example, case studies of electronics, motor vehicles and finance described in Buchanan and McCalman 1989; Rhodes and Wield 1985; and Wickens 1987).

Others are more pessimistic, and question the evidence for such a development. Wood's (1986) study is critical of the extent of such sophistication in selection, arguing that it is the exception rather than the norm. Keep (1992: 331) suggests that 'much of the available evidence tends to indicate that there are real problems in this crucial area of personnel management activity'. In many organizations, recruitment and selection are apparently conducted in a 'haphazard and informal fashion'. Storey and Sisson (1993: 122) echo the differences between the ideal accounts of textbooks and actual problems, noting that the 'not untypical practice in Britain has been to treat resourcing in a very *ad hoc* and peremptory fashion'.

It is none the less clear that selection is receiving increased prominence as an HRM function. It is necessary, however, to provide a more critical assessment of the contradictions implied by a move to a wider range of behavioural and attitudinal qualities identified as important in HRM and in the available methods for assessing these qualities. It is equally critical to disentangle the reality from the rhetoric as to developments in selection practice to distinguish between actual and espoused policies. There is an essential distinction, for example, between some superficial attempts to improve the effectiveness of selection over 'instinctive' methods (for example, graphology) and more considered efforts to define desired attributes and establish new assessment methodologies with acceptable levels of reliability and validity (such as work samples, and job knowledge/ability tests) (Cook 1988; Reilly and Chao 1982).

The traditional model of personnel selection, which has provided the foundation for many of the advances towards greater sophistication in practice, emphasizes rigour in the identification and measurement of job-relevant aptitudes, abilities and behaviour for specific jobs with well-defined notions of what constitutes successful performance. The logic of systematic, standardized, centralized and regular procedures in selection is analogous in many respects to a 'Taylorist' approach to management. This is, essentially, what prompts Sparrow (1994: 14) to argue that 'many currently accepted assumptions in recruitment, selection and assessment will need to be reassessed because they emerged from experiences steeped in organization systems, structures and styles that are rapidly disappearing'. Increasingly, current notions of selection, tend towards a more 'holistic' appreciation of jobs and individual potential (see, for example, Schmitt and Borman 1993). However, within the HRM literature and in practice, there is lack of clarity about what constitutes desirable job performance and the methodology required for its measurement.

This chapter explores the transition from a traditional to an alternative selection model which is consistent with the claimed objectives of HRM. Three lines of argument are followed. First, on the basis of case study and survey evidence, it is shown that the extent and spread of greater sophistication in selection procedures is restricted to a few large corporations. Evidence accumulated from existing surveys, as well as current research conducted by the present authors, is reviewed in an attempt to derive a more accurate account of the range of selection practice and its relevance to differing organisations.

Secondly, whilst large firms may be turning increasingly to a combination of psychological methods of assessment, this does not necessarily imply that they are aware of their basis and limitations. Current practice still shows that many organizations rely on conventional approaches with little emphasis on the principles of measurement underlying selection tools or with regard to a considered appreciation of changing organizational requirements. Reservations regarding the appropriate use of selection methods are exemplified in the relatively recent efforts of bodies such as the British Psychological Society to influence professionalism in workplace psychological assessment and testing through the introduction of certification procedures (Bartram 1991, 1995). In the UK, personnel/HRM staff traditionally have been accorded lower priority and training in personnel issues with the result that there are identifiable gaps in the competency of HRM specialists to deal with the selection problem. A recent survey of Scottish companies found that regular training in 'personnel' was ranked as the least important of six other functions except by companies with over 500 employees, where it was ranked fourth (Lockyer et al. 1994). The chapter argues that the traditional separation between manager, personnel specialist and occupational psychologist as 'selection' scientist is in need of reconstitution to cope with the selection model implied by HRM.

Finally, it is argued that greater conceptual clarity is required with regard to the very nature of the motivational, attitudinal and behavioural characteristics assumed in the HRM approach to be the appropriate foci of selection. The HRM literature on this matter tends to be littered with confusing messages with differing and sometimes conflicting characteristics stressed as important. Is it indeed appropriate for selection to become increasingly rigorous in defining and measuring stable task-specific aptitudes, abilities and skills as championed by the typical selection model of the post-world war years? Broader definitions of successful performance point to motivational and attitudinal traits consistent with a focus on 'company culture', trust, organizational citizenship, or the teamwork philosophy of many HRM approaches (for example, Guest 1987; Peters and Waterman 1982; Kanter 1989; Lawler and Mohrman 1991). Should selection seek employees who are 'both technically competent and potentially trustworthy, as well as loyal and committed to organizational goals' (Hales 1993: 161)? Shifting technological and market conditions and changing management perceptions of job demands (Sparrow 1994) point to qualities such as commitment (Walton 1991), a positive attitude towards learning and flexibility (Peters and Waterman 1982; Shimmin 1989; Townley 1989) and a willingness to take risks and behave entrepreneurially (Kanter 1983). Yet many 'desirable' qualities, such as commitment, remain imprecise concepts which contradict other equally 'desirable' qualities, such as adaptability. Furthermore, neither the psychological nor the HRM literature provides a theoretically coherent account of how employee characteristics influence and are influenced by a changing organizational context. The final section of the chapter identifies the disparity that is beginning to appear between the traditional approach to increasing selection effectiveness and the requirements of the HRM philosophy.

Trends in Selection Practice

An understanding of developments in selection practice requires the separation of two distinct conceptualizations of increased sophistication. These can be summarized as: (a) a more rigorous approach to the definition and interpretation of job components and relevant employee qualities; and (b) the consideration of a broader range of person attributes, including attitudinal and motivational qualities as well as job-specific or technical skills. Typically, the focus of selection research has been towards the advancement of the first notion of 'sophistication', usually centred around issues of reliability of measurement, validity in the prediction of performance criteria and, most influential in terms of recent methodology, the validity generalization of predictors across jobs and employment contexts (Schmdit and Hunter 1977; Schmidt 1993). The second notion of 'sophistication', however, has become increasingly relevant as organizations face more rapid and uncertain change and suggests the need for new concepts and methods of selection (Schmitt and Borman 1993).

In reviews of selection literature and its influence on practice, the more conventional first approach of 'selection as science' predominates as a model for evaluating selection sophistication. This chapter incorporates existing survey evidence with our own study of practice in Scotland (Lockyer and Scholarios 1996). This survey, with responses from approximately 900 establishments, sought to identify the methods used and sources of information regarded as important for four benchmark occupations (managerial/professional, technical, clerical and skilled manual) across a number of sectors (manufacturing, construction, wholesale, retail, tourism and finance). Also of interest was the divergence in practice across firms of different size and ownership. Employing only a broad and simplistic division in terms of size – that is, by grouping all establishments employing more than 100 into one category – marked differences were evident in the selection methods used to select for the four occupations and in the importance attached to different sources of information. The Workplace Industrial Relations Surveys of 1980, 1984 and 1990 also highlighted the relationship between company size and sophistication of selection methods, as did North (1994), reporting on a recent survey conducted by *Personnel Today* on the use of personality, ability and aptitude tests.

Existing surveys, then, have shown continuing reliance on 'mainstream' methods which are relatively inexpensive in terms of time and cost, particularly amongst smaller firms (Guion 1990; Levy-Leboyer 1994; Robertson and Makin 1986; Shackleton and Newell 1994; Smith and Robertson 1989). These include at the initial stages of selection a consideration of application forms and curriculum vitae, often as an indication of educational qualifications and experience (Caplan and Schmidt 1977), as well as some consideration of references and recommendations followed by an interview (IMS 1988: 5).

Indeed, the accumulated survey evidence suggests that the overwhelming majority of firms use the 'classic trio' of application form, references and interview for most vacancies (Cook 1988). The IMS (1988: 6) study reported that nearly 98 per cent of firms used the application form for some of their vacancies, and almost three-quarters for all vacancies. Differing degrees of sophistication, however, can be applied to this initial screening process. At the simplest level it is used as a basis to check whether or not candidates meet predetermined standards of competency, qualification, experience or other personal qualities (such as age). Such standards may be single-factor or may be combined in some subjective impressionistic process. More systematic techniques, such as the weighted application blank (Goldsmith 1992), attribute scores and assign weights to each element of biographical data ('biodata'), the overall score determining whether or not the candidate progresses to the next stage. Such techniques were used, although not consistently or with much success, in the early years of several of the new car factories established under the regional economic policies of the 1960s (see Goodman and Samuel 1966). Multiple predictors used at the Rootes plant at Linwood, Renfrewshire, included rejecting, amongst others, ex-merchant seamen and communists, and giving a higher weighting to married men and those with earnings similar to those offered at the factory (unpublished notes).

The establishment of minimum criteria at these car plants tended to collapse because the high demand for labour and low levels of unemployment forced firms to take on staff who did not meet these minimum standards. This exemplifies the varying effect of environmental context on selection practice and might suggest that the high levels of unemployment which have been a feature since the 1980s have made it more useful for firms to adhere to rigorous criteria (Wickens 1987). Nevertheless, our own study found that the application form was not ranked amongst the most important sources of information, although educational qualifications and experience, each of which is closely related to the application form (Caplan and Schmidt 1977), were among the top three sources of information in all sectors.

Robertson and Makin's (1986) survey of managerial vacancies indicated that more than 90 per cent of firms used references. The IMS (1988) study supports this figure, indicating that use was most common for managerial staff and for filtering out unsuitable candidates. Our own survey indicated that references were not seen as an important source of information, being ranked the least important of six sources across all main sectors. They were, however, seen as slightly more important by smaller than by larger firms, possibly a reflection of the former's inability to use other methods. Recommendations were likewise seen as more important in smaller than larger firms, but were again ranked low in importance (fourth or fifth out of six) as a source of information on applicants. At the sectoral level, recommendations were seen as slightly more important sources of information in retail and construction than in other sectors, although this may be a function of differences in the size of establishment, nature of work and reliance on 'character' and experience rather than formal qualifications.

The interview, as noted by the IMS (1988) study, represents the most significant and visible aspect of the selection process and is almost universal practice (the IMS study noted 99.4 per cent reported use). Our own survey indicated that it was the second most important source of information in making a decision on a candidate; experience was ranked as slightly more important. The importance attached to the interview increased with the size of the firm, possibly a reflection of more formal systems of selection in larger firms, and the smaller firm's ability to rely on informal local networks and personal recommendations to assist in selection decision-making.

Across industry sectors, the use of the interview for clerical staff ranged from 70 per cent in tourism to 91 per cent in finance. For managerial appointments the range was from 84 per cent in manufacturing to 67 per cent in finance. We suspect the lower figure in finance reflects the more broadly based practice of internal promotion and transfer and the far wider use of personality and psychological tests.

The problems of selection using the 'classic trio' are well known (see, for example, Cook 1988) and have prompted a search for alternative more reliable and valid methods of assessment. One approach has been to modify the format of the interview. Evidence cited by Watson (1994) suggests that the single interviewer is typical for selection of manual workers, and a panel combining personnel and line representatives for non-manual employees. Other methods which increase the validity of selection include work-sample tests, such as 'in-basket' exercises for management or trade tests for skilled technical candidates. Tests of cognitive ability also have received increasing attention as the most systematically developed (hence reliable) and valid methods of assessment, as has personality testing, which captures qualities such as leadership, decision-making style, extroversion–introversion, and many other personal traits. (See for example, Landy et al. 1994, for a review of selection method reliability and validity evidence.)

The use of work-sample or in-basket exercises in the selection of managerial staff tends to be relatively low, much lower than for clerical, skilled or manual staff: the IMS study suggested some 5 per cent. In our own survey the range varied from 2 per cent in tourism to 13 per cent in retail. We found, surprisingly, that the use of work samples was slightly higher in the smaller rather than larger firms. We suspect this may reflect differences in the meaning of the term. For smaller firms the work sample may take the form of a test in which managers use their own experience and knowledge to 'test' or 'sample' the work of applicants. In larger firms it is more likely to incorporate exercises which are representative of the range and pressure of work likely to be encountered by the applicant.

There is some evidence of a gradual increase in the use of personality and cognitive ability tests as well as the job categories to which these are applied. In 1963, a British Institute of Management study of 350 members indicated that 2.4 per cent used personality tests while Miller and Hydes' (1971) study of 828 members of the Institute of Personnel Management suggested a figure of 7 per cent. By 1976, a study of 495 respondents from the Dunn and Bradstreet database found some 10 per cent of firms were using personality tests for managers, 7 per cent for technicians and supervisors, 3 per cent for clerical positions and 2 per cent for skilled manual operatives (Sneath et al. 1976). Recent surveys reveal the much higher figures of 67 per cent (MacKay and Torrington 1986) and 64 per cent (IMS 1988: 48) for the use of personality tests for managerial staff. However, the evidence of increasing sophistication is less clear in the selection of skilled manual staff. Tests of trade knowledge or work sampling were far more common (Torrington and Hall 1995), and only 16 per cent were noted as using personality tests for this job category.

The findings of our survey support other recent studies with regard to the increasing use of personality and psychological tests for management. However, this only applies to practice in larger establishments and in particular sectors. In smaller establishments there is much more reliance on traditional methods. An average of 17 per cent over all companies regularly used personality tests in the selection of management, although this figure ranged from 13 per cent in establishments with fewer than 20 staff to 50 per cent in establishments employing more than 100 staff. A similar pattern was evident in the use of psychological tests, whose use ranged from under 9 per cent of firms employing fewer than 20 staff to 59 per cent of firms with more than 100 employees. Likewise, the general level of testing tended to be higher in those sectors dominated by larger establishments, such as finance.

Our survey also supports the view that personality and psychological tests are becoming increasingly popular in the selection of manual staff in larger firms: 10 per cent of firms employing more than 100 staff reported regular use of personality tests and 24 per cent of psychological tests for the selection of skilled manual staff. There was little evidence in the survey of the use of psychological or personality tests in smaller establishments.

Despite these figures for the use of psychological tests, in the selection of clerical and skilled manual staff there remained a far greater reliance on traditional selection methods, such as interviews or work samples. There was much less variation between small and large establishments or between sectors in the use of such techniques. The use of work samples in the selection of clerical staff ranged from 47 per cent in establishments employing fewer than 20 to 51 per cent in those employing more than 100; for skilled manual the range was between 24 per cent and 30 per cent, respectively. The IMS (1988) study indicated some 32 per cent using trainability tests/work samples for clerical and 38 per cent for skilled manual staff (1988: 57). At the sectoral level the percentages regularly using work-sample tests for clerical staff ranged from 30 per cent in tourism to 56 per cent in manufacturing; for skilled manual, use ranged from 19 per cent in wholesale to 30 per cent in manufacturing.

The conclusion drawn from the survey evidence of the past 20 years, including the current research reported here, is that the use of a sophisticated multi-method process of selection is confined to larger companies. The progressive filtering of candidates using a range of techniques incurs increasing costs, making such levels of sophistication prohibitive for smaller employers. The survey of Scottish companies illustrates quite strongly the continuing reliance on less-systematic methods of selection among smaller private sector companies across a range of industry sectors (Lockyer and Scholarios 1996).

Reconciling UK Trends with the Traditional Selection Model

The traditional psychometric model of selection offers substantial validation evidence that psychological tests of intelligence, psychomotor and perceptual ability are among the best predictors of potential performance on most jobs (see reviews by, for example, Reilly and Chao 1982; Hunter and Hunter 1984; Landy et al. 1994; Schmitt et al. 1984; Muchinsky 1986). Yet there is only sparse evidence of their use in Britain, and that is primarily amongst large, overseas-owned companies. Interest in personality testing, particularly for managerial positions, has been more conspicuous; but it is questionable to what extent such practices have followed or been drawn from the psychological literature on the measurement of personality traits for selection. Recent debates in psychology, for instance, focus on the tenability of meta-analytic studies (see, for example, Tett et al. 1991) which infer from moderate validity coefficients in US Army samples using Army job criteria to the use of personality testing across many blue- and white-collar jobs. One extreme position is voiced by Johnson and Blinkhorn (1994: p. 170), who contend that despite the 'widespread and growing' routine use of personality tests, 'there is no body of public knowledge relating scores on personality tests taken as part of a selection procedure to objective criteria of later performance'. On the whole, the paradigm of criterion-related validation has had little visible impact on British selection practice.

The clear divide between UK practice and advances in selection research may be explained partially by contextual variables which have impacted on the degree of selection sophistication adopted by employers. The historical, political, legal and regulatory environment in the US, for example, has been a powerful force shaping testing and HRM practice (see Grant 1984; Schmitt 1989). The focus of selection research, debate and practice in the USA since the Civil Rights Act of 1964 has been on the attainment of validity and fairness in methods, with an emphasis on statistical definitions of fairness involving regression equations and cut scores applied to different applicant groups. Equal employment opportunity legislation in the UK is more narrowly confined to issues of sex and race defined by the Sex Discrimination

Act (1975) and the Race Relations Act (1976), each of which established regulatory bodies (the Equal Opportunities Commission and the Commission for Racial Equality, respectively) and codes of conduct for employers. Selection practice is typified by more qualitative, descriptive approaches which focus on the conduct of the interview, and recognize an absence of validation (Pearn 1989).

In comparison to the American context of HRM practice, these codes of conduct subject employers in the UK to only a limited amount of pressure to hold their selection methods open to scientific scrutiny (Pearn 1989). The consequence of this is that, other than in a few large firms, the established literature on predictive efficiency, validity of assessment methods and 'objectively' defined criteria of successful performance has had little impact on British managers and HRM practice (Robertson and Makin 1986; Anderson and Shackleton 1990). Likewise, the emergence of HRM in Britain has not been accompanied by the particularly American concern for rigorous and scientifically based methods of selection, either in academic texts or in practice. British personnel/HRM texts which offer even the most basic description of testing and its statistical underpinning in issues of measurement remain in a minority (for example, Livy 1988). Rather, the emphasis tends to be that of a 'coaching manual' focused largely on the interpersonal skills and organizational conditions which will improve the reliability of qualitiative methods, such as the interviewing process (see, for example, ACAS 1984).

Our survey, in common with others (such as Millward et al. 1992; North 1994), highlights the relationship between the pattern of selection sophistication and size of establishment. Particularly in smaller companies, traditional methods requiring relatively low levels of technical expertise have been shown to be favoured over more efficient predictors of job performance, such as ability or aptitude tests (Smith and Abrahamsen 1992). Pearn (1989: 161) describes the selection problem for the vast majority of UK employers as one of a 'paper sift of application forms, frequently in the thousands, to smaller numbers to be interviewed'. At best, biodata, some form of self-assessment or the application of a minimum standard for pre-screening may find wider application, rather than expensive and time-consuming cognitive ability tests.

These observations suggest a number of paradigms of 'appropriate' selection. For the small firm, the introduction of 'better' interpersonal skills amongst interviewers, of greater standardization of methods and greater rigour in defining appropriate predictors and criteria may well be the route to improve the reliability and validity of presently used methods of selection (Pearn 1989; Schmidt 1993). In the medium-sized firm, there is a dilemma. 'Better' selection may be achieved either through a more systematic and planned approach to defining the selection problem for specific jobs or through a revised considera-tion of relevant criteria of performance and the search for new ap-proaches and methods for their measurement. Either of these routes, however, requires substantial investment of resources. Large firms in particular require the rigour of traditional selection approaches, and possess both the resources and the need to address the problems of organizational change through new criteria and methods of assess-ment. Amongst these firms, an alternative model of 'selection as strat-egy' (Drenth 1989; Miles and Snow 1984; Snow and Snell 1993) may have some relevance.

On a more pragmatic level, the attainment of either greater scien-tific respectability in selection methods or the consideration of how selection reflects the values of the organization requires a certain level of investment in selection expertise. In many UK companies, the selection specialist functions as no more than a clerk or technician, handing out paperwork and organizing the completion of tests, rather than as a professional who advises and is involved in the design of the selection process, let alone in its contribution to corporate strategy (Miles and Snow 1984). Consequently, understanding of the limita-tions of tests and their use or any statistical appreciation of the prin-ciples of reliability and validity is questionable, particularly in the small to medium-sized firms. '[U]sers of test materials [are] often inadequately trained in their use and application . . . Yet many indi-viduals, with no more than this minimal exposure and little evidence of competence in testing, [have] relatively free access to a whole range of materials' (Henley and Bawtree 1993: 52).

The British Psychological Society (BPS) has endeavoured to re-spond to the lack of general understanding and potential misuse of psychological tests with the introduction of a certification scheme aimed at providing a professional code of conduct for psychologists and minimum standards of competence for training in the use of psychological tests (Bartram 1991; British Psychological Society 1991). The Certificate of Competence in Psychological Testing: Level A was introduced as a requirement for the purchase and use of aptitude and ability tests in personnel or HRM contexts and identifies minimum standards in the knowledge and skills required for fair and profes-sional test use. (Bartram 1995 describes the recent launch of the certificate for personality testing, Level B.) Seven units of competence are identified as essential to Level A certification, including theoretical knowledge of scaling, standardization, reliability and validity; knowledge of types of tests and their suitability for different contexts; practical skills of administering tests to individuals or groups; interpreting test scores, and providing accurate oral and written feedback to candidates; and an understanding of the wider legal and ethical considerations of testing. Each of these reflects attempts to enhance the sophistication of selection practice through greater rigour and knowledge of psychometric principles.

The one severe limitation upon the efficacy of such a certification process is that professional bodies such as the BPS can only monitor and act upon the activities of their members. In Britain, there is no legal compulsion or threat of litigation and damages to encourage employers to adopt these measures (Pearn 1989). The pressures are only ethical and professional. This, then, adds to a situation where the trends reflect increasing scientific rigour only in the largest firms and, even then, only in those with the means to invest in a trained selection specialist.

Selecting the Future?

Personnel selection, particularly amongst firms with an HRM policy, is in the midst of a transition from being an isolated staffing function to becoming an essential component of organizational strategy. The major impetus for this transition has been located primarily in the shifting boundaries between jobs, with the awareness of a need for a new approach to selection tending to parallel the transformation of large, stable bureaucracies to more loosely organized structures. Cultural and changing demographic trends also have contributed to this pressure (Offerman and Gowing 1993; Schmidt 1993).

The key issues for personnel selection in the future are summarized in the following way by Offerman and Gowing (1993: 410):

> The best HR management systems will integrate the traditional personnel functions of recruitment, selection, placement and training into a coordinated total effort. It will not be enough to select people into the skills they currently possess, but rather for their potential to learn and adapt through training as conditions change. It will not be enough to recruit and select diverse individuals, but rather consideration must be given to changing organizational culture, procedures and practices to use effectively the skills provided by this diversity.

Thus, changing organizational conditions highlight the need for a transformation in the established systems of thinking about selection

(Sparrow 1994). The conceptual shift required involves moving from a selection model based on matching individual abilities with specific, well-defined tasks to one in which selection is part of overall company strategy and, even more of a challenge, a component which itself drives competitive strategy (Snow and Snell 1993). If 'strategic staffing' is conceptualized as systemic, then individual qualities related to job suitability can only be understood in relation to other sets of attitudes, behavioural characteristics, personality profiles or the pattern of shared values within organizations. A closed-system view of hiring for precisely defined and static criteria of performance becomes severely limiting and counterproductive and the rigour of measurement implied by the analytic validation framework of criterion-relatedness becomes increasingly complex and evasive.

This review of selection practice has considered the extent to which selection, particularly in the UK, has followed the message of research to strive continuously for improvements in the reliability and validity of methods. Such a survey of reported practice, however, leaves some unanswered questions with regard to a full understanding of the role to be played by selection in realizing HRM goals. First, can HRM define a set of internally consistent desired criteria associated with success and can these criteria of 'successful' job performance be described in more than general abstractions for the purposes of prediction? 'Empowerment, delayering, the creation of new organizational forms and competitive arrangements' (Sparrow 1994) have changed the definition of jobs and have made more ambiguous the definition of successful job performance. In the changing organizations implied by HRM, the interface between jobs is of more interest than the performance of specific tasks (Cascio 1991; Mason and Mitroff 1981) and strategic goals, such as quality or customer service, are added to measures of individual performance as indicators of organizational effectiveness.

Secondly, to what extent can HRM provide a set of policies to restructure the employment relationship, from an assymetrical one of externally imposed control to one of commitment and involvement of employees? Can we define predictor constructs which are theoretically coherent combinations of qualities for particular requirements, which can be translated into empirical as well as conceptual links with performance, and which at the same time are of practical value to employers? The concept of 'whole-person' measurement (Fleishman and Quaintance 1984), whereby motivation, attitudes, interests and values are measured in addition to knowledge, skills and abilities, would in this context 'maximise the prediction of performance' (Offerman and Gowing 1993).

Thirdly, what selection methodology should replace the traditional analytic staffing model of assessing every individuals' job-specific abilities in order to provide the conceptualization of the 'whole person' demanded of an HRM approach? Is it still possible to identify stable individual-job matches when human resource requirements are continuously being reassessed and when selection is broadened to view generalists rather than specialists, at every level, as key human resources? In an increasingly uncertain and insecure context, are HRM recruitment criteria consistent in addressing the lifecycle of a firm, both growth and decline, or is HRM only appropriate in the growth phase of companies (Cascio 1995; Drenth 1989; Snow and Snell 1993)?

Arguably, the HRM approach to selection, by failing to address these issues in any depth, faces some unresolved contradictions. For instance, short-term human resource needs and planning demand that candidate suitability is considered for existing positions; however, strategic concerns require the identification of those individuals who are open to learning and change. The HRM concern with flexible jobs and employee skills also suggests that the assessment of specific job skills should give way to the assessment of more fundamental constructs, such as customer service orientation, team orientation and decision-making styles (Bowen and Greiner 1986; Cascio 1995; Snow and Snell 1993).

The methodology for dealing with general attitudinal or motivational characteristics as opposed to task-specific knowledge, skills or abilities is relatively unrefined (although Anderson and Herriot 1994 provide some recent perspectives on this problem). The paradigm of validation, particularly criterion-related validity, has driven selection research and practice, with a resultant emphasis on testing methods and objective criteria of performance. Guion (1989: 124) lays open to question the assumptions underlying this paradigm: 'In selecting people, we tend to forget their modifiability and concentrate instead on their stabilities, the fact that the characteristics present at the time of hire will continue to characterize them for a long time and will influence their behavior at work.' In its place he suggests a more tailored, person-orientated, almost career-counselling approach to selection which, as a result of its continuous and dynamic re-evaluation, would deal with some of the problems of selecting for changing organizations. Similarly, Offerman and Gowing (1993) predict that greater prominence will be attached to assessment for placement or diagnostic purposes combined with organizational training: 'whole-person' measurement will provide more complete individual profiles which could be matched to occupational responsibilities. Selection thus becomes 'the initial point of measurement in a comprehensive system of evaluation that could be updated regularly to continue matching future jobs with the developing profiles of incumbent workers' (Offerman and Gowing 1993: 403).

These reflections suggest a move away from a traditional validation model, perhaps weakening standardization in order to accommodate a more holistic perspective of people integrated with changing jobs and organizational environments. The implication of this view is a continual reconsideration of job-performance standards as well as the employee attributes deemed to relate to these standards. For the HRM specialist, the problem becomes one of recognizing and defining the criteria of organizational success, understanding the relevant 'general capacities, abilities and skills' (Schmidt 1993) which should be the target of selection, and accessing, developing or gaining competency in the use of selection 'tools' to measure these qualities. The present summary of UK practice indicates that the HRM profession, particularly in the UK, can still only aspire to this model of personnel selection.

Conclusions

A review of British selection practice reveals only limited advances in selection sophistication, either in terms of more-reliable and valid procedures or towards better-integrated HRM practices. There is clearly some discrepancy between the rhetoric and reality. Whilst many HRM/personnel texts claim movement towards more sophisticated selection, such developments appear to be restricted to relatively few companies, usually the largest.

The enduring low status of personnel functions within British organizations and policies of devolving selection decisions to non-HRM qualified staff pose barriers to attempts to enhance professionalism in selection practice. The use of 'vague selection criteria' (Collinson, Knights and Collinson 1990) is evident even in a majority of large companies in sectors where HRM is argued to be the norm. Our evidence supports Keep's (1992: 314) comments that, notwithstanding the reported importance attached to selection, 'in many organisations, recruitment and selection are apparently conducted in a haphazard and informal fashion'.

A more fundamental issue raised in the present review is the dilemmas introduced by a 'strategic selection' notion. The advent of HRM is associated with a potentially fundamental shift in the substance of various essential selection processes: the definition of attributes, such as skill, experience, qualifications, personality, attitude or motivation required to fill a position; the identification of methods to differentiate these attributes within an applicant population; and a means of ensuring the validity of predictors of these attributes for appropriate job criteria. The traditional selection model, in emphasizing a logical matching of ability constructs with clearly defined job components (criterion-related validity), gives way, appropriately, to fundamental issues of construct validity (Landy 1986). The role of selection within an HRM paradigm highlights the need for greater attention to generating theoretical connections between specific and generalizable individual qualities on the one hand and a more ambiguous and changing performance domain on the other.

The continual search for simple panaceas and the resulting variety in practice is better appreciated given the uncertainties and contradictions in the new range of performance criteria being sought. The costs and complexity of developing new methods inevitably lead smaller firms to rely on traditional, informal and often subjective methods of selection decision-making. There is no single way forward; the paths depend not only on developments in HRM and in psychology, but on the ability to relate changing organizational needs to the theoretical and operational definitions of ability and performance constructs which, in turn, can inform HRM practice.

References

ACAS (Advisory Conciliation and Arbitration Service) 1984: *Recruitment and Selection*, Advisory Booklet no. 6. London: ACAS.

Anderson, N. and Herriot, P. 1994: *Assessment and Selection in Organizations: methods and practice for recruitment and appraisal. First update and supplement 1994*. Chichester: John Wiley.

Anderson, N. and Shackleton, V. 1990: Staff selection decision-making into the 1990s. *Management Decision*, 28(1), 5–8.

Arvey, R.D. 1979: *Fairness in Selecting Employees*. Reading, Mass.: Addison-Wesley.

Ballin, M. 1986: How British Steel tempered the job cuts. *Transition*, January.

Bartram, D. 1991: Addressing the abuse of psychological tests. *Personnel Management*, April, 34–9.

Bartram, D. 1995: Implementing the Level B standards: the final steps. Paper presented at the British Psychological Society Occupational Psychology Conference, University of Warwick, January.

Bowen, D.E. and Greiner, L.E. 1986: Moving from production to service in human resource management. *Organizational Dynamics*, 15, 34–53.

Bray, D.W. and Grant, D.L. 1966: The assessment center in the measurement of potential for business management. *Psychological Monographs*, 80(17): whole no. 625.

British Psychological Society 1991: *Psychological Testing: guidance for the user.* Leicester: BPS.

Buchanan, D. and McCalman, J. 1989: *High Performance Work Systems: the digital experience.* London: Routledge.

Caplan, J.R. and Schmidt, F.L. 1977: The validity of education and experience ratings. Paper presented to International Personnel Management Association Assessment Council, 19 April.

Cascio, W.F. 1991: *Applied Psychology in Personnel Management.* Englewood Cliffs, N.J.: Prentice-Hall.

Cascio, W.F. 1995: *Managing Human Resources: productivity, quality of work life, profits.* 4th edn. New York: McGraw Hill.

Collinson, D. 1988: *Barriers to Fair Selection: a multi-sector study of recruitment practices.* London: HMSO.

Collinson, D., Knights, D. and Collinson, M. 1990: *Managing to Discriminate.* London: Routledge.

Cook, M. 1988: *Personnel Selection and Productivity.* Chichester: John Wiley.

Drenth, P. 1989: Psychological testing and discrimination. In P. Herriot (ed.), *Assessment and Selection in Organizations: methods and practice for recruitment and appraisal,* London: John Wiley.

Fleishman, E.A. and Quaintance, M.K. 1984: *Taxonomies of Human Performance: the description of human tasks.* San Diego, Cal.: Academic Press.

Goldsmith, D.B. 1992: The use of a personal history blank as a salesmanship test. *Journal of Applied Psychology*, 6, 149–55.

Goodman, J.F.B. and Samuel, P.J. 1966: The motor industry in a development district: a case study of the labour factor. *British Journal of Industrial Relations*, 4(3), 336–65.

Gospel, H. 1983: The development of management organisation in industrial relations: a historical perspective. In K. Thurley and S. Wood (eds), *Industrial Relations and Management Strategy,* Cambridge: Cambridge University Press, pp. 91–110.

Goss, D. 1994: *Principles of Human Resource Management.* London: Routledge.

Grant, D. 1984: Issues in personnel selection. In *Readings in Professional Personnel Assessment,* Alexandria, Va.: International Personnel Management Association, 67–102.

Guest, D. 1987: Human resource management and industrial relations. *Journal of Management Studies*, 24(5), 503–21.

Guest, D. 1992: Right enough to be dangerously wrong: an analysis of the In Search of Excellence phenomenon. In G. Salaman (ed.), *Human Resource Strategies,* London: Sage.

Guion, R.M. 1989: Comments on personnel selection methods. In M. Smith and I.T. Robertson (eds), *Advances in Selection and Assessment,* Chichester: John Wiley.

Guion, R.M. 1990: Personnel selection, assessment and placement. In M.D. Dunnette and L.M. Hough (eds), *Handbook of Industrial and Organizational Psychology*. Palo Alto, Cal.: Consulting Psychologists Press.

Guion, R.M. 1993: The need for change: six persistent themes. In N. Schmitt and W. Borman (eds), *Personnel Selection in Organizations*, San Francisco: Jossey-Bass.

Hales, C. 1993: *Managing through Organization*. London: Routledge.

Henley, S. and Bawtree, S. 1993: Training standards and procedures for training psychologists involved in selection and assessment in the United Kingdom. In M. Smith and V. Sutherland (eds), *International Review of Professional Issues in Selection and Assessment*, vol. 1. Chichester: John Wiley.

Hunter, J.E. and Hunter, R.F. 1984: Validity and utility of alternative predictors of job performance. *Psychological Bulletin*, 96, 72–98.

IMS (Institute of Manpower Studies) 1988: *Employee Selection in the UK*, Report no. 160. Brighton: IMS.

Johnson, C. and Blinkhorn, S. 1994: Desperate measures. *Psychologist*, 7(4), 167–70.

Johnston, W.B. and Packer, A.E. 1987: *Workforce 2000*. Indianapolis, Ind.: Hudson Institute.

Kanter, R.M. 1983: *The Change Masters: corporate entrepreneurs at work*. London: Unwin Hyman.

Kanter, R.M. 1989: *When Giants Learn to Dance*. New York: Simon & Schuster.

Keep, E. 1992: Corporate training strategies. In G. Salaman (ed.), *Human Resource Strategies*, London: Sage.

Landy, F.J. 1986: Stamp collecting versus science: validation as hypothesis testing. *American Psychologist*, 41, 1184–92.

Landy, F.J., Shankster, L.J. and Kohler, S.S. 1994: Personnel selection and placement. *Annual Review of Psychology*, 45, 261–96.

Lawler, E. and Mohrman, S. 1991: High-involvement management. In R. Steers and L. Porter (eds), *Motivation and Work Behavior*, New York: McGraw-Hill.

Levy-Leboyer, C. 1994: Selection and assessment in Europe. In H.C. Triandis (ed.), *Handbook of Industrial and Organizational Psychology*, vol. 4. Palo Alto, Cal.: Consulting Psychologists Press.

Livy, L. 1988: *Corporate Personnel Management*. London: Pitman.

Lockyer, C. and Scholarios, D. 1996: *Changing Trends in Personnel Selection: an analysis of the Scottish recruitment context*. Manuscript submitted for publication, University of Strathclyde.

Lockyer, C., Malloy, E. and LeTissier, S. 1994: *Recruitment and Training of Graduates*. Report commissioned by Scottish Enterprise.

Mabey, C. and Iles, P. 1993: The strategic integration of assessment and development practices: succession planning and new manager development. *Human Resource Management Journal*, 3(4), 16–34.

Mackay, L. and Torrington, D. 1986: *The Changing Nature of Personnel Management*. London: Institute of Personnel Management.

Mason, R.O. and Mitroff, I.I. 1981: *Challenging Strategic Planning Assumptions*. New York: John Wiley.

Miles, R.E. and Snow, C.C. 1984: Designing strategic human resource systems. *Organizational Dynamics*, Summer.

Miller, K.M. and Hydes, J. 1971: *The Use of Psychological Tests in Personnel Work*. London: Independent Assessment and Research Centre.

Millward, N. et al. 1992: *Workplace Industrial Relations in Transition*. Aldershot, Hants.: Dartmouth.

Moses, J.L. 1973: The development of an assessment centre for the early identification of supervisory talent. *Personnel Psychology*, 26, 569–80.

Muchinsky, P.M. 1986: Personnel selection methods. In C.L. Cooper and I.T. Robertson (eds), *International Review of Industrial and Organizational Psychology*, Chichester: John Wiley.

North, S. 1994: Mind readers. *Personnel Today*, April, 19–22.

Offerman, L.R. and Gowing, M.K. 1993: Personnel selection in the future: the impact of changing demographics and the nature of work. In N. Schmitt and W. Borman (eds), *Personnel Selection in Organizations*, San Francisco, Cal.: Jossey-Bass.

Oliver, B. and Wilkinson, N. 1992: Human resource management in Japanese manufacturing companies in the UK and USA. In B. Towers (ed.), *The Handbook of Human Resource Management*, Oxford: Blackwell.

Parry, J. 1959: The place of personality appraisal in vocational selection. *Occupational Psychology*, 33, 147–56.

Pearn, M.A. 1989: Fairness in employment selection: a comparison of UK and USA experience. In M. Smith and I.T. Robertson (eds), *Advances in Selection and Assessment*. Chichester: John Wiley.

Peters, T. and Waterman, R.H. 1982: *In Search of Excellence: lessons from America's best-run companies*. New York: Harper & Row.

Purcell, J. 1989: The impact of corporate strategy on human resource management. In J. Storey (ed.), *New Developments in Human Resource Management*, London: Routledge.

Reilly, R.R. and Chao, G.T. 1982: Validity and fairness of some alternative employee selection procedures. *Personnel Psychology*, 35, 1–62.

Rhodes, E. and Wield, D. (eds), 1985: *Implementing New Technologies*. Oxford: Blackwell.

Robertson, I. and Makin, P. 1986: Management selection in Britain: a survey and critique. *Journal of Occupational Psychology*, 59(1), 45–57.

Salaman, G. (ed.), 1992: *Human Resource Strategies*. London: Sage.

Schmidt, F.L. 1993: Personnel psychology at the cutting edge. In N. Schmitt and W. Borman (eds), *Personnel Selection in Organizations*, San Francisco, Cal.: Jossey-Bass.

Schmidt, F.L. and Hunter, J.E. 1977: Development of a general solution to the problem of validity generalization. *Journal of Applied Psychology*, 68, 407–14.

Schmitt, N. 1989: Fairness in employment selection. In M. Smith and I.T.

Robertson (eds), *Advances in Selection and Assessment*, Chichester: John Wiley.

Schmitt, N. and Borman, W. (eds) 1993: *Personnel Selection in Organizations*. San Francisco, Cal.: Jossey-Bass.

Schmitt, N., Gooding, R.Z., Noe, R.D. and Kirsch, M. 1984: Meta-analysis of validity studies published between 1964 and 1982 and the investigation of study characteristics. *Personnel Psychology*, 37, 407–22.

Scott, W.D. 1915: The scientific selection of salesmen. *Advertising and Selling*, 25: 5–6.

Shackleton, V. and Newell, S. 1994: European management selection methods: a comparison of five countries. *International Journal of Selection and Assessment*, 2(2), 91–102.

Shimmin, S. 1989: Selection in a European context. In P. Herriot (ed.), *Assessment and Selection in Organizations: methods and practice for recruitment and appraisal*, London: John Wiley.

Smith, M. and Abrahamsen, M. 1992: Patterns of selection in six countries. *Psychologist*, May, 205–7.

Smith, M. and Robertson, I. (eds) 1989: *Advances in Selection and Assessment*. Chichester: John Wiley.

Sneath, F., Thakur, M. and Medjuck, B. 1976: *Testing People at Work*, IPM Information Report 24. London: Institute for Personnel Management.

Snow, C.C. and Snell, S.A. 1993: Staffing as strategy. In N. Schmitt and W. Borman (eds), *Personnel Selection in Organizations*, San Francisco, Cal.: Jossey-Bass.

Sparrow, P.R. 1994: Organizational competencies: creating a strategic behavioural framework for selection and assessment. In N. Anderson and P. Herriot (eds), *Assessment and Selection in Organizations: methods and practice for recruitment and appraisal. First update and supplement*. Chichester: John Wiley, pp. 1–26.

Storey, J. 1992: Human resource management in the public sector. In G. Salaman (ed.), *Human Resource Strategies*, London: Sage.

Storey, J. (ed.) 1989: *New Perspectives on Human Resource Management*. London: Routledge.

Storey, J. and Sisson, K. 1993: *Managing Human Resources and Industrial Relations*. Buckingham: Open University Press.

Tett, R.P., Jackson, D.N. and Rothstein, M. 1991: Personality measures as predictors of job performance: a meta-analytic review. *Personnel Psychology*, 44, 703–42.

Torrington, D. and Hall, L. 1995: *Personnel Management: HRM in action*, 3rd edn. London: Prentice-Hall.

Townley, B. 1989: Selection and appraisal: reconstituting 'social relations'? In J. Storey (ed.), *New Developments in Human Resource Management*, London: Routledge.

Vernon, P.E. 1950: The validation of Civil Service Selection Board procedures. *Occupational Psychology*, 24, 75–95.

Walton, R. 1991: From control to commitment in the workplace. In R. Steers and L. Porter (eds), *Motivation and Work Behavior*, New York: McGraw-Hill.

Watson, T. 1994: Recruitment and selection. In K. Sisson (ed.), *Personnel Management*, 2nd edn. Oxford: Blackwell.

White, M. and Trevor, M. 1983: *Under Japanese Management: the experience of British workers*. London: Heinemann.

Wickens, P. 1987: *The Road to Nissan: flexibility, quality, teamwork*. London: Macmillan.

Wood, S. 1986: Personnel management and recruitment. *Personnel Review*, 15(2), 3–10.

10

Performance Appraisal

GORDON ANDERSON

Introduction

Performance appraisal has been one of the most-debated management practices for several decades. It has generated a wide variety of viewpoints. There are those who see performance appraisal as making an important contribution to human resource management, in that organizations require systematic information on how well employees are performing in their jobs as a key element in ensuring that human resources are used as effectively as possible. Employees at all levels experience a need to know clearly what they should be doing and what is expected of them in terms of quantity and quality of output. In addition most people want to be in a position where they can perform better next time around.

A number of writers, especially during the 1970s, expressed pessimistic views about the future of performance appraisal schemes, and the assumptions on which they are based. Some have tended to write off conventional versions of performance appraisal as backward, simplistic and even counterproductive, arguing that conventional appraisal processes often lead both the manager and employee to approach the performance review with dysfunctional role stereotypes. The employee expects to hear what is wrong with his or her performance, while the manager expects to have to sell the evaluation to a reluctant and possibly hostile member of staff.

Farnsworth (1974) asserts that the history of appraisal systems is one of confrontation and conflict, of poisoned relationships and frustrated hopes. Disagreements about performance, according to Farnsworth, are a major factor in employee turnover, and even when an employee does not leave he or she is frequently embittered by the experience. Levinson (1970) believes that performance appraisal, especially when results-orientated approaches are used, is inherently self-defeating in the long run because it is based on a reward–punishment psychology that serves to intensify pressure on the individual. As long ago as 1957, McGregor expressed the view that managers are often reluctant to carry out appraisals, and Levinson reinforces this opinion by stating that managers perceive their appraisal of others as a hostile, aggressive act which, unconsciously, is felt to be hurting or destroying the other person. More recently Lawler (1994) has highlighted the problem that many performance appraisal systems do not motivate individuals or guide their development effectively. Some, though not necessarily all, of these criticisms have been overcome by the precise specification of appraisal objectives and wide consultation in the design process, together with considerable attention to ensure that implementation is carefully planned.

Lingering doubts have largely been dispelled. The modern viewpoint is summed up in the quotation from Twomey and Twomey (1992): 'The human resource function is increasingly important in shaping the new organisation in which the quality and commitment of people is key to survival. Every aspect of human resource management needs to be reassessed but none is more pivotal or difficult than performance appraisal.'

In recent years there has been considerable growth of interest in performance appraisal, and the great majority or organizations now operate some type of scheme. Bevan and Thompson (1992) carried out a survey of 1,800 employers in the UK. Of the 46 per cent who responded, around 86 per cent were found to be operating a systematic approach in evaluating employee performance; 20 per cent indicated that they were operating more ambitious 'performance management' systems, which will be discussed in a later section of this chapter. While traditionally performance appraisal was applied primarily to managers and supervisors, Long (1986) indicates that it has increasingly been extended to cover clerical and even manual workers. She also dispels the myth that performance appraisal is confined only to large organizations, drawing attention to the growing number of companies with under 500 employees who operate a system of performance appraisal.

In the USA, performance appraisal has for long been established practice in most organizations. McGregor (1957) reported that performance appraisal had become standard practice in American companies during the previous 20 years. A study by the Bureau of National Affairs (1983) showed that, in a sample of 244 organizations, over 90 per cent were operating performance appraisal systems. With the increasing globalization of business, performance appraisal has become an established activity (though in many cases fairly recently) in organizations in most countries of the world. In the Asia-Pacific region, for example, considerable interest in performance appraisal is to be found in countries such as Hong Kong, Malaysia and Singapore.

Performance appraisal can be defined as involving:

• the systematic review of the performance of staff, on a written basis, at regular time intervals; and
• the holding of appraisal interviews at which staff have the opportunity to discuss performance issues past, present and future, on a one-to-one basis, usually with their immediate line manager.

The key words are 'systematic', 'written' and 'regular'. Performance appraisal supplements the informal, ongoing processes of evaluating staff with a systematic approach. Committing evaluative comment about staff and their performance to writing creates much of the distinctiveness, as well as many of the problems and issues, of performance appraisal. The time intervals between appraisals are likely to affect the impact they have on individuals and organizations. The most common corporate practices are to hold performance appraisals every twelve months or every six months, although more-frequent and less-frequent variations can and do occur. For example, in a large corporation specializing in communication systems, appraisals are held every three months. By contrast, in many schools and a number of universities in the UK two years is the time interval between appraisals.

The aim of this chapter is to review the concept of performance appraisal, discuss theoretical and practical issues and consider the changing trends. In this chapter I shall first consider the objectives of performance appraisal and the importance of performance appraisal to human resource management (HRM). I shall then look at the links between performance appraisal and pay, one of the most problematical aspects of the subject. Next there will be consideration of the question 'Who is the appraiser' and of the various alternatives including the recent trend towards 360-degree appraisal.

I shall provide an outline of appraisal methods and of some appraisal issues before examining the human interactions of the appraisal interview. Finally, problem areas and design issues will be identified, with concluding comments about the future of performance appraisal.

Appraisal Objectives

A necessary condition for the effective management of performance appraisal systems in any organization is the need to clarify and communicate to all concerned the objectives which the system is intended to achieve. Typically, performance appraisal schemes are expected to serve multiple objectives. This can often be a strength in that several purposes can be achieved, but it can also prove to be a disadvantage if it leads to a dissipation of effort and lack of focus. It is obviously of crucial importance, and everyone in an organization – especially the key decision-makers – should be fully aware precisely what objectives the system of performance appraisal is expected to achieve, and the priorities within these objectives.

Performance appraisal should lead to the identification of the training and development needs of employees. Indeed, it can be argued that without an appraisal scheme, it would be only accidental if training and development efforts were aimed in the right direction (Anderson 1980). Performance appraisal, by providing feedback to employees on job performance, creates a basis for improvement and development. A key feature of any appraisal system, according to Cameron (1982), is to create a learning experience.

Performance appraisal is centrally linked to the motivation of employees, in that it provides some of the essential components of effective motivational strategies; in particular, feedback that permits an employee to learn how well he or she is performing; goal or objective-setting that specifies what the person should be doing; team-building that allows the employee to participate with peers and their managers in solving problems that impede their productivity; and monetary incentives that reward good performance (see Latham and Wexley 1981).

Performance appraisal has close links with other important areas of HRM – in particular with selection, motivation, succession planning and the training of employees. Performance appraisal data provide relevant information required for validating selection methods, in assessing whether selection methods are bringing high performers into the organization.

The importance of performance appraisal to good HRM is highlighted in Cumming's classification of performance appraisal objectives. According to Cummings and Schwab (1973), the objectives of performance appraisal schemes can be categorized as either evaluative or developmental. The evaluative purposes have a historical dimension and are concerned primarily with looking back at how employees have actually performed over a given time period, compared with required standards of performance. In this respect, performance appraisal carries out a useful auditing function for HRM in providing a mechanism for periodically reviewing the effectiveness of employee performance.

The developmental function of appraisal is concerned with improving the performance of people by identifying areas for improvement, setting performance targets for the future, and agreeing plans for follow-up action. This aspect also involves developing the capacity of people through formulating plans to develop their skills and careers, and helping individuals to reconcile their job and career aspirations with opportunities available in the organization.

Furthermore, there is a certain amount of overlap between the evaluative and development functions, in that the evaluation of past performance will often be an important influence upon the setting of future targets. Brinkerhoff and Kanter (1980) contend that this function is both backward-looking – in the sense of evaluating past performance so as to establish standards – and forward-looking – in that the established standards serve as incentives for future performance improvement through generating peer competition and the desire to best one's own past record.

They argue further that an additional overlapping, but also overarching, purpose for performance appraisal is to ensure that managers are performing a critical management function. Managers should be paying careful attention to the assessment of the past performance of their staff against organizational requirements, and to the development of greater productivity of the human resources available. In my experience, this function of performance appraisal – of encouraging careful and systematic approaches in assessing the performance of employees – is of great importance for practising managers, and its value is often recognized by them.

The possible conflict between the evaluative and developmental dimensions has been much discussed in the appraisal literature. The central issue appears to be: can the manager, acting as appraiser, effectively be both judge and helper without experiencing role conflict? Since future decisions must be based, at least in part, on evaluations of previous behaviour, it could be argued that this conflict is superficial rather than real, and that an effective manager should be able to cope effectively with both roles.

Mohrman et al. (1989) argue, however, that individual employees may have conflicting objectives in being appraised, especially where performance appraisal is strongly linked with the extrinsic rewards they receive. The argument is that employees will place great emphasis on presenting themselves and their performance in the most favourable way possible to their appraisers, because they realize that the results of performance appraisal will have a substantial influence on the extrinsic rewards (especially pay) which they will receive. They will tend to deny problems, attribute areas of deficient performance to others, and claim all aspects of successful performance have been due to their own skills and efforts.

Employees being appraised will wish not only to maximize extrinsic rewards, but also, according to Meyer et al. (1965), to gain accurate and helpful feedback about their performance. They will recognize the benefit of constructive discussions with their appraisers to analyse performance problems, remove barriers to performance improvement and agree plans for personal development and higher levels of performance in the future. Thus an area of conflict among the objectives of the employee occurs: whether to be very open and candid in providing information, parts of which may be unfavourable, in order to receive the feedback they need for growth and development, or whether to withhold some information which they feel could lead to negative interpretations of their performance in order to obtain good extrinsic rewards.

It is easy to overstate the extent to which these conflicts occur among appraisal objectives, especially in the case of high performers. Where unfavourable aspects of performance are slight, the impediments to the interchange of information between appraisers and appraisees are minimal. In dealing with marginal or deficient performers, the conflicts discussed can be a major factor which must be taken into account.

The culture of the organization, and in particular the extent to which relationships are characterized by openness and mutual trust, clearly affect appraisal relationships. Many organizations, to minimize the possibility of conflict among appraisal objectives, are increasingly placing emphasis on climate-setting. They are encouraging managerial styles that will lead to openness and frankness in relationships as a condition for establishing an effective performance appraisal system. The relationship between organization culture and performance appraisal systems is being increasingly recognized as two-way, and Holdsworth (1991) has drawn attention to the modern trend of organisations using their performance appraisal systems to being about cultural change.

Performance Appraisal and Pay

A question of fundamental importance is to what extent, if at all, links should exist between performance appraisal and pay decisions. In the past, different approaches have been advocated by UK and US writers, and have been reflected in different organizational practices, although there is now some evidence to suggest a shift towards more generally held views on how performance appraisal and pay should be related, even though substantial variations in organizational practice remain.

Table 10.1   Purpose of performance appraisal in 510 companies

Purpose	Number of companies n = 510
Determining merit increases	459
Providing basis of feedback on employees' performance	442
Planning goals for job performance with employees	401
Determining training and development needs	352
Identifying promotion potential	346
Identifying employees with specific skills and abilities	236

Source: Peck, C.A. 1984

US literature has consistently articulated the merits of relating performance appraisal to pay. Lawler (1981), while generally advocating close linkages, recognizes that a number of factors will influence the feasibility and the desirability of using performance appraisals in making pay decisions. Data gathered by Peck (1984), and summarised in table 10.1, is illustrative of a number of US surveys highlighting that many US organizations use performance appraisals for pay decisions, to ensure that those who emerge from the system of performance appraisal as high performers receive greater rewards than those considered to be less-good performers.

The traditional UK approach has been to stress the advantages of separating performance appraisal from pay decisions. This approach stresses the existence of conflict among the various objectives that performance appraisal schemes could be expected to fulfil in organizations. Randell (1989) has been putting forward the argument for many years in favour of the separation of the main elements of performance appraisal into three distinct reviews: for future potential, current performance and salary discussions. Randell, in keeping with a number of other British writers, considers that the objective of using performance appraisal ratings for salary decisions is in conflict with other performance appraisal objectives, especially those concerned with improving current performance and identifying the training and development needs of appraisees. Most organizations, even if agreeing to some extent with his proposition in theory, reject it for practical considerations, taking the view that three separate sets of reviews would make unreasonable demands on time and resources.

Research evidence, especially of Lawler (1981) and Prince and Lawler (1986), suggests that there are strong reasons for relating performance appraisal to pay decisions. Furthermore, recent organizational practice in many countries appears to be following the US pattern in this direction. Summarizing their conclusions, the positive advantages in linking performance appraisal and pay are:

- all parties, appraisers, appraisees and reviewers, take performance appraisal more seriously;
- many individuals feel that, for reasons of fairness, there should be a close link between performance appraisal and pay;
- organizations are likely to develop performance-orientated cultures, in which high performers are seen to receive extra rewards, and lower performers receive lower rewards.

Their researches, however, also identify negative factors:

- when pay and performance appraisal are closely linked, the pay issue may overshadow all the other purposes of performance appraisal;
- there may well be a tendency for employees to withhold negative information about performance, leading to a less than frank appraisal discussion;
- employees may try to influence appraisers by seeking to set lower, more conservative goals;
- employees may adapt their behaviour to target on receiving good ratings, rather than to genuinely improve their overall performance.

None of the above problems are necessarily insurmountable but they do indicate clearly that, while there are definite advantages to be gained, the linkages with pay and reward decisions add extra pressures and stresses to any performance appraisal scheme.

Organizations must therefore be fully aware of the risks and issues involved before linking pay and reward decisions to performance appraisal. The advantages all presuppose that a valid performance appraisal system operates. If invalid data emerge from the appraisal system, the damaging effects in terms of loss of motivation and feelings of employee grievance could be substantial. Job design is another important factor. Pay-related performance appraisal is likely to be effective only in organizations where jobs are designed in such a way that allows individual performance to be measured. In situations characterized by high interaction among jobs in achieving results, group-related pay systems may be more appropriate.

Who Conducts Appraisals?

A question of great importance in any performance appraisal scheme concerns who conducts performance appraisals. Not surprisingly, one of the questions of major interest to the average employee – possibly the most important for many – is quite simply: 'Who will be my appraiser?' The answer to this question will impact on individual feelings about the likely fairness of the appraisal process. Managers, too, will have a keen interest in this question, in finding out how many employees they will be expected to appraise. Answering the question of who should conduct appraisals often forces companies to clarify any ambiguities that may exist in the organization's structure.

There are a number of options as to who should conduct appraisals, and these are discussed in the following sub-sections.

The immediate manager

This is overwhelmingly the popular choice in the great majority of organizations. Long (1986) reports that among organizations located in the UK, 98 per cent usually entrust the task of conducting appraisals to the person with direct line management responsibility for the employee being appraised.

The essential argument, long emphasized by US organizations, is that since performance appraisal is an integral part of the managerial role it should be undertaken by the person with immediate management accountability.

The manager's manager

A more traditional approach, formerly used by the UK Civil Service, is for the manager's manager to carry out appraisals. This approach is still used by some organizations: 20 per cent indicate some applications, according to Long (1986), describing the IPM's UK study. The argument in favour of this approach is that it leads to more objective appraisal since the manager's manager should be better able to take a broader, more impartial view of an employee's performance. The difficulties are that this approach tends to erode the position of the intermediate manager, and that the manager's manager may not have a detailed familiarity with the employee's work.

The more common modern approach is for the immediate manager to be the appraiser, with the manager's manager as reviewer. The role of reviewer, if actively carried out, is extremely important in ensuring consistency of standards and valid performance appraisal data.

Self-appraisal

Self-appraisal by the individual is not usually a totally separate option and can, for example, be readily combined with either of the first two examples. One of the major trends in recent years has been the inclusion of self-assessment into the performance appraisal schemes of many organizations. Typically this leads to the development of an extra stage in the appraisal process, with the employee initiating the appraisal through the completion of a self-assessment document, which is passed to the appraiser. The appraiser then responds, commenting on the views of the appraisee, as well as providing independent input.

A number of choices must be made by an organization when utilizing self-appraisal. For example, if the employee's self-assessment is submitted in advance to the appraiser, it becomes one of the inputs into the appraiser's preparation and into the initial formulation of an appraisal report. Alternatively, the appraisee may exchange his or her self-appraisal with the appraiser's draft report at, or just before, the appraisal interview.

Although this latter approach avoids the possibility of a contamination effect, in that the employee's self-assessment cannot distort or have any undesirable influence on the appraiser's evaluation, it can lead to a more difficult and unpredictable situation for the appraiser to handle. Most organizations seem to prefer the first of the two options described, giving appraisers the opportunity to study and consider carefully the self-evaluation made by employees in advance of appraisal interviews.

Upward appraisal

Those who work for a supervisor or manager have a unique perspective of that person, and of some aspects of that person's work performance and contribution to the organization. Some organizations are therefore showing an interest in subordinate assessments as part of the appraisal process.

The main advantages of upward appraisal are that a number of independent viewpoints are introduced. Managers are likely to take very seriously the feedback they receive from their staff, and are likely to make changes based on it. Disadvantages include the fact that subordinates may have a limited vision and understanding of the total role of their managers.

Peer appraisal

Several studies (see, for example, Latham and Wexley 1981; and Thompson 1991) have come to a positive conclusion about the value of peer appraisal, which has for long been used by a number of professional organizations, for example university teachers. The major strengths of peer review include:

- introducing a perspective different from that of line managers;
- obtaining a number of independent judgements;
- obtaining the views of the users of a person's contribution and performance, if they happen to be peers.

The negative factors are:

- possible distortion due to popularity factors influencing peers;
- possible negative reactions towards those who, irrespective of this performance, are seen as unorthodox, inclined to challenge existing practices, and therefore perceived as threatening;
- friendship ratings;
- distortions due to fear of retaliation;
- reliance of peers on stereotypes in making evaluations.

Despite the risks evident from the number of possible negative factors, peer review may well have an increasing role to play in performance appraisal systems of the future, especially in non-hierarchical, team-based organizational structures in which peers are willing to give objective evaluations of one another's performance, and where peers interact sufficiently frequently to be able to develop an informed view of the performance of colleagues.

Multi-appraisal

The limitations of conventional performance appraisal in placing considerable, and sometimes total, emphasis on the judgement of the employee's manager, have been identified and discussed by a number of writers. A pioneering study carried out a number of years ago in Gulf Oil, and described by Stinson and Stokes (1980), highlights an alternative, multi-rater method which overcomes a number of the deficiencies of conventional, manager-orientated appraisal. Gulf Oil based its multi-rater appraisal scheme on the concept of the job network, that is, on those individuals, at more senior, more junior or the same level in the organization (but excluding the immediate manager in the line-reporting relationship), on whom the performance of the employee being appraised has principal impact.

In the Gulf Oil scheme, which was confined to senior managers, those being appraised were invited to nominate between five and eight persons in their job network. These individuals were then asked to complete a rating form that evaluated the manager being appraised by using a number of dimensions of managerial behaviour. A collated summary of their ratings was prepared by the human resource department and passed to both the employee and his or her immediate manager. Anonymity was considered important in encouraging candid and honest ratings, so nothing on the summary feedback sheet could be traced back to any individual. Those being appraised were then asked to complete a self-evaluation, which was also passed to the immediate manager. The immediate manager, equipped with both the summary feedback from the members of the job network and the employee's self-evaluation, then prepared the company's official appraisal document and conducted an appraisal interview.

Although clearly a resource-intensive approach, it led to very specific, constructive feedback from the members of the job network and helped to distinguish between organizational and individual factors which affect performance.

Towards 360-degree Appraisal

Probably the most significant development likely to influence the nature of performance appraisal in the future is the shift away from conventional appraisals undertaken typically by line managers towards the concept of 360-degree appraisal. The concept builds on multi-appraisal and refers to a situation where appraisal data is collected 'all around' an employee, from his or her manager, subordinates, peers and customers, internal and external (where appropriate). A number of factors are encouraging organizations to introduce, or to seriously consider the introduction of, 360-degree appraisal. These include:

- flatter, less hierarchical, more flexible, team-based organization structures;
- awareness of the limited perspective of managers (especially when faced with larger spans of control in flatter organization structures);
- recognition of the value of contributions from other sources, in keeping with trends in human resource management, emphasizing the importance of participation and involvement;
- the advantage of a range of perspectives, given the increasingly complex roles many people play in organizations.

Nowack (1993) suggests additional factors, including the increasing availability of assessment software capable of summarizing data from multiple sources into customized feedback reports.

The element of 360-degree appraisal which is attracting most attention, both in organizations and in the literature, is upward or reverse appraisal (that is, subordinates appraising their managers) discussed in a previous section, largely because of its impact on manager–staff relations and on organization culture. Nicholas (1992) points out that in upward appraisal managers and employees are reversing their roles. Traditionally, the employee's role has been to supply whatever it takes to meet the demands of the manager, who was viewed as the 'customer'. Today, however, many organizations consider the manager as the supplier of direction, resources and coaching advice to 'internal customers' – the employees. In BP Exploration (see Willard and Thomas 1992), upward appraisal, called the Upward Feedback Programme, was introduced in 1990. This has been one of the pioneering examples in the UK, and was introduced in response to a flattening of organization structure and a desire to introduce more open, participative styles of management.

In the Upward Feedback Programme staff complete a questionnaire that addresses the effectiveness of their manager in managing people; subsequently staff meet with the manager to discuss the aggregate results in order to develop ways to overcome problems which have been identified. The implementation of the Upward Feedback Programme has been perceived as a major symbol of change. Initial responses to the first phase which involved 1,400 managers have been largely positive.

In the USA upward appraisal has become, and is becoming, a widely established practice. In Chrysler (see Santora 1992), upward appraisal has been introduced to improve upward communications, develop the skills of supervisors and managers, and generally help its competitiveness in the market-place as effectively as possible.

While 360-degree appraisal may indicate the future direction of performance appraisal, a number of issues need to be addressed. These include:

- ensuring that participation is voluntary: unwilling raters are unlikely to provide accurate or useful feedback;
- deciding whether feedback providers would be identified or remain anonymous: anonymity prevents retaliation, but may encourage bias;
- deciding who should see the feedback, and whether the names of those providing feedback should be shared;
- assessing whether scores should be reported separately or pooled: this will impact on the quality of the feedback, and on whether the person being appraised is likely to be inclined to make changes as a result of it.

Good trust levels, clarity about the objectives of appraisal and a participative team-based culture are likely to be all-important for

Figure 10.1 Components of performance
Source: Mohrman et al. (1989)

360-degree appraisal to be effective. As Ward (1995) points out: 'One of the key principles of 360-degree feedback is that people see you differently.' So for your relationship to be successful, you need to respond differently, depending on the group or individual with whom you are dealing.

Who Should be Appraised?

An important and fundamental question concerns which employees in an organization should be covered by performance appraisal. Increasingly, the answer seems to be 'everyone'; Long (1986) indicates that, while past practice has been to confine performance appraisal to managers and supervisors, there is evidence that most organizations are extending their schemes to include not only secretarial and clerical but also, in some cases, manual workers. Interestingly, Long also reports evidence of extension of coverage in the upper echelons of organizations, to include directors.

Appraisal Methods

A wide range of methods and criteria for appraising performance is used by organizations. The various ways of measuring performance stem directly from the different components of performance (see figure 10.1).

In many early performance appraisal schemes (and still to be found in some) the emphasis was placed on the left-hand side of figure 10.1, the performer, in using personality traits (such as judgement, reliability, initiative) as the basis for assessment. Dissatisfaction with this approach has grown over the years because of difficulties in arriving at common definitions of personality traits and of avoiding very subjective judgements.

There has been a shift towards the right of the figure, with an increasing number of organizations reviewing performance against pre-set objectives. This trend has emerged from the philosophy of 'management by objectives' popularized by writers such as Drucker (1954). Objectives should as far as possible be specific and measurable, and should be challenging to employees, though achievable. The effectiveness of objective-setting or results-orientated appraisal depends to a substantial extent on employee participation in the goal-setting process, since shared goal-setting generally leads to higher feelings of employee commitment to achieve goals that have been jointly agreed.

As it becomes more usual to extend performance appraisal to all organizational levels, there is increased recognition that a number of variants of performance appraisal need to be developed. For instance, objective-setting approaches, defining results to be achieved, are often considered to be more appropriate for managerial than for non-managerial employees. At non-managerial levels, mechanisms focusing on the central part of figure 10.1, the assessment of behaviour, may be more appropriate. The appraisal of job behaviours or competencies implies that these characteristics should be derived from detailed job analysis to determine the most important dimensions for appraisal purposes. Examples of behaviours or competencies used for assessment could include, for example, communications skills, counselling skills, analytical ability, willingness to introduce and accept change.

One behavioural approach, popular in the USA, is called BARS (behaviourally anchored rating scales). This method is an improvement over simple rating scales, in that it provides a set of behavioural descriptions at each point on a rating scale. For example, if a scale measures performance quality, then a set of statements is used to describe the behaviour associated with the worst quality, at one extreme, and the best quality, at the other, with intermediate statements in between.

The wider coverage of appraisal schemes means that many organizations have developed two or more variants of their performance appraisal systems, to address the differing needs of various groups of staff.

Openness in the appraisal process

There has been clear evidence of a trend in recent years towards greater openness in the appraisal process, with the appraisal report and its contents being shown freely to the employee being appraised. The trend towards openness has been encouraged by a number of factors, the three principal ones being identified as:

Table 10.2 Openness of appraisal reports

Degree of openness	% of organisations	
	1977	*1986*
All parts f appraisal reports disclosed	39	64
Some parts not disclosed	35	28
Reports not disclosed	26	8
Total	100	100
n =	236	250

Source: Long (1986)

- the increased use of results-orientated methods of appraisal stemming from management-by-objectives philosophy;
- the changing social climate, emphasizing participation and feedback as a basis for development;
- the growing influence of white-collar unions, stressing the need for mutual trust.

It would be difficult for an organization to operate a results-orientated performance appraisal system without openness, since this type of approach requires the superior and subordinate to identify and set goals that are seen by both as realistic for the subordinate; these agreed goals, where possible translated into measurable objectives, become the basis for the subsequent assessment of the subordinate's performance. Traditional, trait-orientated schemes, by contrast, were sometimes closed to employees.

Table 10.2 shows the changes in this aspect of performance appraisal practice that took place between 1977 and 1986. It highlights that only 8 per cent of organizations in the 1986 survey operated closed appraisal systems in which the individual was not allowed to see the completed performance appraisal report, compared with 26 per cent in 1977. This evidence indicates that an increasing number of organizations recognize the desirability of open communications between appraiser and appraisee in the performance appraisal process. This recognition of the value of openness applies mainly, however, to those aspects that deal with current performance. The undisclosed parts relate mainly, as previously mentioned, to the evaluation of an employee's future potential.

The legal dimension also has to be considered, and this will vary from country to country. In the UK, for example, the Data Protection

Act of 1984 gives individual employees the legal right of access to personal data, such as information about them contained in appraisal documents, if it is held on computer. Personnel data, as defined by the Act, cover both factual and evaluative information, implying that employees could have access to opinions about them expressed in appraisal documents. Any indication of intentions, such as to promote, is outside the scope of the Act. This law does not apply to appraisal documents held in manual systems.

Formal and Informal Appraisal

An area that has often been neglected in the literature has been consideration of the links between formal appraisal – the processes of the organization's performance appraisal system – and informal appraisal, which should be part of the day-to-day management. And yet there is evidence from a variety of sources (see, for example, Fletcher and Williams 1985) to suggest that this is a vital linkage in order for appraisal to be effective and for the organization's official scheme to yield maximum benefits.

One point that has often been stressed by researchers and practitioners is that there should be no surprises at the time of the formal appraisal, when the appraisal interview is held and the appraisal documentation is completed. This implies that those who are appraisers must display a range of skills in their day-to-day management of employees. At least four sets of managerial skills which interact with one another can be identified, to ensure informal appraisal takes place throughout the year, and to provide a sound foundation for the formal appraisal process. These managerial skills are discussed in the following sections.

Diagnostic skills

The appraiser with diagnostic skills has the ability and interest to investigate reasons for specific items of good and bad performance, and changes of trend in performance. This implies a range of skills in focusing on the individual and exploring a number of factors through observation, talking with other managers and users of the employee's services, that explain performance and changes in performance.

Skills in giving and receiving feedback

Any appraiser requires the ability to give employees feedback on specific work items, for example in giving praise and recognition for a task successfully completed and constructive criticism when there has been failure to achieve specific tasks, activities or targets. Thus the formal appraisal should be analogous to a stocktaking or audit, dealing with the overall performance of the individual.

Counselling skills

Although there is likely to be a counselling element in appraisal interviews in discussing career progression and possibly personal problems with appraisees, appraisers should display a willingness and interest, as well as appropriate skills, in conducting counselling sessions with employees whenever the need arises. Willingness to recognize and deal with personal issues that may be affecting employee's performance as and when they occur is more likely to create a situation where the focus can be on performance issues at appraisal interviews.

Coaching skills

An appraiser's coaching skills are important in ensuring willingness to follow up after formal appraisals. This is particularly the case where objective-setting or target-setting methods of formal appraisal are used. Coaching skills (see, for example, Evenden 1994; and Evenden and Anderson 1992) are required to support employees, on an ongoing basis, as they attempt to achieve the targets or objectives agreed in their formal appraisal sessions. These coaching skills involve a number of techniques, such as holding informal mid-term reviews, assisting employees to develop self-evaluation mechanisms, and providing on-the-job training. Another aspect of coaching – possibly even more important – is attitudinal, in investing time and effort in coaching employees and taking a continuing interest in their progress and achievements.

The Appraisal Interview

The appraisal interview is seen by most organizations as the key feature determining the success or failure of the performance appraisal scheme. Most appraisal schemes include provision for holding appraisal interviews which provide an opportunity for managers to inform employees about their performance and to develop plans for the future.

The appraisal interview is one of the most difficult forms of interview which a manager is asked to undertake because:

- the interview can be extremely unpredictable, especially over matters relating to areas of deficient performance and the weaknesses of the individual;
- the manager must display a wide range of interpersonal skills in conducting effective appraisal interviews;
- appraisal interview skills cannot be readily learned from watching other managers in action. Because of the confidential nature of the appraisal interview, it is unlikely that a manager will witness anyone else in the role of the interviewer except his or her own superior.

Objectives of the appraisal interview

The appraisal interview can serve a number of objectives. They should relate to the overall objectives which the organization expects its performance appraisal scheme as a whole to achieve and are likely to include:

- letting the employee know where he or she stands;
- providing an opportunity for a discussion about the employee's job performance over the period under review;
- agreeing action to improve the performance of the employee, including the setting of objectives.

Characteristics of effective appraisal interviews

An examination of the literature suggests that attention has largely focused on the following characteristics of the appraisal interview.

Employee participation   Studies, for example by Wexley (1986), show that the more the employee participates in the appraisal interview, the greater the feelings of satisfaction on the employee's part towards the interview and the interviewer.

Interview support   In general, the more supportive the interviewer, in terms of, for example, showing an appreciation of the employee's point of view, and adopting a constructive approach to problems, the greater the chance that the employee will accept the results of the appraisal and make changes based on feedback.

Identifying and solving problems affecting the employee's job performance
The greater the extent to which emphasis is placed on identifying and solving problems affecting job performance, the greater the likelihood that the employee's behaviour and performance will change in a positive way, compared with situations where appraisers impose solutions. This coincides with Maier's (1976) famous classification of appraisal

interviewing styles, in which he advocates problem-solving styles as opposed to 'tell and sell' and 'tell and listen' approaches.

Emphasizing performance rather than personality Following on from the above, where there is a greater emphasis on job performance rather than on the personality of the employee, more satisfaction with the interview is likely to be generated.

Goal-setting The setting of specific goals which the employee will seek to attain has been shown to have a more powerful effect on subsequent performance than a general discussion about goals.

Limited criticism Effective appraisal interviews contain a minimum of criticism. Mohrman et al. (1989), on the grounds that criticism builds up defence mechanisms, advocate a 'four-to-one' principle – four positive comments for every piece of criticism.

Proportion of interview time when the employee speaks The greater the opportunity the employee has to speak, the more likely it is that he or she will feel satisfied with the appraisal interview. This measure may be an indicator of the level of employee influence on the appraisal process. Anderson and Watt (1988) discovered, however, that appraisers and employees may have very different recollections of the proportion of time each party spoke in appraisal interviews.

Interview processes and outcomes

Anderson and Barnett (1987), studying appraisal interviews and other aspects of the appraisal process for 317 nursing staff, concluded that while, on the whole, positive findings towards appraisal interviews were reported on the basis of the dimensions described above, results were much more mixed and generally poorer in terms of employees' recognition of the importance of making changes and translating the results of the appraisal interview discussions into improved job performance. This suggests that organizations have to face a two-stage challenge: developing, first, sound interview processes, and then, secondly, generating linkages between the interview processes and subsequent outcomes, especially in terms of improvements in job performance.

Problems of Performance Appraisal

Although many organizations have devoted a great deal of time, effort and resources to setting up performance appraisal schemes, the results have often been disappointing. Performance appraisal, in the words of Lawler 1994, 'has been one of the most praised, criticised and debated management practices for decades'.

While there has been considerable progress in improving the instruments of performance appraisal systems, especially by shifting from the more subjective, often simplistic methods to more sophisticated, objectively based approaches, the implementation of performance appraisal still tends to be resisted, if not avoided, by many managers.

One difficulty is the face-to-face situation of the appraisal interview, where the appraiser sits down with the appraisee and reviews his or her performance. When situations are full of positive comments, appraisal is easy. When performance and potential are good, when superior and subordinate have an open relationship, when promotions or salary increases are abundant, when there is plenty of time for preparation and discussion – in short, whenever it is a pleasure – performance appraisal is easy to do.

Frequently, however, and particularly when it is most needed and most difficult to do, when deficiencies in performance are being addressed, performance appraisal refuses to run properly. Beer (1981) suggests three main sources of difficulty:

• the quality of the relationship between appraiser and appraisee;
• the manner and skill with which the interview is conducted;
• the appraisal system itself, namely the objectives the organization expects it to achieve, the methodology, the documents and procedures that make up the system.

The underlying quality of the superior–subordinate relationship has a major impact, since the appraisal process is part of a broader set of interactions between the appraiser and appraisee. Unless there is good mutual trust and understanding, the appraisee is likely to view appraisal discussions with apprehension and suspicion. The appraiser, in turn, is likely to view appraisal time as a daunting experience where employee hostility and resistance are likely to emerge. If regular informal appraisal takes place as previously advocated, the problems of hoarding up points to deal with at appraisal interview and of springing surprises on employees can be avoided.

The appraisal interview is a most difficult type of interview for any manager to undertake. Managers often experience feelings of unease at the prospect of entering a situation with staff in which a more candid and personal set of exchanges is likely to take place than probably at any other time. In addition, the manager may be exposing himself or herself to criticism. If the interview is not well handled, the downside risks are considerable, in terms of potential damage to self-image, motivation and working relationships.

The importance of employee participation and the problems of non-participation have already been highlighted. The Institute of Personnel and Development's (1994) Position Paper, *People Make the Difference*, reinforces in a wider context early findings about the positive aspects of participation, stressing that in the flexible organization of the future employees should be helped to take on more responsibility for their own growth and development.

Other problems may relate to the way the design process and implementation of performance appraisal have been handled in the organization.

Designing and implementing appraisal schemes

Many options are open to an organization in designing and implementing an appraisal scheme. Decisions must be made on a range of important issues, some of which have already been discussed. The following is a summary of major questions which an organization must address in designing or redesigning its system of performance appraisal:

- What categories of employees should be covered by performance appraisal?
- Should any employees be excluded because of organizational status (for example, through membership of the lowest or highest echelons in the organization structure) or on the grounds of age (for example, closeness to retirement age)?
- What criteria should be used to evaluate an employee's contribution to the organization?
- What kind of documentation should be used?
- Who should be the appraisers? Should it be the employee's immediate superior, or someone at a more senior level in the organizational hierarchy?
- Should employees be given an opportunity to make an input to their own appraisal, for example through a self-assessment document or through the inclusion of employee comments in the official appraisal documentation?
- Should the individual's potential, as well as current performance, be evaluated?
- Should the contents of performance appraisal reports be freely divulged to employees?
- What review and appeals mechanisms need to be established?
- Finally, and of paramount importance, what purposes should performance appraisal serve, and what use should be made of the data generated through appraisal documentation?

The list illustrates the many choices and decisions that must be made that, not surprisingly, give rise to substantial variations in practice.

Many organizations experience difficulty in grappling with the problems of deciding what kind of performance appraisal system to adopt or how to improve an ineffective system.

Because performance appraisal is, or should be, a central part of the management process, it is of vital importance that all managers in the organization – and indeed, it could be argued, all employees – should have feelings of ownership of the performance appraisal scheme, and should recognize that their whole-hearted involvement is central to its success. One of the key conditions for successful performance appraisal, design and implementation is consultation. Consultation at the design stage with groups – including directors, senior and middle managers, supervisors, employees, trade unions – should not only help to alleviate anxieties and generate interest and commitment but also stimulate innovative ideas about appraisal methods and implementation procedures which help to ensure that the scheme is effectively tailored to the organization's requirements.

Top management support

The commitment of top management is crucially important, especially as many of the benefits of performance appraisal relate to the medium and long term. Such support and interest will encourage managers at other levels to devote care and attention to the implementation of performance appraisal, especially if it is made clear to them that how objectively and how effectively they appraise their staff will impact on their own appraisals.

Training appraisers

The training of managers and supervisors in appraisal methodology and in the skills of appraisal interviewing is essential for effective appraisal. As Mohrman et al. (1989) point out, performance appraisal is not something that most individuals are genetically or culturally programmed to do well. In fact, some cultural norms work counter to good appraisal.

As performance appraisal systems become more participative, it becomes just as important to train and brief appraisees. This is particularly true in the case of the increasing number of appraisal systems which, as previously noted, involve self-appraisal. Our educational institutions, Fletcher (1984) stresses, do not normally equip people with the skills of self-assessment. Assessment is something that is handed down from above by others throughout the educational system. Thus it is also important to educate and train employees in the skills of self-assessment.

From Performance Appraisal to Performance Management

Connock (1991), *HR Vision*, suggests that in the late 1980s a shift of emphasis began to take place from performance appraisal to performance management. Performance management is essentially a philosophy and a continuous process to which managers and employees need to devote attention 365 days in the year. It encompasses performance and how it is to be improved by engaging in regular dialogue, rather than just focusing on these issues periodically, once every year or once every half year, in formal appraisal sessions.

Performance management focuses strongly on the future. Connock stresses that a major contribution of performance management is to place great emphasis on:

* setting key accountabilities;
* agreeing future objectives in each of these key accountability areas;
* agreeing measures, and standards to be attained;
* assigning time-scales and priorities.

This emphasis on the future represents an evolutionary rather than a revolutionary change since it has for many years been recognized, as long ago as 1973 by Cummings and Schwab, for example, that well-designed systems of performance appraisal should pursue forward-looking, developmental objectives such as the setting of targets for different aspects of job performance for each employee, and the identification of employees' training needs, as well as the historical, evaluative objectives concerned primarily with the assessment of actual employee performance over a given time period of the previous 6 or 12 months. In this respect, performance management builds upon performance appraisal and does not replace it.

Summary and Conclusions

Performance appraisal has been influenced by societal change as well as by business change. It flourished in the UK in the 1980s in a political climate that favoured an individualistic competitive philosophy.

The 1990s has witnessed increasing emphasis on team-based approaches in flatter, less-hierarchical structures (see, for example, Lawler 1994). This implies that organizations need to face up to the challenge of developing new approaches to performance appraisal. Individuals still need encouragement and guidance to develop their skills and direct their efforts towards the achievement of organizational goals.

It is important to stress that there is no such thing as the universal performance appraisal system. What works well in one organization may work badly in another. Appraisal systems must be designed to suit the culture and requirements of each organization. Increasingly, however, the relationship between appraisal and culture is two-way, with organizations expecting their appraisal schemes to contribute to a change in corporate culture that is seen as relevant to the achievement of corporate objectives.

Appraisal systems do not operate in isolation: they generate data that can contribute to other HRM systems – for example, to succession planning and manpower planning.

Despite the desirable objectives that a well-run appraisal scheme can achieve, many problems readily emerge that can impede their achievements (see, for example, Grint 1993). In addition, it must be recognized that there are risks attached to any system of performance appraisal that may be introduced. The benefits can be seen by the employee being appraised in terms of feedback on performance, strengths and weaknesses, an opportunity to clarify training and development needs, and clarification of what is expected in the future; and by appraisers as providing both a better understanding of the employee perspective on a range of issues and also a mechanism to monitor and evaluate performance, providing a basis for actions that will improve employee effectiveness and contribute to corporate performance.

The costs and downside risks are numerous and include negative, defensive employee attitudes towards criticism, a failure by both parties to face up to difficult issues which generates bland appraisals that bear little relationship to actual work performance and, most serious of all, an attitude problem which leads to appraisals being seen as an unpleasant chore to be gone through as fast as possible, with minimal effort and input.

Such problems must be kept in context; increasingly organizations, recognizing how expensive is the time and resource commitment to performance appraisal, are taking steps both to train appraisers and to brief appraisees, and generally to monitor and evaluate more effectively their appraisal systems, so that problems can be identified quickly and corrective action introduced.

References

Anderson, G.C. 1980: *Performance Appraisal in Theory and Practice*, Working Paper 8002. Glasgow: Strathclyde Business School, University of Strathclyde.

Anderson, G.C. and Barnett, J.G. 1987: The characteristics of effective appraisal interviews. *Personnel Review*, 16(4), 18–25.

Anderson, G.C. and Watt, E. 1988: A new context for performance appraisal. *Health Care Management*, 3(1), 27–32.

Beer, M. 1981: Performance appraisal: dilemmas and possibilities. *Organisational Dynamics*, Winter, 24–36.

Bevan, S. and Thompson, M. 1992: *An Overview of Policy and Practice. Performance Management: an analysis of the issues*. London: Institute of Personnel Management.

Brinkerhoff, D.W. and Kanter, R.M. 1980: Appraising the performance of performance appraisal. *Sloan Management Review*, 21, 3–16.

Bureau of National Affairs 1983: *Performance Appraisal Programs*, Personnel Policies Forum Survey 135. Washington, D.C.: Bureau of National Affairs.

Cameron, D. 1982: Performance appraisal and review. In A.M. Bowey (ed.), *Handbook of Wage and Salary Systems*, London: Gower, pp. 197–233.

Connock, S. 1991: *HR Vision*. London: Institute of Personnel Management.

Cummings, L.L. and Schwab, D. 1973: *Performance in Organisations: determinants and appraisals*. Glenview, Ill.: Scott, Foresman.

Drucker, P. 1954: *The Practice of Management*. London: Harper & Row.

Eichel, E. and Bender, H.E. 1984: *Performance Appraisal: a study of current techniques*. New York: American Management Association.

Evenden, R. 1994: Coaching and the development relationship. *Training and Development*, April.

Evenden, R. and Anderson, G.C. 1992: *Making the Most of People*. Reading, Mass.: Addison-Wesley.

Farnsworth, T. 1974: Appraising the appraisals. *Management Today*, November: 103–12.

Fletcher, C. 1984: What's new in performance appraisal? *Personnel Management*, February: 20–2.

Fletcher, C. and Williams, R. 1985: *Performance Appraisal and Career Development*. London: Hutchinson.

Grint, K. 1993: What's wrong with performance appraisals? A critique and a suggestion. *Human Resource Management Journal*, 3(3).

Holdsworth, R. 1991: Appraisal. In F. Meale (ed.), *Handbook of Human Resource Management*. London: Institute of Personnel Management.

Institute of Personnel and Development 1994: *People Make the Difference*, IPD Position Paper. London: IPD.

Latham, G.P. and Wexley, K.N. 1981: *Increasing Productivity through Performance Appraisal*. Reading, Mass.: Addison-Wesley.

Lawler, E.E. 1981: *Pay and Organizational Development*. Reading, Mass.: Addison-Wesley.

Lawler, E.E. 1994: Performance management: the next generation. *Compensation and Benefits Review*, May–June.

Levinson, H. 1970: Management by whose objectives? *Harvard Business Review*, 48(4): 134.

Long, P. 1986: *Performance Appraisal Revisited*. London: Institute of Personnel Management.

Maier, N.R.F. 1976: *The Appraisal Interview*. New York: University Associates.

McGregor, D. 1957: An uneasy look at performance appraisal. *Harvard Business Review*, 35(3): 89–94.

Meyer, H.H., Kay, E. and French, J.P.R. 1965: Split roles in performance appraisal. *Harvard Business Review*, 43: 123–9.

Mohrman, A.M., Resnick-West, S.M. and Lawler, E.E. 1989: *Designing Performance Appraisal Systems*. San Francisco, Cal.: Jossey-Bass.

Nicholas, G.P. 1992: Upward trend continues in appraisal process. *Training and Development*, September.

Nowack, K.M. 1993: 360-degree feedback: the whole story. *Training and Development*, January.

Peck, C.A. 1984: *Pay and Performance: The interaction of compensation and performance appraisal*, Research Bulletin no. 155. New York: Conference Board.

Prince, J.B. and Lawler, E.E. 1986: Does salary discussion hurt the developmental performance appraisal? *Organisational Behaviour and Human Decision Processes*, 37: 357–75.

Randall, G., Packard, P. and Slater, J. 1984: *Staff Appraisal: a first step to effective leadership*, 3rd edn. London: Institute of Personnel Management.

Randell, G. 1989: Employee appraisal. In K. Sisson (ed.), *Personnel Management in Britain*, Oxford: Blackwell.

Santora, J.E. 1992: Rating the boss at Chrysler. *Personnel Journal*, May.

Stinson, J. and Stokes, J. 1980: How to multi-appraise. *Management Today*, June: 43–53.

Thompson, B.L. 1991: An early review of peer review. *Training*, July.

Twomey, D.F. and Twomey, R.F. 1992: Assessing and transforming performance appraisal. *Journal of Managerial Psychology*, 7(3).

Ward, P. 1995: A 360 degree turn for the better. *People Management*, February.

Wexley, K.N. 1986: Appraisal interview. In R. Berk (ed.), *Performance Assessment: methods and applications*, Baltimore, Md: Johns Hopkins Press.

Willard, J. and Thomas, A. 1992: BP exploration and upward appraisal. *Executive Development*, 4(4).

11

Involvement, Empowerment and Commitment

HARVIE RAMSAY

Introduction

The 1970s was the decade of the debate on 'industrial democracy' (ID), symbolized by the bouts of managerial apoplexy surrounding the Bullock Report. In its wake, the 1980s witnessed a sea-change in the flavour and substance of discussions of employee participation in the workplace. A number of aspects of this shift may be identified:

- a change in political climate, which led to a de-emphasizing of 'hard' or power-centred forms of participation (such as information disclosure, works councils, extended bargaining rights, and worker directors); and a move towards 'softer' – in power terms at least – techniques for engendering employee commitment (such as profit-sharing and employee share-ownership, communications and briefing systems, and quality circles);
- a similar and related change in the industrial climate, diverting union attention from demands for ID rights to survival and defence of employment, often requiring them to accept more market-orientated and co-operative views of relations with management;
- a more confident management approach to initiatives in employee relations, including the emphasis of managerial objectives for 'employee involvement' (EI) rather than damage-limitation offers of 'participation' concessions. As confidence grew, management texts even began to risk using the double-edged slogan of 'empowerment';
- growing emphasis on strategic approaches to business matters, extending progressively to the area of human resource management, and so to the role of employee involvement within this.

The 1990s have seen a continuation of many of these trends in the UK, but also some revival in political circles especially of campaigns on employee rights. Thus industrial democracy (ID) has once more challenged employee involvement (EI) approaches to participation. The main engine of this to date has been the Social Charter proposed by the European Commission and agreed in outline by the EU member states (except Britain) in December 1989. Despite the UK government's trenchant opposition to the resulting attempt to include a Social Chapter in the Maastricht Treaty in December 1991, many of the provisions, including those for European Works Councils, will have marked effects in the largest British companies, not least through their subsidiaries in the rest of the European Union. We shall consider some implications of these developments at the end of this chapter.

The main focus of this chapter is the effectiveness of EI initiatives, as seen from a managerial viewpoint. The centrality of 'commitment' and 'empowerment' as objectives to be achieved primarily through EI is embodied in the analysis, and these concepts are subjected to closer scrutiny in the concluding section. However, aspects of 'empowerment' embodied in employee development and appraisal, for instance, or of 'commitment' sought through these and other routes (including rewards schemes) are dealt with in other chapters.

The Importance of Involvement

Figures quoted throughout the discussion of various forms of EI in this chapter will make it clear that it is a widespread and prominent management practice in Britain. The evidence suggests an increasing incidence and variety of schemes over the course of the 1980s. Thus, while the Workplace Industrial Relations Survey (WIRS) of 1980 (Daniel and Millward 1983) found that 24 per cent of managements reported recent initiatives in EI, the 1984 survey (Millward and Stevens 1986) reported that 35 per cent made a similar claim, and that for 1990 (Millward et al. 1992) saw the figure rise to 45 per cent. A Confederation of British Industry (CBI) survey at the very end of the 1980s (CBI 1990), though not strictly comparable with WIRS, records levels of incidence of schemes that imply a continuation of innovation over the decade, a finding reaffirmed by IRS (1993) and by the monitoring of company reports by the Department of Employment (1987, 1988; Hibbett 1991).

It seems likely that this continuing development of EI has a number of sources, varying in importance according to sector and organization, but including labour market pressures, the imperative to improve cost competitiveness, the need to gain co-operation for the introduction of new technology, and the need for enhanced competitiveness through flexibility and quality standards. Each of these proclaims the importance of management paying greater attention to winning the acquiescence or even the active support of their employees; EI is seen as an important means to this end.

The most popular forms of participation have included some which are often more engaged with union organization than management might prefer in an ideal world (though some companies take a more positive view than others of union involvement). These include health and safety committees, pension fund trusteeships and consultative committees. Only the last of these receive detailed attention in this chapter.

The areas of most active innovation in the last decade have undoubtedly been those where union involvement is low, however. The most popular experiments have included team briefings, quality management programmes, teamworking and various forms of financial participation. All of these are analysed in the following pages.

The importance of EI is stressed in a number of studies of management attitudes. In a 1985 CBI survey, it was rated second only to management skill and commitment to industrial relations as a source of improvement in employee relations, well ahead of legislation or government approach, for instance (MacInnes 1987). Similar findings were reported by Edwards (1987), who also found that some form of involvement or communication was seen as the key feature of personnel policy in 46 per cent of establishments he surveyed. This last figure was echoed in turn in Batstone's survey (1984), in which he reports that 47 per cent of personnel managers regarded involvement as the major factor in changing employee relations policy over the previous four years.

The topic of EI is one that has preoccupied managers a good deal in the last decade or more, then. Next we shall consider what they hope to achieve from it, and then assess whether they are likely to realize their aspirations.

The Objectives of Involvement

First, let us consider the main aims which management might entertain for employee involvement. Table 11.1 provides a list, by no means exhaustive, of the kinds of goals which may be sought through employee involvement policies.

The catalogue of possible objectives in table 11.1 highlights a number of things, including:

- the complexity and range of the subject;
- the need for careful definition of objectives. Vague and general terms like

Table 11.1   Possible management objectives for employee involvement

Attitudes	Improve morale Increase loyalty and commitment Enhance sense of belonging/involvement Increase support for management
Business awareness	Better, more accurately informed: stops rumour/'grapevine' Greater interest Improve knowledge and understanding of the reasons for management actions Support for/reduced resistance to management action
Incentive/ motivation	*Passive*: Accept changing work practices Accept mobility across jobs Accept new technology Accept supervisor/management authority *Active*: Improve quality/reliability Increase productivity/effort Reduce costs Identify and solve problems Enhance co-operation and team spirit *Personal*: Greater job interest Greater job satisfaction Employee development
Employee influence/ ownership	Increase job control Increase employee suggestions for improvements and their implementation Increase employee influence on personnel/social/business matters Create/increase employee ownership in the company Increase employee ties to company performance and profitability
Trade unions	*Anti-union*: Win hearts and minds of employees from union influence Fulfil rewards and benefits needs outside union channel Fulfil representative needs outside union channel Restrict scope of union dealings and influence Keep union out of company *With union*: Get union co-operation Draw on union advice Restrain union demands 'Microcorporatism': win over local union representatives (shop stewards, etc.) to management views, detach from national union (where separate)

'improved attitudes' or 'greater incentive' are inadequate for effective targeting and, subsequently, monitoring;
* the potential for objectives to conflict, or at least for there to be a certain strain between them.

To exemplify this last point, a general sense of unity and belonging may sit poorly with the need to sharpen individual competition and incentive, and it may be advisable to use distinct kinds of scheme to achieve each if both require enhancement. Alternatively, aims may have to be prioritized (for example, between incentive-orientated but elitist and possibly divisive executive share-option schemes, and more diffuse but integrative all-employee share schemes).

Most research on managerial objectives suggests that less-substantial aims of general attitude change are more widely sought than more concrete-seeming ones such as direct incentive or motivational effects. To some extent this reflects a poor definition of goals in many companies. Such lack of clarity is sometimes reflected also in a 'catch-all' listing of what schemes are meant to achieve. This exacerbates the problem, since the kinds of objectives stressed, and the extent to which they might be achieved in demonstrable and measurable ways, should vary with the type of scheme under consideration. This general shortcoming is taken up at the end of this chapter when we look at the need for 'strategic' approaches to the subject. Meantime, this chapter turns to an analysis of the types of schemes available.

Types of Schemes

It is possible to construct a detailed typology of involvement and participation schemes, in which managerial approaches such as those we concentrate on in this chapter are shadowed by labour-orientated (ID) initiatives and controls. For our present purposes, though, a few simple parameters will suffice.

First, it is useful to identify the level at which involvement takes place. A focus on the individual or task level includes initiatives such as job enrichment, job enlargement and other work reforms. The work group or department may also experience collective work rearrangements through some form of group autonomy, including that proposed in Japanese-inspired teamworking systems; or the group activity may be more a matter of communication and discussion, as in quality circles or briefing sessions. Higher levels of involvement than this typically entail the election of representatives rather than direct participation for everyone, obvious examples being forms of consultative committee or works council. It is also possible that this representation will be installed at the apex of the organization, through the appointment of employee directors; but in orthodox, private-sector UK companies this is almost unheard of (a study carried out in the late 1970s uncovered just seven such schemes: see Towers et al. 1987).

The concept of levels is not always helpful, however. Communications schemes may be designed to cascade through all levels (as in team briefings, for instance), or to cover all at once (through company magazines or newsletters perhaps). Financial participation, too, can be a pervasive all-employee arrangement, or a group-targeted value-added scheme, or a selective (usually executive) provision for share options. These are schemes which do not allow for decision-making by or active involvement of employees, but instead typically entail passive receipt of information or profit share (though it may be hoped that this will provoke some positive, motivational response), and so are not located in the same identifiable way at a single level.

This makes it apparent that the subject of involvement must be identified. The employee may be offered:

- a feeling-state, such as a sense of belonging or commitment;
- information about the organization and its environment;
- some financial reward;
- a share in decisions.

Where a share in decisions is involved, the topic of involvement must be further specified. It is helpful to distinguish between themes of:

- work organization, including such matters as task controls, the implementation of technical change, or labour utilization patterns in the workshop or office;
- personnel issues, dealing with pay, conditions, staffing levels, employee disciplinary and control questions and the like;
- social matters, such as welfare policy and company facilities;
- business matters, which include policy-orientated decisions on technology, work systems or, most ambitiously, marketing, investment and employment strategies.

Set alongside the list of management objectives provided earlier, these distinctions help us to analyse a variety of types of EI scheme. In this chapter, separate sections will focus on four broad types of scheme, assessing each in turn:

- task and work group involvement;
- communications and briefing systems;
- consultative arrangements;
- financial participation.

The aim throughout will be to summarize the major developments, and to assess the available evidence on the impact of schemes. There is at least as much to be learned from problems as from glistening success stories, so the common practice of providing simplistic recipes or uncritical plaudits for involvement will not be adopted. The chapter will close with a résumé of the main practical findings, and some observations on future developments, including the emergence of strategic approaches to HRM and EI.

Task and Work Group Involvement

Innovations at individual task and work group levels have a long history in the management tradition, largely deriving from the human relations experiments of the 1920s onwards. After the Second World War, the emphasis shifted increasingly from simple leadership style and the need of the individual to belong, to the need for employees to face challenges and have the opportunity to use and develop their abilities.

In the 1960s, individualistic policies pushed for job enlargement and, most ambitiously, job enrichment (the introduction of elements of responsibility into the work task). The pace in group innovations was made chiefly in Scandinavia from the late 1960s onwards, where the idea of the semi-autonomous work group was elaborated, the most publicized examples being in Volvo and Saab. In fact, the pioneering developments here had their origins in the work of the UK-based Tavistock Institute of Human Relations from the 1950s. By the mid-1970s, innovations were being vigorously promoted, often with the encouragement of governments (for example, in the UK the Work Research Unit of the Department of Employment, attached to ACAS since the mid-1980s), in most European countries and also in the United States. Labour militancy and difficult labour market conditions promoted a 'quality of working life' rhetoric which often seemed to fit with ID- as much as with EI-orientated objectives.

The Japanese tradition of work group activity was somewhat different. It also took off in the early 1960s (and also initially as a partial response to tight labour market conditions) but concentrated on the concept of quality, an approach which was to attract the enthusiastic attention of companies in the West from the late 1970s onwards.

Job redesign developments

In the 1980s, with the pressure from below receding and labour markets easing, management attention shifted to the need to compete in a changing and difficult product market environment. Japanese success diverted attention from 'de-alienating' the workers and towards finding some means to improve their performance, above all in terms of quality and flexibility. Enhancement of work experience and skill was often claimed as a by-product of this, or even as a means to achieve it in some cases, but job reform *per se* ceased to be the main impetus of change.

None the less, quite extensive claims were made that reductions in demarcation and extended task flexibility were underway in the 1980s. One study found that nine in ten companies were attempting such changes in 1985 (NEDO 1986), while an ACAS study two years later found that a quarter of companies claimed some success (ACAS 1988). However, other observers have commented that the evidence of major changes in work content, or of significant enskilling in work patterns for a large part of the UK workforce, is at best weak (Pollert 1988; Marginson 1989). The popularity of 'just-in-time' and other methods for ensuring that work effort was more continuous, together with other evidence on labour utilization in the 1980s, suggested that intensification of work might be more common than a genuine break with Taylorism (Elger 1990). The main counterclaims concern teamworking, which is examined more closely below.

Explicit attempts to reform work in a progressive or humanistic way appear to have been rare in the 1980s and 1990s. None are included in the examples of EI in the UK government's exhortatory publication, *People and Companies*, nor in its successor, *The Competitive Edge*, and in a 1985 survey only 3 per cent of companies reported undertaking 'job enlargement/enrichment schemes' (Baddon et al. 1989). Batstone, too, was moved to comment on the absence of individual work reorganization from the initiatives on EI reported by management in recent years (Batstone 1989: 107–8). This may well reflect the relative lack of success and durability of some of the more prominent job-enrichment experiments of the 1970s, and the decision to emulate Japanese practice and focus more on the work group or team.

The rise and fall of quality circles (QCs)

The idea of QCs is commonly attributed to the Japanese, though discussion groups generating suggestions for production improvement were known in the UK and elsewhere in the 1950s and earlier. The first QCs in Japan appeared in 1962, but by the late 1980s optimistic estimates suggested there were one million QCs there, with together about ten million participants.

In the UK, the late 1970s and early 1980s saw an explosion of management interest in QCs. Two surveys at the time found an incidence of 63 per cent (WIRS1 in 1980) and 55 per cent (CBI in 1981), respectively. There are strong signs that the popularity of these schemes was already in decline by the mid-1980s, two studies reporting 19 per cent incidence (Batstone 1984; and the Warwick multi-establishment firm study in 1985: see Marginson et al. 1988), and another just 10 per cent (Baddon et al. 1989). The latest CBI survey in 1989 reports 24 per cent incidence, a marked reduction from their own earlier figure. One researcher who carried out investigations of QCs in practice during the 1980s has described the last years of the decade as 'the tail end of the quality circle movement' from his own observations (Hill 1990).

What, then, happened to QCs? Why did they become so immensely popular – and then go into decline? The popularity of QCs arose from the range of benefits they were claimed to offer. It was said that they not only improved quality, but made cost savings, increased employee commitment and willingness to be flexible, and enhanced supervisory authority and leadership skills.

For this to be achieved, however, it was necessary to do far more than just call a group of employees together to talk over production problems. Research on attempts to put QCs into practice revealed a number of respects in which they were highly vulnerable. Key areas of common neglect included top management support, the need for a facilitator to be appointed to promote and sustain the programme, and getting unions onside (Collard and Dale 1989). There was often a failure to identify and bear the costs of management and employee time spent in running the system, let alone the training time and expenses involved if the participants were to be equipped with a sufficient understanding of the organization to make worthwhile contributions. Resistance was also intensified by middle management indifference or hostility, provoked by additional pressures on their time and often by a perceived challenge to their authority. A failure to follow up QC suggestions frequently resulted, and eventually many schemes lost momentum and faltered.

The decline of QCs may, therefore, be seen as occasioned by the eventual dominance of these problems over the reported advantages. Collard and Dale (1989) report that almost one-third of programmes had been entirely suspended within three years of start-up, while individual QC failures were typical in the others. Other studies have been somewhat more critical of QC achievements on balance (Hill 1986; Bradley and Hill 1987; Wilson 1989).

The cynical will see this as one of the familiar life-and-death cycles of fads and fashions in the world of EI, and view the decline as a general feature of EI rather than as due to anything specific about QCs. A more optimistic view would be that companies have simply moved on to more ambitious and integrated programmes. In particular, it has been argued that to confine quality or other job-related problem-solving to a specific institution is to misconceive the lessons of Japanese experience, which requires that quality-consciousness must suffuse the attitudes of the organization, not just be dealt with in isolation. This leads us to consider teamworking and total quality programmes.

Teamworking

Teamworking in its present guise has its origins in the practices of companies such as Komatsu, Hitachi, Nissan and especially Toyota, all of whom have operations in Britain. Teamworking is seen by its advocates as a vehicle for greater task flexibility and co-operation, as well as for extending the drive for quality. While the application of team principles has not been confined to manual or routine non-manual work, it has been particularly associated with other agendas of Japanized work restructuring such as cellworking, just-in-time (JIT) and so-called 'lean production' systems. Thus a recent survey of 23 automotive component manufacturers found that 19 of the companies operated teamworking and cellworking, and 15 JIT (IRS 1995a).

In fact, the focus on co-operative practices in working groups is not novel. Work group autonomy had been observed by US human-relations and UK socio-technical systems researchers decades before (and a proper history would trace them back to the emergence of industrial production itself), first as a 'problem' (the assertion of worker control from below), and later in the 1950s as a device tamed and harnessed to the goals of management. These notions were pursued especially vigorously in the Nordic countries, most famously in companies including Saab, Volvo and ABB, from the early 1970s. The closure in 1993 of some of the pioneering teamworking factories in Volvo has set off a heated debate on whether the more worker-controlled arrangements there were compromising (Womack et al. 1990) or enhancing (Sandberg 1993; Berggren 1993) efficiency and motivation relative to the Toyotan alternative.

Until relatively recently, companies experimenting with teamworking were few and far between (IDS 1988), but during the early 1990s teamworking became far more prevalent (IDS 1992; IRS 1994). Team sizes are typically seven to ten, though some are much larger. Task flexibility and job rotation is sometimes limited, partly by the sheer range of tasks and partly by the nature of the skills involved. Even with this caveat, the companies undertaking teamworking programmes tend to regard major training programmes as a necessary accompaniment.

There is also a tendency to remove or redefine the supervisory role and to appoint team leaders, both of which create potential dangers as well as savings. The Advisory, Conciliation and Arbitration Service (ACAS) launched a network of companies to share information on teamworking in 1993, and has identified a number of potential problems in the cases it has monitored. These include loss of senior management backing or direction, sometimes through a lack of awareness of possibilities beyond multi-skilling; reluctance of managers to hand over responsibilities to teams; and problems of negotiating changes, particularly when these may be difficult to anticipate, within existing industrial relations climates (ACAS 1993; IRS 1994).

As yet it is too soon to assess the merits and demerits of teamworking and to conclude whether it marks a significant advance on other group-orientated EI techniques. Claims of spectacular benefits abound, but this is nothing new in the EI game. An early study by Cross (1989) claimed that the average productivity improvement from a number of sources in the team activities was 20 per cent. Cross warns, however, that the production system often constrains the degree of autonomy that can be accorded to a team, and that adequate systems for training, rewards, responsibility and performance are all required for success. Gapper (1990) also cautions that management time saved in traditional supervision and control may well be reabsorbed by the need to give adequate support to individuals and groups. This is reportedly borne out by the Courtaulds Grafil case, where support time costs were said to be considerable (IRS 1990a); while in Digital it was claimed that a major workforce criticism focused on the failure of management to give sufficient time and attention to offering praise or information or to consult (IRS 1990b).

More controversial are the criticisms that 'empowerment' through modern teamworking systems is a sham, permitted only on strictly constrained management terms. Considerable worker resistance and disillusionment, occasioned by a primary concern with work intensification at all costs, is reported by some critics, especially in the US (Berggren 1993; Babson 1993; Fucini and Fucini 1990). Garrahan and Stewart (1992) develop the same arguments for Nissan in Washington, UK. Trade unions in Europe and the US for the most part remain suspicious that teamworking is chiefly camouflage for working harder and cutting jobs, and so is more directly shaped by management production priorities than by the union-influenced ID considerations which affected Scandinavian initiatives. From a managerial viewpoint at least, though, the balance of evidence thus far is more positive than for most other EI techniques.

Total quality management (TQM)

Once again, this approach is typically seen as a form of Japanization, but closer attention to history reveals that the Japanese innovation itself was an adaptation of ideas on quality management originating from the visits of two American consultants, Deming and Juran, in the late 1940s and early 1950s. Total quality management programmes derive from a growing belief in the 1980s that commercial success comes not simply from low cost competitiveness but from high and reliable quality, achieved with the associated welding of more stable and mutual relationships between suppliers and customers. This philosophy is seen as unrealizable without the commitment and customer-awareness of employees all the way through the organization, including that to 'internal' customers in the company who use a department's output. The stated aim in pursuit of this is to create a culture of 'continuous improvement'. Pioneers in the UK included Motorola and Xerox, but by the early 1990s quality initiatives were reported in three-quarters of UK companies (Economist Intelligence Unit 1992; IPM 1993), though full TQM probably constituted a minority of these (IPM 1993).

TQM typically purports to subsume QCs or teamwork arrangements into a more integrated approach, and references to EI and empowerment as both means and consequences of such programmes abound (Oakland 1989; Hill 1991; Grant et al. 1994). Yet the objectives of TQM also tend to be 'harder' than for some other programmes, emphasizing performance first and employee satisfaction or development afterwards. Moreover, the whole approach stresses change throughout the entire organizational system. The emphasis by all its gurus (whatever their differences) is on a top-down, management-driven process. As a result, a potential contradiction arises, whereby greater employee influence is declared and yet closely circumscribed to those immediate task-related decisions which do not challenge management control (Wilkinson et al. 1991, 1992; Kerfoot and Knights 1995). Some critics have thus concluded that TQM is in fact a system of management control masquerading as participation, tightening surveillance whilst offloading certain stressful responsibilities (Parker and Slaughter 1993; McArdle et al. 1995; Sewell and Wilkinson 1992).

Evidence on employee satisfaction with TQM-linked changes, meantime, remains fairly mixed.

Early reports of TQM in action were generally positive in their assessments (Hill 1990; IDS 1990a; Wilkinson et al. 1991), but subsequent evidence set the wheels of scepticism in motion. Similar pressures and potential problems to those identified above for other techniques persist. These include middle-management resistance, resilient departmental resistance to integration, a lack of sustained top management commitment, provocation of union resistance, and a failure to achieve the fundamental attitude shift, or 'culture change', generally felt to be essential (Wilkinson et al. 1992; IPM 1993; McCabe et al. 1994). There is also a problem that employee misgivings may be intensified by its frequent coincidence with job rationalization and cutbacks.

It is worthy of note, perhaps, that more recent shifts to business process re-engineering (BPR) have also seen employee involvement as a necessary consequence. However, BPR is far more emphatically management-driven than TQM, and also has far more direct and powerful probable consequences for imposing controls on employees. Thus, any doubts concerning the participative potential for TQM should be writ markedly larger for BPR.

Communications and Briefing Systems

Good communication has been accepted as a touchstone of the effective management of employee relations throughout the living memory of all today's managers. The classical Human Relations School developed an awareness of the importance of giving employees appropriate information to avoid rumour and to secure commitment. It was sometimes argued that management paid little more than lip service to genuine communication, however, and a CBI survey as late as the mid-1970s found that 80 per cent of employees felt that they were not kept informed of corporate developments (quoted in Townley 1989: 329).

Despite this, some companies have long used numerous communication methods to reach employees. ICI began their staff magazine almost as soon as the company was formed in 1927, for instance. Notice boards, newspapers, letters to employees, employee meetings addressed by management, suggestion schemes and numerous other channels were widespread by the 1970s and have continued to proliferate. By 1990, WIRS3 found only 9 per cent of establishments reporting no communication arrangements at all, with an average of 2.4 methods used per company (Millward et al. 1992: 166f), while just over half the companies responding to the CBI's 1989 survey claimed to have a formal communications policy.

Communication may be divided into two characteristic forms: written and oral (though the use of videos partly bridges this gap). Written communication can be shaped and controlled from the top, highly professional in presentation and cheap in terms of its demand on management time. It may not be a good way of getting employee attention, however, particularly in this era of 'junk mail'. According to one recent survey of 400 companies (Vista Communications 1989), management themselves rated notice boards and memos as relatively poor methods of communicating, yet used them more than any other medium.

More time-consuming approaches such as team briefing, employee opinion surveys, and appraisal and development systems were rated far more effective. On the other hand, most of these methods rely on oral communication and are time-consuming. One such – team briefing – saw the most rapid growth of all in the 1980s, and will be examined a little more closely in a moment.

In terms of objectives, communications policies will typically be directed at the ambient, attitudinal aspects of personnel policy, their content depending on whether the primary intent is, for example, to give information *per se*, to create business awareness, to generate a spirit of community, to promote involvement, or to ease the acceptance of change and draw forth ideas from employees. Ascertaining which need is greatest, and how to target it, is one of the key preparatory tasks for any communications policy.

Many companies have begun to provide employee reports, a parallel document to shareholder reports which provide information on the state of the company. Townley (1989) charts the increasing use of this method from the late 1970s, peaking at around three-fifths of surveyed organizations in the early 1980s (though the 1989 CBI survey suggests only 38 per cent were using this means of communication). All surveys confirm that this method is characteristic above all of larger companies.

Section 1 of the 1982 Employment Act requires that companies should make a statement in their annual reports detailing their policy and fresh initiatives in the preceding year on employee involvement. This in itself was expected to promote company action, including readiness to communicate with its own employees. Surveys of subsequent reporting have been carried out by the Department of Employment and the Institute of Personnel Management (IPM), with similar findings. They show that a minority of companies, again particularly the larger ones, complied with all aspects of the requirements, but that most early reports were either deficient or non-existent. Later surveys suggest a high incidence of replication of paragraphs from one year to the next, and so a rather token response by many companies; so the overall result of the legislation has been somewhat disappointing for advocates of involvement.

Team briefings

Briefing systems are not new in British business: 51 per cent of respondents to a 1975 British Institute of Management survey reported that they had such an arrangement (Townley 1989: 331). During the 1980s, however, a carefully formulated cascade briefing group system was promoted by the Industrial Society with considerable success: it proposed, for example, that presentations should be relevant to those receiving them, with only 30 per cent of information relating to wider corporate matters; and that groups should comprise typically from five to fifteen members.

Team briefing systems were consistently found in just under two-fifths of companies in a series of surveys from the mid-1980s (Baddon et al. 1989; WIRS2; Marginson et al. 1988; CBI 1990); more recent studies (ACAS 1991; Marginson et al. 1993; WIRS3) suggest that the proportion has increased to a half or more of companies using a method of this sort. By and large, companies report a high degree of satisfaction with their arrangements; the 1989 CBI survey, for instance, found that 2 per cent of establishments rated their scheme highly effective, 41 per cent effective, and only 29 per cent said it was ineffective or needed improving. However, as this has been the case with other techniques (such as QCs) there is a need for caution in taking such reports at face value.

Team briefing is claimed by its proponents to produce a number of benefits, including increased organizational commitment, avoidance of misunderstanding and 'Chinese whispers', promoting acceptance of change, increasing effort, and reinforcing management legitimacy through the process of information provision. As yet the vast majority of reports on the working of briefings are by managers involved or based almost entirely on management accounts, but one study by Marchington et al. (1989) reported three independently researched case studies, and provided a more balanced assessment.

The authors found that, while benefits were claimed for team briefings, they should not be exaggerated; that a number of difficulties could be identified; and that success depended on context to a significant extent. Briefings were in practice always likely to be seen as dispensable in times of pressure (such as the Christmas rush in a retail organization), and so timing could become irregular and undermine the commitment to hold meetings at all. Irregularity tended to reduce the credibility of the system with employees; and in any case, briefing by itself was unlikely to transform employee attitudes, let alone alter behaviour in ways contrary to their immediate interests. Management scepticism was a sure basis for sabotaging arrangements, and this played a major part in the problems experienced in the National Health Service location studied. Attempts to bypass or weaken the unions might be effective to some degree, but only if other factors were already sapping the union's hold on its members; and where the unions were strong and hostile, this was more likely to be to the detriment of the briefing system itself (a conclusion already familiar from the research on QCs reported above).

Subsequently, a more extensive programme of research (Marchington et al. 1992) reported that 77 per cent of employees in 25 companies felt that team briefings left their commitment to the organization unchanged (while 4 per cent felt it was actually reduced by the system). The system was publicly criticized as overly bureaucratic, liable to decay, and over-reliant on top-down communication only (Jack 1991; Goodhart 1992), though it was not without its defenders who argued that, divested of unrealistic expectations, it retained a bedrock value (Feldman 1993).

Two-way communication

Team briefings were designed as predominantly one-way communication systems. It is widely accepted, however, that employee commitment and involvement would be greater, and the climate of employee relations generally far more positive, if communication worked in both directions, offering employees a chance to express their views and be listened to.

While an attempt to introduce an element of upward flow in communication in team briefings themselves is one of the more notable changes observed in some organizations (IDS 1992), a number of methods may be employed to this end. These include attitude surveys, appraisal systems, open-door and 'speaking out' policies, suggestion schemes, and having senior executives 'walking the floor' to be seen and to listen. QCs and similar arrangements may also be aimed primarily at this objective, though, like suggestion schemes, they may also have a useful efficiency and cost-savings yield.

Two-way communication initiatives were significantly the most popular type of initiative reported by management in the WIRS3 survey (Millward et al. 1992; see also Marginson et al. 1993), with 13 per cent of managers saying that they had been introduced within the previous three years (though representatives typically report such initiatives only half as often, it should be noted). Once again large firms, and particularly those which were foreign-owned, were most likely to report such initiatives. 'Walking the floor' was reported by 65 per cent of companies in the 1989 CBI survey, while 19 per cent (65 per cent of large companies) indicated that they had employee attitude surveys or audits.

While the importance of this type of initiative is widely acknowledged and many companies have sought to move forward in listening as well as telling, the effectiveness of these schemes is again hard to judge and is likely to be heavily contingent on the general atmosphere of employee relations into which they are introduced. A climate of high trust is likely to be a prerequisite for open speaking from below, creating something of a Catch-22 situation; the problems of maintaining momentum in both directions are likely to be formidable.

Problems and lessons

A number of observations on challenges to communications practice in business, each with self-evident implications, may be identified. These include:

- managerial failure to specify the objectives (and the limits thereof) for any given scheme: an Industrial Society survey (1994) found that three-quarters of companies had no written policy on communication;
- loss of momentum after initial enthusiasm;
- too little information – or too much;
- too much 'tell and sell' by management, provoking employee mistrust of the reality of involvement, especially where most news is bad news and accompanied by calls for belt-tightening and restraint;
- attempts to undermine or circumvent a trade union backfire;
- failure to specify those responsible for communicating at all levels;
- lack of training of presenters and of recipients of information both in information handling and presentational skills;
- over-formality: the 1989 CBI survey found that typically informal employee–manager contact was regarded as more effective than any institutional system.

Consultative Arrangements

Joint consultation has been an established channel for employee participation for many decades, with a history stretching back into the nineteenth century and a period of massive popularity in the years immediately following the Second World War, when some surveys suggested that perhaps three-quarters of manufacturing companies had such bodies. During the 1960s, the conventional wisdom (echoed in the Donovan Report and elsewhere) was that consultation was withering, displaced by the growing momentum of shop steward organization and plant-level bargaining. The 1970s saw evidence of a revival, however, with many JCCs having shop stewards in the role of representatives. This led to arguments that consultation not only could co-exist with plant-level bargaining but that it could act as a lubricant for a constructive approach to it.

Available evidence suggests that JCCs survived the 1980s and into the 1990s. Two surveys in the mid-1980s (WIRS2; Baddon et al. 1989) both suggested that one in three companies had formal consultation machinery; WIRS3 suggested some decline, to 29 per cent incidence by 1990. As with most forms of involvement, incidence varies strongly in direct relation to company size, which probably explains why the 1989 CBI survey indicated that 47 per cent of their respondents had such a body, while Marginson et al. (1993) found 57 per cent incidence in their 1992 sample of large corporations, and IRS discovered two-fifths incidence from a survey of member organizations in 1995 (IRS 1995b). The evidence also confirms the prominence of union representation on JCCs; and though there are minor signs of a decline in this practice over the decade (see, for example, Joyce and Woods 1984; Millward and Stevens 1986: 145; Millward et al. 1992: 156–7), the 1989 CBI survey still found just 43 per cent of committees where unions appointed none of the members, and the WIRS3 survey found only 44 per cent.

Apart from these general consultative committees, on which we shall focus here, other similar bodies with more specific remits may exist: *ad hoc* bodies to deal with particular issues as they arise; health and safety committees; and productivity committees, to give examples. In Germany and indeed most other European countries, similar bodies, usually known as works councils, are established by statute or, occasionally (as in Sweden) by national union–employer agreement. The German legislation grants employees through the council a series of rights: to information, to be consulted, and on certain matters of particular direct relevance to employees, the right to co-determination (for example, on payment and recruitment systems, discipline, working hours and work study). In the UK there are no such obligations either to have a committee or to grant it any particular rights – and the likelihood that such a requirement could be one result of the European Commission's Social Charter has caused much bristling in UK managerial circles.

Where management defines objectives for consultation, these may take a number of forms, including:

- straightforward augmentation of communication channels;
- more active co-operation and support in meeting challenges to the organization;
- restricting the scope of the union and collective bargaining, or helping to exclude unions from the company altogether;
- enlisting the union into a more constructive relationship. One variant may seek to win over shop stewards, perhaps against the national union's wishes;
- offering token participation (it should be recalled that this remains a plausible and potentially valid tactic to head off challenges from a management viewpoint).

Clearly the form and allotted capacities of a JCC will be expected to vary to reflect these objectives. Though management may not be able to fashion the constitution and substance of JCC activity in complete freedom, it is normally the case that the initiative will lie primarily with them.

As with other forms of EI, reports on the working of JCCs are usually favourable. Applying our established need for caution in making a balanced assessment allows us to identify a number of possible outcomes, however. Success may entail achieving any of the above objectives, but three characteristic variants involve the attainment of active co-operation and support; the marginalization or exclusion of unions from employee representation; or the complementary operation of consultation and collective bargaining side by side.

On the other hand, there are also three plausible types of failure. In two, the committee has little impact on employee relations, either because it deals only with trivial issues (the 'tea, towels and toilets' syndrome), or because it remains powerless and so attracts little employee interest even when dealing with important matters. The third possibility involves a breakdown of the JCC, either because of the severity of the problems it attempts to deal with, or because of conflicting expectations from the two sides (typically, management seeks discussion and co-operation, while employees seek settlement of grievances and an element of bargaining and influence on important matters). This instability can, in exceptional cases, make labour–management relations worse than before the committee was established.

One review of independent case studies of JCCs (Ramsay 1990) found that problems tended to prevail, in particular triviality and powerlessness, leaving the JCC with a marginal role in labour–management relations. Others are more optimistic (see, for example, Marchington 1987; IRS 1995b), seeing complementary and co-operative outcomes as more probable. It is clear, none the less, that difficulties are not uncommon. Judgements on the operation of works councils in Europe vary also, but frequently identify similar problems of marginality. At the best, schemes may need regular review and revamping if vitality is to be maintained. A number of other comments on approaches to consultation can be added, assuming here that the intention is not simply to make a token concession:

- consultation needs to be genuinely undertaken in advance of decisions being settled, or the exercise may be seen as manipulative;
- an ambitious remit is needed to ensure that the JCC does not lose momentum;
- resourcing is important, including proper research and secretarial backing for employee representatives;
- full and effective reporting back to constituents is necessary if the JCC is not to become detached from and irrelevant to most employees;
- training of members on both sides is again a necessity;
- management representation must be sufficiently senior to carry weight, able to put managerial views authoritatively, and to convince employee representatives that the company takes the process seriously;
- action on agreed proposals should be swift, avoiding the classic weak response of the chairperson who agrees to 'look into things'; rejection of JCC ideas or proposals should not be without good reason, and should be seen to be so;
- it is wise to keep the union informed even if it is not directly involved in the JCC – unless the intention is openly to sideline them, which strategy carries heavy risks.

Financial Participation (FP)

The startling rise in popularity of financial participation (FP) in its various forms since the late 1970s has sometimes obscured the fact that it is not a new idea. The Involvement and Participation Association (as it is now called) was in fact founded in 1884, primarily to promote such schemes amongst business, and the idea goes back at least to the early part of the nineteenth century. Karl Marx can be seen in 1858 strenuously attacking the idea as a pernicious trick played by employers on their labourers (a view which prevailed in the labour movement well into the twentieth century, and has not altogether vanished today).

FP takes two chief forms: employee share ownership (ESO), in which employees gain a direct stake in (usually) the company they work for; and profit sharing (PS), which provides a cash bonus from the revenue surplus. While these schemes are often regarded chiefly as aspects of remuneration (and, in the case of executive share schemes, this may well be a true reflection of their role), research shows that for most managements the main objectives are concerned with involvement, commitment and related attitudinal effects (Baddon et al. 1989).

FP, particularly ESO, has been massively stimulated by UK government encouragement and tax incentives since 1978. Special relief was initially given to schemes for all employees which placed shares donated by the company into a trust for seven (later five) years: that is, Approved Deferred Share Trust (ADST) schemes; by February 1995 there were 1,161 such schemes approved by the Inland Revenue. In 1980 tax relief was also provided for schemes in which employees made a savings commitment over the years, at the end of which they could take shares at the offer price made initially, or, if preferable, the lump sum of savings plus interest: these were Save As You Earn (SAYE) schemes, of which 1,410 had been approved by February 1995. It should be noted that the total number of approved schemes exaggerates current take-up somewhat, since some of the registered schemes have ceased to operate in each of these categories (IDS 1993) – an estimated 244 ADST schemes were thought to be 'dead' by March 1994, for instance (IDS 1995).

In 1984 this special tax relief status was extended to discretionary or executive schemes, and these ironically proved particularly popular with managements: 6,209 schemes had received approval by February 1995. While most of these schemes were targeted on upper management, a few were extended to larger parts of the workforce, notably in the Asda supermarket group. However, the Greenbury Committee on executive remuneration, which reported in July 1995, was critical of the tax holiday they felt executives gained when receiving share options under these schemes, and recommended that they be subject to income tax rather than capital gains tax, a recommendation on which the Chancellor immediately acted. When it emerged that the chief sufferers would be those ordinary employees covered by such schemes (who would rarely be affected by capital gains thresholds, unlike those in senior management), the Greenbury Committee called its recommendation 'a mistake', and the Chancellor was forced to restrict his action to future share options only. This incident was notable for the publicity heat generated by the ESO issue, but also for the near-silence on the far wider employee membership of the alternative schemes (which continued to receive relief as before).

Most recently, in the 1989 Finance Act, Employee Share Ownership Plans (ESOPs) where granted similar tax relief. In these, all shares are retained in a trust and cannot be sold outside the company. ESOPs have largely been activated in management or employee buyouts to date; leaving aside the many schemes which embrace only senior executives, the number of all-employee schemes had probably just stretched into three figures by 1994 (IDS 1994b). Most are small, though they have recently been joined by two sizable employee buyouts of bus companies in South Yorkshire and Manchester (Woodcock 1993).

Other share option schemes exist which, for various reasons, are not eligible for tax relief. The largest obstacles are for smaller, unquoted companies, especially when they wish to avoid any danger of ownership and control slipping out of management hands; for these companies, ESOPs may provide an alternative route (ESOP Centre 1994), though this is not yet widely used.

Profit-sharing schemes that make a cash payment are also widespread in the UK. Few of these are at present eligible for any tax relief, the exceptions being the Profit Related Pay arrangements approved under the terms laid down by the 1987 Finance Act, with up to one-fifth of pay being variable in a specified relationship to company profits. Many employers initially objected to the restrictive definitions in the legislation, preferring for instance to vary wages with what they see as a more relevant, value-added measure of employee performance, and in the first three years the idea attracted little attention. However, with modifications in the regulations and a doubling of tax relief after 1991, interest in PRP did pick up after a slow start (Smith 1993; IDS 1990c, 1994a). The number of employees covered quadrupled to just under one million in 4,149 registered schemes in the two years to the end of 1992, and doubled once more by the end of 1994 to 8,935 schemes covering 2.4 million employees. One view was that some companies were shifting to the more immediate tax-free bonuses for employees which PRP allowed, and so away from the share trusts which required a long wait (IDS 1995).

Survey information confirms that a large proportion of the workforce in the UK are covered by at least one form of financial participation.

Two major surveys taken in the mid-1980s confirm this. The Glasgow/Strathclyde study (Baddon et al. 1989) found that 65 per cent of all respondent companies had some kind of scheme. The most popular form was cash-based profit-sharing (confirmed by the CBI's 1989 survey). This was followed by executive options. Most of the remaining schemes were one of the approved Inland Revenue types (ADST or SAYE), though other share-based schemes still survived in significant numbers. This pattern is roughly confirmed by the Department of Employment survey (Smith 1986; Poole 1989), though the overall incidence of schemes (which are more restrictively defined) is put lower, at 31 per cent of companies. One in five companies in this survey operated all-employee schemes. In interpreting all these figures, it should be noted that it is quite common, in many large companies especially, to operate more than one type of scheme. WIRS3 reported 32 per cent incidence for share-based schemes, and 55 per cent of firms with any type of financial participation (after including the 40 per cent with cash-based payments). Inland Revenue figures suggest that around $3/4$ million employees were allocated shares under ADST plans annually in the early 1990s, over $1/2$ million under SAYE schemes by 1992. Overall, 3.1 million employees and directors were thought to have received shares or options by 1993 (IDS 1995).

Both surveys confirm that publicly quoted, larger companies were markedly more likely than smaller ones to operate share schemes (unless they were foreign-owned: this created other obvious problems for share distribution), but in contrast, cash-based schemes were found not to vary significantly in incidence by size of organization. In short, cash schemes remain more feasible and manageable for small business than share schemes, despite the inducements offered for the latter.

Objectives

As we noted above, attitudinal change is the main objective expressed by managers as their reason for promoting financial participation. Incentive aims may be indicated, but it is generally accepted that schemes of this sort are too weakly linked to employee performance and too far from employee control to have a meaningful effect on behaviour in any direct way. Cash-based schemes may have a greater role in this respect than share schemes.

Other aims have been more prominent, particularly in the past. Anti-unionism was an explicit intention of many of the schemes in the late nineteenth and early twentieth centuries in the UK. While some employers have still sought to use schemes as a disincentive to strike, with penalties built in to the cash or share distribution in the event of industrial action (for example, Hotpoint, Southern Newspapers, British Telecom), this is no longer a common feature, and most companies are at pains to emphasize that their schemes have nothing to do with industrial relations (especially as the last thing they want is for them to become subject to collective bargaining).

The promotion of employee ownership in itself is an important facet of Conservative Party political philosophy but does not seem to be prominent in employer circles. The idea of co-partnership developed in some paternalistic business circles from the late nineteenth century continues to embrace the idea of employees sharing in the benefits of successful business as a means to make society more just. Companies like the John Lewis Partnership or Scott Bader have gone so far as to put all ownership into an employee trust in pursuit of this aim, but for most managements the call of such an ideology is less strong.

Employee influence over business is also sometimes represented as a goal of financial participation. By and large, however, the link is at most a weak one, and the spheres of sharing in profits and sharing in decisions are seen by both sides as unconnected. Companies operating financial participation schemes are more likely to operate other forms of involvement too (Baddon et al. 1989; Poole 1988), but the link is generally rather one of stylistic inclination (that is, managements that see a need for one are also favourable towards experimenting with the other) than of conscious and connected strategy.

In pursuit of a general atmosphere of employee trust, loyalty, commitment, identity and belonging, it appears that all-employee share schemes have a stronger logic than cash-based ones. Arguably an ADST type of scheme, in which the company gives shares, will be most effective. On the other hand, if enhanced business awareness is the primary intention, an SAYE scheme involving employees' own funds might be expected to generate a stronger sense of linked prosperity. The combination of both types of scheme clearly makes a fair amount of sense. However, it should be remembered that take-up rates on SAYE schemes run at around 20 per cent (IDS 1990b; Baddon et al. 1989), with manual workers typically falling well below the average (Baddon et al. 1989: 64; Ramsay et al. 1990), so there may be some danger of divisions emerging.

Performance

The general view of managements operating financial participation schemes is, as with other types of involvement, typically favourable

(Baddon et al. 1989; Jenkins and Poole 1990; CBI 1990). Many of the claims are based on general impressions and faith rather than evidence (which is particularly hard to generate for the objectives we have identified), and take a rather vague and hopeful rather than definite form, however. There is clear evidence, moreover, that in practice financial participation, whether share- or cash-based, may have a rather indirect and dilute influence on employee attitudes.

Cash schemes, in particular, run the risk of being seen as a fancy (though not unwelcome) handout, fairly quickly taken for granted, rather than becoming a source of identification and commitment. Share schemes ensure a longer-term link, especially if the five-year trust minimum for Inland Revenue schemes is operative, and may at least ensure some curiosity about business performance through the medium of share price performance.

This conclusion appears to be contradicted by several studies showing that most employees approve strongly of share schemes, and sizable proportions express the view that they make people work harder, give them greater awareness of management problems, make them more cost conscious, and so forth (see Bell and Hanson 1984, 1987; Fogarty and White 1988; Jenkins and Poole 1990; Baddon et al. 1989). Not only are these findings some way from describing actual behaviour, however, but they also leave out results which indicate less-positive views of such schemes (see Ramsay et al. 1986, for a commentary). Thus more respondents agree than disagree that financial participation is 'just another bonus', and that 'there are better ways of improving benefits', while there is strong agreement that it has nothing to do with worker participation (Baddon et al. 1989; Fogarty and White 1988). Moreover, a detailed study of attitudes both to general issues and to specific perceptions of their employers found that participants and non-participants in SAYE schemes differed only marginally in their outlook (Ramsay et al. 1990). The chief distinguishing feature of the two groups was whether or not they had had money to take up the savings option in the first place.

Proponents of ESO have often expressed concern at the legislation which extends tax relief to executive schemes, seeing these as more likely to accentuate than attenuate the 'us-and-them' divisions at work. Recent developments suggest that this fear is increasingly justified, particularly when large increases in rewards to top executives through share options are publicized. While this is especially true in the privatized utilities in the UK, it is not confined there. In May 1995, employee and other small shareholders in British Gas rebelled *en masse* at the annual shareholders' meeting against executive rewards, though they were formally outvoted by proxy votes exercised by large City institutions. At the same time, strikers in Barclays Bank were reported to be protesting at a low pay-increase offer and heavy staff job losses at a time that coincided with huge profit bonuses for executives which dwarfed profit-sharing bonuses for staff. Clearly, emphasizing selective incentives from financial participation can backfire and damage the quest for unity of purpose which is also so eagerly sought. The débâcle over the 1995 Greenbury Committee Report (see above) further demonstrates the heat in this debate, and also the difficulties in achieving an acceptable solution.

Observations

The findings reported above suggest a number of conclusions concerning financial participation schemes:

*   careful consideration needs to be given to the objectives sought in selecting schemes. Those which maximize incentive and which are discriminating between groups or individuals may well be at odds with those which stress shared identity and co-operation, for instance;
*   a grace-and-favour system that makes payments at management discretion will not only *not* attract tax relief to become a more efficient form of remuneration, but may also generate a sense of arbitrary management decisions, so working contrary to the intended effect;
*   financial participation 'on the cheap' will be most likely to get dismissed as such. But even considerable payouts may come to be seen as welcome bonuses, yet have little meaning beyond this;
*   financial participation is unlikely to be particularly effective in isolation. It may have a stronger effect on attitudes if it is part of a wider, coherent approach to employee involvement than in isolation;
*   overall, perhaps not too much should be expected from an approach which remains somewhat remote from employees' performance and effort, or from their everyday experience.

Concluding Remarks: Lessons and Strategies

Challenging rhetoric

To begin this final section, we should return to the question of words and underlying meanings. The problems which popular but loosely used terminology create for analysis in the area of EI are rife in writings on commitment and empowerment. Both these terms have been included in the title to this chapter because of their currency at the present time: they are to be found liberally daubed over the pages of the fashion-driven and often over-hyped literature which characterizes this field of management. Yet closer scrutiny reveals both ideas as ill-defined and problematical. In particular, both gain manageable coherence only within a unitarist frame of reference, where interests between employee and organization are shared. They also prove, on closer inspection, to be closely intertwined, particularly through contemporary visions of EI.

Scrutiny of the concept of *commitment* reveals a conceptual miasma (Mowday et al. 1982; Reichers 1985; Becker 1992; Meyer and Allen 1991; Iles et al. 1990; Coopey and Hartley 1991). This embodies confusion of attitudinal and behavioural conceptions; between employment, job, career, occupational and organizational commitment; between organizational commitment for affective, normative and calculative/need reasons (often called 'continuance commitment'); and commitment and identification focused at different levels or in different sub-cultures of the organization (work group, department, workplace, company, union, and so on). Not surprisingly, attempts to measure commitment, let alone to assess its effects on other variables (such as absenteeism, labour turnover or work performance), have proved to be plagued with confusion and have revealed rather weak relationships with measures of managerially desired outcomes (Guest 1992).

By and large, conceptions of commitment which fit the aspirations of management HRM policy emphasize a vaguely defined version of organizational commitment, entailing a combination of affective attachment to the organization and internalization of 'its' goals (that is, those defined by top management). Modern orthodoxy in motivation theory (Walton 1985; Lawler 1986) asserts a virtuous circle: between establishing work teams which are given greater capacity to take responsible decisions, more information, and firmer job security assurances on the one hand; and high performance, cohesive and commitment-based relations on the other. Walton's (1985) modern classic paper refers to this as a shift from 'control' to 'commitment', but as the latter system entails vesting greater self-determination, responsibility and trust in all employees, it conforms closely with most definitions of *empowerment*.

Turning our attention to this catch-phrase, we find that it, too, is bedevilled by nebulous or absent definition (Cunningham et al. 1996; Lashley and McGoldrick 1994). 'It is an environment where people want to be responsible and take action', offer Scott and Jaffe (1991: 17), while Brown and Brown (1994: 19) define the process of empowering as 'The reorientation of all these forces, values and beliefs [which determine human behaviour] so that they support and liberate the individual, rather than diminish their range of thought and action.'

Yet despite such assertions as those which claim empowerment is 'a fundamentally different way of working together' (Scott and Jaffe 1991: 14), and 'quite different from the traditional notion of control' (ibid.: 17), we find a far less radical and more constrained reality peeking out from the foliage of effusive proclamation. Scott and Jaffe add: 'in any organisation some things need to be tightly controlled, while other areas of work can be left to individual freedom and initiative' (ibid.); while Brown and Brown (1994: 20) tell us: 'Liberated organisations will continue to have decision-making structures, and will continue to enforce obedience to the general will.' Very quickly in practice it becomes apparent that this is managerial discretion reformulated; the 'general' will is dictated by objectives which top management will continue to define and adjudicate, while empowerment is intended to release active employee engagement only so long as it falls within the parameters for which it was selected as a strategy. In fact, this antithesis of control wavers and transmogrifies: 'In an empowered workplace, paradoxically, people feel *both* freedom and control', suggest Scott and Jaffe (1991: 18), perhaps offering greater insight than they realize. More explicitly, Brown and Brown (1994: 49) tell us, more bluntly, that: 'The core purpose of the organisational process is control', the intended difference being that cultural shaping of a sense of common purpose (that is to say, commitment in its vague sense, to complete the circle) replaces the direct hierarchical exercise of control.

Leaving aside this scepticism concerning the faddish hype in most accounts of empowerment, observation suggests that in practice the degree of control granted to employees by management is highly constrained. Restricted parameters are reported in the studies by Cunningham et al. (1996) and, for the hospitality industry, by Lashley and McGoldrick (1994), often proving to be limited in practice to suggestion schemes, financial participation, or a margin of control over health and safety problem identification, for instance. However, the main expression of empowerment is usually taken to be teamworking, the performance of which was reviewed earlier.

The sense of oversell which comes through from a closer examination of 'commitment' and 'empowerment' is laced also with a strong feeling of *déjà vu*. The exaggerated claims for these methods echo those from the neo-human relations movement of the 1950s and 1960s, or the Quality of Working Life proposals of the 1970s; but then, the theories of motivation and of employee relations behind them, and even the content of the proposed changes, also show remarkably little development from their forebears.

The danger of such faddism and hype will be apparent. It leads to disillusionment with most attempts to apply the changes; but possibly worse still, the general public image of success can lead to a local blame culture: who else could be responsible for failure but employees/managers locally, when everyone else seemingly thrives on these techniques? Thus rhetoric displaces strategy, and 'strategy' itself becomes part of the rhetoric. The danger is that most employees (and many managers) will come to read 'lip-service' where top management promise their own 'commitment' to genuine change.

Practical lessons

It seems better to attend to the less-dramatic but potentially more-effective recognition of the problems of EI identified in this chapter. A number of issues have arisen repeatedly with regard to different approaches to EI, and emerge as broader guidelines for the operation of schemes:

- management commitment should run further than just initiation; many schemes can be costly in management time if they are to be properly run;
- support for EI must be ensured throughout the management system, in preparation for any initiative; one repeated source of failure is lack of support below the top level, especially where (as with workshop or office task-based or briefing schemes) middle- and lower-level managers are pivotal to the implementation of the scheme;
- proper advance consideration of objectives is a necessary preparation for a convincing approach which avoids potential confusion or conflict between schemes;
- training of all involved, both management and participants, is an essential investment, partly to show commitment, and partly to ensure competence rather than disillusionment;
- adequate and impartial monitoring of schemes is also essential wherever possible, and against measuring sticks set by specified objectives, to avoid the prevalence of 'professions of faith' and a public relations image of performance;
- problems and shortcomings are not exceptional but typical of all forms of EI. The mistake (all too common) is to be misled by the prevalence of public relations accounts into believing in panaceas. In particular, the impact of most schemes on employee attitudes and behaviour may be far less profound, and even less permanent, than is usually supposed;
- attempts to bypass or undermine established trade unions by means of EI

schemes are likely to fail, and may even backfire and founder on union hostility. In non-union companies this danger recedes, but this does not erase the other problems of sustaining significant changes in employee responses.

Table 11.1 charted the range of possible objectives for EI. Specific objectives such as incentives to greater efforts and efficiency, co-operation in achieving change and flexibility, or the pursuit of the ever-more-prominent goal of quality, may all find voice in different schemes. The objective of achieving employee commitment (appropriately clarified) and related shifts in attitudes figures most prominently in the profile of management priorities in establishing involvement schemes, however. Other benefits are likely to flow more indirectly from the hoped-for change in the attitude climate in the enterprise.

Strategy in EI

But what of the strategic aspect of EI policy? The requirement for 'strategy' in business has become almost axiomatic. In its pursuit, an integration of objectives and planned action is expected throughout the organization: human resource strategy must be an integral part of business strategy, with labour utilization approaches reflecting production and marketing priorities, for instance. Employee involvement in turn must fit with HRM strategy. More than this, in most 'progressive' management thinking it is accepted (outwardly at least) that involvement is one key to the sort of workforce performance that is essential for achieving a competitive edge.

Within the sphere of EI itself, this requires that various types of scheme are not merely initiated in an *ad hoc* and disconnected manner, but are part of a coherent and linked programme of involvement. It may well be thought that financial participation schemes will only have an impact where they form part of a strategy of EI that includes other, more direct forms of engaging employee support, for instance. Similarly, evidence suggests that the success of Japanese methods is rooted not in any one technique but in their mutual reinforcement within a consistent set of policies.

Research on strategy in HRM is relatively recent, but such as it is, it suggests that claims to be strategic are more often image than reality. While many large companies in particular operate a battery of EI schemes, connected planning of different initiatives with reference to a guiding philosophy, tied further to other elements of business strategy, was found in one study to be a rarity (Baddon et al. 1989:

ch. 5), a view confirmed privately by most seasoned observers of the business community. Whether this will change in the remainder of the century remains to be seen. None the less, EI has become an important element in many companies' HRM strategies. The assessments in this chapter suggest that it should be seen as a range of innovation options, but that these should not be regarded as a panacea for all organizational ills.

However, the future does promise significant changes on the EI front. There are signs that change is being impelled by another shift of climate: the effects of the 'social dimension' of initiatives in the European Union, particularly since the ratification of the Maastricht Treaty in November 1993. The Social Charter proposes a series of employee rights, including initiatives on information, participation and consultation. This approach runs counter to that prevailing in the UK and in government policy throughout the 1980s and early 1990s, which emphasized involvement in forms and degrees determined by management. Yet participation was described by the former President of the EU, Jacques Delors, as the most important element of the Social Charter. Legislation for European Works Councils, which will impact on many large UK firms despite the UK opt-out, has already been passed and will come into force from September 1996.

This and other changes (including the partial resurgence and regrouping of the unions on new platforms, and the possibility of political change) may create fresh pressure from below in the traditions of the industrial democracy debate of the 1970s. The complication of thinking on employee participation is potentially considerable; it certainly implies that strategic thinking can no longer proceed as if employees themselves had no part in shaping it.

References

Advisory, Conciliation and Arbitration Service (ACAS) 1988: *Labour Flexibility in Britain: the 1987 ACAS Survey*. London: ACAS.

Advisory, Conciliation and Arbitration Service (ACAS) 1993: Issues in reinforcing and developing teamworking: interim report of the MOPS research and development project. *QWL*, Winter 1993–4, London: ACAS.

Babson, S. 1993: Lean or mean: the MIT model and lean production at Mazda. *Labor Studies Journal*, 18(2), 3–24.

Baddon, L., Hunter, L.C., Hyman, J., Leopold, J. and Ramsay, R. 1989: *People's Capitalism: a critical analysis of profit sharing and employee share ownership*. London: Routledge.

Batstone, E. 1984: *Working Order*. Oxford: Blackwell.

Batstone, E. 1989: New forms of work organization in Britain. In P. Grootings et al. (eds), *New Forms of Work Organization in Europe*, New Brunswick, N.J.: Transaction Press.

Becker, T.E. 1992: Foci and bases of commitment: are they distinctions worth making? *Academy of Management Journal*, 35(1), 232–44.

Bell, D.W. and Hanson, C. 1984: *Profit-sharing and Employee Share-holding Attitude Survey*. London: Industrial Participation Association.

Bell, D.W. and Hanson, C. 1987: *Profit-sharing and Profitability*. London: Kogan Page.

Berggren, C. 1993: Lean production: the end of history? *Work, Employment and Society*, June, 163–88.

Bradley, K. and Hill, S. 1987: Quality circles and managerial interests. *Industrial Relations*, 26(1), 68–82.

Brown, R. and Brown, M. 1994: *Empowered!: a practical guide to leadership in the liberated organisation*. London: Nicholas Brealey.

Collard, R. and Dale, B. 1989: Quality circles. In K. Sisson (ed.), *Personnel Management in Britain*, Oxford: Blackwell.

Confederation of British Industry (CBI) 1990: *Employee Involvement: shaping the future for business* (study by KPMG Peat Marwick Management Consultants). London: CBI.

Coopey, J. and Hartley, J. 1991: Reconsidering the case for organisational commitment. *Human Resource Management Journal*, 1(3), 18–32.

Cross, M. 1989: Implementing a teamwork philosophy within an existing site. Paper to City University Business School, London, conference on *Teamwork*, October; summarized in *IRS Employment Trends*, 451, 7 November 1989.

Cunningham, I., Hyman, J. and Baldry, C. 1996: Empowerment: the power to do what? *Industrial Relations Journal*, 27(2).

Daniel, W.W. and Millward, N. 1983: *Workplace Industrial Relations in Britain* (WIRS1). London: Heinemann.

Department of Employment 1987: Involving the staff. *Employment Gazette*, March.

Department of Employment 1988: Employee involvement. *Employment Gazette*, October.

Department of Employment 1989: *People and Companies*. London: HMSO.

Department of Employment 1994: *The Competitive Edge: employee involvement in Britain*. London: Employment Department.

Economist Intelligence Unit 1992: *Making Quality Work: lessons from Europe's leading companies*. London: EIU.

Edwards, P. 1987: *Managing the Factory*. Oxford: Blackwell.

Elger, A. 1990: Technical innovation and work reorganisation in British manufacturing in the 1980s: continuity, intensification or transformation? *Work, Employment and Society*, special issue, May.

ESOP Centre 1994: *Non-quoted Companies with ESOPs: 1994 Survey*. London: ESOPC (cited in *IRS Employment Bulletin*, 570, October 1994).

Feldman, D. 1993: Team briefing: kill or cure? *Industrial Society Briefing Plus*, February, 3–4.

Fogarty, M. and White, M. 1988: *Share Schemes: as workers see them*. London: Policy Studies Institute.

Fucini, J. and Fucini, S. 1990: *Working for the Japanese*. New York: Free Press.

Gapper, J. 1990: At the end of the honeymoon . . . *The Financial Times*, 10 January.

Garrahan, P. and Stewart, P. 1992: *The Nissan Enigma*. London: Mansell.

Goodhart, D. 1992: Team briefing has 'little effect on commitment'. *The Financial Times*, 27 July.

Grant, R.M., Shan, R. and Krishnan, R. 1994: TQM's challenge to management theory and practice. *Sloan Management Review*, Winter, 25–35.

Guest, D. 1992: Employee commitment and control. In J.F. Hartley and G.M. Stephenson (eds), *Employment Relations*, Oxford: Blackwell, pp. 111–35.

Hibbett, A. 1991: Employee involvement: a recent survey. *Employment Gazette*, December, 659–64.

Hill, F.M. 1986: Quality circles in the UK: a longitudinal study. *Personnel Review*, 15(3), 25–34.

Hill, S. 1990: Total quality management and new employee relations. Paper to conference on *Flexibilization, Deregulation and Internationalization*, Vienna, 15–16 March, mimeo.

Hill, S. 1991: Why quality circles failed but total quality management might succeed. *British Journal of Industrial Relations*, 29, 541–68.

Iles, P., Mabey, C. and Robertson, I. 1990: HRM practices and employee commitment: possibilities, pitfalls and paradoxes. *British Journal of Management*, 1, 147–57.

Income Data Services (IDS) 1987: *PRP and Profit Sharing*, Study no. 397, April. London: IDS.

Income Data Services (IDS) 1988: *Teamworking*, Study no. 419, October. London: IDS.

Income Data Services (IDS) 1990a: *Total Quality Management*, Study no. 457, May. London: IDS.

Income Data Services (IDS) 1990b: *Profit Sharing and Share Options*, Study no. 468, October. London: IDS.

Income Data Services (IDS) 1990c: *Profit-related Pay*, Study no. 471, December. London: IDS.

Income Data Services (IDS) 1992: *Teamworking*, Study no. 516, October. London: IDS.

Income Data Services (IDS) 1993: *Profit-sharing and Share Options*, Study no. 539, October. London: IDS.

Income Data Services (IDS) 1994a: *Profit-related Pay*, Study no. 564, October. London: IDS.

Income Data Services (IDS) 1994b: *Employee Share Ownership Plans*, Study no. 568, December. London: IDS.

Income Data Services (IDS) 1995: *Profit-sharing and Share Options*, Study no. 583, August. London: IDS.

Industrial Relations Services (IRS) 1990a: Improvement through problem-solving groups at Courtaulds Grafil. *IRS Employment Trends*, no. 470, 4–6.

Industrial Relations Services (IRS) 1990b: Change to cell-based working, multi-skilling and teamworking at Digital Equipment VLSI. *IRS Employment Trends*, no. 475, 5–8.

Industrial Relations Services (IRS) 1993: Employee involvement: the current state of play. *IRS Employment Trends*, no. 545, 3–11.

Industrial Relations Services (IRS) 1994: ACAS and Tavistock aim to develop teamworking in manufacturing. *IRS Employment Trends*, no. 566, 12–15.

Industrial Relations Services (IRS) 1995a: Lean suppliers to lean producers, 1: Changes in working practices. *IRS Employment Trends*, no. 583, 3–9.

Industrial Relations Services (IRS) 1995b: Employee representation arrangements, 2: Company councils. *IRS Employment Trends*, no. 590, 9–16.

Industrial Society 1994: *Managing Best Practice: employee communications*. London: Industrial Society; cited in *IRS Employment Trends*, no. 560.

Institute of Personnel Management (IPM) 1993: *Quality: people management matters*. London: IPM.

Jack, A. 1991: When team briefings tell only half the story. *The Financial Times*, 19 July.

Jenkins, G. and Poole, M. 1990: *The Impact of Economic Democracy*. London: Routledge.

Joyce, P. and Woods, A. 1984: Joint consultation in Britain: results of a survey during the recession. *Employee Relations*, 6(3), 2–7.

Kerfoot, D. and Knights, D. 1995: Empowering the 'quality worker'? The seduction and contradiction of the total quality phenomenon. In A. Wilkinson and H. Wilmott (eds), *Making Quality Critical*. London: Routledge, pp. 219–39.

Lashley, C. and McGoldrick, J. 1994: The limits of empowerment: a critical assessment of human resource strategy for hospitality operations. *Empowerment in Organizations*, 2(3), 25–38.

Lawler, E.E. 1986: *High-involvement Management*. San Francisco, Cal.: Jossey-Bass.

MacInnes, J. 1987: *Thatcherism at Work*. Milton Keynes, Bucks.: Open University Press.

MacInnes, J. 1988: New technology in Scotbank. In R. Hyman and W. Streeck (eds), *New Technology and Industrial Relations*, Oxford: Blackwell.

Marchington, M. 1987: A review and critique of recent research into joint consultation. *British Journal of Industrial Relations*, 25(3), 339–52.

Marchington, M., Parker, P. and Prestwich, A. 1989: Problems with team briefing in practice. *Employee Relations*, 11(4), 21–30.

Marginson, P. 1989: Employment flexibility in large companies: change and continuity. *Industrial Relations Journal*, 20(2), 101–9.

Marginson, P., Edwards, P.K., Martin, R., Purcell, J. and Sisson, K. 1988:

Beyond the Workplace: managing industrial relations in the multi-establishment enterprise. Oxford: Blackwell.

Marginson, P., Armstrong, P., Edwards, P. and Purcell, J. (with Hubbard, N.) 1993: *The Control of Industrial Relations in Large Companies: an initial analysis of the Second Company-level Industrial Relations Survey,* Warwick Papers in Industrial Relations no. 45. Coventry: IRRU, University of Warwick.

McArdle, L., Rowlinson, M., Procter, S., Hassard, J. and Forrester, P. 1995: Total quality management and participation: employee empowerment, or the enhancement of exploitation? In A. Wilkinson and H. Wilmott (eds), *Making Quality Critical,* London: Routledge, pp. 156–72.

McCabe, D. with Knights, D. and Wilkinson, A. 1994: *Quality Initiatives in the Financial Services.* Manchester: Financial Services Research Centre, University of Manchester Institute of Science and Technology.

Meyer, J.P. and Allen, N.J. 1991: A three-component conceptualization of organizational commitment. *Human Resource Management Review,* 1(1), 61–89.

Millward, N. and Stevens, M. 1986: *British Workplace Industrial Relations Survey, 1980–84* (WIRS2). Aldershot, Hants.: Gower.

Millward, N., Stevens, M., Smart, D. and Hawes, W.R. 1992: *Workplace Industrial Relations in Transition* (WIRS3). Aldershot, Hants.: Dartmouth.

Mowday, R., Porter, L. and Steers, R. 1982: *Employee–Organization Linkages: the psychology of commitment, absenteeism and turnover.* New York: Academic Press.

National Economic Development Office (NEDO) 1986: *Changing Working Patterns: how companies achieve flexibility to meet new needs,* report by the Institute for Manpower Studies for the National Economic Development Office in association with the Department of Employment. London: NEDO.

Oakland, J. 1989: *Total Quality Management.* London: Heinemann.

Parker, M. and Slaughter, J. 1993: Should the labour movement buy TQM?. *Journal of Organisational Change Management,* 6(4), 43–56.

Pollert, A. 1988: The 'flexible firm': fixation or fact?. *Work, Employment and Society,* 2(3), 281–316.

Poole, M. 1988: Factors affecting the development of employee financial participation in contemporary Britain: evidence from a national survey. *British Journal of Industrial Relations,* XXVI(1), 21–36.

Poole, M. 1989: *The Origins of Economic Democracy: profit-sharing and employee-shareholding schemes.* London: Routledge.

Ramsay, H. 1990: *The Joint Consultation Debate: soft soap and hard cases,* Discussion Paper no. 17. Glasgow: Centre for Research on Industrial Democracy and Participation, University of Glasgow.

Ramsay, H., Leopold, J. and Hyman, J. 1986: Profit-sharing and employee share ownership: an initial assessment. *Employee Relations,* 8(1), 23–6.

Ramsay, H., Hyman, J., Baddon, L., Hunter, L. and Leopold, J. 1990: Options for workers: owner or employee? In G. Jenkins and M. Poole (eds), *New Forms of Ownership: management and employment.* London: Routledge.

Reichers, A.E. 1985: A review and reconceptualization of organizational commitment. *Academy of Management Review*, 10(3), 465–76.

Sandberg, A. 1993: Volvo human-centred work organization: the end of the road? *New Technology, Work and Employment*, 8(1), 83–7.

Scott, C.D. and Jaffe, D.T. 1991: *Empowerment*. London: Kogan Page.

Sewell, G. and Wilkinson, B. 1992: Empowerment or emasculation? Shopfloor surveillance in a total quality organization. In P. Blyton and P. Turnbull (eds), *Reassessing Human Resource Management*. London: Sage, pp. 97–115.

Smith, G.R. 1986: Profit-sharing and employee share ownership in Britain. *Employment Gazette*, 94(8), 380–5.

Smith, G.R. 1993: Employee share schemes in Britain. *Employment Gazette*, 101(4), 149–54.

Towers, B., Cox, D. and Chell, L. 1987: *Worker Directors in Private Manufacturing Industry in Great Britain*, Research Paper no. 29. London: Department of Employment.

Townley, B. 1989: Employee communication programmes. In K. Sisson (ed.), *Personnel Management in Britain*. Oxford: Blackwell.

Vista Communications 1989: *Annual Survey of Employee Communications*, London: Vista; cited in *IRS Employment Trends*, no. 448, 26 September 1989.

Walton, R.E. 1985: From control to commitment in the workplace. *Harvard Business Review*, 63, 76–84.

Wilkinson, A., Snape, E. and Allen, P. 1991: TQM and the management of labour. *Employee Relations*, 13(1), 24–31.

Wilkinson, A., Marchington, M., Goodman, J. and Ackers, P. 1992: Total quality management and employee involvement. *Human Resource Management Journal*, 2(4), 1–20.

Wilson, F. 1989: Productive efficiency and the employment relationship: the case of quality circles. *Employee Relations*, 11(1), 27–32.

WIRS1, *see* Daniel and Millward (1983).

WIRS2, *see* Millward and Stevens (1986).

WIRS3, *see* Millward et al. (1992).

Womack, J.P., Jones, D.T. and Roos, D. 1990: *The Machine that Changed the World*. New York: Macmillan.

Woodcock, C. 1993: Workers find ESOPs are no fable. *Guardian*, 29 November.

12

Workforce Flexibility

PAUL BLYTON

Introduction

Since the early 1980s the issue of labour flexibility has received considerable attention and has been actively promoted by both governments and employers. Both the European Commission (EC) and the Organization for Economic Co-operation and Development (OECD) have identified the importance of labour market flexibility as a contributor to economic growth (EC 1993; OECD 1989, 1994). Policies such as labour market deregulation, to remove restrictions on the form of employment contracts which employers can offer, have been aimed specifically at increasing flexibility both in the labour market and in employment. In work organizations, practices such as relaxing job boundaries, increasing the number of non-permanent staff, introducing new working-time patterns and wage payment systems, extending the use of self-employed and sub-contract workers, and establishing closer relations between buying and supplying companies, have all been discussed as potentially important sources of flexibility. In turn, this flexibility has been seen as playing a potentially important role in achieving various organizational objectives, including lower labour costs, improved responsiveness to market uncertainties, greater utilization of plant and equipment and higher-quality output. Indeed, the pursuit of greater workforce flexibility is widely regarded as a key policy in the development of human resource management (HRM) and the achievement of a closer relationship between business strategy and personnel practice.

In certain respects the breadth of the discussion surrounding the flexibility issue has been useful, both in underlining the possible links between diverse work arrangements and in identifying the potential contribution of different employment practices to broader organizational objectives. Yet such diversity in the use of a concept also generates its own problems. In terms of flexibility, these lie particularly in the way it has been used as a summary term for a varied set of developments, and in the assumptions commonly made about the degree of uniformity in the nature, extent, pace and consistency of changes taking place, not to mention the factors bringing those changes about.

If securing greater workforce flexibility remains an important issue for HR managers in coming years – and we shall argue that this is likely to be the case – it is necessary to look in more detail at assumptions currently underpinning the flexibility concept and assess how these mesh with other issues high on HRM's agenda. This challenging of assumptions has been made all the more necessary by the 'magic charm' status that workforce flexibility has been accorded in some management literature, which has held that in greater flexibility lies the potential for achieving a host of organizational objectives. Partly, this reflects a tendency to contrast flexibility with rigidity and attribute connotations of adaptability and dynamism to the former and fixed attitudes to the latter.

Yet, even a brief examination of the issues and evidence indicates that in extending various forms of flexibility managers also run certain risks, not least a potential loss of stability, continuity, commitment and quality, as well as possibly creating the grounds for considerable workforce and trade union resistance. To assess these issues and more generally to evaluate the current and future significance of workforce flexibility, the following sections of this chapter examine the factors creating pressures for greater flexibility; the main dimensions of workforce flexibility; the recent patterns of development of these different forms, as revealed by case study and survey findings; the limits to flexibility as it is currently conceived; and finally, the possible future direction of developments in workforce flexibility.

Factors Encouraging Greater Flexibility

The changes in employment and working practices subsumed under the heading of flexibility represent, in the main, an increase in the pace of activities already occurring rather than something wholly new. This begs the questions, however, of what has given rise to this increase in pace, and will these causal factors endure (that is, will the pressure for greater flexibility continue)? In a changing economy it is of course difficult, if not impossible, to measure the relative significance of certain factors compared to others. While acknowledging this, it is nevertheless possible to identify a series of factors said to have encouraged a more intense search for greater workforce flexibility.

First, growing international competition has increased the need among domestic organizations to achieve greater competitiveness. The spread of industrialization into low labour-cost countries such as Taiwan, Korea, Singapore, Brazil and Mexico; the continued expansion of the Japanese domestic economy and the growth of Japanese multinational activity; the shake-out effect of the early 1980s' world recession which reduced the number of less-efficient organizations; and the removal of trade barriers within Europe and North America, all these factors have fuelled a search for greater competitiveness through lower costs (including lower labour costs) and higher quality and specification. In both the private and the public sectors, cost-cutting has been a major initial stimulus to attempts to increase workforce flexibility. Further, with the pressures of increased competition has come greater market uncertainty, partly because particular market segments more rapidly approach saturation due to higher total output, and partly because home markets are becoming increasingly exposed to international competition as the search for markets intensifies. Organizational flexibility (particularly the ability to innovate and diversify) is thus widely seen as increasingly important, and within that, labour flexibility represents a major contribution to overall organizational flexibility.

These two influences of competition and market uncertainty have exerted a particular impact in recent years through the greater prominence of multinational organizations, particularly those originating in Japan. In many instances, Japanese companies have demonstrated an ability to organize more effectively than most of their competitors within the host economy. This is also evident in the Japanese multinationals' ability to establish and maintain a higher degree of workforce flexibility than typifies the majority of domestic organizations. The Nissan plant in the north-east of England, for example, established a wide-ranging flexibility agreement in its early period of operations, which has since acted as a spur to achieving greater flexibility in other car plants in the UK (Wickens 1987).

In some contexts, greater workforce flexibility has also been encouraged by the introduction of new technologies. The ability to reprogramme and retool CNC and other computer-aided equipment rapidly, allows batch sizes to be reduced and a greater variety of work to be undertaken, thereby giving those organizations enhanced scope for responding to particular market trends and changes. Further, advanced equipment can often fulfil in a single sequence what formerly represented a series of discrete tasks. Hence, not only may some new technology require those working with it to extend their range of competences, it can also act to undermine previous occupational structures and give rise to new ones. In this respect, the current generation of technologies is no different from its predecessors in making certain jobs obsolete overnight and giving rise to a series of new ones. Overall, a period of rapid technological change encourages, if not predicates, a greater flexibility both among a workforce and within the organization as a whole, to achieve synergy between operator and machine, output and market.

Also significant in accounting for the growth in flexibility are various political, economic and social factors. Several of these factors have been particularly prominent in the United Kingdom. For example, government policies towards privatization and compulsory competitive tendering in the public services have led to a growth in the number of non-standard and 'external' workers within the public sector. Further, the weakening of trade unions in the 1980s through such means as greater legislative circumscription, reduced the possibility of resistance to changes in employment and working practices which, in earlier periods, had frequently been opposed by the unions (for example, the removal of demarcations between trades and the use of temporary workers and contractors). The creation of a large-scale youth training scheme, based on a comparatively low wage paid to those participating, has also acted to deliver a source of a temporary and inexpensive labour to the market place.

Labour supply factors have also facilitated the growth of flexibility. In the majority of industrialized countries, the continued growth in the number of women with children who wish to secure paid employment, coupled with continuing inequalities in the allocation of domestic responsibilities, has resulted in many women seeking part-time rather than full-time employment. These same domestic commitments also play a part in the preparedness to work 'twilight' and weekend shifts when a partner can take over the domestic responsibilities. Thus, increasing demand by employers for a labour force not comprised solely of full-time employees has been matched by a growth in the supply of labour who are not seeking full-time work. With the decline in the number of young people leaving school, future increases in the labour force are likely to be achieved by attracting more women to, and back to, the labour market. If this is the case, it suggests that any further employer demand for part-time working will not be unduly hampered by the nature of the labour supply.

To expand this last point, in certain situations where employers have experienced shortages of suitable labour they have made greater efforts to attract more women into employment. As part of 'returner' and other schemes, for example, some employers offer working arrangements which fit with home commitments. Hence, different labour market conditions are giving rise to different flexibility patterns: where labour markets are slack, employers are able to shift market uncertainty on to labour via practices such as using self-employed and temporary employees. In tight labour market situations, however, flexibility is again being encouraged, but this time a version which is designed to be more attractive to prospective employees.

What this discussion underlines is that the list of factors encouraging greater workforce flexibility is varied, and that in different contexts particular factors can exert influence in different ways. What is more, at least some of the factors (level of competition, rate of technological change, degree of market uncertainty) show no signs of declining; indeed, if anything they are likely to intensify in coming years. As a result, pressures to continue searching for lower costs and greater flexibility are also likely to remain for the foreseeable future.

The Concept of Flexibility

At its simplest, flexibility denotes pliability, adaptability and a responsiveness to pressure. Its opposite is inflexibility, rigidity and sclerosis. Though the term was not applied to any great extent before the 1980s, the ideas underpinning the notion of labour flexibility are far from new. Casual forms of employment, by the hour or the day, typified many industries in the past (and continue to do so in some cases today). These provided employers with considerable scope to match the volume of labour with the level of demand. In the docks, for example, men were traditionally engaged to load or unload a ship and were likely to be laid off on completion of the task. Overtime, shift-work and short-time working are other long-established sources of flexibility, enabling employers to extend or contract the working day as changes in demand warrant. Yet, while employers have long recognized the importance of labour flexibility, what marks out the present from earlier periods is the added significance being placed on various forms of flexibility as sources of greater organizational efficiency. The greater value is reflected in the range of work patterns and practices subject to review, and an increased pace of change in at least some aspects of workforce flexibility (Hakim 1990).

Much of the recent discussion on flexibility stems from the work of

Atkinson (1984) and his identification of a trend towards the 'flexible firm', comprising different groups of 'core' and 'periphery' workers. In this model the centre of organizations is occupied by a primary or 'core' workforce of full-time, permanent employees who possess key (and scarce) skills, and as a result enjoy relatively high-status positions with good prospects of security and promotion. These core workers are seen to be supported by groups of secondary or 'periphery' workers who are often semi- or unskilled and whose jobs are likely to be less secure, with many on temporary and part-time contracts and with few prospects of advancement. These latter groups of workers are identified as the major buffer against changes in demand. When pressures on output rise, the peripheral workforce is expanded via recruitment from the external labour market. When demand declines the periphery workforce is reduced.

The notion of the flexible firm has a number of similarities to earlier analyses of 'primary' and 'secondary' labour markets which highlighted the extent to which labour markets were segmented, to the general disadvantage of particular groups, notably women, ethnic minorities and youth (Wilkinson 1981). In the more recent debate, the flexible-firm model has been useful in signalling possible areas in which change is taking place, and showing how different types of flexibility may be associated with different work groups; it also has merit as a checklist of the range of developments which could be found within an organization. The flexible-firm model has also attracted criticism, however, including the view that the core/periphery distinction is over-simplistic and can be misleading in terms of the role and strategic significance of different work groups within the enterprise. Some organizations, for example, rely heavily on a part-time workforce and others on contract workers. In these situations the contribution of such groups is often of central rather than peripheral importance to the organizations (see, for example, Malloch 1991). Similarly, it is evident that in many cases ostensibly 'core' groups of skilled workers do not necessarily enjoy the status suggested by the model (O'Connell Davidson 1991). In addition, there is the argument that evidence of flexibility among 'peripheral' groups has been gathered indiscriminately without sufficient attention being paid to its appropriateness as an index of flexibility. The growth of part-time working, for example, has been highlighted by some as an indication of increased flexibility; yet for others it reflects only the continued growth in service sector employment (where part-time working is much more common) with little or no sign of employers switching from full-time to part-time labour to increase flexibility (Pollert 1988). There also appears to be a general lack of appreciation of the continuities also present in the way workforces are hired, deployed and rewarded, and a lack of recognition too that various aspects of the flexible-firm model, such as forms of temporary working, have long existed.

In practice it seems that, while critics are correct in pointing to both the conceptual and the empirical shortcomings of the original model, nevertheless it remains the case that considerable changes have been and continue to be occurring in a large number of work organizations in aspects such as employment patterns, working arrangements and practices, the nature of reward systems and industrial relations, the use of different forms of contract labour and the general organization of production, including relations with suppliers and customers (Blyton and Morris 1991). While the evidence suggests that in many areas (such as multi-skilling, or closer relations with suppliers) developments to date have fallen well short of the 'ideals' of flexibility as expounded in the management literature, nevertheless the picture is one of significant changes in employment patterns and working practices, aimed at securing lower labour costs, tighter staffing levels, higher machine utilization, greater employee mobility and fewer interruptions and bottlenecks in production.

To disaggregate the developments taking place, it is useful to examine the different forms of flexibility separately. Here we focus on four: functional or task flexibility; numerical flexibility; temporal flexibility; and financial flexibility. Later sections will identify the extent of developments taking place, the links and potential conflicts between these different forms, and their relationships to other organizational and HR strategies, such as improving levels of commitment and achieving higher quality.

Task or functional flexibility

This concerns the versatility of employees to undertake a wider range of tasks, and can involve either the horizontal integration of tasks (those formerly undertaken by other employees at the same level) or vertical integration (tasks formerly carried out by employees at higher or lower levels). Much of the discussion surrounding functional flexibility has centred on skilled manual work and the degree to which traditional demarcations are being eroded, to be replaced by 'cross-trade' working and 'multi-skilling'. As we discuss below, the replacement of craft boundaries by multi-skilled workers remains the exception rather the rule, though limited movements in this general direction are widespread.

More common, however, appear to be developments taking place away from the skilled groups, involving both production operatives and non-manual employees. Among production groups, one sign of this has been widespread reductions in the number of job grades within organizations, which in turn facilitate greater mobility and transfer across job boundaries and the introduction of team-working. Among white-collar staff, functional flexibility has been stimulated partly by developments in information technology which cut across previous job classifications such as filing clerk and typist, through the development of electronic equipment designed to input, store, retrieve and transmit information.

Numerical flexibility

This refers to an ability to vary the amount of labour in response to fluctuating levels of demand. This is achievable through such means as the use of non-permanent employment contracts and 'hire and fire' policies. Also relevant here is what some writers have termed 'distancing' strategies, whereby firms use sub-contracting partly as a way of responding to demand fluctuations. While the general evidence indicates a widespread growth in sub-contracting, both for ancillary service activities and certain aspects of production, it now appears that the trend in temporary working has been less marked. The issue of numerical flexibility appears to have attracted more interest in countries such as the UK and Spain than in some other European countries such as Germany and Sweden, where the emphasis has been placed more strongly on achieving greater task flexibility (Brunhes 1989).

Temporal flexibility

This is linked to numerical flexibility; many writers have discussed the two together as aspects of the volume of labour. In the present argument, however, it is useful to distinguish the particular contribution of temporal or working-time flexibility since there are signs that this factor is likely to become increasingly important in many work organizations in coming years. From a management perspective, temporal flexibility refers to the adaptability of working-time patterns to reflect patterns of work pressure. As noted above, shift-working, overtime and short-time working have traditionally been used in this way (Blyton 1985). In recent years, however, new working-time patterns have been devised to reflect specific patterns of demand. For example, part-time schedules have been introduced in retailing and elsewhere to cater for variability in customer activity. In addition, as the duration of the working week has fallen, increasing attention has been given to the arrangement and utilization of working hours as well as their overall duration (Blyton 1994). Further, employers' interest in attracting new entrants, particularly women, on to the labour market is forcing greater consideration of working-time arrangements (such as part-time and flexitime schedules) which allow work commitments to be meshed more satisfactorily with other responsibilities.

Financial flexibility

This involves a shift away from single and uniform payment systems towards more individualized and variable systems. Among other objectives, these seek to establish a closer relationship between performance and reward through such means as performance-related pay, profit-sharing schemes and fee-for-service payments. In the UK and elsewhere, financial flexibility has also entailed an ability to pay lower wages to groups such as young workers. This ability has been secured partly by state action to weaken trade unions, partly by establishing youth employment schemes which reinforced low wage rates, partly via the abolition of Wages Councils, and partly by removing certain conditions (such as Fair Wages Resolutions) and introducing others (for example, compulsory competitive tendering/privatization of services in the public sector) which have further encouraged relatively low wage rates among various sectors and occupations.

It is clear, therefore, that flexibility covers a diverse range of developments. Faced with such diversity, a common tendency has been to assume a high degree of uniformity: that the various developments are occurring at more or less the same pace, in the same places, for similar reasons and with similar outcomes. In practice, however, this is far from the case. Closer examination reveals a much more fragmented and unevenly paced set of developments borne out of a diverse mix of causal pressures. Indeed, at least some aspects of flexibility potentially contradict others and could clash with other organizational objectives. It is to an examination of this evidence that we now turn.

Evidence of Developments

One of the most contentious issues related to workforce flexibility remains its extent: how much flexibility is there and what trends can be distinguished? From this flow a series of supplementary questions:

has flexibility developed in some sectors and occupations more than others? do different forms of flexibility act as alternatives or do they develop in parallel or in sequence? to what extent does flexibility represent part of broader organizational strategies or an isolated development? do current concerns with flexibility represent a real break with the past or merely a redefining of long-established trends? Despite problems such as a lack of agreement on what constitutes flexibility, a dearth of longitudinal studies, and a frequent absence of precision on the extent and depth of change, a view across several studies suggest that:

- there has been a growth in various forms of flexibility in the 1980s and 1990s, in both public and private sectors and in manufacturing and services;
- the extent and pace of this growth are highly uneven both in terms of industrial sector and form(s) of flexibility;
- different types of flexibility are more prominent in different sectors, and similar forms are being pursued for a variety of reasons;
- while flexibility agreements have played a significant role, many of the changes introduced have been introduced by unilateral management action.

Functional Flexibility

Summarizing the available evidence, it is clear that the 1980s and 1990s have witnessed some relaxation in demarcations between crafts and between production and craft workers. However, in the vast majority of cases these distinctions and job boundaries remain. Change appears widespread but, in most cases, relatively shallow: for example, minor maintenance and inspection work being undertaken by production operators; some overall blurring at the margins between crafts; and a greater integration of closely related skills, such as instrument mechanic and electrician. Two further points need to be made, however. First, in a significant number of organizations, the changes introduced have been more far-reaching than the general picture indicates. This is particularly true in (though not confined to) greenfield sites where flexible working practices have been secured partly through extensive selection and recruitment procedures.

Secondly, many of the changes have involved the broadening of non-skilled jobs. A key management aim has been to operate at lower staffing levels and to cover tasks by broadening job responsibilities. This is equally as evident in service industries (such as ancillary workers in hospitals) as in the manufacturing sector. Compared to those involving skilled workers, however, these changes in working practices have received less attention. Partly this may reflect the interest generated around the notion of 'multi-skilling' which has focused attention on craft workers. In addition, the relaxation of craft demarcations has tended to be subject to more formal agreement in the collective bargaining sphere (Marsden and Thompson 1990), while the enlargement of jobs among semi- and unskilled workers has been less subject to formal union–management agreement.

Reviewing the studies of functional flexibility, the difficulty of gauging the extent of change across a diverse range of organizations is marked. What may be judged a major change in working practices in organization A (perhaps due to previously rigidly defended lines of demarcation) could be viewed as a relatively minor change in organization B (possibility because an atmosphere of change has characterized this latter organization for some time).

Despite this difficulty, there is now some agreement on the general pattern and pace of change in this area. Summarizing the evidence from several large-scale surveys and a number of case studies, Storey (1995: 41) for example concludes that 'such functional flexibility as has occurred is a modest and incremental change towards job enlargement and overlapping job descriptions and functions but with little multi-skilling'. Such a conclusion reiterates earlier studies such as that by Cross (1988), who found that the development of anything approaching 'multi-skilling' in the 1980s was limited and that for skilled workers the more common experience was the restricted reform of demarcations, with changes tending to occur at the margins of jobs rather than involving far-reaching reforms.

Turning to non-skilled grades, however, there is 'plenty of evidence . . . to suggest a fairly widespread movement towards enhanced task flexibility' (Storey 1995: 41). This picture appears equally valid for lower-level white-collar occupations as for manual tasks. In their European study of HR practices, for example, Brewster and his colleagues found that 41 per cent of UK organizations had broadened the tasks of their clerical workers over the previous three years, compared to 12 per cent of organizations who indicated that clerical jobs had been made more specific and 43 per cent who reported no change. The corresponding proportions for manual employees were 38 per cent of organizations where the jobs of manual workers had widened, 9 per cent where they had become more specific and 39 per cent where there had been no change over the previous three years (Brewster et al. 1994: 186). Similarly, the WIRS survey found that managers in over one-third (36 per cent) of workplaces reported that over the previous three years changes to working practices had been effected in the form of reduced job demarcations/increased flexibility of working. Certain industries in both manufacturing (such as chemicals, leather, footwear and clothing) and services (for example, banking, insurance and finance, and post and telecommunications) were particularly prominent in effecting such changes (Millward et al. 1992: 334).

Companies cited as being in the vanguard in pursuing functional flexibility have often developed this in conjunction with a 'teamworking' concept, whereby craft workers are typically removed from separate maintenance departments and integrated into production-orientated teams. In Continental Can, for example, the former craftsman's role has been turned into that of 'production technician' who operates on the line, ensuring that maintenance is carried out and machine downtimes are minimized (Incomes Data Services 1988). Similar arrangements operate elsewhere; for example, the drive-shaft manufacturer, Hardy Spicer, where production teams contain 'systems technicians' who carry out tasks such as machine set-up and basic maintenance, as well as bearing responsibility for loading, quality and output (Hendry and Pettigrew 1988). Likewise Ind Coope in Burton, Staffordshire, have devised a teamwork arrangement using 'operator craftsmen' who undertake this twin role formerly demarcated between skilled and production workers. Many other organizations have similarly introduced various forms of teamworking, including Cammell Laird, Cummins Engines, Birds Eye Walls, Shell Chemicals and Cadbury Schweppes (IRRR 1989). Among the most highly developed are those operating in Japanese plants in the UK – notably Nissan, Komatsu and Sony – where an ability to work in teams is an important component in recruitment decisions.

British Steel (BS) represents a useful microcosm of various developments taking place, and in some aspects, the absence of change. The majority of BS plants have reached agreement on 'craft-restructuring' whereby what was formerly a diverse range of individual craft titles have been reduced to two broad craft disciplines: mechanical and electrical crafts. Retraining, however, has largely been confined to within-discipline training (for example, fitters learning other mechanical craft competences) with only a very limited degree of cross-discipline training. As a result, the degree of development of multi-skilling has been modest. Further, several BS plants have also introduced a form of teamworking into parts of their activities, whereby team members together undertake a range of duties and are responsible for production, inspection and routine maintenance. This development mainly represents job enlargement for non-skilled workers. Even where teamworking has not been introduced, the trend within production operations within BS has been towards a broadening of job respon-sibilities partly reflecting a production operation now staffed by only one-quarter of the workforce who were employed in the industry in the late 1970s (Blyton 1993).

There are a number of possible reasons why functional flexibility has not been pursued further in the majority of organizations. Some of these we address in a later section when we consider the limits of flexibility, but among the factors which might usefully be raised here is the provision of training. Functional flexibility rests on an assump-tion that adequate training is provided for workers (either craft or non-craft) to undertake a broader range of tasks. It seems that in many situations the full implications of this in terms of training re-quirements have not been calculated. The size of the issue can be seen from the example of one steel plant in the UK in 1989 where over a thousand craftsmen each had 38 days of retraining (though this re-flects not only the implementation of 'craft restructuring' but also the need to achieve competence in working with new technology). This demand on training for the achievement of functional flexibility is arising in a context where (a) in the past, UK employers have been criticized for their lack of training provision compared to their major international competitors, and (b) continuing financial constraints making additional funding for extra training facilities difficult to secure. A second factor limiting functional flexibility among skilled workers has been the resistance of craft workers themselves to giving up time-honoured job definitions. This was clearly demonstrated in a dispute involving Ford UK in 1988 when one of the points at greatest dispute was the craft workers' unwillingness to undertake production work (Wilkinson and Oliver 1990).

Numerical Flexibility

The pattern of development of numerical flexibility reflects a similar level of diversity to that evidenced in other areas of flexibility, with some elements showing significant change while others have remained static. Tracking the development of numerical flexibility is also com-pounded by the problem that what for many is a major indicator of increasing flexibility – the growth in part-time working – is also shaped by other factors, notably changes in industrial structure.

Turning to the individual elements of numerical flexibility, there is general agreement that there has been a growth in the use of sub-contract labour in Britain. Sub-contracting has long been used for the provision of ancillary services but the use of sub-contracting has increased in the 1980s and 1990s, as a result of organizations contracting out more service activities, the public services contracting out activities formerly undertaken by in-house employees, and, to some extent, businesses contracting out some aspects of production, particularly to cover peaks in demand. In their 1992 study, for example, Brewster and his colleagues found that among the UK organizations, 31 per cent had increased their use of sub-contracting over the previous three years, compared to only 10 per cent who had decreased their use and 31 per cent whose use of sub-contracting was unchanged over that period (the remainder being non-users of sub-contracting) (Brewster et al. 1994: 184). Similarly in the latest WIRS, 38 per cent of financial manager respondents reported that the value of sub-contracted services as a proportion of total costs had risen over the previous three years, while only 8 per cent reported that it had declined (Millward et al. 1992: 340). Among the establishments contained in the WIRS sample, the most common sub-contracted service activities were building maintenance, cleaning and transport, followed by security and printing services. In all, more than seven out of ten establishments sub-contracted one or more services.

This upward trend is not found, however, in relation to temporary working. A comparison of Labour Force Surveys from 1985 to 1993 shows the number of temporary workers fluctuating at between 5 and 6 per cent of the overall labour force during this period (Watson 1994: 241). However, while the overall incidence of temporary employment may have remained static, the distribution of non-permanent employment has shown significant change, with considerable growth in the public sector offset by a decline in use in parts of the private sector. The WIRS survey, for example found that the number of public sector establishments using short, fixed-term contracts increased from 35 to 45 per cent between 1984 and 1990, while in private sector manufacturing the corresponding proportion of establishments declined from 11 to 9 per cent (Millward et al. 1992: 338). Brewster et al.'s study points to a similar conclusion, with the increased use of temporary/casual work and of fixed-term contracts being particularly evident among public sector organizations (Brewster et al. 1994: 180).

The extent of part-time working in the UK has increased steadily. In 1971 the 3.3 million part-time workers in Britain represented less than one in six of the total employees in employment. By 1994 the total number of part-timers had risen to almost 6 million, representing one in four of the total number in employment. Over four-fifths of part-time workers are women and the vast majority (over 93 per cent in 1992) of all part-time work in the UK is located in the service sector, with some parts of that sector (notably retailing, education and hotels and catering) being particularly reliant on part-time working.

It is this location of most part-time working in the service sector which casts doubt on whether the expansion of the part-time workforce truly reflects a growth in flexibility. If it does, there should be evidence of employers switching from offering full-time to offering part-time contracts. In practice, there is some evidence of this happening, for instance in the increased dependence of some retail stores on part-time workers and reductions in the number of full-time workers. However, these cases notwithstanding, the majority of the growth in part-time employment has been due to the increasing predominance of the service sector within overall employment patterns. One analysis of Census of Employment data, for example, concludes that almost three-quarters of the growth in part-time employment between 1981 and 1991 could be accounted for by changes in the industrial composition of the economy – primarily the growth in service sector employment and decline in manufacturing employment (Watson 1994: 241).

One form of part-time working which has attracted considerable comment has been job-sharing, whereby two (or more) people share one full-time job. In 1993 just under 200,000 part-timers (less than 4 per cent of the part-time workforce) were involved in job-sharing. The vast majority of these were women and were mainly located in clerical and secretarial occupations. Half of all job-sharers worked in public administration, education, health or other public services (Watson 1994: 245).

Temporal Flexibility

We noted above how various aspects of temporal flexibility are well-established – notably overtime, shift- and short-time working – and also that part-time working is increasingly being used in retailing and elsewhere as a means of temporal flexibility, allowing work schedules to be created and modified to match peaks in demand during the working day or working week. In addition, it is evident that significant amounts of informal time flexibility exist in many work arrangements. In the main, however, previous discussion on working time have focused on issues of duration rather than on the arrangement and variability of working hours. There are signs, though, that this is changing. As the working week becomes shorter the issue of the effective use of working time becomes correspondingly more significant. Further, with increasing emphasis on optimizing capital utilization and, in the service sector, providing longer opening times, greater attention is being paid to the relationship between individuals' work time and organizational operating time.

In the UK, temporal flexibility has been a prominent issue in the railway industry, stemming from the introduction of 'flexible rostering' in the early 1980s. This entailed the abandoning of a standard eight-hour working day in favour of variable shifts of between seven and nine hours. This variability was designed to improve the match between shift lengths and train running times, thereby increasing the utilization of working time. Though the question of flexible rostering was initially a source of considerable dispute in the industry (see Ferner 1985), it has continued to be a significant issue as management attempts to reduce the high number of hours paid as overtime among groups such as signal workers.

A similar issue of labour utilization was voiced in the 1989–90 engineering dispute in the UK over a shorter working week. However, although during the dispute the employers made various references to increasing the scope to vary weekly working hours, in practice most subsequent agreements left this issue unspecified. Where working time was specifically referred to in these settlements, it was in relation to 'bell-to-bell' working and reductions in the number of tea-breaks in return for a shorter working week (IDS 1990). This pattern varies somewhat with developments in the German engineering industry, where reductions in the working week (from 40 to 38.5 in 1984, to 37 in 1989, 36 in 1993 and 35 by 1995) have been associated with an increase in managerial power to introduce variation in weekly hours depending on the volume of work, provided that an average is achieved over an agreed period (IDS 1990). Other developments in working time in Western Europe also indicate greater consideration being given to the link between working-time patterns and operating times. In the Netherlands, for example, a widespread practice in engineering has been to translate agreed reductions in working time not into shorter weekly hours but into additional free days for employees, so as to maintain operating times at former levels (the free days being rostered into the shift pattern and thus covered by other employees) (Blyton 1988). A number of Dutch enterprises have gone further, and operate shift systems which are longer in periods of heavy demand and shorter during quieter periods. Further, organizations such as the steelmaker Hoogovens operate a shift system with longer shifts in the summer, to cover for employees on vacation, and shorter shifts during the rest of the year to meet the agreed average working week.

These Dutch examples have elements of what is now widely referred to as 'annual hours' systems. These have been discussed increasingly in the UK since the mid-1980s and a number of schemes have been introduced (Hutchinson 1993). Under these systems, agreement over working time is made in relation to the total hours to be worked annually. This gives management greater scope to vary the hours in any given period to match demand. There are signs of growth in the coverage of annual hours schemes. Studies conducted in the 1980s indicated that around 3 per cent of employees had their hours calculated on an annual basis (Marsh 1991). Subsequent studies, however, put this figure at 6.4 per cent by mid-1990 (Wareing 1992) and 9 per cent by 1993 (Watson 1994). The more recent studies also underline the spread of annual hours schemes into the service sector, and show that, while they tend to be more common among those working shifts, annual hours schemes have grown significantly among non-shift workers. In many annual hours contracts, variability is introduced in one of two ways. First, variability of weekly hours may be specified in agreements, such that work periods are longer at specified times and shorter during slacker periods. Secondly, the number of shifts rostered in the annual hours schedule may be less than the agreed annual working time. The difference comprises non-rostered working time, during which employees are effectively 'on call' and can be brought into work at short notice.

An extreme version of temporal flexibility which is attracting attention in some industries (notably retailing) is the concept of the 'zero hours' contracts under which no formal commitment is made by employers regarding the number of hours the contract-holder will work. Instead, the employee is on call, working only those periods which the employer calls for at short notice, for example to cover unforeseen absence. While such arrangements provide a very high level of flexibility for the employer, they offer little in the way of continuity or predictability for the employee. A less extreme version of this model also operates, in which employees are contracted for a relatively small minimum number of hours per week (for example, 16) but are contractually obliged to be available to work up to more than double that number if circumstances require it.

During the 1970s many employers introduced 'flexitime' arrangements, allowing employees to vary their start and finish times within certain limits provided that an agreed 'core' period was worked and that hours worked equated with the agreed working week over a given settlement period. These systems were introduced partly to attract and retain staff, and by 1980 it is estimated that 8 per cent of employees in the UK were involved in flexitime arrangements (Blyton 1985). Overwhelmingly, flexitime has been confined to non-manual employees, although at least one researcher has identified ways in which it can be incorporated into a shift system for production workers (McEwan Young 1978). For employers, these schemes have the potential to offer the added benefits of a greater degree of 'self-supervision' over time-keeping, and a reduction in the number of minor absences. Despite this, there was only limited further expansion of flexitime arrangements throughout the first half of the 1980s. More recently the flexitime appears to have revived to some extent. An ACAS survey found that 14 per cent of responding organizations had introduced or extended their use of flexitime between 1984 and 1987, and a further 11 per cent planned to extend its use in the following year (ACAS 1988). Labour shortages and a desire to recruit and retain women workers appears to have been a major reason for this revived interest. By 1993 the annual Labour Force Survey found that 2.5 million employees in the UK (12 per cent of the total) were working flexible working hours (Watson 1994). Flexitime is more common among full-timers than part-timers and among women than men. It was found still to be much more prevalent in non-manual occupations, particularly secretarial and clerical. In terms of industry, the highest levels of flexitime working are found in financial services and in public administration.

Factors such as reductions in weekly working hours, the increased proportion of part-timers in the workforce and increasing pressures on operating/opening hours are likely to stimulate further managerial efforts in the future to secure greater temporal flexibility. As we discuss in a later section, however, the success of new working arrangements is likely to depend in important part on the extent to which they meet employee preferences for working hours patterns and are consistent with a large body of research evidence on the harmful effects of certain working-time patterns.

Financial Flexibility

As we noted earlier, financial flexibility entails a move away from standardized and collectively agreed payment systems towards variable and individualized systems which seek a closer relationship between individual performance and reward. This has been pursued in a number of ways. For example, in the UK, the state has played an important role in reducing 'obstacles' to financial flexibility, through reducing trade union power, abolishing Wages Councils, removing Fair Wages Resolutions, and so on. The decentralization of collective bargaining has also acted to reduce the prominence of national pay agreements and increase the importance of more locally based settlements. Further, management's introduction of new elements in reward, including merit or performance-related pay (PRP), profit-sharing and share option schemes, has contributed to greater financial flexibility. The extent of such developments has not been fully recorded and there are indications that management discussions and advocacy of financial flexibility continue to run significantly ahead of practice. However, Kessler (1995: 259) points out that by the end of 1992 there were in excess of 4,000 approved profit-related pay schemes, covering almost one million employees, and over 2,000 employee share-ownership schemes covering around three million workers. Estimates of performance-related pay schemes indicate a greater prevalence among senior management; however, the latest WIRS survey indicates PRP being used for clerical and administrative staff in one-third of establishments and for skilled manual workers in one-quarter of establishments (Millward et al. 1992).

The signs are that aspects of financial flexibility will develop further in coming years. First, the extension of other forms of flexibility will bring about a greater diversity in organizational payment systems. Much sub-contracting, for example, is undertaken on a fee-for-service basis. Further, as organizations continue to modify their structures around the notion of local cost and profit centres, the emphasis on decentralizing collective bargaining arrangements is likely to remain, as managers seek to achieve greater local control over labour costs.

The Limits of Flexibility

Workforce flexibility has been identified as an important component of broader organizational flexibility, which in turn is widely viewed as a major ingredient in achieving and maintaining organizational success. Yet flexibility is not the only characteristic regarded as important to that success. The 1980s 'excellence' literature, for example, also emphasized the importance of organizational cultures which embodied commitment and pursuit of quality as important goals (Peters and Waterman 1982). Similar arguments have been put forward in subsequent HRM texts. Yet if numerical flexibility is pursued via high levels of temporary working, this is unlikely to produce sustained levels of commitment and quality output. There is a fundamental inconsistency between the simultaneous pursuit of 'dependable' and 'disposable' labour (Legge 1990; Blyton and Turnbull 1992). Commitment can be secured by a variety of means but important elements in this are usually reasonable salary, job security and/or access to promotion; most temporary workers have none of these. In addition, the very nature of temporary working normally precludes anything other than minimal training, which could further hinder the achievement of high-quality output. An additional clash of objectives could be the pursuit of harmonization and single status with the maintenance of diverse employment contracts, some permanent others embodying different degrees of temporariness.

Guy Standing (1986) has remarked that another possible pitfall of flexibility is that it may undermine stability and continuity within organizations. The short-term nature of fixed contracts, for example, contrasts with the continuity embodied in more-permanent employment relationships. These potential clashes with other organizational processes and objectives relate particularly to numerical flexibility. Many numerically flexible strategies have been pursued for their cost-cutting and control potential rather than for any deeper contribution to the organization. However, if continued heavy reliance on numerical flexibility impedes the achievement of other objectives and runs contrary to managerial thinking regarding employee development, teamworking, and so on, we can anticipate less emphasis on numerical flexibility in the future and more on other forms of flexibility.

In principle, there is potential for areas of common interest between management and workforce in achieving greater flexibility. This is an issue which so far has been largely unaddressed, reflecting the weaknesses in the position of trade unions and workers in the overall labour market. On working practices, for example, broader training and the attainment of greater competences could not only improve levels of job satisfaction but also employees' earnings potential. In addition, new working-time schedules could represent a means for existing employees to achieve a better match between work and non-work commitments. There is considerable evidence, for example, that many workers would prefer a time schedule which offers more free days (as in the Dutch example quoted above) than one which translates any reduction in hours into a slightly shorter working day (Blyton 1985). For management, too, this potentially offers greater flexibility since it ensures the maintenance of longer operating times.

If managers' pursuit of time flexibility translates into more-extensive shift-working, it will be important that research is taken into account which highlights the dysfunctions of some forms of shift-working. In particular, the social, psychological and medical problems associated with night-working are well documented (see, for example, Carpentier and Cazamian 1977). Not only do workers function much below their optimum during night shifts, but the extent to which they adjust over time is limited, if at all. On top of this are the marked social and family disruptions which can be caused by shift-working. The overall implication is that while round-the-clock working may look at first sight an extremely efficient use of resources, there are considerable drawbacks; these were a major reason for the general reductions in the 1960s and 1970s in the proportion of shifts containing night-working (NBPI 1970; Bosworth and Dawkins 1980).

Summary and Conclusion

Various aspects of workforce flexibility have been pursued in most industrialized countries in recent years, though to varying extents and at different rates. Managerial arguments in favour of increasing flexibility have focused largely on its potential contribution to lowering labour costs, increasing responsiveness to change and improving utilization of equipment.

Flexibility has developed within particular sets of circumstances, reflecting not only general pressures such as increased competition and greater market uncertainties, but also specific conditions such as persistently high levels of unemployment in many countries, growing female participation in labour markets and, in many contexts, weakening trade union power. In some countries at least, these conditions have given rise to forms of flexibility that emphasize primarily the cost-cutting and control aspects of numerical flexibility. If flexibility is to become part of a long-term strategy, however, rather than reflecting short-term opportunism, it will be necessary for management to address the possible inconsistencies arising between flexibility strategies and other HR objectives, and also to accept the need for greater investment in flexibility (in training, enhanced payment for skills, and communications, for example). It will be important, too, that greater recognition is given to employee interests in the creation of new working arrangements and practices. Failing this, flexibility is likely to become progressively marginalized rather than remaining a central aspect of HRM policy in the late 1990s.

References

Advisory, Conciliation and Arbitration Service ACAS 1988: *Labour Flexibility in Britain: the 1987 ACAS survey*, Occasional Paper 41. London: ACAS.

Atkinson, J. 1984: Manpower strategies for flexible organisations. *Personnel Management*, August, 28–31.

Blyton, P. 1985: *Changes in Working Time: an international review*. London: Croom Helm.

Blyton, P. 1988: *Labour Flexibility in the EEC: the growth of new working time patterns*, report for the European Commission. Available from the author.

Blyton, P. 1993: Steel. In A. Pendleton and J. Winterton (eds), *Public Enterprise in Transition*. London: Routledge, pp. 166–84.

Blyton, P. 1994: Working hours. In K. Sisson (ed.), *Personnel Management*, 2nd edn. Oxford: Blackwell, pp. 495–526.

Blyton, P. and Morris, J. 1991: A flexible future: aspects of the flexibility debates and some unresolved issues. In P. Blyton and J. Morris (eds), *A Flexible Future? Prospects for employment and organization*. Berlin: De Gruyter.

Blyton, P. and Turnbull, P. (eds) 1992: *Reassessing Human Resource Management*. London, Sage.

Bosworth, D.L. and Dawkins, P.J. 1980: Shiftworking and unsocial hours. *Industrial Relations Journal*, 11, 32–40.

Brewster, C., Hegewisch, A. and Mayne, L. 1994: Flexible working practices: the controversy and the evidence. In C. Brewster and A. Hegewisch (eds), *Policy and Practice in European Human Resource Management*, London: Routledge, pp. 168–93.

Brunhes, B. 1989: Labour flexibility in enterprises: a comparison of firms in four European countries. In Organization for Economic Co-operation and Development, *Labour Market Flexibility: trends in enterprises*. Paris: OECD, pp. 11–36.

Carpenter, J. and Cazamian, P. 1977: *Nightwork*. Geneva: International Labour Organization.

Cross, M. 1988: Changes in working practices in UK manufacturing, 1981–1988. *Industrial Relations Review and Report*, no. 415, 2–10.

European Commission (EC) 1993: *Growth, Competitiveness, Employment: the challenges and ways forward into the 21st century*. Brussels: Commission of the European Communities.

Ferner, A. 1985: Political constraints and management strategies: the case of working practices in British Rail. *British Journal of Industrial Relations*, 23(1), 47–70.

Hakim, C. 1990: Core and periphery in employers' workforce strategies: evidence from the 1987 ELUS survey. *Work, Employment and Society*, 4, 157–88.

Hendry, C. and Pettigrew, A. 1988: Multiskilling in the round. *Personnel Management*, April; 36–43.

Hutchinson, S. 1993: *Annual Hours Working in the UK.* London: Institute of Personnel Management.

Incomes Data Services (IDS) 1988: *Teamworking,* Study no. 419. London: IDS.

Incomes Data Services (IDS) 1990: *The Shorter Working Week,* Study no. 461. London: IDS.

Industrial Relations Review and Report (IRRR) 1989: Labour flexibility re-assessed. *Industrial Relations Review and Report,* November, 7–10.

Kessler, I. 1995: Reward systems. In J. Storey (ed.), *Human Resource Management: a critical text,* London: Routledge, pp. 254–79.

Legge, K. 1990: Employment relations in the enterprise culture. Paper presented at Employment Research Conference, Cardiff, September.

Malloch, H. 1991: Strategic management and the decision to subcontract. In P. Blyton and J. Morris (eds), *A Flexible Future? Prospects for employment and organization,* Berlin: De Gruyter, pp. 191–210.

Marsden, D. and Thompson, M. 1990: Flexibility agreements and their significance in the increase in productivity in British manufacturing since 1980. *Work, Employment and Society,* 4, 83–104.

Marsh, C. 1991: *Hours of Work of Women and Men in Britain.* London: HMSO.

McEwan Young, W. 1978: Flexible working arrangements in continuous shift production. *Personnel Review,* 7, 12–19.

Millward, N., Stevens, M., Smart, D. and Hawes, W.R. 1992: *Workplace Industrial Relations in Transition.* Aldershot, Hants.: Dartmouth.

National Board for Prices and Incomes (NBPI) 1970: *Hours of Work, Overtime and Shiftworking,* Report no. 161, Cmnd 4554. London: HMSO.

O'Connell Davidson, J. 1991: Subcontract, flexibility and changing employment relations in the water industry. In P. Blyton and J. Morris (eds), *A Flexibile Future? Prospects for employment and organization,* Berlin: De Gruyter, pp. 241–58.

Organization for Economic Co-operation and Development (OECD) 1989: *Labour Market Flexibility: trends in enterprises.* Paris: OECD.

Organization for Economic Co-operation and Development (OECD) 1994: *The OECD Jobs Study: unemployment in the OECD area, 1950–1995.* Paris: OECD.

Peters, T. and Waterman, R. 1982: *In Search of Excellence.* New York: Harper & Row.

Pollert, A. 1988: The flexible firm: fixation or fact? *Work, Employment and Society,* 2, 281–316.

Standing, G. 1986: *Unemployment and Labour Market Flexibility: the United Kingdom.* Geneva: International Labour Organization.

Storey, J. (ed.) 1995: *Human Resource Management: a critical text.* London: Routledge.

Wareing, A. 1992: Working arrangements and patterns of working hours in Britain. *Employment Gazette,* March, 88–100.

Watson, G. 1994: The flexible workforce and patterns of working hours in the UK. *Employment Gazette*, July, 239–47.

Wickens, P. 1987: *The Road to Nissan*. London: Macmillan.

Wilkinson, B. and Oliver, N. 1990: Obstacles to Japanisation: the case of Ford UK. *Employee Relations*, 12, 17–22.

Wilkinson, F. (ed.) 1981: *The Dynamics of Labour Market Segmentation*. London: Academic Press.

13

Human Resource Management and Flexibility in Pay: New Solutions or Old Problems?

CLIFF LOCKYER

How much work employees can do and what will motivate them to complete a task have been the two core problems confronting all employers since earliest days. Work measurement and pay are central issues in any attempt to motivate employees.

Currently performance pay, 'the explicit link of financial reward to individual, group or company performance' (Armstrong and Murliss 1991: 21), is arguably 'one of the most dynamic issues in human resource management' (Kessler 1994: 465). Secondly, and of equal concern, is the current trend towards increasing flexibility in pay, the widening occupational, sectoral and spatial differentials stemming, in part, from the declining proportion of employees whose pay is either influenced or determined by collective bargaining (Beatson 1993: 406), and the increasing managerial preference for treating each employee as an individual with individualized pay rates. A third and further significant feature of the current trends in pay methods has been the introduction of a range of new and non-traditional payment schemes, adding to the already existing diversity in the objectives and methods in these schemes.

Arguably, this pursuit of pay flexibility and diversity reflects much of human resource management – 'the least disciplined of disciplines; a market place for every pedlar of far fetched ideas; an amalgam of theory and practice, personalised fantasy, shrewd application of experience' (Braham 1982: xi) – and its relationship to pay. It has ignored the lessons of the history of payment schemes, the relationship of payment schemes to particular production and organization requirements, and neglected those other features essential to effective performance (Storey and Sisson 1993: 139).

The multiple agendas of HRM – individualism, reinforcing a performance culture, flexibility, team methods of production, cultural change, motivation and change, increased commitment and management control – lead to images of confusion, contradiction and superficiality in modern payment schemes. Traditional typologies of payment schemes appear ill equipped to provide the bases to assess and compare different schemes systematically. The complexity and time required in many of the current schemes to complete the assessment of performance and to link it to pay inevitably leads to parallels with many of the complexities of payment-by-results schemes of the 1950s and 1960s, and with their demise.

This chapter reviews current typologies of payment schemes to locate and categorize the current diversity in payment schemes. The second section examines the links between payment schemes and production systems and a categorization of those factors which have traditionally influenced the appropriateness and effectiveness of particular schemes. Thirdly, current pay agendas are discussed to indicate developments and likely trends in HRM related schemes. The chapter concludes with a review of the changing topography of payment schemes and the potentially short life of many HRM varieties.

Typologies of Payment Systems

Traditionally payment systems have been classified by whether pay is fixed or variable (IDS 1980). This typically leads to a division based on the degree to which pay relates to output/effort or to time. Salary grades, measured day work, time or flat-rate schemes are based on the number of hours spent at work. There is no relationship between effort and reward. Conversely piece work, performance- and profit-related pay relate pay levels to effort.

Variable or output/effort schemes can be further classified by the extent to which pay varies directly or indirectly with output/effort. Piecework and payment-by-results schemes have a close relationship to individual effort; in contrast, share ownership, profit-related pay and establishment-wide schemes have only an indirect or remote relationship to individual effort. Such traditional classifications have been of limited use in encompassing a number of the newer schemes – skill-based, merit- or performance-related pay – or in providing a means to contrast differences between traditional and newer payment schemes.

An alternative has been to survey the use of different schemes for different occupations. Casey et al. (1992) sought to measure the use of a broad range of schemes by employers for different occupational groups. Others have developed typologies distinguishing between traditional and non-traditional payment schemes. Mahoney (1993) identifies the domination of job-based or fixed compensation that arose with industrialization and the development of the factory system, a payment system consistent with Scientific Management. Mahoney recognizes that this fixed rate of pay can be augmented by a range of performance/output elements. Non-traditional payment schemes include those based on attributes of the individual – skill, seniority and so on – and with performance. He links his threefold categorization of job rates, person and performance, to work (the degree of standardization or variation) and organizational characteristics (the range of technology or product variation). One advantage of this typology is an ability to locate sets of hybrid schemes, such as merit – a combination of job rate plus a performance element.

Performance measures are central to much of HRM and pay. Kessler (1992 and 1994) categorizes performance-related pay by the nature and assessment of the performance measures and criteria. Such measures and criteria vary considerably, but tend towards combinations of quantifiable (output) or more qualitative (behavioural) factors (Kessler 1994: 466). These can be organized and further differentiated in terms of a series of inputs and outputs at different levels in the company. Inputs reflect the attributes of the individual employee, including a range of traits, skills, competencies and discretionary share/profit schemes. Outputs include production, reaching objectives, commission, profit-related pay and a range of constitutional share/profit schemes.

These dimensions of type of payment scheme, definition of performance and the level in the organization at which some varying element of pay is determined can be combined to provide a typology of basic payment schemes, as is illustrated in table 13.1.

Job or fixed schemes remain the dominant form of payment: some 75 per cent receive either the rate for the job or are paid according to a pay scale (Casey et al. 1992: 32), although the percentage is declining slightly. The percentage of establishments in 1990 relying on fixed rates was 68 per cent for manual and 71 per cent for non-manual (Millward et al. 1992: 259). Job or fixed-rate schemes are those where there is no reward or incentive for achieving higher than set production levels. The desired level of production may be based on the results of work study, as in measured day work, or simply a time rate. The basis for pay ranges from a rate set either by market

Table 13.1   A typology of payment schemes

	Individual/job	*Group*	*Enterprise*
Job or fixed	Hourly rate, measured day work, job rate or salary range		Standard job rates and grades, either hourly or salary
Performance input person	PRP, seniority or merit-based pay, skill-based pay, competency- or qualifications-based pay, suggestion schemes	Skill, contribution-based, peer assessment schemes	Discretionary profit-sharing, share option and ownership
Performance output	Piece-work, payment by results, performance-based pay	Team bonus	Constitutional share option ownership, profit-related pay, cost-reduction schemes

or by negotiation with the trade union (the rate for the job), or it can take the form of a range of pay for a particular grade of work. The level at which the pay is set can be the individual, or more commonly the job, the group, the company or the industry; the latter applies when industry-wide or national bargaining prevails. The common feature of all job or fixed schemes is the absence of any requirement or incentive to produce to or above the established production/work levels.

Performance input or person-based schemes are those in which the basis for additional reward depends upon the *characteristics* of the individual. Additional reward can reflect length of service with the company, the acquisition and use of a range of skills, competencies, behaviour patterns or abilities which facilitate the work process and which the company believes are important to its success. More traditional forms of reward such as suggestion schemes fit into this category. At the group level, this can include peer assessment schemes and contribution-based pay, again reflecting the contribution of the individual to the work of the team or group. At the company level, input or person schemes are a range of discretionary profit-sharing, share option and ownership schemes.

In contrast, performance output schemes reward employees on the basis of achieving pre-set standards, objectives or production and work-related levels. The oldest and simplest of such schemes is piecework, or payment by results. Performance-related pay schemes which are based on quantifiable output-related criteria – output, quality, target-based – fit here. At the group level, it is the team bonus, and at the company level, constitutional share option, profit-related pay and cost reduction schemes.

Such a typology follows Kessler and Purcell (1992) in distinguishing performance-related pay by the nature of the performance criteria and how the assessment is linked to pay. Performance output schemes tend to be 'mechanistic' and put greater emphasis on achieving pre-set and established performance levels, rather than a more 'organic' and qualitative emphasis on individual performance.

Clearly, each category in this classification is subject to a number of influences. All are influenced by factors in the labour market, pay and rates, demand for labour and supply of particular occupations and skills. Cost of living, economic performance and labour market issues were identified by Millward et al. (1992: 238) as the three most common influences. Secondly, the payment system may be the product of collective bargaining. Special questions added to the New Earnings Survey in 1985 suggested that 64 per cent of full-time employees' pay was affected by collective bargaining (Beatson 1993: 407). The Workplace Industrial Relations Survey indicated figures of 48 per cent for manual employees and 43 per cent for non-manual employees in 1990 (Millward et al. 1992: 219). Thirdly, at the enterprise level, taxation law may shape the form of the profit, share option and ownership schemes; the rise of profit-related pay affecting some 1.9 million stems directly from legislation in 1987.

The typology classifies pure types, but does not indicate the bases of hybrid schemes, such as are indicated by Mahoney's (1993) model, nor does it indicate the link between the performance element and pay. Kessler (1994) identified three different linkages of pay to performance that reflect whether or not the payment is consolidated, and the level at which the bonus is determined. The performance element can vary between consolidation into the basic pay and non-consolidation in which a lump sum varying in size from year to year is paid. Nevertheless, the typology is a useful starting point to consider in more detail differences between particular schemes, reasons for and extent of the shift in popularity of different schemes and levels of operation both generally and for particular occupational groups. It facilitates a more constructive breakdown of performance-related pay based on the focus on either inputs or outputs and the level at which performance is measured.

Job, Fixed or Time Rates and Grades

The first reference to job or fixed pay schemes – measured daywork – was in the printing trade in the fourteenth century. Master printers were expected to produce sufficient sheets of paper which, when stacked, would reach a predetermined mark, a 'day werk', on a wall. By the 1600s published tables of day werkes (how much an agricultural labourer could be expected to produce under different conditions) were available for landowners as an early form of manpower planning and labour costing. Clearly, the introduction of clock time and, more recently, time and motion study offered a solution to many of the problems of defining 'effort' or 'reasonable' performance by employees.

Gospel's (1983) account of the history of payment schemes provides a valuable account of the relationship of pay to production methods, and the emergence of both job and simple output schemes. With the Industrial Revolution employers faced major problems in motivating and controlling employees. The traditional alliances between master and servant seemed ill-suited to the new methods and pace of work, and the problems of generating and maintaining a sense of co-operation appeared harder, especially after the formation of trade unions.

Initially many employers, after abandoning experiments with model villages, turned to the putting-out system. The employer provided raw materials and sometimes tools to a dispersed labour force. This cheap system of production avoided the need for the conventional factory; it reduced capital investment and spread the risk of production. Secondly, it was a flexible system of production: the employer could alter production levels by varying both the amounts of materials put to outworkers and the numbers of outworkers. Thirdly, production efficiency was partially assured through the rational economic assumptions of motivation.

Home- or outworking is the contemporary version of the putting-out system. Employees or self-employed people work at home on material delivered and collected by the employer. It flourishes in sectors such as clothing, light and low-value assembly work, maintenance, data inputting and areas of computer programming. When linked to assumptions of employee motivation which stress the discretion of individuals to plan and schedule their own work and the freedom of working at home, it becomes a respectable HRM technique and a recognized part of the flexible working force. It can be an efficient technique, as its flexibility enables rapid readjustment to changed levels of demand, and it reduces long-term non-wage labour costs. In many respects it parallels the practice of large firms of interlocking their sub-contractors to their production.

Larger-scale production and the need to reduce costs associated with stocks of work-in-progress favoured the factory system of production. Gospel (1983) notes that as work became located within the factory, different methods of group payment systems emerged, including the butty system, gang working and sub-contracting. These schemes, which emerged in the early nineteenth century, contain within them many of the elements of modern motivation theory. All, to a varying extent, stressed elements of both economic incentives (scientific management) and social needs (human relations).

In addition to the motivational benefits, these schemes placed the onus for efficiency and resolution of production problems on employees (frequently the skilled workers or gang boss). Such schemes tended to operate best where there was high manual skill, a low level of mechanization or non-standard and non-recurring tasks. As production became integrated and more sophisticated a greater degree of planning and hence co-ordinated control was necessary.

Increasing mechanization and much of automation necessitated routine regular tasks which were less suited to the freedom and variable pacing of such group production methods. Nevertheless, recent technological and organizational developments in a number of industries have enabled firms to return to such concepts, within an HRM framework, to organize their production around group production concepts for motivational reasons associated with productivity and quality; for example, job enlargement, autonomous work groups and cellular production schemes.

By the mid-nineteenth century employers in the textile industries had lists of piece-work prices; these spread to common lists for towns and then for districts. The rise of such town and district rates gave an important role to employers' associations. Additionally, the impact of piece-work contributed to the rise of trade unionism and attempts to reduce the worst effects of the evident exploitation between the piece rates and prices.

Elsewhere time or fixed rates prevailed. The end of the nineteenth and first part of the twentieth centuries witnessed frequent attempts by management to introduce piece-work systems into industries and occupations traditionally paid on the basis of time or hourly rate. But at the same time Fordist production methods – mass production, scientific management and standardization – were emphasizing the 'job' as the basis for pay, recruitment, training and trade union negotiation and collective agreements (Mahoney 1993: 339). For both time and piece-work rate systems the pressures to improve efficiency led to the progressive introduction of work study or time and motion study to establish the most efficient methods of work and the time necessary to complete standard tasks; this progressed to time standards as the basis of the pay system. A variant of time systems incorporating work study is measured day work (MDW).

In measured day work systems, the pay of the employee is fixed on the understanding that a specified level of performance is maintained and that pay does not fluctuate in the short term. This arrangement relies on some form of work measurement as a means both of defining the required level of performance and of monitoring the output level (Office of Manpower Economics 1973, quoted in Burchill 1976: 74). Measured day work schemes are appropriate when output is machine- or process-controlled, when operations are closely linked and when management seeks high and consistent production from a rigid sequence of operations.

In the UK, MDW was seen as a payment system which overcame many of the industrial relations difficulties associated with payment-by-results (PBR) schemes. It was claimed that it would lead to improved flexibility of labour and higher productivity (National Board for Prices and Incomes 1967; IDS 1979); hence it was sometimes described as a 'high day rate system of payment'. While it generally led to fewer disputes over pay rates, these were replaced by more disputes over effort and 'manning levels'. In reality the gains were often less and the problems greater. Operationally the schemes relied on work study arrangements which were often complex and difficult to understand. The lack of an incentive to improve output led to effort drift and minimum acceptable effort, and later schemes often had a bonus element added to encourage either performance or quality. Furthermore, there was no incentive for production employees to maintain production, or to assume responsibility for undertaking additional tasks. Above all, the scheme required a much greater degree of competency among management to programme work efficiently, to maintain sufficient levels of stocks and components and to organize adequately to reach and maintain satisfactory production schedules.

Fixed, job or time rates and grades – either hourly, weekly, monthly or yearly – have been and continue to be the dominant form of payment and the basis upon which most performance-based payments are made. Frequently, merit and performance pay and skill-based pay take the form of additional increments to the established pay grading structure. They remain the norm for most white-collar staff and are popular in smaller organizations and/or where the work is varied or non-standard and hence it is difficult or costly to apply work study techniques. Typically and traditionally, much of personnel and trade union activity has been organized around the requirements of the job: job analysis, descriptions and evaluation, selection, training and work organization.

However, the extent to which such pay was established by multi-employer, industry-wide bargaining has declined. By the 'mid-1990s over 90 per cent of private sector employees will have pay bargained or otherwise determined by the enterprise that employs them' (Brown and Walsh 1994: 448). Between 1985 and 1990 the proportion of employees who had their pay determined by collective bargaining fell to below 50 per cent (Beatson 1993: 405).

Time, rate and grade systems illustrate many of the requirements for a successful payments scheme. They are simple and cheap to operate and are easily understood by all. Many of the schemes have both the advantages and disadvantages of scientific management and Fordist principles. Standardization of the work and the task led to simplification of training, selection and payment. It led to detailed job descriptions and often large numbers of rates of pay and/or narrow grades and to job rigidity. It frustrated attempts to introduce functional flexibility and formalized systems of team working. Manual job rates have become broader, more general and with fewer rates of pay (IDS 1992a), and rigid salary structures have increasingly given way to more flexible pay spines. Thus the move from Fordist production systems of standardized production and mass markets to more flexible production systems and niche markets has led to increased flexibility in time- and grade-based systems of payment.

Performance-based Schemes

Performance output-based payment schemes

Both traditional and modern schemes have an established relationship between performance or output and reward. At the individual or job level, piece-work schemes are the oldest and simplest form of output incentive. Pay is proportional to effort, the more produced the larger the reward. The scheme rests on 'rational economic' assumptions about motivation, and as such invokes a degree of criticism from the human relations tradition, the source of much of HRM. However, there are clear parallels between piece-work and the newer forms of performance-related pay. It is easy to argue that performance-related pay is the designer version of piece-work for white-collar and managerial staffs.

Payment-by-results (PBR) schemes are defined as payment systems which attempt to establish a formal relationship between pay and output or effort. Such systems have one underlying assumption: namely, that where the worker can vary output according to the effort put into work and this can be related to earnings in an understandable manner, the prospect of increased earnings will induce greater effort. (National Board for Prices and Incomes 1968a: para. 8).

Operationally, the simplicity and some of the motivational value are lost for four reasons. First, the scheme needs some method to determine appropriate performance levels. This usually implies the introduction of some form of work study or rate-fixing. Secondly, notions of fairness, equity and expectation demand that techniques should ensure that workers of similar skills and economic value should earn approximately the same (ACAS 1983). Thirdly, the need for some security of earnings imposes the need for a minimum level or fall-back rate. This can range from 30 per cent to 70 per cent. Most schemes tend to have a form of guaranteed earnings when operators cannot work for lack of materials, machine breakdowns, and so on. Fourthly, there is much evidence that employees endeavour to work to informal limits and restrict their pace of work.

Most payment schemes are work-measured schemes. A set time is allowed to complete a task. The bonus depends upon the difference between actual time taken and allowed time, that is, the amount of time saved. Standard times can be established by actually measuring the task, or synthetically, by the use of previously established measurements. The incentive element can be varied in four ways. First, proportionally, where the bonus increases in direct proportion to output. Secondly, progressively, where the bonus increases at a faster rate above a particular level. Thirdly, regressively, where the bonus increases at a slower rate than output. Finally, variably, where the relationship between payment and output differs at different levels of output.

The 1990 Workplace Industrial Relations Survey (Millward et al. 1992) suggested that some 32 per cent of workplaces have PBR schemes for manual staffs. New Earnings data, albeit generated on the basis of a slightly different question, indicate a slight fall in the percentage of manual employees in receipt of incentive payments. However, this decline may reflect the declining numbers employed in those industries which have been the traditional strongholds of PBR schemes.

Schemes can seek to reward quality and other items as well as output. For employers, piece-work systems put the onus for efficiency on operators and are a well-proven system of motivation. However, such schemes tend not to provide short-term control over production levels or wages. Incentive schemes can have an adverse effect on the quality of work and can lead to considerable negotiation over changes in methods, materials and volumes of output and their effects on earnings. Particularly in engineering, the ability of production workers under piece-work schemes to increase output as compared with those, such as skilled staffs, under time systems of pay, led to issues of relativities and differentials becoming issues of dispute. In times of a high demand for labour, piece-work schemes can lead to increases in labour costs as employees seek to maintain average earnings when new times, methods or materials are introduced.

Traditionally, bonus payments have been introduced at either the individual or group level to encourage employees to maintain or improve on standard production and/or quality. These can take the form of either a fixed payment or a scheme in which the payment varies according to sustained changes in achievement levels. While such schemes appear to introduce a degree of incentive, they tend to become more costly and complex to administer. Significantly, there is little evidence to suggest that such bonus schemes have a measurable motivational impact.

In recent years attention and developments have tended to be concentrated at the enterprise level with the development of share ownership and profit-related pay schemes. The UK government has pursued a policy of wider share ownership, and has influenced both the type of scheme and their popularity by a series of legislative innovations and changes. Measures in 1978 led to tax relief for 'approved profit-sharing'. Approximately three-quarters of a million employees currently participate in Inland Revenue-approved schemes which can, depending on the length of time the shares are held, incur no tax liability when the shares are finally sold. Administratively such schemes can be complex (IDS 1993, 1994c).

Employee share-ownership plans vary widely, and it is estimated that up to a third are in reality forms of executive share option schemes (IDS 1994c), and hence are based more on the position and status of the employee than a function of the output of either the individual or the organization. The concept is based on establishing a trust to hold a proportion of the enterprise's shares on behalf of employees. The proportions vary from 100 per cent in a number of road haulage and bus companies to 30 per cent elsewhere (IDS 1994c). Unless the majority of employees vote otherwise, shares can only be sold back to the trust. The PSI payment systems survey results suggest that up to 24 per cent of professional and some 15 per cent of craft employees have share plans operated for them (Casey et al. 1992: 21).

Academically, profit-related pay schemes derive from the ideas of Weitzman and Meade, that employment would be increased and wage-induced inflation reduced if a significant proportion of pay was based on a fixed percentage of a profit-sharing pool. In practice, 1987 tax legislation and the opportunities to minimize tax exposure of up to 20 per cent of pay or £4,000 have made such schemes attractive. Under such schemes pay is formally linked to company profits, and can vary depending on whether or not profits are made. It is a means of subsidizing or raising take-home pay at low cost (Labour Research Department 1994) and of reducing tax exposure, well illustrated by the 1993 Budget changes which removed the 'guaranteed' profit-related pay schemes. The original measures have undergone a number of changes, but at June 1994 some 1.9 million, or one in ten, of private sector workers were covered by between 7,000 and 7,500 registered schemes (Labour Research Department 1994; IDS 1992a, 1994a). Such schemes have tended to be in the financial services sector, limited areas of retailing, banks and building societies.

Profit-sharing is more broadly based. The PSI payment systems survey suggested that 29 per cent of managers and administrators, 19 per cent of clerical, 12 per cent of craft, and 7 per cent of personal and protective staffs had some form of profit-sharing (Casey 1992: 21). Profit-sharing can be a new element in the reward package, or be a substitute for part of pay or for a pay increase, or to retain staff. There is some evidence that profit-sharing is spreading to manual employees, specially in the recently privatized utilities, where the motive may relate to a broader policy of reducing the role of collective bargaining.

More traditionally, enterprise bonus schemes lead to an additional payment for all employees based directly on the total volume of output, profit, or the sales value of goods produced in a given period. Other schemes (Rucker and Scanlon plans) have been based around ideas of reducing costs as well as increasing output. Typically, a bonus will be paid when production exceeds a predetermined level. The bonus can increase when further production and/or quality targets are reached. The advantages of such schemes echo much of the human relations literature: increased employee involvement, enhanced teamwork, a more co-operative and collaborative atmosphere, an ability to use employees' knowledge and skills to reduce costs, improve efficiency and lead to an increased sense of unity of purpose.

Where there is gradually rising demand and a slow rate of product and technical change, such schemes can have an influence. However, the direct incentive effect on individual employees is weak since they cannot see any clear and direct relationship between their work, overall performance and the bonus paid. Drawing on expectancy theory, we can see how an employee may feel increased resentment because increased effort has not resulted in an increase of the bonus. There is little evidence of sustained success of such schemes in large organizations.

Performance input or person-based schemes

Schemes in which the size of the performance payment depends upon some assessment of the input of the individual or the characteristics of the individual can be defined as performance input or person-based schemes. This category includes a mixture of both traditional and new schemes.

Traditional and popular schemes include additional payments, usually increments in a salary grade, for length of service or age, or a variable starting salary based on qualifications and experience. Merit payments, either constitutional or discretionally based assessments of performance, have been increasingly used in preference to service increments (IDS 1988c).

Skill- or competency-based pay likewise has both traditional and modern features. Pay differentials on the basis of skill have been a traditional feature in engineering, both between skilled and non-skilled workers and between different skills (Armstrong 1993: 99). Recent developments have sought to both deepen and broaden employee skills to facilitate both vertical and horizontal functional flexibility, and hence target rewards towards the acquisition of 'new' or 'additional' skills (IDS 1992a, 1994a). The basis for skill-based pay may be national qualifications or company-specific skills and competencies, 'groups of skills which the organisation is willing to reward with extra pay' (ibid.: 102). The order of the acquisition of skills may be defined and based on assessment of the individual, but the costs of such training and monitoring competency levels is frequently high (Cross 1992).

Suggestion schemes are a traditional form of additional reward.

Typically, schemes offer some economic reward for ideas which aid production. The reward can be made to the employee who makes the suggestion or be added to the bonus scheme paid to all staff. Plant- or enterprise-wide schemes have been advocated by human relations writers, who stress the collaborative and co-operative atmosphere that can be engendered by such schemes, which encourage all employees to contribute to improving performance or reducing costs and hence share in a reward.

Undoubtedly the symbolic payment system of HRM is performance-related pay (PRP). In this chapter performance-related pay is divided into two broad types – output and input focused – reflecting differences in the nature of the performance criteria. There is some evidence of a move away from an emphasis on personal qualities inherent in conventional merit rating towards an assessment of performance against managerially established objectives (Fowler 1988). In practice many schemes combine both, sharing the general principle of the abandonment of general, annual pay increases for all and a move towards schemes in which all increases are based on the performance of the individual. The popularity of schemes which qualitatively assess a range of behavioural criteria for both non-manual and manual staffs warrants a separate review. While PRP has a high priority according to personnel managers, the incidence of such payment schemes is somewhat less. Merit pay, financial participation and individual PBR schemes remain the most common forms of performance-related pay (Beatson 1993: 413).

It is difficult to fault the aims of PRP: 'to improve performance by converting it from an indiscriminate machine to a more finely tuned mechanism, sensitive and responsive to a company's needs' (Brady and Wright 1990: 1), The principles – rewarding the right staff and targeting effort where the organization wants it – appear equally sound.

A major element in the popularity of performance-related pay has been its widespread introduction in the public sector. During the 1980s and 1990s the UK government endeavoured to move away from the traditional wage and salary principles of equity of treatment – that all government employees doing the same job should receive the same pay – towards basing pay on a combination of local labour market rates and individual performance. The trend has been to inject a more managerialist/commercial approach. Putting performance pay into the various areas of the public service has been as much an act of political will as of new employment policy, and affects in varying forms more than 500,000 non-industrial civil servants.

Four reasons are most frequently cited to explain the spread of performance-related pay: first, it is seen as an element in a wider strategy of changing employee attitudes towards those which stress high performance and a new corporate culture. It can be coupled with more sophisticated and complex performance appraisal schemes and constitute a central element in a policy for training and development. Secondly, in terms of expectancy theory, it stresses the link between individual performance and reward. The basis for expectations of reward change from those of cost of living, comparability and other factors external to the organization, to the individual's own efforts and the success of the organization. Thirdly, to relate to employees on an individual basis is seen as contributing to a reduction in the influence of trade unionism and collective bargaining. It underpins a unitarist view of the enterprise and a teamwork approach to management. Fourthly, it can minimize increases in labour costs since it replaces annual increases for all employees with a system of targeting increases to those employees who contribute more, in some way, to the organization.

However, there is a gap between many of the aims and reality. It has proved hard to establish performance criteria and to assess staff without unacceptable levels of subjectivity and inconsistency. The 'signs are that in many organisations individual PRP is leading to major problems' (Storey and Sisson 1993: 139). Contradictions emerge between the objectives and behaviours, the links between performance and levels of pay are not always clear and effective, and may contradict other policies (ibid.: 140–1).

The success of such schemes depends upon sustained low inflation (Fowler 1988); management trust, commitment and ability (IPM 1990; Kinnie and Lowe 1990); simplicity (Fowler 1988 cites the example of a scheme which had a 34-page management manual and required the completion of a six-page appraisal form for each employee); being an integral part of the company's total reward strategy (IPM 1990); an acceptable means to translate appraisal into pay (Kinnie and Lowe 1990); and considerable preparation and revision (IDS 1988b).

As employers face continued pressures to cut costs and manage to engineer out the need for some of the behaviour patterns rewarded in PRP schemes, there is an incentive to simplify the payment schemes or to use sub-contractors to assemble products. Recent developments in the electronics industry suggest that the 'golden age of PRP' may well be over for an increasing proportion of staff in the industry.

The history and development of payments schemes indicates that to be effective a system needs to relate to a number of factors. These are illustrated in table 13.2. There is much to suggest that a number of

Table 13.2 The traditional contexts of pay

Factors internal to organization	Environmental factors	General principles
Need to control labour costs	Relationship to market rates	Easy and cost-effective administration
Equity between jobs of equal worth	Trade union policies and industry practices	Easy to operate
Rewarding the good employee	Legislation, equal pay and value provisions	Easy to understand
Personnel management policies	Product markets and competition	Perceived as fair
Technological and organizational constraints		Solves problems and achieves aims
Product cycle and changes		

HRM payment schemes have ignored several of these basic considerations in their concern to increase the commitment of the individual.

Human Resource Management and Pay

Intellectually HRM, with its humanistic image of the employee, derives largely from human relations and neo-human relations. As such it draws on the concept of the work group, leadership styles, communication and job content to generate a range of motivational techniques and associated payment and reward systems to improve and reward enhanced performance. This element of HRM focuses on the behavioural elements as a basis of pay systems.

The aim of human resource strategy is: 'The expanded utilisation of human resources primarily through measures for enhancing motivation, tapping shop floor knowledge of production and corresponding measures for training and work organisation' (Jurgens et al. 1986: 259). The objective of improving quality and efficiency via a behavioural, more human or individual-centred approach is largely based on a reworking of a number of ideas from the 1940s to the 1960s.

Efficiency underlies the second strand of HRM, namely a focus on employees as the human assets of the firm and an increased focus on the costs of employees. In contemporary HRM literature we note the concern and investment in 'core' employees and the simultaneous search for more-effective 'flexible' patterns of employment. This leads to a number of contradictions. On the one hand, HRM presents itself as developing payment systems which link individual performance to career development and salary advancement, yet at the same time it debates the cost benefits of flexibility of working hours and reduced earnings for employees. Simultaneously it is concerned with developing reward and payment techniques to overcome the problems of motivating part-time or fixed-contract staff.

With its focus on increasing employee performance and commitment, HRM has to be seen as part of a wider strategy which includes:

- the reduction of labour costs through more-efficient and flexible patterns of work organization and division;
- the introduction of more-flexible and efficient technologies;
- increased control over the employee, to reduce the gap between potential and actual performance, to generate employee commitment rather than compliance;
- a move towards the individualization of employment relations.

The HRM techniques of pay and rewards can only be understood from this wider, and not always internally consistent, set of objectives, and form an appreciation of the power relations of work.

Goodrich's (1922) concept of the 'frontiers of control' envisaged work as a continual struggle in which the employers seek new schemes of motivation and work measurement to extend their control. Employees respond to such tactics by a variety of collective acts – organization, collective action and restrictions of output – to assert their control. The response of HRM to collectivized relations is to seek to reassert a unitary perspective. Crucial to most HRM pay schemes is a direct relationship between the individual and the organization. Individualized pay rates, usually based on some management assessment of performance, behaviour and attitudes, reinforce this link and act to reduce the sense and value of collective action amongst employees. Within the public sector there are examples in health, transport and local government of the introduction of performance-related payment schemes associated with the simultaneous ending of established collective-bargaining arrangements.

The response of HRM to the issue of control at work is to introduce a set of techniques which reduces the gap between employee performance and potential, and which increases employer control of the employee (Townley 1990). Control can be achieved by motivational methods (as in payment schemes), by leadership styles (through new work organization and communication methods that stress the work group), or by using technologically advanced forms of work monitoring and control. Frequently strategic HRM uses the interaction of a number of these aspects. Thus we can understand Peters and Waterman's (1982) contribution to HRM as an attempt to alert management to the unused potential performance of employees.

The response of HRM has been to look to organizational and involvement schemes to reinforce monetary-based schemes. The emphasis on the integrated work group, the possible introduction of quality circles and briefing groups along with a range of other involvement schemes have been used to buttress MDW schemes. These have tended to replace the older human-relations approach which stressed the adoption of plant- or enterprise-wide schemes. The human relations theories of motivation, of the value in developing a sense of teamwork, or, to use the more modern terminology, 'a corporate culture', led to the emergence of schemes which seek to improve overall performance and engender a sense of working together.

Summary and Conclusions

It is clear that there is no one best payment scheme. As table 13.3 illustrates, the broader context influences the suitability of a system. The technology of production and the particular problems experienced, the characteristics of the labour market, the extent and nature of competition and the attitudes that employees bring to work (Lupton and Gowler 1969), all influence the relevance of particular schemes. The history of payment schemes should lead us to be cautious of the claims of motivational theorists, as there is little evidence from the past that motivational schemes, apart from those based to a large degree on economic rewards, are successful. However, pay, the amount, relativities and pay differentials between individual or between groups are evidently of major importance in issues of motivation and satisfaction (National Board for Prices and Incomes 1968b). Equally, any motivation scheme must be cheap and easy to administer – a requirement which disqualifies many of the modern schemes. Additionally, we have focused on the immediate economic rewards of work: attention should be given to the other economic incentives – bonuses, facilities,

Table 13.3 Pay and contexts

Basis for pay	Method	Measure	Technology work method	Management
Job	Hourly rate salary grade	Standardised procedures	Taylorist systems	Mass production, stable technologies and work systems
Performance input	Skill-based pay	Qualifications, competency	Teamwork, variable technology and work flows	Variable production and technology, flexible organizations
	PRP	Behavioural, attitudes, etc.	Teamwork, individual work, where quality, effort, manner are important	High time cost in appraisal; management vulnerable to pressures to reduce costs
Performance output	PRP	Targets, quantifiable measures		
	Piecework	Need to identify work	Batch, short assembly lines, independent operations	Limited supervision, but time to set and monitor rates

perks, pensions, and so on, all of which constitute an element in the employee's assessment of the economic rewards of work.

Furthermore, any payment system must not only be simple, cheap to manage and effective, it must also relate to the methods of production and to labour market conditions. The concern of HRM for greater control of employees has created payment systems with a tremendously long administrative tail. The time to complete the appraisal system properly (especially if the scheme is linked to other personnel policies such as development and training, to allow for meaningful dialogue between the appraiser and appraisee) may well be regarded as excessive by line management. As such the scheme may fall into disrepute.

These contradictions and the neglect of technological contexts mean that developments in payment and reward schemes have operated, for the majority of firms, at the level of rhetoric rather than of substantial changes. Whilst there have been considerable developments in the introduction of performance-related payment schemes (IDS 1988a,b), and in some industries of the interrelationship of pay to new organizational structures and new policies towards trade unions, elsewhere the schemes have had only a limited effect, and have been rapidly modified or abandoned.

Any cursory review of the personnel journals leaves the impression that individual performance input versions of PRP are frequently promoted with evangelical zeal rather than logical argument (Brewster and Connock 1985). There is mounting evidence to suggest that there are few links between improving company performance and performance-related pay (Bevan and Thompson 1991). 'The positive effects of PRP have been, at most, very modest among Inland Revenue staff' (Marsden and Richardson 1991). Skill-based pay or performance output schemes, with their greater reliance on objective and quantifiable measures, may well prove more durable in most sectors than the behavioural and more subjective schemes.

References

Advisory, Conciliation and Arbitration Service (ACAS) 1983: *Job Evaluation*, Advisory Booklet no. 1. London: HMSO.

Advisory, Conciliation and Arbitration Service (ACAS) 1985: *Introduction to Payment Systems*, Advisory Booklet no. 2. London: HMSO.

Armstrong, M. 1993: *Managing Reward Systems*. Buckingham: Open University Press.

Armstrong, M. and Murliss, H. 1991: *Reward Management*. London: Kogan Page.

Beatson, M. 1993: Trends in pay flexibility. *Employment Gazette*, September 101(9): 405–28.

Bevan, S. and Thompson, M. 1991: Performance management at the crossroads. *Personnel Management*, November: 36–9.

Brady, L. and Wright, V. 1990: *Performance Related Pay*, Fact Sheet no. 30. London: Personnel Management.

Braham, J. 1982: *Practical Manpower Planning*. London: Institute of Personnel Management.

Brewster, C. and Connock, S. 1985: *Industrial Relations: Cost effective strategies*. London: Hutchinson.

Brown, W. and Walsh, J. 1994: Managing pay in Britain. In K. Sisson (ed.), *Personnel Management*, 2nd edn. Oxford: Blackwell.

Burchill, F. 1976: *Introduction to Pay Systems and Pay Structures with a Note on Productivity*. P881 Industrial Relations Course. Milton Keynes: Open University Press.

Casey, B., Lakey, J. and White, M. 1992: *Payment Systems: a look at current practice*. London: Policy Studies Institute, Employment Department.

Cross, M. 1992: Skill-based pay. Unpublished research paper produced for the IPM/NEDO working party.

Fowler, A. 1988: New directions in performance pay. *Personnel Management*, November, 30–4.

Goodrich, C.L. 1922: *The Frontier of Control*. London: Bell (republished 1975 by Pluto Press).

Gospel, H. 1983: The development of management organisation in industrial relations: a historical perspective. In K. Thurley and S. Wood (eds), *Industrial Relations and Management Strategy*, Cambridge: Cambridge University Press, pp. 91–110.

Incomes Data Services (IDS) 1979: *Guide to Job Evaluation*. London: IDS.

Incomes Data Services (IDS) 1980: *Guide to Incentive Payment Systems*. London: IDS.

Incomes Data Services (IDS) 1981: *Guide to Profit Sharing*. London: IDS.

Incomes Data Services (IDS) 1985: *Improving Productivity*, Study no. 331. London: IDS.

Incomes Data Services (IDS) 1987: *PRP and Profit Sharing*, Study no. 397. London: IDS.

Incomes Data Services (IDS) 1988a: *Integrated Pay*, Study no. 411. London: IDS.

Incomes Data Services (IDS) 1988b: *Paying for Performance: Top Pay Unit*. London: IDS.

Incomes Data Services (IDS) 1988c: *Bargaining*, Report no. 71. London: IDS.

Incomes Data Services (IDS) 1990: *Profit Related Pay*, Study no. 471. London: IDS.

Incomes Data Services (IDS) 1992a: *Teamworking*, Study no. 516. London: IDS.

Incomes Data Services (IDS) 1992b: *Profit Related Pay*, Study no. 520. London: IDS.

Incomes Data Services (IDS) 1993: *Profit Sharing and Share Options*, Study no. 539. London: IDS.

Incomes Data Services (IDS) 1994a: *Multi Skilling*, Study no. 558. London: IDS.

Incomes Data Services (IDS) 1994b: *Profit Related Pay*, Study no. 564. London: IDS.

Incomes Data Services (IDS) 1994c: *Employee Share Ownership Plans*, Study no. 568. London: IDS.

Institute of Personnel Management 1990: *Performance Related Pay*, Personnel Management Fact Sheet no. 30. London: IPM.

Jurgens, U., Dohse, K. and Malsch, T. 1986: New production concepts in West German car plants. In S. Tolliday and J. Zeitlin (eds), *The New Automobile Industry and its Workers*, Cambridge: Polity Press.

Kessler, I. 1991: Workplace industrial relations in local government. *Employee Relations*, 13(2), pp. 2–31.

Kessler, I. 1992: *Pay Determination in the Professional Civil Service*. Templeton College Management Research Paper. No. 1, January.

Kessler, I. 1994: Performance pay. In K. Sisson (ed.), *Personnel Management*, 2nd edn. Oxford: Blackwell.

Kessler, I. and Purcell, J. 1992: Performance related pay: objectives and application. *Human Resource Management Journal*, 2(3): 34–59.

Kinnie, N. and Lowe, D. 1990: Performance related pay on the shop floor. *Personnel Management*, November: 45–9.

Knowles, K.G.J.C. 1952: *Strikes: a study in industrial conflict*. Oxford: Blackwell.

Labour Research Department 1992: *Performance Related Pay*, Report series. London.

Labour Research Department 1994: *Profit Related Pay*, Booklets series. London.

Livy, B. (ed.) 1988: *Corporate Personnel Management*. London: Pitman.

Lupton, T. and Gowler, D. 1969: *Selecting a Wage Payment System*. London: Routledge & Kegan Paul.

Mahoney, T.A. 1993: Multiple pay contingencies: strategic design of compensation. In G. Salaman (ed.), *Human Resource Strategies*, London: Open University/Sage Publications.

Marsden, D. and Richardson, R. 1991: *Does Performance Pay Motivate? A study of Inland Revenue staff*. London: London School of Economics.

Millward, N. et al. 1992: *Workplace Industrial Relations in Transition*. Aldershot, Hants.: Dartmouth.

National Board for Prices and Incomes 1967: *Productivity Agreements*, Report no. 36. London: HMSO.

National Board for Prices and Incomes 1968a: *Payment by Results*, Report no. 65. London: HMSO.

National Board for Prices and Incomes 1968b: *Job Evaluation*, Report no. 83. London: HMSO.

Office of Manpower Economics 1973: *Measured Daywork*. London: HMSO.

Peters, T.J. and Waterman, R.H. 1982: *In Search of Excellence: lessons from America's best run companies*. New York: Harper & Row.

Royal Commission on Trade Unions and Employers' Associations 1968: *Two Studies in Industrial Relations*, Research Paper no. 11. London: HMSO.

Sisson, K. (ed.) 1994: *Personnel Management in Britain*. Oxford: Blackwell.

Storey, J. and Sisson, K. 1993: *Managing Human Resources and Industrial Relations*. Buckingham: Open University Press.

Townley, B. 1990: Foucault: power/knowledge and its relevance for HRM. Paper presented to a conference on *Employee Relations in Enterprise Culture*, Cardiff Business School, September.

14

Training and Development: the Employer's Responsibility?

JEFF HYMAN

Introduction: the Context for Training

In the first edition of this book this chapter noted that the broad environment within which organizations operate had undergone considerable changes over the 1980s. The main changes were represented by advances in technology and increased competition, underpinned by the climate of free-market individual enterprise embraced and promoted by the Conservative government. In turn, these contextual influences were associated with industrial restructuring, union decline and the influx of overseas operations, which collectively and individually presented domestic organizations with a complex of challenges. It was argued that these challenges could be met, in part at least, by employers adopting systematic training and development programmes.

From the perspective of the mid-1990s, there is no doubt that the same processes have continued and, indeed, accelerated throughout the early part of the decade, thereby sharpening the profiles of both challenges and opportunities to enterprises. It is clear, for example, that the pace of industrial restructuring is continuing unabated as manufacturing and extractive industries continue their long decline, public utilities and services become transformed into commercial operations and private sector services extend their coverage (see Hyman and Mason 1995). Moreover, union decline in terms of membership and influence has continued (McLoughlin and Gourlay 1994: ch. 1) and overseas companies, perhaps tempted by freedom from regulatory requirements in Britain, have expanded their operations (Oliver and Wilkinson 1992).

What is more questionable, however, concerns the extent to which the majority of British employers have taken responsibility for strategically training and developing their employees. Ashton and Felstead (1995: 248) conclude, for example, that there is no systematic evidence in support of 'transformation of training activity at the company level'. Though a more optimistic view is offered by Greenhalgh and Mavrotas (1994: 31), they also express concern at the 'firefighting' emphasis of much contemporary employer training practice. Finally, there is considerable uncertainty whether the much-vaunted government targets for company training will be met: by March 1994, only 600 companies had achieved the Investors in People standard and very few companies had been persuaded to adopt NVQ accredited training (*Guardian*, 3 March 1994).

The manifold tensions noted above have continued to stimulate close interest by researchers into the processes, strategies and practices of management and in particular the management of employee relations under conditions of turbulence in both product and labour markets. It has become apparent that changed circumstances do not lead to uniform responses by employers; indeed, under unregulated market conditions we can note considerable variation in the actions of managers in response to circumstances facing the organizations for which they are held accountable.

Examination of labour relations practice provides evidence of this variety of response. Attempts to manipulate the employment relationship have been allocated somewhat arbitrarily into either the hard or soft manifestations of human resource management (HRM), the former calculative and based upon rational deployment of organizational assets, both human and capital, to serve immediate organizational ends. In contrast, the soft approach, with its emphasis on motivation through communication and consultation, can trace its immediate ancestry to the human-relations traditions espoused by Mayo and adopted, more recently by Hertzberg, Argyris and others. Implicit in the soft approach is recognition of a long-term mutual commitment between employer and employees, a relationship which is lacking in the hard-edged version of HRM.

Though it is difficult to embrace these somewhat diverse trends within a universal model of HRM, there are common features. Both promote the supremacy of individual employee relationships over the collective, either implicitly or through overt emphasis; both link employee management with the broader operational directions to be taken by companies; accordingly, each stresses the need for an appropriate organizational culture within which these features can flourish. Researchers differ, though over interpretations of the extent to which migration towards either (or both) of these HRM poles has occurred.

In particular, doubts circulate as to the nature and extent of benefit attributable to contemporary HRM-driven employment relations (Fernie et al. 1994). As part of this re-evaluation, commentators have questioned whether specific and embracing personnel policies are actually enacted beneath the superficial highly polished HRM gloss (Marginson et al. 1988). Flexibility, a key component of either approach to HRM, seems to be rather more elusive in its functional form than is suggested by proponents of a multi-skilling revolution (MacInnes 1987: 113–24).

Training and development form a special case owing to their centrality in changing the performance potential of employees and managers; this importance is confirmed by the continuing attention afforded to these processes by government throughout the 1980s and 1990s (see, for example, White Paper 1988; *Labour Market and Skill Trends 1995/96*: 1994); by representative bodies of practitioners and employers; and by management consultants.

The problem has been, however, that training continues to hold insufficient attraction for individual employers. Following a succession of damning comparative studies of UK industrial performance, realization has hardened that British workers not only lack the skills and qualifications of their continental, American and Japanese counterparts (NIESR 1989; Mason and van Ark 1994), but that managers in the UK are sadly deficient in qualities found in abundance elsewhere and that insufficient is done by their employers to help managers to acquire qualifications and competence to enable them to manage better (Handy et al. 1988). It is true that numerous voluntary initiatives, such as the Management Charter Initiative and Opportunity 2000, have been launched in subsequent years, but nevertheless, the management development movement in Britain has been authoritatively typified as remaining in a 'fragile' state (Storey 1994: 394).

As British employers are consistently failing to train their staff and managers, or at least not training them sufficiently to close the gap on our trading partners (see, for example, Greenhalgh and Mavrotas 1994), it is difficult to see how they can be realistically pursuing an HRM approach which is dependent upon learning as the vital route to effective work, organizational performance and continuing adaptability. At the conceptual level, Thurley's (1990: 55) point that the 'HRM model tends to focus on skill development' confirms the centrality of training to HRM but fails to address the sort of model we are left with if opportunities for learning and skill enhancement are not offered in practice. The assumed links between HRM, training and performance again appear prominently in the diagrammatic representation of the

HRM process presented by Storey (1989: 7). Even in its hard manifestation, short-term market forces would lead rational employers to
train for immediate job requirements in the absence of alternative
sources of labour. There is some evidence that limited training opportunities are being offered by employers for that reason (Training Agency
1989). Nevertheless, limited is the key word; the same report points
out that two-thirds of economically active people aged between 19
and 59 claimed to have received no formal training over the previous
three years. Moreover, many of the respondents held scant expectations of receiving training, and, reflecting the 'anti-learning' cultural
context typified by so many organizations in the UK, pathetically few
saw any point in seeking it in the future.

The Failure to Train

But why have British employers failed to train and develop their staff,
when ample evidence exists that to do so offers them clear benefits?
In an illuminating article, Keep (1989) identifies a number of barriers
which must be surmounted if a genuine training climate is to be
adopted. One problem is that the surmounting must be performed by
personnel and training specialists, neither of whom have been well
equipped for such activity. Moreover, the barriers are substantial and
firmly rooted; only a minority of senior managers are educated to
levels enjoyed by their overseas counterparts and few have been recipients of sustained developmental programmes (ibid.: 118). Consequently, training for their employees has not received high priority.
Corporate objectives have tended to be short-term with strategies
defined by short-term profit and financial criteria, thereby constraining any longer-term developmental aspirations held by personnel specialists for their employees, and encouraging the acquisition of required
skills through poaching (ibid.: 121). Indirectly related to the imme-
diacy of domestic commercial activity, the continuing attachment of
British managers to informality in their employment practices miti-
gates against the adoption of HRM. Moreover, training the workforce
within an HRM framework could jeopardize the authority (and con-
ceivably, the jobs) of poorly equipped managerial staff by widening
the scope of tasks performed by subordinates. For this reason, resistance by line managers to some manifestations of HRM can be anticipated, and, as later research has established, has indeed emerged
(Hunter and Beaumont 1993; Cunningham et al. 1996).

Somewhat understated in Keep's classification are the effects of government policy, though this is an essential influence upon employer orientations towards training. Traditionally voluntarist in direction, government policy in the UK eschews legislation or other formal requirements imposed upon employers to train their workforces systematically. Voluntarism has culminated in the market-driven approach that has defined and dominated the Conservative period of office which began in 1979, in which training provision passed exclusively to employers to allocate on the basis of market need. The result has been that the imperatives of market uncertainty have, in combination with the other factors outlined above, conspired to loosen employer commitment to long-term training. (Coopers & Lybrand Associates 1985: 7). This abstentionist approach is in great contrast to the directions taken by the UK's leading trading partners: the Coopers & Lybrand report demonstrates that economically successful 'training countries' have real controls, legal, cultural or both, on training provision. Here, other than regular doses of exhortation, regulation is largely absent, and company executives feel little sustained pressure to change their ways.

If neither senior executives nor line managers can be relied upon to provide a positive environment for the development of employees, what is the scope for personnel specialists presumably more sensitive to the long-term consequences of such neglect? While they may wish for a stronger developmental orientation (and many HR managers would be schooled in the corporate advantages to be gained from policy-making openly formulated and consistently implemented), they frequently find themselves in a less than strategic position to push their preferences. We have seen that many organizations adopt limited time horizons for the realization of their objectives, leading to the managerial ascendancy of the financial specialist and the supremacy of cost controls as the mainspring of managerial action. And as Armstrong (1995: 151) has pointed out, accountants experience severe difficulty in accounting for investments in people; one consequence is that training expenditure is regulated very much according to cost rather than developmental investment criteria. Further, personnel would find it difficult to justify training expenditure owing to the acknowledged difficulties in measuring its return in financial terms. Not surprisingly, training evaluation beyond that of measuring its near-immediate impact upon individual recipients is rarely undertaken even in the most training-conscious organizations (Hussey 1988). The Training Agency (1989), which arrived at its conclusions through the careful aggregation of survey data, was nevertheless forced to rely largely upon anecdotal material to illuminate the beneficial effects of training, an approach which, by neglecting to highlight failures, quantify effects or illustrate trends, represents an easy target for the corporate accountant intent upon cost-reduction exercises.

Compounding the institutional weakness of the personnel department have been its associations with employee welfare; its range of superficial and unrelated activities; and, until recently, a uniformly inferior position within the managerial hierarchy. A high proportion of personnel practitioners appear to have lacked professional and relevant qualifications, itself an interesting observation, bearing in mind that the same people would be expected to act as the prime organizational advocates for the benefits of education, training and formal qualifications for employees. Equally serious, survey work indicates that formal and professional qualifications are held by limited numbers of training specialists. Moreover, the limited priority afforded to training was demonstrated in the same survey by the high proportion (two-thirds) of designated training specialists who were reported to spend less than one-tenth of their time on training activities (Hyman 1992).

Opportunities for Training

The analysis so far makes sombre reading for the HRM specialist convinced of the value of systematic development policies for the workforce and wishing to convert, confirm or increase an organization's commitment to this vital activity. At this point, we can state that all is not gloom: there are a number of favourable signs. Indeed, it could be argued that a combination of factors have currently converged to provide a more highly favourable context for promoting employee development than has been evident for some years, providing the human resource practitioner with scope to apply the specialized 'expert' skills associated with the function (Torrington 1989) in this direction.

As we shall see, these favourable signs are clearly interrelated but, for purpose of analysis, can be located within structural and occupational categories. The structural factors include the following: continuing problems of skill shortages and the need to recruit, grow, retain and motivate key employees in a climate where head-count reductions are prominent; enterprise reformation towards learning, empowered and lean organizations; increasing sophistication of technology; pressures of competition; quality of products and services. These factors combine to ensure a need for greater employee flexibility, involvement and adaptability, all of which are dependent upon the provision of systematic and continuing training and development.

Positive occupational indicators derive from a growing recognition by senior management of the relevance of the personnel function in confronting the structural and market challenges outlined above. There is, finally, growing acknowledgement of the importance of management education and development as expressed through the Management Charter Initiative (MCI), enthusiastic acceptance by many senior managers of responsibilities offered to them to co-ordinate training and enterprise in the government's employer-dominated regional training bodies (see p. 320), rising numbers of personnel specialists with formal occupational qualifications, and the apparent recent growth in the number of personnel managers at senior director level. The trends to some sophisticated personnel techniques, such as performance appraisal, also point towards a more consistent and integrative approach to employee management. A further favourable impetus has been provided by the publication of government aims to meet specific workplace training targets. The expanding significance of Europe on employment matters may also reinforce the need for personnel expertise. HRM specialists should now be considering how they can exploit the favourable tilt in their direction to establish a lasting organizational commitment to employee development.

In this chapter we next examine in more detail each of the structural factors identified above. This is followed by an exploration of the underlying occupational factors which might support HRM ambitions to establish a more strategic developmental orientation to employee management. The final section concludes that the UK's future competitiveness will be further undermined by a failure of employers to invest in employee skills enhancement and to utilise these investments to best advantage.

Structural Factors

Skill and labour shortages

A persistent threat to companies in the 1980s was posed by the prospect of the demographic downturn. To some extent, this threat has been offset by the economic recession of the early 1990s, combined with the strenuous efforts taken by many enterprises to restructure their organizations to operate with smaller core workforces.

Nevertheless, these downsizing operations can also expose serious skill deficiencies as existing employees and managers attempt to take on additional and extended responsibilities (see Clark 1993). Also, shortages of young entrants to the labour market are likely to continue owing to the growing pressure on, and tendency of, young people to continue in education: government intentions to bring the UK's modest higher education participation rates into line with other countries is being reflected in the growing numbers of young people continuing with their education beyond the compulsory leaving age. By 1991, the British entrant rate into higher eduction had reached 41 per cent of the relevant age range, more than double the figure of five years earlier (*The Times Higher Education Supplement*, 25 February 1994; Hyman 1992: 62). One outcome of these trends could be that better-educated and -qualified people will have high expectations of training and development once they enter the labour market, particularly if their future career prospects are dependent upon acquisition of transferable skills.

The related problem of labour shortages, though not as acute as during the 1980s, is still restricting economic performance (see, for example, *Skills and Enterprise Briefing*, August 1994: *Financial Times*: 1996). This problem derives directly from the UK's historical and continuing failure to train systematically and continuously. We are still in the paradoxical situation of witnessing persistently high levels of unemployment co-existing with critical shortages of essential skills.

These problems could well be exacerbated now that the European Union presents few barriers to the mobility of valuable skills across national boundaries; the signs are that more qualified people can be enticed to work on mainland Europe than will be attracted to come and work in the UK. Employers are beginning to recognize the gravity of the situation and HRM specialists are in a unique position to push claims for an integrated human resources policy offering high priority to employee development. The fact that most young graduates who leave their first positions after less than two year' service do so through lack of fulfilment and opportunities for self-development provides the HRM specialist with valuable ammunition. The scope, and challenge, facing HRM is demonstrated by a survey reported recently in which over one-quarter of graduate recruits considered that their organizations did not show interest in their careers. Even worse, over one-third replied that their managers had not been trained to look after graduates, while a further 55 per cent were unable to say whether their managers had received this training (see *Personnel Management Plus* 1990).

New technology

The potential impact of new technology on work has been much examined in recent years (see, for example, Cooley 1987; Daniel 1987; Baldry 1988; Webster 1990; Clark 1993b) and is highly pertinent to the skills shortage issue outlined above, in that the full productive capacities of new technology cannot be fully exploited in the absence of skills to operate and service it. Without the required familiarity, employers will either shrink from introducing technology, or, if introduced, only part of the potential of the new technology will be realized. In either case, the consequence will be a lack of competitive edge. A National Institute of Economic and Social Research (NIESR) study into the manufacture of kitchen furniture in the UK and Germany provides startling evidence of how a highly skilled workforce interacts with technology to produce high-quality goods and a wide choice of output without compromising productivity. Needless to say, this represented the German rather than British workforce; in the former, nine out of every ten manual employees were qualified skilled craft workers, in contrast to the one in ten found in the UK factories (Steedman and Wagner 1987). A recent paired comparison study of Dutch and UK engineering companies arrived at similarly depressing conclusions. Whilst the UK companies concentrated on producing semi-skilled workers carrying out a narrow range of tasks, a much higher proportion of Dutch workers were trained to craft level and above, and these employees were able to adapt rapidly and effectively to the introduction of new technology, leading to a productivity advantage over the UK companies of 25–30 per cent in output terms alone (Mason and van Ark 1994).

If British employers are to move away from the 'low added-value–low skills equilibrium' label ascribed to them so appropriately by Finegold and Soskice (1988: 22), technology must be embraced and the skills to operate and manage it must accompany its introduction and development. Evidence shows that most workforces readily accept new technology and that introduction is most successful when the human implications of its introduction, in terms of participation, communication, security of employment through training and safety, are given full and open consideration by management (Daniel and Millward 1993; Fogarty and Brooks 1986: 9). The human resource specialist must, therefore, be familiar with technology and be in a position to insist to line colleagues and superiors that these 'human' conditions be fulfilled prior and subsequent to the implementation of the technology. Managers who, generally speaking, are themselves not technologically literate should receive new-technology training as an integral part of their own development: a survey by Brown and Coopers & Lybrand in 1988 disclosed that, while two-thirds of managers had access to a computer, only two-fifths used a computer on a regular basis. Over half of the managers surveyed had received no training at all in the application of computer technology.

Pressures of competition

Competition can take many forms. Traditionally, product or service competition is based on cost to the consumer; *ceteris paribus*, in a competitive market, the least-expensive product or service will prevail. In reality, of course, products serving the same market can vary considerably not only in terms of cost but in other factors as well. Quality of produce can vary, so that output from some sources or countries is automatically associated with value and quality, such as Marks & Spencer, or Japan as a quality producer country. Conversely, other products can be tarnished with the tag of poor quality or reliability (for example, in 'finish' or in attention to detail). Availability is another potential source of difference, coupled with punctuality in delivery times and after-sales service. As we saw with the kitchen furniture example cited above, choice available in terms of model range or services offered is also likely to influence consumers.

Product competition between companies and between producer countries is becoming more heated with the emergence of the global economy and the rise of developing countries to challenge the dominance of established producers. A major plank of the Conservative government's economic strategy to ensure economic stability has been to introduce or strengthen the operation of market forces in the public sector through privatization, compulsory competitive tendering, market testing and, more generally, through liberalizing the labour market.

The disciplines of competition are forcing organizations to examine closely their methods of manufacture, quality, service and customer relations as key components of their service to consumers (see Saggers 1994). *In Search of Excellence* (Peters and Waterman 1982) and its flood of derivative publications have been widely influential among management circles in stressing the values of a service- and quality-based corporate culture. While technical innovation will be a major feature in ensuring quality, choice and output, this must be combined with the required human inputs along the entire chain of production. Effort, attention to quality, adaptability and cost-effectiveness will be the necessary components of the productive mix. These demand not merely a level of technical competence, but also the commitment of all employees concerned and the challenge to the employer of retaining commitment over time.

In these situations, training, in the broad sense of encouraging continuing positive orientations to the organization, becomes crucial, for this should help to establish and reinforce the crucial value-system base upon which the development of commitment can be built. But positive orientations do not, and will not, simply emerge from the organizational infrastructure; they need to be planned for and systematically implemented throughout the workforce. No greater contrast with earlier images of training, restricted to a tiny minority of skilled craftsmen or the rare management course offered 'when conditions allow', could be envisaged.

The drive for quality

We saw above that competition is expressed strongly through attention to quality. A number of factors have contributed to this concentration on quality. First, new technology for production and services is able to perform consistently to the highest standards. Consumers now expect these standards to be met or exceeded. Secondly, higher levels of disposable income mean that consumers are more concerned with quality than with price alone. The quality expectations of people grow in line with ever-improving standards and the publicity given to these through publications such as *Which* and growing numbers of televised consumer programmes. Thirdly, low-cost production can take place where labour is relatively inexpensive, as in some developing countries and the emergent economies of Eastern Europe. Advanced economies cannot easily compete on labour cost criteria and aim to seek out appropriate market opportunities, possibly requiring smaller batch production at high quality and supported by continuing product innovation. Fourthly, production and provision of services are now heavily internationalized. Developments made in the parent country can rapidly be reproduced in satellite operations, requiring competing producers to respond with equivalent or superior innovations, thereby stimulating further competitive reaction.

The emphasis given to quality in production and in service provision has clear implications for provider organizations in their approaches to employee management and in particular to training and development programmes. Hence, following the example set by Japanese producers, many organizations are now experimenting with built-in quality programmes such as 'zero-defect' and 'right-first-time' manufacture. The infusive effect of this approach throughout the workforce can be seen from the account given by Peter Wickens (1987) of the Nissan production system. In a chapter entitled 'Quality – above all', Wickens makes reference to the commitment given to quality in the company's 'philosophy statement': 'We aim to build profitably the highest quality car sold in Europe.' He stresses that the positive commitment to quality permeates all levels of the company and is especially prominent in management, whose attitudes and knowledge derive from 'their education level, the seniority system, continuous in-house training, development and rotation and sheer dedication' (ibid.: 63).

Encouraging employees to become their own quality controllers, implementing total quality programmes, team-building, or introducing and sustaining a 'quality culture' into the organization have far-reaching implications for the training and development of the entire workforce, particularly as it is almost impossible to impose quality requirements on employees. As Wickens points out, concern for quality must emerge from the relationship between employee and product. Hence, training for quality consciousness needs to be a continuous and inclusive part of the work of each manager, and should be integral to the relationship between them.

Management style

If a concern for quality cannot be instilled by coercion into employees who are expected to assume greater responsibility for their work, there are additional implications for the employee–management relationship. In these conditions, managers need to learn to co-ordinate and advance the talents and skills of specialized staff. Key employees must be encouraged to use their own discretion to arrive at speedy and effective solutions to problems surfacing in their spheres of activity. However, they need access to the resources, informational and physical, required in order to resolve these issues. This approach to management calls for a 'high-trust' (to quote Fox 1985) relationship between the parties. Such a response cannot be forced from employees but needs to be part of an agreed equation, in which management are willingly prepared to share information with subordinates, to delegate work and share responsibility (and rewards) whilst maintaining their overall authority on the basis of applied knowledge and organizational contribution rather than through titular status. The 'empowered' organization, which is expected to apply these principles, is a current example of moves in this direction (Stewart 1994; Cunningham et al. 1996).

Participative management cannot take place within a vacuum. It requires to be adopted as part of an overall philosophy endorsed and applied throughout the organization. Many managers have an understandable fear of releasing valuable information to colleagues (let alone subordinates), fearing that to do so will dilute their responsibility or deprive them of authority. As Keep (1989: 123) has pointed out, the prospects of greater employee self-reliance can be threatening to an under-educated and potentially vulnerable management team. Training can help managers to overcome these fears, as well as offering them the opportunity to develop their own abilities for closer involvement in management affairs (see Kanter 1983).

Practically, in the participative organization, managers will need to learn how to disclose and share information, possibly through formal consultation or communication networks; they will need to learn how to provide opportunities for individuals and groups to use their talents, and to encourage their development through appraisal and appropriate reward systems. These are not easy changes to contemplate for managers accustomed to a culture of protective secrecy, anxious to safeguard existing command structures for fear of losing face or status. Change of this sort can only be considered when senior management itself is prepared to take the lead in adapting its management style rather than concentrate on reliance upon the artificial and self-defeating protections of hierarchy and secrecy.

The human resource function can provide a catalytic service in helping to bring about a more participative management style. Nevertheless, fears of sharing can only be genuinely dispelled when the sharers know that the consequences to them (there might be genuine and well-founded fears that jobs are at risk from redundancy as tiers of the organization structure are removed through de-layering) will not be unfavourable. Managers can learn, but the organization must prepare secure ground for the learning to take place.

Enterprise Restructuring

Other factors also pointing to the importance of management style include the considerable changes occurring to the framework of organizations. Though the directions and extent of structural modification have varied, they are linked by a common strand in that change has been sought as a direct or indirect response to market pressures. Changes include moves to flexibility through sub-contracting various activities to external agencies, thereby helping to minimize otherwise fixed labour costs; decentralization of activities into product or geo-graphical divisions (multi-divisional or 'M' form); development of 'organic' structures to respond to market and process change; decen-tralized decision-making accompanied by devolution to enterprise-, division- or establishment-level bargaining in organizations that recog-nize trade unions. Decentralization might also be accompanied by an abandonment of collective bargaining procedures and their replacement by a more individualistic style of employee management (McLoughlin and Gourlay 1994: 15).

The second factor is the move, in some organizations at least, to-wards forms of work flexibility (ACAS 1988). Functional flexibility is associated with more responsibility (Cunningham et al. 1996). Em-ployees gain increased discretion over their work, and in so doing become more valuable to the organization, which may introduce tech-niques such as performance appraisal and performance-related pay in order to monitor and stimulate work performance. Deficiencies can be remedied by supplementary training; high performers should receive regular opportunities to develop and extend their capabilities through training and development. It should also be added that appraisers will almost certainly require training in order to assess the work of subor-dinates systematically and fairly.

These structural shifts have also led to calls for more profound organizational and managerial shifts towards lean production (Womack et al. 1990), business process re-engineering and, in its most recent manifestation, 'lean enterprise', which combines elements of flexibility, teamwork, multi-functionality and 'learning organization' processes (*The Financial Times*, 11 March 1994).

The shifts taking place within the broader context in which organ-izations operate and the complementary developments taking place within organizations themselves have clear implications both for HRM generally and specifically for training and development, until now the least-advanced and most-neglected of all HRM activities.

However we define and describe HRM, it is clear that these changes are leading to re-evaluation by managers of employment relationships within a broad framework which gives priority to the attainment of organizational objectives. A significant outcome for managers and employees has been the rise in performance appraisal, new remunera-tion and bargaining arrangements and other significant changes to terms and conditions of employment. Nevertheless, if this re-evaluation is going to engage fully with the challenges facing organizations, it is imperative that full weight be given to training and development to accompany these initiatives. Further neglect will not only increase the

distance between ourselves and competitor nations but rapidly bring
into question the motives of management towards restructuring employment relationships. The costs of change will have been borne by
employees through job loss and continuing insecurity, and the benefits, in terms of subsequent mutual commitment between the parties,
will be largely illusory.

Occupational Factors

The HR function is going to have to fight its own corner in converting
the potential noted above into developmental reality for managers and
employees. But at least they will be so engaged at a time when conditions for advance are relatively favourable. We can point to at least
seven areas which coincide with the structural factors noted earlier
and which could place HR specialists in a more favourable position
to promote their case for continuing investment in employees and
managers.

First, we can note the positive reception by employers of the wide-
ranging criticisms contained in the reports of Handy et al. (1988) and
Constable and McCormick (1987) on management education, development and training. Positive action emerged quickly through the
establishment of the Management Charter Initiative: increasing numbers of employers have committed their organizations to follow a code
of good practice for their managerial employees. By July 1991, over
900 organizations, employing in excess of one-quarter of the workforce,
had committed themselves to the Charter (Storey 1994: 381).

A second favourable sign of senior management endorsement of the
links between training and performance has been the enthusiastic
response and committed involvement of senior executives (including
directors of HRM) as members of the Training and Enterprise Councils (TECs, in Scotland Local Enterprise Companies – LECs) established by the government to assess, co-ordinate and deliver training
on a regional basis throughout the country.

A third factor concerns the status of HRM, reflected in specialist
contributions to management and, relatedly, to its place within the
managerial hierarchy. At the beginning of the 1980s Daniel and
Millward (1983) noted that many personnel practitioners were not
specialists in the function. Only about one-quarter had occupational
personnel qualifications and only an equivalent proportion worked
exclusively in personnel. Some recent signs indicate that managers
with HRM responsibilities are becoming better qualified, both in terms

of basic education and occupational qualifications (Torrington 1989: 57, 63; Whittaker 1989; Millward et al. 1992: 35–6). While HRM is unlikely to establish the credentials usually associated with professional status (see, for example, Sisson 1994: 21), greater specialization demonstrated through occupational qualifications should allow HR specialists more scope to offer 'expert' employment management authority in its relations with their line, other functional and senior management counterparts. Moreover, recent studies do indicate that the presence of HRM specialists can 'make a difference' to organizational performance (Guest and Hoque 1994).

Also emerging from the 1980 WIRS survey was the minority (42 per cent) of establishments with specialist personnel practitioners represented at board level, where they might be in a position both to influence organization-wide issues and to incorporate personnel matters for consideration at the highest levels of the organization. A subsequent WIRS survey, conducted at the height of a recession and amid high unemployment in 1984, provided a stable figure of 43 per cent main board personnel or industrial relations representation (Millward and Stevens 1986: 35). The most recent WIRS study, conducted in 1990, confirms that this proportion for specialist personnel practitioners has been maintained (Millward et al. 1992: 49). In a large-scale survey conducted in the winter of 1989, a more favourable picture emerges: over 60 per cent of 'heads of personnel' were reported to have a place on the main board of directors, and in organizations with more than 5,000 employees this proportion rose to three-quarters (Price Waterhouse/Cranfield 1990).

Fourthly, though as yet signs of a more profound approach to training and development by employers are limited, there are indications of change in related aspects of employee management which should provide some leverage for HR specialists, especially those with strategic and board responsibilities, to link these changes with employee development. Performance appraisal, with its intent to change individual behaviour at work (Randell 1994), and employee development are clearly closely related, particularly as one strand of the purpose of appraisal is geared towards identifying and furthering employee potential. Performance appraisal unaccompanied by formal and implemented training opportunities will rapidly signal to employees the 'contractual' as opposed to the commitment (or 'social': see Streek 1988) orientation of their relations with managers.

A fifth factor is that training targets have been introduced and supported by both CBI and the government. National targets for education and training were first proposed by the CBI in 1991. In

March 1993, a national advisory body to monitor progress was established. Two sets of targets have been introduced: foundation targets, which aim to raise initial educational vocational qualifications through the National Vocational Qualification (NVQ) system; and lifetime targets, which aim to enhance the skill qualifications of the workforce. For lifetime targets, it is expected that all employees will participate in training and development activities by 1996 and by the same year, a half of medium and large organizations are expected to have gained the Investors in People (Iip) award. Since publication of these targets, there have been repeated calls to raise both NVQ standards and the proportions of people gaining qualifications (*Employment Gazette* 1994; *Guardian*, 3 March 1994). Particular concern has been voiced about the slow progress of the Iip programme. The Chairman of the programme, Sir Brian Woolfson, has stated that if the 50 per cent target is not met, the consequences would be 'catastrophic' for Britain (*Employment Gazette* 1994: 274). These targets should provide HR specialists with ideological resources to persuade their organizations to engage in targeted programmes.

A sixth factor concerns the moves towards European integration. Thurley (1990) has suggested that tension between the competition implied by the European Union and the requirement that member states compete on equal terms within an agreed structure of employment regulation could lead to the development of a 'European Model' of personnel management. This model would encompass the principles of employee rights and obligations as laid down in the Social Chapter, overlaid with a respect for cultural and national differences and values. Achieving this balance in the management of the international enterprise emphasizes key roles for education and staff development: 'European integration will result in the demand for new international education and training courses to develop specialists to help shape the policies that will make such international firms actually work' (Thurley 1990: 57). Though Britain has opted out of the Social Chapter provisions, it is becoming clear that UK companies with European interests are adopting a pragmatic line on their employment policies and practices; this would have implications for training and development to be adopted consistently throughout their operations (see Ramsay, ch. 11 in this volume).

Finally, we return to our earlier observation that training and development are central to an HRM approach to employee management. We also pointed out that organizations which purported to recognize their staff as assets, but then failed to invest in these assets, could scarcely be following an HRM approach. The apparently high levels of disaffection expressed by graduate recruits regarding their advancement prospects seem to confirm the presence of a gap between organizational intent and practice. Conversely, there are companies with expressed policies which fit the 'committed' HRM profile and for which training and development form an inclusive part of both organizational philosophy and practice. It is perhaps not surprising that many of these organizations show senior management commitment to training, expressed possibly through subscription to the Management Charter Initiative and Investors in People programme, and have energetic and influential HRM departments to pursue the training ideal.

Concluding Comments

Evidence from diverse sources shows that changes are taking place to and within organizations; size, differentiation of structure, control systems, allocations of responsibilities are all under corporate scrutiny as organizations in the public and private sectors alike face up to the implications of a threatening and uncertain economic climate. In these circumstances, with competitive pressures mounting and prompted by financial advisers intent on preserving shareholder dividends, managers may be tempted to see cost-cutting as their primary route to survival. In the UK there are few signs that physical investment is growing following emergence from the 1990s recession (Hutton 1995a; the same author provides a sustained critique of British investment policy in capital, technology and people in his recent book: see Hutton 1995b). If physical investment is in a precarious state, what might be the fate of human investment through development, an area continuously neglected by UK managers in this country, even under favourable conditions?

An alternative response to the developments taking place at present concerns the need to plan or to invest for the future, an aspect of management totally at odds with the short time-span approach which seeks to achieve immediate shareholder gratification. Companies which operate in such countries as Germany and Japan, with supportive financial institutions and consequently less threat from corporate predators, can plan their activities according to more distant time horizons, diversify their activities and seek out new markets in the confidence that their managers and workforce are capable of adapting to new conditions (see Hutton 1995b: ch. 10). The evidence shows that UK managers persist with their shrinking world, successively cutting back those areas where developmental costs might be incurred, even though competition has to be faced, in terms of quality, productivity and service. Yet, despite constant publicity and government exhortations, there have been few signs that companies are training and developing their employees at the levels and depths necessary to meet these challenges. Even the Confederation of British Industry (CBI), though implacably opposed to most areas of state regulation in employment affairs, has recognized that the training problem has not been resolved and has established a working party to test member reactions to the possibility of an imposed training levy (*Personnel Management*, December 1994: 11).

Training and development, therefore, should not and *must not* be seen simply as a desirable component of HRM but, as evidence from comparative studies shows, as an essential contributor to organizational objectives. The fact that it is difficult to identify a specific contribution should not deter the HR specialist from pressing claims for investment in employee development. As we stated above, many successful organizations integrate their developmental activities within a broader HRM perspective in such a way that making an attempt at evaluation of training's contribution in isolation from these other factors (and from the effects of technological investments) becomes a highly questionable exercise. It is interesting that in Japan the level of integration of training into management processes makes for difficulty in estimating training budgets, which tend to exclude major indirect expenditure items (Dore and Sako 1989: 81).

For too long, UK employers have ignored and rejected training and development; but through a conjunction of relatively favourable structural and occupational factors, the 1990s HR manager is now in a stronger position to press the case for human investment as a concomitant to physical investment. Existing employees and educated entrants to the workforce will also harbour high expectations for career growth. If these are not met, organizational performance will be further undermined, first, through operating at sub-optimal levels of skill; secondly, through lower employee motivation; and thirdly, through high labour turnover, as frustrated employees migrate to companies able to satisfy their needs. After many years during which companies which trained faced and had to contend with poaching from non-trainers, we are beginning to move into a 'reverse-poaching' direction, in that non-training companies, albeit those that pay well, may well risk losing valuable staff to the minority of domestic organizations and the growing ranks of incoming overseas-owned enterprises which offer career prospects and full opportunities for advancement to men and women. This is not to suggest that poaching by low-training firms from high trainers will not continue: but rather, that the ability of such companies to retain educationally sophisticated employees in an environment where lifetime learning (as opposed to traditional front-loaded training) is on offer elsewhere, is unlikely to be sustained.

It is immaterial whether employee investment is undertaken as part of an explicit HRM orientation or independently as an expression of effective management of people towards securing organizational objectives. Nevertheless, the ultimate responsibility for the training investment presently rests with employers, and the HRM specialist must mobilize the resources available to communicate to employers the probable consequences of not meeting this responsibility. If the training challenge remains unanswered by industry, we should debate whether it would be in the interests of all parties to allocate responsibility to the state to adopt a more interventionist role in enhancing workplace skills and qualifications.

References

Advisory, Conciliation and Arbitration Service (ACAS) 1988: *Labour Flexibility in Britain*, Occasional Paper no. 41. London: ACAS.

Armstrong, P. 1995: 'Accountancy and HRM'. In J. Storey (ed.), *Human Resource Management: a critical text*, London: Routledge, pp. 142–66.

Ashton, D. and Felstead, A. 1995: Training and development. In J. Storey (ed.), *Human Resource Management: a critical text*, London: Routledge, pp. 234–53.

Baldry, C. 1988: *Computers, Jobs, and Skills: the industrial relations of technological change*. New York: Plenum.

Brown, R. and Coopers & Lybrand 1988: *Managers and Information Technology Competence*. London: British Institute of Management.

Clark, J. 1993a: Full flexibility and self-supervision in an automated factory. In J. Clark (ed.), *Human Resource Management and Technical Change*, London: Sage, pp. 116–36.

Clark, J. 1993b: Managing people in a time of technical change: conclusions and implications. In J. Clark (ed.), *Human Resource Management and Technical Change*, London: Sage, pp. 212–22.

Constable, J. and McCormick, R. 1987: *The Making of British Managers*. London: British Institute of Management/Confederation of British Industry.

Cooley, M. 1987: *Architect or Bee?* London: Hogarth Press.

Coopers and Lybrand Associates 1985: *A Challenge to Complacency*. London: Manpower Services Commission/National Economic Development Office.

Cunningham, I., Hyman, J. and Baldry, C. 1996: Empowerment: the power to do what?. *Industrial Relations Journal*, 27(2).

Daniel, W.W. 1987: *Workplace Industrial Relations and Technical Change.* London: Frances Pinter/PSI.

Daniel, W.W. and Millward, N. 1983: *Workplace Industrial Relations in Britain.* London: Heinemann.

Daniel, W.W. and Millward, N. (1993): Findings from the Workplace Industrial Relations Surveys. In J. Clark (ed.), *Human Resource Management and Technical Change,* London: Sage, pp. 43–77.

Department of Employment 1990: *Labour Market and Skill Trends 1991/92.* London: HMSO.

Department of Employment 1992: *Labour Market and Skill Trends 1993/94.* London: HMSO.

Dore, R.P. and Sako, M. 1989: *How the Japanese Learn to Work.* London: Routledge.

Employment Gazette 1994: Updated national targets proposed. August, 271–5.

Fernie, S., Metcalf, D. and Woodland, S. 1994: *Does HRM Boost Employee–Management Relations?,* CEP Working Paper. London: London School of Economics.

Financial Times 1994: The rise of lean enterprise. 11 March.

Financial Times 1996: Skills shortage is holding us back, employers say. 6 May.

Finegold, D. and Soskice, D. 1988: The failure of training in Britain: analysis and prescription. *Oxford Review of Economic Policy,* 4(3), 21–53.

Fogarty, M. and Brooks, D. 1986: *Trade Unions and British Industrial Development.* London: Policy Studies Institute.

Fox, A. 1985: *Man Mismanagement,* 2nd edn. London: Hutchinson.

Greenhalgh, C. and Mavrotas, G. 1994: Workforce training in the Thatcher era: market forces and market failures. In R. McNabb and K. Whitfield (eds), *The Market for Training,* Aldershot, Hants.: Avebury, pp. 19–57.

Guest, D. and Hoque, K. 1994: 'Yes, personnel does make a difference'. *Personnel Management,* November, 40–4.

Handy, C., Gordon, C., Gow, I. and Randlesome, C. 1988: *Making Managers.* London: Pitman.

Hunter, L.C. and Beaumont, P.B. 1993: Implementing TQM: top down or bottom up. *Industrial Relations Journal,* 24(4), 318–27.

Hussey, D. 1988: *Management Training and Corporate Strategy.* Oxford: Pergamon.

Hutton, W. 1995a: Money before machines. *Guardian,* 3 January.

Hutton, W. 1995b: *The State We're In.* London: Jonathan Cape.

Hyman, J. 1992: *Training at Work: a critical analysis of policy and practice.* London: Routledge.

Hyman, J. and Mason, R. 1995: *Managing Employee Involvement and Participation.* London: Sage.

Kanter, R. Moss 1983: *The Change Masters: corporate entrepreneurs at work.* London: Routledge.

Keep, E. 1989: Corporate training strategies: the vital component? In

J. Storey (ed.), *New Perspectives on Human Resource Management*, London: Routledge, pp. 109–25.

Labour Market Skills and Trends 1995/6, 1994: Nottingham: Skills and Enterprise Network.

MacInnes, J. 1987: *Thatcherism at Work*. Milton Keynes, Bucks.: Open University Press.

Mangham, I. and Silver, M.S. 1986: *Management Training: context and practice*. Swindon, Wilts.: Economic and Social Research Council.

Marginson, P., Edwards, P.K., Martin, R., Purcell, J. and Sisson, K. 1988: *Beyond the Workplace*. Oxford: Blackwell.

Mason, G. and van Ark, B. 1994: Vocational training and productivity performance: an Anglo-Dutch comparison. In R. McNabb and K. Whitfield (eds), *The Market for Training*, Aldershot, Hants.: Avebury, pp. 335–55.

McLoughlin, I. and Clark, J. 1988: *Technological Change at Work*. Milton Keynes, Bucks.: Open University Press.

McLoughlin, I. and Gourlay, S. 1994: *Enterprise without Unions*. Buckingham: Open University Press.

Millward, N. and Stevens, M. 1986: *British Workplace Industrial Relations, 1980–1984*. Aldershot, Hants.: Gower.

Millward, N., Stevens, M., Smart, D. and Hawes, W.R. 1992: *Workplace Industrial Relations in Transition*. Aldershot, Hants.: Dartmouth.

National Institute of Economic and Social Research (NIESR) 1989: *Productivity, Education and Training*. London: NIESR.

Oliver, N. and Wilkinson, B. 1992: *The Japanization of British Industry*, 2nd edn. Oxford: Blackwell.

Pearson, R., Pike, G., Gordon, A. and Wecgman, C. 1990: How many graduates in the twenty-first century? Summarised in *IMS Report*, no. 177.

Personnel Management Plus 1990: Poor interviewing puts off graduates. 1(3), 4.

Peters, T. and Waterman, R. 1982: *In Search of Excellence*. New York: Harper & Row.

Price Waterhouse/Cranfield 1990: *Project on International Strategic Human Resource Management: Report*. London: Price Waterhouse.

Randell, G. 1994: Employee appraisal. In K. Sisson (ed.), *Personnel Management*, 2nd edn. Oxford: Blackwell, pp. 221–52.

Saggers, R. 1994: Training climbs the corporate ladder. *Personnel Management*, July, 40–6.

Sisson, K. 1994: Personnel management: paradigms, practice and prospects. In K. Sisson (ed.), *Personnel Management*, 2nd edn. Oxford: Blackwell, pp. 3–52.

Skills and Enterprise Briefing, August 1994.

Steedman, H. and Wagner, K. 1987: A second look at productivity, machinery and skills in Britain and Germany. *National Institute Economic Review*, no. 122, 84–96.

Stewart, A.M. 1994: *Empowering People*. London: Institute of Management/ Pitman.

Storey, J. 1989: Introduction. In J. Storey (ed.), *New Perspectives on Human Resource Management*, London: Routledge.

Storey, J. 1994: Management development. In K. Sisson (ed.), *Personnel Management*, 2nd edn. Oxford: Blackwell, pp. 365–96.

Streek, W. 1988: The uncertainties of management in the management of uncertainty. *Work, Employment and Society*, 3(1), 281–308.

Thurley, K. 1990: Towards a European approach to personnel management. *Personnel Management*, September, 54–7.

Times Higher Education Supplement 1994: 25 February.

Torrington, D. 1989: Human resource management and the personnel function. In J. Storey (ed.), *New Perspectives on Human Resource Management*, London: Routledge, pp. 56–66.

Training Agency 1989: *Training in Britain: Main Report*. London: HMSO.

Webster, J. 1990: *Office Automation*. Brighton, Sussex: Harvester Wheatsheaf.

White Paper 1988: *Employment for the 1990s*, Cm 540. London: HMSO.

Whittaker, J. 1989: Institute membership: passport or profession? *Personnel Management*, August, 30–5.

Wickens, P. 1987: *The Road to Nissan*. London: Macmillan.

Womack, J.P., Jones, D.T. and Roos, D. 1990: *The Machine that Changed the World*. New York: Rawson Associates.

15

Human Resource Management and Women: the Vision of the Gender-blind?

JEAN WOODALL

Introduction

The debate in the UK about human resource management (HRM) has taken little interest in women, either in terms of textbook space or in terms of evaluating what HRM policy prescription and practice has actually meant for the employment of women. Excluding research monographs, over 15 academic textbooks on HRM have been published since 1989. Only one of them, the first edition of this text (Towers 1992) has included a separate chapter on women, and another, the more recent second edition of an earlier text (Dickens, in Sisson 1994), contains a critical review of equal opportunities in employment in general. Several other texts on HRM do not even have an index reference to women. This apparent oversight is understandable in that other dimensions of employment diversity such as ethnicity, age and disability receive similar treatment, so why should gender be singled out for special consideration here? Perhaps the gender issue is not really salient to the debate on HRM?

This chapter will argue that, to the contrary, there is a great deal to be discussed in respect of the implications of HRM for women. However, to be fair, the responsibility for omitting any discussion of women and human resource management to date does not lie only at the door of the writers and editors of HRM textbooks. Indeed, most writing on women's experience of the employment relationship tends to focus upon broad themes that are not directly related to the HRM debate, such as describing and explaining patterns of labour force participation (especially the reasons for the under-representation of women in management); women in trade unions; the social construction of sex roles at work; or upon providing empirical evidence and explanation of the limitations of a formal equal opportunity policy within organizations. This was the main thrust of the chapters in the two texts cited above, with some glancing acknowledgment of the 'apparent contradictions' of HRM: namely, that commitment to the effective utilization of human resources can coexist simultaneously with a tolerance of their waste, as exemplified in the underutilization of women. Yet this acknowledgment apart, neither of these chapters really engages with the debate on HRM and its significance for the employment of women.

This chapter will endeavour to take the debate forward by examining what HRM means in both prescription and practice for the employment of women in organizations. Excellent reviews of labour market participation, equal opportunity policy, and so on, are cited in the annotated references at the end of this book. After a brief résumé of what HRM actually involves, the discussion will move on to consider the implications of some of the key features of HRM: its strategic integration with business strategy; flexibility in employment contracts; high-commitment work systems and cultures; and managing quality and performance.

What is Human Resource Management?

Defining HRM is no mean feat, and it is debatable whether it is consciously practised in full or in part by more than a minority of organizations in the UK (see Guest 1987; Storey 1992). As Karen Legge has recently pointed out (1995a, b) rhetoric and reality intermingle with bewildering confusion. For a start, claiming a distinction between HRM and personnel management is problematic because of the difficulties of precise conceptual clarification. For example, 'personnel' can refer either to an activity or to a specialist department with a general lack of coherence and low status. There is also little consensus about its purpose. The personnel function can be seen as an instrument of corporate control, the 'maintenance crew for the human machinery', and even as the 'consensus negotiator'. Not only do all of these aspects make personnel management vulnerable to ambiguity and paradox, they also make it very difficult to be conceptually clear – an essential prerequisite for any comparative activity.

If we abandon the search for a clear benchmark of personnel management and turn to examine HRM in its own terms, the paradoxes and ambiguities are present to an even greater extent. From the time when the earliest models of HRM were articulated, over ten years ago in the USA, there has been an observable distinction between the 'hard' business-led HRM of the Michigan model (Fombrun et al. 1984) and the 'soft' human-relations focus of the Harvard model (Beer et al. 1985). This tension persists, and has been remarked upon throughout the UK debate on HRM. However, as Legge points out, these distinctions are mainly at the rhetorical level and the different emphases are not necessarily incompatible, the actual approach adopted being contingent upon an organization's business strategy. So 'soft' HRM seems appropriate to a strategy of producing high-value-added goods and services in a knowledge-based industry, while 'hard' HRM may be more appropriate in a labour-intensive, high-volume, low-cost industry. In the light of this it becomes very difficult to draw up a shopping list of distinctive features of HRM, be it as long as 27 items (Storey 1992) or as short as four (Guest 1987).

None the less, a frame of reference is needed in which the prescription and practice of HRM can be examined from the perspective of women's employment. The framework adopted for this chapter approximates to Guest's list of four features of HRM that could be present in both 'hard' and 'soft' models: integration, flexibility, high-commitment culture, and rewarding quality and performance. What each of these means is now briefly summarized.

- Integration has three aspects: the 'fit' of human resource policies with business strategy; the internal coherence and complementarity of specific HRM policies; and the acknowledgment of the importance of HRM by line managers.
- Flexibility in Guest's (1987) original model related to organizational design, job design and employee attitudes and motivation. However, there is the additional aspect of labour market flexibility and flexible employment contracts.
- Commitment is associated with the 'soft' HRM policies of participation, team working and briefing, multi-skilling and career development.
- Quality has three dimensions in Guest's model: quality of staff, quality of performance and reputation for quality in HRM policies.

Each of these will be examined in turn to determine whether the HRM 'vision' really does address the gendered nature of employment.

Strategic Integration and Corporate Policies for Women

Strategic integration implies that a concern with equal opportunities complements both overall business strategy and other HRM policies, and that those managers charged with its implementation will do so in a committed manner. However, the gap between rhetoric and reality is wide, as can be seen through a more detailed examination of formal equal opportunity policies within organizations. Equal opportunity policy development has a very recent history. In the 20 years since the UK Sex Discrimination and Race Relations Acts came into force, very few organizations have got beyond making a general statement of commitment to equal opportunities. The lead was taken in the early 1980s by public sector organizations – especially Labour-controlled local authorities and also health authorities. There were a few beacons of 'good practice' in the corporate sector, but a survey to discover which companies were the 'best' employers of women (McGuire 1992) found that they were mainly in retail trade, the media, financial services and local authorities (with one or two surprising exceptions in petrochemicals and engineering).

The reasons for the low level of commitment can usefully be illustrated by reviewing conventional approaches to equal opportunity development. Within the framework of the 1975 Sex Discrimination Act, the 1986 Race Relations Act and subsequent legislation recognized that good practice involves making this the responsibility of all staff, but with oversight at senior management level, and ensuring back-up administrative support. Usually this means allocating responsibility to the personnel/HRM department, but occasionally to a specialist equal opportunities unit, both of which may or may not report to the main board. The approach usually follows the guidance of the two equality commissions' codes of practice and, as with other personnel work, tends to be bureaucratic (Aitkenhead and Liff 1991).

The first stage is to agree a policy that establishes the organization's aims regarding equal opportunities, and then to draw up procedures which prescribe how the policy is to be implemented, for example with respect to recruitment and selection, promotion and discipline. The main function of the personnel/HRM department (or equal opportunity unit) is to design and disseminate good practice policy; to monitor and evaluate these procedures and policy outcomes in relation to the human resource profile of the organization; to ensure legal compliance on the part of the organization; and to provide a source of advice and support to those who feel they have experienced discrimination. Thus the approach is bureaucratic and formalistic in that it assumes policy change is brought about by means of formal (rather than informal) processes agreed by committees and cascading down a bureaucratic hierarchy. This sits uneasily with current developments in organizational structure and the location of wider HRM policy-making. In addition, the overall spirit of equal opportunity policies is to 'increase' opportunity rather than 'maintain' it. It is thereby more suited to a time of organizational growth than one of retrenchment.

Outside large unitary organizations a corporate-wide 'fit' between HRM and business policy is at the worst non-existent or at best of a 'loose–tight' nature (Purcell and Ahlstrand 1994). Multi-divisional organizational structures and other 'newer', more fluid 'network' or 'boundaryless' structures are a manifestation of the drive to be closer to the market. Given that both sets of organizations may well be serving several different markets, it is usual for HRM policy development either to be devolved to business-unit level or be a diffuse responsibility. Often there may not be a corporate HRM function, or what exists may well be a skeleton staff team with or without a token presence at main board level. In these circumstances, broad-brush HRM corporate policy frameworks may be developed in which business unit managers have a great deal of discretion over their implementation to meet the needs of local circumstances. This poses all sorts of problems for equal opportunity policy implementation, where the emphasis is upon 'best practice' and 'professionalism' in human resources rather than business integration and variation with different business-unit needs.

Recent research evidence on equal opportunity implementation within multi-divisional companies and in organizations which are undergoing corporate restructuring (Woodall et al. 1995) has shown that the disturbance of the bureaucratic chain of command creates a gap between the development of a common corporate equal opportunity policy and its implementation by relatively autonomous business units. In these circumstances, the HRM department or the specialist equal opportunity unit have difficulty acquiring accurate monitoring data, let alone enforcing policy compliance. Furthermore, as so much of the corporate sector is currently cutting staff overall and taking out layers of management, it becomes extremely difficult to monitor the equal opportunity effects, as the original baseline data are no longer useful for benchmarking. As internal departments, units and job grades are changed, the equal opportunity effect of cutbacks is difficult to discern (Woodall et al. 1995). Consequently, equal opportunities becomes even more marginal to the overall business.

The marginality of HRM and equal opportunity units as the champions of equal opportunities has been recognized as a major obstacle, and provided the inspiration behind the Opportunity 2000 campaign launched in 1991. This promoted the business case for equal opportunities for women, without being overly prescriptive. The primary focus was upon obtaining board-level commitment, analysing where women were under-utilized as a business resource, and finally setting goals for change. This was a much more relaxed approach than the prescriptions of codes of practice. By the end of 1994, 275 organizations from both the public and the private sector had joined (Opportunity 2000 1994), over a quarter of them being members of *The Times* Top One Hundred Companies.

But does equal opportunities make good business sense? As Dickens (1994) has pointed out, this depends upon the motivation of the individual organization. Organizational self-interest may be served by equal opportunities, for example, if it assists with recruitment in difficult labour markets, and with the image projected to customers (as exemplified by the human resource practices of many high street retail banks). On the other hand the business case for equal opportunities may not be served if the organization is pursuing a strategy of low-cost employment (such as with catering or cleaning contractors), or if the main employee relations concern is redundancy and redeployment. Thus in the same way that HRM policies are contingent upon business strategy, in practice, so might a commitment to equal opportunities.

For some organizations the management of 'diversity' rather than 'equal opportunity' is preferred. The management of diversity has been hailed as a move beyond the traditional equal treatment and opportunity measures of the 1970s (Kandola and Fullerton 1994; Herriot and Pemberton 1995). It involves recognizing that there are many other dimensions of inequality at work besides gender or even race in general. Differences within ethnic minorities are as extensive as those between them and white majorities. Physical disability and mental disability (including learning difficulties) and even age can all be dimensions of disadvantage. However, it rests upon an extremely weak concept of organizational justice. It remains to be seen whether as a result of diversity management 'all shall win and all shall have prizes', and it should not be forgotten that enthusiasm for diversity management was born in a climate of male backlash in the 1980s, and the irritation of US business with federal contract compliance conditions in respect of equal opportunities.

The second aspect of integration claims that HRM is about achieving coherent and internally consistent policies, but in the case of equal . opportunities is not proven. As Dickens (1994) has commented, practices associated with HRM may be at odds with the promotion of equal opportunities for women. For example, the growing prevalence of individualized compensation, and merit and performance-related pay in particular does not in general serve women well (Bevan and

Thomson 1992). As a policy it also conflicts with the principles of equal pay based on systematic job evaluation. At another level, the emphasis upon formal procedure enshrined in equal opportunities can conflict with the increasing emphasis upon responsiveness and flexibility of recruitment, selection and assessment. Moves towards staffing arrangements to achieve flexibility deny part-timers and other peripheral employees (who are mainly women) equitable treatment in employee terms and in conditions and benefits.

Turning to the third aspect of integration, placing HRM responsibility more firmly on the line manager, especially the first line manager/supervisor and middle manager, there is again little evidence to provide grounds for optimism. On the one hand, this could provide the opportunity for increasing the legitimacy of the services provided by the HRM function in general, and concern with equal opportunities for women in particular. On the other hand, it aggravates the perennial difficulty of persuading line managers to take HRM seriously and comply with (let alone commit to) policy. Again there is much research evidence that line managers can deliberately evade equal opportunity monitoring (Collinson et al. 1990; Jewson and Mason 1986; Liff and Dale 1994). Middle managers in particular are under increasing work pressure. Their jobs are becoming more generalist with greater responsibilities, a wider range of tasks, an increasing span of control and responsibility for a wider mix of staff. Above all, as their performance has become more visible through the availability of better, computer-based information, they have become more accountable and are required to take on wider business responsibility (Dopson and Stewart 1990). This may include more responsibility for recruitment and selection and for performance management (including appraisal, setting objectives and determining individual performance-related pay, and identifying development needs and opportunities). However, there is abundant evidence that responsibility takes second place to achieving performance targets, and a short-term focus means that longer-term off-the-job development in general, and equal opportunities in particular, become a 'luxury' to be pursued when time, resources, and inclination permit. Add to this the glass ceiling effect whereby very few women hold middle management positions, and it is not surprising that there is little commitment to equal opportunities at this level.

All this indicates a fundamental and enduring contradiction between the pursuit of equal opportunity and the embrace of HRM. Equal opportunities is principally concerned with the rights and social needs of employees, but HRM is concerned with business needs and with employees as resources to achieve this. A unitarist philosophy under-pins HRM whereby employee interests are held to be identical to those of employers, but equal opportunities rest on the foundation of pluralism, starting from the premise that employees have independent rights and interests which may very well be infringed by employers. Consequently there is always a potential contradiction between equal opportunities and business-driven HRM.

Flexibility in Employment and Equal Opportunities for Women

Guest's (1987) original consideration of flexibility related to organ-izational design, job design, and employee attitudes and motivation. As he acknowledges, the first two are closely related to the existence of a highly committed workforce, and this will be considered in the next section. However, developments in labour market flexibility and their effect upon organizational employment practices are of the greatest significance to women. The debates surrounding external and internal labour market flexibility are well-rehearsed, and there is considerable research into the employment effects of flexible manufacturing sys-tems (see chapter 12). Both of these are seen as integral elements in HRM, and the gender dimension is particularly apparent here. Wom-en's employment patterns are much more likely to exhibit numerical, temporal and the more disadvantageous aspects of financial flexibility, than the functional flexibility central to flexible manufacturing sys-tems (Beatson 1995; Legge 1995b).

Starting with labour market flexibility, over ten years ago forecasts of the changing structure of employment in the UK predicted that there would be an increase of 1.7 million jobs by 1995, but that 90 per cent of these would go to women. This has been borne out, and women now constitute 44 per cent of the employed workforce in the UK (see table 15.1). What was not widely admitted at the time was that most of this increase in employment opportunities would be in the form of non-standard employment contracts: primarily part-time and short-term contracts: 38 per cent of all employees (27 per cent of men and 52 per cent of women) were part of the flexible workforce by 1993 (Watson 1994). However, the composition of this flexible workforce shows a strong gender difference. While the rate of increase of males in part-time employment has greatly outstripped that of females (see table 15.2), between 1984 and 1993 the total increase in the numbers of men in part time work was 320,000 compared with

Table 15.1 Changing economic activity rates of women and men, 1979–93 (%)

	1979	*1984*	*1990*	*1993*
Women	63	66	71	71
Men	91	88	88	66

Source: Sly (1993: 484)

Table 15.2 Rate of change in economic activity by type of employment, 1979–93

	1979		*1984*		*1990*		*1993*	
	%	*'000s*	*%*	*'000s*	*%*	*'000s*	*%*	*'000s*
Full-time employees								
Women	—	5,603	−7	5,221	19	6,200	−5	5,896
Men	—	14,321	−9	12,987	5	13,701	−9	12,433
Part-time employees								
Women	—	3,426	15	3,935	13	4,475	4	4,676
Men	—	117	253	413	40	580	26	733

Source: Sly (1993)

730,000 women who constitute about 85 per cent of all part-time employees (Sly 1993). In contrast women account for 56 per cent of all temporary workers, and here the number of males has increased by 21 per cent since 1990 (in contrast to a fall of 6 per cent for women). Events have shown that the growth in women's participation in the labour force has been primarily in part-time employment.

Much of this is due to three factors: the primary responsibility for childcare resting on women; the segmentation of the female labour market (Scott MacEwen 1994; Sly 1993); and the difference between less-qualified women (who are more likely to be employed in part-time, low-paid, low-skilled jobs) and more highly qualified women. Of mothers with children under 16, 64 per cent work, and since 1984 the number of working women with children under the age of five has risen from 37 to 52 per cent (Sly 1994). It is thus not surprising that 63 per cent of all working mothers are in part-time employment: the presence of dependent children within a family has a profound effect upon women's economic activity.

Turning to labour market segmentation, women are more likely than men to be employed in the service sector (83 per cent of women as opposed to just 56 per cent of men: Sly 1993). This means that women are to be found mainly in personal services (such as catering, cleaning and hairdressing), in retail and clerical work (in all sectors, but particularly financial services), and in certain areas of manufacturing such as food, textiles, and also in chemicals and electronics. At the professional and semi-professional level, women are concentrated in health, welfare and education. So, many of the service sector occupations in which women are concentrated are dominated by part-time employment, and have been increasingly prone to numerical flexibility. The introduction of internal markets and subcontracting in healthcare and local authority services, and the tailoring of staffing to respond more flexibly to customer demand in the increasingly competitive environment of retail and financial services, all these factors have actually increased the proportion of women employed on part-time contracts. Full-time, mainly female workforces have been replaced by 'flexible' employment – again largely composed of women. Even though there are reports that the rate of increase in employment on non-standard contracts is much greater for men than for women, in absolute terms the reverse is the case (see table 15.2). Furthermore, part-time working is inversely related to educational attainment (Corti and Dex 1995): only 11 per cent of highly qualified women managers and 25 per cent of women professionals (mainly in health and education) work part-time, but this increases to 29 per cent of secretaries/clerical workers; 30 per cent of those in retail, and 45 per cent of those employed in personal services occupations (hairdressing, cleaning and so on).

Financial flexibility has also had an adverse effect upon women. By 1990, less than 50 per cent of UK employees were covered by collective bargaining (Beatson 1995), compared with nearly 60 per cent in the early 1980s. Where collective bargaining has remained, there has also been substantial decentralization, and it is estimated that as many as a third of employees are covered by performance-related pay of some kind. This move away from standardized and collectively agreed payment systems towards variable and individualized arrangements works in men's favour (Bevan and Thompson 1992). For a start, most merit pay and individualized performance-related pay has been introduced at management levels (mainly senior and middle management). As women constitute only an estimated 27 per cent of all managers and between 4 and 8 per cent of middle managers, they are largely excluded from such systems. In addition, research comparing pay data for women across 13 OECD countries (Whitehouse 1992) has shown a strong association between high relative earnings for women, strong centralized wage-fixing arrangements and extensive public sector employment. Corporate moves towards financial flexibility have been greatly assisted by UK government legislation, despite European Union directives to equalize terms and conditions of employment for employees on non-standard contracts (including part-time workers). The weakening of wages councils and the rescinding of the Fair Wages Resolution have particularly affected women, since they constitute the majority of low-paid employees. It would thus appear that financial flexibility has little to offer women.

Finally, the much-trumpeted spread of functional flexibility across core workforces has not happened (see chapter 12). The erosion of traditional craft skill demarcations in manual work and their replacement by multi-skilling has been the exception; in any case, because of labour market segmentation, it would have had a marginal effect upon women. While skill boundaries have been eroded, as in clerical work and in social and healthcare, it is debatable whether this has led to upskilling rather than to intensification of work with overlapping job descriptions, job enlargement and sometimes deskilling. In all cases it has been accompanied by growing uncertainty for the employees involved.

This highlights the major weakness of all forms of external and internal labour market flexibility: flexibility is seen from the perspective of the business and not the employee. There is considerable speculation over whether the pursuit of flexibility is a conscious corporate strategy or an *ad hoc* pragmatic response, but in both cases the outcome is seen from the vantage point of the organization. Flexibility should also be seen from the point of view of the employee. Apart from choosing whether or not to accept insecure employment with poor benefits but with convenient work hours, there is little to commend non-standard contracts of employment to the employee. If such employment is seen as 'family-friendly', it is by default.

The reverse of flexible employment is the intensification of working time. Officially recorded hours of those in full-time employment have been slowly declining throughout the 1980s, but have started to rise again in the 1990s (Sly 1993). For those in full-time employment, officially recorded working hours are not a true reflection, especially for those employed in managerial positions. As we shall see below, long work hours are central to the HRM rhetoric of commitment, despite the contradictory emphasis upon output as the basis of reward. Flexible working practices such as job-sharing, term-time working, fractional permanent appointments (especially after maternity leave) and so on, that could assist those employees (mainly women) with dependant care responsibilities are usually seen as benefits to be individually negotiated rather than as a matter of entitlement (Cooper and Lewis 1995). The interrelationship between private and public life receives limited acknowledgment in either the rhetoric or the practice of HRM. It might be expected that 'soft' HRM would endorse family-friendliness, but, a very few cases apart, HRM has underwritten public policy principles that see family-friendliness as a benefit and not an employment right. Thus many employees who are job-sharing are also part-time, and job-sharing is only available to professionals after formal consideration of whether the job can be split. The prevailing assumption is that it is highly undesirable at higher levels of management responsibility, and that at lower levels, substitution by part-time employees is the preferred option. Conversely, the availability of part-time or fractional appointments at professional or managerial level is constrained and carries the cost of losing out on career development. Flexibility concedes family-friendly employment to women at a high price. Yet it need not do so, and indeed the reorganization of work time to meet the needs of both men and women is possible (Bailyn 1994).

The UK has an outstanding record for officially endorsing the least family-friendly employment practices in Europe, and underwriting them within its social policy. While the UK does give the most maternity leave (40 weeks) in the European Union, because full entitlement rested upon two years' service and employment for a minimum of 30 hours per week (until prompted to change in 1993 by a European Union directive), about half of working women in the UK did not qualify, as they worked less than 30 hours a week. All women employees are now entitled to maternity leave, regardless of their length of service and hours of work, but the level of entitlement varies accordingly. The absence of an official entitlement to parental leave (as the UK opted out of this in its rejection of the European Union Social Charter), and the scarcity of either public or corporate childcare provision for pre-school and school-age children throughout the year, reinforces the impression that these are matters that belong in the private domain. In addition there is little acknowledgment that women constitute the majority of carers of the elderly and of disabled dependants, and that this responsibility is extremely difficult to combine with employment. Despite some notable exceptions in financial services, most organizations have very few schemes to attract women returners. Above all, it could be argued that family-friendly policies 'play around at the margin' of work, allowing employees with family commitments to adapt to but not challenge traditional work structures.

Thus the one-sided employer perspective on flexibility has little to offer women. Numerical, temporal and financial flexibility offer the opportunity to respond to domestic commitments at an unfavourable rate of exchange. The focus is upon policies which enable women to enter and remain in a workforce constructed by men for men without primary family commitments (Lewis 1995).

Women Working in a High-commitment Culture

Commitment is associated with the 'soft' HRM policies of participation, team-working and briefing, multi-skilling and career development. Indeed, we would expect it to be associated with the creation of a core of functionally flexible employees. Survey evidence shows that the factors directly associated with high commitment are confirmed job expectations, work involvement, scope for responsibility and self-expression (Legge 1995b), and, more alarmingly, increasing age and lower levels of education. Obviously, this explains why organizations consciously endeavouring to achieve corporate culture change share a common concern to inculcate values such as initiative, autonomy, innovation, team-working and so on. The hope is that these will lead to the holy grail of a highly committed workforce. Again, it is necessary to probe behind the rhetoric to discover what this means for women.

First, there has been a persistent popular assumption that women in general exhibit lower commitment at work than men. This underlies the pervasive discriminatory practices surrounding promotion, whether in manual or service sector employment or as managers. Assumptions about women's biological clock, the consequent need to avoid 'wasting' investment in their development, and their perceived lack of mobility or unwillingness to work all hours are often the implicit reasons why women are not offered the development opportunities to make them fit for promotion. The assumption is that they are not committed to the organization, and this assumption is both logically and empirically flawed (Alban-Metcalfe 1989; Wilson 1995).

There is no empirical survey evidence to suggest that gender is a significant explanatory variable. At junior management level, at least, women exhibit lower labour turnover than their male equivalents. Also, over half of all working women who leave to have a baby have returned to work within three years (albeit longer if they have other children). This is hardly indicative of a lack of commitment. There is also considerable debate over the way in which organizational commitment is measured. A pluralist rather than the traditional unitary model of organization would assume that it is normal for there to be competing foci of commitment: the job, work team, department, trade union and family. It then becomes obvious that both women and men exhibit variable patterns of commitment; neither are totally committed just to overall organizational values and objectives. Others would argue that commitment is a two-way street – namely, that it is an exchange relationship, and that any analysis of employee commitment should examine the balance of what is offered and received on both sides. This can explain why in the presence of glass ceilings women may be more prone to labour turnover at middle management levels and above. So has HRM honoured its side of the bargain by clarifying job expectations, providing means for effective work involvement, and scope for responsibility and self-development for women?

HRM may have led indirectly to a relative increase in women's commitment, if we look at changing patterns of employee involvement. Traditionally, trade unions have been male-dominated organizations. However, the combination of changes in employment law and the changing structure of the economy and employment have led to a substantial increase in women's participation and the recognition of 'women's issues' as mainstream concerns, particularly by service sector unions with a high female membership, such as Unison. Table 15.3 shows the membership composition of the top ten unions in 1993, five of whom have an overwhelming majority of female members. This factor accounts for the high priority currently placed upon minimum wage legislation and employment rights for members. At the same time, the marginalization of traditional industrial relations as a forum for employee involvement has opened up new forms of involvement. In particular, high-performance work systems have spread from manufacturing to services. From insurance to restaurant chains and the health service, the rhetoric of team working and 'empowerment' has now become a key feature of women's employment at all levels. It has thereby provided the means for many women to enter first-line management and team-leadership roles in particular. Indeed, most of the expansion of recruitment of women into management can be said to have occurred at this level.

So women are more involved and display little difference in levels of commitment compared with men. But as a result, are they getting more in return? The 'soft' side of HRM with its emphasis upon the full utilization of human resources by developing their potential suggests that this should increasingly be the case. Certainly, as such organizations are experiencing more frequent and radical change, there

Table 15.3   Membership of top ten UK unions in 1993

Union	Membership ('000s)	Men (%)	Women (%)
Unison	1,465	38	62
Transport and General Workers Union	949	82	18
Amalgamated Engineering and Electrical Union	835	94	6
GMB	809	62	38
Manufacturing, Science and Finance Union	516	74	26
Royal College of Nursing of the UK	303	8	92
Union of Shop, Distributive and Allied Workers	299	41	59
Graphical, Paper and Media Union	250	83	17
National Union of Teachers	232	25	75
National Association of School Masters and Union of Women Teachers	207	47	53

Source: Bird (1995): membership of trade unions based on information from the certification officer, *Employment Gazette*, May, 208

has been a greater emphasis upon training and development, and particularly upon competence-based development. Survey evidence shows that over the last ten years the number of female employees receiving training has doubled to 15 per cent, and in fact is one percentage point higher than that for men (Gibbins 1994). This surprising fact is explained by patterns of labour market segmentation in that the majority of employees in craft and engineering operations (which have a very poor record for training) are male, and women are concentrated in public and private sector services which devote more resources to training. At the same time, women were far more likely than men to have had their fees paid by a government agency or local authority or to be self-financed.

Yet the demand for off-the-job training and development often outstrips the organization's ability to provide it, and the need for speed and relevance means that development 'opportunities' are increasingly work-related, and that the line manager is the main point of access. Development measures such as job enrichment, job rotation, internal secondments, but above all allocation to special development projects or membership of high-profile task forces, are the main means of developing skills and visibility. In most of these cases the line manager is the main point of access, but research evidence frequently confirms reports that women managers seldom receive positive support from their immediate line manager and often have to acquire mentors and sponsors at a senior level elsewhere in the organization (White et al. 1992; Woodall et al. 1995); they become a key means of access to opportunities to 'prove oneself', take on a challenge, and ultimately acquire the visibility necessary for career progress (Sturges and Vinnicombe 1995). This becomes particularly evident in relation to the persistent under-representation of women as international managers, where prejudice and unreasonable hurdles are the main obstacles (Harris 1995).

But what of increased scope for responsibility and self-development? If we look at how women enter managerial positions, most have worked their way up from administrative or operational-level positions into the increasingly important supervisory positions that now constitute first-line management. However, while it is reassuring that women do stand a better chance of entering lower-level management positions, they still face considerable difficulties in progressing to middle and senior positions. For women to be successful in management, they need to 'jump through hoops' (Hirsh and Jackson 1989); they need to enter management at an early age through training schemes or with appropriate qualifications; they need to have experience in functions which are seen as central to the core business of the organization and move into generalist managerial roles; they need to be continuously employed; they need to be able to work long hours; they need to conform to the organization's age-related concept of careers; they need to be geographically mobile; and they need to manage the promotion process by conforming to the promotion criteria. Where women are located in the labour force, the manner and timing of the entry into managerial jobs, stereotypes of the desirable traits required for management as well as the problem of domestic responsibilities and childcare are the main reasons why women have not done well in the past.

There is also evidence that continuing structural change in management due to downsizing and delayering may be exerting a disproportionate effect on women, especially where they have managed to break through the glass ceiling into middle management positions. There has been little research to date on what has happened to women as a result of organizational restructuring, and seldom does equal opportunity monitoring cover this (Woodall et al. 1995). However, organizational case studies do show that the effects of such restructuring can fall disproportionately upon women because of where they are located in the managerial labour market. Women have traditionally tended to enter management through 'functional chimneys' and professions such as personnel, marketing, advertising, public relations and, more recently, the law and accountancy. Once there, they are less likely than men to enter general management and build up a wide portfolio of experience. We have already noted that lack of support from line managers is a contributory factor here. However, functional career paths have been considerably eroded by downsizing and delayering, and the previous career moves may no longer be there as staffing in corporate headquarters is radically reduced. This is of particular significance to women's presence in the HRM profession, the majority of whose members are women but whose history exhibits their marginalization by men at senior levels.

Again, we can see how the HRM espousal of commitment belies a unitarist and one-sided interpretation. The 'greedy' demand for unlimited commitment and the blindness to several other legitimate objects of employee commitment are particularly evident in relation to the employment of women. Furthermore, as HRM is silent and inactive over the persistence of biased stereotypes of women's commitment to work and career, its claim to a 'soft' human-relations focus rings hollow.

Managing Quality and Rewarding Performance: Are Women Included?

Guest's (1987) model stresses three dimensions of quality in HRM: quality of staff, quality of performance, and reputation for quality in HRM policies. As Legge (1995b) points out, it spans both the hard and soft versions of HRM, because there are various approaches. The hard approach stresses conformation to specification, value for money, and waste reduction, while the soft approach stresses fitness for use or conformation to customer requirements. Quality of staff is closely linked to the achievement of a high-commitment workforce, and thus investment in staff development. We have already seen the extent to which women are covered by this. The other two dimensions will be dealt with together, as they are very closely related. At the centre of this is the emergence of performance management and emphasis upon 'scientific' rigour in selection and assessment techniques.

The last ten years have provided wonderful business opportunities for occupational psychologists in two major areas: the design, administration and analysis of psychological tests, and the specification of behavioural competences. Both are central to HRM. Properly validated and reliable test instruments are the central plank of many large organizations' HRM policies from selection to assessment and development centres – and more recently for 'outplacement' (redundancy). Hard HRM requires standardized employees for TQM operations, and soft HRM is concerned to build upon behavioural strengths and to address weaknesses in a planned developmental way. At first glance, it would appear that these new systematic approaches to assessment could not possibly have a gender dimension, due to the very rigour of the underpinning professional psychological knowledge. However, Alimo-Metcalfe (1995) challenges this on three counts: the skills, behaviours and qualities sought for effective management; the methods used to assess; and the judgements of assessors.

Despite the overall methodological rigour, much managerial job-role analysis to establish the behaviours, skills and traits associated with effective managerial performance has focused upon managerial positions that until relatively recently were almost exclusively occupied by men, and by surveying only male respondents. Recent research carried out on matched samples of local authority housing managers and NHS managers (Alimo-Metcalfe 1995) has shown that the perceptions of the characteristics required of managerial jobs differs quite strongly between female and male respondents. One example of potential difference is the psychological construct of leadership. This relates to earlier research on gender differences in leadership style. Earlier research in the United States has shown that men's preferred leadership style can be described as predominantly 'transactional' which is concerned with exchanging rewards and punishments for performance, and by using power derived from their organizational position, expertise and control over resources. In contrast, women exhibit a preference towards a 'transformational' leadership style which is very different, based upon encouraging participation, sharing power and information, and managing performance through encouragement and positive reinforcement. Women were less likely to use position, expertise and resource power in favour of personal power. This was echoed in similar studies based upon subordinate's perceptions of their leaders.

There has been a great deal of debate as to whether a tendency for gender differences in leadership style is universal (Wilson 1995), and there is plenty of anecdotal evidence of the 'iron ladies' who got to the top primarily by means of a transactional leadership style. However, what is at issue here is that the constructs of leadership, and therefore the behaviours, skills, traits and so on sought from potential or actual job incumbents may exhibit a gender bias, no matter how rigorous the method of job-role analysis used. The drive towards high-quality HRM policy and practice in this area has led to the widespread use of competence-based assessment in many organizations, and there is a potential for gender bias in the apparently androgenous qualities listed, especially in respect of high-performance management competences. In general, it is ironical that studies in a wide variety of organizations have demonstrated that the use of a transformational leadership style has resulted in staff who show the highest effort, performance and job satisfaction, and high-performing, high-commitment management teams (Alimo-Metcalfe 1995). Thus transformational leadership is espoused by a number of organizations moving away from hierarchical to flatter management structure with responsibility decentralized to teams. This means that the dominant leadership qualities required are more likely to be those associated with women managers. Will this mean that more women than men will be recruited into these new job roles? Past experience suggests that this is unlikely unless there are changes in the way in which these behaviours and traits are assessed.

Again 'quality' HRM policies and practices have exhibited a move towards more rigorously validated and reliable selection and assessment instruments. This can be seen in the structure of the interview process as much as in the identity and training of interviewers. Situational or behavioural event interview techniques are increasingly used as a means of avoiding the personal bias and snap decisions that lead to the stereotyping of applicants according to whether the position has traditionally been held by a male or female applicant. High-quality selection also exhibits a move away from reliance upon a single selection device, and psychological tests are increasingly used as part of a package of selection techniques. Again, research (Alimo-Metcalfe 1995; Wilson 1995) suggests that even some of the most scientific test instruments are grounded in theories drawn from research on exclusively male samples (especially those studies carried out before the 1980s). This is particularly the case with personality testing and can be illustrated with reference to the concept of 'achievement motivation' which, because it was developed from exclusively male samples, unsurprisingly generates very different responses when used to measure males and females. It took a while for further research to come to the conclusion that achievement motivation was defined and valued differently by males and females. Thus even the scientific rigour of personality test construction is not impervious to gender bias; furthermore, the same problems of construct validity and measurement are held to be present in tests of ability, although the most notorious examples leading to industrial tribunal cases have related to ethnicity rather than gender.

The highest-'quality' HRM selection and assessment instrument is of course the assessment or development centre. While they usually have various designs to meet their various purposes, meta-analysis of these centres has shown that they have the highest validity and reliability of all. Yet even here, there are grounds for concern about gender bias, in terms of the behavioural indicators that the trained assessors (usually senior managers) are given, if these indicators have emerged from a predominantly male sample, even though there may be research evidence of sex difference in behaviour. Another potential source of sex bias arises in the context of the group dynamics that are exhibited in the course of assessment and development activities, such as leaderless group discussions, simulations of board meetings, and so on (Alimo-Metcalfe 1995). In this situation it can be too easy to jump to the conclusion that female compliance indicates poor leadership skills, or that forceful assertive behaviour is aggressive. Sadly, this research does not yet appear to have been incorporated into the design and operation of assessment and development centres.

Finally, there are grounds for thinking that gender bias is very common in the judgements of assessors. Even if rigorous job-role analysis and selection and assessment instrument design has eradicated potential sources of gender bias, assessment decisions can be arrived at that do not take all the evidence into account, and additional extraneous criteria come into play. Excuses can be found, and again Alban-Metcalfe (1995) cites research evidence that this factor comes into play in the way that others attribute the causes of success and failure. A man's success is usually attributed to his ability, while for a woman it is more likely to be attributed to luck or effort. Conversely, a failure for a man is more likely to be attributed to bad luck, but for a woman to lack of ability. There is a great deal of evidence that women who have equivalent experience and qualifications to men receive lower evaluations in respect when applying for jobs or promotions, particularly where they are applying for positions in non-traditional female occupations, especially at a professional level. It also explains the evidence that women are disadvantaged by appraisal judgements in relation to pay and development. Again, Alban-Metcalfe (1995) reports recent research evidence on junior managers in the NHS, that twice the proportion of men get top appraisal ratings compared with women, and that women tend to occupy the lower bands.

Thus this lengthy consideration of assessment processes indicates that rewards for high-quality performance in terms of pay and career are not equally available to men and women, and that high-quality HRM policies and practices lack sufficient rigour to eradicate sources of gender bias. Where does this leave women in the high-performance, high-commitment culture of HRM? It leaves them very stressed! Much has been written about the pressures of executive stress at senior level, but the diffusion of stress throughout organizations, and in particular to middle and junior management levels, makes women more vulnerable. In particular, women managers with children are more susceptible to work stress and overload due to the multiple role demands inherent in running a career, home and family. Although this is the single most important factor, other research cited in Davidson and Cooper (1992) has highlighted other stressors faced by women, such as coping with prejudice and stereotyping, overt and indirect discrimination, lack of role models, feelings of isolation, being the 'token' woman, and so on. So, while women and men managers often share common experiences of stress, women often face additional pressures.

The achievement of quality and the reward of high performance is not as scientifically based as is claimed, and again, gender bias is present in many of the supposedly rigorous HRM instruments in selection and assessment.

Summary and Conclusions

Far from being merely androgenous, HRM is gender-blind. Its underlying features are insensitive to the gender aspects of employment. Flexibility in employment contracts, high-commitment work systems, the pursuit of quality and strategic integration are 'motherhood' concepts: they tolerate no challenge, and you cannot get enough of them. They are elements of a rhetoric that simultaneously sanctions intensification of work, but in practice wastes nearly half the human resource in employment. At the centre is a unitarist managerialism that cannot admit the diversity of a plurality of workforce interests. At the same time, an unequal exchange relationship means that little is offered to the employee in return for unlimited flexibility, commitment and high quality. This low rate of return is even more apparent with HRM's refusal to address institutionalized stereotypes and bias that do not just affect a minority. Women are nearly half the UK workforce, and one day may even be more than half. Admittedly, the very looseness of the HRM vision and the difficulty of identifying organizations which intentionally espouse and 'live' it, make it impossible to claim conclusively that HRM has aggravated the position of women in employment. However, 'shifty' concepts should not be let off lightly. While it would be foolhardy to argue that HRM alone has proved an obstacle to equality in employment, its conscious pursuit will not guarantee the eradication of labour market segmentation, working practices centred around a male model of working time, and the persistence of stereotypes and biased assessments. This makes it doubtful whether HRM will find a cure for its own gender-blindness.

References

Aitkenhead, M. and Liff, S. 1991: The effectiveness of equal opportunity policies. In J. Firth Cozens and M.A. West (eds), *Women at Work: psychological and organizational perspectives*, Milton Keynes Bucks.: Open University Press.

Alban-Metcalfe, B.M. 1989: What motivates managers? An investigation by gender and sector of employment. *Public Administration*, 67(1), 95–108.

Alimo-Metcalfe, B. 1995: Leadership and assessment. In S. Vinnicombe and N.L. Colwill, *The Essence of Women in Management*, Hemel Hempstead, Herrs.: Prentice-Hall.

Bailyn, L. 1994: *Breaking the Mold: women, men, and time in the new corporate world*. New York: Free Press.

Beatson, M. 1995: Progress towards a flexible labour market. *Employment Gazette*, February, 55–66.

Beer, M., Spector, B., Lawrence, P., Quinn Mills, D. and Walton, R. 1985: *Human Resource Management: a general manager's perspective*. Glencoe, Ill.: Free Press.

Bevan, S. and Thomson, M. 1992: *Merit Pay, Performance Appraisal and Attitudes to Women's Work*, IMS Report 234. Brighton: Institute of Manpower Studies.

Bird, D. 1995: Membership of trade unions based on information from the certification officer. *Employment Gazette*, May: 208.

Cameron, I. 1993: Formulating an equal opportunities policy. *Equal Opportunities Review*, 47, January–February, 16–20.

Collinson, D., Knights, D. and Collinson, M. 1990: *Managing to Discriminate*. London: Routledge.

Cooper, C.L. and Lewis, S. 1995: *Beyond Family Friendly Organisations*. London: Demos.

Corti, L. and Dex, S. 1995: Highly qualified women. *Employment Gazette*, March, 115–22.

Davidson, M.J. and Cooper, C.L. 1983: *Stress and the Woman Manager*. London: Martin Robertson.

Davidson, M.L. and Cooper, C.L. 1992: *Shattering the Glass Ceiling: the woman manager*. London: Paul Chapman.

Dickens, L. 1994: The business case for women's equality: is the carrot better than the stick? *Employee Relations*, 16(8), 5–18.

Dopson, S. and Stewart, R. 1990: What *is* happening to middle management? *British Journal of Management*, 1(1), 3–16.

Fombrun, C., Tichy, N.M. and Devanna, M.A. (eds) 1984: *Strategic Human Resource Management*. New York: John Wiley.

Gibbins, C. 1994: Women and training: data from the Labour Force Survey. *Employment Gazette*, November, 391–402.

Guest, D.E. 1987: Human resource management and industrial relations. *Journal of Management Studies*, 24(5), 503–21.

Harris, H. 1995: Organizational influences on women's career opportunities in international management. *Women in Management Review*, 10(3), 26–31.

Herriot, P. and Pemberton, C. 1995: *Competitive Advantage through Diversity*. London: Sage.

Hirsch, W. and Jackson, C. 1989: *Women into Management: issues influencing the entry of women into managerial jobs*. Institute of Manpower Studies Paper no. 158. Brighton: IMS.

Jewson, N. and Mason, D. 1986: Modes of discrimination in the recruitment process: formalisation, fairness and efficiency. *Sociology*, 20(1), 43–63.

Kandola, R. and Fullerton, J. 1994: Diversity: more than just an empty slogan. *Personnel Management*, November, 46–50.

Legge, K. 1995a: HRM: rhetoric, reality and hidden agendas. In J. Storey (ed.), *Human Resource Management: a critical text*, London: Routledge.

Legge, K. 1995b: *Human Resource Management: rhetorics and realities*. London: Macmillan.

Lewis, S. 1995: 'Family friendly' employment policies: a route to changing organisational culture or playing about at the margins? Paper presented at Opportunity 2000 and University of Cambridge conference on *Culture Change in Organisations*, Lucy Cavendish College, Cambridge, 26–27 June.

Liff, S. and Dale, K. 1994: Formal opportunity, informal barriers: black women managers within a local authority. *Work, Employment and Society*, 8(2), 177–98.

McGuire, S. 1992: *Best Companies for Women*. London: Pandora Press.

Opportunity 2000 1994: *Third Annual Report*. London: Business in the Community.

Purcell, J. and Ahlstrand, B. 1994: *Human Resource Management in the Multidivisional Company*. London: Oxford University Press.

Scott McEwen, A. (ed.) 1994: *Gender Segregation and Social Change*. London: Oxford University Press.

Sisson, K. 1994: *Personnel Management: a comprehensive guide to theory and practice in Britain*, 2nd edn. Oxford: Blackwell.

Sly, F. 1993: Women in the labour market. *Employment Gazette*, November, 483–502.

Sly, F. 1994: Mothers in the labour market. *Employment Gazette*, November, 403–13.

Storey, J. 1992: *Developments in the Management of Human Resources*. Oxford: Blackwell.

Sturges, J. and Vinnicombe, S. 1995: How do you make it to the top? A study of the influences on men's and women's managerial careers. Paper presented at the conference on Culture Change in Organizations, organized by Opportunity 2000 and University of Cambridge, Lucy Cavendish College, 26–27 June.

Towers, B. 1992: *The Handbook of Human Resource Management.* Oxford: Blackwell.

Watson, G. 1994: The flexible workforce and patterns of working hours in the UK. *Employment Gazette,* July, 239–47.

White, B., Cox, C. and Cooper, C. 1992: *Women's Career Development: a study of high flyers.* Oxford: Blackwell.

Whitehouse, G. 1992: Legislation and labour market gender inequality: an analysis of OECD countries. *Work, Employment and Society,* 6(1), 65–86.

Wilson, F.M. 1995: *Organizational Behaviour and Gender.* London: McGraw Hill.

Woodall, J., Edwards, C. and Welchman, R. 1995: Organisational restructuring and the achievement of an equal opportunity culture. Paper presented at conference on *Culture Change in Organisations* convened by Opportunity 2000 and the University of Cambridge, Lucy Cavendish College, Cambridge, 26–27 June.

16

Human Resource Management in the Public Sector

CHRIS MOORE

Introduction

The aim of this chapter is to explore the relevance of HRM to public sector organizations. The argument is that HRM models developed in the private sector may be inappropriate for the different context and purposes of public sector organizations. Thus the chapter addresses key issues which reflect not only the relevance of business HRM to this sector, but more generally the applicability of business management practices to it. Are there universal models and practices which can be transferred across sectors? It is the contention of this contribution that when reviewing the development of HRM in the public sector we should first address the purpose and processes of the public sector, and only then review appropriate managerial practices to fit these defined purposes and processes.

What is HRM? Debates and Definitions

On reading the literature one is struck by the continuing debate on what human resource management (HRM) actually is. Many commentators emphasize the heterogeneous nature of the beast. For example, Goss (1994: 1, my emphasis) says it is 'a diverse body of thought and practice, largely unified by a concern to *integrate* the management of personnel more closely with the core management activity of the organisation'. It is the linkage between personnel management and corporate strategy which for many marks the transition from traditional personnel administration to HRM. One helpful summary of the key features of HRM and its distinction from more traditional personnel

Table 16.1 Contrasts between human resource management and
personnel management

Features	HRM	Personnel management
Focus of management	Long-term Strategic	Short-term *Ad hoc*
View of the organization	Unitarist Individuals unified by common identity, commitment to organizational goals and shared values	Pluralist Groups engaged in bargained co-existence and commitment within overt rules and structures of collective bargaining
Organizational structures and processes	Organic flexibility	Bureaucratic rule and role bound
Attitude towards employees	High trust Resource to be developed and maximized Search for commitment Self-control	Low trust Cost to be contained and minimized Search for compliance Imposed control
Responsibility for staff	Line managers Delegated	Specialist personnel practioners Centralized
Outputs of production emphasize:	Quality	Quantity

Source: Guest (1987)

management is provided by Guest (1987) and is summarized in table
16.1.

Guest makes the point that these characteristics represent stereotypes and do not necessarily imply that one approach is better or more
effective than the other. He makes the interesting point about adapting practice to the particular context: 'For example, in public service
bureaucracies, or in organisations with a strong tradition of adversarial
industrial relations, personnel management might more successfully
contribute to achievement of organisational goals' (Guest 1987: 508).

It is important also to emphasize the problematic aspects of HRM. For example, Guest says that HRM is based on 'high trust', yet there is evidence that organizations sometimes seen as exponents of HRM practice, such as Nissan, in fact use the latest production line technologies allied to job redesign and group-based work to exercise intensive control of their workforce (Garraghan and Stewart 1992; Delbridge and Turnbull 1992).

Assuming these features as outlined by Guest are core elements of HRM, why are they being emphasized at this time? The primary driving force seems to lie in the external environment of organizations. In particular, competitive forces are seen as generating an inexorable pressure to restructure with the emphasis on continuous innovation, organizational and individual flexibility and responsiveness to customer demands. This economic dimension of the environment which is creating pressures for change might not in itself lead to HRM practices since changes need to be implemented. Thus socio-economic conditions need to be receptive, and here writers point to the shifts in the balance of power between management and workers. The reassertion of managerial authority is linked to the relative decline of organized labour. This decline can be explained by the combination of several factors: shifts in the structure of economies; changes in the labour market; levels of unemployment; employment and trade union legislation.

Many of the ideas lying behind identified HRM-related concepts and practices are not in themselves new. As Towers (1992) observes, we can trace the ideas propounded in many versions of HRM some way back in managerial thinking. There seem to be divergent models or approaches as to what HRM constitutes which lead to apparent inconsistencies. One often-quoted dichotomy is that of Storey's 'hard' and 'soft' versions of HRM (Storey 1991), the key elements of which are outlined in table 16.2.

Again, as with Guest's presentation, we need to acknowledge the stereotyping inherent in this and the contingent nature of HRM in practice. So it is likely that organizations will develop a mix of approaches and even differentiate employees internally on the basis of perceptions of utility to the attainment of corporate goals. The growth of core and periphery labour markets within organizations illustrates this kind of variation in the treatment of workers in the same company. Also the distinction between 'hard' and 'soft' does not necessarily imply a normative preference for one over the other. If what really distinguishes HRM from personnel is its strategic focus, then either version may be perfectly rational depending on the organization's particular circumstances.

Table 16.2   Typologies of human resource management

Features	Hard	Soft
Orientation	Instrumental Quantitative Resource utilization	Identification Qualitative Human development
Theoretical antecedents	Scientific management (F.W. Taylor)	Human relations (Elton Mayo)
Management of employees	Control and compliance through external means, e.g. performance measures, performance-related pay, staff appraisal	Search for commitment and identity through shared values, common interests and self-control (e.g. quality circles)

Source: Storey (1991)

The picture which emerges from the literature is that HRM does seek to embody a particular set of practices which at some level are consistent and mutually reinforcing although still revealing the essential contradictions, ambiguities and tensions which define management as a practice (Hales 1993). So bearing in mind the problems outlined above in offering clear definitions of HRM, what implications does it have for public sector management?

Management in the Public Sector

There is a fairly long-standing debate within the literature on public sector management as to how far it should reflect the management ideas and practices found in business. In the UK, and in other countries such as the USA and New Zealand, there have been significant shifts in the rhetoric and substantive practices of public sector management. The concept of the 'new public management' has emerged which is seen as presenting a distinctive form of managerial ideology and practices in contrast to the more traditional models embodied in the concept of 'public administration' (Hood 1991; Gunn 1987).

The new public management (NPM) emphasizes flexibility, performance, value for money and cost effectiveness. In contrast, public administration is traditionally based on due procedures reflecting an emphasis on equity, probity and a public service ethos. Within this framework management was not viewed as a high-level activity (Metcalfe and Richards 1990; Hennessey 1989). The term 'administration' rather than 'management' symbolized this emphasis. Administration implies routine implementation of predetermined orders. This was reinforced by a standardized bureaucratic provision of public services allied with strong professionalization in certain key areas of the welfare state such as health, education and social services (Hoggett 1991). In contrast, management was seen as something that happened in the business world and emphasized innovation, change and performance. This is what the NPM attempted to incorporate into the public sector during the 1980s.

NPM emerged due to a combination of factors. One was economic. The 'fiscal crisis' of the public sector economy from the mid-1970s led to cutbacks in management. The second driving force was political and ideological, reflecting particular values, beliefs and ideas concerning the appropriate relationship between the state and society, collective public provision and individual private decisions. The market was seen as the most efficient and effective allocator of goods and services and as a means of pursuing choice and freedom based on individual responsibility. Thus privatization and reduction in public service provision were key items of policy, but where these were not seen as feasible or appropriate, the aim was to introduce private business management ideas and practices into the public sector. This importation was personalized through the contribution of business managers and management consultants in reforming public service management (Flynn 1993).

In addition, the popularization of certain ideas about what constituted good management began to filter through into the public sector. Of particular significance was the 'excellence literature' represented by Peters and Waterman (1982). In the USA the more recent publication of Osbourne and Gaebbler's (1992) *Reinventing Government* served as a blueprint for President Clinton's reform of the federal administration (Margetts 1994) This book can be viewed as the public sector version of *In Search of Excellence*. In the UK even writers who would not identify themselves with the Thatcherite project were drawing upon the excellence literature in seeking to develop an alternative approach to public sector management reform (Stewart and Clarke 1988). The link between this body of writing and HRM is apparent, with its emphasis on flexibility, cultural values, people management and user or customer satisfaction.

Hood (1991) provides a definition of the NPM by reviewing key themes which have emerged in public sectors across Western Europe, North America, Australia and New Zealand. These themes include:

- professionalization of management and the development of accountable management;
- performance measurement which is the adjunct of accountable management, emphasizing objectives which can be quantified;
- output control which scrutinizes the link between resources used to provide services and the results obtained;
- disaggregation of producer/supplier units and the development of a network of contractual relationships;
- competition which is linked to efficiency gains and improvements in service standards;
- discipline and parsimony which emphasizes cost-cutting and efficiency.

Stewart and Walsh (1992), in reviewing developments in the British public sector during the 1980s, make similar points. In key parts of the public sector there has been a separation or disaggregation of providers and purchasers, for example the internal market in the National Health Service (NHS). This has been based on the development of contractual arrangements which specify performance objectives and targets. The disaggregation of the public sector has also provided the basis for flexibility and variations in the pay and conditions of employees. Under arrangements for executive agencies working under contracts (framework agreements) with central government departments, hospital trusts in the NHS and opted-out schools, responsibility for HRM has been devolved to unit-level managers with power to move away from standard national terms of pay and conditions of service. Elected politicians continue to establish strategic objectives, distribute overall resources and evaluate performance, but operational management is contracted to identifiable units within the public sector or increasingly to private providers. Hence markets either of the external type or internal to the public sector emerge. Finally, these arrangements are seen as improving service to a customer/user. Stewart and Walsh contrast these developments with the old culture and practices of public administration based on hierarchy, bureaucracy and professionalization.

It should be emphasized that these developments are not peculiarly British. Boston (1987) describes the reforms of the New Zealand public sector initiated by a Labour government during the 1980s as 'one of the most comprehensive re-organisations initiated anywhere in the West in the post war period'. The reforms included change to the system of wage-fixing with moves away from centralized pay determination based on comparability with the private sector, annual general adjustments, standardized conditions and fixed relativities towards more flexible decentralized enterprise-based bargaining. This was designed to give senior managers greater autonomy over resource use, including staffing levels. Established conventions governing personnel policy such as security of tenure were breached. Other key aspects of reform included greater emphasis on performance as opposed to following established processes. In a later study Boston describes how this focus developed into a system of performance-related pay for departmental chief executives with appointments on five-year contracts (Boston 1992).

The NPM and the UK Civil Service

In order to illustrate some of the implications of these developments we shall look at the key changes that have occurred in the UK Civil Service over the last 20 years. When Margaret Thatcher assumed office in 1979, one of the priorities was to reduce the size of the public sector. The Civil Service came under sustained pressure, with targets set for cuts in staff numbers and pressures to control and cut public spending programmes (Drewy and Butcher 1991).

However, it would be simplistic to see the Thatcherite project for the Civil Service simply in terms of crude cutback. Alongside the emphasis on curtailing costs was the aim of making the service more cost-effective in its use of resources and to shift the culture of civil servants towards a managerialist focus. Various phases of an emergent change strategy can be identified (Richards 1988). First, the efficiency scrutinies spearheaded by Mrs Thatcher's official adviser on management in the Civil Service, Derek Rayner, who combined some previous experience of working in government with his commercial expertise with Marks & Spencer. The scrutinies were a series of short-term projects throughout Whitehall designed to identify areas of waste, improve use of administrative resources; but perhaps more significantly, to begin the longer-term process of changing values, attitudes and behaviour of civil servants so that they saw themselves as managers responsible for the cost-effective use of substantial resources. One of the outputs of the scrutinies was a project pioneered by Michael Heseltine, a minister unusually interested in management. This project was the Management Information System for Ministers (MINIS) which focused on the development of an information system enabling top managers to have sophisticated data on departmental activities, resource inputs and performance outputs at a highly disaggregated level. The aim was to improve internal planning and control mechanisms. The third phase of the programme was essentially the systematic adaption of MINIS throughout Whitehall under the umbrella of the Financial Management Initiative (FMI). Each department had to come up with its own version of MINIS as part of a move to specify objectives, measure performance, delegate management responsibilities and develop managerial skills. In 1988 Robin Ibbs, Derek Rayner's successor, conducted a review of progress. Ibbs said that, whilst much had been achieved, there were still important blockages to managerial change.

His report, which became known as *The Next Steps*, recommended a major structural reorganization of central government around the concept of executive agencies. The principle was that responsibilities for operational management, the day-to-day delivery of public services, could be separated out from policy and strategic management responsibilities. Whilst the latter would remain the province of ministers and senior civil service advisers within Whitehall departments, the former would be hived off into a series of separate agencies each headed by its own chief executive. Agencies would enter into contracts, known as framework agreements, with their sponsoring departments. These contracts would specify what the agencies were supposed to provide within the resources allocated to them. Significantly, from the perspective of HRM in the Civil Service, each agency would employ its own staff with the aim of developing agency-specific pay, conditions of service, promotion and personnel policies. Whilst staff would come from civil service departments and would remain defined as civil servants, there would over time be a disaggregation of common national employment practices and experiences. The government accepted the Ibbs Report and agreed with its basic argument that the Civil Service was too big and complex to be treated as a single homogeneous entity which had to be subject to universal management practices. In some ways the Civil Service was undergoing a massive programme of decentralization which paralleled the divisionalization of large business corporations (Purcell 1991).

In 1994 the government published a White Paper which set out its aims in relation to the Civil Service (HMG 1994). This emphasized the principle of delegated management, including responsibility for pay and gradings, whilst at the same time arguing that the Civil Service should remain a coherent entity. It noted that since the Ibbs Report some 97 executive agencies had been established employing 340,000 civil servants, or 64 per cent of the total employed. The government acknowledged important differences between public and private sector contexts, particularly in respect of public accountability and access to services on the basis of entitlement, but also said that greater competition and a focus on economy and efficiency were ingredients of a more effective public management. The delegation of pay and gradings was being promoted in order to reflect the diversity of tasks and services within central government and to introduce greater management freedom to meet local needs. At the time of publication, 60 per cent of civil servants had delegated pay bargaining arrangements. Responsibility for grading and pay systems had been delegated to 20 agencies, including the Inland Revenue, Customs and Excise and the Health and Safety Executive. It was intended that this should grow as the Treasury became satisfied that agencies had the capacity to take on full responsibilities in this area. In addition, the government was aiming to reduce staffing levels in the Civil Service to below 500,000 over a four-year period. Alongside this 'downsizing', the White Paper also referred to equal opportunities, training and management development and leaner managerial structures. Continuing moves towards individually determined pay and performance-related pay at senior levels were to be made.

There seems to be a lot in this which would fit quite easily with HRM ideas and developments in business management. Key concepts and themes include delegation, including the management of personnel, flexibility of pay and conditions, and the decentralization of organizational structures within a set of core values and a common culture. The emphasis on cost control and productivity gains connect with aspects of the hard HRM model as defined by Storey (1991). At the level of particular agencies, some recent studies of practice show how these principles are being implemented. Greer (1994: 103) suggests that the diversity set in motion by the *Next Steps* report is likely to lead to the fragmentation of the Civil Service despite the government's claims that the service remains unified: 'The term "Civil Servant" will become increasingly meaningless and people will instead identify more with their particular role, for example an employee of a particular agency.'

She thinks that this may have implications for security of employment, loyalty and the commitment to a public service ethos. Plowden (1994) documents the increasing difficulties in attracting and retaining good people in the senior Civil Service. By 1992, of the 1,700 entrants to the service coming through the selection board procedure between 1972–82, only 800 remained. Continuous cuts in staffing levels combined with pay limits have made the service less attractive. Growing insecurity of employment and worsening of terms and conditions due to the contracting-out of services through 'market testing' is also cited as undermining the concept of a career. Plowden contrasts this with the situation in Canada, where government through its Public Service 2000 programme, which formally has many of the same aims as the British government's reform programme, has placed more emphasis on people management and career development. Even in areas of equal opportunity the Civil Service faces problems. Although half the total workforce are women, only 9 per cent of senior posts are occupied by them.

A recent study of two of the larger executive agencies, which focused on the impacts of the reforms from the perspective of the labour process, presents a picture of intensification of managerial control and work, casualization of employment conditions and fragmentation of bargaining arrangements (Fairbrother 1994). Pollitt (1993) has described the changes in public services management more generally as a movement towards 'neo-Taylorism' with 'contrasting flashes of culture management'. Leach et al. (1994: 207) highlight contradictions in these developments:

> On the one hand there are pressures to build up a more responsive organisation in which staff are conscious of the needs of the service user and are able to act on their initiative to meet them. This sort of organisation implies that staff are strongly committed and self-motivated. On the other hand there are pressures towards less security, closer monitoring of work and cuts in pay and conditions of service.

The divisions of the workforce into core and periphery labour markets is also developing within public services through contracting-out, internal markets and more flexible modes of employment contract. Leach et al. say that HRM initiatives are more likely to occur where the workforce is predominantly composed of skilled, high-discretion workers. But, as in the private sector, flexibility has its hard rationalistic push in the form of reducing employment levels, increasing both numerical and functional flexibility, as well as the 'softer' side aimed at securing co-operation and commitment from key workers, albeit on managerially determined lines.

HRM and the Public Sector

Transferring business practices

Certainly, we can find developments across the public sector which seem consistent with many of the features of HRM, but whether this is an appropriate transference of ideas and practices is another question. This is not simply or even primarily a technical issue about good management practice or organizational efficiency and effectiveness. These developments involve more fundamental value judgements about organizational aims and purposes and social relationships both within organizations and in relation to their external environments, including service users.

An important development in the UK during the 1990s has been the Citizen's Charter which stresses the importance of public service organizations being more responsive to their users through such means as setting open performance targets, the development of redress procedures and greater user choice about forms of service provision (HMG 1991). Of particular interest in relation to HRM is the stress on quality and customer focus paralleling the language of the business world. However, critics argue that viewing users of collective public services as customers is highly inappropriate due to a range of factors, including the limited choice of particular service providers available to users. The collective nature of public goods and services means that these are provided not simply to satisfy individual preferences and demands but on the basis of social need as determined through the political process. Fundamentally, it is argued that users of public services are better viewed as citizens with rights and responsibilities in relation to publicly provided services, including the opportunity to directly, or indirectly through their elected representatives, participate in decisions about what services are provided, to whom, how, and at what level of provision. This leads to a much more complex and engaged relationship with service providers than would typically be found in the market place (Stewart and Ranson 1988).

There are several distinctive features of employment within the public sector, although many of the changes made in the UK during the 1980s are aimed at convergence with business management practices. The role of the state impinges on the relationship even where people are employed by disaggregated units of service delivery such as executive agencies, hospital trusts or opted-out schools. The state acts as the funder through public expenditure and has used this as a tool of macroeconomic management, whether in the form of Keynesian demand via an expanding public sector, or more recently through monetarist deflationary policies where the public sector and its workers are seen as a source of inflationary pressure to be controlled. Hence, during the 1990s in the UK public sector pay has been held in check by cash limits and the insistence that increases be tied to efficiency gains and productivity; this translates as job losses, greater flexibility and intensification of work. Further, it reflects the influence of politics, policy and ideology on public sector employment practices – for example, contracting-out and competitive tendering.

In the context of developments in the way public services are financed and delivered, the notion of competitive advantage in a market is not an unreasonable way for public managers to look at their organizations. A hospital trust manager seeking contracts from the local health authority or general practitioner fundholders may well begin to think in terms of business planning, competitive edge or differentiation in 'product services' offered and the implications for resource use, including the key component of unit costs, namely staff. Whether this is viewed as a 'good thing' crucially depends on how we conceive of public services and what they represent.

It is possible to argue that management is largely a set of generic principles, activities and functions which differ in practice due to contingent circumstances and contexts. Thus we would not necessarily expect management practices in Japan to translate into the different sociocultural context of the UK without some adaption and adjustment. This does not render Japanese management principles and practices irrelevant in the British context, but it means that transference is likely to involve modifications to fit local circumstances. Similarly, we would not necessarily expect a business employing ten people to exhibit the same management practices as a multinational corporation employing 10,000 people. Both might engage in planning, budgeting and people management, but how they do these things is likely to differ substantially. Thus, on this perspective, why should we expect public management to be practised in the same way as business management if public services provide a different context for management (Gunn 1987)?

There is a danger of setting up business management as a model of good practice to be studied by public managers for lessons to learn and, where appropriate, to apply. The exponents of the NPM go further. They clearly believe that business management must be inherently superior to public management because businesses are driven by competitive market pressures and are thus more efficient in their use of resources, more innovative in managerial practices and more responsive to customers, who can exit to an alternative supplier if their demands are not satisfactorily met. Therefore either public services should be transferred to the private sector or, where this is not possible, business practices should be imported as far as possible into the public sector. This approach does not explore the argument for a model of public management which operates on distinctive principles

Table 16.3 Competing approaches to public sector management

Feature	Public administration	New public management	Public service orientation
Basic principles	Distinctiveness of public sector	Superiority of business management	Distinctiveness of public services
Organization	Bureaucratic Standardized Equitable	Decentralized Variations Flexibility	Decentralized Diversity within agreed commonality
Accountability	Political process Representative democracy	Markets User choices	Political process Direct democracy
Relations with service users	Users as subject Loyalty Producer as professional bureaucrat	User as consumer Exit Producer as satisfying user needs	User as citizen Voice Producer as partner working with user
Employment relations	Paternalistic Collectivist Security within commitment to career bureaucracy	Performance-orientated Individualistic Flexibility within commitment to competitive consumer-orientated 'business'	Participative Collegiate Flexibility within commitment to collective service

(Stewart and Ranson 1988; Ranson and Stewart 1994). We can present three basic models of public sector management with implications for HRM (see table 16.3).

The traditional approach identified with classical public administration emphasizes the distinctive nature of the public sector. The predominant model is of a highly bureaucratized service providing standardized goods and public services on the basis of equity. Service providers work within a constitutional framework of political accountability which stresses the responsibility of elected politicians for the overall management of public services and their ultimate answerability to the electorate. Users of public services are viewed as subjects with legal/political entitlements to those services but very much as subjects who show loyalty to these services. The providers are a mix of bureaucrats and professionals who define what is most appropriate for the service user. Employment relations are characterized by paternalism within a bureaucratic context which provides security of employment over a career. Industrial relations are based on collective national agreements negotiated through recognized formal procedures with trade unions representing the workforce.

We can see the marked contrast between this traditional model and the emergence of the NPM during the 1980s–90s. Farnham (1993) sums up the shifts succinctly in terms of three broad developments. First, 'the move away from a predominantly "soft" welfare-centred "model" employer approach . . . to a "harder" market-centred human resource management approach'. Secondly, the breakdown of the industrial relations model based on national collective bargaining (the Whitley model) to a much more flexible decentralized bargaining. Thirdly, the weakening of the collectivist approach to the management of people based on common standards and joint machinery to what he terms 'factional individualist initiatives'. He concludes his review of developments across the public sector thus:

> Public service employers can no longer universally claim to be model or good practice employers setting an example for other employers to follow. They, like their private sector counterparts, are now far more likely to be concerned with efficient human resource utilisation, effective employee performance, flexible working arrangements, widening pay and benefits differentials amongst employee groups. (Farnham 1993: 122)

Under the emergent NPM model, the organization and resourcing of public services increasingly is based on market arrangements either through the contracting-out of service provision (or aspects of such provision such as hospital catering or local government computer services) or the development of internal markets within a publicly owned and managed service, such as the National Health Service. Accountability begins to assume market forms where performance and rewards are based on winning contracts and customers (patients, pupils). Users are given more choice so that exit options become available, thereby reinforcing the importance of producers satisfying consumer preferences (Flynn 1993).

The development of the NPM was driven by a powerful critique of public services as bureaucratic and therefore inflexible, unresponsive and inefficient. Producers were viewed with deep suspicion. It was felt that they were primarily motivated by the desire to satisfy their own interests in the form of job security, big budgets and power over the service user (Niskanen 1973). Whilst this representation may be criticized as being a caricature, it seemed to contain enough truth to connect with popular experience and conceptions of remote bureaucratic services. The absence of any well-worked alternative which acknowledged the problems of public service management but sought reform within a context of collective provision rather than markets allowed the NPM to dominate. However, over time an alternative set of ideas did emerge, largely associated with the writings of John Stewart and his colleagues at Birmingham University's Institute of Local Government Studies. This drew upon emerging practices in several local authorities and was reinforced by Stewart's role as a consultant and management trainer within the UK local government scene (see Stewart 1986; Stewart and Ranson 1988; Ranson and Stewart 1994).

The term public service orientation (PSO) was coined to describe this alternative view. PSO, like classical public administration, emphasized the distinctive nature of public sector organizations but emphasized more acutely the focus on providing services for citizen users. Stewart observed that public sector organizations needed to stress service *for* the user, not service *to* them, thereby pointing to a different relationship between users and providers than seemed to be the case with traditional models of public administration. Thus, similarly to the NPM, we see under this model the commitment to decentralization and flexibility, albeit within a commitment to collective public provision. In contrast to the NPM's belief in the efficiency of markets, PSO emphasizes the political process as the basis for accountability and decisions about public services but, in sharp contrast to classical public administration, encourages forms of direct democracy in terms of user participation in service design and delivery. This has been most extensively developed within local government in services such as housing, where tenant groups are involved in estate management (Burns et al. 1994; Lowndes and Stoker 1992). Thus the user of public services is viewed as an active citizen rather than as a loyal and largely passive recipient of services, or as an individual consumer shopping around in a market for the best buys. The relationship between service providers and users is seen in different terms as users are empowered through participation. Within public service organizations the key employees are the front-line staff who deliver the services to the public and have direct contact with users. The emphasis on decentralization is partly about empowering these staff to be more responsive to users but also to increase employee satisfaction and commitment. Employment relations practices relate closely to the 'soft' HRM practices identified by Storey.

It might be argued that PSO is largely a theoretical model associated primarily with a few academics, although these individuals have been closely involved with local government so that there is empirical evidence of PSO as a practice. However, given the highly centralized nature of the UK political system, the dominant model during the last 15–20 years has undoubtedly been the NPM.

Conclusions

What we have seen in the UK over the past 20 years is a progressive lessening of public sector distinctiveness and a growing convergence with business management ideas and practices which sees the transferability of these as a desirable and necessary project. The problem with this is that whilst the *content* of management *may* have some universal characteristics, the *context* in which these take concrete shape as practices are substantively different because public service organizations pursue fundamentally different goals and have different purposes and values.

Public services, unlike business in a market place, cannot be simply orientated towards the preferences of individual users; first, because services are based on collective decisions and choices about what to provide, how much to provide within the context of the resources made available, and who is entitled to receive them; secondly, because the interests of the wider community in the services provided is a relevant factor in decision-making. Thus the non-using taxpayer has an interest in the various services and this interest is typically represented by the elected politician. This raises issues of accountability and control and of reconciling conflicting demands, which generally do not apply to private enterprises in a market place. In the context of public services, employees are also citizens and have a legitimate interest in how services are provided as well as being a 'resource' in terms of service provision. Many employees would lay claim to professional status, and this places them in a different kind of relationship both to their managers and to service users. Any management of 'human resources' in the public sector needs to bear this kind of complexity in mind.

The collective organization of employees in the public sector, whether in the form of trade unions and/or professional associations, is likely to render certain aspects of HRM problematical, although the reforms in public service management during the 1980s–90s illustrate the poss-ibilities of making significant changes to employment relations even within a relatively highly unionized/professionalized context. Beaumont argues that there are several constraints on the development of HRM in the public sector besides union density (Beaumont 1992). He cites the heterogenous nature of the workforce, limited education and train-ing of managers, the political nature of strategic objectives and the distinctive nature of public sector management. It seems to this author that some of these constraints are not peculiar to the public sector – in particular, many large private organizations would have a diversity of staff to deal with and many commentators have pointed out the relative poverty of British management in terms of education and training. However, the political nature of the public sector and its distinctiveness in terms of management make more sense in develop-ing an argument for a distinctive public sector HRM. Pollitt (1993) builds on this argument. He argues that key principles within the public service have included the concept of meeting social needs, the importance of professional standards in helping to determine needs and decide on how best to meet them, the provision of collective services and an equitable distribution of services. He goes on to argue that

> historically they played little or no part in the development of manager-ialist ideologies. Thus the transfer, during the last decade or two, of managerialism from private sector corporations to welfare state services represents the injection of an ideological 'foreign body' into a sector previously characterised by quite different traditions of thought. (Pollitt 1993: 11)

In his view, the neo-Taylorism of the NPM with its emphasis on targets, performance indicators and measurement and rewards linked to performance far outweighs any emphasis on human relations and corresponds in many ways to the hard instrumental version of HRM. He sees the dominant view of public servants that has developed under the NPM as fundamentally at odds with any positive commit-ment to employee development. If public service workers are por-trayed largely as self-interested and inefficient (although ironically perhaps somewhat efficient at promoting their self-interest), then the overriding emphasis in managerialist terms becomes one of control whether through bureaucratic rules or market forces.

Leach et al. (1994) argue that this negative view cannot provide a good basis for improving public services or HRM within the public sector, where 'labour is more than simply a means of producing the service but is a basic part of the service'. The separation of operational management responsibilities for service production and delivery from more politicized strategic decision-making may offer opportunities for some longer-term strategic management at the operational level. However, the changing context of public service delivery with market or 'quasi-market' arrangements may simply drive operational unit managers into cutback management or opportunistic behaviour in order to win 'market share' from competitor units. This may be the outcome of internal markets in the NHS or the education system and of contracting-out in various parts of the public services. Pressures to maximize resource inputs or minimize various costs, especially labour, are likely to be major factors in managerial decision making (Flynn 1994).

There is however, no *a priori* reason why public sector HRM should be modelled on practices from business enterprise. To follow this logic is to articulate an ideological view of the public services, their management and the role of employees. This view is certainly arguable but should not be presented as a universalist rationality. The appropriateness of this model can certainly be questioned on the grounds of principle as well as on aspects of its practice.

References

Beaumont, P.B. 1992: *Public Sector Industrial Relations*. London: Routledge.

Boston, J. 1987: Transforming New Zealand's public sector: Labour's quest for improved efficiency and accountability. *Public Administration*, 65(4), 423–42.

Boston, J. 1992: Assessing the performance of departmental chief executives: perspectives from New Zealand. *Public Administration*, 70(3), 405–28.

Burns, D., Hambleton, R. and Hoggett, P. 1994: *The Politics of Decentralisation: revitalising local democracy*. London: Macmillan.

Delbridge, R. and Turnbull, P. 1992: Human resource maximization: the management of labour under just-in-time manufacturing systems. In P. Blyton and P. Turnbull (eds), *Reassessing Human Resource Management*, London: Sage.

Drewy, G. and Butcher, T. 1991: *The Civil Service Today*. Oxford: Blackwell.

Fairbrother, P. 1994: *Politics and the State as Employer*. London: Mansell.

Farnham, D. 1993: Human resource management and employee relations. In D. Farnham and S. Horton (eds), *Managing the New Public Services*, London: Macmillan.

Flynn, N. 1993: *Public Sector Management*. Hemel Hempstead, Herts: Harvester Wheatsheaf.

Flynn, N. 1994: Control, commitments and contracts. In J. Clarke, A. Cochrane and E. McLaughlin (eds), *Managing Social Policy*, London: Sage.

Garraghan, P. and Stewart, P. 1992: *The Nissan Enigma: flexibility at work in a local economy*. London: Mansell.

Goss, D. 1994: *Principles of Human Resource Management*. London: Routledge.

Greer, P. 1994: *Transforming Central Government: the Next Steps initiative*. Buckingham: Open University Press.

Guest, D. 1987: Human resource management and industrial relations. *Journal of Management Studies*, 24(4), 503–21.

Gunn, L. 1987: Perspectives on public management. In J. Kooiman and K.A. Eliassen (eds), *Managing Public Organisations: lessons from contemporary European experience*, London: Sage.

Hales, C. 1993: *Managing Through Organisations*. London: Routledge.

Hennessey, P. 1989: *Whitehall*. London: Fontana Press.

Her Majesty's Government (HMG) 1991: *Citizen's Charter*, Cm 1599. London: HMSO.

Her Majesty's Government (HMG) 1994: *The Civil Service: continuity and change*, Cm 2627. London: HMSO.

Hoggett, P. 1991: A new management in the public sector. *Policy and Politics*, 19(4), 143–56.

Hood, C. 1991: A public management for all seasons? *Public Administration*, 69(1), 3–19.

Leach, S., Stewart, J. and Walsh, K. 1994: *The Changing Organisation and Management of Local Government*. London: Macmillan.

Lowndes, V. and Stoker, G. 1992: An evaluation of neighbourhood decentralisation. *Policy and Politics*, 20(1), 47–61.

Margetts, H. 1994: The national performance review, the Clinton presidency and the future shape of American government. Paper presented to the Political Studies Association Annual Conference, Swansea, April.

Metcalfe, L. and Richards, S. 1990: *Improving Public Sector Management*. London: Sage.

Niskanen, W. 1973: *Bureaucracy: servant or master?* London: Institute of Economic Affairs.

Osbourne, D. and Gaebler, T. 1992: *Reinventing Government*. Reading, Mass.: Addison-Wesley.

Peters, T.J. and Waterman, R.H. 1982: *In Search of Excellence*. London: Harper & Row.

Plowden, W. 1994: *Ministers and Mandarins*. London: Institute for Public Policy Research.

Pollitt, C. 1993: *Managerialism and the Public Services*. Oxford: Blackwell.

Purcell, J. 1991: The impact of corporate strategy on human resource management. In J. Storey (ed.), *New Perspectives on Human Resource Management*, London: Routledge.

Ranson, S. and Stewart, J. 1994: *Management for the Public Domain: enabling the learning society.* London: Macmillan.

Richards, S. 1988: Turning civil servants into managers: strategies for cultural change. Paper presented to the Royal Institute of Public Administration conference, University of Kent, September.

Stewart, J. 1986: *The New Management of Local Government.* London: Allen & Unwin.

Stewart, J. and Clarke, M. 1988: *Understanding Local Government.* Harlow, Essex: Longman.

Stewart, J. and Ranson, S. 1988: Management in the public domain. *Public Money and Management,* 89(112), 13–18.

Stewart, J. and Walsh, K. 1992: Change in the management of public services. *Public Administration,* 70(4), 499–518.

Storey, J. 1991: Introduction: from personnel management to human resource management. In J. Storey (ed.), *New Perspectives on Human Resource Management,* London: Routledge.

Towers, B. 1992: Introduction. HRM: an overview. In B. Towers (ed.), *The Handbook of Human Resource Management,* Oxford: Blackwell.

17

Managing Human Resources in the Information Age

JOHN A. TAYLOR AND HELEN D. MCINTOSH

Human Resource Management and Information Resources

Human resource management (HRM) is profoundly information-intensive, both conceptually and in its practice. It is, equally, a boundary-challenging concept, for in its full-blown normative expression HRM presumes that information will flow around the organization in ways which sustain the integrative and holistic management thinking by which HRM is underpinned. For example, if the line manager is viewed as a point of integration and decision for all resource deployment in the organization, including human resources (Legge 1989), as normative HRM presumes, then that manager has to be supported by substantial information resources. For the line manager in an HRM environment, information must provide more than functionally specific data; it must also provide possibilities for 'data-matching' – for setting data about employees, to take one example, alongside data on business performance, thereby making more visible the contribution of human resources to the value-adding processes of the organization.

This information-intensiveness of HRM can be illustrated further if we take Guest's (1987) 'ideal type' perspective on HRM which sees it as laying emphasis upon the attainment of four main organizational and managerial objectives: organizational integration; employee commitment; flexibility; and quality.

Improved information resources can secure higher degrees of integration at both strategic and operational levels of the organization, as well as between those levels. At strategic level the case for functionally integrated approaches to business planning and analysis is now well accepted; and a key part of this integrated holism is that information planning should be central to it as the existence of the business process re-engineering (BPR), which we review below, testifies (Hammer 1990; Hammer and Champy 1993; Davenport 1993). Thus the development and deployment of information resources in support of general business planning is seen as a crucial prerequisite for the achievement of strategic integration. Equally, these arguments apply to operational levels of the organization. For example, the new emphasis upon BPR emanates from a fundamental concern to deconstruct the compartmentalized, functional organization, recognizable by its restricted flows of information, and to replace it with a model of organization within which the integrating, cross-cutting theme of *process* predominates. Information flows are afforded enormous significance in the achievement of this process model of organization (Davenport 1993; Hammer and Champy 1993) for the way in which they can facilitate the lateral integration so central to a process perspective.

Employee commitment (Guest's second objective for HRM) also has important informational components. If we interpret 'employee commitment' as essentially meaning commitment by the employee to the organization's goals, then information resources can be critical to its realization. Providing employees with an information-rich or 'informated' (Zuboff 1988) environment – both in the narrow sense of the employee being more informed about the immediate task environment, as well as in the wider sense of the employee understanding better the overall organization – brings forward the potential for a sense of engagement with work which may well have been lacking hitherto. Thus an information rich environment has the potential 'to increase the intellectual content of work at virtually every organisational level, as the ability to decipher explicit information and make decisions informed by that understanding becomes broadly distributed among organisational members' (Zuboff 1988: 243). As one white-collar worker in Zuboff's study put it:

> The best part about having this new system is knowing what is in the unit and being able to feel like I have control over the work. That is one of my responsibilities but I never felt like I had control before. . . . Now that I can see the total functioning of the office, I feel more ownership towards all of the units, not just my own. I do more coordination of the work flow with my peers. I finally feel like I am really doing my job. I am not just a record keeper, but I can really use my brain.

This theme of employee commitment, when seen from an informational perspective, coincides to an extent with what Guest suggests should be a further objective of HRM: that of improving the quality of working life in the organization, including the enhancement of its human capabilities. Thus the provision of information resources can both reduce or eliminate the mundanity of some types of work (as the above quotation suggests), allow for the greater exploitation of human intellect and professional expertise (Taylor and Williams 1989, 1992, 1994), and thereby result in quality improvements both for and of the workforce.

The HRM-orientated organization, according to Guest, should also seek to secure a fourth strategic objective, that of high levels of employment flexibility. It can do so in line with its strategic preferences to introduce more flexibility into its procurement, design, production and delivery systems (Piore and Sabel 1982; Pollert 1991; Clegg 1990). Thus the challenging of demarcated job roles through teamwork and multi-tasking; the 'contractorization' of some elements of the workforce; the use of teleworking (in all of its forms – see pp. 382–4); the adoption of performance-related and time-specific payment systems; and the change from internally sourced activities to ones which are 'outsourced', are all elements of an HRM strategy which is in keeping with an integrated corporate strategy whose emphasis is upon the attainment of new levels of corporate flexibility.

As with Guest's other core objectives of HRM, flexibility requires significant information resources for its realization. Corporate concern with lowering transaction costs through production and delivery flexibilities, for example, can be assuaged by the development of information flows between supplier and buyer organizations which are designed to link orders to production and delivery schedules. In service industries, too, new 'customer-handling' facilities in the form of information-intensive organizational units and systems suggest the need for the development of a range of employment flexibilities. In telephone or electronic banking, for example, where a 'we never close' policy is in operation, as well as working in shifts designed around the peaks and troughs of customer calls, employees are working flexibly in handling customer enquiries, routing customers electronically, as necessary, to points of the organizational network where their business can be handled effectively. A further dimension of flexibility is revealed in the adoption by organizations of computerized 'attendance management systems', and of production control systems which monitor product quality levels, both of these systems supplying information to human resource managers which hence provides the basis for flexible rewards (Li 1995).

Information and Communications Technologies (ICTs) and Human Resources

Digital networks

To this point of the chapter we have sketched the connectedness of *information* resources to the concept and practice of HRM. Focusing primarily upon information has been deliberate as we wish to escape from any charge of technological determinism in bringing forward the arguments of this chapter. Whilst the technologies are powerful in the management capabilities which they bestow, they are not so autonomously. The deployment of computers and telecommunications in and around the workplace (the digital networks of the information age), and the design and implementation of information systems which run on them, are the consequences of human choices and actions. These technologies bring forward new capabilities for information management and for additional forms of communication, but they do not determine them *per se*. As Nicholas Negroponte (1995) has recently observed, the information revolution is not about *atoms* (physical objects) but about *bits* (packets of more and less structured information). For social scientists interested in analysing and explaining the information age, it is the digitized information (the bits) – its construction and communication – which should be the core focus. Whilst the physical machinery – the computerized machinery of the factory, the PC/word processor of the office, the ubiquitous telephone, the near-ubiquitous fax, forms of mobile communications technology, and the local and wide area telecommunications networks – is the common-sense focus of attention, it is its manner of deployment in the workplace, its *informational* significance for work organization and workers which should be deemed of primary importance.

The informational importance of ICTs becomes clearer when we examine the fiercely polarized debates which have surrounded the introduction of new technologies (including ICTs) into organizations. Technology is idealized or reviled, its potential beguiles or revolts, its consequences are to emancipate and empower or to enslave and dehumanize. The debate about ICTs follows these themes – implicit and explicit forms of Utopianism contend with pessimistic and dystopian concerns – and in so doing serves at one level to point up the complexity involved in determining the consequences for the workplace of the introduction into it of ICTs.

The remainder of this chapter draws out this tendency to work with polarized views such as those to be found in contemporary debate surrounding ICTs in the workplace. It does so in two ways; first, by looking generically at some of the key points of contention in this polarized academic debate; and secondly, by looking in detail at two specific applications of ICTs which are of crucial importance for HRM in the contemporary workplace: those of 'teleworking' and 'business process re-engineering'. This examination is used as a backdrop for that possibility to which we allude above of refashioning management thinking for the information age.

The Utopians

In late industrial society we stopped worrying about food. In late communicative society we will stop worrying about material resources. And just as the industrial economy eliminated slavery, famine and pestilence, so will post-industrial economy eliminate authoritarianism, war and strife. For the first time in history the rate at which we solve problems will exceed the rate at which they appear. This will leave us to get on with the real business of the next century: to take care of each other; to fathom out what it means to be human; to explore human intelligence; to move into outer space.   (Stonier 1983)

This resounding celebration of the post-industrial information society is typical of a genre of academic thinking and journalistic commentary which interprets ICTs and the 'revolution' which they herald as, undifferentiatedly, a 'good thing' (see, for example, Toffler 1980). From within an HRM perspective such Utopian thinking translates into the realization of desirable workplace values such as managerial openness and transparency; a shift away from the 'authority of hierarchy' and towards the 'authority of knowledge', fostered and sustained by new information resources at the disposal of the empowered employee; and the changing scale of organization from the mass to the 'de-massified' (ibid.) as organizations take on new networked forms, both within themselves and between themselves and others (Taylor and Williams 1991; Jarillo 1993; Davidow and Malone 1992). Facilitating these changing values are ICTs and the information resources and flows which they permit. Openness and transparency presume widespread access to high-level management information – the information commons of the organization is greatly extended; the ascendancy of the 'authority of knowledge' presumes strong information resources at the disposal of individual knowledge workers; and the changing scale of organization is attendant on changes in transaction cost structures allowing for strategically determined downsizing, internal fragmentation and outsourcing.

The dystopians

'Control' is a key word in the lexicon of those who argue against these Utopian views, and information technologies, old and new, are inherently bound up in its realization (Beniger 1986). The industrial age set in train the speeding up of economic processes in capitalist economies. Technical innovations around the provision of information resources are said to have underpinned the era of mass production, for example, including the bureaucratic forms of organization by which that era was characterized. Uncertainties are endemic in economies experiencing transformation, and technological innovation around the development of information resources brings with it the alluring promise of greater capabilities for control. Such a view fits with the 'labour process' perspective on the introduction of technology. Here technology is to be understood 'not as the servant of humanity but as the instrument of those to whom the accumulation of capital gives ownership of the machines' (Braverman 1974).

Thus a Bravermanesque interpretation of the widespread diffusion of ICTs into the contemporary workplace is that they are designed to be used to garner greater degrees of control into the hands of those responsible for capital accumulation. Thus, on both Beniger's and Braverman's accounts, the case is established for seeing ICTs as being incorporated into business processes so as to accommodate and advance business interests through enhanced forms of process and human control.

This perspective on control through technology remains dominant. It shapes interpretation of management action, suggesting that it must be interpreted as the search for new forms of Taylorized control (Giordano 1993), and it raises the spectre of the fundamentally dehumanizing effects on the organization of the adoption of ICTs. Whilst normative HRM brings forward positive visions of the information-intensive workplace, here we see the reverse being proffered in a critique which is wholly negative.

Characteristics of new technology

But to what extent are ICTs different from other technologies? If we are to take forward this negative thesis of the workplace in the information age, then we have to consider the properties of these information and communication technologies and of the information which they are making available. What is it about them which might lead us to a view about their effects which we might call Bravermanesque?

There are two aspects of the technologies, each heavily related to the other, which help us to answer this question. First, we have to ask what it is that fundamentally differentiates these technologies from other forms of (non-information-based) workplace technology. Zuboff (1988), to whom we have already referred, answers this question by arguing that IT (she does not use the term ICT) introduces 'an additional element of reflexivity: it makes its contribution to the product but it also reflects back on its activities and on the system of activities to which it is related'. IT therefore, unlike other technologies, allows workers to reflect upon the process of work in which they are engaged. It is not simply a technology designed to speed up and otherwise improve production processes, for example. Rather, it is a generic technology which has important additionality in the form of its reflexiveness. The earlier quotation which we used from Zuboff brings home this point very clearly. There the newly informated worker is ostensibly emancipated and empowered by a machine which can reveal so much about the whole activity within which that worker is embedded.

The second characteristic of ICTs, to which we now turn, helps to explain however why, none the less, a dystopian perspective can be sustained when we look at the workplace application of ICTs. This second characteristic is identified by the 'C' of ICTs. Computer networks in the modern organization open up the possibility not just of the realization of enhanced control of work by the individual but of control of that work by others. The work of data-input clerks, for example, can be communicated to management at a distance and thereby monitored. Whilst those clerks may know their own workrate from their own computer so, equally, that machine will provide workrate information to supervisory management, possibly without the knowledge of the employee. A further example is provided by the 'checkout' worker in the information-intensive supermarket who need not be aware that her (usually) transaction-processing activities are providing management with information about their workrate and their honesty (Taylor and Williams 1994). The computerized machinery at the checkout is performing the specific and self-evident functions for which it was designed – speeding the flow of goods through the store and reducing the labour content of transaction processing. What it may also be doing in more or less covert ways is supplying productivity and honesty data to remote management through its 'surveillance' capabilities. These systems provide information on the workrate of each checkout worker, relating that information to store and company norms. Management can thus identify whether a particular individual is working at the desired rate.

This is one aspect of the reflexivity of these in-store information technologies, but these systems also allow for a further level of reflexivity. In addition to productivity data, the systems supply information from each bar-code scanner on the number of items cancelled in any given period. Such data are scrutinized closely by management employees, again matching it against the norm for the store. For, if a particular employee is cancelling higher than average numbers of trans-actions, the suspicion is that they may be colluding with 'customers' to steal goods from the store. Where this suspicion arises, in some supermarkets the reaction of management staff is surreptitiously to use another form of ICT – in-store cameras – to watch the behaviour of that individual.

ICTs in Employment: Two Ways of Seeing

These then are examples of how the distinguishing characteristics of ICTs allow them to be incorporated into the control of workers through forms of computer and telecommunications-intensive surveillance. Their reflexive qualities can therefore work simultaneously in each of two ways. On the one hand, we have seen how these qualities can enable higher degrees of self-control in the workplace, allowing indi-vidual employees to pursue organizational goals through wider under-standing of the processes in which they are a part, enabling them to take on more self-direction. Alternatively, the reflexive qualities of ICTs can supply high levels of surveillance and control data to super-visors and management, denying individual employees autonomy in their work and eroding their personal privacy at work.

Control and surveillance, threatening, respectively, the onset or consolidation of the workplace as sweatshop (Iacono and Kling 1991; Perrolle 1991) and the workplace as panopticon (Lyon 1994), are clearly at odds with the more optimistic scenarios for the future of employment conditions. Here, therefore, we have the qualities of ICTs drawn out so as to display the antagonism of their potential effects on the organization. The Roman god Janus – the god of portals, of arrivals and departures, and thereby of communications – faced two ways at the same time. Our contemporary god of communications, made manifest in the form of ICTs, also 'looks' simultaneously in two directions – one look filled with optimism, the other with pessimism.

This thesis can be extended with further examples of these polarized perspectives. There are, for example, inconclusive debates about the centralizing or decentralizing effects on organizations of ICTs (Rose 1988); and about their effects on management hierarchies (Dopson and Stewart 1993). Equally, there are broader debates which surround the diffusion of ICTs in the workplace; for example, the debate on the effects of these technologies on the gender division of labour (Cockburn 1985). Is the world of the modern supermarket, to return to our example, a well-preserved patriarchy in which (largely) male managers dominate the work of (mainly) women employees through new information resources?

These antagonisms and ambiguities are added to by yet another dimension of these debates: the spatial or geographical impact of ICTs upon working patterns. Computer networks are spatial networks, allowing for flows of information resources between more and less distant places, and removing the pre-exiting need either for the co-location of capital (fixed investment) and labour or for the co-location of the organizations' functions, including its front and back office structures. Business activities, whether we are considering the functional base of the single organization or the complex *filières* which exist amongst groupings of organizations, can be geographically scattered and attenuated, yet at the same time can be 'held together' through flows of electronically conveyed information. This spatial characteristic of ICTs can lead to dramatic effects on the way organizations make locational choices both for whole functions or units *and* for individual employees. 'Teleworking', using the term at this point in the broadest of senses, is not a new concept, but advances in technology and changing public policy regimes are offering new possibilities for teleworking in the context of strategic HRM.

The New Geography of Human Resource Management

When a department of government devises plans to separate its customer-facing activities from its back-office administration and to use ICTs to hold the two parts of the organization together (as some of them presently are doing), it is, in a very broad sense, committing both workforces to a regime of teleworking. The back-office support functions for the Department of Social Security's operations in London are run from Glasgow yet, by design, the front-office worker in London is able to provide a service to claimants equivalent to when the two organizational elements were conjoined. The information needed to service a claim for benefit should be as available and reliable when administered from Glasgow as when it was administered from London itself. Similarly, when a business firm which operates from a number of geographically dispersed sites decides, to take one example, to relocate and consolidate its administrative and clerical support staff on a single site, it does so with the expectation that 'working across the wires' can be equally effective as a strategy of decentralized administrative support. The firm also knows that in choosing to aggregate specific functions in this way it will gain economies of scale as well as potentially gaining from lower labour and accommodation costs.

HRM, with its emphasis upon integrated business strategy, will inevitably take forward these kinds of options and opportunities for the relocation of work. Where a separated personnel function might well have resisted such transformations in the workplace design, modern HRM is predisposed by its core philosophy to working with them.

Examples such as these are becoming commonplace (Goddard 1991; Li 1995) and they represent just one of the categories of teleworking which have been identified and towards which we now turn. A recent study (Gillespie et al. 1995) has identified five major categories of teleworking, each opening up additional possibilities for HRM. They are:

- ICT-supported repatterning of the organizational design, as in the examples cited above;
- ICT-supported homeworking: the most common view of teleworking. It tends to assume that home has become the sole locus of work. In practice it is more usual to find employees working in part from home and in part from other locations, including their employers' premises. It is this view of teleworking which has given rise to its strongest opposition. The negative effects of this form of teleworking can include loss of full-time employee status, with the attendant problems of loss of conditions of service, fewer opportunities for staff development and promotion, and in general the potential for exploitation, particularly in the lower-waged sectors of the economy;
- ICT-supported local offices or 'telecottages': these ventures are designed to provide infrastructure to independent, one-person businesses and to employees of larger organizations. They are usually found in rural and peripheral parts of countries;
- ICT-supported peripatetic employees: a group of teleworkers characterized by its use of portable ICTs which enable them to perform their tasks in many different locations. This form of working is being encouraged by

some firms through the introduction of 'hot-desking'. IBM, for example, has developed its own application of 'hot-desking' under the SMART acronym (Space, Morale and Remote Technology). IBM's sales and field engineering staff were using allocated office space on average for 40 per cent of the time available. SMART has differentiated employees according to their need for desk and office space, and desks are made available accordingly, but they are not allocated to individuals.

• ICT-supported distributed and *ad hoc* team working: perhaps the best examples of this form of teleworking (otherwise known as Computer Supported Co-operative Working, or CSCW) come from research and development groups with their emphasis upon enabling knowledge workers to communicate with each other on a regular basis during the lifecycle of a project, and thereby establishing 'virtual' knowledge communities.

These five categories of telework provide a strong sense of the options increasingly becoming available to the modern business organization for the distribution of its work. The 'drivers' behind such new patterns of employment and work include labour flexibility; reductions in accommodation and other costs; attentiveness to quality-of-life factors in the life and workstyles of some kinds of employee; and a variety of technological factors surrounding advances in the capabilities of new ICTs.

Two other factors add further to these drivers of change, reinforcing our argument that telework options will play a growing part in future HRM strategy. The first of these concerns the kind of work to which teleworking might be applied. Evidence on the practice of teleworking in the UK and elsewhere remains patchy, but one study has examined this question of which types of work ICT-supported homeworking applies to (Huws 1993). Figure 17.1 illustrates the wide range of occupations which are the subject of teleworking from home, as well as the surprisingly even distribution of them.

A second important factor likely to add significantly to the drivers towards teleworking is the shift in public policy stances towards high-quality telecommunications infrastructures (the so-called 'superhighways' debate) and, included in those stances, the prospect of enlarging the numbers of teleworkers. One of the core technological restrictions on each form of teleworking, particularly as it relates to forms of knowledge work, is the quality of telecommunications infrastructures available in different locations (Taylor and Williams 1995). In an argument which now has the status of cliché, advanced telecommunications overrides geography, for it permits the transmission of data and information almost instantaneously, regardless of the distance involved. Our argument, however, is that the growing importance of the capabilities which advanced telecommunications brings forward,

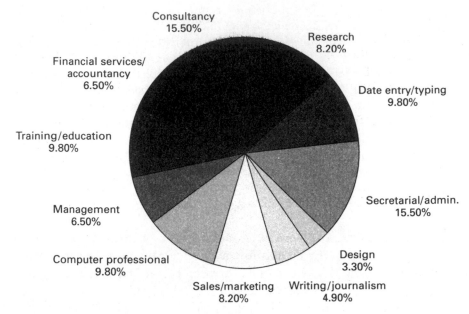

Figure 17.1   Occupations of teleworkers
Source: Huws (1993: 55)

raises serious questions about its uneven geographical presence. It is clear that the current low-level approach to the concept of universal service in telecommunications in the UK, for example, means that the quality of infrastructures required for much that we might define as teleworking is far from ubiquitously available. One of the thrusts of the superhighways debate, as it is emerging from the European Commission, in particular, is that infrastructures need to be developed which will enlarge the teleworking communities of Europe:

> We need to promote working from home and in decentralised offices, so that employees do not travel long distances to get to work. . . . In addition, telecentres should be opened in the 20 cities by the year 1995 for at least 20,000 workers. Telework will increase by 2 per cent in white collar jobs by 1996 and to 10 million telework posts by the year 2000.   (Bangemann 1994)

Business Process Re-engineering

Business process re-engineering (BPR), like HRM, represents a fundamentally integrationist and therefore holistic approach to the strategic management of organization (Davenport and Stoddard 1994). It brings forward, from a strategic perspective, a critique of existing organizational design, arguing for a more aggressive use than hitherto of ICTs in the recasting of the organization. The BPR movement, whose origin is generally put at 1990 and the appearance of a seminal article in the *Harvard Business Review* (Hammer 1990), embodies a number of distinctions from that of the teleworking movement though, ultimately, both movements seek to bring about radical shifts in organizational design. Both these movements have profound significance for the future of HRM. We now turn to a brief comparison designed to contrast their key features.

BPR and teleworking

As we have seen, teleworking raises questions for human resource managers about the appropriate location for different kinds of work, holding out the prospect of advantages for both worker and employer alike. BPR, on the other hand, comes at the question of organizational design from an entirely different perspective. BPR places *primary* emphasis upon relating the organization to the satisfaction of customer needs rather than upon the employment location issues by which teleworking is driven. The fundamental critique of existing organization from a BPR perspective is that the vertical structures of business functions work to the detriment of the horizontal *process perspective* required to enable the organization to respond satisfactorily to its customers' demands (Davenport 1993; Hammer and Champy 1993). The fundamental organizational critique from a teleworking perspective is that existing arrangements do not provide sufficiently for efficiency-inducing employment flexibilities, that is the geography of the organization needs to be loosened up.

Like teleworking, BPR assumes a powerful role for new ICTs. For too long, say its proponents, ICTs have been used to sustain traditional business processes. It is now imperative that they are used to support the new horizontal (process) arrangements which will dramatically improve service quality as well as drive out costs. Teleworking has no such specific critique of existing use of ICTs *within* organizations. Rather, it is a movement which is seeking to benefit from *advances* in ICTs, particularly from advantages which might flow from public provision of enhanced forms of telecommunications.

BPR also differs from the teleworking movement in its approach to employees. Amongst mainstream advocates of BPR there is, presently, scant regard for its employment consequences (for this critique, see

Willmott 1995). In the teleworking movement there has been a continuing concern for such issues as the quality of working life (see, for example, Kinsman 1987).

Whereas telework has garnered the strength it has as a movement from its intermittent support by public policy-makers, many of them concerned with regional policy issues, BPR draws its strength largely from two powerful sources unconnected to public policy. First, the rationalist claims which advocates of BPR make for the delivery of radical improvement in business organizations – the promise that BPR can solve the 'IT productivity paradox' (Strassman 1990) – is celebrated by IT professionals and the wider strategic coalitions in organizations which are increasingly at pains to demonstrate the value to the business of their huge IT investments. Secondly, and equally, the BPR movement draws strength from the power of the industrial complex which is promoting it, which centres upon the telecommunications and computing industries and is supported by large management consultancies. Until now, teleworking has lacked such concerted and powerful advocacy. Teleworking persists as an alternative organizational strategy for both firms and individuals and, as we have seen, is once again receiving much attention from European policy-makers. BPR, on the other hand, is taking the corporate world by storm and looks set to have a deep and lasting place in management techniques.

BPR: a radical movement?

From the rhetoric surrounding BPR, with its strong core utterances about the delivery of radical organizational transformations which are linked to the aggressive use of ICTs, BPR might appear to be offering up a new 'information age' management paradigm. It is argued elsewhere, however (Taylor 1995), that this is not the case; for BPR, as it is conventionally advocated, is largely a re-expression of industrial-age management thinking, with its rationalist concerns, on the one hand, to adduce universalistic principles for organizational design and, on the other, with its relative lack of concern for employment conditions in the transforming organization. The dominant expressions of BPR are essentially Taylorist (when Taylorism is interpreted generically to cover the scientific management and administration movements of the early twentieth century). Thus whilst, in its apparent holism, BPR seems to provide a thoroughly post-modern approach to organizational change, in its rhetoric and practice it fails to move beyond a narrow and universalist machine model perspective reminiscent of the classical adminstration movement of the 1920s and 1930s.

The rhetorical core of BPR provides many clues to its underlying philosophy. 'Don't automate, obliterate' (Hammer 1990) has become axiomatic for the BPR movement. The existing 'cowpaths' of the organization must not be 'paved over' (that is, supported and sustained by information systems) but dug up, with new ICT-supported organizational processes replacing them. At the same time, this 'obliteration rhetoric' is redolent of assumptions from the machine model of organization, seemingly showing little if any regard for the human fallout from 'obliteration'. There is little concern in dominant expressions of BPR either for employee welfare or for the functional value of the organization's existing human resources.

The hallmark of classical administration is stamped upon the BPR view of organization. The organizing principles brought forward in the 1920s and 1930s are now, in the 1990s, reduced to one: process linked to customer. Thus the modern business process is a work flow which can extend beyond the formal boundaries of the organization, back into its suppliers or forward into its customers or clients. A strong requirement within a BPR perspective is that these new business processes will be supported by ICTs and systems designed to integrate the organization, including, in some instances, its suppliers and end customers. The *primary* task for BPR, therefore, is to identify the business processes within the organization, and the *secondary* task is to identify the new information needs attendant on those processes and to build the information systems which will then support them. The technologies and systems are thus deemed to *enable* desirable change in the organization.

BPR is therefore interpreted as largely a technical process. The identification and precise delineation of new business processes, the first step on the path to BPR, is seen as technically rationalist and thus as untrammelled by human aspects of the organization. That particular technical exercise is then supplemented by a second step – one which puts in place the ICTs and systems which together secure the new business process.

HRM and ICTs: the Transformation of the Organization in the Information Age

To summarize: the main arguments of this chapter so far are that HRM is an information-intensive phenomenon, in large part dependent on the adoption and diffusion of ICTs and the new information resources which they make available. Furthermore, we have argued that the adoption by organizations of new technologies (ICTs or other technologies) has tended to excite fiercely polarized debate, as Utopian and dystopian accounts vie for dominance. Moreover, we have sought to explain the polarized arguments of this debate, as they relate to ICTs, by reference to two centrally important characteristics of these technologies which, when taken together, help to explain how both these views can be sustained by their proponents. The combination of the *reflexive* and *network* characteristics of the technologies provides opportunities for informational support for new forms of HRM which might move the organization towards greater or lesser degrees of employee control and surveillance. Finally, to this point, we have brought forward analysis and argument about two powerful movements for organizational transformation – teleworking and BPR – focusing in particular on the signal importance of ICTs to both of them, and arguing that, for different reasons, both these movements hold profound significance for the future of HRM.

We finish this chapter by offering a perspective on radical organizational change in the information age which we argue is of central importance to human resource management. We develop this perspective through two strands of argument. First, it seems clear, particularly from examining movements such as BPR and teleworking, that ICTs will play a powerful support role in the future of HRM. Equally, it seems clear to us that it is misguided to take up strongly held positions on the impact of ICTs on organizations. Polarized views on the organizational impact of ICTs, the fierceness of oppositional debate, contain serious limitations for the quality of our understanding of management in the information age. These views have high value in raising specific, empirically derived issues for celebration, investigation, vigilance and condemnation: they have low value if what they are doing is to create twin Procrustean beds. These powerful and opposing ways of seeing *technology* in organizations may well be serving to lock successive generations into ideas which are fundamentally irrelevant when investigating *ICTs*. The heady challenges of polarized debate must not crowd out the development of new ways of thinking. As we move to a new management era, within which these technologies will play an important part, we shall need to undergo a degree of intellectual divestment. The intellectual fashions of the Utopians and dystopians should now be deemed *démodées*.

At the root of the problem with these twin, though polar-opposite perspectives, lies their basic technicism – their willingness to ascribe a deterministic role, for good or ill, to technologies such as ICTs. Our contention is that it is not the technologies which should provide the central focus in the study of ICTs but the technology-borne information. Two important consequences for HRM flow from this informational focus. First, it should alert HRM specialists to the nature of information flows, actual and proposed, in the organizations in which they have responsibilities. Such a focus should go beyond formal systems development – though it would need to embrace that – and into the informal world of the organization. Information systems have the potential to deliver both intended and unintended consequences. Information designed for one purpose can become of value in other ways, some of which might be detrimental to organizational well-being. Thus, as we have seen, information derived from checkout systems in supermarkets, which may have been designed primarily for effective inventory management, can go on to be used for powerful forms of employee control.

The second consequence of this informational perspective is that it should help to alert HRM specialists to the nature of the organization within which they are employed. Where empirical work on 'electronic sweatshops' has been undertaken, it seems clear that organizations are largely predisposed culturally to use information in one way rather than another (see, for example, Attewell 1987). Thus there is no *causal* relationship between ICTs and employee control and surveillance, on the one hand, or between ICTs and employee emancipation and empowerment, on the other. A contingency view of information use, rather than an absolutist view of technology impacts, suggests that HRM specialists need to develop clear awarenesses of the values which are being embedded in the development of information resources within their own organization, and to make these values explicit.

Our second strand of argument in this concluding section concerns the importance of knowledge resources in contemporary organizations, recognizing the centrality of human knowledge to the effective performance of organizations and recognizing too the potential damage to existing knowledge bases which approaches to 'transformation' such as BPR can wreak.

The technically rationalist, industrial-age paradigm within which the discourse of BPR has largely occurred, and within which practical advice and consultancy is taking place, is in essence ignorant of the human aspects of organization, including its politics and its embedded human knowledge (Taylor 1995). Because of this ignorance BPR is, in practice, likely to lead to deep frustrations, on the one hand, as proposed transformations are reduced by organizational politics to the status of incremental change, or to operational disasters, on the other, as axe-wielding BPR consultants damage the organization's intellectual base. The business processes of the organization, whether long-established or new, are embedded *in* organizational politics and *with* organizational knowledge. The first will act to shape proposed changes, diverting them from any technically rationalist scheme which originated them, and the second must be protected, nurtured and developed (though not preserved) if the organization is to thrive. The argument here is that organizations should be *made ready* for radical changes, where such changes are deemed necessary, and that one key to this preparation lies in the creation of a radical information and communication strategy for the organization.

Whereas the mainstream BPR literature favours all-out obliteration strategies, the view taken here is that careful and thoughtful preparation should be seen as an essential prelude to deep organizational change. This preparation must be directed so as both to reshape the politics of the organization and to recognize fully the value of the existing human asset base.

The paradox at the heart of these injunctions to act sensitively in respect of organizational change programmes lies in the way in which the highly functional human knowledge base of the organization is acting simultaneously so as to frustrate programmes of deep transformation. In the complex world of the organization, politics is intruding upon knowledge, and knowledge is supporting and sustaining politics.

Taking further, therefore, the arguments of this chapter, we ask how management can best proceed so as to prepare the organization for change and to create a situation of readiness from which strong transformation programmes, such as BPR and some aspects of teleworking, can subsequently occur. An answer to this question in the so-styled 'information age' lies in breaking down the political structure of the complex organization, in part by the use of new systems which are designed to give shape to an organizational 'information commons'. Information structures often act to secure the political structure of the organization. Investment in new systems, designed to provide pathways around previously discrete information holdings, thereby enabling wider use of hitherto domain-specific information, can be one tool for developing readiness to change. Similarly, laying emphasis upon common data specifications across the organization, developing organization-wide communications infrastructures and boosting cross-functional working will help to prepare the organization for the possibility of change. Indeed, measures such as these may well give rise to bottom-up pressures for change in the organization as the knowledge- and information-intensive workforce establishes new perceptions of ways to 'do things better'.

Information system developments in organizations have, typically, given rise to limited rather than extensive access to information. Organizations and their employees remain largely in a state of 'information poverty'. Creating readiness for organizational change must spring, not from an industrial age paradigm which proceeds in ignorance of the human content of organization – its knowledge bases and its political structures, for example – but from an information age paradigm in which the emphasis moves away from the 'machine model' of organization. Instead, the emphasis must be upon the need simultaneously to lower internal barriers to organizational change, to develop the 'intelligence' of the organization and to manage an information strategy aimed an 'information empowerment as a form of "unplanned" reengineering of management processes' (Teng et al. 1994).

References

Attewell, P. 1987: Big Brother and the sweatshop: computer surveillance in the automated office. *Sociological Theory*, 5, 77–89.

Bangeman, Martin et al. 1994: *Europe and the Global Information Society: recommendations to the European Council*, Brussels, 26 May.

Beniger, J.R. 1986: *The Control Revolution*. Cambridge, Mass.: Harvard University Press.

Braverman, H. 1974: *Labor and Monopoly Capital: the degradation of work in the twentieth century*. New York: Monthly Review Press.

Clegg, S.R. 1990: *Modern Organisations: organisation studies in the post modern world*. London: Sage.

Cockburn, C. 1985: Caught in the wheels: the high cost of being a female cog in the male machinery of engineering. In D. MacKenzie, and J. Wajcman, *The Social Shaping of Technology: how the refrigerator got its hum*, Milton Keynes, Bucks: Open University Press.

Davenport, T.H. 1993: *Process Innovation: re-engineering work through information technology*. Boston, Mass.: Harvard business School Press.

Davenport, T. and Stoddard, D. 1994: Reengineering: business change mythic proportions? *MIS Quarterly*, June, 121–7.

Davidow, W.H. and Malone, M.S. 1992: *The Virtual Corporation*. New York: HarperCollins.

Dopson, S. and Stewart, R. 1993: Information technology, organisational restructuring and the future of middle management. *New Technology, Work and Employment*, 8(1), 10–20.

Gillespie, A., Richardson, R. and Cornford, J. 1995: *Review of Telework in Britain: implications for public policy*. Report prepared for the Parliamentary Office of Science and Technology, CURDS, University of Newcastle, February.

Giordano, L. 1993: *Beyond Taylorism*. London: Macmillan.

Goddard, J. 1991: New Technology and the geography of the UK information economy. In J. Brotchie, M. Batty, P. Hall and P. Newton (eds), *Cities of the 21st Century: new technologies and spatial systems*, Harlow, Essex: Longman.

Guest, D. 1987: Human resource management and industrial relations. *Journal of Management Studies*, 24(2), 503–21.

Hammer, M. 1990: Re-engineering work: don't automate, obliterate. *Harvard Business Review*, July–August.

Hammer, M. and Champy, J. 1993: *Re-engineering the Corporation*. New York: HarperCollins.

Huws, U. 1993: *Teleworking in Britain*, Employment Department Research Series no. 18. Sheffield: Employment Department.

Iacono, S. and Kling, R. 1991: Computerization, office routines, and changes in clerical work. In C. Dunlop and R. Kling (eds), *Computerization and Controversy*, San Diego, Cal.: Academic Press.

Jarillo, J.C. 1993: *Strategic Networks: creating the borderless organization*. Oxford: Butterworth-Heinemann.

Kinsman, F. 1987: *The Telecommuters*. Chichester: John Wiley.

Legge, K. 1989: Information technology: personnel management's lost opportunity? *Personnel Review*, 14(3), 19–40.

Li, F. 1995: *The Geography of Business Information*. Chichester: John Wiley.

Lyon, D. 1994: *The Electronic Eye: the rise of surveillance society*. Cambridge: Polity Press.

Negroponte, N. 1995: *Being Digital*. London: Hodder & Stoughton.

Perolle, J.A. 1991: Intellectual assembly lines: the rationalization of managerial, professional, and technical work. In C. Dunlop and R. Kling (eds), *Computerization and Controversy*, San Diego, Cal.: Academic Press.

Piore, M. and Sabel, C. 1982: *The Second Industrial Divide: possibilities for prosperity*. New York: Basic Books.

Pollert, A. 1991: The orthodoxy of flexibility. In A. Pollert (ed.), *Farewell to Flexibility?*, Oxford: Blackwell.

Rose, H. 1988: Constructing organisational forms for flexible computing'. In D. Boddy, J. McCalman and D. Buchanan (eds), *The New Management Challenge*, London: Croom Helm.

Stonier, T. 1983: *The Wealth of Information: a profile of the post-industrial economy*. London: Methuen.

Strassman, P. 1990: *The Business Value of Computers*. New Canaan, Conn.: Information Economics Press.

Taylor, J.A. 1995: Don't obliterate, informate! Business process re-engineering in the information age. *New Technology, Work and Employment*, 10(2), 82–8.

Taylor, J.A. and Williams, H. 1989: Telematics, organisation and the local government mission. *Local Government Studies*, 15(3), 75–93.

Taylor, J.A. and Williams, H. 1991: The networked firm. In B.C. Williams and B.J. Spaul, *Information Technology and Accounting: the impact of information technology*, London: Chapman & Hall.

Taylor, J.A. and Williams, H. 1992: Police management, office automation and organizational change. *New Technology, Work and Employment*, 7(1), 44–53.

Taylor, J.A. and Williams, H. 1994: The 'transformation game': information systems and process innovation in organizations. *New Technology, Work and Employment*, 9(1), 64–75.

Taylor, J.A. and Williams, H. 1995: Superhighways or Superlow-ways. *Flux*, 19, March, 45–54.

Teng, J.T.C., Grover, V. and Fiedler, K.D. 1994: Business process reengineering: charting a strategic path for the information age. *California Management Review*, Spring, 9–31.

Toffler, A. 1980: *The Third Wave*. New York: William Morrow.

Willmott, H. 1995: The odd couple? Reengineering business processes, managing human resources. *New Technology, Work and Employment*, 10(2), 89–98.

Zuboff, S. 1988: *In the Age of the Smart Machine: the future of work and power*. Oxford: Heinemann.

Part III
Cases

18

'Honey and Vinegar': Ford Motor Company's Move to Human Resource Management

ALAN MCKINLAY AND KEN STARKEY

It used to be so easy to hate [Ford] managers because they were so awful. It is a bit more difficult these days because the company have become a bit cleverer. The company seems to have realised that you catch more flies with honey than with vinegar.
Jimmy Airlie, Engineering Union, *The Financial Times,*
10 November 1987

Introduction

Jimmy Airlie's colourful imagery captures the tension at the core of Ford Motor Company's transition from tough managerialism, a management philosophy based on the uncompromising pursuit of tight control over all employees, to a strategy of willing participation and involvement. But such profound challenges to deeply embedded management practices and employee expectations are protracted, subject to reversal and always qualified. It is the tension between 'honey and vinegar' in Ford's strategy that we explore in this chapter.

Guest (1987: 503) argues that if the term 'human resource management' (HRM) is to have any social scientific value 'it should be defined in such a way as to differentiate it from traditional personnel management'. He then proposes that HRM constitutes one of our models of best personnel practice, that few UK organizations practice HRM, but that there might be a slow trend in that direction, as evidenced by the increasing adoption of HRM policies such as employee involvement. The definition of HRM is as a set of policies designed to maximize organizational integration, employee commitment, flexibility and quality of work. The HRM model is characterized as being people-orientated with an emphasis on the maximization of individual talent and consultation with the workforce. For Guest, the only companies practising this model completely in the UK are IBM and Hewlett-Packard.

The three other major personnel models Guest describes are:

- the *paternalist welfare* model, characterized by careful selection, training and treatment of staff, with a strong customer focus, a prime example of which is Marks & Spencer;
- the *production model*, based on tough, consistent industrial relations practice, focusing on the maintenance of efficient continuity of production, exemplified by Ford Motor Company;
- the *professional model* which emphasizes professionalism in four core activities: selection, training, pay and industrial relations. Firms such as ICI, Unilever and some of the major oil companies are cited examples of this model.

This approach to HRM categories, which is far from atypical, has at its centre a contingency view of personnel practices. The effective adoption of the various models depends on the appropriateness of particular practices to particular industrial settings.

Guest suggests that the HRM model is significantly different from traditional personnel practices, which has more in common with the elements of the other three models. In this chapter we critically examine these distinctions in an analysis of personnel practices in Ford Motor Company, a paradigmatic example of Guest's 'production model' of personnel management. We argue that if a longitudinal perspective is adopted, it is possible to discover key points in company evolution in personnel practices where the traditional model of personnel management becomes inadequate for the changing strategic situation of the company. At such moments, the changing strategic needs of the company make a shift toward HRM practices – with all their associated risks – more attractive. For executives charting this transition, it is never a simple 'either/or' calculation but a complex, multi-faceted series of choices based on a changing balance of advantage between established personnel practices and emerging HRM policies. Accordingly, we also argue that it is possible to identify elements of more than one model coexisting more or less comfortably in the same company setting.

The nature of this coexistence raises the issue of whether or not the presence of apparently contrasting – if not contradictory – models of personnel practice constitutes a transitory phase. And, if so, whether the next evolutionary step in personnel practice will involve a return to traditional models, as, for instance, 'cycles of control' theorists such as Ramsay (1983) would argue; or whether we are witnessing the slow emergence of a new general model of personnel practice based on HRM. The chapter begins by reviewing the pressures for radical changes in personnel practice before considering the case of Ford Motor Company in detail. In many ways, Ford exemplifies the difficulties associated with a shift from what Guest labels a 'production' paradigm towards HRM. We argue that Ford, as indeed are most major western companies, is in the throes of a long-term transition and displays features common to more than one of Guest's ideal types.

Pressures for Change in Personnel Practice

A central premise of Torrington's analysis of the relationship between HRM and personnel management is that the nature of HRM is 'not yet clear' (Torrington 1989: 60). By this, Torrington is hinting that the functional implications of moving to HRM for the role of personnel specialists remains unclear. The pressures driving such changes, however, do seem clear. A key policy goal underpinning HRM practice is to 'maximize organizational integration' which 'refers to the ability of the organization to integrate HRM issues into its strategic plans' (Guest 1989: 42); HRM assumes strategic importance when the need for employee commitment becomes central to the implementation of corporate strategy, for example, commitment to strategic goals concerning efficiency, quality and innovation. The management of the human resource becomes a critical factor in the search for competitive advantage (Porter 1987).

The increased attention paid to the human factor in the 1980s can be traced to three main issues: the success of Japanese firms in the West, the publication of Peters and Waterman's *In Search of Excellence* and ensuing debates concerning the nature of 'excellent' organizations, and the growing awareness of the importance of the management of the human resource in strategy implementation. In the USA interest in HRM was also stimulated by the launch of an HRM module as a compulsory subject in the Harvard Business School Master of Business Administration degree courses in 1981.

The debate about the roots of Japanese success has focused on a variety of factors that are seen as distinguishing the Japanese enterprise from the Western. The sources of Japanese success have variously been described as:

- the Japanese ability to redefine the nature of industrial markets through product price, reflecting their efficiency, quality of product and innovation. The Japanese have proved themselves able to resolve the 'innovation-efficiency' dilemma (Lawrence and Dyer 1983) and achieve both while, in the West, we have concentrated on efficiency in the strategy of large-scale production of standardized products (that is, in Porter's terminology, a cost leadership generic strategy). This is now outmoded. It has led to inflexibility and, ironically, inefficiency (Abernathy et al. 1981);
- the Japanese strategy of production flexibility to match a marketing strategy of product differentiation, as seen, for example, in the fragmentation of the market for standard cars into a set of distinct sub-markets, to generate a more diverse range, updated more frequently. This production flexibility is sustained by the skilled use of new manufacturing technologies, product development based on simultaneous engineering, with product design and manufacturing working in tandem, rather than the just-in-time (JIT) relationships to facilitate the prompt response to fluctuation in demand;
- the Japanese social organization or production based on teamwork, job rotation, learning by doing, skill flexibility, the use of workers' tacit knowledge, culture, trust, respect, long-term employment, self-management and the philosophy of continuous improvement. Broader job definitions have a major impact in terms of reducing the need for indirect workers to support production and self-certification of quality and self-control require fewer tiers of lower-level managers to monitor and discipline;
- Japanese industrial structure, particularly Japanese corporations' rejection of the vertical integration of Western companies. Japanese strength lies in scope and durability of horizontal integration, networks of firms established in long-term co-operative relationships (the *keiretsu*) rather than in conglomerates, long-term manufacturing competitiveness rather than financial engineering is the organizing principle of the *kaisha*;
- the role of the Japanese government in supporting key industries through the Ministry of International Trade and Industry (MITI).

All these factors obviously have some effect on the competitiveness of Japanese firms, and analysts are divided in giving priority to any one factor. From the HRM perspective, it is the social organization of production that has proved most influential. There have been strong claims, backed by empirical research, that it is its management of its human resource that is the key factor in understanding Japanese success (Abernathy et al. 1981). Certainly, this view is at the root of the phenomenon of Japanization, the attempt to emulate Japanese production practices in the West, an approach that has proved successful in companies such as Xerox (Giles and Starkey 1988). The core of the argument is, according to Deming (1982), a key protagonist in teaching the Japanese how to manufacture quality products, the stress on purpose at work and worker self-respect as sources of competitiveness. The conventional Western approach, in comparison with the new competition, creates obstacles so that 'the hourly worker is deprived of his right to do good work and to be proud of himself'. This, according to Deming, 'may be the single most important contribution of management to poor quality and loss of market' (Deming 1982: 166). The main theme of the critique of the conventional Western approach based on scientific management is that people need identity and meaning in work and that work arrangements should, therefore, emphasize trust, teamwork and the opportunities to develop creative, problem-solving and co-operative capabilities. The alternative to scientific management is to create, as in Japan, opportunities for the pursuit of meaning in work (Best 1990: 161).

Peters and Waterman were also crucial in bringing human resources (HR) concerns to the forefront of the management agenda with their *In Search of Excellence* (1982). Their '7's framework' has as its central idea the claim that organizational effectiveness stems from the interaction of not just strategy and structure, the traditional concerns in organization design (Chandler 1962), but also from the 'relationship between systems, management style, as seen in an organization's culture, the organization's skills base, its staff and its superordinate goals'. HRM, in other words, shares central concerns with the 'excellence' movement. HRM also emerges as a key concern in the strategic management literature in:

- the view of strategy as a process to be managed rather than an exercise in rational planning and execution (Quinn et al. 1988);
- the view of strategic management as a form of organizational learning;
- the increasing awareness in the strategic management literature of the problems of implementing strategy; and the importance in strategy implementation of continuous attention to the fine-tuning of strategies as they evolve incrementally (Beer et al. 1984; Hamel and Prahalad 1989; Prahalad and Hamel 1990).

Guest (1988: 10) also suggests the embracing HRM principles may significantly enhance a company's image: 'A company seen to be in the forefront of the management of human resources may gain advantages in the market place. First, it may attract sales through an image of social responsibility and quality.' Ford, for instance, launched crucial new products between 1990 and 1992 with advertisements whose central image was employees participating in personal development programmes. The implicit message was that a progressively managed workforce guaranteed high quality products. Secondly, Guest continues, burnishing a company's HR image may help in attracting – and retaining – high-quality recruits.

From Traditional Personnel Management to Human Resources Management

Guest (1987) contrasts HRM with a 'production model' approach to personnel management. In this section we examine changes in personnel practice in Ford Motor Company both in the USA and in Europe. Ford is Guest's ideal-typical example of the production model approach which is based on tough, consistent industrial relations practice, focusing on the maintenance of efficient continuity of production. This approach has much in common with Purcell and Gray's (1986) 'traditional/consultative' style of employee relations in which 'labour is viewed as a factor of production and employee subordination is assumed to be part of the "natural order" of the employment relationship'. According to this view, unions are accepted as inevitable, employee relations policies centre on the need for stability, control and the institutionalization of conflict, management prerogatives are defended through highly specific collective agreements and careful administrative attention is paid to the implementation of agreements at the point of production. The importance of management control is constantly emphasized with the aim of minimizing or neutralizing union constraints on both operational (line) and strategic (corporate) management decisions. To support such an approach there is a strong emphasis on the central personnel control function (Purcell and Gray 1986: 242–5).

In crucial respects, the 'production/traditional/consultative' approach to personnel management differs fundamentally from that espoused in the HRM perspective. The HRM model is characterized as people-orientated with an emphasis on the maximization of individual skills and motivation through consultation with the workforce so as to produce high levels of commitment to a company's business goals. Labour is more than a factor of production to be minimized: it is an asset to be invested in. The emphasis is on fostering working conditions that encourage 'responsible autonomy' rather than the need for 'direct control'. Labour provides potential, not constraint. It is a resource to be used to its fullest capacity. The traditional 'production model' is based on the negotiation and enforcement of collective agreements, an emphasis on the need for closed managerial definition of the nature of work and forms of control that support this definition and behaviours that conform to it, employee compliance rather than commitment, and a relationship of low trust between management and labour (Fox 1973).

Under the 'production' paradigm of personnel management, order and stability are seen as key issues in producing for stable markets. When markets change, so does the emphasis in management:

> the need to meet rapid and continuing change in markets shift the emphasis away from formality, and the imperatives of juridification (Storey 1989) and arbitration (Littler 1987), as the focus of employment management. This [change] does indeed require a difference of emphasis and skills among personnel professionals (Kochan and Capelli 1984) and is why top management has seemingly begun to take an active interest in HRM.   (Hendry and Pettigrew 1990: 36)

Ford Motor Company in the 1980s provided a powerful example of major changes in personnel practice. We chose to concentrate on Ford for two reasons: (a) because of its paradigmatic importance as progenitor of the traditional 'production' approach; and (b) because of the magnitude of the change it initiated during the 1980s which reflected a critical re-evaluation of the production approach and a significant move in the direction of HRM for strategic reasons.

Ford is synonymous with the creation of a particular management style – Fordism – based on hierarchial decision-making with strict functional specialization, tightly defined job design and specialized machinery to mass produce a standard product for mass markets (Starkey and McKinlay 1989, 1993). A conjunction of market and technological factors stimulated Ford's continuing efforts to redesign jobs, its mode of organization and its prevailing culture. The organizational model for Ford's rethinking of its approach to personnel management was, in part, Japanese-inspired. The company's close links with Mazda, in which it owns a 25 per cent stake, serves as a source of competitive bench-marking. This bench-marking formed the basis of its long-term strategy. The pre-existing Fordist system provided important elements of continuity:

> The attempt to reconcile Ford's short- and long-term objectives has meant that the company is currently negotiating a major transition period; on the one hand, striving to introduce aspects of 'Japan-like' industrial organization in preparation for future strategic change, whilst, on the other hand, maintaining established managerial practices and work organization patterns essential to current competitiveness.   (Starkey and McKinlay 1989: 94)

The change process of the last 15 years in Ford UK had two main sources: first, the recognition that structural reforms of internal bargaining procedures were insufficient to generate the necessary step-change in productivity and quality; secondly, in response to change initiatives emanating from the US parent company. Drawing on the US parent company's experience, Ford UK's change process was markedly more programmatic than the *ad hoc*, essentially pragmatic approach adopted by the majority of UK companies (Storey 1992). The context was of emerging overcapacity in the global auto industry and a growing awareness of Japanese competitive advantage – both in the USA and Europe. The new competition posed the threat of radically new standards of efficiency, quality and design. Ford UK's poor manufacturing performance was highlighted, not just when compared to the new Japanese competition but also to the corporation's continental factories within an integrated pan-European production system. The strategic agenda for Ford UK centred on the long-term development of a co-operative industrial relations process to improve its capacity for continuous change in work organizations. Ford's strategy has been paralleled by all the main players in the European auto industry (Mueller 1992). Indeed, the speed at which corporations can embed HRM is emerging as a critical factor in determining comparative advantage in an intensely competitive industry.

In the USA a key role in Ford's return from the brink of disaster at the end of the 1970s was played by the Employee Development Strategy and Planning Office which was responsible for developing HRM policies based on principles of participative management (PM) and employee involvement (EI) in support of the company's most pressing strategic issues: improved quality of design and manufacturing. In 1979, this group was instrumental in developing a policy letter that sanctioned EI. Company policy hinged on mobilizing all employees behind business objectives. This required a major culture change in order to develop a work climate in which employees at all levels could achieve individual goals and work satisfaction by directing their talents and energies towards clearly defined company goals. This policy was also sanctioned in a letter of understanding with the United Auto Workers (UAW). Over the years EI came to play a central role in the improvement in quality of the company's products and also contributed to other major changes of central strategic importance (Johnson 1988: 194–5).

Employee involvement is defined as 'the processes by which employees at all levels have the opportunities to participate actively in the key managerial processes affecting job-related matters' (Banas 1984:

2). The processes offering opportunities for participation include consultation (to maximize information and commitment), collaboration (based on a norm of consensus) and delegation (the manager assigns responsibility for an agreed outcome to an individual or group). The joint aim of management and unions was to make work a more satisfying experience, improve the overall work environment, enhance creativity, contribute to improvements in the workplace, and help to achieve quality and efficiency and reduce absenteeism. Participative management, the other side of the coin to EI, is defined as 'the techniques and skills which managers use to provide employees with opportunities to participate actively in key managerial processes affecting job related matters' (ibid.: 1). Techniques include job redesign, team-building, task forces and problem-solving groups. Skills include contracting (establishing clear expectations), and rewarding and modelling participative skills.

Company strategy is embodied in the 1984 mission statement, *Mission, Values and Guiding Principles*. Ford's mission is to be a worldwide leader in automative and related products and services and in newer industries such as financial services. Its basic values are described as people, products and profits. The guiding principles form a code of conduct that encapsulates policy towards employees, customers, dealers and suppliers. These guiding principles include commitment to: quality in all aspects of the business; customers; continuous improvement; EI teamwork at all levels; specified levels of competitiveness and return on assets. Ford strategy is underpinned by its strategic vision of being a low-cost producer of the highest-quality products and services which provide the best customer value. All strategic issues such as quality improvement, customer satisfaction and cost reduction have one common denominator:

> They all depend on the capacities, competencies, and commitment of our people. Although marked improvement has been made in changing our corporate culture, the issue, now and into the future, is how to create and sustain a 'right-sized', flexible work force with the capacities, competencies, and commitment (including the technical and managerial leadership) that gives us a competitive edge in a turbulent, uncertain world marketplace. (Johnson 1988: 196)

The marked improvements associated with these changes in the USA in the 1980s include major improvements in earnings, profitability, market share, productivity, product design, quality and customer satisfaction. The company perceives itself as having gone through a major transformation in management style and, with the help of the UAW, having generated a recognition by employees, unions and management alike that their common interests are best served when there are agreed common goals and mutual benefits (Banas and Sauers 1988). Employee involvement has been embraced as company policy, so managers are expected to act accordingly. The other side of the coin to EI is PM: skills that managers use to provide employees and fellow managers with opportunities to participate in key managerial decision-making processes. A major goal of the change initiative, therefore, was managerial behaviour. The company had accepted Deming's assessment of their quality problems as primarily rooted in management practices and not, as management had previously believed, worker failure to conform to management dictates. A major aim was to tap into 'the competencies (depth), capacities (breadth), and commitment (motivation) of the workforce at all levels':

> Reduced to its essentials, EI is the process by which employees are provided with the opportunities to contribute their minds, as well as their muscles, and hopefully their hearts, to the attaining of individual and Company goals. Through a variety of techniques – such as problem solving groups, new product launch teams, ad hoc quality and scrap involvement teams – opportunities have been created, for hourly employees to contribute their ideas, their analyses, and their solutions to job-related problems. Since 1979, virtually every hourly employee, either directly or indirectly, has been affected by this process. Today EI is functioning in virtually all major Ford facilities. (Banas and Sauers 1989: 3)

In the USA the crises of the early 1980s were seen as rooted not just in problems of the business cycle and in the new competition but in lack of trust between management and labour, a lack of clear corporate values and sharply defined goals and in a turbulent history of adversarial labour–management relations. In the UK the move towards an HRM culture was not stimulated by a crisis to that experienced by the American parent company. In fact, Ford of Europe played a vital role in providing the finances which sustained the parent company through these troubled years. The contrasting fortunes of Ford US and its European division, particularly the cash-cow Ford UK, were factors shaping the trajectory of the change process in the two organizations.

For almost 40 years Ford UK has been a wholly owned subsidiary of Ford Motor Company USA. From the formation of Ford in Europe in 1967 the US parent has exercised an increasing degree of strategic control, notably through budgetary controls. And although Ford UK retains operational responsibility, including pay bargaining, performance is closely monitored against financial targets set in Detroit. Two major change initiatives have dominated Ford UK since 1979. The first, 'After Japan', sprang from a study trip to Japan by the company's vice-president of manufacturing. 'After Japan' represented the company's acknowledgement of the threat posed by that country. Its limited success was due to management mistakes in the attempted implementation of some of the HRM initiatives proposed, most notably in the unilateral imposition of quality circles, and to union resistance. The second change initiative centred around the HRM policies and practices emanating from the US parent under the EI/PM banner. EI failed to win the formal agreement of blue-collar unions but was endorsed by the staff unions for a period.

Central to 'After Japan' was the view that the roots of Japanese success could be traced to a management style that was diametrically opposed to the Fordist model. The essence of the Japanese approach was seen to lie in management by consent rather than by control, and in the mobilization of commitment rather than the elimination of worker discretion. The need for change was communicated to the workforce with the results of a competitive bench-marking exercise against Japanese productivity standards and strategic targets set in terms of return on investment, market share, efficiency measure and reduction in head count. The cumulative effect of exposing shop-floor trade unionists to business information should not be underestimated. Initially, bench-marking was received sceptically by a UK workforce accustomed to being criticized for relatively poor productivity. However, over time bench-marking – combined with continued rationalization – slowly infused 'new realism' into the lay leadership of Ford UK's shop-floor unions (Darlington 1994: 213–14). The strategic goals of quality, customer satisfaction and cost competitiveness became part of the discourse of management–union negotiations. Elements of the Japanese system of JIT inventory management were introduced as well as a new quality philosophy of 'right first time'. At the same time, the production model of personnel management was refined in the introduction of more rigorous cost control systems (Marsden et al. 1985: 188).

Initially, Ford envisaged the introduction of quality circles as the first step in the rapid 'Japanization' of the company, a process that was to include training the workforce in problem-solving and interpersonal skills to enhance teamwork, JIT and more stable relations on a long-term basis with preferred suppliers who could meet the company's exacting design and quality standards. The failure of the quality circle initiative was a watershed in the development of Ford UK's approach to HRM. This chastening failure compelled Ford executives to recognize that a gradual processual approach to modifying a deeply adversial company culture was essential.

The successor to the failed quality circle initiative was the adoption of the American process of EI and PM, an approach to management that has been incorporated into mainstream pay and working condition negotiations. Only the staff unions agreed to formal involvement in the EI process, but the philosophy and practices underlying EI have been diligently pursued by Ford management informally at the local level. For example, problem-solving work groups, similar to quality circles, flourish in Ford UK facilities. For Ford management, the 1985 Pay and Working Practices Agreement was a breakthrough in the informal diffusion of employee involvement, versatility and flexibility, the acquisition of new skills and the elimination of inefficient demarcation lines in both craft and production work. The principles of the 1985 Agreement were reinforced and extended in 1988 when involvement and flexibility initiatives were defined as issues for plant- and national-level negotiation.

One of the main goals of PM is changing managerial attitudes and dismantling the tight 'chimney' structure designed to maximize control, irrespective of the negative impact on information-processing or innovative capability. PM began a process of simplifying managerial control, devolving authority and breaking down the barriers between managerial groups erected – and zealously protected – to ensure functional specialization. The key goal of EI/PM was to achieve a major cultural change, to embed co-operation as a way of life rather than a specific, finite burst of corporate restructuring. Ford UK executives regarded the withdrawal of the staff unions from the formal EI agreement with equanimity, satisfied that sufficient of the programme's principles had been internalized to make further progress more a matter of evolution than formal accommodation. The successor to EI is the Employee Development and Assistance Programme (EDAP) which introduced non-pay non-job-related benefits, principally funding for personal development through education (Mortimer 1990). Through EDAP Ford has successfully opened up a second front in its ongoing 'battle' to win employee hearts and minds; a battlefield, moreover, in which it sets the terms of engagement. EDAP has been a major success: first year figures were doubled in year two, and reached 44 per cent in 1991: around 20,000 Ford UK employees had taken part in EDAP (TURU 1991: 8). Over 80 per cent of Ford UK employees regarded EDAP as a joint management–union initiative while only a small minority perceived it as exclusively a management or union programme (TURU 1993).

Education and personnel development has emerged as a neutral arena for the development of co-operative labour relations. During the 1980s product quality played a similarly 'neutral' role. Peter Drucker (1990) argues that the introduction of statistical quality control (SQC), based on the work of Deming and Juran, is radically changing thinking about manufacturing management and the social organization of the factory. By aligning information with accountability, Drucker argues, SQC resolves the apparently irreconcilable conflict between 'scientific management', based on the work of F.W. Taylor and Henry Ford, and the 'human relations' approach founded by Elton Mayo. Both traditions aimed at improving quality and productivity but, according to Drucker, it is only with the advent of SQC that the management of manufacture becomes truly scientific, the dream of Taylor, and that worker pride and knowledge, the key factors in the human relations approach, can be fully realized:

> Without SQC's rigorous methodologies neither scientific management nor the assembly line could actually deliver built-in process control. With all their successes, both scientific management and the assembly line had to fall back on massive inspection, to fix problems rather than eliminate them.
>
> The human-relations approach sees the knowledge and pride of line workers as the greatest resource for controlling and improving quality and productivity . . . But without the kind of information SQC provides, you cannot readily distinguish productive activity from busyness. It is hard to tell whether a proposed modification will truly improve the process.   (Drucker 1990: 96)

Statistical quality control provides the knowledge technology to design both quality and productivity into the manufacturing process by giving responsibility for the process and control of it to the only people who can assure quality – the machine operators. Ford has relentlessly pursued the introduction of SQC, initially using Deming as a consultant (Pettigrew 1985). Beside its impact on product quality and productivity, a consequence of the new emphasis on quality has been the emergence of a common language for both management and employees. Based on mutually agreed definitions of terms, 'quality' has functioned as a vehicle to develop a common understanding of the strategic issues facing the company. Crucially, negotiations, from the shop floor to the national level, are now legitimized by management and unions in terms of competitiveness. The language of quality, therefore, has provided an important source of, and impetus to, consensus.

The legacy of 'After Japan' and the lessons from the US EI/PM initiative is a twin-track change strategy. On the one hand – and demonstrating the resilience of the production model within Ford – is the strong defence of managerial prerogatives and its strict disciplinary code. While, on the other hand, management pursues a more complex, longer-term approach aimed at building more consensual management–labour relations. The tensions between these two approaches become more apparent the closer one examines the practices of front-line management – the pressure point of the change process.

Conclusion

We started this chapter by looking at one of the more sensitive analyses of recent developments in HRM (Guest 1987). We begin our conclusion by suggesting that Guest has perhaps been too sensitive to distinctions between his four models of personnel management. Such strong distinctions do suggest an either/or choice for management, certainly between the production and the HRM models. In practice, different approaches will tend to coexist, at least during those often lengthy transition periods when firms move from one model of personnel management to another. And, as our Ford example illustrates, even having negotiated such a transition period, traces of previous models may not be fully displaced among operational management or shop-floor trade union leaders. As the Ford experience demonstrates, the administrative heritage of a company will determine the trajectory and speed of the change process. Understanding the historical dimension to corporate change highlights the limitations of the conventional contingency approach to strategy and structure.

For managers socialized into a company with a powerful Fordist culture, breaking with past assumptions about, for instance, the possibilities for industrial relations to deliver an open-ended HR agenda may be the single biggest obstacle to change. To understand the present we have to be sensitive to the constraints rooted in companies' histories. The majority of firms find themselves faced with a complex transition period in which to negotiate and experiment with the exact balance between continuity and change. They cannot afford the luxury of throwing away the rule-book and recommencing *ab initio*. Only firms setting up on greenfield sites start with what approximates to a *tabula rasa* (Guest 1989). Sensitive handling of change involves the reassessment of the existing system for strengths that can still prove useful, experiments with new practices to establish which of them have the potential for broader dissemination, and the acceptance that, such is the weight of history and tradition, some established practices may be too strongly embedded to remove in the short term. Theoretically, the need is not for more-refined categories of personnel and HR models but, rather, for the processes of change between different employment and management practices.

The current growth of interest in HRM reflects the past failings of the personnel function: 'a persistent failure of personnel departments to innovate on personnel policy and therefore to contribute to the pursuit of competitive advantage' (Guest 1988: 10). In many respects, HRM is the policy agenda of a profession – personnel management – in search of a new role and even a justification for its continued existence. At the very least, it presents us with a radical rethinking of the function. Legge (1989) argues that HRM has three key features that distinguish it from previous approaches to personnel management. Traditional personnel management was couched in terms of something performed on subordinates by managers; HR focuses not only on the development of employees but also on the development of managers themselves (ibid.: 27). In the Ford case, a prerequisite for effective employee involvement was the development of participative management. With HRM there is, according to Legge, a far tighter integration of personnel practices into the pursuit of strategic goals. In the Ford case, the mission statement emphasized the symbiotic relationship between strategy and a strong culture in promoting a sense of purpose and commitment in the organization. Guest (1988) makes similar points when he answers the question: what is needed to install HRM? But he is pessimistic about the skill of British firms to operationalize the HRM agenda. He argues that much recent change in the UK has focused on cost-cutting, but that, when the limits of such rationalization are reached, we may see stronger moves towards HRM.

Perhaps the key distinguishing feature of HRM is its evolving strategic role. Miller (1989) depicts traditional personnel management as non-strategic, separate from the business, reactive, short-term and constrained by a limited definition of its role as dealing with unionized and lower-level employees. Personnel management becomes strategic when employees are managed in ways which recognize their key role in strategy implementation, and when employee motivation becomes critical to competitive strategy. This view fits with the literature on strategic leadership, where the most important top management function is to motivate employees to exceptional effort by fostering a sense of commitment to institutional purpose – a long-standing theme (Selznick 1957; Wrapp 1967; *Strategic Management Journal* 1989). Strategic leadership and HRM come together in strategic HRM. For an HR specialist personally involved in Ford's employee development programmes in the USA, it is an important task for the personnel specialist:

> To better identify where our HR systems impact and support corporate strategic issues . . . to demonstrate its competence in strategic planning and implementation. We need to clearly specify the value-added benefit of the HR function in formulating and implementing business strategy. We need to be able to surface the Human Resources implications of strategic alternatives and provide options for handling HR issues that are directly related to strategic planning issues . . . In short, we need to evolve the role of Human Resources from an administrative role to a consultant one in running the business.   (Johnson 1988: 199)

Other authors are less optimistic about this possibility. Purcell (1989) claims that the whole thrust of current developments in corporate strategy, geared to expansion by acquisition and diversification and/or an emphasis on short-run returns on investment and tight financial controls, is inimical to the very principles of an employee-centred HRM. Such an approach to strategy marginalizes employees as stakeholders in weighing strategic issues:

> The criticism of diversified, multi-divisional companies on employee relations presented here is another twist of a familiar story. It is odd, then, that the current wave of interest in human resource management is so optimistic and implies that a major reconsideration of personnel practice is underway. The belief is that corporate executives and line managers have discovered the need to encourage employee involvement, team work, and integrated reward systems . . . as a crucial element of their corporate and business-unit strategies. Changes are, of course, taking place . . . But in many diversified firms, in Britain at least, the material conditions for these to be translated into long-run strategic decisions placing human resource management as the, or even a, critical function in corporate strategy, do not exist. What ought to happen, as prescribed by the burgeoning literature, is a long way from being realized.   (Purcell 1989: 90)

It is odd that Purcell can reconcile this view of the move towards HRM as being, at best, marginal and yet can also state that the old order is crumbling. Into what, one wonders, if the old verities no longer apply and there is no new paradigm to replace them? Equally odd is that Purcell's contribution is within a text which provides examples of HRM practices from a variety of firms, including Bejam, BMW, British Airways, BP, British Rail, British Steel, Ford, GE, General Motors, Hewlett-Packard, IBM, ICL, Lucas, Jaguar, Komatsu, Matsuchita, Mercedes, National Westminster Bank, Nissan, Rover, Shell, Toshiba, Whitbread and Xerox. In another recent overview of the field (Evans et al. 1989), multinational examples of HRM practice include SAS, Peat Marwick, Xerox, Olivetti, ICL, Philips, Unilever, Nissan, Shell, Exxon, Nestlé, Honeywell, BP, IBM, Hewlett-Packard, Volvo and Marks & Spencer. The variety of these companies surely signals a strong trend towards HRM practices. Purcell, though, is correct to the extent that his view counsels against too simplistic an acceptance of the inevitability of HRM in a pure form, sharply distinct from previous practice. This chapter has demonstrated that it is by no means an unlikely occurrence, that some aspects of the old order will survive with the emerging new order.

References

Abernathy, W.J., Clark, K.B. and Kantrow, A.M. 1981: The new industrial competition. *Harvard Business Review*, September–October, 69–77.

Banas, P. 1984: *The Relationship Between Participative Management and Employee Involvement*. Dearborn: Ford Motor Company.

Banas, P. and Sauers, R. 1988: *Participative Management and Employee Involvement: model and application*. Dearborn: Ford Motor Company.

Banas, P. and Sauers, R. 1989: *The Relationship Between Participative Management and Employee Involvement*. Dearborn: Ford Motor Company.

Beer, M., Spector, B., Lawrence, P.R., Mills, D.O. and Walton, R.E. 1984: *Managing Human Assets*. New York: Free Press.

Best, M.H. 1990: *The New Competition: institutions of industrial restructuring*. Cambridge: Polity Press.

Chandler, A.D. 1962: *Strategy and Structure*, Cambridge, Mass.: MIT Press.

Darlington, R. 1994: *The Dynamics of Workplace Unionism: shop stewards' organization in three Merseyside plants*. London: Mansell.

Deming, W.E. 1982: *Quality, Productivity and Competitive Position*. Cambridge, Mass.: MIT Center for Advanced Engineering.

Drucker, P. 1990: The emerging theory of manufacturing. *Harvard Business Review*, May–June, 94–102.

Evans, P., Doz, Y. and Laurent, A. (eds) 1989: *Human Resource Management in International Firms.* London: Macmillan.

Fox, A. 1973: *Beyond Contract: work, power and trust relations.* London: Faber & Faber.

Giles, E. and Starkey, K. 1988: The Japanization of Xerox. *New Technology, Work and Employment,* 3(2), 125–33.

Guest, D. 1987: Human resource management and industrial relations. *Journal of Management Studies,* 24(5), 503–21.

Guest, D. 1988: Human resource management: is it worth taking seriously? London School of Economics, First Annual Seear Fellowship Lecture.

Guest, D. 1989: Human resource management: its implications for industrial relations and trade unions. In J. Storey (ed.), *New Perspectives on Human Resource Management,* London: Routledge, 41–55.

Hamel, G. and Prahalad, C.K. 1989: Strategic intent. *Harvard Business Review,* May–June, 63–76.

Harvey-Jones, J. 1988: *Making it Happen: reflections on leadership.* London: Collins.

Hendry, C. and Pettigrew, A. 1990: Human resource management: an agenda for the 1990s. *International Journal of Human Resource Management,* 1(1), 1–7.

Johnson, R.H. 1988: How Ford's HR staff supports strategic planning. In Y.K. Shetty and V.M. Buehler (eds), *Competing through Productivity and Quality,* Cambridge, Mass.: Productivity Press, 189–99.

Jurgens, U., Malsch, T. and Dohse, K. 1993: *Breaking from Taylorism: changing forms of work in the automobile industry.* London: Cambridge Unversity Press.

Kochan, T.A. and Capelli, P. 1984: The transformation of the industrial relations and personnel function. In P. Osterman (ed.), *Internal Labour Markets,* Cambridge, Mass.: MIT Press, 133–62.

Lawrence, P.R. and Dyer, R. 1983: *Renewing American Industry.* New York: Free Press.

Legge, K. 1989: Human resource management: a critical analysis. In J. Storey (ed.), *New Perspectives on Human Resource Management,* London: Routledge, 19–40.

Littler, C.R. 1987: The social and economic relations of work. *Labour and Industry,* 1(1), 1–7.

Marsden, D., Morris, T., Willman, P. and Woods, S. 1985: *The Car Industry.* London: Tavistock Publications.

Miller, P. 1989: Strategic industrial relations and human resource management: distinction, definition and recognition. *Journal of Management Studies,* 24(4), 347.

Mortimer, K. 1990: EDAP at Ford: a research note. *Industrial Relations Journal,* 21(4), 309–14.

Mueller, F. 1992: Flexibility working practices in engine plants: evidence from the European automobile industry. *Industrial Relations Journal,* 23(3), 191–204.

Peters, T. and Waterman, R.H. 1982: *In Search of Excellence*. New York: Harper & Row.

Pettigrew, T.J. 1985: Process quality control: the new approach to the management of quality in Ford. *Quality Assurance*, 11(3), 81–8.

Porter, M. 1987: From competitive advantage to corporate strategy. *Harvard Business Review*, May–June, 43–59.

Prahalad, C.K. and Hamel, G. 1990: The core competence of the corporation. *Harvard Business Review*, May–June, 79–91.

Purcell, J. 1989: The impact of corporate strategy on human resource management. In J. Storey (ed.), *New Perspectives of Human Resource Management*, London: Routledge, 67–91.

Purcell, J. and Gray, A. 1986: Corporate personnel departments and the management of industrial relations: two case studies in ambiguity. *Journal of Management Studies*, 23(2), 205–23.

Quinn, J.B., Mintzberg, H. and James, R.M. 1988: *The Strategy Process*. Englewood Cliffs, N.J.: Prentice-Hall.

Ramsay, H. 1983: Evolution or cycle? Worker participation in the 1970s and 1980s. In C. Crouch and F.A. Heller (eds), *Organizational Democracy and Political Processes*. Chichester: John Wiley, vol. 1, 203–26.

Selznick, A. 1957: *Leadership in Administration*. New York: Harper & Row.

Starkey, K. and McKinlay, A. 1989: Beyond Fordism? Strategic choice and labour relations in Ford UK. *Industrial Relations Journal*, 20(2), 93–100.

Starkey, K. and McKinlay, A. 1993: *Strategy and the Human Resource: Ford and the search for competitive advantage*. Oxford: Blackwell.

Storey, J. 1992: *Developments in the Management of Human Resources: an analytical review*. Oxford: Blackwell.

Storey, J. (ed.) 1989: *New Perspectives on Human Resource Management*. London: Routledge.

Strategic Management Journal 1989: Special Issue: *Strategic Leadership*, 10 (1–3).

Torrington, D. 1989: Human resource management and the personnel function. In J. Storey (ed.), *New Perspectives on Human Resource Management*, London: Routledge, 56–66.

TURU 1991: *Employee Development and Assistance Programme*. Oxford: Ruskin College.

TURU 1993: *Evaluation into EDAP Participation and Non-participation: general observations and preliminary findings*. Oxford: Ruskin College.

Wrapp, H.E. 1967: Good managers don't make policy decisions. *Harvard Business Review*, September–October, 9, 1–9.

19

Culture Change through Training: the Case of Sainsbury

ALLAN WILLIAMS AND PAUL DOBSON

Introduction

Changing the culture of an organization is a fashionable topic in management circles. However, the difficulties involved in changing culture are frequently played down. This makes it a suitable and rewarding topic for a case study. The case to be described below was originally one of 15 cases we studied as part of a research project aimed at identifying the methods organizations used to bring about culture change (Williams et al. 1989). One of the findings to emerge from our study was the ubiquitous role of training in any attempt to change organizational culture. In this chapter we shall summarize some of the findings of the study, and present a case study of an organization which was trying to change aspects of its culture primarily through training. When the case study is used as part of a classroom exercise, students may want to make their own analysis before reading the conclusions.

Concept of Culture

The concept of culture has been enriched by the work of social anthropologists, sociologists, organizational psychologists, management consultants and others. Unfortunately, the variety of meanings given to the term, and the variety of situations in which the term is used, complicate the task of the researcher trying to study culture change. A working definition of organizational culture which we used in our study, and which conforms to some of the more authoritative definitions in the literature, is the following: 'Culture is the commonly held and relatively stable beliefs, attitudes and values that exist within the organization' (Williams et al. 1989: 11).

Things to note about this definition include: firstly, to change culture you need to change the beliefs, attitudes and values underlying behaviour; secondly, since it is concerned with commonly held beliefs, the target for change needs to be the organization as a whole or a fairly autonomous part of it; thirdly, the beliefs, attitudes and values associated with a culture will have achieved stability over a long period of time, and therefore are likely to be deep-rooted. If one is prepared to accept these assumptions it follows that planned culture change is an uphill battle requiring leadership, time and plenty of resources!

Methods of Culture Change

Given the potential problems of trying to bring about planned culture change, what methods do we actually find organizations using? Our research indicates the main categories as listed in the headings below.

Changing people

This may be subdivided into two categories: the individual differences approach and the learning approach. The former approach recognizes that some individuals will already hold beliefs close to the desirable ones, while others will not. This approach is reflected in recruitment, selection, transferring employees and releasing them.

The learning approach, on the other hand, recognizes that an individual's beliefs are malleable, and can be changed under appropriate conditions. This approach is reflected in the purposeful use of role models (e.g. using senior managers with participative styles as trainers), of group methods (e.g. quality circles), of formal training programmes and of formal communication channels.

Changing structure

We identified four types of structural changes:

1 restructuring involving changes to the composition of the organization's stakeholders;
2 decentralization;
3 job redesign to increase role flexibility;
4 introducing new structures to cater for new needs (e.g. a new quality unit).

Changing management systems

The two areas where change was most frequent were budgeting and control systems, and HRM systems. Our case studies abounded with examples of the latter. This is not surprising given the HRM systems impinge directly on the beliefs, attitudes and values of employees.

Changing other variables

Although not illustrated by our case studies, it is clear from our knowledge of the literature that changing certain other variables will also have an impact on an organization's culture. For example, a change in an organization's dominant technology from a mechanized office paper system to a computerized information technology system, or a change in the geographical location of a plant from an urban to a rural community, will almost certainly have implications for the type of person employed and therefore for the beliefs, attitudes and values of new recruits.

Dynamics of Culture Change

Knowledge of the methods used by organizations to bring about culture change is only part of the equation for successfully changing beliefs, attitudes and values. To overcome the self-reinforcing properties of culture, any planned change must generate sufficient forces for change, and simultaneously reduce the forces against change. Kurt Lewin's (1951) force-field model is a particularly useful aid in helping one to identify the positive and negative variables which are most likely to result in a pattern of forces conducive to change. On the basis of our research there appear to be three important sources from which forces for culture change are generated:

1   *Some precipitating event or crisis* (e.g. dramatic fall in market share). This condition seems necessary for an organization to question some of the fundamental beliefs which have influenced the way it has done things in the past.
2   *Organization strategy.* A culture change programme needs to be strategy-led if it is to be integrated with other changes, allocated the required resources to achieve success, and gain the long-term support of the 'dominant coalition' or top management.
3   *Powerful change agents.* To expect external consultants to take on the role

of primary change agents is a naïve assumption to make within the context of culture change. Their power base is far too brittle and temporary. What is required is the combined resources of a range of change agents such as the chief executive officer, the personnel director, senior line managers, as well as the specialist expertise of internal or external consultants. Above all it is the chief executive officer who has to take on the role of change agent, because it is he or she who will normally have the most power to influence culture change.

As already mentioned, a successful change programme will attend to forces pushing against change as well as those pushing for change. Useful guidelines in dealing with the former include:

1 The need for change should be recognized by those who will be affected by the change. In our study management attempted to achieve this condition through training, formal communications, and involvement or participation in the decision-making processes associated with the planning and implementation of change.
2 Steps should be undertaken to reduce the uncertainties accompanying change, particularly those threatening the security of jobs and existing rewards. A variety of methods can be employed here, including: training, keeping people informed through effective communications, the direct participation of individual employees in the decision-making processes accompanying change, and where appropriate the early consultation and negotiation with employee representative bodies.
3 Care needs to be taken to ensure that the right behaviours (i.e. those compatible with the desired beliefs, attitudes and values) are being reinforced on the job. It is a well-established fact that the transfer of learning from a formal training course to the job situation is often adversely affected by the lack of appropriate on-the-job reinforcements. Similarly, resistance to change is sometimes the result of traditional, but no longer appropriate, reinforcements being allowed to persist, thus inadvertently continuing to reinforce previously accepted behaviour. The mechanisms through which reinforcements operate include these variables already referred to, that is, role models, organizational structure and management systems.

The Role of Training in Culture Change

From this brief summary of methods used by organizations to bring about culture change, and our knowledge of the conditions conducive to successful change, it will be noticed that training can play an important role. However, training must not be viewed in isolation. It should be clear from the ideas presented above that (a) the processes whereby training is initiated, planned and implemented, and (b) the conditions which are present in the post-training phase, will determine the extent to which training is effective in contributing towards a planned culture change programme. In order to explore the practical implications of these statements, the following case study is presented. It is in two sections: Sainsbury A was researched during May and June 1988 as part of a series of case studies on culture change (Williams et al. 1989), and is presented as written at that time; Sainsbury B reports the results of a follow-up some two and a half years later, in December 1990.

Case Study: Sainsbury A

Background

J. Sainsbury was established as a family business in Drury Lane in 1869 and to this day it retains strong family ties. It is a long-established company with a traditional non-participative management style with clear reporting lines and accountability. Productivity targets are used as a means of management control. While there are exceptions, a typical Sainsbury manager would be described as being primarily task oriented.

The company is one of the largest food retailers in the UK. In 1987, it had 270 supermarkets, 6.5 million customers per week, annual sales exceeding £4,000 m. and pre-tax profits of £268 m. Sainsbury's has over 69,000 staff of whom 40,000 work part-time. The full-time staff include 6,500 managers. The majority of the performance indicators suggest that Sainsbury's is a successful company. Profitability, sales, productivity and market share have all increased significantly over the last five years. Over 19,000 jobs have been created over the same period and, in an industry known for its high labour turnover, 12 per cent of the staff have been with the company for over ten years. The organization continues to expand and develop. It has opened 15–17 new stores a year for the past seven years and has branched out into the DIY market through its Homebase subsidiary. There are four associated companies: Savacentre, Brecklands Farms, Haverhill Meat Products and, in the USA, Shaws supermarkets.

The retail operation of Sainsbury's is organized in five geographical areas, each with a training department providing specialist training services to the stores. At the London head office there are training managers who develop and administer the retail training programmes for staff and managers and more general training programmes for managers at head office and in the distribution depots. Each store has a personnel manager who co-ordinates training and a number of store instructors carry out the day-to-day training of sales staff.

Changing culture

The early and middle 1980s saw an increase in customer expectations and competitors began to respond by introducing customer service programmes for staff. Most of these were rather gimmicky short-term 'Smile' and 'Have a nice day' type programmes where there was no attempt to try to change the attitudes of sales staff.

The board recognized that there was a need for Sainsbury's to have a customer service training programme. Six months were spent working by personnel on a proposal for the board. It was realized that ideally such a programme needed the support of management as role models for the change in behaviour. But it was also recognized that a top-down approach would not be acceptable given the existing culture. Consequently, a bottom-up approach was planned. The training department's initiative 'Building better business' (BBB) was thus focused on customer service training for branch sales staff. The board recognized that they were geared to business needs and supported the initiative with the proviso that the training of the checkout and counter staff in such things as bag packing preceded the softer attitudinal training elements. The training was sponsored by the director of branch operations.

Customer Service Training Ltd were brought in as consultant to develop a training package for use in the induction of new staff and the development of existing staff. It was recognized from the outset that the key to changing the behaviour of sales staff was to change their attitudes towards the customer, the job and colleagues. The training had to be aimed at the discretionary part of the job and not the mandatory parts given in job descriptions. That is, the training was required to concentrate on how staff did their job and not on what they did.

Two videos, one called *Out in front* which concentrates on the role of the front-end checkout team, and the other *Counting on service* aimed at counter sales staff, formed the basis of the BBB programme which was piloted in five stores in May 1986. The initial programme was primarily concerned with developing behavioural skills and product knowledge and was less explicitly attitudinal than later developments. After some fine-tuning the programme began to run through all 270 branches, 25–30 branches at a time. This approach kept the resources required to manageable proportions and also served to reinforce and keep the programme alive.

Directors and senior managers were given a one-day course describing BBB. Area trainers were trained in the philosophy and then they ran a two-day course for the branch management team and a three-day course for the store instructors. The latter trained the sales staff who received six hours' off-the-job in-store training.

Each branch was given 12 weeks to get all the sales staff through the programme. This was not difficult in small stores, but in those of 300 staff or more, considerable resources were required. A large number of hours were invested in training and an allowance of 4.5 hours was given to branch managers on their productivity targets. This has created a precedent for more recent initiatives and follow-ups.

In May 1987 a further three videos and a new introductory video began touring the branches. *Look at it this way* puts across the message you only get out what you put in, and encourages positive attitudes towards self, job and colleagues. *You've got what it takes* introduces FRESH – the five essential qualities to make people choose Sainsbury's rather than another store – Friendliness, Responsiveness, Enthusiasm, Sincerity and Helpfulness. *In just three seconds* shows how important are first impressions. It addresses the care that should be taken with presentation – self and store; it looks at body language and explains how to deal with complaints using the three A's – Apologize, Analyse, Act.

The training programme that was developed explicitly explored the nature and significance of attitudes as determinants of behaviour. For example, participants were asked to consider how their attitudes colour their views, how attitudes affect work, and the importance of positive attitudes in determining success. The training methods used are a combination of case study, video presentation, role playing, role modelling and group discussion. The following description of the training programme was given in the Sainsbury's in-house journal in July 1987 (p. 4):

> Building Better Business is not merely a course or a video or an exercise, it's an attitude.
>
> Training for the scheme revolves around six videos which are designed to act as food for thought. Breaks are incorporated into the

videos to allow discussion of points raised and participants are encouraged to examine their attitudes to customers and colleagues.

The videos often show the right and the wrong ways of doing things. Participants are asked to use their experience to decide which is the best approach. We all know the difference between getting good and bad responses from people and these videos show how to improve the way you communicate with others.

In addition to taking part in group discussion, each participant completes a booklet which asks questions about his or her working methods; how they deal with customers in a variety of situations, and general attitudes, as well as how things are done in his/her particular department.

The booklet allows staff to stand back and assess themselves and their department in the light of what they are learning.

The BBB initiative has been supported by internal marketing – the BBB logo is given constant exposure in the in-house journal, and in presentations – and by gaining the visible support of the director of branch operations. Monthly reports are made to the board on progress, and BBB is kept on the management agenda. In addition, a number of specific designed activities have been undertaken.

A poster competition was devised where employees were asked to design posters for the BBB programme. The response was so good that a winner and runner-up were selected each month for 12 months. All entrants received a BBB pen or mug and the winners received a £25 cash prize and had their poster professionally printed and circulated on the notice-boards of all branches. The winners also received a 'Certificate of Commendation', signed by the director of branch operations and the senior manager, management training and development.

A Christmas BBB competition was run where entrants had to complete a quiz (designed to test and improve product knowledge), undertake a word search game and a crossword, both closely linked with BBB concepts, and make as many words as possible from the phrase 'BBB training our most valuable asset – you'. Every entrant received a BBB Christmas mug or pen; the first 50 entrants received BBB slimline diaries; and the winner £50 cash, a certificate and an autographed copy of the Sainsbury's *Book of Wines*.

The purpose of these two competitions was to reaffirm and reinforce the customer service and BBB message. The BBB programme has now become a vehicle for more than customer service training. Product knowledge, customers with special needs, and telephone training videos have been developed and run under the BBB banner. As it is stated in the Sainsbury's in-house journal (July 1987: 5): 'There is no real end to building better business. It is an ongoing training programme which is to be developed for the future and will grow to encompass different areas.'

The product of change

Customer service training was introduced because there was a clear business requirement for it. One of the pilot store managers summed up the effects of the programme in the following way (July 1987: 5):

> It was hard work being a forerunner of the scheme. Many people on the administration side were hearing about BBB for the first time. There were lots of feedback sessions to attend. My staff now have more confidence to deal with customer queries and to cope with the jobs they are given. It has created a better working atmosphere. We had a good set up here from the start so it was a case of building on what we already had. Now we have the task of keeping the momentum going and we are doing well on that score.

The programme was targeted at the sales staff, and while the managers are involved in the programme no direct attempt has been made to change their attitudes. Branch managers are required to support the training initiative. They write to all the staff outlining its purpose and attend introductory or summary group discussions. The requirement for managers to adopt a more participative style and discuss such things as being helpful and developing a positive attitude towards colleagues, has had some interesting effects. Branch managers have expressed difficulty in dealing with staff in this way and have requested training in briefing and presentation skills. There is also a rather obvious point of conflict between sales staff who are being asked to become helpful and positive towards customers and colleagues, and the traditional style of the branch manager. The impact of the programme has been variable. In some cases the BBB programme is having a knock-on effect up the the line, while in others the manager's style is inhibiting the impact of the programme. This situation is exacerbated because more senior managers who have not been closely involved in the programme are presenting a traditional role model to their subordinates. While it was initially recognized that a top-down approach was desirable, it was also recognized that in a successful company there is little rationale for changing management style.

Sainsbury B

Background

Sainsbury's success has continued. Group sales have increased to £7.3 bn (compared to £4 bn in 1987), with sales per square foot increased to £17.26 per week (£15.43); profit before tax has increased to £450 m. (£268 m.); market share has increased to 11.6 per cent (10.2 per cent); and earning per share has increased to 19.64 p (11.34 p). Since 1987 the number of employees employed by the group has increased to over 100,000 (62,000 part-time), from 69,000 (40,000 part-time).

The joint presidents of the company remain Lord Sainsbury of Drury Lane and Sir Robert Sainsbury, and the chairman remains Lord Sainsbury of Preston Candover. Of the 19 board directors, 17 were either board or departmental directors in 1987. The two newcomers are both from outside the company, one of them is the personnel director who was appointed in 1989.

Since 1987 the personnel function has been restructured with the intention of clarifying its roles and responsibilities.

'Building better business' 1990

The original BBB fanfare and supporting competitions and initiatives created a lot of interest among shop staff, and BBB is still a topic of discussion in the stores. However, no new initiatives have been used to support it since its introduction; and more recent training programmes, such as a major programme of retail hygiene (in response to new European legislation on retail hygiene), have not been run under the BBB label. Surveys undertaken by outside consultants indicate that customer service has improved over the years, but it is not possible to determine BBB's contribution to this result.

In general, branch management have been fully committed to the customer service aspect of the BBB programme, and have given it full support. However, some groups felt that it overemphasized the softer attitudinal aspects of customer service training, and encouraged some staff to consider its message as being optional rather than a job requirement. These subjective impressions have led the retail division, with its new director of branch operations, to initiate and develop 'phase 2' version of BBB.

Following concerns expressed by senior management a directive was issued to branch personnel managers in January 1990, setting out the main aspects of the revised approach. Recruiters are now required to assess the customer skills of job applicants during interview. During induction, the employee is allocated a 'guardian' and receives a 30-minute training session on customer skills ('customercare briefing') by the branch manager. This includes a new video and support material entitled 'Building better customer care', or BBCC as the new initiative is known. The video was introduced in 1989 and adopts a more autocratic and hard-hitting style than the previous BBB videos; employees are told what they must and must not do in order to improve customer service. The video is followed by a statement of the importance of the customer to the success of the business, and then by a clear statement of job requirements by the manager:

> Although I am sure that most of you do treat customers correctly, to ensure that EVERY employee operates correctly, I am INSTRUCT-ING you that from today, everyone must operate to the following minimum requirements: . . . When asking for payment etc., you MUST say 'PLEASE'. . . . If a customer asks where an item is displayed, you MUST offer to take them to the display (Emphasis given in the original material.)

The revised approach is also more formalized than previously: ratings of customer service skill are part of new employee appraisal during the six or ten-week probationary period and adequate performance is a prerequisite to confirmation of employment; managers are required to confirm that the employee has undergone customer skills training; the employee is required to confirm that he or she had received the training; and a formal plan and record of the training are held on personnel files. The original BBB videos are now included as part of post-induction training. Existing staff and management are also required to attend the 30-minute customer care briefing session, and to notify the district manager that they have done so. Managers and supervisors are requested to monitor customer service in stores, and to act as role models in order to 'set a first class example'.

Line management initiated and developed the new programme without involving divisional personnel. The retail division added the programme to the front of the existing BBB training materials. Initially this created some difficulties: there were procedural inaccuracies in the video that tended to undermine its credibility, and its approach was inconsistent with some of the existing videos. Divisional personnel have now been involved, and three of the original BBB videos (*Look at it this way*, *You've got what it takes*, and *In just three seconds*) have been withdrawn, and training revamped to present a more coherent package.

The BBB programme is still running, but in a drastically altered form. The original idea for BBB to act as a vehicle for introducing widespread bottom-up change has disappeared. Its role has been reduced to improving customer service. The training has been shortened, become less participative, and more focused on behaviour rather than attitudes. Greater emphasis has been placed on the monitoring and formal control of training and behaviour. It is too early to tell whether the new approach is going to be more successful than the original at changing customer service behaviour. Certainly it would appear to be more compatible with existing management culture.

Mention has already been made of a major training programme which has been introduced on retail hygiene as a result of European legislation. Two other training initiatives are worth noting: 'Resourcing the business' which is designed to encourage line managers to own their human resource (HR) problems; and there are plans to introduce a programme aimed at developing a more consultative style of management. Compatible with the latter intention was a recently completed job evaluation exercise which had a significant consultative element, and the current consultative approach which the retail division is adopting in arriving at a new uniform.

Conclusions

In this chapter we have summarized the findings derived from a series of case studies concerning the methods of culture change. We have also outlined some of our knowledge relating to successful organizational change. Finally, we have described a case study of culture change which was spearheaded by training. This case study was undertaken at two points in time, and provides us with a 'live' example in which to apply the findings covered earlier in the chapter. A number of issues emerge for discussion, and we should like to conclude by commenting on three of these: culture and customer service; behaviour and attitudes; and culture change.

Culture and customer service

Skilled individuals and efficient management systems provide some of the key elements needed for creating and maintaining competitively superior customer service. If durability for this quality is sought, then the attitudes and values which underlie the behaviour must become an inherent feature of the organization's culture. Only when this process of internalization has taken place will staff feel that it is 'right' and 'normal' to behave towards customers in certain desirable ways.

Improving customer service has become one of the main strategies for enhancing the competitiveness of service organizations in the recent past. The almost evangelical work of individuals such Crosby (1979) under the label of total quality management, have given a significant fillip to this development. It is therefore not surprising to find that many large organizations have been trying to reorientate their culture in order to achieve greater quality in customer care. In common with others Sainsbury's is conforming to this trend, and is using training as the pivotal tool for changing culture.

Behaviour and attitudes

Is improved customer care more likely to be brought about by a training programme which emphasizes changing behaviour or changing attitudes? Phase 1 of the BBB programme emphasized the latter, phase 2 the former. Theoretically, attitudes, values and beliefs underlie much of our behaviour. The main reason why research findings often contradict this relationship, is because behaviour is powerfully influenced by situational factors. Thus, although you may have negative attitudes towards rude customers, you may continue to deal with them in a polite manner in the presence of your supervisor for fear of being reprimanded! The answer therefore is that both behavioural skills and attitudes need to be targeted during training. They will each reinforce one another.

A further reason for attending to attitudes as in the original BBB programme is to do with our understanding of the nature of culture. The culture of Sainsbury is the commonly shared attitudes, values and beliefs of those employed within the company. A subset of those attitudes/values/beliefs relate to customer service. To change this subset means influencing the attitudes of all employees, not just those whose jobs brings them in direct contact with the public. Managers may rarely come into contact with customers, but their attitudes towards customers will be communicated to subordinates who do, either through modelling or through their selective reinforcement of behaviour. Undoubtedly Sainsbury managers will have a positive attitude towards customers, but what they may not be predisposed to do is to encourage staff to give priority to helping a customer find a product as opposed to keeping the shelves fully stocked. It is in these choice situations where priorities have to be determined that attitudes and values often come to the fore, and where cultural cues are exposed. Intentionally or unintentionally managers will have a dominant influence on this aspect of the company's culture. It is therefore important that they should be subjected to the attitudinal training experienced by the sales staff.

Culture change

On the basis of objective information it is not possible to give a categorical answer to the question: has the culture of the retail division changed as a result of the BBB programme? On the basis of our knowledge of the nature of culture and the conditions under which cultural change takes place, it is unlikely that Sainsbury's retail culture has changed. This is not to say that there have not been improvements to the quality of their customer service; only that these observable behaviours may not as yet be reflected in the stable attitudes, values and beliefs which underpin these behaviours and determine their durability.

In analysing the case study in the light of the earlier generalizations made with regard to cultural change, the reader will note that those factors which could be identified as facilitating change include:

- BBB phase 1 targeted attitudes as well as skills;
- it was system-wide, in that managers were introduced to the programme as well as sales staff throughout the country;
- a systematic approach was used in implementing the programme in that senior managers were given a one-day course, trainers were trained and then ran a two-day course for branch management and a three-day course for store instructors, and the latter then trained the sales staff;
- outside experts were used to help in the initial development and implementation of the package, but ownership and responsibility for the main implementation rested with the company;
- the messages communicated in training were reinforced through other media such as house magazines and competitions.

Those factors which may have been inhibiting change include:

- when the programme was initiated the company was a successful business and has remained so, and therefore there was no immediate and strong pressure to change culture;
- the initial phase 1 programme seemed to be more the 'baby' of personnel and training than of the board and line management;
- the traditional 'tell and sell' management style sat uneasily against the softer and more participative style underlying the BBB phase 1 programme.

It is interesting that in the follow-up visit to the company, two noticeable changes have taken place: the programme has been modified so that it sits more comfortably within the traditional management style embedded in the Sainsbury culture; and the current phase 2 version of the programme is the result of an initiative of line management. It is for the reader to surmise whether the company is still on course for a genuine change in its culture.

Postscript

During the past five years there have been no dramatic changes with respect to our knowledge relating to organizational culture change, the role of training in this process, or to the contextual situation that an organization such as Sainsbury finds itself in. Nevertheless, it is worth making some selected observations on each of these themes.

The original study in which Sainsbury was one of the cases has been extended by incorporating further cases of organizational culture change in the second edition of Williams et al. (1993). In the Preface to this new edition we noted that academics had continued the debate about the discrepencies and gaps in our knowledge of organizational culture (for example, Furnham and Gunter 1993), and that practitioners and managers appeared to be adopting a more thoughtful and focused approach to culture change. This approach incorporated the current state of knowledge in the area, particularly by recognizing: that cultural change should be seen as a route to strategic change rather than an end in itself; the importance of 'unfreezing' the existing culture (often through revolutionary rather than evolutionary change); the appropriateness of a bottom-up as well as a top-down approach to change, depending on situational factors (that is to say, the ownership of change and the power to make change happen should be mutually reinforcing); the need to adopt an holistic or systems view of culture change (so that, for example, training efforts are supportive of strategic goals, technological innovations and restructuring as well as of cultural change goals); and that success in a dynamic environment requires a continual process of adaptation rather than a once-for-all change effort.

Training will almost inevitably be an integral part of any culture change programme. Given the nature of culture (see the definition at the beginning of this chapter), it can readily be argued that training should focus on both behaviour (that is, skills) and attitudes so that each can reinforce the other. Without this mutual reinforcement there is a danger that the softer attitude approach will result in dissatisfaction or compliant behaviour (that is, a consequence of external rewards and punishment rather than internal beliefs and commitment), and that the harder behavioural approach will only result in attitudinal change if the newly learnt behaviours are rewarded over a significant period of time.

Sainsbury remains a successful retail organization, but so are its main competitors. They all have focused attention on customer service in its widest sense. This not only means being helpful to the customer in face-to-face situations but meeting their needs through free parking, childcare facilities, shorter queues, restaurant facilities, one-stop shopping centres and so on. Retail organizations are also making greater use of the potential for information technology to benefit the customer and the organization. The full realization of this potential will depend to a significant extent on management's willingness to invest in its people. One of the most effective ways of achieving this is to build training into the culture of the organization, and thereby to lay the foundations for the learning or adaptive organization.

References

Crosby, P. 1979: *Quality is Free*. New York: McGraw-Hill.

Furnham, A. and Gunter, B. 1993: Corporate culture: definition, diagnosis and change. In C. Cooper and I.T. Robinson (eds), *International Review of Industrial and Organisational Psychology*, vol. 8, London: John Wiley.

Lewin, K. 1951: *Field Theory in Social Science*. New York: Harper & Row.

Williams, A., Dobson, P. and Walters, M. 1989: *Changing Culture: new organisational approaches*. London: Institute of Personnel Management.

Williams, A., Dobson, P. and Walters, M. 1993: *Changing Culture: new organisational approaches*, 2nd edn. London: Institute of Personnel and Development.

20

Business and Human Resource Management Strategies at Rosyth Dockyard

JAMES KELLY AND JOHN GENNARD

Introduction

This chapter analyses the business and human resource management (HRM) strategies adopted at Rosyth Dockyard over the period 1990–5 and the contribution of HRM to the devising and implementing of these strategies which were designed to secure organizational survival and growth through increased competitiveness. Our contribution to the previous edition of this book analysed the same issue for the first stage of the contractorization of the Dockyard and covered the period 1987–90. Until April 1987 Rosyth Dockyard was owned and managed by the Ministry of Defence (MoD); but on that date, in compliance with the Defence Services Act 1986, the management of its assets was taken over by Babcock Thorn Ltd (a private consortium) which had won the seven-year contract to manage the largest single industrial site in Scotland employing 5,600.[1]

Contractorization was to maximize competition, to reduce the costs of repairing and refitting Navy vessels, including submarines, and to provide greater value for money for the tax-payer. Under contractorization 70 per cent of Rosyth's work was to be allocated by the MoD in the form of ship refit work for the Navy. A further 20 per cent of such work was to be gained in competition with the Devonport Naval Dockyard and private ship repair companies.[2] A further 10 per cent of work, to secure the maximum utilization of the Rosyth Dockyard capacity, was to be gained from the commercial sector. In undertaking allocation and competitive work the Dockyard managers were to adopt risk pricing and accept full responsibility for both losses and profits on contracts. Against this economic and political environment Rosyth's new managers needed to improve efficiency and to develop HRM policies to facilitate the achievement of this objective.

The HR strategy adopted put in place a number of personnel/ employee relations policies designed to provide institutions and procedures which would enable a quicker response to market changes and achieve a greater utilization of labour than was possible under the Civil Service procedures and institutions the Dockyard had operated previously. A new institution, the Dockyard Joint Industrial Council, made up of senior management and full-time trade union officials but including conveners of shop stewards, was established to negotiate company-wide agreements. An Enabling Agreement contained a joint commitment to participation in the development and implementation of change programmes designed to ensure the best use of Dockyard resources. It contained agreed common objectives of the company and its trade unions, and spelt out the commitments both would enter into to achieve these joint objectives. Terms and conditions of employment of the Dockyard employees were negotiated outside the national Whitley Committee: a joint management and trade union institution with a history dating back to 1919. A new code of behaviour (entitled 'Working Together') set down rules for high standards of performance, safety and behaviour expected of employees and what they in turn could expect from the company. In addition, new communications policies and a formal change programme based on employee involvement in improving performance sought to promote joint benefit. This was all in stark contrast to the previous Civil Service environment which offered job security, reasonable terms and conditions of employment, a paternalist management style which was nevertheless rule-driven, autocratic, impersonal and slow, whilst inefficient decision-making structures resulted in a multiplicity of informal distortions, including extra allowances, excessive overtime working, and so on, to cope with local circumstances.

The first three years of contractorization saw positive, if moderate, progress in improving the efficiency of the Rosyth Dockyard. There had been improvements in labour utilization, the introduction of more flexible working practices, the advent of performance-related pay, a modest reduction in absenteeism, no lost working time from industrial disputes, and the overcoming of resistance to contractorization from the Yard's trade unions based on their fears of what might happen with private sector managers, for example that large-scale enforced redundancies would ensue. However, the thawing of the Cold War in 1989–90 changed significantly the economic and political environment and also the product markets in which the Rosyth Dock-yard had previously operated. The economic and political changes in Central and Eastern Europe meant a reduction in MoD demand for naval refit work. This expected downturn in business would not only require the 1987 business strategy to be changed but would put strain on the HRM framework and the co-operative relationships developed between management, unions and employees over the period 1987–90. How Rosyth Dockyard management responded to, and overcame, the problems stemming from the end of the Cold War is the central theme of this chapter.

Furthermore, although a UK case, Rosyth Dockyard is part of a broader trend towards agency management, contractorization and privatization of government defence establishments generally, and has a wider international significance. The Levene Report (1984) high-lighted the variable methods of navy ship repair work in various coun-tries, particularly the USA, although all retained significant public sector control. With the end of the Cold War all major industrialized countries, including the NATO and Warsaw Pact members, have an interest in effecting reductions in public expenditure and the size of their armed forces (Lovering 1991). Coupled to globalization of the private enterprise culture, direct public agency control over such es-tablishments is being eroded, and the UK government is further down this road than most others.

This chapter consists of four sections, starting with an account of Rosyth's new business strategy to remain competitive and to develop the business in the changed economic, political and product market environments of the early 1990s. Secondly, it examines the HRM strategies and policies developed to deliver the new business strategy. Thirdly, the extent to which the HR institutions and procedures set up in 1987 have withstood the pressure of these changes is investigated. The final section considers possible future HRM developments at Rosyth Dockyard as it moves towards complete privatization in 1996.

The Business Strategy and Environmental Change

Options for Change

In July 1990 the defence review, *Options for Change*, announced, in the light of the diminishing Soviet threat, reductions in the Navy's com-plement of ships. It reduced the number of surface vessels, destroyers and frigates, from 50 to 40, submarines from 17 to 12, and minor war and support vessels proportionately. Subsequently the number of destroyers and frigates was reduced to 35 ships. In addition, the review proposed longer periods between ship refits; they were to be cheaper in the future and would increase the percentage of naval work subject to direct competition between the two naval dockyards and private ship repair yards from 20 per cent to 30 per cent. These reductions in defence expenditure held severe implications for the size, and even the survival, of Rosyth, because it meant the extent of allocated core work from the Navy would continue to diminish during the first half of the 1990s. The experience during the period 1987–92 had been of allocated work continuously falling short of that promised, whilst HMS *Southampton* had been refitted in a private yard to standards acceptable to the Navy.

Allocation of Trident Work and Phasing Out of Allocated Work

A second major setback to the planned workload at Rosyth was the government announcement in June 1994 that the Trident nuclear submarine would be refitted at Devonport and that all allocated Navy work would be phased out. Rosyth would be a facility capable of refitting a full range of surface vessels with an allocated work programme from the Navy to last until 2000 for large vessels and to 2005 for small ships such as mine sweepers and Royal Fleet Auxiliaries. This programme represented over the time period some 50 per cent of the anticipated surface vessel refit programme.

Rosyth had refitted Polaris nuclear submarines, but Devonport had not – it repaired only conventional submarines. However, the two yards required extensive investment of several million pounds in new facilities if they were to be capable of completing Trident work. In 1984 the MoD had announced that such a facility at a cost of £550 million would be provided at Rosyth and work had been commissioned to build the necessary huge dry dock.

However, by mid-1994, with the diminishing threat from the Soviet bloc, the major priority of naval chiefs had become speed across the Atlantic. The south-west coast of the UK met this objective better than the east coast of Scotland. Rosyth no longer had the best strategic location, even though Trident's home port was Gareloch at Faslane, Scotland. The government justified its decision to favour Devonport, and thus a one-dockyard option, on grounds of cost:

Devonport's bid was £64 million lower than that of Rosyth. The latter's bid for Trident included constructing a new facility whereas the Devonport bid only involved upgrading existing facilities. However, Rosyth suspected that the decision was motivated by political considerations, in that the Conservative government feared the loss to the Liberal Democrats of marginally held parliamentary seats in south-west England. However, with respect to surface ships, the government continued to prefer a two-dockyards option due to the larger number of such ships, the need for competition to bring down costs and a lack of confidence in the private repair yards to compete effectively due to their lack of experience of refitting ships for the Navy.

The new business strategy

The above changes meant reductions in the core refit programme and increased competition for a diminishing share of the unallocated Navy refit work. Rosyth Dockyard saw little alternative but to adopt a business strategy for the first half of the 1990s of diversifying the business and improving its competitiveness in all its markets (allocated, competitive, commercial sector) by cost reduction. Moves towards such a strategy had begun during the period 1987–90 when the promised core allocated work did not materialize. The 1990–5 strategy was based upon building on the Dockyard's strengths to gain additional opportunities to generate profits and to divest from areas of weakness which absorb scarce resources. Up to 1990 opportunities had been developed in railway carriage refurbishment, which offered work similar to ship cabin renovation but at reduced costs because the process is nearer to mass manufacturing rather than to the unit production required in ship repair. From this period other commercial opportunities, including manufacturing, had been developed in joinery work, steel fabrication, off-shore design, high-quality pipe work, the marketing of skills in dockyard facilities management in the UK and other parts of the world, and in maintenance work on the Forth Bridge. In addition, Rosyth had developed the capacity to build new small ships, including catamarans and Coastguard vessels. This was work gained in competition with private shipbuilders. Many of these activities involved joint ventures with other enterprises that possessed expertise in these product markets. At the same time divestment had taken place from textiles, electroplate fabrication and foundry activities; these were areas where the Dockyard could not compete with the private sector but they absorbed resources that could be used for more-productive activities.

This proactive business strategy of growing the business through product diversification and cost reduction was based on producing high-quality products which provided a high added value on a low volume of output. High margin and high unit cost naval work would be balanced against more competitively priced private sector work requiring low labour and other costs if work, and associated employment, was to be secured by Rosyth. The strategy thus forced the Dockyard management to seek work in high value-added products, but at the same time pressure continued to be exerted by the Navy to reduce the costs of naval work by making them comparative to the cost the Dockyard worked on when competing for work in the private commercial sector. Cost reductions on all the Dockyard's work in the first half of the 1990s was to be achieved by reducing the size of the workforce, obtaining greater flexibility in the use of labour, reducing working time lost from absence and grievance handling, reducing premium payments such as shift premiums, and the self-financing of improvements in terms and conditions of employment.

The 1992 internal reorganization

A central part of this strategy of growing and developing the business through diversification and cost reduction was the 1992 internal reorganization of Babcock Thorn, based on the creation of profit centre businesses to give a sharper focus to the targeted market segments. Thorn EMI withdrew from the consortium, repositioning itself out of electronic weapons systems and into other industrial sectors. Rosyth Royal Dockyard is still the employing company, although presently in the process of sale. The Babcock Facilities Management Division of Babcock International has been established with a number of stand-alone profit centres each with its own board of directors. The largest of these is Babcock Rosyth Defence Ltd, whose mission is to compete successfully for naval ship repair work. Other profit centre businesses were Babcock Rail, Babcock New Zealand, Babcock Joinery Products and Babcock Rosyth Fabricators. All employees are transferable between the various business units.

Babcock Facilities Management Division is the organization at the Dockyard to which the managing directors of these businesses report. This organization is responsible for the overall strategic direction of all these businesses. The reorganization was not only designed to provide a more focused product market orientation but was also to gain for the 'new businesses' credit with potential customers who otherwise might not take them seriously (for example, their capability to deliver a job to the right quality and standards and on time) in their bids for work outside the traditional areas of the Dockyard's operations. Given the new business strategy and objectives established after 1990, what contribution did human resource management strategies and policies make towards attempting to achieve the business objectives?

Human Resource Management Strategies and Policies

These have been designed to achieve cost reduction through the achievement of a smaller workforce, a more efficient use of labour, a reduction in the loss of working time from absence, grievance and industrial disputes, and so on, the stricter control of overtime working, a change in shift patterns and record systems and an increasing focus on management development through team-building techniques. Many similar changes in business and HR strategies have been recorded in both the HRM literature (Storey 1992) and in single case studies of particular industries (Colling 1991; McKinlay and Taylor 1994), the latter dealing, respectively, with HR changes resulting from privatization of electricity distribution and at Yarrow Shipbuilders.

A smaller workforce

Since 1987 employment in the Dockyard has fallen from 5,600 to 3,600 in 1995. Most of the reduction has been amongst the manual workforce, although a number of staff grade employees have suffered redundancy. Volunteers have taken advantage of the relatively generous Civil Service voluntary severance scheme. Redundancy compensation payments arising from reduction in the core (allocated) workload are the liability of the MoD. To date, all severance costs have been reimbursed by the MoD, although the Term Contract does require a threshold of commercial workload which, if not met, would require the managers of the yard to bear some of the cost. In the period 1990–95 all the voluntary redundancies were as a result of falls in the anticipated allocated work from the Navy. According to the House of Commons Public Accounts Committee Report 39 (1992/93), redundancies at Rosyth over the period 1987 to 1992 had cost the MoD £42 million. Despite the reduction in the numbers employed at Rosyth, what has not happened, unlike in the privatized public utilities, is a significant delayering of management.[3] This absence of significant numbers of compulsory redundancies has helped to maintain a positive employee relations climate in the Dockyard. The management has been able to adopt a policy of 'incremental' change rather than one of radical and rapid change. Sustaining workloads through high-value submarine work and through commercial work has provided a cushion to soften the need to improve costs radically and rapidly. Rosyth's management style contrasts markedly with that reported by McKinlay and Taylor at Yarrow Shipbuilders, where privatization led to an aggressive interventionist style in pursuit of cost reduction and increased business efficiency.

More-flexible working

The period 1990–5 has seen the significant increase, relative to 1987–90, in the functional and numerical flexibility of the workforce. Craftsmen have been equipped with secondary skills to enable them to progress jobs without having to wait around for other craftsmen. In this regard the Dockyard has moved towards the concept of a steel fabricator and away from the multiplicity of narrow boilermaking skills of past job demarcations. Mechanical and electrical fitters have developed additional skills to enable them to undertake tasks in both mechanical and electrical fitting. Joiners have been trained to undertake painting tasks. However, there has not just been relaxation of job demarcations between crafts trades. Craftsmen have taken on cleaning and fetching duties which were previously the preserve of the lesser-skilled manual workers. One result of this is that in the period 1990–95 over 1,000 semi- and unskilled jobs were lost. Previously, the unskilled and semi-skilled workers (a Transport and General Workers Union job territory) had resisted craftsmen's attempts to take over their jobs on the grounds that it would reduce their overtime opportunities as well as their employment opportunities. This widening of the craft workers' jobs had been initially resisted by the shop stewards of the lesser-skilled, but their full-time officials persuaded them that this policy was not sustainable if the Dockyard were to survive. Worker resistance was overcome by a combination of absence of support from the Transport and General Workers Union national officials and generous severance payments which undermined the shop stewards' position.

This situation, of craftsmen taking over the tasks of the lesser-skilled, is to be found in many other British industries, including general engineering and general printing. Moreover, competitive business pressures have increased task flexibility in the USA, where Conti (1992) reports widespread efforts by employers to change restrictive works rules in union contracts in the engineering industry. But relaxing US job demarcations, unlike those in the UK, is hindered by seniority rules, with even narrower job classifications supported by the legal status of their collective agreements.

Numerical flexibility has been increased relative to 1987–90 to match staffing needs to cope with fluctuations in workloads without adding to the core workforce. However, although the employment of temporary and agency employees in both manual and non-manual areas has now become accepted in principle, it remains small as a percentage of the total workforce. For example, in January 1995 only 9.5 per cent of manual workers on site were temporary or agency employees. Recruitment of temporary employees and employees on short-term contacts is the norm when workloads increase. For temporary employees, usually recruited about 12 at a time, the dockyard contacts the agency and uses its own register of former employees who have security clearance. Even at the highest levels of the employment hierarchy, fixed-term contracts are not uncommon; redundant senior managers from private ship repair companies have been recruited on a fixed short-term contract basis. In 1995 there were between 15 and 20 senior managers employed on this basis. To this extent Rosyth is following a trend widely established in both UK industry and throughout other European countries (Brewster 1995). Most of the flexible working has come in functional rather than in numerical flexibility.

Compared to the 1987–90 period, when functional flexibility was in its infancy, changed working practices have been accepted by the trade unions and the employees with little or no resistance from the various manual trades.

However, uncertainties and fluctuations in workloads require Rosyth Dockyard to retain skilled workers if the naval refitting work is to be fulfilled. This means that the company must operate a labour-hoarding strategy since if, in the short-term absence of Navy work, the skilled labour is laid off and moves to other employers, the company may not be able to recruit a sufficient supply of skilled labour when the Navy work returns. Labour hoarding is not without costs, but these are met by the MoD. During 1990–1 and 1991–2, the Ministry paid £47 million plus a 3 per cent disruption fee to Rosyth. It considered that paying for labour underutilization was a cheaper option than redundancy since a subsequent rise in workload would give rise to the need to rehire.

Collective agreements

During the period 1990–5 the Dockyard management sought to control labour costs by obtaining self-financing improvements in terms and conditions of employment. For example, the introduction of the 37-hour working week in 1991–2 was financed by the reduction of shift premiums, particularly those for the 16.15–00.45 hours shift, and a change in shift working patterns so that the double day shift was abolished, with the majority of employees becoming employed on a traditional day shift. There remains, however, a night shift of 23.30–07.30 hours. Additionally, a four-night shift was introduced, between 21.00 and 07.30 hours, bearing a premium of 37 per cent. The same shift patterns now apply for both manual and non-manual employees. In the 1993–4 wage negotiations the company did not make an across-the-board pay offer on the grounds that labour costs were too high by competitive standards in the markets into which the Dockyard was seeking to diversify. Instead, it paid a £650 *ad hoc* bonus to each employee that was financed from the profits of the businesses but not subject to overtime and shift premiums.

The Dockyard management also attempted to reduce costs by bargaining out overtime premiums via a lump sum payment. This was rejected by the workforce as overtime payments count in the calculation of redundancy compensation payments and pension entitlement. Given this sensitivity, the management did not push the issue. To date, the management has not sought to end the anomaly stemming from the Civil Service whereby non-manual employees are in receipt of ten more days holiday than manual workers. A reduction in labour costs, however, has been achieved by employing sub-contractors on site to complete work which otherwise might have been undertaken by the Dockyard's own labour force. This has also had a learning effect in that Dockyard employees have seen at first hand that employees with the same skills as theirs are employed by companies in competition with the Dockyard on inferior terms and conditions of employment. The discipline of this learning effect may have a wider application; research by Nolan and O'Donnell (1995) in the UK coal industry shows that one-third of the 15,000 miners are contractors competing with those on employment contracts, and use this as part of their explanation for cost reduction and improved labour productivity.

Employability

The trade unions at Rosyth were concerned about the reduction in numbers employed but accepted through joint agreement the necessity to secure the greatest number of jobs within a product market which was outside their control. Management's communications policies and mechanisms have been of the highest standard and they discussed the business strategy with the unions through regular quarterly meetings of the Dockyard Joint Industrial Council and at occasional mass meetings where the senior management addressed all employees on all aspects of the performance of the company. Trade unions accepted that to remain in the Civil Service would not guarantee employment as the naval fleet was further reduced. Like management, they saw future employment security as lying in the private commercial sector.

In 1990, in response to the government's policy to have all Navy refit work open to competition by the year 2005, management adopted the policy that they could not guarantee to their employees lifelong employment at the Dockyard but would help them to acquire skills to make them employable when they could no longer be employed in the Dockyard. In short, the company would provide its employees with 'employability'. This depended on employees being willing to learn new and updated skills so that they could secure work both inside the Dockyard and outside, should they have to leave. In this way internal dockyard functional flexibility is extended to encompass the external labour market.

The introduction of this concept of 'employability' meant that management now gave top priority within the HR function to the training and development of both manual and managerial personnel. Employees are trained to meet the national standards of competence set by National/Scottish Vocational Qualifications (NVQs/SVQs), thereby not only broadening skills but having them recognized beyond the Dockyard. Not all employees are undertaking training because some 800 already have the necessary level of competence and experience to be certificated. 'Employability' opens up the opportunity for workers to gain access to craft and supervisory jobs previously denied to them because they did not serve an indentured apprenticeship at the appropriate age or left school too early with inadequate qualifications. In this way employment is to be found by removing the barriers that have previously obstructed certain employees.

Management development

The period from 1990 to 1995 has also seen, relative to 1987–90, a greater focus on management development through team-building by involving senior managers in real business projects aimed at developing the organizational capability of the company in pursuit of its commercial strategy of diversification. This has led to greater interaction between directors and senior managers and to building personnel management issues into business problem-solving. However, the absence of line management ownership of employee relations issues has remained a problem. In this context performance appraisal, management succession planning and employee participation are discussed with line managers rather than being left to the personnel department. In this way the integration of all personnel processes has been improved and their relevance as part of the total business more clearly appreciated by line managers.

Role of personnel in the development of the business strategy

In the period 1987–90 the personnel director had secured considerable authority and influence on the board of Rosyth Royal Dockyard. He had been part of the small team which worked on the Babcock Thorn tender to manage the Dockyard assets and which negotiated the seven-year term contract with the MoD. It is widely accepted that the personnel director showed considerable vision in planning and putting down the basic institutions and agreements which governed employee relations during that period. With his untimely death in 1990 the company appeared to allow the leadership of the personnel function to change direction by appointing as personnel director a retired part-time director from Babcock International plc.

However, following the reorganization of the company and retirement of the part-time director, the industrial relations manager was appointed director of personnel, reporting to the managing director of Rosyth Royal Dockyard (also MD of Babcock Rosyth Defence Ltd), because this business employed all of the dockyard workers. Both these directors operated with an industrial relations bias, leaving line managers increasingly marginalized in the management of people. Indeed, during the early 1990s, the training and development activity was transferred out of the personnel department and located in management services.

The authors' wider research on the authority and power of personnel directors suggests that this is influenced by a number of variables, including a personnel director who has a strong business orientation, an MD supportive to the personnel function who has established a high trust relationship with the personnel director, high professional standing for the personnel department's and the directors' work in the eyes of other directors and senior managers, and well-developed interpersonal social skills in solving business and HR problems (Kelly and Gennard 1996). In the period 1990–4 personnel directors at Rosyth were less all-round business-orientated than the director for the period 1987–90, and they returned to a more traditional industrial-relations approach, acting as a buffer between line management and the trade unions. Professional respect for the function fell in the eyes of other managers and there was a move by directors of other management functions to lessen the influence of personnel during the personnel director's illness in 1990.

The changes to business strategy highlighted in previous sections led to the appointment in August 1994 of a new human resource director to the board of Rosyth Facilities Management Division, restoring and reinforcing the business orientation of the personnel director and the department. The training and development activity has again been put directly under personnel's control and become a critical function to the achievement of the business strategy. HR and business strategies have again been integrated to solve business problems by securing line management ownership. In addition, the new human resource director is also responsible for information technology, again assisting the integration of human resources into business strategy. In this way, personnel's professional credibility had been restored, with other directors' involvement in personnel being upgraded at the same time. Industrial relations remains an important activity of the personnel function as the company prefers to manage by making collective agreements with the trade unions. However, it is seen, in football parlance, as the defence of the three functions, with the 'strikers' (forwards) as the training and development function and the 'mid-field' as line management carrying out basic personnel processes of recruitment, selection, discipline, and so on.

Change programme and profit-related pay

The change programme has been incorporated in the Rosyth 2000 Challenge programme to improve performance and reduce costs. It could be argued that the change programme, established in 1987 and aimed at generating suggestions to improve performance through employee participation, became bogged down in a bureaucracy of hierarchical committees, resulting in diminished enthusiasm and commitment by workers and line managers. The point was made above that line manager ownership of HR aspects had been in decline in the period 1990–4. There is no longer a specialist change manager dedicated to the programme's success. Notwithstanding, the HR strategy aimed at reducing labour costs to competitive levels by the year 2000 is well understood.

Profit-related pay, established in 1987, has also been abandoned. As a form of financial participation it failed because workers could not identify with the bonuses of approximately £50 paid twice per annum. As there was no motivational effect, the payment was consolidated into the pay structure at the end of 1989. Except for individual performance-related pay for some very senior managers, the pay structure at Rosyth Dockyard is a simple graded one that contains no extra financial incentives.

Human Resource Institutions and Outcomes

Institutions

The HRM institutions and procedures established in the Dockyard over the period 1987–90 were in a different political, economic and product market than that of 1990–5. However, the creators of this HRM infrastructure saw them as capable of surviving in an alternative situation. The evidence from the Dockyard between the years 1990 and 1995 inclusive showed this to be the case. There was no significant change to the content of the Enabling Agreement nor to the operation, functions and authority of the Dockyard Joint Industrial Council, except that the latter has been used more intensively in the last year. The Code of Conduct has remained effective and withstood on separate occasions the scrutiny of two industrial tribunals. The number of full-time shop stewards continued to decline from 36 under the MoD, to eight in 1990 and to four by 1995. However, since 1987 the numbers employed have also fallen considerably and the ratio of shop stewards (full-time) to full-time employees remains favourable compared with the late 1980s. The institutions have stood the test of time with changes in business and HR strategies. However, the status quo agreement, which was fudged over in the disputes clause of the Enabling Agreement, became a source of friction in the early 1990s but was clarified to management's satisfaction, so that nowadays, if business demands are urgent or there is a work emergency, the changes in working practices are implemented, but if the unions wish to object, their grievance goes into procedure to await a constitutional outcome. The changed working practice remains in operation until the procedure results in a decision.

Outcomes

Productivity outcomes in the Dockyard in 1990–5 were more difficult to measure, although Babcock Thorn informed the House of Commons Committee of Public Accounts that unit cost savings of 20 per cent had been effected, and a reduction of £13 million per annum had been achieved between 1987–8 and 1990–1. Nevertheless, the MoD accepted that it was difficult to assess improvements in output and productivity from the Dockyards. Given the one-off jobbing nature of ship repair, where the work involved was often not known accurately until the job was secured, no means of measuring real output had been developed. Management HRM indices revealed a general improvement in performance, although management conceded that labour costs remained too high to compete successfully in the commercial sector.

Over the period 1990–5 Rosyth retained its record of no working days lost due to strikes, although there was an occasional overtime ban imposed by a section of the workforce. Redundancies amongst non-craft Transport and General Workers Union members resulted in mass meetings, but the potentially 'explosive' issue was contained and a stable industrial relations environment was maintained. Overtime working was tightly controlled by the managing director of Babcock Facilities Management Ltd, who personally monitored, approved or rejected claims from senior management that overtime working was necessary to meet work priorities of the various business units at Rosyth.

In the first half of the 1990s the number of recorded group grievances was no greater than in the period 1987–90. There were only three external conferences and six local conferences during the period. An external conference involved the participation of national trade union officials, whereas the local conference involved the full-time union district official. The Dockyard continued to maintain a stable employment relations environment in the early 1990s despite the management of the Yard having to deal with a different external environment.

Sickness absence had always been a major problem at Rosyth, as it had been in other ex-MoD factories such as Royal Ordinance. It was an established part of the previous Civil Service culture that employees took a specified number of sick days in the year, regardless of whether the sickness was genuine. It was regarded as an entitlement, and management had been reluctant to investigate and to take action against the employees concerned. In the period 1987–90 a modest improvement in sickness absence rates had been made at Rosyth, but achieving the target reduction of below 8 per cent of working time had proved extremely difficult. However, by 1995 the sickness absence rate for manual workers (that is, days lost as a percentage of scheduled working days) had been reduced to 5 per cent and at one point in 1994 stood at 4 per cent. This compared favourably with similar work environments in Scotland, for example Kvaerner Govan Shipbuilders Ltd, whose average absence rate over the same time period had been reduced to 6 per cent. Individual employees with an absence problem were dealt with by utilizing the Code of Conduct, which management judged to be working as effectively in the early 1990s as it had in the latter years of the 1980s.

Shift patterns have been modified by agreement with the trade unions to provide more cost-effective staffing cover. The 16.15–00.45 hours shift premium of plus 16 per cent was reduced. Moreover, the agreement of 1991–2 transferred workers to a normal day hour pattern of 08.00–16.00 hours, although the Dockyard continued to retain a night shift, 22.30–07.30 hours, plus a small back shift on 16.15–00.45 hours. These amendments to the shift pattern also enabled an agreed reduction in the length of the standard working week to 37 hours on a full cost recovery basis.

Conclusions

The business strategy (1990–5) at Rosyth Dockyard combined product diversification with cost reduction to achieve improved competitive performance. It recognized that ship refit work for the Navy was only part of its business portfolio, and a diminishing one at that. Management therefore established an organizational structure to give sharper focus to the different market segments outlined in the strategy. However, although significant progress has been made, Rosyth management readily acknowledges that there is still some way to go to achieve commercial competitive standards in its cost-centre-based businesses. The implementation and acceptance by the workforce of the business strategy has been helped in that the pace of change has been positive but incremental. Both external and internal pressures for change have impacted, but not in any 'big bang' or radical manner. The sustained allocated MoD workload, which is highly profitable, and the preparedness of the MoD to support a policy of labour hoarding to even out fluctuations in workload, has enabled management to adopt an evolutionary rather than a revolutionary approach to business and organizational change. Even the failure to gain the

Trident contract was compensated for by a guarantee of 50 per cent of the Navy's surface vessel refit programme to the year 2000 and beyond.

Despite these positive advantages, the Rosyth business strategy was devised in an environment of political uncertainty. During 1987–90, Rosyth management had been led to believe that they would gain the contract to refit the Trident nuclear submarine. However, the politicians decided in 1994 to put such work to its rival yard at Devonport. The Minister of Defence justified the decision on the grounds that Devonport had submitted a cheaper tender and not, as suggested by some at the time, as the Government's desire to retain political support in south-west England, where it was under challenge from the Liberal Democrats. However, at the time of writing (mid-1995), Devonport was experiencing difficulty in obtaining a safety licence for its dock to refit Trident and it was seriously being discussed that a political decision might be made to reallocate Trident work to Rosyth.

The question arises as to whether labour hoarding at Rosyth has wider application for other industries in a period of numerical flexibility and short-term contracts. The argument of Rosyth management, accepted by the MoD which met the cost, is that it costs more to declare significant redundancies amongst established employees during lulls in the naval programme and then to recruit when the workload picks up. The cost-benefit outcomes of such a strategy appear to depend on a number of factors particular to Rosyth, such as the length of lull in the allocated programme, a generous Civil Service severance package, and doubts over the availability of the skilled workforce as a pool of labour once unemployed. Generally the benefits arise for organizations of having greater control over a permanent workforce on hand to cope with fluctuations in demand for the product. Even companies in that most flexible of industries, building and construction, offer 40 per cent of employees significant stability for reasons of continuity in knowledge and skill, product quality and commitment to organizational goals (Winch 1986). With regard to Rosyth, we can only speculate that the figure of 10 per cent of employees presently on short-term and temporary contracts will rise with the onset of privatization and the phasing out of allocated MoD work by 2005.

The HR strategy at Rosyth was seen by management, including the managing director of the holding company, as an integral part of business policy. Although there are different businesses (profit centres), all employees are employed by Rosyth Royal Dockyard and are completely transferable between and within the different 'businesses'.

The style of management has been co-operative and collaborative, working with the trade unions much as in the 1987–90 period. The dual system of communications with employees continues through line management and trade unions, although forms of employee participation through profit-sharing and the change programme have either been abolished or have diminished in importance. The combined strategies of incrementalism in the implementation of change and of collaborative management style have been supported by management's offering generous severance payments for voluntary redundancies as the means of downsizing the labour force. If enforced redundancies had proved necessary, due to a more severe reduction in naval refit work and to less success with product diversification, then the management style would probably have been more hard-nosed, inviting a reciprocal response from the trade unions, as happened at Yarrow Shipbuilders on the Clyde.

Notwithstanding a strategy of cost reduction, there has been no delayering of middle management grades at Rosyth despite the run down in the number of manual workers. The 'gift' of being able to adopt an incremental strategy enabled management the 'luxury' of not having to deal with this question. However, there have been a few voluntary redundancies amongst staff grades but not on any significant scale. Change, as it has affected middle management, has been through the promotion of team-working and through middle managers accepting greater HR responsibilities in the management of their subordinates.

Significant differences between 1987–90 and 1990–5 concerned functional flexible working and the new concept of 'employability'. Both these were complementary as relaxation of job demarcation between crafts engendered job insecurity which was partly offset by enhancing the skills of craftsmen through training. Moreover, because the training was tied to recognized labour market qualifications (NVQs/SVQs), craftsmen and their trade unions accepted that their best interests were served by the management's 'employability' policy since this would provide survival in the external market when Rosyth could no longer offer them lifelong employment security. In addition, 'employability' helped to reduce trade union resistance to voluntary redundancies within Rosyth as the unions and their members saw that it gave them skills which were more widely marketable than just to ship repairers.

The personnel function has again taken on a proactive role at Rosyth with the appointment in 1994 of a new human resource director who is also responsible for information technology at the Dockyard. During the period 1987–90 the personnel director established the framework for the stable conduct of employee relations and was also a progressive change agent for the business as a whole. He was very influential. The early 1990s witnessed a change in direction with the personnel director playing a more traditional industrial relations role and giving priority to the maintenance of a stable employment relations environment. As a result, line managers were marginalized from HR decisions and the credibility of the personnel department declined. Since 1994 the 'strike force' of personnel became the training and development activity at the manual worker level and within management, through team-building, with line managers playing a larger part in driving the implementation of personnel policies.

In 1987 Babcock Thorn negotiated at Rosyth Dockyard a stand-alone site enabling agreement, having rejected membership of the Scottish Engineering Employers' Federation; the company has subsequently joined as a non-conforming member regarding Federation agreements. The enabling agreement established the Dockyard Joint Industrial Council and appropriate union recognition and disputes procedures. This joint arrangement has withstood the test of time and was able to cope with the changes arising from the implementation of the 1990–5 business strategy. The operation of the agreement has delivered outcomes to the parties which both have found beneficial in terms of employment conditions and the necessary changes to working practices and procedures to facilitate product diversification and to improve cost reduction. Indeed, the reorganization into various business units has seen the Dockyard Joint Industrial Council being used more intensively than previously and has provided the forum in which the proposed changes to the businesses were discussed with representatives of the workforce. The institutional arrangements established in the late 1980s have not been challenged by management, who have also seen no commercial advantage in attempting to de-recognize or bypass trade unions or to narrow the scope of collective bargaining. This position, contrary to alleged general trends in industrial relations, can be explained by the values of senior management referred to in the 1992 edition of this book; and the commercial market pressures of the early 1990s still meant that competitive improvement could be acquired by evolution, rather than revolution which would have required management to be more 'aggressive' in its approach to regaining product market competition.

It is too early to judge whether the influence of trade unions has been weakened at Rosyth. They continued to participate in joint regulation of the Dockyard via making collective agreements on behalf of their members. In turn they have accommodated and accepted major changes in work organization and a significant reduction in numbers employed at the Yard arising from management's implementation of its business and HR strategies. There was no 'across-the-board' pay increase in 1994, although a one-off payment of £650 was made by the company. Since the introduction of 'contractorization', the unions have not imposed serious industrial sanctions in opposition to management's planned changes. The changes in the labour force, especially the significant reduction in numbers of non-craftsmen, has reduced the influence of the Transport and General Workers Union, once dominant, compared to that of the Amalgamated Engineering and Electrical Union and the craft section of the General, Municipal, Boilermakers and Allied Trades Union. Amongst the staff unions, the three existing in 1987, namely the Institute of Professional Civil Servants, the Civil and Public Services Association and the Society of Public and Civil Servants, have been reduced to one, the Institute of Professionals, Managers and Specialists, whose members still retained a strong Civil Service orientation. However, as we saw above, such staff attitudes, including those of middle managers, have not been seriously challenged by delayering or redundancies. The unions at Rosyth have behaved pragmatically in responding to the changed circumstances of the 1990s, accepting that government policy and management's business strategy takes them ever more into the private commercial sector but at the same time offers the best option to sustain employment at the Dockyard. Like any organization, they have seen that survival and continuing influence requires adaptation and a flexible response, not a principled and inflexible ideological stand.

By 1996 the government plans to change the status of Rosyth and Devonport Dockyards from 'contractorization' to privatization via the sale of their assets to private sector companies. Contractorization meant that the land, buildings and heavy equipment were retained, for strategic defence reasons, by the Ministry of Defence. Babcock International and DML are the only bidders to become the new owners of the respective Dockyards. There is a view that privatization will act as a catalyst to force management to implement more radical business and HRM changes at Rosyth and to depart from the existing change strategy of incrementalism. We can only speculate as to the HR implications of privatization. Other organizations have found the adjustment difficult. For example, when Kvaerner brought the British Shipbuilders yard at Govan on the Clyde there was resistance to management's attempt to change the attitudes and culture of the workforce to one that was more compatible with the private sector. This was only achieved after a major dispute in which management successfully resisted the unions' opposition to its HRM policies designed to improve the competitiveness of the Yard. However, Rosyth may avoid such an outcome: it has had nine years of contractorization, during which time a collaborative approach to HRM policies has been adopted to adjust to changing commercial pressures. The authors will continue to observe and analyse HRM policies, practices and institutions at Rosyth as the Dockyard is privatized.

Notes

1   In the 1980s Rosyth was one of five dockyards catering for the needs of the British Navy. The others included Fleetwood, Portsmouth, Chatham and Devonport; only Devonport and Rosyth remain open. First World War preparations led to the establishment of Rosyth Naval Dockyard on the River Forth adjacent to Scotland's east coast as a defence against German naval access to the North Sea and the Atlantic. This strategic geographical location resulted in a modern, well-equipped yard capable of repairing a wide range of vessels, from small mine sweepers to capital ships. During the inter-war period the yard was placed on a care and maintenance basis, then reopened, with the approach of the Second World War, in 1938. After cessation of hostilities in 1945 the dockyard retained an important strategic role during the Cold War period with the threat from Warsaw Pact countries. In the 1960s the yard's repair capability was further extended to cover nuclear submarines, the first of which was HMS *Dreadnought*, commissioned in 1963.

2   Devonport Dockyard, located at Plymouth in south-west England, employed 11,460 in April 1987. It has a more ancient history than Rosyth, having operated as a naval dockyard since the late Middle Ages. It has the capacity to refit all naval vessels except nuclear submarines, although, as an older yard, it has carried the encumbrance of history, including some outdated facilities that add to its financial overheads. Notwithstanding, Devonport's historical association with the Royal Navy and its traditions are very strong, securely based on a strategic location in defence against England's old enemies in the form of the French and Spanish fleets. In more modern times the wars in Europe have favoured Rosyth as the main strategic location, but this may have changed in the 1990s with the reduction in the size of the fleet and greater reliance on Trident nuclear submarines as the main weapon of defence.

3   Delayering of grades in managerial hierarchies has become popular in British organizations throughout the 1990s, with manufacturing enterprises in particular taking out three to four levels between first line supervision

and senior production management. This reduction in middle management grades applies not only to line management, but also to functional specialists including personnel/human resource managers. The trend is linked to a battery of ideas contained in the management literature, giving greater autonomy to sub-organizational units, decentralization and the establishment of profit centres, a stronger customer focus in dynamic product markets and on the shop floor, with the empowerment of work teams/groups in either autonomous work patterns or cellular production units.

References

Brewster, C. 1995: HRM: the European dimension. In J. Storey, *Human Resource Management: a critical text*, London: Routledge.

Colling, T. 1991: Privatisation and the management of IR in electricity distribution. *Industrial Relations, Journal*, 22(2), 117–29.

Conti, R.F. 1992: Work practice barriers to flexible manufacturing in US and the UK. *New Technology, Work, and Employment*, 7(1), 3–14.

Gennard, J. and Kelly, J. 1992: HRM and managing change: the case of Rosyth Royal Dockyard. In B. Towers (ed.), *The Handbook of Human Resource Management*, Oxford: Blackwell.

House of Commons. Session 1992–93 1993: Committee of Public Accounts 39 Report. *Ministry of Defence: Operation of the Royal Dockyards under Commercial Management*, 24 May 1993. London: HMSO.

House of Commons. Defence Committee 7 1993: Report 829. *The Royal Dockyards*. London: HMSO.

Kelly, J. and Gennard, J. 1996: The role of personnel directors on the board of directors. *Personnel Review*, 25(1), 7–24.

Levene, P. 1984: Future of the Royal Dockyards: a preliminary report (mimeo).

Lovering, J. 1991: The British defence industry in the 1990s: a labour market perspective. *Industrial Relations Journal*, 22(2), 103–16.

McKinlay, A. and Taylor, P. 1994: Privatisation of industrial relations in British shipbuilding. *Industrial Relations Journal*, 25(4), 293–304.

Nolan, P. and O'Donnell, K. 1995: New industrial relations and performance of the British coal industry, 1985–95. Research paper delivered at BUIRA conference, Van Mildert College, University of Durham, July.

Storey, J. 1992: *Developments in the management of Human Resources*. Oxford: Blackwell.

Winch, G.M. 1986: The labour process and labour market in construction. *International Journal of Sociology and Social Policy*, 6, 301.

21

Human Resource Management Change at Bayer Diagnostics Manufacturing Ltd

P.B. BEAUMONT AND L.C. HUNTER

Introduction

The notion of 'organization culture' has been a useful metaphor for illuminating the processes of organizational change 'since it recognizes the truly human nature of organizations and the need to build organizations around people rather than techniques' (Morgan 1986: 138). However, beyond this sort of highly general statement (that is, that organizational change is about changing people, and not just about changing organizationzal structures) a great deal of controversy exists among both practitioners and researchers concerning the role of HRM in the processes of organizational change.

For instance, important debates and disagreements centre around the following sorts of questions and issues. What is the appropriate model of HRM change? Should it be a top-down, senior management-led process or a more decentralized, incremental process of change? Secondly, which are the most powerful HRM policy instruments for bringing about change, and what is the appropriate order in which they should be used? Thirdly, does an HRM programme of change fit comfortably with existing industrial relations arrangements in unionized organizations?

The present case study is designed to offer some insights into these sorts of questions and issues. Accordingly, in what follows we introduce the case study organization, and then examine in turn the incentives for change, the processes of change, the nature of the change, and finally, some outcomes (to date) of the change process.

The Organization

The organization concerned is Bayer Diagnostics Manufacturing Ltd, which is based at Bridgend in South Wales. This manufacturing plant was originally established in the late 1940s and was known until June 1995 as Miles Ltd.[1] Until 1977, it was owned by the US-based Miles Inc. which had manufacturing outlets in some 21 countries; the Bridgend plant was the largest manufacturing plant outside the USA. It was originally a pharmaceuticals manufacturer, although diagnostic products have (from the 1960s) become the major element in its product lines over time and currently account for some two-thirds of its output. It has traditionally pursued a rather mixed competitive strategy with its individual product lines comprising both high-volume/low-margin and low-volume/high-margin ones. In 1977 it was acquired by the well-known German company, Bayer AG.

The peak employment level at Bayer Diagnostics (as we shall refer to it) was some 450 in the late 1970s, and the current workforce consists of some 300 employees, 50 of whom have been recruited in the last six months. It has always been a very highly unionized organization (close to 100 per cent up to lower management levels), with three unions (Transport and General Workers Union (TGWU), the Amalgamated Engineering and Electrical Union (AEEU) and the Manufacturing, Science and Finance Union (MSF)) being recognized for collective bargaining purposes, for production, skilled and technical workers respectively. The historical union–management relationship has been described as 'an adversarial one, but not a particularly militant one'. The key elements in this description are as follows:

1 There has only ever been one strike involving a plant-specific issue. This occurred in 1982, when TGWU members were on strike for about a week and a half in protest at an AEEU (as it is now) attempt to establish a pre-entry closed shop.
2 Industrial relations matters were almost exclusively dealt with through the medium of members of the personnel department meeting on a weekly basis with six shop stewards from the three unions; line management traditionally had little responsibility or interest in such matters. It was thus fairly typical of what Storey defines as a regulatory personnel function: formulating, promulgating and monitoring observation of employment 'rules . . . operating within the traditional paradigm [as] managers of discontent' (Storey 1992: 168–9).
3 Bayer Diagnostics was traditionally a 'good payer' in the local labour market, with pay rates invariably being in the top quartile. This encouraged a long-service tradition among the workforce, but was associated

with a tendency to 'buy off' the negotiating demands of the unions; long-serving union representatives and members of management still refer to the 'top pocket' payment approach of a former managing director at the plant (that is to say, something extra could always be found at the last minute to break a bargaining deadlock).

As a background to the organizational change programme, the following points should also be noted. First, there has been a long-standing works committee, involving representatives from the three unions, although historically it never operated and acted as an 'integrative bargaining' body (Walton and McKersie 1965). Secondly, following the 1982 strike, single-table bargaining arrangements were introduced. Thirdly, the early 1980s also witnessed an experiment with quality circles; a number were introduced in 1982 and produced some useful initial recommendations, but the programme was discontinued in 1982–3 in the face of some inter-union disagreement as well as middle management subversion. More generally, it is important to see Bayer Diagnostics as historically an organization which was very much a microcosm of the pharmaceutical manufacturing industry. Its structure, management orientation and working arrangements very much mirrored the traditional industry emphasis on quality assurance via 'controlling batches and products'. This emphasis inevitably meant in the 'politics of the organization' that the traditional centres of power were the skilled craftsmen (AEEU members) and the science-based jobs in the laboratories. The importance of this observation will become apparent as we turn to the details of the change programme.

The Incentives for Change

Some earlier research has noted that an HRM-based programme of organizational change is stimulated and facilitated by a combination of product market/performance pressure and a change of senior management personnel (Hendry et al. 1988: 38). Bayer Diagnostics fits this scenario closely, with the arrival of a new plant director (PD) who acted as a top-level champion with commitment to the change process.

In the late 1980s the US parent organization (within the larger Bayer set-up) acquired another organization as part of the process of expanding the diagnostic products side of the business. However, this added further to an existing problem of duplication of capacity within Bayer and rationalization was needed, putting the future of the Bridgend plant at serious risk. Rationalization task forces were established, and senior managers from Miles in the USA visited the Bridgend plant, conveying the message that the plant might not fit into the new portfolio of business activities. The concern that it might be closed and its profitable business lines transferred to France was given additional credence by the fact that in 1989 the Bridgend plant recorded a loss of £2.46 million. This loss was the immediate background to the appointment of a new plant director who was charged with turning the company around, and ensuring that the plant fitted better with the larger competitive strategy of the corporate organization. Thus internal competition within the organization acted as the trigger for the changes which ensued, and the strategic aim of the change programme had to be initially survival and subsequently the development of a wider and more profitable product base.

The new PD has been described as a very production-orientated individual who holds strong views on employee motivation and management (McGregor 1960). In March 1990 he presented his vision for the future of the plant to the works committee. The key points involved are listed in figure 21.1. A number of major elements in this vision underline the key role to be played by human resources in the change programme, with operator knowledge of and involvement in planning and improvement, training for analytical problem-solving and quality management, and effective communication.

In recent years there has been considerable criticism of senior management-led, top-down, organization-wide programmes of HRM change; instead, a bottom-up, incremental process of change has been increasingly favoured (Beer et al. 1990). The major criticisms of the former type of change programme are essentially: (a) the difficulty of maintaining and institutionalizing the change if the senior management 'champion' leaves the organization; (b) the likelihood of 'big change' encountering, not to say stimulating, big resistance, particularly from the middle ranks of the organization who may see their own positions threatened. Criticism (a) is not currently an issue for Bayer Diagnostics. How they have sought to deal with criticism (b) will be examined by considering the processes of change and the phasing of the change process. However, before considering these matters, it is important to ask whether the new PD's 'vision' for change (figure 21.1) was injected into a 'relatively receptive' context for change (Pettigrew et al. 1992). To some extent, the answer is 'yes'. There are three major points in support of this judgement:

1   The size of the plant losses in 1989 were certainly widely known and the possibility of the plant being closed was extensively discussed. This being

1   Beliefs about people
- Treat people as mature adults who, if expectations are defined, will discipline themselves as a group to follow rules.
- People want more than just money from working and would like to grow and develop and contribute their ideas.
- The majority of people enjoy working in an environment where they are challenged to acquire new skills which are reflected in a progressive compensation structure.

2   Organizational structure
- Simple flat structure with the minimum number of levels, with a simple and effective communication system in place.
- Minimum number of job categories.
- Decentralized budgeting and decision-making.
- Clearly defined roles.
- Senior manager as coach and counsellor, thinking and planning up to a year ahead.
- Management thinks and plans up to three months ahead, solving issues in a proactive manner.
- Operator solves day-to-day issues on the line, knows and is committed to weekly line expectations, is aware of and involved in future improvements and plans for the plant.

3   Administrative systems
- Decentralized administrative responsibility with operators writing standard operating procedures and involved in filling batch manufacturing records.
- Well thought out and consistently administered training programmes for all employees in group dynamics, project management, group problem-solving and quality expectations in the pharmaceutical industry.

4   Physical facility
- Logic material flows.
- Minimum work in progress.
- Built-in surge (the ability to cope with unforecast demand).
- Flexible lines (easy change-over between product batches).
- Pharmaceutical standards required for compliance with the Medicines Act.
- Meaningful operator-administered preventative maintenance.

Figure 21.1   The new plant director's 'vision' for Bayer's Bridgend plant
Source: ACAS (Wales), *Best Practice in Industrial Relations*, 1994

said, there were sections of both management and the workforce which felt that closure was never a real likelihood due to the resource capacity of Bayer to cross-subsidize individual operations and help them out of short-term operating difficulties. That view perhaps failed to reflect the reality of widespread organizational rationalization in manufacturing, such as had been experienced in Britain in the early 1980s.

2   The new PD's vision of or model for change was grounded in his previous employment experience in a Miles plant in North America. In other words, he offered a 'solution' based on a viable model in the same industry, indeed, in the same organization. The importance of the (same) industry context in 'selling' organizational change programmes has been noted in existing research (Cappelli and Rogovsky 1994: 217–18).

3 There was some 'fertile ground' for his message in that the TGWU had long been arguing that the ideas and experience of the operators should be increasingly drawn upon in the production process. The senior representative of the TGWU in fact became an important, natural ally of the PD in the cause of selling the programme.

Nevertheless, some resistance was anticipated, and a great deal of attention was given to the processes of the change programme. In reviewing what happened it is perhaps worth observing another criticism of the top-down approach to change. Thomas (1992) observes that top decision-makers operate at some remove from the proposed changes and hence are isolated from the political 'contest' for resources (or organizational power) which exists further down the line (for example, between line management and staff departments, or between supervisors and technically minded engineers). They will also be more remote from the reality of the social system of the workplace. It then becomes important, if the change process is to succeed, 'to take into account the knowledge, interests and aspirations of those who are the object of change' (ibid.: 295). In that respect, developing a sense of ownership within the social fabric of the workplace may be essential to neutralize the desire to resist or challenge the change process itself. How this was resolved in the Bayer Diagnostics case is the matter to which we now turn.

The Processes of Introducing Change

One of the standard characterizations of Japanese v. British/US organizations is that the former take a relatively long time to make a decision, but then implement it quickly, whereas in the latter, the opposite position prevails. The new PD at Bridgend sought to depart from this characterization of the typical British organization. Although he insisted that the four individual elements of the vision or model were not negotiable, he initially presented the rationale for the model to the works committee. This body currently consists of 18 people (including six union representatives), is chaired by the PD, and meets on a monthly basis, typically for two hours or so. Moreover, he made it clear that this body was to become *the* decision-making body for translating the broad elements of the vision into detailed operational policies and practices. Very little use has been made of outside consultants throughout the change programme. (The exception was in the provision of training for shop-floor workers in analytical problem-solving techniques (Kepner-Tregoe), where a systematic training needs analysis was undertaken, and external consultants were brought in to train facilitators who then became the trainers for the remainder of the shop-floor training programme.)

This aside, the absence of external influences and the direct involvement of a representative body which incorporated the three unions together with management in a single unit effectively transferred the opportunity (or responsibility) for ownership of the design of the change programme much closer to the shop floor and to the social context of work rules and norms. The works committee then became the medium by which details of the change process were articulated. For example, the terms of the multi-skilling grids (see next section) had to be 'cleared' by this body.

A series of workforce meetings was initially convened on a variety of bases (that is, department, management level, union, supervisors). In the early stages these involved the PD, sometimes accompanied by the head of the personnel department, speaking about the need for and the broad nature of the change programme. As anticipated, a number of the meetings, particularly with the craftsmen and to a lesser extent with the laboratory-based groups, were 'very fiery' in nature; such groups obviously had the most to lose in the change process (given their previous power positions) and often reacted angrily to the strong production orientation of the PD. The craftsmen's concerns were two-fold: the change would involve a squeeze on wage differentials over the production workers (as indeed transpired); and secondly, there was a 'macho' concern that the TGWU members were receiving priority of attention – and the T&G workers were women, while the AEEU members were predominantly men. However, the responsiveness of the TGWU to the vision of change and what it promised to them proved a valuable asset which helped to isolate the AEEU interests, and to a lesser degree the MSF. Eventually the resistance dissolved because the prospect of remaining in permanent opposition within the Works Committee appeared unattractive.

As the extensive communication programme has continued throughout the various stages of the change exercise, the initial problems have subsided and it is the Works Committee, rather than the PD personally, that has become increasingly responsible for cascading down information.

The Nature of the Change Programme

The initial step in the change programme (1990) was the complete elimination of the supervisory level and a general reduction in the

- **Level 1**: for new recruits for a probationary period
- **Level 2**: basic skills (existing job functions plus analytical trouble-shooting training)
- **Level 3**[a]: intermediate skills for routine operations (skills broadly equivalent to those of chargehands under the previous management structure)
- **Level 4**[b]: the multi-skilling level. There were five groups of skills ('grids'):

Grid 1 = administration
Grid 2 = machine/mixing operation
Grid 3 = material receipt/handling
Grid 4 = computer operations
Grid 5 = truck

To be multi-skilled, employees had to be capable of performing Grids 1 and 2, together with two out of the other remaining grids.

Figure 21.2 The multi-skilling production arrangements at Bayer Diagnostics
[a] Paid £13 per week over basic rate.
[b] Paid £30 per week over basic rate.
Source: ACAS (Wales), *Best Practice in Industrial Relations*, 1994

number of levels of authority and responsibility. For example, the previous six levels of reporting in both engineering and production were reduced to three levels in both cases. In total, some 70 employees were made redundant, 15 of these being enforced redundancies; the latter were very much individuals who could not or did not want to fit into the new way of doing things. A number of senior managers also left at this time. An extensive upgrading of the physical facilities and conditions at the plant also took place.

During the 1991 wage negotiations the company introduced the possibility of something like a 20 per cent wage premium for multi-skilling. This prospect resulted in a strong push from the TGWU for the development of such a programme. The result was the establishment of a working group to develop multi-skilling in the production area, reporting to the works committee. The agreed results of their deliberations are set out in figure 21.2.

The introduction of multi-skilling/pay-for-knowledge arrangements has had a major impact on the previous pay structure. Around 34 separate pay rates have been reduced to nine in total, with a 17 percentage point difference now existing between the top AEEU rate and the top TGWU rate; ten years ago this differential was of the order of 40–50 per cent. The development of a core of multi-skilled operators (currently about 70 individuals) has provided the basis of the latest stage of development in the change programme, namely the movement to cell manufacturing arrangements.

Cellular manufacture has two main advantages over a more conventional functional layout: (a) the effect on the flow of materials within the plant, minimizing travelling time for materials and products and ensuring their flow along a well-defined route; (b) workers within a cell, concerned with a complete set of operations, tend to develop a greater sense of ownership, there is recognition of the need for flexibility and interchange, and a heightened concern for quality.

In early 1994 cell arrangements were successfully pilot-tested and then introduced more extensively in the middle of the year. There are basically four cells which range in size from 80 to 15 employees. The cell groups consist of a cell manager, to whom all operators and fitters report directly; a packaging technologist and a quality assessment section manager with dotted line responsibility to the cell manager but a direct line responsibility to the quality assurance (QA) director. However, the cell structure arrangements have had to be modified in the light of a decision by the medicine inspectors (Medicines Control Agency). The inspectors are generally unhappy with cell manufacturing arrangements in the pharmaceuticals industry because the reportage arrangements run to line management; the traditional arrangements involved quality assurance as an independent staff function. The concern seems to be that line managers are likely to respond more strongly to production volume pressures than to quality considerations, and that if there is not an independent quality assurance function the pharmaceutical standards may be jeopardized. As a consequence, Bayer Diagnostics have recently removed the technicians from the cells.

Some further initiatives and developments are being contemplated and discussed at Bayer. For example, a profit-related pay scheme is likely to be introduced in 1995, and the Bayer group as a whole is committed to going down the competencies route. In another Bayer plant discussions are under way to try to identify a range of key competencies (such as customer service, personal development) but at this stage the Bridgend plant is not involved. There may, however, be some need for review of the skill grids at Bridgend to allow for inclusion of a competencies dimension. This and the implications of competencies for management are likely to be items for the agenda of the future.

The Outcomes of the Change Programe

It is obviously difficult to make a final judgement about the programme at this stage because it is still on-going, but there are evident signs of a significant turnaround in performance. Turnover for 1993 increased by over 20 per cent, resulting in a pre-tax operating profit

Table 21.1   Bayer Diagnostics: diagnostic product line statistics, 1989–94

	1989 (actual)	1991 (actual)	1994 forecast (including US volume)
Total manufacturing volume ($£$'000s)	6,940	9,253	22,065
Manufacturing overheads ($£$'000s)	3,195	3,561	4,290
Headcount (allocated to diagnostics)			
(a) Total labour	162.8	120.2	169.0
(b) Direct labour	61.0	53.0	90.0
(c) Indirect labour	101.8	67.2	79.0
Productivity			
(a) Units (i.e. bottles)/direct	114	175	245
(b) Units (i.e. bottles)/indirect	69	138	279

of $£$5–6 million. (See table 21.1 for a more complete set of performance indicators which bear out the improved performance overall.)

In the same year, further investment was made to upgrade physical
facilities, and a number of new product lines were pilot-tested and
introduced. Two other changes in an ever-changing environment
deserve to be noted. One is that the role of the personnel function has
changed. We noted earlier that before the change it was a characteristic
'regulator', but (in Storey's classification) it has now moved nearer to
an 'adviser' role. This is seen as non-interventionary but more strategic, in the sense that the smooth running of operations and personnel
issues is increasingly the responsibility of line and general managers,
but the service-advisory function is related to helping set the 'tone' for
the new labour–management interface, and for providing the support
in terms of training and management development to enable the successive changes to be implemented. This kind of approach, too, seems
to be consistent with the consolidation of ownership feeling among
those centrally affected without the interposition of the personnel function as a go-between. Personnel now has a more constructive role.

The second point is related to a growing concern that the abolition
of clocking on/off arrangements and the development of self-directed
work teams (arising out of the multi-skilled programme) has involved
some loss of a sense of urgency on the shop floor. In the Bayer
Diagnostics context of largely self-managed teams, the evidence indicates to management that where an individual deviates sharply from
normal practice (by taking excessive breaks or cutting hours of work)

peer group pressure has been an effective force of control. However, it may be that the self-directed ethos and the absence of supervision leads to a marginal shading off of individual effort, the cumulative effect of which may be significant. In a sense the organizational slack or 'X-inefficiency' which effective supervision can control may be more difficult to handle under self-management. The concern is that production and scheduling deadlines could be put at risk by individuals who take advantage of the trust shown by the company in relation to breaks and hours of work.

The problem now being recognized at Bayer Diagnostics is that it is hard to determine whose problem this is and how it can be resolved. If management intervenes to restore a degree of hierarchical control, that will run counter to the ethos which the change programme has sought to build up. But because the individual contribution to slack is marginal it may be difficult for the work group to monitor that slack or to tighten the norms of working practice. This matter is arguably an example of what Lawler (1982: 302) has described as (in management's eyes) participation shading over into permissiveness. The plant director has sought to handle the problem personally. He has discussed the issue extensively in cell meetings and has achieved some success, which was due to be reinforced by his presentation of an end-of-year review to small groups (December 1994). Success in this was considered vital to the introduction of new product lines in 1995, an important step in the fulfilment of the strategy of broadening the product base.

Conclusions

There are many useful lessons in this account of a continuing change process which appears on the evidence of the performance indicators to be going ahead successfully, though not without problems on the way. This reflects the reality of change, which will seldom be smooth and free from conflict. The determinants of success are the extent to which challenges to the process can be foreseen and countered, and whether the conflicts can be handled.

In the Bayer Diagnostics case, the disadvantages of the top-down model of change seem to have been neutralized, not by compromise on the part of the new PD, who was clear about the vision and the objectives, but by the use of the Works Committee as the crucible in which design features could be worked out and approved, and which, in the later stages, became part of the communication medium for the process itself. This appears to have controlled some of the conflicts which a 'political' model of change would lead us to expect, and of which there are clear symptoms here. The main form this took was the craft versus production tension, as a result of the threat to the craftsmen's position; but there was also some tension on the part of the lab-based workers (MSF members) who had a 'professional' concern that the notion of product quality would be endangered by the loss of supervision – and the quality ethos was strong among the lab-based personnel.

But secondly, there was also a receptivity factor which played its part. The credibility of the vision was given weight by the previous experience of the PD in a similar context. The ability to win over the support of the TGWU to the programme by providing a means to greater employee involvement in decisions and planning (which the union had been pressing for) was undoubtedly important also. The responsiveness of the TGWU to the change vision gave a positive drive to change which neutralized the initial resistance of the AEEU and (to a much lesser extent) the MSF. And the threat of closure may also have acted as a trigger to generate a more positive response.

From the HR perspective, the key point is the underpinning of the change programme by a recognition of the value of the organization's human resources, which needed to be given greater responsibility if they were to develop greater commitment to organizational goals. This was already clear in the PD's initial vision, but the process itself involved a transfer of ownership to the management and workforce representatives and led on to greater involvement as the phases of change proceeded. This appears to have been effective in overcoming the points of resistance from those key groups who saw their status, their pay relativity or their organizational authority in danger of being undermined.

Again, the programme of change also brought about significant shifts in the responsibility of line management, who were increasingly involved directly in the interface with the shop floor, and also in the role of personnel and IR management which, as we have seen, found its firefighting intermediary role converted into a more strategic, supportive and service role. It was not, however, the 'change-maker' – that role was enacted by the PD and the Works Committee.

Lastly, as we have noted, the process of change has to deal with the unexpected as well as the problems that can be foreseen (for example, the internal resistance in key areas). Thus the requirements of the pharmaceutical standards agency forced a modification of the cell structure. And the development of a degree of organizational slack in the context of self-directed teams has posed another problem which has still to be fully resolved. But these problems aside, the case represents an interesting example of successful change producing tangible results. The plant has survived the initial threat to its continued existence, and building on this it has attracted trial batches of new product lines to the plant. These have been produced more quickly and efficiently under the new production arrangements than in sister plants, and as a result Bridgend has consolidated on a broader product base, including a new generation of products with strong market prospects. This seems likely to stabilize the plant's position within the corporate enterprise and enhance its longer-term competitiveness with other plants in the Bayer organization.

Note

1   This organization was one of the case studies featured in ACAS (Wales), *Best Practice in Industrial Relations* (1994). This ACAS report did not involve the present authors and it deals with different features of the company.

References

Beer, M., Eisenstat, R.A. and Spector, B. 1990: Why change programs don't produce change. *Harvard Business Review*, Nov.–Dec.: 158–66.

Cappelli, P. and Rogovsky, N. 1994: New work systems and skill requirements. *International Labour Review*, 133(2): 205–20.

Hendry, C., Pettigrew, A. and Sparrow, P. 1988: Changing patterns of human resource management. *Personnel Management*, November 37–41.

Lawler, E. 1982: Increasing worker involvement to enhance organizational effectiveness. In P.S. Goodman (ed.), *Change in Organizations*, San Francisco, Cal.: Jossey Bass.

McGregor, D. 1960: *The Human Side of Enterprise*. New York: McGraw Hill.

Morgan, G. 1986: *Images of Organisations*. London: Sage.

Pettigrew, A., Ferlie, E. and McKee, L. 1992: *Shaping Strategic Change*. London: Sage.

Storey, J. 1992: *Developments in the Management of Human Resources*. Oxford: Blackwell.

Thomas, R.J. 1992: Organizational change and decision making about new technology. In T. Kochan and M. Useem (eds), *Transforming Organizations*, London: Oxford University Press.

Walton, R.E. and McKersie, R.B. 1965: *A Behavioral Theory of Labor Negotiations*. New York: McGraw Hill.

22

Commitment and Conflict: Worker Resistance to HRM in the Microelectronics Industry

ALAN MCKINLAY AND PHIL TAYLOR

Introduction

Critical studies of the impact of human resource management (HRM) techniques have been hampered by a lack of longitudinal empirical research. With few exceptions, existing studies of worker reactions to HRM are snapshots, report *managerial* perceptions of changes in employee commitment, or are based on extremely limited qualitative research (Scott 1994). Our analysis is based on the experience of a greenfield microelectronics plant – Pyramid – which commenced production at its new factory in 1992, in the booming global cellular phone market. The Pyramid plant is owned by an American multinational – PhoneCo – which has deliberately encouraged a high degree of experimentation in work organization and labour regulation. The cornerstone of the corporation's unitarist ideology is individual commitment to personal growth and collective pursuit of total quality. But we shall argue that the apparent liberal humanism of the corporate mission statement is derived from a reading of the demands of a business which straddles high-technology and mass consumer electronics. In the final analysis, innovatory personnel policies are seen by PhoneCo as an essential precondition for securing competitive advantage in a growing but highly competitive and fragmented global market. Interestingly, PhoneCo's experimental approach to teamworking at Pyramid was not one which was shared by the company's practices in the USA, where more traditional methods prevailed, so that developments at Pyramid in Scotland must be seen as an innovatory departure from core company policy and culture.

Three complementary methodologies were used to chart the development of the greenfield plant: extensive interviews with managers and shopfloor employees; participant observation; and four surveys of employee attitudes to work, supervision and teamworking over a three-year period. A series of face-to-face interviews were conducted with key corporate, divisional and operational managers at critical moments in the plant's development. Extensive interviews were also conducted with shopfloor employees. Participant observation involved both researchers going through the standard induction process for new employees and daily contact with two production teams. Finally, we administered four surveys which included, for instance, standard questions on commitment, pace of work and attitudes towards specific innovatory personnel practices. This combination of methodologies allowed us to construct an intimate record of the *process* of change rather than a series of static snapshots of work experience.

The chapter is in four sections. The first reinforces criticism of some of the major assumptions underlying sympathetic expositions of human resource management. Further, it makes a brief reassessment of studies which have emphasized the coercive and authoritarian (as opposed to 'empowering') realities of HRM regimes. The second section reviews the dynamics of discipline within the team-based organization and culture. This is followed by an examination of peer review, a formal process designed to force workers to rate each other's work performance and adherence to PhoneCo's cultural norms. In particular, we lay stress upon workers' resistance to the peer review process. Finally, we examine management's attempts to revive a peer review process whose original version had been fatally wounded by passive and active worker opposition.

Human Resource Management: Empowerment or Surveillance?

Much of the literature associated with human resource management has utilized a powerful rhetoric of unitarism. Within regimes characterized by flatter managerial hierarchies, stress is placed upon the existence of common goals and shared objectives between employees and managers. The assumption is that teamworking leads to increases in responsibility, decision-making and, ultimately, trust in the ranks of workers previously habituated to following top-down directives and performing routinized, deskilled tasks. 'Empowerment' was and remains the managerial buzz word most associated with what has been perceived as a transformation in the experience of workers at the point of production. Underlying the bulk of prescriptive HRM texts is an assumption that what has been wrought are changes which are enriching and liberating for the individual worker. A classic early statement is that by Richard Walton:

> Under the commitment strategy, performance expectations are high and serve not to define minimum standards but to provide 'stretch objectives', emphasise continuous improvement, and reflect the requirements of the marketplace. Accordingly, compensation policies reflect less the old formulas of job evaluation than the heightened importance of group achievement, the expanded scope of individual contribution . . .   (Walton 1985: 77)

There is thus no contradiction between the successful pursuit of profit and the job satisfaction of employees at all levels.

This highly optimistic, if not idealistic, reading has been challenged by a minority of critical authors whose ranks include Sewell and Wilkinson (1992a, 1992b, 1993) and Delbridge et al. (1992). Their studies have led them to see 'empowerment and trust as rhetoric and the centralization of power and control as the reality' (Sewell and Wilkinson 1992b: 102). Collectively their writings describe an antithetical experience of HRM in which disciplinary mechanisms based on the surveillance and control capacities of quality monitoring systems are dominant.

These writers draw theoretical sustenance from Foucault's extended metaphor of the panopticon. In *Discipline and Punish* (1977), Foucault conceptualizes Jeremy Bentham's plans for a prison in which isolated individuals would never know if they were being scrutinized from a central observatory. Crucially, the carcereal gaze is based upon one-way visibility which objectifies the individuals under scrutiny. The gaoler peering through the 'judas hole' is simultaneously exercising power *and* consolidating a knowledge base of what constitutes normal or acceptable behaviour. In this way, power and knowledge are mutually reinforcing. For these writers Foucault's panopticon is clearly a seductive metaphor.

Developing Foucault's discussion of the architectural panopticon as a metaphor for surveillance, they argue that computer-based monitoring makes for near-total systems of observation and control. What exists is 'an Electronic Panopticon, where a disembodied eye can overcome the constraints of architecture and space to bring its disciplinary gaze to bear at the very heart of the labour process' (Sewell and Wilkinson 1992a: 283). The 'constant scrutiny of a Panoptic gaze which penetrates to the very core of each member's subjectivity' (ibid.: 284) ensures that team members, undergoing peer pressure, themselves carry out the necessary disciplinary functions.

Much of this body of writing has, in its successful exposure of the realities of work intensification, tight discipline and strict monitoring, proved a valuable corrective to earlier, glowing accounts of HRM. However, despite this significant contribution, we contend that versions of the argument tend to a one-sidedness. In effect, this critical research is simply the obverse of the Utopian capitalism of HRM, an image of emerging factory regimes in which workers lose even the awareness of their own self-exploitation. We agree with Sewell and Wilkinson that one of the *aims* of total quality management (TQM) is 'Total Management Control', but we disagree with the extent to which even the most powerful and sophisticated surveillance system achieves near-total control in the workplace. To ignore or underestimate the possibilities of workers' resistance to these forms of control is to neglect a contradiction at the core of teamworking: the concept of self-managed teams is premised on opening up an unmanaged social space for worker activity, not passivity.

In their study of an electronics plant in South Wales, Sewell and Wilkinson go so far as to suggest 'a seemingly unquestioning acceptance' (1992b: 110) of the operation of a particularly oppressive surveillance system by workers. The picture is rather Orwellian, with workers conscious of the scope of the scrutiny but incapable of challenging this ubiquitous 'carceral gaze'. Even the authors of this bleak scenario concede that, however unlikely worker resistance is in practice, it remains a theoretical possibility (Delbridge et al. 1992: 105).

Our main contention is that, no matter how advantageous the circumstances for management to erect a system of surveillance, peer review and self-discipline within a team structure, worker resistance remains a daily reality. Admittedly, it can operate at differing levels of consciousness, effectiveness and strength across a workplace and over time. From our research, it would be a serious mistake to see management as possessing a free hand in implementing and developing forms of control. Even low levels of worker resistance can modify managerial behaviour and create currents of opposition to those most seductive of company cultures which embrace the most powerful rhetoric of empowerment.

PhoneCo: the Power of Teams?

For PhoneCo, the cellular phone market epitomized the conflicting pressures of intense price competition within a fragmented marketplace. The harmonization of cellular networks across Europe and their rapid introduction in developing economies such as China resulted in an explosive growth in demand for portable phones from the late 1980s. In the Western economies, the shift from luxury to mass market was paralleled, moreover, by rapid product innovation and the continuing fragmentation of demand, by functionality and design. Equally, the market rapidly became fiercely price competitive with the entrance of global players in microelectronics, notably NEC and Sony. In the five years from 1990 to 1994, prices have tumbled by between 20–25 per cent per year. If PhoneCo's decision to open a new plant to service non-American markets reflected buoyant global demand, then its choice of work organization reflected intensifying cost and customization pressures. In contrast to its conventionally organized American sister plant, the new Pyramid plant was to test the viability of teamworking rather than hierarchy, of commitment rather than control. The importance of the new plant's output for PhoneCo's global strategy and its novel organization ensured that Pyramid's performance was closely monitored by corporate headquarters. Pyramid was attempting to go far beyond PhoneCo's existing employee involvement initiatives in its American plants (Lawler 1986).

PhoneCo was one of a number of leading American microelectronics multinationals which located in Scotland's 'Silicon Glen' between 1965 and 1975. The description 'Silicon Glen' conjures up images of both the Highlands of Scotland and California's 'Silicon Valley'. In both senses its usage is misleading since, in reality, 'Silicon Glen' amounts to the dispersed location of these companies within the central industrial belt of Scotland which occurred, in part, as a result of policies designed to counteract the decline in the traditional industrial base.

American multinationals in the sector have consistently prohibited trade union organization (Findlay 1993). PhoneCo's 'direct dealing' policy places an absolute priority on the psychological, as well as the legal, contract between the *individual* and the corporation, to the exclusion of trade unions. In its rigorous selection process to search for clusters of psychological types to form production teams, flat organizational structure and application of HRM techniques, phoneCo is atypical of electronics plants in Scotland. Innovation in process technologies or the social organization of production is confined to American-owned electronics plants rather than characteristic of the sector as a whole (Findlay 1990: 213–16). Even within this group new production concepts such as just-in-time (JIT) and innovatory HRM practices were only gradually introduced through the 1980s (Webb and Dawson 1991: 194). The trigger for changes in patterns of labour regulation was market fragmentation and increased price competition. A central objective behind the introduction of JIT, total quality management and problem-solving workgroups was to increase plant responsiveness and efficiency. But step gains in productivity did not necessarily result in work intensification. Indeed, by producing only to order and not for stock, such firms freed time for workgroups to work on quality or process improvements (Dawson and Webb 1989: 233). This reorientation towards work organization constituted a radical change in labour regulation. The autonomy and creativity of the worker is no longer an obstacle to the enterprise's success to be cowed – as in Taylorism – but 'a central economic resource' to be mobilized (Miller and Rose 1990: 26).

The assumption by workgroups of technical and co-ordinative roles normally confined to management fundamentally altered the nature of authority on the shop floor. Managerial authority is derived from interpersonal skills and technical competence rather than office or hierarchy. But if the authority of the individual manager was opened up to scrutiny from below through employee involvement, then managerial power *per se* became more opaque. By dispersing the functions of management, efficiency, flexibility and quality were suffused as the rationality of the organization as a whole rather than the prerogative of specific functionaries (Cressey et al. 1985: 53–4). The authority of the individual manager becomes more personalized and contingent as the factory's power structure becomes more anonymous and unquestioned. Organizationally, PhoneCo's Pyramid plant was to extend these trends towards dispersed control: the social processes of teamworking were to be continuously monitored, evaluated and engineered.

Prospective managers, immersed in an intensive induction process, were impressed with the need to perform in ways that were radically different to traditional roles. Managers were, above all, facilitators who in developing self-directed teams were expected to 'step back and allow teams to manage day-to-day activities'. Guarding against haste and unrealizable expectations, managers were reminded: 'This is a long-term process . . . [which] requires patience, understanding and support' (PhoneCo Internal Training Document 1990, no. 06069-019). More important than any lessons drawn from the parent corporation or from previous managerial experience was a year-long period of experimentation in a small pilot plant – Stewartfield – employing approximately 100 workers whilst the new facility was under construction. The pilot plant concentrated on a single product using well-established technology to minimize technical uncertainty. Production schedules were secondary to the process of social experimentation. Technological, product and marketing choices were selected so as to focus managerial and employee attention on the social dynamics of production. No external or corporate consultants were hired to provide blueprints. Rather, the implicit assumption was that Stewartfield would yield an organic organizational strategy deeply embedded in managerial and employee experience, and that this intense socialization would form a bedrock of collective commitment for the new, much larger facility. Self-managing teams encompassed a range of productive and organizational functions. Each month every team member was required to assume one of a number of rotating co-ordinating roles: component supplies, liaison with other teams, holiday rotas. Teams were allocated a range of support staff – personnel, technical and facilitative. Such 'staff associates' were to have no authority within the teams, and their roles were designed to be supportive rather than directive.

At the outset, management anticipated that the Stewartfield workforce would play a pivotal role in the new Pyramid plant scheduled to employ 2,000 within two years of opening. The Stewartfield workers were to act as the bearers of the teamworking culture, spearheading the diffusion of behavioural norms in the new plant. In practice, however, the employees socialized into the team culture of Stewartfield played an ambiguous role in extending the principles of teambuilding. Such workers found themselves juggling unfamiliar responsibilities for vetting potential new recruits, training new starts, and ensuring that the teamworking culture was not diluted by the flood of new arrivals. The hiring and training roles, coupled with their knowledge of the principles of the teamworking culture, consolidated the informal authority exercised by Stewartfield veterans on the assembly lines. Pyramid expanded from a single production line to 14 in under two years. Against a background of constantly expanding production targets and chronic material shortages the teams were forced to improvise, shifting between work stations in an attempt to compensate for successive droughts and surges in components. In the context of bearing great responsibilities in a rapidly changing workplace, the Stewartfield cohort found their first months insider Pyramid immensely stressful. One influential worker, a member of the original Stewartfield cohort, expressed the sentiments of many:

You can't stop thinking about your job. The tension comes from the pressure they put on you, the obligation you feel about what you are doing. I remember when the machine broke down one time and the Factory Manager said, 'It's up to you to fix it.' The onus is on you to run things as a team . . . when it suits them.   (Interview with Elsa, line worker, 16 February 1993)

From being the bearers of a managerially sanctioned team ideology, a significant minority of Stewartfield veterans increasingly conceived of themselves as guardians of a set of norms which they had played an active role in creating. Paradoxically, the diffusion of the teamworking culture in Pyramid assumed a defensive quality in which workers resented any deviation from the practice of collective decision-making established in Stewartfield. Any team member or manager whose actions crossed the line separating facilitative from directive behaviour was openly criticized. The Stewartfield veterans articulated a vision of the 'factory of the future' in which teamworking always took precedence over production norms and targets. For one exasperated manager this friction was based on experienced employees 'making the mistake of thinking PhoneCo is a team-driven organisation. It's not: it's a *business*-driven organisation' (interview, HR development manager, November 1993).

At Stewartfield managers had been deeply impressed by the tight discipline maintained by the teams. Indeed, for management the success of self-policing absenteeism, time-keeping and less-tangible 'cultural' indices of team-building reaffirmed their belief that flexible volume production was best 'managed through culture not structure' (interview, HR director, May 1992). That a visiting corporate executive was upbraided by a line worker for breaking an elementary safety rule or that an absent worker was confronted by his fellow team-members symbolized the potency of team-based control. In Pyramid, however, the lack of clear factory-wide rules quickly led to wide variations in disciplinary actions in different teams. The fast-changing composition of the teams highlighted the differing propensities of teams to take 'corrective action' against individuals. 'Corrective action' was the generic term for any sanction imposed by a team to improve an individual's performance or as punishment for an infraction of quality, efficiency or behavioural standards. The Pyramid teams varied widely in their interpretation of the broadly defined behavioural standards laid down by PhoneCo. The 'corrective action' imposed for absenteeism without alerting the team ranged from a mild rebuke at a team meeting to a suspension of overtime for three weeks.

Discipline was rapidly perceived as *ad hoc*, arbitrary and distorted by personality clashes. A further complication was added by management's decision to hire temporary workers rather than relax their stringent recruitment procedure. The use of temporary workers was always regarded as a temporary expedient – 'a necessary evil' – rather than the creation of a permanent layer of 'peripheral' workers (interview, production manager, May 1993). Temporary workers were excluded from the internal decision-making processes of the teams and restricted to the most deskilled tasks on the line. Control of temporary workers rested with permanent members of PhoneCo teams. Experienced employees were gate-keepers in the company's recruitment process. After successfully negotiating psychometric and dexterity tests, prospective employees were interviewed by a representative of the team they would join. At this stage, the team delegate could veto the appointment of an applicant. In the case of temporary workers, the teams played an even more important role. Temporary workers could apply to become permanent employees. However, they still had to go through the full selection process, irrespective of their length of service on the line. More than this, to fail any stage of the recruitment process was to have one's contract immediately terminated, with no right of appeal. Temporary workers were, therefore, in an extremely vulnerable position. Divisions emerged among the group of Stewartfield veterans over the treatment of temporary workers. On one hand stood a minority who enforced extraordinarily tight discipline on temporary workers and gained a reputation for rejecting all but a few applicants for permanent employment. On the other hand was the majority of experienced employees, who considered such draconian discipline a breach of the teamworking ethos by individuals determined to bring themselves to the attention of management. In these circumstances, the majority of permanent workers became increasingly protective towards temporary workers. For management, the net result was that fewer temporary workers applied for permanent status while the teams became indiscriminate in their support of transfer applications.

The result of this complex process was that the teams gradually withdrew from their disciplinary role. Even where easily remedied flaws in routine tasks caused frustrating disruptions to work flows and the teams maintained the façade of peer review, this did not mean that effective 'corrective actions' were imposed. One line worker explained that the lack of basic discipline was damaging efficiency and corrosive of personal relations within his team: 'You'd just be getting in to the swing of production and – bang! – you'd discover two or three wrong spools [of components had been loaded]. The team would meet and "Willie" would promise not to do it again. But next week it was the same story' (interview, line worker, April 1994). At the same time a wide layer of workers became increasingly reluctant to exercise *any* form of corrective action as team decision-making became subordinated to the compulsion to deliver production targets.

In turn, this compelled shopfloor managers to intervene to enforce discipline. Inevitably, such interventions drew heavy criticism from the teams as yet another sign of the emergence of traditional managerialism. Within the first year of Pyramid's existence, both management and workforce were confronted with the disintegration of the original conception of a team-based organization.

Team-based work organization and an empowerment ideology does not eliminate the control imperative from the workplace. Nor does it necessarily smother worker dissent and resistance. Rather, even in this non-union environment, opposition, particularly for those workers steeped in the original teamworking vision, was articulated *through* the empowerment ideology. Equally, the disciplinary purpose of team-based organization can be deflected, moderated or completely thwarted by a tacit campaign of non-co-operation by the workforce. Even this mildest form of protest posed serious questions for a work regime whose whole rationale was not just to manufacture consent but to sustain the positive commitment of the workforce.

Resistance to Peer Review

Kenney and Florida (1993: 27–8) argue that peer review is perhaps 'the most important element of social control in the Japanese transplants [in the USA] because it does not involve a direct confrontation between management and labour'. Teams and peer pressure act both as the first disciplinary line and as a conduit for informing management.

Peer review was pioneered in microelectronics by Digital and Motorola (Katzenbach and Smith 1993: 187). Even in these corporations, however, peer review had been introduced in only a few locations and in a highly circumscribed fashion (Hodson and Hagan 1988: 121). Beyond noting a general – and durable – dissatisfaction with peer review, particularly in terms of annual wage adjustment, no study has yet examined the dynamics of the process in detail (Buchanan and McCalman 1989: 165).

For PhoneCo management, the success of peer review was the key to gauging the embeddedness of the team culture. Peer review had a dual purpose: to provide managerial knowledge *and* to provide a forum for the teams to reflect individually and collectively on the teambuilding process. It is difficult to exaggerate the importance management attributed to understanding the dynamics of team development through constant monitoring of 'the subjective process at work through the Peer Review process' (PhoneCo, *Corporate HR Manual*, 1994).

Peer review was conceived as the critical arena of the disciplinary process within the production teams. This involved each team member rating every other member on ten dimensions of individual behaviour and attitudes, ranging from behaviour which indicated their assimilation of the teamworking culture to assessments of an individual's conscientiousness and readiness to pioneer innovations in work organization. To 'be a good team member' is defined thus:

> Is a good listener, cares about team's purpose and goals, builds friendships in team, generous towards other team members, sees the factory as one big team, assists other team members, cares for and helps team members when unwell or has a problem, co-ordinates team towards targets, takes on team roles enthusiastically, works well with others. (*Definition of Behaviours*, internal document, May 1993)

Other definitions captured a tension at the heart of the peer review process. To 'show a positive attitude' involved not just encouraging other individuals and the team as an entity; each individual was also asked to assess each other's readiness to encourage *and* criticize. In other words, peer review was conceived as a microscopic disciplinary process which would lay bare individual and collective shortcomings in team development. Indeed, management made a direct link between the effectiveness of peer review as a disciplinary practice and corporate competitiveness:

> The rating placed on anyone's contribution is important. However, what is more important is the prior discussion of the views of the team, the agreement on the ratings, the recognition of effort and the carrying out of corrective actions. These are essential in order to improve performance and ensure we develop to be world class. (*Using the Peer Review Rating Scale*, internal document, June 1993)

Peer review was seen by management as a continuous process of self-assessment and improvement. It was not an adjunct to teambuilding but was, rather, integral to it. Although in the final analysis the ultimate purpose of peer review was to facilitate the development of mature teams capable of fulfilling the requirements of quality production, the peer review meetings were to be insulated from the demands of production. Meetings were not to be contaminated with discussion of output targets. The ideal was to hold monthly meetings at which the relative scores of all permanent team members would be displayed on graphs and subjected to extensive discussion. The monthly meeting was the formal and symbolic expression of the constant and collective nature of discipline within the workgroup. In itself, this open forum at which detailed comparisons of three individuals' performances were the sole topic was the first level of corrective action. Simply exposing weaknesses in individual performance to collective scrutiny was intended to increase the team member's motivation to comply with expected behaviour and norms. The monthly peer review meeting was not only the moment at which internal tensions were to be dispersed and the team ideology reinforced, but also when disciplinary issues were explicitly confronted by the team. This was the opportunity to exercise collective discipline over individuals with, for instance, poor time-keeping records or suspect attitudes towards co-operation.

Successive surveys of the PhoneCo workforce revealed a deep and pervasive distrust of peer review. In our first survey, two-thirds of the respondents affirmed that they understood peer review's objectives but at the same time they were critical of it in practice. Fewer than 20 per cent of respondents favoured assessing – or being assessed by – their co-workers. Indeed, the workforce's attitudes were the exact opposite of management's intention: it drained individual and team confidence, was an intimidating experience, created or sharpened tensions in the teams, and, most of all, workers intensely disliked reviewing their team-mates. Broadly speaking, the level of antipathy to peer review was greatest among those with an employment history outside microelectronics and those who had previous membership of a trade union. For all categories, however, the distrust of peer review hardened over time and the most profound opposition was displayed by the longest-serving employees.

As production pressures intensified and team meetings increasingly concentrated on issuing top-down instructions and exhortation to the virtual exclusion of team development, the culture, practices and norms nurtured in the days of Stewartfield and during the early days of Pyramid were seriously undermined. Physical constraints became more apparent as the workforce expanded. Team meetings grew ever more chaotic, as around 40 people struggled to hear, let alone participate in, the proceedings. Even the formalities of peer review slowly collapsed under the strain. In those teams in which peer review continued, it proved an incredibly divisive practice, often embittering personal relationships. The erosion of peer review forced management to intervene in an attempt at revival. In doing so they succeeded only in deepening the level of opposition. One experienced line worker recounted:

> Kathleen [management facilitator] said to us that we were the only team that didn't like peer review. I know for a fact that's not true. Nobody likes them. She's always trying to get us to argue with each other. She even says we should take notes on each other. Imagine that. You're sitting there, doing your work and you're keeping notes on somebody which you then bring to the meeting. Two of them were doing it yesterday. Idiots! You work as a team but they try to split you off when it comes to these reviews.   (Interview with Martha, line worker, 21 January 1993)

Retaliatory scoring, marking down someone who had scored you low in the previous month, was not uncommon. This was often almost a counterdisciplinary form of action where the enthusiastic low marker would be taught a lesson by others. 'There was one time when Jackie went on a course to teach you about peer review. He came back knowing what peer review was all about and started giving people 1s and 2s and being more critical. But after a while he settled back into giving people 3s and 4s, (Jim C., line worker, 9 February 1993).

Individuals trying to maintain the managerial intention of peer review were well aware of the prevalence and potency of retaliatory scoring. One line worker noted in the summer of 1993: 'The peer review is not something I like because when I make the reviews I am very honest about it and that sometimes does not go down too well – it puts you on the spot rather than the person you have reviewed' (Questionnaire 2/43).

This practice of tacitly trading monthly scores, negating the discriminartory intent of the system, became quite widespread throughout Pyramid. It was a commonplace to hear workers saying that to keep things 'fair' they gave each other 3s and 4s. Workers were subverting the individualization that lay at the heart of peer review. Appropriating the rhetoric of collectivism that accompanied teamworking, workers engendered forms of real collective activity on their own terms in response to what they felt was an unfair and discriminatory process.

Our surveys showed that workers drawn from outside the micro-electronics sector were particularly hostile to peer review and quickly learnt to subvert its surveillance objective. In addition, the most-experienced workers in Pyramid were responsible for spreading oppositional practices throughout the plant as established teams were broken up to form the basis of new lines: equalized scoring became the norm among all categories of employees. Ironically, the subversion of peer review was justified through an identification with Pyramid's team-based culture. That is, if teams were meeting their output and quality targets then it was widely considered unfair for any individual team-member to receive a negative peer review. This shift in employee opinion was paralleled by a deterioration in the formal disciplinary processes of the teams. While informal pressures continued to be applied to any recalcitrant team member, it was rare for individuals to be exposed to the full glare of peer review.

Both responses to peer review undermined its dual purpose of team development and discipline. The most obvious instances of tit-for-tat scoring simply led to a corrosion of morale and bad feeling within the teams. Collectivized score trading struck at the heart of the process, rendering peer review a formalistic routine in the minority of teams where it still took place on a regular basis.

Managerial facilitators were acutely aware that the disciplinary content of peer review was being collectively exorcised by the workgroups but were powerless to reverse the trend. Opposition to peer review involved a complex series of responses by individuals and teams. The strength of opposition varied across a spectrum of responses, ranging from individual jokes and moans at one extreme to quite hard, persistent and collective resistance at team level at the other. Limitations to opposition did, of course, exist. As has been noted, opposition was often expressed *through* the company culture and, given the absence of any representative body amongst the workers in the form of trade union or works council, there was no mechanism for articulating overt opposition. Hostility was clandestine but effective. At the same time, hostility to peer review coexisted with widespread, if not unqualified, endorsement of the principle of teamwork and the rotation of secondary jobs, co-ordinative roles normally performed by front-line management.

The immobilization of the peer review process forced management to revamp the system towards the end of 1993. Peer review was not to be abandoned but continued in a different form. The first step involved the rationalization of the workers' annual pay review. The collapse of the existing peer review process had left management with no mechanism to rank workers' performance. Confronted with this vacuum in their knowledge, management considered that they had little option but to classify the workforce arbitrarily into five bands, each receiving a fixed percentage rise ranging from zero to 8 per cent.

The announcement of the individual bands created a reaction amongst workers which dwarfed any previous opposition to peer review. The most extreme reaction came from one line which halted work completely for a shift. Throughout the day, workers congregated in small groups and, when asked, told anxious plant managers that they were considering production issues. This silent strike was followed by what the workers involved called a three-week 'go-slow' (interview, line worker, January 1994).

The following comment is typical of the workers' reaction during the early days of 1994:

> The way they've given out the bands is dividing people up. You ought to have seen the arguments between people after they gave out the bands. 'Why did you get that and I only got that?' As far as I can see that's it, there's nothing left of the teams. They don't decide anything any more and they're putting worker against worker. It's alright for the bosses. They just sit there and play people off against each other. On this shift it's different because we've decided to take them on together. (Interview with Vera, line worker, 14 January 1994)

That there would be dissatisfaction at a grading exercise which identified only 10 per cent of workers as Band A was entirely predictable. The extent of dissatisfaction, however, was staggering: more than two-thirds of the permanent workforce lodged a complaint about their grading. For the core workers who had been socialized into the PhoneCo culture in Stewartfield – 'the elect' – the grading awards simply confirmed the profound shift away from the original team culture (Geary 1992: 48). On the shop floor the consensus was that the gradings were arbitrary and reflected the ill-informed judgements of inexperienced line leaders rather than the continuous and, above all, transparent appraisal promised through peer review.

The grading process was widely criticized as arbitrary, ill-informed and divisive: the death-knell of the team culture:

> I'm part of this team and we are always hitting our targets. My attendance has been good, my time-keeping is good. I've got a secondary job and I got a C. So I'm appealing. He [points to another 'loyal' worker] got an A. What do you expect? There are people on the line who have got worse attendance than me, who don't do a secondary job and they got B's. That's not fair. (Interview with Lynn, line worker, 18 January 1994)

For management, a prime virtue of the peer review process was its transparency. There would be no surprise gradings: workers would be constantly informed of their colleagues' opinion of their performance and conformance to PhoneCo culture. Line leaders usurped the team's disciplinary purpose and compromised the internal transparency of the team-based reward system. A B-graded assembler who was satisfied with her award explained that her secondary jobs increased her visibility: 'Take me. I get a B because I do secondary jobs and the bosses can see me doing them. That takes me off the line. The girls who replace me got a D and an E. That's not right at all' R (interview, line worker, January 1994).

The link between worker visibility and grading also systematically discriminated against 'back-end' workers who were quite literally invisible to management. Similarly, the vital training roles routinely assumed by Stewartfield veterans kept them on the line, and this was widely perceived as a main reason for their disappointing gradings.

One line worker summed up the cultural change that many of the older cadre of workers felt was responsible for their marginalization:

> What they've managed to do is seriously demotivate a lot of people. I've got no incentive to work hard any more . . . What's annoyed me is some of the people who have been given the good scores. They are the ones who are in and out of the office with tittle tattle . . . But many of us who got ordinary marks have been here for a bit and we know how to do our job. So we get on with it and we do it well. So they never hear us or see us in the office. Because of this I would say there has been a lot of people who have been given a slap in the face.   (Interview with Andrea, line worker, 20 January 1994)

Reviewing Peer Review

Even before the pay award fiasco, management was acutely aware that peer review had fallen into abeyance, but, given the centrality of peer review, there was no way that it could simply be scrapped. Rather, management redesigned peer review around a rating process which forced employees to discriminate between their fellow team-members. A major failing of the original system was that management had no systematic knowledge of its collapse under the weight of production pressures or subversion by reciprocal scoring within teams. The depth of opposition to the pay award was a watershed moment, precipitating managerial strategy. Peer reviews became quarterly rather than monthly events, compulsory rather than voluntary, and team scoring was automated to permit management to monitor its implementation and minimize the opportunities for retrospective manipulation of scores. In essence, the new rating system was designed to prevent team members tacitly trading scores. Each employee, under the new system, is given a fixed quota of points to allocate between her or his team members. The individual's score is multiplied by a factor allocated by management to reflect overall team performance. The manager who designed the new rating system emphasized that the objective was to sharpen the disciplinary dimension of teamworking:

> The changes to the peer review process will force the teams to confront the discipline issue. We're trying to force the issue. People in the past have used the scoring scale as a way out, give everyone 4. Now we're going to force distribution but not about the norm. We're not interested in normalising the scores. What we're interested in is forcing people to take responsibility. Each team member has only a limited number of points to distribute. In other words, if I give you a 4 then I have to give someone else a 3. (Interview, HR director, November 1993)

In contrast to the *ad hoc* nature of the initial peer review process, in the new system the roles of all participants are more tightly specified. Detailed documentation now codifies management's expectations of each person's role in the process and the scope of the actual review meeting. Each individual must sit silent while the team explains how his or her behaviour is reflected in the scoring: all team members must contribute at this stage. As the instruction manual states, 'the person being reviewed remains silent during this part of the review until each person has taken their turn to give recognition and feedback'. The individual under scrutiny then explains his or her self-assessment and asks for 'clarification' from any of the scrutineers. The content of the exchanges are noted for future reference. This time the tension at the core of such highly charged exchanges is explicitly recognized: facilitators are warned that they have to tread a fine line between ensuring that the team is judgemental in its scrutiny of the individual yet avoids alienating the team from the process itself.

Despite the closing of the loopholes, it is highly debatable whether management will succeed in its objectives for at least two reasons. First, the damage done to morale, trust and perceptions of team culture by the awarding of pay bands was massive. Any managerial innovation was destined to be treated with caution if not outright cynicism by layers of previously co-operative workers. Secondly, by the end of the research period evidence was beginning to accumulate that workers were developing new ways of subverting the modified version of peer review. An initial response by workers was to arrange to give each other the same average score of 3. When this option was forbidden by management, workers began to discuss quite sophisticated marking systems where low marks would be awarded one month followed by higher marks the next for one worker, and vice versa for another. There would be no discernible pattern of reciprocal marking but the scores for each worker over a number of months would tend to equivalence. What is most striking is not just the complexity of these calculations and the inventiveness of workers' responses, but also the fact that workers have rejected the legitimacy of attempts to connect individual performance to peer review. What matters most is the workers' desire to remain fair to each other and to resist attempts to assess each other to anyone's detriment. The teams, in other words, reasserted their own definitions of responsibility, trust and autonomy which ran counter to those of management and the corporate vision.

Conclusion

We began by suggesting that the power of HRM techniques to defuse employee resistance and channel their individual and collective aspirations through corporate agendas had been greatly exaggerated. PhoneCo employees created a variety of methods to subvert the disciplinary intent of innovatory HRM practices. In terms of surveillance, the teams shifted from a tight self-policing *internal* regime to protecting the integrity of the team concept from *external* – managerial – intrusions. The teams' first line of defence against an emerging managerialism was the managerially sanctioned rhetoric of empowerment. When management intervened in team matters, their most potent defence was to make the disciplinary processes inoperable. Furthermore, we argue that there is a danger that insensitive application of Foucauldian concepts of surveillance and discipline risk overstating the reach of panoptic organization. There is never simply a stark alternative between 'empowerment' and 'emasculation' nor is this categorization conclusive and irreversible. Pyramid employees endorsed key elements of teamworking as an ideology and as a practice while decisively rejecting its disciplinary objectives. The nature of teamworking itself becomes a contested issue through workers constantly probing the depth of management commitment to maintaining the integrity of devolved decision-making. If the disciplinary intent had been undermined slowly by the work-groups' refusal to enforce the peer review system, the ideology of the managerless organization was punctured by the first annual pay evaluation. The visible, sovereign power of management was re-established at this critical juncture. The revamped peer review system was designed not just to rescue peer review but was also aimed at reviving the disciplinary edge which management wanted to occupy the heart of the self-empowered teams.

It is our contention that radical critiques of HRM are often flawed by their readiness to accept management objectives as accomplished facts. Due to the dynamic of capital accumulation, the factory can never be a prison or an asylum, no matter how beguiling the metaphor might be. No matter how 'total the surveillance and monitoring system and no matter how favourable the circumstances – a non-union, greenfield site in the context of high unemployment – worker resistance remains a reality. The attitudes of workers at PhoneCo were neither uniform nor fixed in time. Elements of acceptance and rejection of PhoneCo culture and practices intermingled in complex patterns. Workers' opposition to what was seen as the erosion of empowering culture was often couched in a vocabulary that management had once proselytized. Yet opposition could go much further: witness the scale of protest at the plant's first comprehensive pay review. Far from eliminating individual disobedience and collective resistance, peer review became the focal point of worker opposition to managerial attempts to appropriate the spontaneous, mutual control of the work group. Our observations at PhoneCo uncovered a plethora of disobedience behaviour amongst workers subjected to a system of peer review in which the disciplinary function was to be exercised by workers against themselves.

One consequence of worker resistance was to provoke a refinement of management's attempts to construct mechanisms able to provide them with continuous information about the internal dynamics of teamworking. But rather than leading to a closed panopticon which nullifies disobedience, it simply ushered in a different phase of worker resistance to managerial initiatives. The topography of teamworking and peer review remains contested terrain.

Acknowledgements

We gratefully acknowledge the financial support of the Leverhulme Trust. Our greatest debt of gratitude is to those who have worked and continue to work at PhoneCo.

References

Barker, J.R. 1993: Tightening the iron cage: concertive control in self-managing teams. *Administrative Science Quarterly*, 38(2), 408–37.

Buchanan, D. and McCalman, J. 1989: *High Performance Work Systems: the digital experience*. London: Routledge.

Cressey, P., Eldridge, J. and MacInnes, J. 1985: *Just Managing: authority and democracy in industry*. Milton Keynes, Bucks.: Open University Press.

Dandeker, C. 1990: *Surveillance, Power and Modernity: bureaucracy and discipline from 1700 to the present day*. Oxford: Polity Press.

Dawson, P. and Webb, J. 1989: New production arrangements: the totally flexible cage? *Work, Employment and Society*, 3(2), 221–38.

Delbridge, R., Turnbull, P. and Wilkinson, B. 1992: Pushing back the frontiers: management control and work intensification under JIT/TQM factory regimes. *New Technology, Work and Employment*, 7(2), 97–107.

Findlay, P. 1990: What management strategy? Labour utilisation and regulation at Scotland's 'leading edge'. Unpublished DPhil thesis, Oxford University.

Findlay, P. 1993: Union recognition and non-unionism: shifting fortunes in the electronics industry in Scotland. *Industrial Relations Journal*, 24(1), 28–43.

Foucault, M. 1977: *Discipline and Punish: the birth of the prison*. Harmondsworth, Middx: Allen Lane.

Foucault, M. 1979: *The History of Sexuality*, vol. 1. Harmondsworth, Middx: Allen Lane.

Foucault, M. 1980: *Power/Knowledge: selected interviews and other writings, 1972–1977*, ed. C. Gordon. Brighton: Harvester.

Garrahan, P. and Stewart, P. 1992: *The Nissan Enigma: flexibility at work in a local economy*. London: Mansell.

Geary, J.F. 1992: Pay, control and commitment: linking appraisal and reward. *Human Resource Management Journal*, 2(4), 36–54.

Goldstein, N. 1992: Gender and the restructuring of high-tech multinational corporations: new twists to an old story. *Cambridge Journal of Economics*, 16(3), 269–84.

Hodson, R. and Hagan, J. 1988: Skills and job commitment in high technology industries in the US. *New Technology, Work and Employment*, 3(2), 112–24.

Katzenbach, J.R. and Smith, D.K. 1993: *The Wisdom of Teams: creating the high performance organization*. Cambridge, Mass.: Harvard Business School Press.

Kenney, M. and Florida, R. 1993: *Beyond Mass Production: the Japanese system and its transfer to the US*. London: Oxford University Press.

Lawler, E. 1986: *High Involvement Management: participative strategies for improving organizational performance*. San Francisco, Cal.: Jossey-Bass.

Miller, P. and Rose, N. 1990: Governing economic life. *Economy and Society*, 19(1), 1–31.

Rose, N. 1990: *Governing the Soul: the shaping of the private self.* London: Routledge.

Scott, A. 1994: *Willing Slaves? British workers under human resource management.* Cambridge: Cambridge University Press.

Sewell, G. and Wilkinson, B. 1992a: 'Someone to watch over me': surveillance, discipline and the just-in-time labour process. *Sociology*, 26(2), 271–89.

Sewell, G. and Wilkinson, B. 1992b: Empowerment or emasculation? Shopfloor surveillance in a total quality organisation. In P. Blyton and P. Turnbull (eds), *Reassessing Human Resource Management*, London: Sage, 97–115.

Sewell, G. and Wilkinson, B. 1993: Human resource management in 'surveillance' companies. In Jon, Clark (ed.), *Human Resource Management and Technical Change*, London: Sage, 137–55.

Townley, B. 1993: Performance appraisal and the emergence of management. *Journal of Management Studies*, 30, 221–38.

Walton, Richard E. 1985: From control to commitment in the workplace. *Harvard Business Review*, 63, 77–89.

Webb, J. and Dawson, P. 1991: Measure for measure: strategic change in an electronic instruments corporation. *Journal of Management Studies*, 28(2), 191–206.

23

Managing in Different Cultures: the Case of Ghana

KATHERINE M. GARDINER

Introduction

Very little of what has been written about 'what managers do' or managerial work is truly and fully reflective of the nature of managing in cultures which differ significantly from those in which most of the research on managerial work has originated.

In fact, with a few exceptions (Carlson 1951; Kotter 1982; Martinko and Gardner 1990), one of the major limitations of the literature on managerial work (for example, Burns 1954; Guest 1956; Jasinski 1956; Copeman 1963; Luijk 1963; Stewart 1967, 1976, 1982; Hinrichs 1976; Mintzberg 1973; Luthans et al. 1988; Hannaway 1989) is that the role that the societal environment plays in shaping and defining the nature of managing and managerial work has been largely over-looked or glossed over – the interests of the researchers appearing to be elsewhere.

Many of these studies, therefore, are not stated to be clearly set within any particular socio-cultural or socio-economic context which influences directly the observations being made and the theories which are subsequently proposed. They have, nevertheless, been assumed to have universal relevance and application, despite the fact that no cross-cultural comparisons were made. As such, they are in reality reflective only of the particular social environment in which they were con-ducted and should not be seen to be necessarily authoritative.

In other instances, the emphasis has been on the creation of catego-ries for purposes of classification (for example, Mintzberg 1973; Stewart 1976), which has resulted in significant details, including those per-taining to the environment, being completely lost.

The erroneous impression that this can create for the reader, there-fore, is that the job of the manager, which includes his behaviour, how he spends his time and the conditions under which he works, is similar across national boundaries, is unaffected by the nature of the social environment he operates within rather than to some extent being determined by it, and can, therefore, be discussed in isolation from it.

One striking exception to this is Sune Carlson's (1951) work *Executive Behaviour*, in which he sets his study clearly within a particular social context and attempts to explain his findings in terms of that context. He does not attempt to propose any theories, but suggests rather that future research on managerial work should study managers in different countries with a view to identifying any similarities and differences that may exist in their working behaviours. This suggestion is significant in that Carlson recognized the fact that the external environment will cause there to be differences in managing across cultures.

This lack of recognition and research into the influences of the social environment on managerial work is particularly glaring in view of the existence of contingency theory and the fact that organizations have long been viewed as open systems in which the economic, informational, technical and social environments influence, and in turn are influenced by, the organization (Lawrence and Lorsch 1967; Thompson 1967; Hall 1987; Reed 1992).

Cross-cultural researchers and comparative management theorists have also long studied the influences of the external environment on the firm's management (Farmer and Richman 1964; Ajiferuke and Boddewyn 1970; Negandhi 1974), and have focused on the behaviours of people from different cultures in organizations.

All these fields of management recognize that environmental influences do not remain outside the organization but penetrate it, making its character felt in various ways throughout the system. Why, therefore, these same influences have not been shown to be reflective in so much of the research conducted into managerial work is a mystery.

Some works, such as Martinko and Gardner (1990), Stewart (1982) and Kotter (1982), have ascribed some importance to the effects of the environment on what the manager does, even though the discussion and elaboration of its influences are severely limited and hardly comprehensive enough for the reader to fully grasp their nature and importance.

The Socio-cultural Environment and Managing

Action theory (Silverman 1987) is supportive of the view that features of the wider social environment can be observed within the organization, not least in what managers do, their style of managing and leadership, but also in how they behave and respond to situations generally. This is because they do not perform their work in a cultural vacuum but within a society whose values they have themselves imbibed and from which meanings of situations and events are derived and understood. Likewise, the people they work with or come into contact with will display attitudes, values and beliefs at work which are again reflective of this same culture. Managing will, by necessity, mirror characteristics of the culture within which it is practised. It is of concern, therefore, that so much research in the area of managerial work has been undertaken without explicit cognizance having been taken of the subtle and not so subtle influences of the wider social environment on the findings documented.

Using Ghana as a case study, therefore, this chapter illustrates in depth distinctive features of managing in a different cultural environment. It identifies the conflicts and challenges facing the manager due to differences in the value systems and behaviours that are acceptable within the social environment and those of many of the larger organizations which operate within it: a problem that would not obtain in many of the more industrialized countries. It details features which could not have been suspected to exist by reading the existing literature on managerial work. Ghanaian managers see these as being part of what it means to be a manager since they account for their use of time and in some instances constitute the *conditions* under which they must work – an important dimension of managerial work first mentioned by Carlson (1951) but one which is still largely ignored. The emphasis will be on the cultural, as opposed to the economic or political characteristics and influences of the environment on managing.

Ghanaian Society

Influences of colonialism and internationalization show Ghana to be in transition from a traditional to a modern society. As such, traditional Ghanaian behaviours, beliefs, practices and attitudes exist alongside the modern Western-orientated society. In varying degrees Ghanaian managers, and to some extent expatriates working in Ghana, therefore, have the unique challenge of having to interact in both these sharply contrasting and often conflicting arenas in the course of carrying out their managerial duties. They will, furthermore, need to resolve the problems created by this clash of cultures as well as withstand the stresses caused by it.

The main cultural features – 'the traditional' – experienced by any manager working in Ghana concern:

- traditional practices and institutions;
- elements of Ghanaian culture;
- other socio-cultural features.

These would have to be managed alongside 'the modern' – whatever principles of managing and organizing, patterned along Western-orientated lines, are in operation.

Traditional Practices and Institutions

Regardless of the level of education of managers, their degree of exposure to Western ways of life and thought, or the nature and sophistication of the organizations they work for, at some time or the other they will come into contact with traditional practices, beliefs and institutions. These will sometimes originate from employees or from the wider society and will account for the use of some managerial time and be reflected in the content of managers' work.

Traditional beliefs and witchcraft

Wiredu (1980: 11) suggests that a still strongly surviving feature of Ghanaian culture is the belief in 'witchcraft and a variety of spirits, fetishes and powers, both good and bad'. Such beliefs often reach the desk of the manager either because they involve his workers, or because these behaviours in members of the general public are adversely affecting the company's operations and require some action, decision or response on his part. Managers have been known, for example, to authorize the pouring of libation and the sacrifice of chickens, sheep, goats and cows by the local chief priest at the request of workers in order to ensure their safety at work, especially when accidents, particularly fatal accidents, occur.

Many Ghanaian and expatriate managers working in Ghana have had some contact with, or experience of, these traditional beliefs in spirits, fetishes and gods – it is not an uncommon experience. The attitude of many managers, however, in dealing with such beliefs is that if the vast majority of workers believe in them and if performing the necessary rites gives the workers the peace of mind to work, they will not prevent these activities from taking place since no harm is caused. They will not show outright disregard for these beliefs and rarely, if ever, are they physically present when they are being performed. It is essential, however, that they put these beliefs into the right perspective from the organization's point of view, looking at their cost-benefit and being able to refuse to acquiesce where to do so would clearly be to the detriment of the company, financially or otherwise.

The chief executive of a company whose generators continually developed mechanical problems, for example, refused to have them moved to a new location on the advice of local people who claimed that the problem was due to the fact that the generators were sited on an old burial ground. To do so would have cost the company a substantial amount of money and the CE knew, furthermore, that the fault was of a purely mechanical nature.

Funerals

Funerals and 'elaborate rituals of mourning' (Wiredu 1980) are another cultural feature which impinge rather heavily on work, put pressure on managers' time and create problems and dilemmas for them. Because of the extended family system and the importance attached to funerals, but also because Ghana is still a comparatively small and closely knit society where people tend to know one another, funerals generally draw a huge crowd. This social activity affects managers in four ways:

1   As successful members of their families, heads of their organizations, members of several other boards and just by being long-standing members of a closely knit society, managers come to know many people and are known by them. Many managers, therefore, feel obliged to attend funerals on several weekends a month and often have to travel quite long distances in order to put in an appearance. In addition, on each occasion, they must make a respectable donation to the bereaved family and this, over a period of time, adds up to quite a substantial sum of money.
2   Their subordinates also have similar obligations and will often ask for time off to attend funerals of extended family members and close friends. This can affect productivity. One chief executive interviewed observed that workers see nothing wrong with asking for two or three days off work in order to participate fully in the various activities associated with the funerals. On many a Friday afternoon, therefore, a significant number of people are not at their jobs because 'they are attending a funeral'.
3   The organization is further affected because the workers frequently ask for loans to help with their funeral expenses. In addition, companies have a legal obligation, incorporated into their collective agreements, towards the employee who dies in the service of the company or who loses a close relative. They must contribute towards a coffin or actually provide one,

give a cash donation, and in addition make transport available to enable mourners from the office to attend the funeral which invariably is miles away from the company's offices. The company's obligations often extend to cover the death of a wife, husband, father, mother or child of a serving employee.

4 The fourth way in which managers are affected by funerals relates to third parties. Not infrequently, people he may need to consult urgently in government ministries or elsewhere are not available because they are 'attending a funeral' and are unlikely to return to post for the next few days.

An expatriate manager working in Ghana said of funerals that 'they take a lot of getting used to' in terms of the importance attached to them and the inordinate amount of time and money spent on them. Summing up the situation, Wiredu (1980: 11), says in a footnote: 'The lively survival of this cultural practice in present-day Ghanaian life is an anachronism with some quite unhappy economic consequences.'

Many Ghanaian managers find that funerals are becoming increasingly burdensome: in terms of the precious time that they take up at weekends, when they would rather have time to unwind after a stressful week or think about more serious work-related issues. One CE went as far as to describe them as a 'nuisance'. Funerals add to the hectic life of the CE and create more stress and exhaustion, particularly when they involve a journey by road of several hours. Despite these pressures, many still feel obliged to attend them because it is generally considered to be socially unacceptable not to put in an appearance.

With regard to keeping the attendance by workers at funerals under control, many organizations are adopting the strategy of deducting any days off from annual leave so that the worker is encouraged to attend only those funerals that are important to him and therefore he is absent for a shorter time. This is another way of arriving at a practical solution to a cultural problem.

It will be difficult to change the importance currently attached to funerals in Ghana, notwithstanding the inconvenience and loss of productivity that they cause. People complain but still accept them as a normal part of life in Ghana.

Chieftancy

Another important feature of Ghanaian culture which the Ghanaian manager and, for that matter, any manager working in Ghana is also likely to come across relates to chieftancy. Because of 'the attachment of a religious significance to the office of a chief, with reverence for and complete obedience to his authority' (Wiredu 1980: 11), managers must accord it due respect by doing the right sort of things.

The location of the business has a lot to do with the extent of interaction with chiefs, the areas outside the capital, Accra, generally having the greatest contact. Also, the greater the significance of the company's line of business to the community, the greater will be the relationship. Some 'stools'[1] are of far greater importance than others, so where the company operates in an area with an important and powerful chief, a number of their activities will necessarily include him.

A typical meeting between a chief executive and a chief or queen-mother, for whatever purpose, would always be conducted along very traditional lines and would be in sharp contrast to the brisk format of normal business meetings. The purpose of the meeting would be arrived at only after very prolonged pleasantries have been completed which would include such ceremonies as the pouring of libation and the exchanging of gifts – most often drinks such as whisky and schnapps. Each side of the meeting would include several other people, including a person who would act as the chief's spokesman.

The manager must be properly prepared for such meetings, both from a cultural point of view but also from his organization's business viewpoint. From a cultural point of view, he must know, or find out if he is unsure, the correct way to receive such a delegation and he will often need to get someone to speak on his behalf as custom demands. From the business perspective, he must always remember that he has responsibility for running a business efficiently and must not concede to every demand made by the visiting delegation. At the same time, he has, in this case, a social responsibility which he must fulfil. In such a situation, saying 'no' outright to a request is considered impolite and disrespectful. Attaching conditions to the granting of the request is one way of getting round the problem. On the other hand, where the need to say 'no' is unavoidable, the diplomacy and tact of the local languages enables this to be done gently, without any loss of face.

The Ghanaian or expatriate manager will inevitably come into contact with the institution of chieftancy in the normal course of his work and must do the right customary things; these will vary according to the importance of the chief and the ethnic group he belongs to. Managers must also be capable of playing in two diametrically opposing arenas, switching from a modern Western business orientation in one situation to a very traditional one in another. The Ghanaian manager can generally make this switch fairly comfortably since he will have been brought up in an environment where it is not at all unusual to have both the modern and the traditional existing side by side. As regards the right thing to do, he may often need to consult someone knowledgeable if he is unsure, in order to be adequately prepared and to follow the correct traditional protocol.

Other Elements of Ghanaian Culture

There are a number of other elements of Ghanaian culture with which the manager is bound have contact. These features and behaviours again exert pressures and create problems that must be dealt with and which take time to resolve.

The extended family

The extended family is an important feature of Ghanaian society; it refers to family members beyond those who would normally be considered the nuclear family and includes even distant relatives. Because families in Ghana have traditionally been large, this web of relations can be extensive.

Much as the extended family system is valued in Ghana, it does have a negative side in that members often come to see the manager in the office asking for all sorts of favours which they fully expect that their uncle or cousin will be capable of carrying out. Many put a lot of pressure on the manager to employ them or their children regardless of their qualifications or whether the company has any need for them. Again, because of the relative poverty of the rural population, many of them also come to the manager expecting money which he often feels obliged to give, particularly since he is better placed and better off financially than many of them and, therefore, feels a sense of responsibility towards 'the family'. Many managers also help with the school fees of the children of their less well-placed brothers and sisters. They face added stress when they pay visits to their villages or home towns because people expect to be given gifts of money. Over a period of time the manager will have given away quite substantial sums of money.

Yet other members of the extended family, and sometimes members of the public who the manager may not even know, come seeking help to obtain scholarships or passports. Still others come wanting to discuss very personal matters, ranging from marital problems to difficulties at work. The manager is often made out to be wicked and unfeeling when he does not or cannot offer them assistance. The collapse of many a business in Ghana has been attributed to the inability to manage 'the family' in relation to the business effectively, with the result that the needs and interests of the organization become secondary to the needs of the family.

'Begging' and mediation

The habit of 'begging' for forgiveness when one has transgressed is an accepted mode of behaviour in Ghanaian culture. In the workplace, it is considered that, regardless of the seriousness of the transgression, whether theft or drunkenness at work, once the transgressor goes to 'beg' all should be forgiven. So a driver who is sacked for theft prostrates himself in front of the CE to beg for forgiveness. The situation is made even worse if the transgressor brings along or sends another person to beg on his behalf, again usually an elderly person – a father or an uncle – who may also prostrate himself in front of the CE. He may even ask a politician or member of government to mediate on his behalf.

Culturally, this is the usual procedure and one that is well known to the CE. Coupled with the great societal respect for the elderly, an uncomfortable and stressful situation is created. Sometimes he may forgive and offer a last chance or may mitigate the punishment, but he must be very careful not to set a precedent which will act to the detriment of the company he is managing.

An unusual situation, therefore, obtains between codes of behaviour that are culturally acceptable in the wider society, but which are unacceptable in many large organizations whose members are, nevertheless, a part of this wider society.

Attitude to authority

Another feature of Ghanaian culture that often manifests itself in the workplace is the general attitude to those in authority. Ghanaian culture emphasizes respect for age, which has to some extent become synonymous with status. This attitude to the elderly or those in authority could be described as almost subservience – certainly a little more than just respect.

The tendency, therefore, is not to question those in authority. In addition, people often find it difficult to speak their minds openly but do so behind the person's back or in private. The autocratic tendencies of many governments in Ghana have served to reinforce this behaviour and have made people cautious about expressing their disagreement with those in authority or with power. The fact that Ghanaians are brought up to be polite and courteous makes it even more difficult to be blunt when necessary.

The concern about 'loss of face' by another compounds the problem, thus making it difficult for people to disagree with their seniors. This feature of Ghanaian culture creates even more awkwardness when a younger supervisor or manager has subordinates who are older than he is but to whom he must nevertheless give instructions and discipline if need be.

The enduring, but gradually changing practice in many Ghanaian organizations, especially those in the public sector, of basing promotion on seniority rather than on merit could also be a manifestation of this respect for those older than oneself.

This cultural characteristic found in much, although by no means all of the Ghanaian workforce, will have implications for managing and for the manager, making it different from what it is likely to be in other countries.

Attention to detail

Yet another aspect of behaviour which has its roots in the culture concerns poor attention to detail and a general lack of precision in doing many things, including their jobs. Wiredu (1980: 11) is of the view that the traditional mode of understanding, utilizing and controlling external nature and of interpreting man's place within it is mainly intuitive and is essentially unanalytic and unscientific. The effect of this is that many people will instinctively make a guess rather than try to resolve an issue scientifically.

Many a CE, therefore, often has to do the work of his supervisors in order to ensure that things are properly done, and in particular done straight where straightness may be essential. He has, in addition, the task of teaching people the necessity and importance of being accurate.

Other Socio-cultural Features that Affect the Manager

There are a number of other features which will simply be described as socio-cultural since they are either cultural, social or a mixture of both.

Conflict between the raison d'être *of the business and the perceptions of the average Ghanaian*

The perception that the Ghanaian public has of the business concern as opposed to the business's own *raison d'être* also has a profound effect on the CE. Many Ghanaians do not understand that everything that is done in a company should further that company's interests and safeguard its survival and that it has a separate life of its own. They do not understand that there is, and should be, a dividing line between their personal needs that they expect the company to satisfy and what the company can realistically satisfy. That dividing line in the perception of many a Ghanaian is blurred, with the result that much pressure and therefore stress is put on the chief executive to satisfy needs that he should not in all honesty commit the organization to. This behaviour is again illustrative of the conflict between 'the traditional' and 'the modern'.

Furthermore, according to Peil, Ghanaian workers are better satisfied with the less formal style of social organization than with the more bureaucratized, impersonal management styles characteristic of modern organizations (cited in Twumasi 1973: 20) where decisions are supposed to be made according to rules. Sentiment, passion and sympathy are presumably irrelevant to carrying out the purposes of bureaucratic organizations.

A conflict immediately arises since fundamental aspects of Ghanaian culture are steeped in sentimentality, passion and sympathy. Rather than permitting the bureaucracy to be impersonal and faceless, the Ghanaian unconsciously tries to make it personal, since this is the only way he or she knows how to function. Several of the cultural features observed in the workplace, such as mediation, funerals, appeals to the top, reluctance to discipline, respect for authority, all contravene bureaucratic principles and serve to make the bureaucracy very personalized.

In addition, because the majority of Ghanaians are illiterate, they depend on the goodwill of a familiar person to help them gain access to the civil administration. So deeply ingrained has this personal intervention become that Ghana has been said to have a 'face-to-face' culture, in that many organizations will themselves only respond to situations when a personal contact has been made.

This infiltration of traditional values into the workplace can and often does create problems for the organization and for the manager in particular. Unchecked, the extreme situation arises when company property is treated as though it were personal to the worker and can, therefore, be distributed to friends as an act of goodwill. So the worker employed by the municipal authorities to collect the 'toll' in a public car park does not demand payment consistently from everyone but only from those with whom he has not struck up a friendship.

G.P. Hagan (1984: 1) has observed that: 'In the light of African Cultural values, the work situation is an all-embracing social fact.' This has religious, social, legal, economic and political implications for the worker. He elaborates by saying:

> A close study of Ghanaian traditional values would reveal that the use of time accords to the following scale: First, religious duties; second, social duties; third, economic duties . . . What it does mean is that where the African perceives a conflict between his religious, social and economic duties, he is likely to relinquish the economic first and the social second in order to fulfill the religious.   (Ibid.: 18–19)

Hagan points out that such behaviour is in sharp contrast to Western cultures which tend to give first priority to the economic, second to the social and the last priority to the religious.

Clearly, with constraints and attitudes such as these, the work of the manager often becomes more arduous as he struggles to introduce and maintain a work ethic that often runs counter to the cultural orientation of a significant number of his employees.

Appeals to the top

Many chief executives complain that virtually everyone coming to the company tries to see them personally rather than going to the person responsible for dealing with the issues they wished to discuss. It seems, therefore, to be 'normal' for the chief executive to have a steady stream of people, the majority from outside the company, coming to see him about one thing or another during the course of the day. This seemingly endless stream of 'visitors' appears to be a greater problem for the Ghanaian CE than for his expatriate counterpart working in Ghana. The situation is partly caused by the fact that much of the Ghanaian public does not appear to know about, understand or take seriously appointments. Very few people, therefore, come to see the chief executive with an appointment. It has been suggested that this could be cultural.

Secondly, many chief executives tend to keep an 'open door' policy and rarely turn people away, even though a few do. This obviously tends to encourage this particular behaviour. The humaneness of the Ghanaian and his sympathy for his fellow countryman tends to make it difficult for the chief executive to turn people away.

At the same time people often prefer to see the chief executive himself because they do not get satisfactory answers from people lower down the hierarchy and do not feel confident that their problem is being adequately taken care of.

Amoa and Marfo (1977), in an interesting study of this phenomenon in the Civil Service in Ghana, came to the conclusion that both cumbersome and over-elaborate procedures for handling petitions in the Civil Service as well as the traditional system of settling issues have considerably influenced people's attitudes to seeking redress in the modern administrative system (p. 65). With respect to the traditional social milieu, Marfo and Amoa quote an Akan proverb, '*Ade da opanim anim a enyera*', which means that when a matter or an issue is before an elderly person it does not get ignored. They conclude that 'the belief in direct communications and bringing an issue directly to the elderly person accounts for the tendency in the Ghanaian to appeal directly to the man at the top in modern administration' (ibid.: 62). Deeply ingrained in the Ghanaian culture is the 'belief in the wisdom of age' (Wiredu 1980: 4). Age, to all intents and purposes, is synonymous with organizational status.

Unless he takes positive steps to prevent or minimize it, the Ghanaian chief executive will be besieged by people from all walks of life and with all sorts of missions. The effect of their physical presence, to say nothing of the purpose of their visit, is often harrassing to the chief executive and puts pressure on his time. To make matters worse, the siege can continue in his home – either early in the morning or in the evenings – unless he puts a firm stop to it.

When asked the purpose of the visit a typical response is 'Personal'. Rarely do people state precisely why they want to see the chief executive, and this is often a great source of irritation. Chief executives have been known to react to such situations by refusing to take any such 'personal' visits in the office. In other cases companies have had to redesign their visitors' form so that it was impossible to write only 'Personal' on it.

One CE interviewed classified the 'stream' of people from outside the company coming to see him into three groups:

- those connected with the job or which are in some way work-related;
- visits by the extended family;
- people he does not know at all or very distantly, but who need some personal assistance.

'You are not just managing your business', said one chief executive. 'You are managing the whole b— Accra.'

In some cases, people who do not work in the organization but who are from the same ethnic group as the CE will go to great lengths to try to see him or her – again, usually on purely private missions. They feel free to do this primarily because they speak the same language or are from the same town or region. Such visits can often be a nuisance to the CE and a waste of time. The strategy used by one CE to get round this problem was to speak to these visitors in English. By so doing she made her visitors feel less at ease and they left quicker.

Ethnic problems

It has been documented that Ghana has about 26 different languages, each more or less corresponding to a different ethnic group. The dominant ethnic groups, however, are about four in number, and each of the languages and dialects spoken within each group, as well as aspects of their culture, differ completely from the next.

It is natural that people from the same ethnic group will gravitate to each other; even though English is the working language in Ghana, it does not bind people together. The bringing together of people from these different ethnic groups under one roof, however, can sometimes create problems and the CE must often intervene and adopt strategies to keep it under control.

Problems created by ethnic feelings come in many forms. With respect to recruitment, the tendency could be for the personnel officer to recruit people from the same ethnic group as himself unless steps are taken by the CE or some other person to prevent it. It is not considered to be healthy to have any one particular ethnic group dominating the working environment since it tends to reinforce ethnic differences which can have undesirable side-effects. Occasionally, such a state of affairs may arise where, due to the location of a company within a particular region of the country, more of the locals will be employed.

Making a conscious effort to get a good balance often diffuses ethnic tensions and enables workers to see that the manager himself is being fair and is not collaborating with any particular ethnic group. Quite often, however, when a worker is disciplined by his supervisor, he sees the cause to be their different ethnic backgrounds. Such feelings can exacerbate tensions in the factory or office, and the wise manager, therefore, goes out of his way to diffuse them.

In other situations, a supervisor from one ethnic group can create problems for those working beneath him, particularly when they are from another ethnic group. On the other hand, he may be at the receiving end of such ethnic feelings. Whatever the case, problems of discipline are often the outcome of such behaviours.

A number of CEs reported being fortunate enough to have no serious ethnic problems in their organizations. The seriousness of such situations varies and in many cases amounts to little more than comments or jokes about people from various other ethnic groups, which still goes to show that such feelings do exist, albeit beneath the surface.

Women in the Ghanaian culture

In theory, Ghana appears to be very progressive with respect to the status of women and has ratified a number of ILO Conventions including Convention 100 on *Equal Remuneration for Women*; Convention 45 on *Underground Work (Women)* and Convention 103 on *Maternity Protection for the Working Woman*. Ghana is, in addition, a signatory to the United Nations Convention on the *Elimination of all Forms of Discrimination against Women*, which was ratified by the Ghana government in September 1985.

Despite the fact that many women now hold very senior positions in both the public and the private sector and can be found in most, if not all, the professions, in the minds of the majority of men they are still considered to be second-class citizens who should play second fiddle to the men.

On closer examination, this appears to be a serious misrepresentation in view of the resourcefulness of Ghanaian women, their strong entrepreneurial ability, particularly the powerful women traders known as 'mammies', and the fact that many women are the backbone of the family. In the organization, therefore, even though a Ghanaian woman holding the same appointment as a man earns the same pay, she often, although not always, becomes the target of their displeasure, more so when she has men working under her.

It is not unknown, for example, for female CEs to be heckled at meetings by their well-educated male colleagues whenever they make a contribution. Others have had their contributions belittled and laughed at by their male counterparts, regardless of how useful they were. The impression these women had was that many men just could not accept women in high positions either rubbing shoulders with them or telling them what to do, even though the men recognized their expertise and competence. The fact that the numbers of women in such positions are so small does nothing to enable the men to get used to the idea.

Fortunately, several women have encountered no difficulties at all in working with their male counterparts. At the other extreme, however, men have been known to resign their jobs rather than suffer the indignity of having a woman for a boss.

The time factor

Generally speaking, the African's attitude to time is well known and is another potential source of conflict and frustration for the manager trying to run his organization efficiently. Jokingly referred to as 'African punctuality', the situation applies as much in Ghana, even though it is changing slowly.

Hagan (1984: 15–18) provides an interesting explanation of the concept of time and the Ghanaian (or African generally). Stating the obvious, he says that the clock is not an African invention, implying that if the African had had need of it he would have invented it. Instead, the movement of the sun, the crowing of the cock, seasonal changes, or the appearance of the moon – all imprecise indicators of time – guided human activity. 'The precise division of the day into hours as a means of regulating and, especially, synchronizing human activity represents a revolutionary cultural innovation in most African cultures' (ibid.: 15).

Hagan goes on to explain that lateness is often given a superior value since it is the prerogative of a chief or elder. Also, he says, 'a punctual worker might even be described as one who has nothing to do at home . . . The Ghanaian worker thus sees sanctions for lateness as unconscionable' (ibid.: 17). From Hagan's explanation, we can again see how the economic activity of work comes secondary to the social – in this case, the home. He goes on to say that in Africa 'Time is made to extend to accommodate work; work is not compressed to fit into time' (ibid.: 18), as it is in the Western world.

This cultural perception of time can either be encouraged or discouraged by the organization. Since precision of time is essential for viable economic activity, but because culturally the tendency to be lackadaisical and over-relaxed about time is inherent in the vast majority of Ghanaians, more stringent efforts need to be made by top managements to instil into people the necessity of keeping good time. Generally speaking, the less educated the person, the less he realizes the value of time.

This lack of awareness of the importance of time often manifests itself in the absence of a sense of urgency about most things. This can prove exasperating for the manager who has to work with people who have such an attitude.

Another irritating manifestation of this lack of appreciation of time is the lateness with which scheduled meetings often actually start. This becomes a waste of time for the person who is punctual, and when he complains people invariably fail to sympathize.

With respect to lateness generally, leadership can and should set a good example for others to follow. Having a good and operational control system which records the arrival and departure times of categories of workers is often essential. Where the organization has been able to develop a culture of discipline generally in all aspects of its activities, this culture has the effect of influencing the behaviour of employees, and they will tend to make a greater effort to arrive at work on time. Where there is instead a culture of laxity and indiscipline, as in many government organisations, lateness becomes more endemic.

Inability to discipline

The unwillingness of managers or supervisors to discipline subordinates and to tell them when they are doing something wrong also makes the CE's job more difficult since that difficult and often unpleasant task is left to the CE more often than it should be.

In some instances, the reason could be fear of reprisals but the most likely explanation for the unwillingness of managers to discipline is again the extended family. The culture of caring and sympathy for one another, of being each other's keeper, and the fact that Ghanaian society is still comparatively closely knit, makes it very difficult for a manager to be hard on another person, knowing full well the implications that taking a tough line will have for him. This is particularly the case because Ghana has no unemployment benefits. People are also reluctant to take hard decisions which may adversely affect others because to do so means risking becoming unpopular, which many managers would rather not be.

The perception of an expatriate CE who has worked in Ghana for several years is that Ghanaians are 'too nice': they do not like confrontation. Neither do they like harassing people. As a result they find it difficult to sack or discipline and would rather that someone else did it.

Because of this tendency, which works its way down the entire organization, criticism is frequently behind the back of the person concerned. Anonymous letters are also written informing the CE about the unacceptable actions and behaviour of someone in the organization and requesting an investigation. Several CEs interviewed reported receiving anonymous letters. One of them even described it as a 'Ghanaian thing'. This tendency also affects the usefulness of performance appraisals since rarely are they honestly and critically done. Invariably, middle-of-the-road assessments such as 'satisfactory', 'fair' or 'average' are used to describe a person's performance. The experience of some CEs was that supervisors would often complain to them about the behaviour of some member of staff, but when it came to writing an assessment on that person's performance, they would not put their complaints on paper. In one instance, the CE had asked that the performance appraisal form be modified so as to make the information more useful.

A CE's explanation of the situation was that, in assessing a person, he or she is invariably thought of, not in terms of business output, but in very personal terms.

Attitude to expatriates

A sensitive and perhaps controversial issue that can also be observed in the workplace concerns the attitude of Ghanaians to expatriates. Years of colonial rule have left their mark with the result that in many, though by no means in all, situations, Ghanaians often accord white expatriates far more respect than is often necessary, even when they hold positions lower than the Ghanaians'. For this season, the Ghanaian often has difficulty asserting himself, even in the face of misconduct from a white subordinate. The proverbial Ghanaian hospitality and generosity to visitors may also have a part to play in this tendency. Indeed, it is often felt that Ghanaians tend to discriminate against themselves in their own country. Furthermore, Ghanaians working for an expatriate will often take their work more seriously than if they are working for a Ghanaian and are often more willing to take orders from an expatriate than from a Ghanaian.

On the other hand, it may be that Ghanaians prefer working for an expatriate because he or she has no tribal affiliations or family connections and in that sense, therefore, is fairer. They may take their work more seriously because they know that if they want to keep their jobs they have no choice but to work hard, since the expatriate would not have any qualms about sacking them. Neither would the expatriate have any pressures put on him by outsiders to reconsider his decision.

The very revealing and well-known Ghanaian (Akan) expression, '*Oye Boronyi n'edwuma*' (It is the white man's work), carries with it the implication that it should be taken seriously. Quite often the reason given why one should not break one's back over a job but take it easy is that it is '*Aban edwuma*' (It belongs to the state).

Many CEs recognize the advantages of having expatriates in their organizations. First, they help to keep ethnic differences down, probably without even realizing it; and it is easier for them to discipline, since they have fewer and less-intense social connections with Ghanaians and, therefore, hardly any pressures from the public. Again, because of this regard that Ghanaians tend to have for expatriates, workers tend to work harder, which is another positive aspect. At higher levels in the organizational hierarchy, where Ghanaians are better-educated, experienced and confident, this belief in the superiority of the expatriate disappears almost entirely.

The expatriate manager working in Ghana, may, therefore, encounter fewer difficulties in the first instance with his staff than would a Ghanaian manager, who may need to make far greater efforts to assert himself than his expatriate counterpart will ever have to. An expatriate CE of a multinational company said, for instance, that people wishing to see him always made appointments. He also had far fewer people coming to see him than his Ghanaian counterpart had.

Conclusion

It is clear that aspects of the manager's job, and managing generally, will differ between cultures simply by virtue of the characteristics of the particular political, economic and cultural environment he or she is working within. This environment will affect the organization and the manager directly, thereby creating a set of conditions which will be unique to that particular country alone. The manager's natural response to these circumstances, which could come in the form of constraints or demands placed upon him, will also be conditioned by the environment. Managing, as such, will differ in some aspects between cultures.

It is crucial, therefore, that more cross-cultural comparisons of managerial work should be done in order to determine where any similarities and differences lie. Only after this has been done will it be possible to propose theories that are authoritative and that accurately reflect the situation in different countries. Before this can be done, however, definitions of what constitutes managerial work, or simply what managing is, will have to be agreed upon by researcher and practitioner. Between practitioners from different countries it will need to be defined and understood, since agreement between them may not be possible. The Ghanaian manager, for example, may view his or her interactive role with the general public in the ways described as being very much a part of his job as a manager, whereas his American or European counterpart may have an entirely different opinion, which would influence his reactions to any such situations. Definitions of managing are likely to differ among managers even though there will probably be clusters of similarity if enough cross-cultural comparisons are made. It is important to point this out in a discussion of managing in a different culture lest the situation in one country be dismissed by the manager from some other culture as 'not managing at all'.

The fact that many Ghanaian managers found aspects of their responsibilities, such as funerals, perceptions of Ghanaians with respect to the organization, or 'visitors' to his office, as problematic to them is also significant. It is again reflective of the basic conflict that exists between codes of behaviour which derive from the cultural environment and which are acceptable within that environment and those that are found within many foreign and larger Ghanaian owned organizations which, by necessity and good reason, have adopted codes of practice and behaviour that have originated in the Western world but which to some degree clash with those of the social environment it operates within and from which it draws its employees.

The Ghanaian, or for that matter any indigenous CE, is at the meeting point of these two cultures and, therefore, on the receiving end of that clash. In many respects, he is the best person to manage the conflict since in most instances he understands both cultures. At the same time, by virtue of his position he is put under tremendous stress to keep the organization going under such circumstances and in particular to keep cultural behaviours under control. The challenges, therefore, that managers face by virtue of this conflict will differ between cultures. Such a conflict and all the problems it creates will be found in countries where much of the largest investment is foreign – as it is in Ghana, and where, therefore, the two cultures differ markedly from one another. It will also be evident in the larger Ghanaian companies whether state owned or private. The conflict will be less marked where the business is smaller and indigenous and is, therefore, adhering less strongly to any foreign-derived organizational values and practices. For this reason, many foreign-owned companies generally employ a local person in a high-ranking position who will be able to advise appropriately the foreign CE, where they have one.

Problematic as some of the socially derived cultural tendencies may be, they still represent the nature of managing on the ground now, and therefore should form part of the picture as it is realistically. What then remains the challenge to the manager is to look for creative solutions with respect to these problems such that they become less problematic for him. To set the objective of eliminating them altogether could be a mistake. Exceptions to this will be those that clearly impede the company's ability to be competitive, such as the lack of precision and attention to detail and general attitudes to time and work.

The ideal situation would be to work towards a state of affairs that reflects the culture and that is acceptable within that culture, but one which at the same time does not impede the organization competitively. Convergence, internationalization and education will, with the passage of time, modify behaviours within particular cultures, but the solution is not to copy blindly and assume that what pertains in one particular country should automatically be applied in another. It may not fit. Like the Japanese, the aim should be to work towards a style and system of managing that sits comfortably within the particular culture but which will, at the same time, not impede the company's efforts towards becoming competitive internationally.

Acknowledgements

My sincere thanks and appreciation to Colin Mair and Dr Chris Baldry for useful discussions.

Note

1   A stool is the traditional wooden chair that a chief sits on. In this context, 'stool' refers to the area of the chief's jurisdiction.

References

Ajiferuke, M. and Boddewyn, J. 1970: 'Culture' and other explanatory variables in comparative management studies. *Academy of Management Review*, June, 153–63.

Amoa, S.A. and Marfo, E.O. 1977: Appeals to the top: an emerging administrative problem. *Greenhill Journal of Administration*, 4(1–2), 59–65.

Burns, T. 1954: The directions of activity and communications in a departmental executive group. *Human Relations*, 7, 73–97.

Carlson, S. 1951: *Executive Behaviour: a study of the work load and the working methods of managing directors*. Stockholm: Strombergs.

Copeman, G. 1963: How British executives spend their day. In G. Copeman, H. Luijk and F. Hanika (eds) (1963), *How the Executive Spends his Time*, London: Business Publications.

Farmer, R.N. and Richman, B.M. 1964: A model for research in comparative management. *California Management Review*, 7(2), 55–68.

Guest, R.H. 1956: Of time and foremen. *Personnel*, 32, 478–86.

Hagan, G.P. 1984: Culture-derived management problems: the bane of African development. Paper delivered at a Conference organized by PAID-ESA, Zambia.

Hall, R.H. 1987: *Organizations: structure and outcomes*. Englewood Cliffs, N.J.: Prentice-Hall.

Hannaway, J. 1989: *Managers Managing*. New York: Oxford University Press.

Hinrichs, J.R. 1976: Where has all the time gone? *Personnel*, 53, 44–9.

Jasinski, F.J. 1956: Foremen relations with the work group. *Personnel*, 33, 130–6.

Kotter, J.P. 1982: *The General Managers*. New York: Macmillan.

Lawrence, P.R. and Lorsch, J.W. 1967: *Organisation and Environment: managing differentiation and integration*. Cambridge, Mass.: Harvard University Press.

Luijk, H. 1963: How Dutch executives spend their day. In G. Copeman, H. Luijk and F. Hanika (eds), *How the Executive Spends his Time*, London: Business Publications.

Luthans, F., Hodgetts, R. and Rosenkrants, S. 1988: *Real Managers*. Cambridge, Mass.: Ballinger.

Martinko, H.J. and Gardner, W.L. 1990: Structured observation of managerial work: a replication and synthesis. *Journal of Management Studies*, 27(3), 329–57.

Mintzberg, F. 1973: *The Nature of Managerial Work*. New York: Harper & Row.

Negandhi, A.R. 1974: Cross-cultural management studies: too many conclusions, not enough conceptualization. *Management International Review*, 6, 59–67.

Reed, M. 1992: *The Sociology of Organisations*. London: Harvester Wheatsheaf.

Silverman, D. 1987: *The Theory of Organisations*. Aldershot, Hants: Gower.

Stewart, R. 1967: *Managers and Their Jobs*. Maidenhead, Berks.: McGraw-Hill.

Stewart, R. 1976: *Contrasts in Management*. Maidenhead, Berks.: McGraw-Hill.

Stewart, R. 1982: *Choices for the Manager*. Englewood Cliffs, N.J.: Prentice-Hall.

Thompson, J.D. 1967: *Organisations in Action*. Maidenhead, Berks.: McGraw-Hill.

Twumasi, P.A. 1973: Dysfunctions of bureaucracy: the Ghanaian experience. *Journal of Management Studies (Ghana)*, 6(2), 20–4.

Wiredu, K. 1980: *Philosophy and an African Culture*. Cambridge: Cambridge University Press.

24

Managers' Work Values in Different Cultures: the Case of the Korea Electric Power Corporation

YOUNG-HA LEE

Introduction

This study examines how Korean managers' work values differ from those of UK managers and how work values affect their working hours. Specifically, the study considers culture as the most important factor which differentiates both managers' work values and their working hours. The study concludes that there is a considerable difference in work values between Korean and UK managers. Korean managers rate their work and career as more important than their family relationships, whilst the opposite is true for UK managers. This difference in work values between Korean and UK managers also has a considerable influence on their working hours.

This is the first large-scale study to compare Korean managers' work values with those of managers in the West. It offers an interesting aspect of the Korean managers' social value system which has largely remained unknown, especially to management writers and practitioners in Western countries. The findings of the study may provide valuable information for Western managers in learning how to work harmoniously with managers from Korea in today's multinational business organizations. It will also contribute to reducing the cultural shock that managers in Western nations may face when moving to work in Korea or other Far Eastern countries, such as China, Japan or Taiwan, whose people seem to have a similar work-orientated social value system.

The case study was drawn from the author's doctoral thesis at the University of Glasgow, UK (Lee 1994).

Research Methods and Data Collection

The data for the study were collected by both observation and questionnaire methods. The observation was conducted over three working days for each manager, that is, a total of 30 days for ten managers, in the Korea Electric Power Corporation. During the observation, the author acted as a participant observer. This was possible because he was a manager in the company, which enabled him to observe almost all work activities in which the sampled managers engaged, reducing the possibility of being prevented from observing things they might be ashamed of or which were confidential or contradictory to what was expected of them. The data obtained from the observations were not susceptible to computer or statistical analysis. Hence, they have been calculated and analysed manually and required only simple statistical techniques in the analysis.

Meanwhile, the Managerial Work Activity Description Questionnaire (MWADQ), which was designed to measure both managers' work values and working hours, was circulated to a large number of top, middle and first-line managers in various functions in the sampled company. The data collected through the questionnaire were analysed using the Statistical Package for the Social Sciences (SPSS). The major statistical techniques employed in the analysis were cross-tabulation tables and Student t-tests (an independent sample).

Sampled Managers

The subjects of the study were divided into two groups: one for observation and the other for questionnaire survey. The managers for observation were composed of ten 'effective' managers from a variety of hierarchies (three senior, three middle, four first-line), functions (two finance, two operations, six sales and marketing) and geographically dispersed areas in South Korea.

In the study, 'effective managers' meant those (a) who achieved a high organizational performance; and (b) who had subordinates with high satisfaction and commitment. To choose effective managers as the sample, the study first selected those with the best performance from the Performance Evaluation Report published yearly by the company, which was designed to determine the incentive rate for organizational units and individuals. Next, their subordinates were interviewed to see whether their satisfaction and commitment to their superior were high or not. Through this process, the researcher could find ten effective managers who fully met both of these criteria.

The researcher observed details of activities carried out by the subjects, and recorded them on the observation log, which consisted of three main parts: the chronology, the contact, and the correspondence records. Specifically, the chronology record was designed to provide information about managers' working hours, which was the major issue to be discussed in the study.

The questionnaire survey involved more numerous and diverse groups of individuals. The target was 281 managers from various levels and functions. They consisted of 46 senior, 91 middle, and 144 first-line managers by managerial hierarchy, and 47 personnel, 26 finance, 113 production, 65 marketing, and 30 other managers by function. The sample represented 5 per cent of all managers within the company. Respondents were randomly selected from the list of managers prepared annually by the company.

Representativeness of the Korea Electric Power Corporation

The sample company in which the study was carried out is the Korea Electric Power Corporation, which is generally regarded as a typical Korean firm. The company was established in the late nineteenth century and celebrated its centenary in 1987. It is a quasi-public organization involved in processes from the generation to the distribution of power. The company has nearly 36,000 full-time employees throughout South Korea. It is owned by both the Korean government (70 per cent) and a large number of individual shareholders (30 per cent).

The reason for choosing the power company for the study was primarily because of its representativeness. It is regarded by the Korean people as representative of Korean firms in terms of its history, size, characteristics and influences on other companies in Korea. First, the power company has the longest business history in Korea, as noted earlier. Secondly, it is one of the largest business organizations in the country. Thirdly, it has dual characteristics that can be found in both public and private sector organizations, given its semi-public nature. Fourthly, it has influenced almost all large Korean firms in the private sector in the course of the country's rapid economic development.

In the 1970s and 1980s, the majority of large firms in the private sector which had suffered great shortages of skilled managerial per-

Table 24.1   Comparison of factors of importance to Korean and UK managers (%)

Factors	British managers	Korean managers
Family relationships	62	41.6
Work and career	28	54.1
Religious beliefs and activities	5	3.7
Leisure time and recreational activities	4	0.3
Political or community activities	1	0.3
Total	100	100

sonnel (such as Samsung, Hyundai, Goldstar and Daewoo) invested their utmost efforts to headhunt skilled managers from the Korean Electric Power Corporation because it was the only firm with skilled managerial manpower in the country. This headhunting led the private sector to import the management system practised in the company. In effect, the new managers applied the managerial skills gained from the company across almost all managerial activities. As a consequence, they played an important role in narrowing the difference in management practices between the power company and the private sector organizations. Thus, it can be anticipated that managers' work values and their activities in the power company are unlikely to differ greatly from those of private companies. This means that managers in the Korean Electric Power Corporation are highly representative of the majority of managers working in large business organizations in both the public and private sectors in South Korea.

Comparing Korean and UK Managers' Work Values

In their empirical study, Nicholson and West (1988) asked UK managers to rank the following five key factors in order of importance to them in their lives: (a) family relationships; (b) work and career; (c) religious beliefs and activities; (d) leisure time and recreational activities; (e) activities relating to political or community activities.

The most obvious difference between Korean and UK managers lies with their attitudes to their work and families, as seen in Table 24.1. More than half the sampled Korean managers rated their work and career as the most important factor in their lives, whereas less

Table 24.2 Differences in attitudes to work and family, by age of manager

Factor	Older n (%)	Middle-aged n (%)	Younger n (%)
Work and career	62 (74.7)	59 (50.9)	31 (44.3)
Family relationships	21 (25.3)	57 (49.1)	39 (55.7)
Total	83 (100.0)	116 (100.0)	70 (100.0)

$\chi = 16.93$
D.F. = 2
P < 0.005

than a third of their UK counterparts had this attitude to their work. Likewise, nearly two-thirds of UK managers rated their family relationships as the most important thing in their lives, whilst less than half of Korean managers did the same. This shows that Korean managers regard their work and career as more important than do their British counterparts.

Additionally, the other difference in the order of importance between Korean and UK managers lies in their attitudes to leisure time and recreational activities: 4 per cent of UK managers rated leisure time and recreational activities as the most important aspect of their lives; but only 0.3 per cent of their Korean counterparts had the same attitude. Both percentages are small, but this difference is also in line with the *Scotsman* (1992) report, which revealed that no Korean employee said that he would spend money on leisure if given an unexpected fortune. This finding also corroborates the finding that Korean managers are less interested in leisure time or recreational activities compared to UK managers, that is, they have a lower leisure orientation.

Finally, in order to examine whether there was a change in Korean managers' attitudes towards their work and career with age, the researcher compiled a cross-tabulation, as shown in table 24.2. For the analysis, he recoded the sample into three different age groups: under 40 years as younger managers; 41–50 as middle-aged; and over 50 as older; he also reclassified the responding values into two categories: work and career, and family relationships. The other minor values such as religious, recreational and political activities were treated as missing values.

Table 24.2 shows the relationship between Korean managers' ages and their attitudes towards their work and families: 74.7 per cent of older managers, 50.9 per cent of middle-aged managers and 44.3 per cent of younger managers rated their work and career as more important than their family relationships, whilst 25.3 per cent of older managers, 49.1 per cent of middle-aged managers and 55.7 per cent of younger managers showed the opposite attitudes to their work and families. This finding strongly suggests that the younger the manager, the greater the concern for family, whereas concern for work and career increases as managers' age increases. Younger managers are more concerned with their family relationships than are older managers. This implies that younger managers in the Korean power company must be getting closer to their UK counterparts than are older managers in their attitudes to their family relationships. This is, in fact, likely, since the younger generation's work values are becoming more Westernized compared with those of the older generation in Korean society. This implies that there is a certain type of convergence in the social value system between Korean and UK managers, especially younger ones.

Management writers (for example, Ralston et al. 1992; Kyi 1988; Adler 1991; Luthans 1989; Hofstede 1983; England 1973; Whitely and England 1977; Hofstede and Bond 1988; Hamilton and Biggart 1988; Ueno and Sekaran 1992; Dubinsky et al. 1992) identified considerable differences in management culture between the East and the West. However, managerial culture seems neither totally isolated nor halted in time. The adoption of Westernized education systems in Far Eastern countries, the rapid development of communication and transportation systems and the more frequent exchange of people than ever before seem to have accelerated the pace of convergence in social value systems across countries. Luthans (1989) and Huczynski and Buchanan (1991) maintained that Korean and Japanese cultures had become Westernized, and that Anglo-Saxon culture had moved closer to Eastern culture. For example, the recent widespread labour strikes in South Korea, in which workers demanded their share of economic gains, were an indicator of such rapidly shifting attitudes and values as the harmonious spirit becomes less dominant. Another example of Western culture moving to the East lies in large Japanese companies recently laying off permanent staff in favour of contract workers, constituting a partial abandonment of lifetime employment models.

Specifically, this type of change in the social value system in Korean society seems to be more evident amongst the younger generation than the older. This is because the young are more easily influenced by Western cultures than older people, who tend to be more loyal to their traditional ways of life, philosophy and social value system. The

Table 24.3 Results of t-test on differences in weekday working hours between work-orientated and family-orientated managers

Types of manager	No. of cases	Mean	Std dev.	t-value	D.F.	P
Work-orientated managers	152	10.77	0.94	11.78	267	< 0.001
Family-orientated managers	117	9.39	0.81			

other reason may be that the younger generation has more opportunity to be exposed to Western cultures than older people, due to both Westernized education and the nuclear family system introduced into Korea since the Korean war in the 1950s. Recently, younger employees' increasing family orientation is one of the most important issues facing almost all Korean companies. The majority of younger employees tend to be reluctant to work extra hours in order to spend more time with their families, even when there are workplace emergencies. This tendency is scarcely understood by older managers, who have been ready to sacrifice their family relationships for their work and career.

How Do Work Values Affect Working Hours?

So far, we have discussed how Korean managers rate their work more importantly than their family relationships, whereas their UK counterparts put their family relationships ahead of their work and career. This finding leads us to consider the relationship between managers' work values and their working hours. Can we assume that if a manager regards his work as more important than his family relationship he is more likely to work longer hours?

In order to examine the relationship, the sampled Korean managers were recategorized into two main groups: those who thought that their work was more important than their family relationships, and the others who rated their family relationships as more important than their work. The few respondents who rated recreational, religious or political activities as the most important factors in their lives were treated as missing values. Table 24.3 summarises the results. It shows that the average working hours for those who rate work as more

Table 24.4 Results of t-test on differences in Saturday working hours between work-orientated and family-orientated managers

Types of manager	No. of cases	Mean	Std dev.	t-value	D.F.	P
Work-orientated managers	152	5.08	1.09			
				1.83	267	0.069
Family-orientated managers	117	4.85	0.92			

important are 10.77, whereas those managers who regard family relationships as more important are 9.39 (P < 0.001).

In a similar context, the Korean managers' Saturday working hours
were also found to be influenced by their work values, as were weekday working hours. Table 24.4 indicates that the figure for Saturday
for work-orientated managers is 5.08 hours, whilst that for family-
orientated managers is 4.85 hours. The P value (0.069) of this analysis is much smaller than P < 0.1, the maximum limit that we can
accept. This means that there is a significant difference in Saturday
working hours between work- and family-orientated managers.

These two findings confirm that the working hours for the work-
orientated managers are longer than those for the family-orientated
managers. This difference suggests that managers' personal values
relating to their work are an important indicator of their working
hours. Based upon the finding, we can conclude that managers who
consider their work as more important than their family relationships
work longer hours than those who regard their family relations as
more significant than their work. This outcome is in accord with our
earlier assumption, that there is a positive relationship between managers' work values and their working hours.

Differences in Working Hours between Korean and UK Managers

With regard to UK managers' working hours, major studies conducted in the United Kingdom reveal that they are unlikely to work
long hours. As shown in table 24.5, UK managers were reported to
work, on average, 42.6 hours a week, ranging from 41.5 to 44 hours
(8.5 hours per day).

By contrast, the data on Korean managers' working hours obtained

Table 24.5 UK managers' working hours

Study	Working hours per week
Burns (1957)	41.5
Stewart (1967, 1988)	42.5
Horne and Lupton (1965)	44.0
Wilkie and Young (1972)	42.5
Average	42.6 (8.5 per day)

Table 24.6 Ten Korean managers: weekday working hours, by observation

Day	Senior managers			Middle managers			First-line managers			
	Kwon	Shin	Cha	Paik	Chang	Kim	Ha	Choi	Park	Kang
1	9.7	9.25	9.05	9.5	9.33	13.0	10.0	9.67	9.32	10.33
2	9.17	9.5	9.25	9.2	9.08	10.25	10.17	9.23	9.75	12.52
3	9.37	9.0	9.08	9.6	9.17	11.87	9.53	10.27	9.22	12.58
Mean	9.41	9.25	9.13	9.43	9.19	11.71	9.9	9.72	9.43	11.87

Overall mean = 9.9 hours

from both observation and questionnaire methods in the study, confirmed that Korean managers in the power company worked much longer hours than did UK managers. First, table 24.6 discloses that the ten Korean managers observed by the author each for three working days worked, on average, 9.9 hours a day (49.5 hours per week)

Secondly, the data obtained through the questionnaire on 281 Korean managers shown in table 24.7 gives an average figure of 10.16 hours a day, ranging from 8 to 13 hours (median = 10, mode = 10). The majority of the sampled managers (72.8 per cent) answered that they worked 10 hours or more a day. This result is very similar to that obtained from observation (mean = 9.9 hours). From these two findings, we can draw the conclusion that Korean managers work on average 10 hours a day. This means that they work nearly one and half hours longer than do UK managers every day.

Furthermore, these Korean managers' working hours do not involve their post-work activities which take place after business hours, and in which the majority of Korean managers tend to engage on an almost daily basis. These events usually happen in the form of informal

Table 24.7   Weekday working hours, obtained from questionnaire

Working hours	Frequency	%	Cumulative %
13	6	2.1	2.1
12	33	11.7	13.8
11	58	20.6	34.4
10	108	38.4	72.8
9	50	17.8	90.6
8	26	9.4	100.0
Total	$N = 281$	100.0	
Mean = 10.16	Std dev. = 1.29	Median = 10	Mode = 10

group meetings with their subordinates, superiors, peers or colleagues either in a pub or in a restaurant. In practice, they are hardly distinguishable from their normal working activities, since most of their conversations during the meetings focus on work-related topics. Whilst conducting the field study, the researcher found that the majority of the sampled managers in the observation took part in these kinds of group activities after work. Nevertheless, it was very difficult to provide an exact number of hours devoted to them since they occurred on an irregular, *ad hoc* basis with variations in their duration.

Reasons for the Higher Work-orientation of Korean Managers

We have thus far examined the difference in working hours between Korean and UK managers. It reveals that Korean managers work much longer hours than do UK managers. Why should it be so? The reason is likely to be closely associated with their attitudes to their work. As discussed earlier, managers who consider their work and career as more important than their family relationships work longer hours compared to those who have the opposite attitudes to their work and families (see tables 24.3 and 24.4). This finding seems to offer an appropriate answer for the difference in working hours between Korean and British managers, that is that Korean managers, having value systems which are more work-orientated, tend to work longer hours than do their British counterparts who have a lower work-orientated social value system.

The reason why Korean managers are more work-orientated can be explained in terms of difference in their cultural, social and economic environments. First, the gap in living standards seems to be an important factor. Although Korea has made remarkable economic strides over the last three decades, living standards are still behind those of the United Kingdom. Since Korean managers' average living standards are lower than those of UK managers, they appear to be more concerned with Maslow's 'physiological or security needs' (making money through hard work) than their British counterparts, who are more concerned with the higher 'love needs' (more time with the family).

Secondly, as noted by Luthans (1989) and Adler (1991), the difference in the 'time dimension' between Korean and UK managers also appears to contribute towards differentiating between their attitudes towards their work and career. According to these writers, Western people (UK, US, Canadian) have a present or near-future orientation, whilst Far East Asian people (Korean, Japanese, Chinese) have a long-term future orientation. UK managers, who are present time-orientated, may consider that current happiness with their families is more important than that in the future, which is more uncertain in its realization, whereas Korean managers, whose time dimension is more future-orientated, are likely to prepare for future happiness through current hard work, rather than enjoying the present with their families.

Thirdly, Korean people's work ethic, stimulated by Confucianism, may be a further reason. Liu (1959) and Song (1990) maintain that Korean people's hard work culture is basically derived from the teaching of Confucius, in which diligence, thrift and hard work are emphasized. Confucianism has been established as both a religion and a philosophy in Korea for the last 600 years, following its introduction from China. Chu (1991: 229) describes the influence of Confucianism on Korean society in the following terms:

> Although Buddhism was the official religion for centuries in many of the states of ancient Korea, and it is still widely practised there, Confucianism, both as a religion and a philosophy of social order, played a more fundamental role in the development of Korean values.

Fourthly, the work ethic seems partially attributable to the small, hilly and agriculturally unproductive nature of the country. Korea has the third-highest population density in the world after Bangladesh and Taiwan. Furthermore, the total land per capital is only 0.58 acres with two-thirds of this area being hilly and unsuitable for either agricultural or urban use. This unproductive territory has encouraged Korean people to work hard to avoid starvation and has established itself as the corner stone of the social value system.

Fifthly, Korean managers' long tenure with their firms appears to contribute to differentiating their work values from those of UK managers, whose tenure is relatively short. According to Lee (1994), Korean managers were found to stay longer with their companies than UK managers, because of the lifetime employment system that the majority of Korean firms adopt. Due to their strong loyalty to their companies, stimulated by their long period of service, they are unlikely to complain when they are forced to work longer hours. In many cases, Korean managers (particularly, middle-aged and older ones) do not seem reluctant to work extra hours if they have something to do, whether extra benefits are paid or not for such overtime activities. Mr Choi, one of the managers who participated in the field study, put his view of overtime work in the following way:

> If I have something to do, I try to finish it as soon as possible. In effect, I have many experiences to work throughout the night until the following morning to this end. However, my company's compensation system for the overtime work does not stimulate my motivation for such hard work. Rather, my strong commitment to my work and my concern for my company lead me to do so. The work for which I am responsible is my own work rather than the company's one.

Finally, the Korean people's desire to overtake developed countries also seems to encourage their work-orientation. Although Korea has experienced an enviable achievement in its economic development in recent years, thanks to the nationwide campaign to encourage hard work initiated by both the Korean government and the private sector, it still has to go a long way to catch up with advanced countries. This will have some effect on the work-orientation of Korean managers compared with their UK counterparts.

Summary and Conclusions

The study has examined how Korean managers' work values differ from those of UK managers, and how managers' work values affect their working hours. It shows that Korean managers rate their work as more important than their family relationships, whilst the opposite is true for UK managers. This implies that Korean managers' social value system is more work-orientated than that of their UK counter-parts. In addition, the study also reveals that managers' attitudes to their work and career strongly influence their working hours. Managers who consider their work as more important than their family relationships work longer hours than those who have the opposite attitudes to their work and families.

The reason why Korean managers have a higher work orientation seems to be closely associated with the cultural, social and economic environments in which they have been brought up and educated. The most likely reason may be due to the gap in living standards between Korean and UK managers. Secondly, the difference in hours worked also seems to be explained by their future-orientated time dimension. Thirdly, the teaching of Confucius emphasizing diligence and hard work appears to encourage their work orientation. Fourthly, their small, hilly and agriculturally unproductive territory may be an additional influence. Fifthly, Korean managers' long service within their company is likely to differentiate their work values from those of UK managers, whose tenure is relatively short. Lastly, Korean people's desire to catch up with major industrialized countries in a relatively short period may encourage them to have a higher work-orientated social value system.

References

Adler, N.J. 1991: *International Dimensions of Organisational Behaviour*. Boston, Mass.: PWS–Kent.

Burns, T. 1957: Management in action. *Operational Research Quarterly*, 8(2), 45–60.

Chu, C.N. 1991: *The Asian Mind Game*. New York: Rawson Associates.

Dubinsky, A.J., Michaels, R.E., Kotabe, M., Lim, C.U. and Moon, H.C. 1992: Influence of role stress on industrial sales people's work outcomes in the United States, Japan, and Korea. *Journal of International Business Studies*, First Quarter, 77–99.

England, G.W. 1973: Personal value systems and expected behaviour of managers: a comparative study in Japan, Korea and the United States. In D. Graves (ed.), *Management Research: a cross-cultural perspective*, Amsterdam: Elsevier Scientific Publishing Company, 25–48.

Hamilton, G.G. and Biggart, N.W. 1988: Market, culture, and authority: a comparative analysis of management and organisation in the Far East. *American Journal of Sociology*, 94, Supplement, S52–94.

Hofstede, G. 1983: The cultural relativity of organisational practices and theories. *Journal of International Business Studies*, Fall, 75–89.

Hofstede, G. and Bond, M.H. 1988: The Confucius connection: from cultural roots to economic growth. *Organisational Dynamics*, 16(4), 4–21.

Horne, J.H. and Lupton, T. 1965: The work activities of middle managers: an exploratory study. *Journal of Management Studies*, 2, February, 14–33.

Huczynski, A.A. and Buchanan, D.A. 1991: *Organisational Behaviour: an introductory text*, 2nd edn. Hemel Hempstead, Herts.: Prentice Hall International (UK).

Kyi, K.M. 1988: APJM and comparative management in Asia. *Asia Pacific Journal of Management*, 5(3), 207–24.

Lee, Y.H. 1994: A cross-cultural comparison of work activities between Korean and western managers. Unpublished PhD thesis, University of Glasgow.

Liu, H.C.W. 1959: An analysis of Chinese clan rules: Confucian theories in action. In D.S. Nivison and A.F. Wright (eds), *Confucianism in Action*, Stanford, Cal.: Stanford University Press.

Luthans, F. 1989: *Organisational Behaviour*, 5th edn. Maidenhead, Berks.: McGraw-Hill.

Nicholson, N. and West, M.A. 1988: *Managerial Job Change: men and women in transition*. Cambridge: Cambridge University Press.

Ralston, D.A., Gustafson, D.J., Elsass, P.M., Cheung, F. and Terpstrs, R.H. 1992: Eastern values: a comparison of managers in the United States, Hong Kong, and the People's Republic of China. *Journal of Applied Psychology*, 77(5), 664–71.

Song, B.N. 1990: *The Rise of the Korean Economy*. Hong Kong: Oxford University Press.

Stewart, R. 1967: *Managers and Their Jobs: a study of the similarities and differences in the ways managers spend their time*. London: Macmillan.

Stewart, R. 1988: *Managers and Their Jobs: a study of the similarities and differences in the ways managers spend their time*, 2nd edn. London: Macmillan.

Ueno, S. and Sekaran, K. 1992: The influence of culture on budget control practices in the USA and Japan: an empirical study. *Journal of International Business Studies*, 23(4), 659–74.

Whitely, W. and England, G.W. 1977: Managerial values as a reflection of culture and the process of industrialisation. *Academy of Management Journal*, 20(3), 439–53.

Wilkie, R. and Young, J.N. 1972: Managerial behaviour in the furniture and timber industries. *International Studies of Management of Organisation*, 1, 65–84.

Annotated Further Reading

Books

Abo, T. (ed.) 1994: *Hybrid Factory*. New York: Oxford University Press. A rather dry but thoroughly researched piece on Japanese transplants in the USA.

Anderson, G.C. 1993: *Managing Performance Appraisal Systems*. Oxford: Blackwell.
This book focuses on the management of performance appraisal in organizations, and covers issues relevant to those who are subject to performance appraisal in organizations, to managers who conduct appraisals and to personnel/human resource specialists who co-ordinate performance appraisal systems.

Ashton, D. and Felstead, A. 1995: 'Training and development'. In J. Storey (ed.), *Human Resource Management*, London: Routledge.
A useful review of past and contemporary training policies and practices in Britain.

Bamber, G.J. and Lansbury, R.D. (eds) 1989: *New Technology: international perspectives on human resources and industrial relations*. London: Routledge.
A series of studies on technological and organizational change from Australia, Canada, Denmark, Italy, Sweden, Switzerland, UK and USA.

Bamber, G.J. and Lansbury, R.D. (eds) 1993: *International and Comparative Industrial Relations: a study of industrialised market economies*. London and New York: Routledge.
An industrial relations context for HRM in nine advanced industrialized countries: Australia, Canada, France, Germany, Italy, Japan, Sweden, UK and USA, including a useful analysis of economic and labour market data.

Barham, K. and Wills, S. 1992: *Management Across Frontiers*. Berkhamsted: Ashridge Management Research Group and Foundation for Management Education.
The result of a qualitative research study of practising international managers, this report highlights the competencies, both behavioural and psychological, required for this role.

Beatson, M. 1995: *Labour Market Flexibility*, London: Department of Employment and Education.
Provides an excellent summary of all the available surveys.

Beaumont, P.B. 1992: *Public Sector Industrial Relations.* London: Routledge.
This book looks specifically at the industrial relations context of the public
sector.

Blyton, P. and Morris, J. 1991: *A Flexible Future? Prospects for employment and
organization.* Berlin: de Gruyter.
Many of the chapters in the collection report studies of developments in
flexibility in different industrial and national locations.

Brewster, C. and Hegewisch, A. 1994: *Policy and Practice in European Human
Resource Management: the evidence and analysis from the Price Waterhouse/
Cranfield survey.* London: Routledge.
The Price Waterhouse/Cranfield Survey represents the richest descriptive
database on HRM across Europe. This volume reports in depth on the
contours of HRM across Europe and identifies some of the major trends.

Brown, A. 1995: *Organisational Culture.* London: Pitman Publishing.
A fairly comprehensive textbook covering the broad area of organizational
culture, including managing culture change.

Brown, W. and Walsh, J. 1994: Managing pay in Britain. In K. Sisson (ed.),
Personnel Management, Oxford: Blackwell.
A discussion not entirely focused on the ethics of pay, but which never-
theless deals with some of the issues surrounding fairness and effort.

Cassels, J. 1990: *Britain's Real Skill Shortage.* London: Policy Studies Institute.
A succinct and worrying analysis of Britain's skills profile is followed by a
highly authoritative plea for greater government training and intervention
and labour market regulation.

Chandler, A.D. 1962: *Strategy and Structure.* Cambridge, Mass.: MIT Press.
A classic study of the rise of the 'managerial enterprise', the form of
business organization which dominated the era of mass production.

Davidson, M.J. and Burke, R.J. (eds) 1994: *Women in Management: current
research issues.* London: Paul Chapman.
A useful collection reflecting the different research interests and their policy
implications.

Davidson, M.J. and Cooper, C.L. 1992: *Shattering the Glass Ceiling: the
woman manager.* London: Paul Chapman.
A good overview of the research on women in management covering employment patterns, stress, work roles and relationships, plus a discussion
of strategies for change.

Davidson, M.J. and Cooper, C.L. 1993: *European Women in Business and
Management.* London: Paul Chapman.
A concise and detailed country-by-country summary focusing upon a
number of common themes.

Dickens, L. 1994: Wasted resources? Equal opportunities in employment. In
K. Sisson (ed.), *Personnel Management: a comprehensive guide to theory and
practice in Britain,* Oxford: Blackwell.
A well researched review of the factors that might encourage organizations
to take equality action, and the reasons for uneven outcomes. Also contains

a clear explanation of the limitations of equal opportunity prescriptions of 'good practice'.

Dunphy, D. and Stace, D. 1990: *Under New Management: Australian organizations in transition.* Sydney: McGraw-Hill.
Discusses organizational change and HRM and includes several models.

Evenden, R. and Anderson, G.C. 1992: *Management Skills: making the most of people.* Wokingham, Berks: Addison-Wesley.
This book aims to help managers to develop practitioner skills to master the people side of their roles in modern organizations. 'Making the most of people' is the theme, and the book combines the spectrum of skills from recruitment, through achieving positive relationships, to training and developing people.

Farnham, D. 1993: Human resource management and employee relations. In D. Farnham and Sylvia Horton (eds), *Managing the New Public Services*, London: Macmillan.
This chapter, in a very useful edited collection, focuses specifically on recent developments in public sector HRM.

French, S.W. and Bell, C. 1990: *Organization Development*, Englewood Cliffs, N.J.: Prentice-Hall.
A useful and comprehensive text dealing with the various approaches to organizational change.

Fucini, J.J. and Fucini, S. 1990: *Working for the Japanese.* New York: Free Press.
Colourful account of life at Mazda's factory at Flat Rock in the USA.

Furnham, A. and Gunter, B. 1993: Corporate culture: definition, diagnosis and change. In C. Cooper and I.T. Robinson (eds), *International Review of Industrial and Organisational Psychology*, vol. 8, London: John Wiley.
A useful overview and critique of the literature on corporate culture.

Gardner, M. and Palmer, G. 1992: *Employment Relations: industrial relations and human resource management in Australia.* Melbourne: Macmillan.
This discusses IR and HRM, the concept of strategy to explore the possibility for integration between IR and HRM practice. It is a text book supplemented by case studies.

Hammer, M. and Champy, J. 1993: *Re-engineering the Corporation.* New York: HarperCollins.
Though details of government policy have subsequently been altered, the voluntarist traditions examined in these highly accessible papers have been sustained and reinforced. The Finegold and Soskice 'low-skill equilibrium' associated with non-intervention, which has subsequently generated substantial discussion, is included. Undoubtedly the most widely referenced book on business process re-engineering. It is characterized by its relative indifference to the subtleties involved in human resource management.

Her Majesty's Government 1994: *The Civil Service: continuity and change*, Cm 2627. London: HMSO.
The UK government's official statement on the future of the Civil Service,

covering implications of key reforms such as Next Steps agencies and the Citizen's Charter for personnel management in the service.

Herriot, P. 1989: *Selection and Assessment in Organizations*. In N. Anderson and P. Herriot, *Selection and Assessment in Organizations, 1994 Supplement*, London: John Wikey.

Hochschild, Arlie, 1989: *The Second Shift: working parents and the revolution at home*. New York: Viking.
Deals with the stresses faced especially by working mothers and the kinds of adjustments they must make to deal with these.

Hofstede, G. 1991: *Cultures and Organizations*. Maidenhead: McGraw-Hill.
The 'doyen' of cross-cultural researchers, Gert Hofstede is the author of the seminal study in the field. This more recent book contains all his basic arguments, but in a more readable form than the original research monograph.

Hutton, W. 1995: *The State We're In*. London: Jonathan Cape.
A popular but analytical account of the multiple failures of British employers and government approach to investment in human, capital and technological resources. The dire consequences of this continuing neglect are spelt out in suitably apocalyptic terms. An alternative economic agenda is presented.

Hyman, J. and Mason, B. 1995: *Managing Employee Involvement and Participation*. London: Sage.
This text gives a wide-ranging and intelligent review of the area, with plenty of contemporary material and information. Judgements are generally sound and reliable and link into wider debates.

Kirkbride, P.S. (ed.) 1994: *Human Resource Management in Europe: Perspectives for the 1990s*, London: Routledge.
The result of a major international conference on international HRM, this edited collection addresses the questions of European cultural difference, Eastern European development and the creation of pan-European managers, in a series of papers.

Kochan, T.A. and Osterman, P. 1994: *The Mutual Gains Enterprise*. Cambridge, Mass.: Harvard Business School Press.
The contents of Chapter 6 of this book illustrate the increased desire of unions to favour a joint partnership approach to HRM in the USA.

Kochan, T. and Useem, M. 1992: *Transforming Organizations*. New York: Oxford University Press.
A collection of articles dealing with the conditions necessary for organizational change.

Lawler, E.E. 1990: *Strategic Pay: aligning organizational strategies and pay systems*. San Francisco: Jossey-Bass.
Discusses the advantages and disadvantages of a wide variety of compensation schemes.

Legge, K. 1995: *Human Resource Management*, London: Macmillan.
This adopts the same format as the chapter by Guest but provides more detail. It gives a provocative and critical view of developments in HRM in the UK.

Li, Feng 1995: *The Geography of Business Information*. Chichester: John Wiley.
A book which usefully develops a wide range of perspectives on information and communications technology and organizations.

Lucio, M.M. and Weston, S. 1992: Human resource management and trade union responses: bringing the politics of the workplace back into the debate. In P. Blyton and P. Turnbull (eds), *Reassessing Human Resource Management*, London: Sage.

Marchington, M. 1992: *Managing the Team*. Oxford: Blackwell.
More technique-orientated and practical in style, this text has a less-ambitious analytical sweep than Hyman and Mason, but benefits from the author's extensive knowledge of examples. An alternative, and in some ways more valuable as a research document, is the Department of Employment-sponsored study involving Marchington and others, 1992: *New Developments in Employee Involvement*. London: HMSO.

Marginson, P., Armstrong, P., Edwards, P., Purcell, J. and Hubbard, N. 1993: *The Control of Industrial Relations in Large Companies: an initial analysis of the Second Company Level Industrial Relations Survey*, Warwick: Industrial Relations Research Unit, Warwick University.

Millward, N., Stevens, M., Smart, D. and Hawes, W. 1992: *Workplace Industrial Relations in Transition*. A ldershot, Hants.: Dartmouth.
The most recent workplace survey is reported in this book. The most authoritative sources of trends in employment relations in the UK continue to be the Workplace and Company Level Industrial Relations Surveys. Unfortunately the Workplace Surveys omit important areas of human resource management but they are very valuable none the less (see also Other Sources).

Oliver, N. and Wilkinson, B. 1992: *The Japanization of British Industry*, 2nd edn. Oxford: Blackwell.
Account of the adoption of Japanese methods in the UK, covering both Japanese transplants and the emulation of Japanese practices by UK firms.

Organization for Economic Cooperation and Development (OECD) 1989: *Labour Market Flexibility: trends in enterprises*. Paris: OECD.
Analyses the components of flexibility and identifies the degree to which different aspects have been emphasized in different countries.

Patrickson, M.G., Bamber, V.M. and Bamber, G.J. (eds) 1995: *Organizational Change Strategies: case studies of human resource and industrial relations issues*. Melbourne: Longman.
Contains 27 relevant detailed case studies of the interrelationships between management strategies, industrial relations, human resources, quality and other issues.

Roomkin, Myron (ed.) 1990: *Profit Sharing and Gain Sharing*. New York: Scarecrow.
A series of articles discussing the organizational and motivational impacts of a variety of forms of contingent compensation.

Schein, E.H. 1985: *Organization Culture and Leadership*. San Francisco: Jossey-Bass.

An important contribution to the theoretical literature. Offers useful insights into difficulties of coping with the concept of culture.

Sheppard, B.H., Lewicki, R.J. and Minton, J.W. 1992: *Organisational Justice: the search for fairness in the workplace.* New York: Macmillan.

A readable book; one of the few which concentrates on employment issues.

Schuler, H., Farr, J.L. and Smith, M. (eds) 1993: *Personnel Selection Assessment: individual and organizational perspectives.* Hillsdale, N.J.: Lawrence Erlbaum: Associates.

This volume covers both individual and organizational perspectives of personnel selection, with contributions from established researchers and writers from the USA, the UK and Europe. It provides much-needed consideration of the neglected aspects of personnel selection research relating to individual perceptions and reactions to the selection process.

Smith, M. and Robertson, I.T. 1993: *The Theory and Practice of Systematic Staff Selection,* 2nd edn. London: Macmillan.

Detailed account of the stages in the selection process, including some less-traditional material on applicant reactions and ethical issues, and a comprehensive review of the scientific evidence relating to designing and evaluating selection systems, including chapters on psychometric measurements and meta-analysis.

Snape, E.J., Redman, T. and Bamber, G.J. 1994: *Managing Managers: strategies and techniques for human resource management.* Oxford and New York: Blackwell.

Most managers are also employees who need to be managed. This book shows that their effective management is a key ingredient of organizational success.

Starkey, K. and McKinlay, A. 1993: *Strategy and the Human Resource: Ford and the search for competitive advantage.* Oxford: Blackwell.

In depth study of Ford's attempt to break with its past, in terms of strategy, structure and management style. Focuses on the design and executive processes as well as shopfloor industrial relations.

Storey, J. and Sisson, K. 1993: *Managing Human Resources and Industrial Relations.* Buckingham: Open University Press.

A text which admirably locates performance-related pay with the related HRM employment policies, and which raises issues of individualism versus collectivism.

Taylor, R. 1994: *The Future of Trade Unions.* London: Andre Deutsch. Chapter 5 outlines the position of a number of unions in Britain towards HRM.

Torrington, D. and Hall, L. 1995: *Personnel Management HRM in Action.* Hemel Hempstead, Herts.: Prentice-Hall.

This latest volume reviews the personnel/human resource processes in organizations that are regarded as leading to effective management. It illustrates a range of practical approaches to recruitment and selection. It represents a reasonably comprehensive view of how, in practice, issues of reliability and validity are considered. It illustrates the emphasis on personal skills rather than other methods of selection.

Trompenaars, F. 1993: *Riding the Waves of Culture: understanding cultural diversity in business*. London: Nicholas Brealey.
Whilst not as rigorous in his research methodology as Hofstede, Trompenaars writes very well and his scenario method offers some interesting insights into cross-cultural differences across Europe.

White, T.I. 1993: *Business Ethics: a philosophical reader*. New York: Macmillan.
A large book with readings and cases covering the spectrum of the ethical issues in business. An American focus, but this is where much of the literature originates.

Williams, A., Dobson, P. and Walters, M. 1993: *Changing Culture*: new organisational approaches, 2nd edn. London: Institute of Personnel and Development.

Wilson, F.M. 1995: *Organizational Behaviour and Gender*. Maidenhead: McGraw-Hill.
A refreshing reminder that so much received wisdom about motivation, leadership, personality, etc. was based on research carried out by male academics on male samples and either ignored possible gender differences, or assumed, unjustifiably, that these differences existed.

Womack, J.P., Jones D.T. and Roos, D. 1990: *The Machine that Changed the World: the triumph of lean production*. New York: Rawson Macmillan. Very readable account of lean production methods in the auto industry.

Zuboff, S. 1988: *In the Age of the Smart Machine: the future of work and power*. Oxford: Heinemann.
A powerful presentation of argument and evidence which derive from several years of research into new patterns of work resulting from the introduction of new technology.

Journals

Atkinson, J. 1984: Manpower strategies for flexible organisations. *Personnel Management*, August, 28–31.
In this short article the author sets out his 'flexible firm' and defines the different aspects of flexibility ('functional', 'numerical', etc.) which have since become widely debated.

Beatson, M. 1995: Progress towards a flexible labour market. *Employment Gazette*, February, 55–66.
A useful recent overview of the development of flexibility in Britain.

Curtain, R. and Mathews, J. 1990: Two models of award restructuring in Australia. *Labour and Industry*, 3(1), 58–75.
Includes propositions useful for analysing labour market reform. It outlines a dichotomy of approaches and contributors to debates about post-Fordism, in the Australian context.

Economic and Industrial Democracy provides a heavier read for the more academically minded, though managerial studies are scattered across a very wide range of academic publications.

Education, training and economic performance 1988: *Oxford Review of Economic Policy*, 4(3).

Though details of government policy have subsequently been altered, the voluntarist traditions examined in these highly accessible papers have been sustained and reinforced. The Finegold and Soskice 'low-skill equilibrium' associated with non-intervention, which has subsequently generated substantial discussion, is included.

Grint, K. 1993: What's wrong with performance appraisals? A critique and a suggestion. *Human Resource Management Journal*, 3(3).

Labour and Society, 1987: 12(1). This journal issue is devoted to labour market flexibility, developments in Europe and North America are analysed, with discussion at enterprise and national labour market levels.

Lawler, E.E. 1994: Performance management: the next generation. *Compensation and Benefits Review*, May–June.

This article gives an up-to-date, balanced and on the whole positive view about the current state of performance appraisals, and identifies future issues to be addressed.

New Technology, Work and Employment 1995: Special issue on business process re-engineering, 10(2).

This is a collection of articles written by social scientists which critically examines the phenomenon of business process re-engineering.

Olson, C., Levine, D., Strauss, G. and Ichniowski, C. (eds) 1996: What works at work. *Industrial Relations*, 35(3).

A series of studies, in a variety of industries, concerned chiefly with two questions: which firms are most likely to adopt new forms of work organization, such as teams, and what is their likely impact on organizational performance?

Pollert, A. 1988: The flexible firm: fixation or fact? *Work, Employment and Society*, 2, 281–316.

This article offers a critique of the flexible firm model, identifying both conceptual and empirical shortcomings.

Stewart, J. and Walsh, K. 1992: Change in the management of public services. *Public Administration*, 70(4), 499–518. This article provides a good summary review and critique of the key changes in public services management during the 1980s–90s.

Verma, A. 1989: Joint participation programs: self-help or suicide for labor? *Industrial Relations*, 28(3), 401–10.

Considers both the potential benefits and costs to unions of involvement in HRM practices.

Ward, P. 1995: A 360-degree turn for the better. *People Management*, 9 February.

The introduction of 360-degree appraisal into a growing number of organizations is one of the most significant developments shaping the future of performance appraisal, and this article gives a clear account of many of the issues involved.

Other Sources

Her Majesty's Government, 1994: *The Civil Service: continuity and change*, Cmnd 2627. London: HMSO.
This is the UK government's official statement on the future of the Civil Service. It covers in particular implications of key reforms such as the Next Steps Agencies and Citizen's Charter for the personnel management of the service.

Incomes Data Services: A range of reports and studies which provide an updating of the current pay policies and schemes in operation in both the public and private sector. Also for a regular updating on techniques and approaches reviewed in Chapter 11.

Labour Market and Skill Trends 1995/96, Nottingham: Skills and Enterprise Network.
An annual review, sponsored by the government, of the changes in demand and supply within the labour market with particular emphasis on changing skill needs.

Labour Market Trends (formerly *Employment Gazette*) is the regular source of government research and official viewpoints.

Marginson, P., Armstrong, P., Edwards, P., Purcell, J. and Hubbard, N. 1993: *The Control of Industrial Relations in Large Companies: an initial analysis of the second company level industrial relations survey*, IRRU Warwick University.
Company-level survey reported here.

Index

For reasons of space, single mentions of companies and countries have been omitted.